D1561507

The Gunstocker

From a painting of the late and great Al Linden (who died in 1946) at work in his shop at Bryant, Langlade County, Wisconsin.

Showing Ole Skratch giving a few final scrapings to the inletting on the blank intended for one of his peerless gunstocks.

GUNSMITHING

A Manual of FIREARMS DESIGN, CONSTRUC-
TION, ALTERATION *and* REMODELING. *For*
AMATEUR *and* PROFESSIONAL GUNSMITHS
and USERS *of* MODERN FIREARMS

By ROY F. DUNLAP

Author of
Ordnance Went Up Front

Drawings by PAUL WEBB

STACKPOLE BOOKS
HARRISBURG, PENNSYLVANIA

Standard Book Number 8117-0770-9

Library of Congress Catalog Card Number: 63-21755

Printed and bound in the United States of America

683.4
D u n
31844

Contents

1. The Workshop   1
2. Basic Tools   9
3. Extra and Special Tools   25
4. Reference Books and Sources of Supply   37
5. Shop Practice   65
6. Helpful Gunsmithing Knowledge   75
7. Soldering and Brazing   92
8. Welding   102
9. Heat Treatment of Metals   116
10. Making and Fitting Sights and Accessories   129
11. Making, Fitting and Heat Treatment of Parts   146
12. Cartridge Information for the Gunsmith   167
13. Rifle Barrels and Barrel Information   180
14. Chamber and Barrel Work   206
15. Rifle Action Work   231
16. Pistol and Revolver Work   266
17. Shotguns and Shotgun Work   287
18. Twenty-two Rim Fire Arms   348
19. Browning, Blueing and Blacking of Metal   366
20. Fitting Commercial Metallic Sights   404
21. The Mounting of Telescopic Sights   419
22. Wood for Gunstocks   452
23. Design of Gunstocks   471
24. Stockmaking: Layout and Inletting   489
25. Stockmaking: Shaping and Fitting   509
26. Stockmaking: Finishing   526
27. Stockmaking: Checkering   539
28. Finishing Semi-Inletted Stocks   556

29. Stock Repair and Alteration   568
30. Styling the Custom Rifle   584
31. Custom Metal Work   590
32. Ornamentation of Wood and Metal   609
33. Target Rifles   625
34. The Garand Rifle   651
35. Testing Facilities and Apparatus   668
36. Tables of Mechanical Reference   685
    Appendix I (1963): Synthetic Bedding   713
    Appendix II (1963): Cartridge and Chamber
    Drawings and Data Sheets   722
    Index   735

Credit

I wish to thank the following men and credit them for the very valuable information which they so willingly allowed me to use in this volume.

Parker Ackley
J. R. Buhmiller
F. K. Elliott
John Hearn
Leonard Mews
Joe Pfeifer
Tom Shelhamer
W. A. Sukalle
Bliss Titus

Drawings by PAUL WEBB, *Tucson, Arizona*

Introduction

THIS VOLUME is intended as a working guide for gunsmiths, professional and amateur, and I have attempted to make it as complete and understandable as I could, without undue emphasis on highly technical matters of interest to only a few professional men. Above all, it is meant to help the general gunsmith—the man in every town who is called upon to do almost all types of gunwork. Since I do this kind of work myself, the lack of a good book on modern gunsmithing has been very evident, and I hope *Gunsmithing* will fill the void to some extent. The specialists—the pistol technicians, barrelmakers, custom gunstockers and others limiting their work to a particular line—may find this book lacking in detail in their specialty, but they undoubtedly know more about their jobs than I do!

No one man—myself included—can be thoroughly versed in all areas of the field of gunsmithing. I have not hesitated to call upon others for information to supplement my own experience and knowledge, nor to repeat worthwhile data previously printed. Therefore please do not credit me with knowing everything, or condemn me as a copyist. I believe this work to be the most complete, modern and practical of its kind and hope it will be of as much use to the gunworkman of today as Baker's *Modern Gunsmithing* has been to us for some 20 years past.

If *Gunsmithing* can save the average American gunsmith some of the years myself and others spent learning many of the operations described, and help him to do better work, both the publisher and the author will feel well repaid for the three years spent on its preparation and writing.

Sincerely,

ROY F. DUNLAP

2319 Ft. Lowell Road
Tucson, Arizona
September, 1950

Publisher's Note

THIS BOOK has become a classic in the gunsmithing field. Roy Dunlap learned gunsmithing through many years of working with guns and became a top custom gunsmith. He made beautiful stuff, doing things most other gunsmiths only dreamed about. He now specializes in match rifles. In this book Roy Dunlap has sought to pass on his wide experience for the benefit of other gunsmiths.

In this new edition Mr. Dunlap has written a special chapter on the use of fiber glass and other synthetics in bedding rifles, which will be of special interest to all gunsmiths who are seeking a method of inletting which does not require special equipment, is relatively inexpensive and easy to use, and gives lasting results including increased shooting accuracy. See Appendix I, page 713.

We also include in this new edition additional specification sheets covering new cartridges brought out since the first edition of this book was published. See Appendix II, page 722.

CHAPTER 1

The Workshop

LUCKY is the man who has complete power over the location and equipment of his place of work. Few of us ever can pick and choose our workshop, but we can try to make it into one which suits us. The unfortunate who lives in a small apartment or furnished room in a big city may have a tough time if he likes to work on even his own guns. Maybe the landlady will let him setup and keep a small, sturdy table to use, and maybe not. There is one practically sure-fire way out for such individuals, however, and if you are one, wander up and down the alleys close by until you find a garage for rent. Said rent is seldom over a sawbuck per month, sometimes less by half, and besides, every guncrank knows at least three other such characters, any or all of whom probably need little persuasion to come into the corporation and cut down expenses. The garage owner may want a buck or two extra for the electric bill, should you put in big lights and power equipment, but in ninety-nine out of a hundred cases he will not care what kind of benches you build, how many shavings you spread around, or what variety of blueing solution you spill on the floor.

The amateur gunsmith need not worry about location or business address and can pursue his hobby anywhere he can conveniently setup a bench. The professional needs a location reasonably easy of access by customers, and as good a setup as he can afford, with space for as much equipment as he can use. He should have ample gunracks for display of new guns and for safe storage of repair jobs, as well as display cases to show handguns, scopes, mounts, sights and accessories.

The most important item to be considered first is a *good* workbench —good meaning steady. It will have to be heavy and should be anchored to both floor and one wall, or better, set with one end in a corner of the shop room and braced so that it will not move in any direction if you apply all your strength to it. Length can be from four to eight feet, width, two to three feet—30″ is the perfect medium—

I

and height, from 36″ to 42″. Most of your work will be done while standing and, although a stool is quite restful, you will shift about so much that to use a low bench will become very tiring. I prefer a bench with drawers in it somewhere along one side or just under the top, with a full-sized shelf a few inches above the floor, where tools and materials may be stored. The elaborate thick-edge maple tops are naturally highly desirable, and also highly expensive. You can get along just as well with a level top made of any kind of 2″ or 3″ lumber, covered with one of the almost indestructible compositions available, such as Masonite. Tip: make it as light in color as possible.

Legs and frame under the top should be of 2″ x 6″ stock—legs can be heavier—braces and shelves of 1″ or thicker wood. Around the top, or at least along the front of the bench, put a little low molding to keep pins, screws and small parts from being accidentally brushed off. (If the bench is level, they will not roll off!) The aluminum counter-edging sold by hardware stores and mail-order houses is excellent for the purpose. The 30″ width is not really needed for working space, but you can set small cabinets, tool racks and mount small shelves on the wall at the back of the bench, or next to the wall, to provide equipment within easy reach from the front of the bench. And no matter how big it is, it will always be crowded.

The first tool, which goes with the bench for consideration, is a vise. Get as big and as good a swivel-base machinist's vise as you can afford. It will handle anything you may run into, excepting removal and replacement of barrels on bolt action rifles, for which jobs only the clamp-type vise is proper anyway. Location should be on a free corner of the bench for full freedom of movement and, an important point too many people do not see until too late, it must be so close to the edge that the inner jaw will be beyond the limit of the bench top in at least one position. Otherwise, you cannot clamp vertically barrels, rods, or bar stock without having them bear against the bench. So, check the frame of the bench and the bolt holes in the vise base, making sure of such a mounting. To be on the safe side, it might be well to buy the vise first and build the bench to accommodate it.

The swivel-base type of vise is not as strong as the rigid base style, especially in the lighter and cheaper makes, but its handiness in all the ninety-nine percent of shopwork requiring a vise makes up for the slight loss of strength necessitated by the movable base. For all normal operations encountered you will find no fault. In size, jaw width and jaw opening should be at least 4″. Vises made by Reed, Morgan or Wilton are considered top grade, although there are a few less-known makes that are every bit as good. Check by weight—good vises are heavy. If a dealer tries to peddle you one just as good and cheaper, yet!—find out how it compares in poundage with a standard cataloged brand.

In addition to the large bench vise a shop needs one or two smaller vises, which can be the cheapest cast-iron junk store breed. These you will maltreat anyway, using them to hold parts for soldering or even welding, and for filing parts, in some instances filing flush with or into the jaws to prevent rounding surfaces.

Purchase or make a tool cabinet for storage of small tools and parts, and obtain a chest with three or four drawers, the ordinary bedroom type, for the keeping of large tools, sandpaper, abrasive cloth, steel wool, pistols in for repair, and so on. The large drawers permit good-sized equipment and keep dust from papers and oiled tools. Also, the top makes a light auxiliary workbench.

A power grinder is a necessity for anyone contemplating any work in metal at all, and any of the small ¼ or ⅓ HP electric double-shaft bench grinders on the market is satisfactory, in 1,750 RPM. Keep a wire brush wheel on one side and a medium-coarse carborundum cutting wheel on the other. For precision grinding of drills and small items a slower speed and finer stone is to be preferred, but for all around work, when only one grinder can be setup, the medium stone is best. It is possible to do quite accurate and controlled grinding on coarse stones by utilizing the side of the wheel, rather than the face, when touching up taps and drills. The medium-coarse and coarse grained wheels are much less likely to burn steel than the finer grades, though of course this is no reason to use them. For some jobs, such as manually grinding down 1917 rifle receiver bridges, the coarse stone is desirable, but this is about the only job in the business really requiring it.

If at all possible, the shop should have a 14″ or 16″ bench or floor type drill press, with chuck capacity for ½″ bits. A bench drill press, set on one end of a narrow but steady table or bench about four feet long, is very efficient, since adjustable rests can be set or built on the bench to hold barrels and complete guns steady and level while drilling. A Palmgren #000 all-angle drilling vise is extremely useful in general, and literally a "must" for any shop doing much mounting of metallic receiver sights or telescopic sights.

A motor sander is vital in the professional shop, and to some extent in the amateur setup. By motor sander I mean a single or double-shaft electric motor, 1,750 RPM, using abrasive-cloth discs backed

.22 LONG RIFLE

MAXIMUM CARTRIDGE

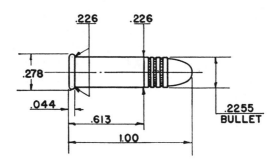

.226   .226

.278

.044

.613

1.00

.2255
BULLET

MINIMUM CHAMBER

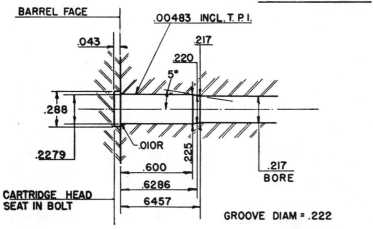

BARREL FACE

.00483 INCL. T. P. I.

.043

.217

.220

5°

.288

.010R

.225

.2279

.600

.6286

6457

.217
BORE

CARTRIDGE HEAD
SEAT IN BOLT

GROOVE DIAM = .222

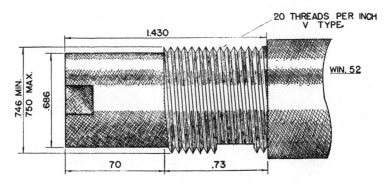

20 THREADS PER INCH
V TYPE

1.430

.746 MIN.
.750 MAX.

.686

WIN. 52

70

.73

by semihard rubber plate. All cutting is done on the side, of course, the work held at right angles to motor shaft. I know of no better way to fit rubber or neoprene recoil pads properly than to use such cutting discs. Also, they save an immense amount of time and labor in shaping up the outside of stock blanks.

Now, for the big item—that lathe. A lathe can be the most important tool in a shop or the least, depending entirely upon the skill of the operator. The skilled machinist or toolmaker who goes into gun work has a great advantage over the average gunnut or even gunsmith, who probably has to teach himself as he goes along. If you cannot cut threads or tapers or any of the usual turning operations, but want to make a firing pin or punch now and then, you can get along by getting a chuck to fit on one of the grinder shafts, holding the material in it and doing the shaping with a file.

However, the gunshop lathe should be large enough to handle a bolt action rifle—receiver with a 26″ barrel—and should have a 1¼″ hole through the head, so that any barrel or blank can be put through for

---

THE .22 LONG RIFLE

I was almost thrown for a loss when I started to get information on the .22 Long Rifle chamber. It seems that there are no standard dimensions anywhere anyhow and besides, every manufacturer uses a different chamber for each type of arm. You can therefore prove me a liar on any of these chambers, but they are suitable to the type of arm listed.

The match cartridge is supposed to be the same in dimensions as the standard, but after using the micrometer on all makes of match .22 ammunition, I have reached the conclusion the manufacturers hold the precision stuff close to the minimum.

The standard chamber has no shoulder at the end of the cartridge case, but it is long enough to freely accept the bullet, which at the lubrication rings is approximately case diameter.

Note: For specifications and drawings of other cartridges, see Appendix II, page 722.

cutting off and crowning. Bed should be not less than 36", although swing does not need to be large. Both three- and four-jaw chucks are needed, two or three lathe dogs, and a drill chuck for the tailstock. Automatic features are naturally desirable of course, but all work can be done manually. Because of the infinite number of off-standard threads and diameters found in gun screws, it is a good idea to get all the threading gears you can. Unless you are specializing in barrel work, only a few draw-in collets are really needed—these in the more common drill rod diameters used for firing pins and screws.

There are half a dozen or more manufacturers of lathes suitable for gunshop use. I cannot attempt to recommend any particular company, since I have not had experience with all makes. South Bend will sell you any small capacity lathe from the little basement home-workshop ones (not recommended) to fancy toolroom equipment costing thousands of dollars. Their bench models in the $400 class are very acceptable for general work, though not large enough for all barrel work. The Sheldon lathe, advertised and recommended for gun work, and capable of handling all barrels, costs over $1000. The Hardinge lathes are long-established in machine shops and toolrooms and have a fine reputation. All in all, talking about lathes is difficult due to the price angle. Good ones cost money, even second-hand, and guncranks and smiths never seem to have much! All I can say—get the best you can.

One of the best buys in the lathe line is the Clausing, made by the Clausing Manufacturing Company, Ottumwa, Iowa. Their 100 series line is listed with $\frac{3}{4}$" bore through spindle, but actually have $1\frac{3}{16}$". This is important because it means that the small lathe will take Enfield, Springfield and Krag military barrels far enough through the head to permit cutting the muzzle back for the short-barrel addicts. About $500 will set one of these, with 36" bed and necessary attachments, including motor, in your shop. The 200 series has $1\frac{3}{8}$" bore and, fully equipped for the gunshop, will run around $1000. These lathes are very well made, with the most modern features, such as enclosed drives, sealed gear box and quick-change gears.

If you are just starting to buy equipment and do not know the score, try to find a machinist who knows something about guns and get him to figure out the size and type lathe most useful in the long run to you. And maybe help you operate it, if you are cautious about starting cold. You can teach yourself, if no trade school or instructor can be found. I know of several men who did just that and who became expert workmen in a very few years. They were of careful temperament, however, the type who think out every move before barging

Author's stockmaking bench. In usual state of disarray, except that there aren't any shavings.

Checkering cradle setting in foreground. Being primarily a metal-worker, I prefer the machinist's swivel-base vise for wood-working.

This bench top is three inches thick, and covered with Masonite, as are all my benches.

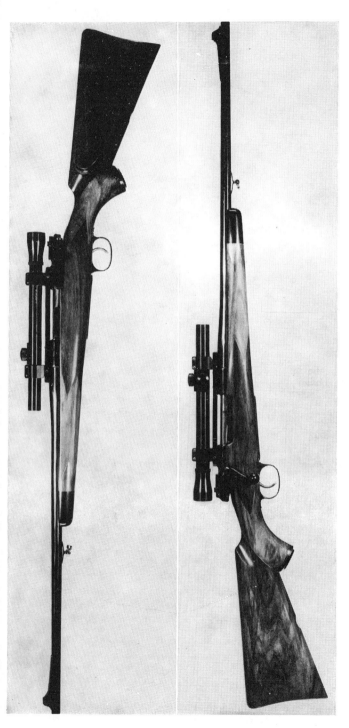

A Bob Owen Sporter

A .270 Mauser, fitted with a 22-inch barrel. This stock was made from a very dense piece of Circassian walnut, of the type known as "cloudy." As in some of my other rifles, the rather large cheekpiece was an attempt to get away from the little thin ones seen on most rifles, the use of which is mainly ornamental.

Many years ago, some well known authors stated there should not be any sharp lines on a sporting stock. I differ with them. The thin sharp lines around a cheekpiece must be left sharp and not dubbed off with sandpaper, as such lines are the signs of careful workmanship. Witness the sharp clean lines around the lock plates of good English shotguns, the drop points, then take a look at the rounded edges of some of our domestic productions.

Perhaps the best examples of American gunstocking were to be found on the old Parker double shotguns, or the old original Dan Lefever guns, but these guns are no longer made and most of the artists who worked on them have passed on to the Great Beyond.

ahead. Personally, I do not qualify myself as a machinist, although I use a lathe and can do most operations. Funny, too—I was once a machine-tool assembler and finisher, did extreme precision work, yet hardly ever used a lathe.

Blueing equipment is the last thing to consider in the gunshop, because it should not be in the shop. I know of only one blueing solution which can be used close to tools and machines without fouling up the atmosphere and rusting everything not coated constantly with cosmoline. If you must have the blueing tanks in the same shop area, put up some sort of partition and install a small exhaust fan to keep fumes away from the shop proper. You will need three tanks and two sets of burners for them, and a polishing layout on either direct drive or polishing heads, presenting for use felt and cloth cutting wheels for rough polishing; more felt and cloth for finer polishing and buffing; and fine steel wire wheels for removing rust incurred in various processes. It is possible to get along with less, but I think five soft "wheels" and one wire brush are the minimum for working efficiently, not having to stop and change from coarse to fine charged wheels every few minutes. One motor can be set to operate a drive shaft and so power two or three polishing heads, but the double-shaft motor, which handles two wheels only allows more freedom of movement.

Lighting a shop is of the utmost importance. You must have the very best possible light to work in, and do not stint on the artificial light. Even the brightest sunlight often is not enough, and take care of dark days and night work with large bulbs. I am against fluorescent lighting. With the large four-tube units it is possible to get enough light if close over the bench, but if suspended even five feet above, they will strain your eyes in time. I had three fluorescents in my shop for about six months, apparently giving wonderful illumination. Then I began to notice my nose getting closer to the work and not seeing so clearly and I developed the choicest case of eye-strain west of the Mississippi—lots of light, but low intensity. So I threw out the fluorescents, put in 300 watt bulbs and worked happily in the glare. Do not stint on the size of the light bill—the few cents more large bulbs cost are not much compared with the cost of a new pair of glasses each year. Gun work is hard on eyes under any circumstances, so give yourself a break on the lights.

You will find use for all the shelves, odd cabinets and racks of various kinds you can think of and for which you can find room. If you go to the expense of having made or you make a very large drawer cabinet, with perhaps 30 drawers, the drawers having an inside dimension of 4″ x 12″ x 24″ you will be going a long way toward an orderly shop.

This chapter has been hard to write, for there are so many items which are at times very useful that could be mentioned, yet can be done without by a resourceful man. Being a Scotsman—though five generations removed—it is painful to mention the expensive gadgets involved. The necessary items are tough enough for the average man starting out. The price of that three-jaw universal chuck alone will buy many good steaks!

CHAPTER 2

Basic Tools

SO FAR the advice has been on just a place to work and the main pieces of equipment required for general gunsmithing. The small tools are the ones used most, either by themselves or in conjunction with lathe or drill press. Here the sky is the limit—you can buy enough hand tools and gimcracks to fill a warehouse—if you have no sales or catalog resistance. As in all phases of life, what you need and what you want do not necessarily coincide. It is hard to resist buying that special micrometer or that set of extra wood-carving chisels, when you can get along very well without them. My weakness is files—I cannot get enough. To be absolutely honest, you do not need a great many tools in a gunshop. You can have endless variety, but you will find that you do not use very many similar items. I will try to cover the tools needed to accomplish the general work encountered in gun repair and alteration, without going very far into the specialized field of barrelmaking.

Measuring tools are probably the first consideration, and the micrometer caliper is the first measuring tool. Get either Starrett, Lufkin, or Brown & Sharpe, 1″ capacity, graduated for ten-thousandths. Whether it has the ratchet handle, or a lock, is up to you. I prefer the plain type myself. Besides the mike, you will need a 6″ narrow steel rule, or scale—as is the proper nomenclature. Also a 12″ steel scale, a steel carpenter's square and a five or six foot steel measuring tape. I find a lot of use for a 6″ vernier caliper and a little—not much —for regular inside and outside calipers. A thread gage can be considered a necessity and a drill gage a luxury. The thread gage, or by its true name, screw-pitch gage, should have a range great enough to cover practically all gun screws; the Starrett Bicycle Screw Pitch Gage No. 157 fills the bill on small screws, and their No. 4 takes care of coarser threads, up to 32 per inch. The No. 157 will handle nearly everything you want it to, however, as most gun screws come in fine thread. And as long as the micrometer works, you have a drill gage.

9

One absolute necessity is a good level suitable for use on gun receivers, sight bases and scope mounts. The Starrett No. 134 is practically perfect. Made like a little try-square, it measures 2" x 3", has three leveling "bubbles" and is so accurately made that it will serve as a try-square itself. Having glass-bubble vials in both arms, it will level vertically as well as horizontally; that is, one arm can be held against a vertical surface and the level read on the right-angle arm. Starrett lists this little tool as "Cross-Test Level and Plumb."

Numerous files are necessary. The ordinary mill-cut file in 8", 10" and 12" lengths probably sees more service than others. Vixens, commonly called auto-body, are useful in the smaller sizes, and a modern Nicholson variation of the vixen type, called super-shear, is very useful. In the special files, I like the 6" and 8" narrow pillar (smooth edge) files, and the same lengths in slim round taper types. Large round files, up to ¾" in diameter are needed, say one 16" and one 12". One 10" half-round file will take care of most large inside curved surfaces. In the small sizes, get a set of die-sinkers files—come in sets of a dozen, all shapes—preferably in 5" length, and, if you think you need them, a set of needle files, 4". The die-sinkers will do nearly everything the needle files will, and much that they will not. The cut of the files is important: get none of the large files in finer than oo, the 6" pillar in o, the die-sinkers in #1, and the needle files in #2. Get two or three odd half-round and pillars in #4 and #6 cut, 5" or 6" for testing metal and making fine finishing cuts. A screw-slotting file, 6", will take care of your narrow slots and cuts. One 10" triangular #0 cut, with teeth ground off for four inches on one side back from tip, is needed for sight dovetail slots.

For working on wood, a small and a large half-round bastard cut are useful, and also a couple of mill-files. These files for wood should be kept separate and never under any circumstances used on metal. One pass across iron or steel and they will not again cleanly cut wood. I do not go for the use of a cabinet rasp on stocks or stock blanks. Anything you can do with a rasp can be done better with files or a sanding disc, with less danger of tearing wood you do not want torn up.

Rifflers, or the specially shaped bent files with teeth only on end portions such as are used by tool and die men, have limited use in general gun work. You should have three, the V, half-round, and flat types. The best rifflers I have seen for gun work are those made by Grobet, of Switzerland. Nicholson makes similar tools, but not in the small sharp-edge types most useful in gun work on V notches or in sharp corners. These are small tools, not the larger silversmith rifflers which are better suited to wood or soft metal. However, a half-round silversmith riffler is quite useful in removing burrs from around holes drilled into rifle receivers, on the inside, of course. Grobet also makes checkering files for checkering or lining metal, cutting parallel grooves. The files vary in length, the 8″ or 10″ being the commonest sizes available. Number of lines to the inch run from 18 to 50. The 24-line is probably the most useful, although the very fine files are better for checkering buttons, triggers, grips and the like.

FILE SHAPES

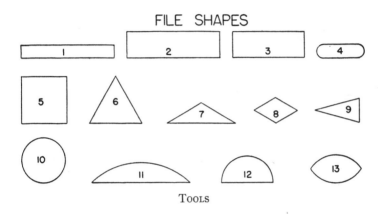

Tools

File Shapes: 1. Thin file—may be either mill or double cut. In the smaller
              sizes, these are somewhat flexible and can be bent or sprung
(Cross-Section) while working, and therefore round off flat surfaces.
          2. The ordinary mill file proportions.
          3. Narrow file, either standard or pillar. Available in almost
             all sizes, widths and cuts, these are the most useful large
             files in the gunshop.
          4. Round edge file. Very useful in rifle action work.
          5. The square file.
          6. The standard triangular file, with faces at 60° angles. (Re-
             member, most dovetails are 45°, so a standard file must be
             ground to different shape.)
          7. Cant file. Teeth on all sides. The barette file is similar, but
             has cut only on bottom.
          8. Slitting, or diamond file.
          9. Knife file. Both this and the cant file are very useful.
         10. Round file.
         11. Half round file.
         12. Pit saw file—this is truly half round. Today usually avail-
             able only in machine saw type.
         13. Pippen file.

In the general run of the files mentioned, I prefer the American Swiss brand, although Nicholson and Disston make good quality files also. American Swiss seems to have the most complete line of special shapes. A file card for cleaning the coarser files is needed and should be used constantly while filing, after every pass or two. Fine-cut files can be cleaned by using the edge of a thin piece of brass or aluminum pushed across the file, paralleling the line of cut of the teeth.

The file has often been acclaimed the most useful of tools, as it is theoretically possible with it to make all other tools. Experience will teach you which types you need and use most. In the larger items, occasionally you may find excellent ones in the local five and dime store, almost always "seconds" from reputable manufacturers which have gone wrong somewhere in the making. The brand names are usually ground off, and most often the cause of rejection is merely a few teeth cut shallow or incorrectly. These cheap pickups can be used for rough work, to save your good files.

Most modern gun steel is soft and tough which makes filing difficult due to the file clogging on almost every stroke. For that reason I seldom use the very fine-cut files, preferring to handle the coarser ones which can be cleaned easier and then finishing with abrasive cloth wrapped around the file, to give a good surface. Just plain use does not bother files as much as you would think—it takes a long time to dull a good one—but improper care can give you headaches. Files should not touch each other, particularly large files. Diamonds cut diamonds, you know, and files damage each other in a hurry if banged together. Best bet is to get a 2″ block of wood, perhaps 6″ x 20″, drill some ¼″, ⅜″ and ½″ holes through it, spaced 1½″ apart, nail it to the top of the bench back by the wall, and set your files therein—the tangs in the holes. This keeps files within reach, visible at all times, and they will not contact each other. The same system can be used with the small files. Should you prefer to use files with handles attached, cut slots in the edge of a narrow board and nail it on the end of the bench or on the wall close by. Handles make filing easier on the fingers, but I lose the "feel" of the file with a handle, and so very seldom use one so fitted.

Unless specialization in stockmaking is anticipated, two planes will be ample—a 12″ smooth plane and a very small one-hand block type (Stanley No. 100). The drawknife is not much use on stocks, but the spokeshave, or cabinet scraper, is quite useful on straight-grained stocks or blanks. You can get started without a brace and bit, although a good brace and a set of screwdriver bits can be quite handy at times.

BASIC TOOLS 13

A good breast drill is a necessity. It must handle up to and include ½″ bits. I use a two-speed Millers Falls model and find it very satisfactory.

The screwdriver problem is always with the gunsmith. The best are none too good, and no matter how many you have, a screw is forever turning up with a different slot. I finally surrendered and now try to keep only four or five good screwdrivers, in the most useful sizes of blades, and from six to a dozen cheap ones of all sorts, which are constantly being ground and filed to fit individual jobs. When a fancy shotgun or scope mount comes in with very tight screws, it is often necessary to file a good blade to fit. *Making* good screwdrivers requires some real knowledge of steel and how to work it. Blades must be forged and tempered just right, for maximum strength without getting them brittle. There are some modern tool steels which can be filed to shape and used without tempering, with pretty fair results. Often blades can be made of heat-treated steel and remain serviceable without treatment after shaping. Overseas, during the war, I made several very good small and medium-sized drivers from Starrett drift punches, which had broken tips. The blade was simply filed on the *head* of the punch, and a handle installed.

Excepting the largest screwdriver, used for removing stock bolts, all gun drivers should have short or medium length shanks, from 1″ to 3″, and large handles, preferably hexagonal or octagonal in cross-section. Both Starret and Brown & Sharpe make good small screwdrivers with removable bits, very handy for revolver screws. Get two or three extra bits and narrow them down for sight and other small screws, also filing the wedge profile out at tip. (Obtain the pocket-type with wooden handle, both small and large size, not the smaller jeweler's screwdrivers.)

The long stock-bolt remover can be a large electrician type, with plastic handle. Drill a ¼″ hole through the handle somewhere, at right angles to shaft, so that a short section of rod can be inserted to make a cross-handle and give added leverage on tight bolts. The shank should be from 8″ to 10″ long.

I think you need three hacksaws—one conventional pistol-grip style, one narrow-frame type of the 10″ size, and one of the small affairs using 6″ blades, for fine work. These little frames are usually made of a single length of rod bent into shape. Only trouble is, you can seldom find extra blades available. Most of your sawing will be done with the narrow-frame 10″ model, which holds the blade much more rigid than the ordinary frame. You will need to keep high-speed blades on hand, in the 18, 24 and 32 teeth-per-inch cuts, and possibly occasionally have

.22 HORNET

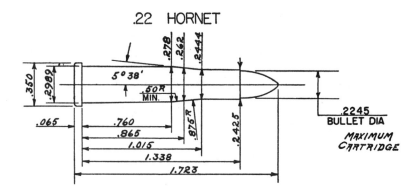

5° 38'
.278 .262 .2444
.350 .2989
.50 R MIN.
.876 R
.065
.760
.865
1.015
1.338
1.723
.2425

.2245
BULLET DIA
MAXIMUM CARTRIDGE

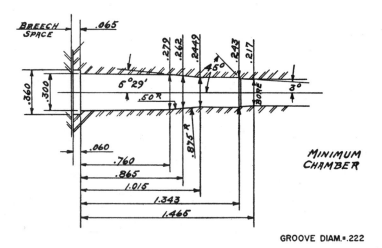

BREECH SPACE
.065
.272 .262 .2449
45°
.243 .217
.360 .300
6° 29'
.50 R
BORE
3°
.060
.760
.865
.875 R
1.015
1.343
1.466

MINIMUM CHAMBER

GROOVE DIAM.=.222

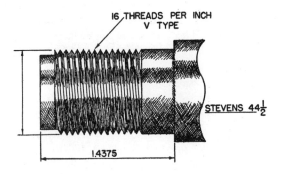

16 THREADS PER INCH
V TYPE

STEVENS 44½

1.4375

use for a coarser blade. One of the very best blades I have used is the "Griffen" brand, of all-hard type. These will cut through Mauser barrels and Enfield ears without losing sharpness and teeth en route. Adkins and Disston make good blades, as well as the other better-known toolmakers. There is a wide variety to choose from—silver, steel, tungsten, the all-hard types, the flexible-back hard edge type and others. Best to buy one of every kind you locate and try them out, settling on that which suits you best. Get some of the ⅝" wide, all-hard, heavy duty blades for the tough jobs. These are really light power-saw blades.

The only wood saw required is the mitre-box backed type, complete

---

THE .22 HORNET

Our smallest commercial center-fire rifle cartridge, the Hornet has a curious history. Winchester brought it out many years ago in black powder, low-velocity form, as the .22 W.C.F. or .22 Winchester Center-Fire. The Germans took it up and during the 1920s began pepping it up, eventually getting around 2300 FPS with metal-jacketed bullets, naming the cartridge the 5.6mm Vierling. A little later some American experimenters, notably Grosvenor Wotkins, began the same process, stepping up the .22 W.C.F. to high velocities in modern steel barrels which would stand jacketed bullets. (Original .22 WCF barrels were nearly all of softer steel.)

Eventually the Hornet name was applied, the cartridge became known as the .22 Hornet, and became entirely separated from its predecessor. Factories adopted it and made strong, heavy-based cartridge cases with thick rims, to prevent its use in old rifles chambered for the .22 W.C.F. or even the 5.6 Vierling, which might not stand the respectable pressures developed by the Hornet loadings. The Hornet cartridge was loaded and sold commercially before any commercial rifle was made in the caliber, incidentally. Winchester first brought out the Model 54 for the Hornet, and then Savage developed the models 23D and 19H. All were bolt actions, and all are now discontinued. Today the Hornet is available in the Winchester 70 and 43 models, and in the Savage 219 singleshot and the Stevens 322 bolt action.

The Hornet loadings can run pressures up to around 40,000 lbs. or better, so require strong actions. The small, tapered case develops considerable back-thrust, and many of the older single-shot actions are liable to set back and develop headspace. The Stevens 44½ action is considered suitable by most barrel men, after a good job of bushing the old block for the modern small rifle primer has been done. The Hornet is rather tricky to reload, in that a combination of loose chamber and tight sizing die can work the brass case excessively and promote ruptures on a third loading. With a little care the individual can of course avoid unnecessary sizing and get along all right.

The .22 Hornet is extremely accurate up to 175 yards and while designed for vermin extermination, is considered quite satisfactory for wild turkey hunting. Handloading can naturally cut the velocity down to whatever is best for other small game shooting and so avoid meat destruction.

with metal mitre-box. Of course, you can get along with a homemade wood mitre, but the metal type, instantly adjustable to any required angle, is so much handier that the greater investment is worth while. The saw itself should not be shorter than 16″ and have not less than 22 teeth-per-inch. Ninety-nine percent of its use will be on buttstocks, changing pitches or shortening for recoil pads, and the finer teeth cut cleaner and tear less wood.

Chisels and gouges are rather hard to procure at the present moment, but some of the gunsmith supply houses have a few from time to time. The English-made carving chisels are the best, made of Sheffield steel. Regardless of shape, the proper name for the wood tool is "chisel" but in this country the term "hand gouge" has appeared, so ask for both when in the hardware stores. The "Acorn" brand, made by Henry Taylor, Ltd., is very good, and the usable tools of the line of Wm. Marples & Sons, Ltd., are excellent. I do not know whether the Addis line is now on the market. If you cannot locate what you want, get your hardware or local tool dealer to contact Alfred Field & Co., Inc., 93 Chambers Street, N. Y. who are the importers of these and other foreign tools.

I would recommend the following, for a minimum set of chisels for stock-making: No. 1, straight, ½″; No. 1, straight, ³⁄₁₆″; No. 10, straight, ½″; No. 10, straight, ¼″; and No. 19, long bent, ½″. This is based on the rather complicated British chart, which allows all sizes and many variations of each type. The No. 1 chisels are ordinary straight, flat wood chisels, the No. 10, curved-edge types, and the No. 19 a curved-edge, curved shank type. A ⁵⁄₁₆″ V-chisel is useful, and this would be a No. 39 straight parting tool. A long-bent parting tool, usually called a veining tool, can be used in cutting borders in checkering. Get the No. 40 in ⅛″. Your curved chisels should all have inside bevel, excepting the largest, a ½″ or ⅝″, which should be altered to outside bevel so that you can use it in barrel channels. In American-made wood chisels, the Buck Brothers brand is excellent, but the line is limited. Get the octagonal wood handles available for the chisels from the makers.

Wood chisels come with edges ground, but not stoned. This you do yourself, using a medium-coarse small round Arkansas stone for the rounded or curved-edge tools, and an oil stone for the flat chisels. For most gunstock work the edges are to be kept razor-sharp, and many expert stockers like to bevel the edge slightly on the back side also.

For sharpening and keeping sharp the edged tools, nothing is better for the flat edges than an old-fashioned natural oil stone. Such stones are almost unobtainable today—indeed, the only concern listing them I know of is the Central Scientific Company, of Chicago. And they probably do not have any in stock. The small 5″ or 6″ hard Arkansas stones, the bonded artificial stones which come in round, square, triangular, half-round and all sorts of shapes, with and without tapers and the white natural Arkansas stones, or "slips" also are used in the smoothing of gun actions.

Before leaving the chisels, better make a note to get a pair of cold chisels, one ¼″ wide, one ½″.

Hammers go with cold chisels (not wood chisels, though) so figure

WOOD CHISELS

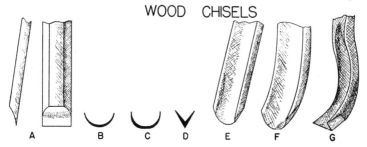

A   B   C   D   E   F   G

Wood Chisels: A. The common straight chisel, available from ⅟₁₆″ to 2″ in width.
B. Curved chisel, or gouge cross section at tip: this is the medium curved type, most useful in stock work.
C. The deep curved chisel, of limited value to the gunsmith.
D. Veining, or parting chisel; in the long bent style, these are used by expert stock men for putting borders on checkering patterns.
E. The straight gouge, or carving chisel.
F. The long bent style, useful in stock work.
G. Short bent, or spoon gouge. Not much good to the gunsmith except in special stock work.

on several. Lead hammers are useful, but do not get or make too large a one. A one-pound head is plenty heavy for your work. Zinc makes a good soft-metal hammer head. Brass and copper have long been favorites in most shops, but I do not particularly like them, due to the fact that they will mark a blued finish to some extent, and even dent very soft steel. A small, light steel hammer, usually found only in the ball-peen type, will find a great deal of use, as will the heavier steel machinist's hammer. My favorite large hammer is one of the type used by blacksmiths in very light forging—its weight, complete with hickory handle is only 12 ounces. The rubber mallet is handy in stock work for tapping actions and guards into stocks, but a rawhide mallet will serve

that purpose and many others. I use the rawhide mallet almost exclusively to remove and replace dovetail sights. No punch, no drift,
no nothin'—just beat happily on the side of the sight itself till it is in
or out, whichever is desired. No chance whatever of marking barrel or
sight base finish as with punches.

The accepted shop practice has been to use brass or copper punches
or drifts on finished steel to avoid marking, but they usually do not
avoid it. Aluminum or duralumin is much better. Get a couple of feet
of $\frac{1}{4}''$ rod, round or square, and cut into $3''$, $4''$ and $6''$ lengths, file tips
to desired shapes and you will have little trouble. Marks left by alumi-
num on steel can be rubbed off with an oily patch, and the blue itself
is not disturbed in the least. On easily-moved parts, fiber drifts can
sometimes be utilized, with no danger of disfiguring a finish. Your real
set of drift or pin punches, for use on gun pins, should be Starrett or
Brown & Sharpe, modified so that the taper will not affect use through
gun receivers, in the smallest sizes made, $\frac{1}{16}''$, $\frac{3}{32}''$ and $\frac{1}{8}''$. Smaller
diameters are made by other companies, but are hard to find. Better
make them, using short lengths of drill rod set into sections of larger
diameter. The Pacific Gun Sight Company furnishes a set, consisting
of several punches with replaceable tips and a nice light little hammer.
Punches larger than $\frac{1}{8}''$ see little use and are easily made of drill rod.
It does not pay to expend great effort in making really good drift
punches, for it seems to me that a good one lasts no longer than a poor
one. The pin part must be tough but not brittle, so it is always getting
burred and must be touched up. For starting very tight pins, drifts
with short points should be used, or a nailset employed. The true drift
punch should not be called upon to do particularly hard work.

Drills should be in complete sets, with at least two extras carried in
the most-used sizes. Get "Number" drills, with a good stand, high
speed type, sizes 1 to 60, extras in Nos. 28, 29, 30, 31 and 34, and
"Fractional Sizes" $\frac{1}{16}''$ to $\frac{1}{2}''$, by 64ths, and if you can afford it now,
the "Letter" series, which will give you a very complete range of sizes.

Taps and dies cost money and you may want to start with just two
or three sets. The 6 x 48 thread is the most widely used, being standard
on most receiver sights and telescope mount bases, so get several taps
and a die. Frank Mittermier supplies adjustable dies, which are the
only type to have, in this size as well as the larger diameters for the
Enfield and Mauser guard screws. Get the one for the Enfield screws,
at least. The 8 x 32, 8 x 36, 8 x 40 and 10 x 32 are threads also encountered in different gun jobs, so taps should be carried in these
sizes. The 8 x 40 is used on the popular Weaver scope mounts, so extra

taps should be obtained. It is now possible to obtain 6 x 48, 8 x 36 and 8 x 40 taps in the two-flute type which is much stronger than the standard three- and four-flute jobs. The two-flute tap is widely used in industrial threading operations and is sometimes called a "gun" tap, not because of any connection with firearms, but because in fast power-driven threading it "shoots" a shaving forward from each cutting edge.

There are also widely-advertised "gun drills" for the purpose of drilling holes in hard receivers without annealing. These are usually Stellite or other hard-face material, and will drill hardened steel. They anneal their way into the metal. The catch is, they require considerable pressure in a good drill press to work, and as most usage would be on case-hardened rifle receivers, drilling into curved surfaces, the problem of holding material rigid so that the drill would not skid or walk away from the desired center is almost unsolvable. If a center is made for the drill, this is not so bad, but if you can make a good crater for a center, you usually can get the hole in with a regular drill. For drilling mounting holes into the tops of rifle receivers, such as the hard Eddystone Enfields, where the action can be supported directly under the drill pressure, the hardened gun drill has some value, but in general, it contributes to more incorrect sight and scope mountings than anything else.

Heat will be needed in many operations, from quick-blueing a screw-head to tempering a spring. An ordinary two-burner gas plate will do a lot of work, and you can lay out from fifty to two hundred and fifty bucks for a little heat-treating unit which may or may not ever pay for itself, but will be just what you need every once in awhile. You will need a small soldering "iron"—copper, that is—and blowtorch too. Personally, I love my welding outfit and do nearly all of my hot jobs with it, one way or another. Most gunsmiths in the past have not done their own welding, having it done by an outside welding shop. This I consider a very great mistake. There is nothing at all difficult about the welding operations connected with gunsmithing if the barest semblance of common sense is applied. The professional welder, however great his experience and skill, seldom can do a perfect gun job because he rarely, if ever, understands what the desired finished result is to be in use and appearance.

The welding unit I find to be perfectly satisfactory for gun use is the Smith Aircraft Torch, with just three tips—Nos. 20, 25 and 27. I have six tips, but the three mentioned are the only ones ever used. The cost of torch, tips, hose, regulators and accessories such as lighter, cleaners and goggles, will be not over $70.00, with the acetylene and oxygen

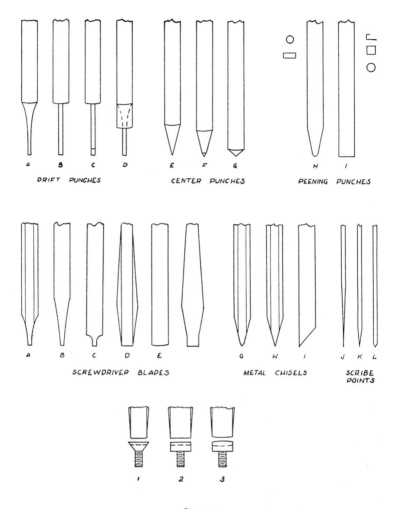

DRIFT PUNCHES   CENTER PUNCHES   PEENING PUNCHES

A   B   C   D   E   F   G   H   I

SCREWDRIVER BLADES   METAL CHISELS   SCRIBE POINTS

A   B   C   D   E   G   H   I   J   K   L

1   2   3

POINTS

I started to title this "Points of Interest," then decided puns were out of place here. These are important.

On the top row we have punches. . . .

A. Standard pin punch. Not good because of taper, which wedges in holes. This is the strongest form of drift punch, however.
B. Straight pin drift. Best for gun work, although not strong.
C. Ditto, with brass tip, for use on soft pins.
D. Standard commercial punch, same as A, with copper or brass sleeve over tapered portion. This is about the best for gun use.

available from local welding supply establishments. Four kinds of welding rod should be kept on hand—3½% nickel-steel, very hard to obtain; vanadium steel; ordinary low-carbon rod; and any of the patented hard-surfacing rods. The nickel-steel rod, in ⅛" diameter, will do for 95% of all gun-welding. It alloys perfectly for bolt handle alterations, flows easily, and blues well. Later on in the story we will go into welding further, and indeed, in all phases of specialized gun work and bring into print the extra tools needed for such operations.

E. Prick punch, or sharp center punch. Used only for locating the centers of holes.
F. Ordinary center punch.
G. Shallow, or wide cone center punch, to enlarge marks of the other tips.
H. A peening punch, which can be made as cross section of tip is shown— both hemispherical tipped, and rounded straight edge.
I. Round, square and rectangular flat end peening punches. These should be made of tool steel, hardened and polished.

On the bottom row we have a few edges. . . .

A. The better type of commercial screwdriver, shown in profile. These are okay for much gun work.
B. Ordinary commercial screwdriver, with wedge profile. Not so good as these slip, tear and burr up screw slots.
C. The strongest tip available, shown in cross section. You will have to make these and they can be made of round tool steel stock.
D. Face view of commercial blade, with wedge visible. These will bevel screw head countersinks unless care is observed.
E. Correct gun screwdriver edge, for milled slot screws. The edge should be straight for cut slots.
F. Commercial blade with edge cleared for gun use. Can be used for counter sunk heads safely.
G. The standard cold chisel.
H. Sharp metal chisel—can be used only for light work on steel, but best shape for soft metal.
I. Sharp single bevel chisel. Very useful for cutting burrs or extruded metal away inside receivers, when the metal cannot be peened back in place.
J. Needle point scribe. The most accurate, but the most fragile.
K. A stronger tipped scriber, with better proportions.
L. Scriber with shallow cone tip, not so good.

Figures 1, 2 and 3 show the three most common types of screw head and slot, with the appropriate screwdriver blade for most efficient use on each. Note that in 1 the blade must only be as wide as the *bottom* of the slot in the screw head. If wider it will gouge into the countersink first, then be lifted higher in the screw slot and not give much holding or turning effort through lack of full engagement with the slot.

The foregoing items are those to be considered needed to start a gun-shop and do the general run-of-mill jobs encountered. In the matter of supplies to be carried, the type of work to be expected must influence buying. If woodworking is heavy the shop should have a wide assortment of sandpaper, linseed oil, tung oil, Japan drier, turpentine, dry shellac, prepared white shellac, orange shellac, spar varnish, color in oil (burnt umber, sienna, and such) varnish remover and practically everything else found in a paint store except paint! If stock work is only occasional or done only in conjunction with fitting of recoil pads, you will not need so much. Sand or garnet paper in o, 2–o, 4–o, 6–o and 8–o, linseed oil (boiled), spar varnish, coloring agents, both white and orange shellac, shellac sticks, and dark mahogany stain will take care of you.

Steel wool is needed in both stock and metal work, in oo and oooo sizes; the oooo or 4/o is hard to locate, costs about $1.oo a pound (one pound goes a long way) and is made by the SOS Company, of Chicago. Its great value is its ability to remove fine rust from blued arms without scratching the finish.

Abrasive cloth comes in grits up to 600 fine and the gun shop should have sheets and strips in Nos. 120, 150, 240 and 320 at minimum, and finer if available. The 240 and 320 grit will see more service than the others. Emery cloth is not so good compared to the newer aloxite and carborundum types. Crocus cloth is needed for polishing, and at least one cutting powder should be kept on hand for lapping holes and miscellaneous jobs. I use emery "flour" for such work, some old stuff I have had for years. Today you can buy patented lapping compounds which are no doubt better, since you can pick and choose for whatever jobs you have to do. Best thing to do is get literature from the companies making or selling toolroom equipment and see what they can furnish at the moment. Norton and Behr-Manning make a great variety of grinding components, and their lapping compounds, in powder form, can be had for any type of metal or finish.

Wood dowels should be available locally, in $\frac{1}{2}''$ and $\frac{5}{8}''$ diameters for making repeating shotgun magazine plugs, and in smaller sizes for odd jobs.

Drill rod must be carried in stock for making pins, screws, firing pins and small tools. In round rod, get as many different small sizes, under $\frac{5}{16}''$, as you can, and also one rod each in $\frac{3}{8}''$, $\frac{1}{2}''$, $\frac{5}{8}''$, $\frac{3}{4}''$ and $1''$. In flat drill rod—yes, it comes round, flat and square—get $\frac{1}{32}''$ by as wide as is available at the time, $\frac{1}{16}'' \times \frac{1}{2}''$, $\frac{3}{16}'' \times \frac{1}{2}''$, wider if you can obtain it, $\frac{1}{8}'' \times \frac{1}{4}''$, $\frac{1}{8}'' \times \frac{3}{4}''$, and some $\frac{3}{16}''$ and $\frac{1}{4}''$ square.

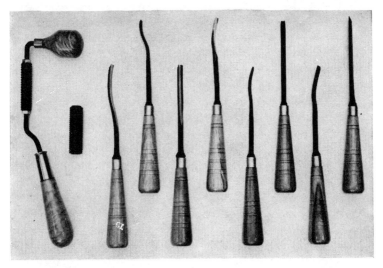

Z. S. Denman's handmade stock chisels and gouges, and barrel channel rasp. Excepting the straight veining tool, all are forged to maximum strength. Made of the best steel, these are the best tools of the kind made in America today and equal in quality to English wood-carving chisels. Mr. Denman is conscientiously trying to improve them constantly, so we may expect to have excellent inletting tools available from here on out. The barrel rasp can be had with cutters from $\frac{1}{2}$ to $\frac{3}{4}''$ diameter, for smoothing various diameters of barrel channels.

A SMALL AND MODERN GUNSHOP

Main working section of author's shop. We cleaned up the counter enough to see over it, but that's all. The drawer-cupboards contain most of the small items usually found on the backboard of the gunshop bench.

This room is approximately eighteen feet square and is just about right for the amount of equipment in it, for a one-man shop. A power saw and air-compressor are concealed by the high counter in foreground.

At the opposite end of building are blueing room and polishing equipment, the former being enclosed to prevent moisture damaging guns or equipment in the main shop. In the center of the building is the store section, where the camera was set up. This has showcase, wall shelves and gun racks, etc. The working areas of the shop are blocked off by breast-high counters which allow the customers and visitors to see everything without getting their fingers against anything hot or sharp! Drill press, grinder and barrel vise are mounted on a small heavy table in center of the main shop area.

Drill rod is definitely not the best material for pins and screws, but it is often the only easily-obtained steel of known characteristics obtainable. And while tool steel firing pins are better, there are probably five times as many repair or replacement jobs in the field today with drill-rod pins than those of all other materials combined.

In tool steels, carry the ground flat stock made by the tool companies such as Starrett, Brown & Sharpe, or Disston. Only a few sizes are needed, and the expense is not great. You will need $\frac{1}{16}''$, $\frac{3}{32}''$, $\frac{1}{8}''$, $\frac{5}{32}''$, $\frac{3}{16}''$ and $\frac{1}{4}''$. Get the thinner sizes in as wide widths as available; $\frac{1}{32}''$ flat stock is useful in making laminated-head checkering tools. In round tool steel, get $\frac{1}{4}''$, $\frac{5}{16}''$ and $\frac{1}{2}''$, buying other sizes as you need it. The round stock will not be finished on the outside, and the surface must be turned off before anything can be made. In other words, you need $\frac{5}{16}''$ steel to make a $\frac{1}{4}''$ diameter pin or screw. Be sure you find out the hardening and tempering characteristics of the round stock.

Get whatever cold-rolled steel you can pick up besides $\frac{1}{4}''$, $\frac{3}{8}''$, $\frac{1}{2}''$ and $1''$ round. Hit the nearest large machine shop or steel warehouse and prowl through their scrap box to find the short cut-off ends and odd lengths discarded in regular sale. In this way you can save cutting charges at least, and the general run of prices will be a little lower.

For spring stock, purchase untempered flat spring stock in $\frac{1}{32}''$ and $\frac{1}{16}''$ thickness, $\frac{1}{4}''$ and $\frac{3}{8}''$ widths, some clock spring stock—as many sizes as you can find, and an assortment of finished coil springs of as much variety as possible, from $\frac{5}{16}''$ diameter on down. Large hardware stores and mill supply houses carry these, in lengths from $2''$ to $6''$, as a rule. If good spring wire is available, get a supply of this, too.

CHAPTER 3

Extra and Special Tools

THE preceding chapter lists the general equipment needed to get along on, but there are quite a few additional tools which simplify many jobs and should be added to the shop sooner or later—preferably sooner.

Clyde Baker went to some lengths to popularize the dental engine as a light power tool capable of many types of work in cutting, grinding and polishing. If a dental engine can be obtained, it can be extremely useful in metalworking. The burrs are hard enough to cut steel, and when no longer sharp enough for the dentist, still useful to the gunsmith. So talk to your dentist not only about his rounding up an old dental engine for you, but about his saving up his used burrs for you. A new outfit will cost from $75.00 up, today. Basically, the dental engine is a light flexible shaft grinder, with a trick head.

Burrs come in various types and in sizes from No. ½ to No. 11, ranging from about .023″ diameter. No. 6 is .067″, a handy size for countersinking sight apertures, or straight drilling. Round-end burrs can be used as light center punches, since they will not slip or skid, and on occasion you can use them to eat through a thin case-hardening. Figure 7, the inverted cone shape, makes a fine little milling cutter for hard surfaces, and the fissure burr, plain in Figure 8A and crosscut in Figure 8B, is good for working inside small holes, clearing slots, or enlarging. Reamers, large burrs, mandrels for holding polishing wheels, and of course the wide selection of mounted grinding wheels are sold by dental supply houses, such as the S. S. White Dental Manufacturing Company. The dental engine has a peculiarity all its own. Remember the "hammered fillings" in your back teeth? It hammered 'em, with the head adjusted to give a very rapid, short hammering or punching movement instead of rotation. This hammering or peening motion can be utilized when matting ramps, riveting small pins in place, or even stippling.

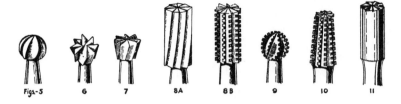

Figs.-5   6   7   8A   8B   9   10   11

The modern competitor of the dental engine in the gunsmithing field is the ubiquitous hand grinder. These little direct drive hand tools are found in almost all workshops today. Made by a half-dozen different companies, in prices from ten to thirty dollars, usually sold with a small case and an assortment of wheels, burrs, sanding discs, little carborundum cut-off wheels and countless other gadgets, the hand grinder can be a great help. *But don't try to inlet stocks with it!*

My own hand grinder is one of the most popular makes. It is the "Handee" made by the Chicago Wheel Company, 1101 W. Monroe, Chicago, Illinois. It is available with either $\frac{1}{16}''$ or $\frac{1}{8}''$ collets, or chucks—better get both—and will take any attachment with $\frac{1}{16}''$ or $\frac{1}{8}''$ shank. Not all attachments are available in either shank size, so be able to use any of them. The little cut-off wheels and differently-shaped bonded rubber polishing heads are invaluable when altering bolt notches and the cylindrical stones almost a necessity for cutting the recess in receiver for altered bolt handles. The little brushes are not much use—the speed of the tools is too great for wire brushes—but the tiny sanding drum with its replaceable coarse, medium and fine carborundum and aloxite bands really *is* useful. Not only for polishing in small radius curved surfaces in general, but for cleaning the toolmarks from bolt sleeves prior to blueing, where the ordinary polishing wheels and mandrels do not reach. The very small diameter cylindrical stones, with $\frac{1}{16}''$ shank, are excellent for getting in notches and holes.

The steel burrs usually furnished with the tools are for wood and plastic, not steel, but special tool steel burrs for steel are made today. They cut a little faster than the stones and the pointed type will get into a corner.

Hand grinders must be used with discretion. They cannot be pushed very hard, as the low-powered universal electric motors heat up rapidly. Used sensibly, they are a great help. I use mine as a last resort—after I cannot do the job with files or the large bench grinder—and so far have not burned out anything but one set of bearings.

Comparing the hand grinder with the dental engine, each has individual advantages. The dental engine is variable speed, which is a valuable factor, and is perhaps easier to manipulate. It will not do as heavy work as the hand grinder, nor take as many special accessories. The hammering or peening action is valuable. A special hand-tool on the market, the Burgess Vibro-Tool, does have the peening motion and can be used in matting and stippling.

Sharpening drills is a little art in itself, and since the gunsmith uses small drills predominantly, a drill-grinding attachment for the bench grinder is a good gadget to have around. The commercial models will barely handle drills as small as No. 31, which the gunsmith uses most, but they can be fixed up and adjusted to do the job. It is important that this drill not cut oversize. In that tool-assembly job I had once, I had to drill and tap fifty-six holes, of several sizes, in one fairly small casting, and I learned quite a bit about hand grinding drills. More than most gunsmiths and machinists ever learn—and I still do not trust my eye and hand to do a perfect job.

I do not believe the average gun shop absolutely requires a surface plate. If you want to lay out mounting jobs, tools, or sights on something flat, head for the biggest auto junk yard you know of and buy the biggest old-fashioned plate-glass windshield they have. On the surface plate deal, a good one of the size required by the gunsmith, which is a minimum length of 30″, will cost more than it will be worth to you. I remember one I made years ago; the casting was seasoned three years; it was milled and shaped as close as machinery could get it; and then I spent eleven working days finishing the surface, to one thirty-thousandth of an inch. Our instruments would not check any closer. It was 30″ x 42″ in area. Now do you understand why surface plates cost so much?

Your little toolmaker's level and some leather vise jaws will take care of all the leveling necessary in sight and scope mounting.

Several sets of "soft" vise jaws, or false jaws, will be absolutely needed. Lead jaws push out of shape so quickly I have quit using them for the most part. Instead, I keep some thin sheet lead on hand, both $\frac{1}{16}$″ and $\frac{3}{16}$″, and when lead jaws are needed, snip out enough for the immediate job. Sheet copper, about $\frac{1}{8}$″ thickness, is very useful and jaws are easiest made by cutting a piece to exact width of the vise jaws proper, and the opposite dimension to measure $1\frac{1}{2}$″ above top of vise when jaws are clamped together, and as deep as the steel faces of the vise. Just hammer the exposed portion down over the vise, repeat the process to make another false face for the steel, then close the vise with both copper jaws in place and beat the whole surface with the steel hammer. This will produce a pair of jaws to protect your work which will not fall on the floor when you open the vise. A pair of protecting jaws which *will* fall on the floor, but are perhaps the most useful of all types are those made of a single strip of heavy sole leather, bent in the middle to form a "U." I use this type more than any other. Good for either wood or metal.

Wood vise jaws are limited to special purposes, such as grooved to hold round stock, or tongue-and-grooved or mortised to hold odd shapes without distortion, such as triggerguards. I believe one of the handiest jaw arrangements would be to have perfectly flat polished steel false jaws, which could grip flat gun parts without marring. These I have not tried, but am going to some day.

Plain wood vise jaws can easily be made to fit your vise, with either felt or leather gripping surface. I prefer leather to felt, as it is possible to check the leather at a glance for filings or anything which might mar a gun part, and clean the surface with a pass or two from a wire brush.

BOTTOMING TOOLS

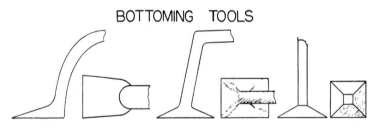

Bottoming Tools: Here are shown three types of bottoming tools, which are really chisels with shanks so located as to permit use of the tool in the inletted portion of a stock, to clean out corners and level off the receiver bed. The type at right has vertical shank, with blade sharpened on all sides, so that the tool will cut in any direction. The middle tool is designed to cut on the front and the side edges, and the tool at left to cut on the front edge only.

Special rasps and bottoming tools speed up the stockmaker's work, and while most useful sizes are available commercially, from Mittermeier and others, it is not particularly difficult to make what you need if you have more time than money. Barrel inletting rasps are very easy to make with the lathe. Just turn a section of steel to whatever length and diameter is wanted, cut the teeth, drill and thread one end for a handle and finish it up to your own desired specifications. Naturally, hardened tool steel is best, but plain cold-rolled round stock, cut to shape and case-hardened, will do very well.

Bottoming tools are simply specially-shaped wood chisels to cut in out-of-the-way spots, to get down and level off the bottoms of stock inletting cuts without bothering the edges. You can have as many shapes as you wish, but one or two are all you will need. I consider a bottoming tool useful only for cleaning up corners and smoothing sunken surfaces, not for any real cutting or inletting.

A woodworker's vise and a checkering cradle are further aids to the stock man, although an ordinary swivel-base machinist's vise seems more useful to me than the wood vise. The checkering cradle can be made like the illustration, adjustable for one-piece rifle stocks, or buttstocks only, either rifle or shotgun.

Checkering tools of similar design are put out by several men in this country. All use a minimum of two cutting heads, one for lining, or laying out the checkering pattern, and one for cutting the grooves. Checkering is actually sawed into wood, not cut as with a chisel. Most, if not all, of the commercial tools are descended from the old German type and try to cut two or even three grooves at a time.

None of the commercial tools will do better than a third-rate job of checkering, nor will any tool ever be sold which will do fine work. For really good checkering, the tool must have very fine, shallow teeth: hardened or unhardened, these dull rapidly, so that often a tool must be sharpened before it finishes a single job on a stock of good hard wood.

All the expert stock men I know, without exception, use a two-line layout tool, or liner, to mark the checkering pattern, cutting shallow grooves, then deepen these grooves, or lines, with the single-edge checkering tool, which they make and sharpen themselves. Curved triangular files and die-sinker's V rifflers have been used to do good checkering, and the handmade tools approximate the blades of these. The good American custom stocker usually makes his tool of drill rod or tool steel, shaping it to his taste, cutting simple cross teeth without much rake or individual edges, and uses it as is, without hardening or tempering. It cuts only wood, and when dulled can be sharpened in a couple of minutes with very fine file or chisel.

The bordering tool, sometimes used to outline the edges of the checkering pattern, can be of two or three different designs, to cut a single deep half-round groove, or two narrow V grooves with a wider low-relief raised rounded center. The border is often used to disguise a few spots where the checkering tool overran the edges of the pattern,

CHECKERING TOOLS

but a really good border adds to the appearance. And, contrary to some past printed words it is harder to turn out a nice pattern with a border than to do the highly-touted "borderless" checkering. Thomas Shel-

---

CHECKERING TOOLS

Here we have something worth while. I show only the blades and the principles—the shape of your handle and styling of the shanks is up to your own prescription. Scale, approximately 4-1.

A. Side view of layout tool. (Also called spacer and liner.) Note that there is no rake or saw effect, and that the edge is curved slightly.
B. Cross sections of spacers, giving you your choice of notches to file along the middle. X and Y show the amount of the teeth that do the work. In other words, no greater depth than limited by the dotted lines is permissible with this tool.
C. Approximate full size sketch of a checkering tool, of the type made and used by Shelhamer in his matchless work. (No, he will not make you a tool.)
D. The actual checkering tool, used to deepen the layout lines made by the spacer. This is the type with file cut teeth, raked as shown. The teeth are to be approximately .001" deep. I like a slightly curved edge for this also, so that some of the teeth besides the pair on the front end do a little cutting.
E. This is the ticket—same as above, but with chisel cut teeth. The edge is really a tiny hand cut file, or riffler. The dotted lines represent a low angle handle, which is very useful on forend checkering.
F. Now, here is something the boys never bothered to tell you before—the angle of the checkering tool edge. It is important, too. For good wood—hard, close textured—make it 100°. The diamonds in your checkering will not only be stronger, but will look a lot better.
G. A 110° or 115° angle tool should be used for softer woods, to make shallower diamonds, which of course are stronger. This permits 20 line checkering on ordinary American walnut, as a rule.
H. A bordering tool, in cross section, which is to be made in the same way as a checkering tool. It is used to cut a rounded groove around the pattern.
I. Another bordering tool, which is to be sharpened all the way across the bottom—in the shallow hollow and on the edges. Hard to make.
J. Profile of the chisel used to cut teeth on the tools. You may have to experiment to find out exactly which angle of tip suits you best—it all depends on how you hold the chisel when cutting the teeth.
1. Section of checkering as done by two groove commercial tool. These, or the three groove type cut only on the tips of the teeth.
2. Ditto, with commercial single tool or bent file for tool.
3. Sharp checkering—okay except that diamonds break off easily.
4. Correct checkering, in proportion of the height of the diamonds to the width.

hamer does the most perfect checkering I have ever seen, though John Hearn turns out some beautiful jobs.

Both bordering and lining tools, also called spacers, can be purchased, rather than made. To make a plain V groove for a border, a small curved veining tool, or V-edge wood chisel can be used. Should you desire to make your own lining tools, it is wise to use drill rod for material, for these can be hardened and so remain sharp for some time as they see little use. A laminated tool can be made, using $\frac{1}{32}''$ steel for blades and whatever spacer or shim stock is required to obtain the desired distance between the two edges. Make nothing but two-line spacers. The common sizes are $\frac{1}{16}''$, $\frac{1}{18}''$, $\frac{1}{20}''$, $\frac{1}{22}''$ and $\frac{1}{24}''$, to give either 16, 18, 20, 22 or 24 lines of checkering to the inch. If a solid tool is made, the head is forged thick enough and center slot or groove cut with file or milling cutter. The illustrations show the types of heads to be shaped up.

I personally have little use for the characters who think they have to put 28 line checkering on stocks, even when the wood is hard and close-grained enough to hold it. They think fine checkering looks nicer than coarse. It does—when second rate on both. A mediocre job in fine lines does not show the slips and uneven diamonds visible in a similarly slipshod coarse line pattern. Very little stock wood today, even imported walnut, will hold finer than 22 line checkering perfectly, and the average American walnut blank is best off with 18 line. Some wood is so soft as to require 16 line spacing.

The checkering tool itself can be made by filing from drill rod, tool steel, or metal cut from an old file, after annealing. Make the edge like the illustration, so that a cross-section would show an approximate angle of 100 degrees. This will give each diamond a slope of approximately 50 degrees, which will make it strong enough to hold in good wood. For soft wood, the angle should be increased, so that diamonds will be shallower and therefore stronger. The best-cutting edge will be cut with a chisel—the teeth, I mean—exactly as a hand-cut file is made. The chisel cross-section is shown, and this chisel is used to cut single teeth on each side of the checkering tool edge. The teeth are actually only small burrs raised on the face of the tool. Some little practice is necessary to be able to sharpen the tool in a hurry, but when the knack is attained, a dulled tool can have its teeth filed off and new ones cut in a very short time.

If the chisel routine seems too hard, you can attempt to cut deeper teeth with a sharp file. A needle type three-square with teeth ground off one side, will do fairly well. It should be 6 cut, which is the finest normally available. The teeth are to be filed with slight angle to the rear, so the tool will cut on the forward stroke more than on the rearward, and are not to have much rake. Do not attempt to get a saw-like edge in the center—just plain little serrations will do. As mentioned before, the men who do a lot of checkering seem to prefer to keep this tool unhardened, and touch up the edges frequently. Probably the fact that it would be rather difficult to heat and harden the blade without dulling the tiny cutting edges is the main reason.

The beading punch, also a German idea, has little merit. It is a punch on the order of a nailset, with hollowed tip, so that when placed on wood and tapped with a light hammer, it leaves a round dot. This is generally used to cover up uneven lines or diamonds at the border of the checkering pattern, often at the corners. I have seen quite a few old German-made sporter stocks with the points of the pattern beaded, but do not believe even the Germans have used the idea for twenty-five years.

If you want to play with one, just buy a large nailset—$3/32''$ or so diameter at tip—turn a bit of brass rod $1/8''$ in diameter to a rounded end, not quite hemispherical, and with lapping compound polish out a rounded hollow in the end of punch. Chuck the nailset in the lathe and the lapping rod in the tailstock, to do the job in a hurry; practically painlessly.

Today every gunsmith should have headspace gages in .30–06 and 8x57mm Mauser, whether he does any barrel fitting or not. By charging half a buck for checking the souvenir German rifles and N.R.A. Enfields and Springfields the careful customers bring in, the price of gages can be made up in a short time. The intelligent men will not mind in the least paying for safety. So get gages, from Wilson or Forster Brothers.

You can find use for many machinist's gages and should add them to the shop inventory as you go along. Combination squares, telescoping gages to measure shotgun barrels and chokes, inside transfer micrometers (actually expandable steel gadgets which are inserted into openings, adjusted to size then measured with the regular micrometer, a depth micrometer (for checking firing pin protrusion and making snap-gages for the same purpose), center and dial indicators for the lathe, thickness or feeler gages and whatever other items in the Starrett, Lufkin or Brown & Sharpe tool catalogs for which you find a need. Something is always attractive—right now I see a Starrett tool I think I will get—their Universal Scraper, No. 194. An inexpensive little cabinet scraper with adjustable handle and blade guard. It will be

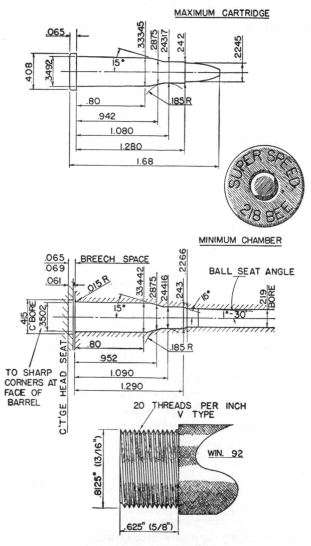

THE .218 WINCHESTER BEE

The popularity of the .22 Hornet and the .22/3,000 Lovell cartridges prompted Winchester to bring out the .218 Bee, and the Model 65 lever action rifle for it. The rifle was not accurate enough to get the best out of the cartridge, and is now obsolete. No factory rifle except the Winchester M43 bolt action is now available.

The Bee is slightly faster than the Hornet, and a much better cartridge for the reloader. Winchester ballistics for the .218 give it 2,860 FPS at the muzzle.

very handy for cleaning factory varnish off shotgun stocks before refinishing and for squaring up the backs of recoil pads.

All the tool manufacturers mentioned make one type of gizmo no
bench should be without—the automatic center punch. These are
spring-loaded double-action punches, used without a hammer. The
point is placed on the work and the handle pressed down, compressing
the spring to a certain point when the force is released and delivered
to the hardened point, driving it down. I have all three sizes, small,
medium and large, but the middle number, a Starrett No. 18A, is all
that is really needed. I find it possible to do a great many jobs with it
easily which would be difficult with the old hand-and-hammer method.
Most important, it is easy to keep in place while punching, and as the
force of the blow is adjustable through regulation of the tension on the
spring, a light mark can be made first on delicate jobs, checked for
position, then corrected if necessary and deepened. For positive location, most toolmakers make their initial centers with prick punches,
which are plain center punches with long, tapered, sharp points. The
true center punch has a shallow cone point and it is wise to make a
few punches with varying cones. You want a wide crater, comparing
width to depth, to start the drill point. No drill is ever as pointed as a
punch at its very tip.

Scribers can be made of drill rod ground and stoned to needle-sharp
points, hardened, then stoned again. You can buy scribers with handy
knurled handles and replaceable tips very reasonably, but I believe
it best to make your own. I have a Starrett, but seldom use it any more.
I honestly believe that it is more practical to deliberately *not* make
really good scribers. That sounds silly when spoken, and looks odd on
paper, I know. But—if you make a good scriber you will be forever
tempted to use it after it gets dull and will always be putting off sharpening it, while if you just clip off a four-inch section of $\frac{1}{16}''$ drill rod,
point it up and use it, when it dulls you will not stop for a second be-

---

Any action suitable for the Hornet is also suitable for this cartridge, and
many large bolt actions have been altered for it, for use as vermin rifles in
settled country, where the violent report of the larger .22 center-fires is
objectionable. The Winchester Model 65 rifle was essentially a dolled up
Model 92, and old '92s can be made into Bee rifles by the installation of a
Model 65 .218 barrel. The barrel shank dimensions are the same on both
models.

The .218 Bee is based on the .25–20 repeater cartridge—it withstands
repeated reloading much better than does the Hornet case.

fore repointing it. And you can make half a dozen in fifteen minutes, so always have a couple of sharp spares ready.

Toolmaker's parallel clamps are vital to scope and sight mounting, and a pair of the 2½″ or 3″ jaw length should be purchased, and also one small clamp, the 1⅝″ jaw length, or smaller, opening to ¾″. These items are usually sold in pairs, but many hardware houses will break a set. Pin vises come in extremely handy and a complete set should be acquired, to hold round material up to .187″. Get the knurled-round-handle type, all metal, and you can clamp these handles in the three-jaw lathe chuck when necessary. Although they seldom center perfectly, they are quite useful for holding small short screws for reshaping or polishing heads, without burring the threads.

So far I have omitted mention of pliers, for the reason you really do not need as many as a filling station, in spite of most writers on gunsmithing. The Bernard #402 parallel-jaw type sees more use in my shop than any other single tool, I believe. The type of jaw enables round work to be held firmly, and the tool is indispensable for inserting pins, holding bolt action firing assemblies, small parts for grinding and so on. A good pair of side-cutters, for snipping off soft wire and pins, and a good quality needle-nose pair for springs will take care of the plier problem, with a pair of the common dime store cast steel or iron pliers thrown in to handle hot metal and pans. The Bernard tool really is indispensable, and I even make little brass and lead jaws for it, as for the vise, to protect finished work.

Many of your small bench accessories will be made up as you need them. Wood blocks for sandpaper and abrasive cloth, slotted mandrels for the drill press to take a strip of the cloth and polish holes, arbors to fit the bolt runways of rifle receivers and shotgun chambers, plugs for removal of barrel dents in shotguns, shaped wooden wedges to hold stocks level in the mitre-box—a thousand and one little things to help you work better and faster.

In machine tools you can add a milling machine; the small bench type takes up less space and handles nearly all gun jobs. Indeed, a milling attachment for the lathe will do most of them, without costing very much. A small shaper—not the bench type—has some purpose, especially for removing the "ears" on Enfield receivers, which are tough on milling cutters. However, a shaper should be considered strictly a "luxury" tool for the small shop. The tool-post grinder is necessary for making reamers, but you are better off buying your chambering reamers. It is not too difficult to rig up a tool-post holder for the small hand grinder, for light inside grinding and polishing.

CHAPTER 4

Reference Books and Sources of Supply

A SMALL shop library is of considerable use to the gunsmith. It is not possible to remember everything, and the customers are liable to look down on you if you cannot answer questions on any type of arm they hear about. The shop should have not only instructive books on gunsmithing, but reference works on modern and recently obsolete guns, tool, gun parts and supply catalogs. Many tool and hardware supply houses put out postcards and folders every time they receive a stock of small items, and it pays to get on the mailing lists. I will try to list references and suppliers of value in the gunsmithing field who are most likely to remain in business for many years to come.

Reference and Technical Books

The Rifle in America (Sharpe): Lists practically all American rifles and cartridges up to 1940 developments. Valuable for identification of old arms. Published by Wm. Morrow & Company, New York.

Professional Gunsmithing (Howe): An extensive work, mainly devoted to the type of repair jobs which come into the general gunshop. Very complete in this respect and covers all types of firearms. Published by T. G. Samworth, Georgetown, South Carolina.

Advanced Gunsmithing (Vickery): Especially useful to the skilled man, for metal work. Published by T. G. Samworth, Georgetown, South Carolina.

The Book of Pistols and Revolvers (Smith): The standard work on handguns. Published by The Stackpole Co., Harrisburg, Pa.

The Book of Rifles (Smith): A companion work on rifles. Published by The Stackpole Co., Harrisburg, Pa.

Small Arms of The World (Smith): The current authority on military small arms of the world. Published by The Stackpole Co., Harrisburg, Pa.

Book of the Springfield (Crossman): Devoted to the 1903 Springfield, much of the information can also be applied to other bolt actions. Published by T. G. Samworth, Georgetown, South Carolina.

37

Firearm Blueing & Browning (Angier): A book of formulae and processes for finishing metal, with considerable useful information on various chemicals and acids. Published by T. G. Samworth, Georgetown, South Carolina.

Book of the Garand (Hatcher): Devoted to the M1 rifle, this is a very well illustrated book which will be of value when the M1 rifle becomes more easily available to shooters. Unless the gunsmith has had army armorer experience with the M1, he is going to need this book. Available from N.R.A., Washington, D. C.

Gunstock Finishing and Care (Newell): The first work on this subject, this book is a very complete job of describing just about every known type of finish possible for a stock, with directions for making your own fillers. sealers and finishing compounds. Published by T. G. Samworth, Georgetown, South Carolina.

The Gunsmith's Manual (Stelle & Harrison): A reprint of one of the earliest gunsmithing books, quite valuable for general information in working on obsolete arms. Published by T. G. Samworth, Georgetown, South Carolina.

Catalogs and Handbooks

Lufkin (The Lufkin Rule Company, Saginaw, Michigan): Makers of all types of mechanical measuring devices and precision tools.

Starrett (The L. S. Starrett Company, Athol, Massachusetts): Makers of precision tools and equipment, similar to Lufkin.

Winchester Ammunition Guide (Winchester Repeating Arms Co., New Haven, Connecticut): Lists all Winchester ammunition, with ballistic tables.

Western Ammunition Handbook (Western Cartridge Co., East Alton, Illinois): Same as above, covering Western ammunition.

Parts Catalogs: Put out by the arms manufacturers, covering current available parts for arms of their own manufacture:

Winchester Repeating Arms Co., New Haven, Connecticut.

Remington Arms Co., Inc., Ilion, New York.

Savage Arms Corp., Chicopee Falls, Massachusetts (includes Fox and Stevens brands).

Harrington & Richardson Arms Co., Worcester, Massachusetts.

O. F. Mossberg & Sons, Inc., New Haven, Connecticut.

Marlin Firearms Co., New Haven, Connecticut (includes L. C. Smith line).

Smith & Wesson, Springfield, Massachusetts.

High Standard Mfg. Corp., New Haven, Connecticut.

Colt Mfg. Company, Hartford, Connecticut.

Firearms International Corp., 1522 Connecticut Avenue, N. W. Washington, D. C.

W. A. SUKALLE

Bill Sukalle has had more than 27 years experience in the making and fitting of fine rifle barrels, starting out in 1923 with the hand turning of a new barrel for an old 7mm Mauser rifle. Prior to that time he operated an automobile repair shop and did considerable repair work on lever action rifles of the .30/30 class.

Once that 7mm job was completed, the Sukalle repair shop rapidly developed into a full-fledged rifle manufacturing plant and the automobile end of the business soon petered out.

This Arizona riflemaker also shoots rifles as well as making them. He has been a member of two Arizona State Rifle Teams at Camp Perry and held the offhand championship of the state for many years. In addition, he is a good handgun shot.

"Sukalle is a master of machine work with firearms" wrote Rex Stanley in a *Rifleman* article. "His gun rebuilding—'one part know-how to ten parts midnight oil and sweat'—is legend to riflemen. But barrels figure first with Sukalle. 'One sure way to shooting more accurately' he says 'whether you are aiming for the ten-ring on a range or the heart of a hell-bent buck, is a better barrel.' "

BLISS TITUS

This Utah barrel and riflemaker is another avid hunter and rifleman who went into the gunmaking business because he was so fond of guns and shooting.

Bliss' gunsmithing started out after the First World War with a few barrel shortening jobs done for hunting friends and rapidly developed into a full-time occupation. During the Second World War he worked in several Government Arsenals and studied barrel making at Rock Island Arsenal; his duties included the making of considerable ballistic and testing equipment, in the construction of which his past experience as a tool and diemaker stood him in good stead.

Ithaca Gun Company, Ithaca, New York.

Iver Johnson Arms & Cycle Works, Fitchburg, Massachusetts.

Browning Arms Company, St. Louis 3, Missouri.

Supply Catalogs for Gunsmiths:

Gunsmith's Mart—Brownell Industries, Montezuma, Iowa.

Frank Mittermeier, 3577 East Tremont Avenue, Bronx 61, New York.

Stoeger Arms Corp., 507 Fifth Avenue, New York.

Driver Equipment Co., 1152 Valencia St., San Francisco 10, California.

Victor Machinery Exchange, Inc., 251 Centre St., New York 13, New York. (Small tools & accessories for the shop.)

Magazines & Periodicals:

Machinery (Industrial Press), 148 Lafayette St., New York 13, New York.

American Rifleman (National Rifle Association), 1600 Rhode Island Avenue, Washington 6, D. C.

American Machinist, 330 West 42nd Street, New York 18, New York.

Heat Treating & Forging, 108 Smithfield Street, Pittsburgh, Pennsylvania.

National Hardwood Magazine, P.O. Box 1721, Memphis, Tennessee.

There are numerous trade magazines pertaining to metal working, machine tools and other items of interest to the gunsmith, but it is better to take a few hours off every couple of months to check over these at the public library, rather than subscribe to several. Subscriptions to such publications cost money.

Special Parts Suppliers:

Firearms International Corp., 1526 Connecticut Avenue N. W., Washington, D. C. (Mauser parts.)

N. F. Strebe, 5215 R Street SE, Washington 19, D. C. (Mauser, foreign pistol parts.)

R. F. Lovell, 4622 North Wolcott, Chicago 40, Illinois. (Foreign rifle parts, also pistol parts.)

Western Gun Exchange, 441 South Greenleaf Avenue, Whittier, California. (Foreign pistol parts.)

John P. Gschwind, 4124 North Leamington Avenue, Chicago 41, Illinois. (Springfield, Garand parts and tools.)

James E. Serven, Santa Ana, California. (Obsolete Colt revolver parts.)

Barrelmakers:

J. R. Buhmiller, Kalispell, Montana. (Blanks only, all calibers.)

James D. Adair, Rt. 1, Box 161, Roseburg, Oregon. (Blanks, barrels, .22, .25, .270 & .30 caliber.)

G. R. Douglas, Rt. 3, Box 297-A, Charleston, West Virginia. (Blanks and barrels, all calibers.)

P. O. Ackley, Trinidad, Colorado. (Blanks, barrels, complete rifles.)

40 GUNSMITHING

W. A. Sukalle, 1120 East Washington Street, Phoenix, Arizona. (Barrels, all calibers, custom gunsmithing.)
Pfeifer Rifle Corporation, 11252 Penrose Street, Roscoe, California. (Barrels, blanks, complete rifles, all calibers.)
W̦eatherby's, Inc., 8823 South Long Beach Boulevard, South Gate, California. (Barrels, blanks, complete rifles.)
Eric Johnson, 115 Carleton Street, Hamden, Connecticut. (Match barrels, .22 & .30 caliber.)
Johnson Automatics Arms, Inc., P.O. Box 1512, Providence, Rhode Island. (Barrels, blanks, remodeling military rifles.)
Bliss Titus, Heber, Utah. (Custom barrels, centerfire calibers.)
Gregoire Engineering Co., P.O. Box 3114, New Haven, Connecticut. (.22 barrels and blanks.)
Vernor Gipson, Box 156, North Salem, Indiana. (Barrels, chambering, cartridge development and supplies.)

Metallic Sight Manufacturers:
Redfield Gunsight Co., 3315 Gilpin Street Denver, Colorado.
Lyman Sight Corporation, Middlefield, Connecticut.
Vaver Corporation, 2439 South Kolin Avenue, Chicago 23, Illinois.
Pacific Gunsight Co., 355 Hayes Street, San Francisco 2, California.
King Gunsight Co., 667 Howard Street, San Francisco 5, California.
Marble Arms & Mfg. Co., Gladstone, Michigan.
Leroy Rice, 316 Masonic Temple, Elyria, Ohio.
Williams Gun Shop, Inc., 7387 Lapeer Road Davison, Michigan.
C. A. Dahl, 1133 Balmoral Avenue, Chicago 40, Illinois. (Ramps only.)
W. P. Spofford, 720 Ogden Avenue, Swarthmore, Pennsylvania.
Harris Machine Co., Rivera, California. (Sweat on Ramps.)
Merit Gunsight Co., 6144 Monadnock Way, Oakland 3, California.
John R. Speer, 7428 Richland Manor Drive, Pittsburgh 8, Pennsylvania. (Band-type front ramp blanks.)
Armstrong Gun Accessories Corp., 475 Fifth Avenue,.New York 17, New York.
Goss Engineering & Sales, Lincolnwood 45, Illinois.
Micro Sight Co., 5813 Mission Street, San Francisco 25, California. (Target pistol sights.)
Maynard P. Buehler, 697 Vernon Street, Oakland 10, California. (Auxiliary sights for Buehler & Redfield Scope Mounts.)
Christy Gun Works, 875 57th Street, Sacramento 16, California.
Terhaar Gun Works, 3108 Main Street, Jacksonville, Florida.
Dockendorff & Co., Inc., Oronoque, Connecticut. (Rifle front sights.)

Target Telescopic Sight Manufacturers:
John Unertl Optical Co., 3551 East Street, Pittsburgh 14, Pennsylvania.
Lyman Sight Corporation, Middlefield, Connecticut.

J. W. Fecker, Inc., 2016 Perrysville Avenue, Pittsburgh 14, Pennsylvania.
R. A. Litschert, Winchester, Indiana.
O. F. Mossberg & Sons, 131 St. John Street, New Haven 5, Connecticut.

Hunting Telescopic Sight Manufacturers:
John Unertl Optical Co., 3551 East Street, Pittsburgh 14, Pennsylvania.
Lyman Sight Corporation, Middlefield, Connecticut.
W. R. Weaver Co., El Paso, Texas.
Stith Mounts, 500 Transit Tower, San Antonio 5, Texas.
Leupold & Stevens Instruments, 4445 North East Glisan, Portland, Oregon.
Carl Zeiss, Inc., 485 Fifth Avenue, New York 17, New York. (Handle Zeiss and Hensoldt equipment.)
Norman-Ford Company, Tyler, Texas.
The Maxwell Smith Co., Los Angeles 25, California.
Bausch & Lomb Optical Co., Rochester 2, New York.

Hunting Telescopic Mount Manufacturers:
W. R. Weaver Co., El Paso, Texas. (¾" & 1" sizes only.)
Leupold & Stevens Instruments, 4445 North East Glisan, Portland, Oregon.
Redfield Gunsight Company, 3315 Gilpin Street, Denver, Colorado.
Stith Mounts, 500 Transit Tower, San Antonio 5, Texas.
Maynard P. Buehler, 697 Vernon Street, Oakland 10, California.
Tilden Mfg. Company, 2750 North Speer Boulevard, Denver 11, Colorado.
Williams Gun Shop, 7387 Lapeer Road, Davison, Michigan.
Paul Jaeger, Jenkintown, Pennsylvania.
Mykrom Company, 1335A South West Morrison Street, Portland 5, Oregon.
Pachmayr Gun Works, 1220 South Grand Avenue, Los Angeles 15, California.
P. O. Ackley, Trinidad, Colorado.
Kesselring Gun Shop, Route 2, Sedro Wooley, Washington.
Clarence Hill, Dixon, Illinois.
E. C. Herkner Company, Boise, Idaho.
Griffen & Howe, Inc., 202 East 44th Street, New York 17, New York.
Mashburn Arms Co., Inc., 1220 North Blackwelder, Oklahoma City, Oklahoma.
E. W. Lehman, Chula Vista, California.

Dot Reticules:
T. K. Lee, P.O. Box 2123, Birmingham 1, Alabama.

Optical Coating & Repair Firms:
John Unertl Optical Co., 3551 East Street, Pittsburgh 14, Pennsylvania.
Optical Coating Laboratory, Inc., 711A Eighth Street, N. W. Washington 1, D. C.

Spotting & Observation Telescope Manufacturers:
Bausch & Lomb Optical Company, Rochester 2, New York.
Carl Zeiss, Inc., 485 Fifth Avenue, New York 17, New York.
John Unertl Optical Co., 3551 East Street, Pittsburgh 14, Pennsylvania.
Tinsley Laboratories, 2524 Grove Street, Berkeley, California.
Argus, Inc., Ann Arbor, Michigan.
Kollmorgen Optical Corp., 4 Franklin Avenue, Brooklyn 11, New York.
Davidson Mfg. Co., 5146 Alhambra Avenue, Los Angeles 32, California.
O. F. Mossberg & Sons, 131 St. John Street, New Haven 5, Connecticut.

Semi-Inletted Stock Blanks:
E. C. Bishop & Son, Inc., Warsaw, Missouri & 3638 Dam Road, San Pablo, California. (Also fully-inletted stocks. American black walnut only.)
Central Pattern Works, Inc., Racine, Wisconsin. (Black walnut.)
Herter's, Waseca, Minn. (Also fully-inletted stocks and stock blanks in the rough. All available woods.)
Flaig's, Millvale, Pa. (Black walnut and maple.)
W. R. Hutchings, 4504 West Washington Boulevard, Los Angeles 16, California. (Also finish-inletted, finished and custom stocks. Black walnut, California-English walnut, maple, birch and other woods. Also, laminated blanks and stocks. Is a rifleman to boot.)
D. W. Thomas, Vineland, New Jersey. (American walnut and maple.)

Fully-Inletted Stocks (Not including above suppliers):
Weatherby's, Inc., 8823 Long Beach Boulevard, South Gate, California. (All available domestic and imported woods.)
Parker-Whelen Co., Inc., 827 14th Street, N. W. Washington 5, D. C. (American walnut, for 1917 rifle only.)
Stoeger Arms Corp., 507 Fifth Avenue, New York, New York. (American and French walnut.)

Stock Blank Suppliers:
D. W. Thomas, Vineland, New York. (American walnut and maple.)
Herter's, Waseca, Minnesota. (American walnut, maple, myrtle: South American Mahogany, French walnut.)
John Hearn, 35 S. 50th Street, Philadelphia, Penna.
Gilbert Arms, Manlius, New York. (French walnut.)
Continental Arms Corporation, 697 Fifth Avenue, New York 22, New York. (Italian walnut.)

Paul Jaeger, Jenkintown, Pennsylvania. (French walnut.)
Frank Mittermeier, 3577 East Tremont Avenue, Bronx 61, New York. (French walnut.)
R. Vail, Warwick, New York. (French walnut, also American woods.)
Howard Clark, Stevens Point, Wisconsin. (French walnut, American walnut, hard maple.)
Mitchell, Bosly & Co., Ltd., Little Shadwell Street, Birmingham 4, England. (European walnut, usually French.)

Gunstock Finishing Compounds, Varnishes, Shellac, Stains and Supplies:
A. Donald Newell, 14,586 Archdale Road, Detroit 27, Michigan.

Stockmaking Chisels:
Z. S. Denman, 423 West 136th Street, Hawthorne, California. (Hand Forged chisels and gouges, barrel inletting rasps.)
Frank Mittermeier, 3577 East Tremont Avenue, Bronx 61, New York. (German and British chisels and gouges, Swiss rifflers.)
Stoeger Arms Corporation, 507 Fifth Avenue, New York, New York.
Brownell Industries, Montezuma, Iowa. (Buck Bros. Chisels.)

Checkering Tools:
Frank Mittermeier, 3577 East Tremont Avenue, Bronx 61, New York. (Grobet Swiss tools.)
Warner Products Co., Baldwinsville, New York.
Franz Metal Specialties, 625 North 22nd Street, Allentown, Pennsylvania.
Dem-Bart Company, P. O. Box 700, Tacoma 1, Washington. (Hand and electric checkering tools.)

Checkering Files:
Driver Equipment Co., 1152 Valencia Street, San Francisco 10, California.
Frank Mittermeier, 3577 East Tremont Avenue, Bronx 61, New York.

Shotgun Choke Devices:
W. R. Weaver Co., El Paso, Texas. ("Weaver Choke.")
Lyman Gunsight Co., Middlefield, Connecticut. ("Cutts Compensator.")
PolyChoke Company, Hartford, Connecticut. ("PolyChoke.")
Pachmayr Gun Works, 1220 South Grand Avenue, Los Angeles 15, California. ("POWer-PAC.")
Shooting-Master Corp., Gardner, Massachusetts. ("Shooting-Master Choke.")

Recoil Pads:
Pachmayr Gun Works, 1220 South Grand Avenue, Los Angeles 15, California. (Screw attaching pads & solid neoprene non slip rifle plates.)

.219 ZIPPER

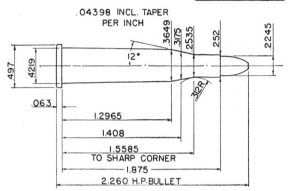

.04398 INCL. TAPER PER INCH

12°

.3649 .3175 .2535 .252 .2245

.497 .4219

.063

1.2965

1.408

1.5585
TO SHARP CORNER

1.875

2.260 H.P. BULLET

3/12 R

MINIMUM CHAMBER

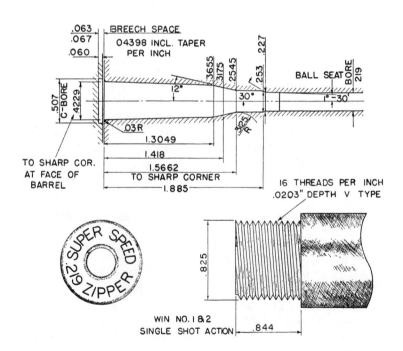

.063
.067
.060

BREECH SPACE

.04398 INCL. TAPER PER INCH

12°

30°

1°-30'

BALL SEAT

.227

.3655 .3175 .2545 .253

BORE .219

.507
C-BORE
.4229

.03 R

3/12 R

1.3049

1.418

1.5662
TO SHARP CORNER

1.885

TO SHARP COR.
AT FACE OF
BARREL

16 THREADS PER INCH
.0203" DEPTH V TYPE

SUPER SPEED
.219 ZIPPER

.825

.844

WIN NO. 1 & 2
SINGLE SHOT ACTION

Mershon Company, Inc., 511 East Broadway, Glendale 5, California. (Screw attaching pads & non slip "White Line" rifle plates.)

Jostam Mfg. Company, Peotone, Illinois. (All types of pads, including leather-covered lace-on type.)

Southwest Cutlery & Mfg. Co., Inc., 1307 Olympic Boulevard, Montebello, California. (Screw attaching pads.)

Rifle Buttplates:

Niedner Rifle Corp., Route 5, Niles, Michigan. (Checkered steel plates. Recommended.)

Pachmayr Gun Works, 1220 South Grand Avenue, Los Angeles 15, California. (Neoprene plates.)

Mershon Company, Inc., 511 East Broadway, Glendale 5, California. (Neoprene plates.)

Herter's, Waseca, Minnesota. (Plastic plates.)

Stoeger Arms Corp., 507 Fifth Avenue, New York, New York.

THE .219 WINCHESTER ZIPPER

Winchester's contribution to the single shot rifle boys—intended as a lever action vermin rifle and cartridge combination—the .219 Zipper was foredoomed to failure because of the comparative inaccuracy of the lever action factory rifle, but was rescued from oblivion by its adaption to the stronger obsolete single shot arms beloved by many vermin hunters.

The standard cartridge is capable of excellent accuracy in such rifles as the heavy Winchester single shot, the Sharps-Borchardt and the Farquharson, although the excessively tapering case and long shoulder are not in line with modern ideas. Winchester, of course, designed the case for maximum ease of feeding and extraction in their repeating lever action.

The flat tip bullet profile (hollow point) is necessary for safety in the tubular magazine of the Model 64 Winchester, which was the only factory or commercial rifle ever made for the Zipper cartridge. It is a slightly improved model of the old but still present '94 action. Handloaded ammunition with pointed bullets can be used only for single shot loading. (One cartridge to be loaded and fired only.) In the tubular magazine, the bullet tip of one cartridge contacts the primer of the cartridge ahead of it, so that recoil or a severe jolt to the butt of the rifle may possibly fire the cartridges in the magazine. For this reason, spitzer (pointed) bullets are never loaded for lever action or other rifles with tubular magazines. Remington developed a crimped tube for their 14 pump action, intended to hold the cartridges at an angle in the magazine tube, so that the bullet tips will not contact the primers of the preceding cartridges.

The Zipper is a good step ahead of the .218 Bee in velocities—the factory cartridge with 46-grain bullet now being rated at 3,390 FPS and the 56-grain bullet at 3,050 FPS, both figures muzzle velocities.

The No. 3 Winchester heavy single shot action uses a barrel shank .935″ in diameter, with the same thread pitch and approximately the same length as the Nos. 1 and 2 illustrated.

Rifle Forend Tips:
E. C. Bishop & Son, Warsaw, Missouri. (Plastic tips, black & white.)
Herter's, Waseca, Minnesota. (Plastic tips.)
Frank Mittermeier, 3577 East Tremont Avenue, Bronx 61, New York.
D. W. Thomas, Box 184, Vineland, New Jersey. (Ebony and plastic blocks.)
Schmidt Precision Products, 3027½ Delores Street, Los Angeles 41, California. (Fancy woods for tips and caps.)

Custom Riflemakers:
Pfeifer Rifle Co., Inc., 11252 Penrose Street, Roscoe, California.
Pachmayr Gun Works, 1220 South Grand Avenue, Los Angeles 15, California.
Griffen & Howe, Inc., 202 East 44th Street, New York 17, New York.
Weatherby's, Inc., 8823 South Long Beach Boulevard, South Gate, California.
P. O. Ackley Company, Trinidad, Colorado.

Custom Stockmakers:
R. G. Owen, Box 131, Port Clinton, Ohio. (Bob Owen, the original.)
Thomas Shelhamer, 513 Spruce Street, Dowagiac, Michigan.
Leonard Mews, 932 W. Summer St., Appleton, Wisconsin.
John Hearn, 35 South 50th Street, Philadelphia 39, Pennsylvania.

Short Action Alteration:
Roy F. Dunlap, 2319 Ft. Lowell Road, Tucson, Arizona.
Arthur Shivell, Box 300, Route 2, Saugus, California.

Left Hand Action Alteration:
Naval Company, Doylestown, Pennsylvania.
Arthur Shivell, Box 300, Route 2, Saugus, California.
Roy Gradle, 205 West Islay, Santa Barbara, California.

Bolt and Action Work and Alterations:
Harold G. Rowe, R. R. 2—Box 155, Three Rivers, Michigan.

Rifling Tools:
H & M Tool Company, 250 East Nine Mile Road., Ferndale 20, Michigan.

Chambering Reamers:
F. K. Elliott, Ramona, California. (The original "Red" Elliott.)
H & M. Tool Company, 250 East Nine Mile Road, Ferndale 20, Michigan.
Wright Gun & Tool Shop, Bloomsburg, Pennsylvania.
Driver Equipment Co., 1152 Valencia Street, San Francisco 10, California.
Fuller Tool Company, 3950 West Eleven Mile Road, Berkley, Michigan.

Headspace Gages:
L. E. Wilson, Cashmere, Washington. (.30–06 only.)
Forster Bros., Lanark, Illinois. (All gages for centerfire.)
H & M. Tool Company, 250 East Nine Mile Road, Ferndale 20, Michigan.
(All caliber gages.)

Engraving Tools and Supplies:
Swartchild & Company, 29 East Madison Street, Chicago, Illinois.

Files:
Frank Mittermeier, 3577 East Tremont Avenue, Bronx 61, New York.
Swartchild & Company, 29 East Madison Street, Chicago, Illinois.
Stoeger Arms Corp., 507 Fifth Avenue, New York, New York.
American Swiss File Co., Elizabeth, New Jersey. (Manufacturers.)
Nicolson File Co., 19 Acorn Street, Providence, Rhode Island. (Manu-
facturers.)
Brownell Industries, Inc., Montezuma, Iowa.

Electric Hand Grinders:
Chicago Wheel & Mfg. Co., 1101 West Monroe Street, Chicago, Illinois.
Dremel Mfg. Company, Racine, Wisconsin.

Electric Hand Tool:
Burgess Battery Co., 176 North Wabash Avenue, Chicago, Illinois.
(Burgess Vibro-Tool.)

Drill Presses:
Canedy-Otto Mfg. Company, Chicago Heights, Illinois.
Atlas Press Company, Kalamazoo 13, Michigan.
South Bend Lathe Works, 452 East Madison Street, South Bend, In-
diana.
Walker-Turner Division, Kearney & Trecker Corp., Plainfield, New Jer-
sey.
Delta Mfg. Div., Rockwell Mfg. Company, 600 East Vienna Avenue,
Milwaukee, Wisconsin.

Lathes:
Clausing Mfg. Company, Ottumwa, Iowa.
Atlas Press Company, Kalamazoo 13, Michigan.
South Bend Lathe Works, South Bend, Indiana.
Sheldon Machine Co., Inc., 4243 North Knox Avenue, Chicago 41, Il-
linois.
King Machine Tool Division, American Steel Foundries, Cincinnati 29,
Ohio. (Sebastian Lathes.)
Monarch Machine Tool Co., Sidney, Ohio. (Engraving Lathe.)

Heat Treating Furnaces and Equipment:
  Stewart Industrial Furnace Div. Chicago Flexible Shaft Co., 5600 West
    Roosevelt Road, Chicago, Illinois.
  Frank Mittermeier, 3577 East Tremont Avenue, New York 61, N. Y.
  Gilbert S. Simonski, 401 North Broad Street, Philadelphia 8, Penna.
  Colloid Equipment Co., 50 Church Street, New York 7, New York.
  Cooley Electric Mfg. Corp., 38 South Shelby Street, Indianapolis, In-
    diana. (Electric furnaces only.)

Abrasives:
  Simonds Abrasive Company, Philadelphia 37, Pennsylvania.
  The Carborundum Company, Niagara Falls, New York.
  The Norton Company, Worcester, Mass.

Steels:
  Timken Roller Bearing Co., Steel & Tube Div., Canton 6, Ohio. (Graphitic
    Tool Steels.)
  Allegheny Ludlum Steel Corp., Pittsburgh, Pennsylvania. (High Speed
    Drill Rod.)
  Republic Steel Corp., Alloy Steel Div., Massilon, Ohio. (Alloy steels.)
  Carpenter Steel Company, 105 West Bern Street, Reading, Pennsylvania.
    (Stentor Tool Steel.)
  Columbia Tool Steel Company, Chicago Heights, Illinois. (Tool Steels for
    all purposes.)
  (For special steels, contact the above manufacturers, who will refer you
    to your nearest sales point.)

Hard Surfacing Material:
  Haynes Stellite Company, Kokomo, Indiana.
  Gorham Tool Company, 14400 Woodrow Wilson Avenue, Detroit, Mich.
  The Carboloy Company, Inc., 11147 East 8 Mile Road, Detroit 32, Mich-
    igan.

Acetylene Welding Equipment:
  Linde Air Products Co., New York, New York. (Manufacturer.)
  Smith Welding Equipment Corp., 2633 Southeast 4th Street, Minneapo-
    lis 14, Minnesota. (Manufacturer.)
  Johnson Welding Equipment Co., 2640 West Van Buren Street, Chi-
    cago 12, Illinois. (Jobbers & Dealers.)
  Alloy Rods Co., York, Pennsylvania. (Welding rod and electrodes.)

Electro Welding Equipment:
  Hobart Brothers Company, Troy, Ohio.
  Lincoln Electric Company, Cleveland, Ohio.
  John H. Graham Co., Inc., 105 Duane Street, New York, New York.

Hardness Testers:
Wilson Mechanical Instrument Co., Inc., 230-D Park Avenue, New York 17, New York. (Rockwell & Tukon machines.)
Shore Instrument Mfg. Company, 9025 Van Wyck Avenue, Jamaica 2, New York. (Shore Schleroscope.)

Phillips Screws:
Phillips Screw Manufacturers, C/o Horton-Noyes Company, 1800 Industrial Trust Building, Providence, Rhode Island.
American Screw Company, Providence 1, Rhode Island.

Drills:
Cleveland Twist Drill Company, 1242 East 49th Street, Cleveland 14, Ohio.
Greenfield Tap & Die Company, Greenfield, Massachusetts.
Morse Twist Drill Company, New Bedford, Massachusetts.

Toolmaker's Microscope:
George Scherr Co., Inc., 199 Lafayette Street, New York 12, New York. (Wilder microscope.)

Special Grinders:
Dumore Company, Racine, Wisconsin. (Tool Post, Machine and powerful hand grinders.)

Wood-Working Machinery:
Walker-Turner Division, Kearney & Trecker Corporation, Plainfield, New Jersey.
Delta Mfg. Division, Rockwell Mfg. Company, 600 East Vienna Avenue, Milwaukee, Wisconsin.
Mead Specialties Co., 4114 North Knox Avenue, Chicago, Illinois.
Barron Tool Company, 370 Architects Building, Detroit, Michigan.

Lead Hammers:
S & H Soft Hammer Products Co., 15410 Stoepel Avenue, Detroit 21, Michigan. (Lead hammer parts, head molds, et cetera.)

Shotgun Specialties:
Safeties: AB Engineering Co., 4303 N. Sawyer Avenue, Chicago 18, Illinois. (For Winchesters 12 & 25.)
John Crowe, 2713 Duncan Street, St. Joseph, Missouri. (For Winchesters 12 & 25.)
Don Lowery, 34 West Adams Street, Tucson, Arizona. (Tang safeties for Winchesters 42, 12, and others.)

Dent Raisers: Alex J. Thill, Camp Simms, Washington 20, D. C.

Barrel Ribs: Simmons Gun Specialities, 1426 Walnut, Kansas City 6, Missouri.
Don Lowery, 34 West Adams Street, Tucson, Arizona.

Rifle Safeties, for Telescopic Sights:
Tilden Mfg. Company, 2750 North Speer Boulevard, Denver 11, Colorado. (M70 & Mauser.)
Anderson Gun Shop, 1203 Broadway, Yakima, Washington. (Tang type, for most bolt actions and Savage M99.)
Eads Mfg. Company, 2502 Larimer Street, Denver 5, Colorado. (Mauser, Springfield, Winchester 54.)
Redfield Gun Sight Company, 3315 East Gilpin Street, Denver, Colorado. (Mauser, Springfield, Winchesters 54–70.)
Maynard P. Buehler, 697 Vernon Street, Oakland 10, California. (Mauser, Springfield, Krag, Winchester 54.)
P. O. Ackley, Trinidad, Colorado. (Springfield, and both right and left hand for Mauser.)
W. A. Sukalle, 1120 East Washington Street, Phoenix, Arizona. (Springfield and Mauser.)
Paul Jaeger, Jenkintown, Pennsylvania. (Conventional and side safeties for most bolt actions.)
Firearms International Corp., 1526 Connecticut Avenue, Washington 6, D. C. (Left hand Mauser only.)

Set Triggers:
John R. Speer, 7428 Richland Manor Drive, Pittsburgh 8, Pennsylvania. (Double, forward setting.)
Firearms International Corp., 1526 Connecticut Avenue, Washington 6, D. C. (Double, supplied in Mauser triggerguards only.)
Paul Jaeger, Jenkintown, Pennsylvania. (Single Set.)
M. H. Canjar, 4476 Pennsylvania Street, Denver 16, Colorado. (Single Set.)
Miller Single Trigger Mfg. Co., Millersburg, Pennsylvania.

Single Stage Trigger Mechanisms:
Paul Jaeger, Jenkintown, Pennsylvania.
Pfeifer Rifle Company, Inc., 11252 Penrose Street, Roscoe, California.
Dayton-Traister Co., 34 Southeast 66th Ave., Portland 16, Oregon.
M. H. Canjar, 4476 Pennsylvania St., Denver 16, Colorado.
Allen Timney, 5832 Oliva Avenue, Bellflower, California.
Mashburn Arms Co., 1220 North Blackwelder Street, Oklahoma City, Oklahoma.

Cartridge Loading Tools:

Pacific Gun Sight Co., 353 Hayes Street, San Francisco 2, California.

Lyman Gun Sight Company, Middlefield, Connecticut.

L. E. Wilson, Cashmere, Washington.

Hollywood Gun Shop, 6116 Hollywood Boulevard, Hollywood 28, California.

Modern-Bond Corp., 813 West 5th St., Wilmington, Delaware.

Masters Machine Works, Brookville, Pennsylvania. (Jordan press.)

Belding & Mull, Philipsburg, Pennsylvania.

Meepos Machine Shop, 135 North Western Avenue, Los Angeles 4, California.

Star Machine Works, 418 Tenth Avenue, Los Angeles, California.

A. A. Easton, 624 Tenth Avenue, Salt Lake City, Utah.

Potter Engineering Co., 10 Albany Street, Cazenovia, New York.

Powder Measures:

Lyman Gun Sight Corporation, Middlefield, Connecticut.

Belding & Mull, Philipsburg, Pennsylvania.

Modern-Bond Corp., 813 W. 5th Street, Wilmington, Delaware.

Pacific Gun Sight Company, 353 Hayes Street, San Francisco 2, California.

Santa Anita Engineering Co., 2435 East Colorado Street, Pasadena 8, California.

Hollywood Gun Shop, 6116 Hollywood Boulevard, Hollywood 28, California.

Powder Scales:

The Redding Co., Box 524, Cortland, New York.

Pacific Gun Sight Co., 353 Hayes Street, San Francisco 2, California.

Brown & Sharpe, Providence, Rhode Island.

Bullet Lubricators:

Lyman Gun Sight Corp., Middlefield, Connecticut.

Meepos Machine Shop, 135 North Western Avenue, Los Angeles 4, California.

L. E. Wadman, Mill Valley, California.

Star Machine Works, 418 Tenth Avenue, Los Angeles, California.

Blueing Supplies (Dealers):

Frank Mittermeier, 3577 East Tremont Avenue, Bronx 61, N. Y. (Brushes, wheels, pipe burners.)

Gunsmith's Mart, Brownell Industries, Montezuma, Iowa. (Brushes, wheels, tanks, compounds, salts.)

Driver Equipment Co., 1152 Valencia Street, San Francisco 10, California. (Brushes, wheels, tanks, general supplies.)

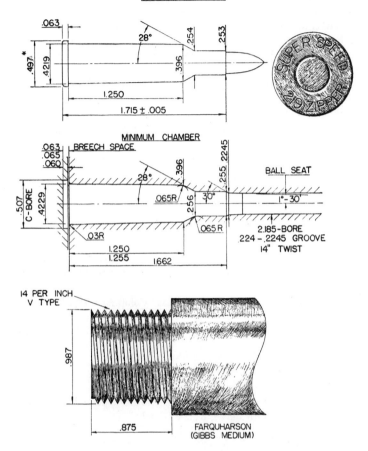

MAXIMUM CARTRIDGE

MINIMUM CHAMBER

BALL SEAT

2.185-BORE
224 - .2245 GROOVE
14" TWIST

14 PER INCH
V TYPE

.875   FARQUHARSON
(GIBBS MEDIUM)

*NOTE : RIMS MAY BE TURNED TO .473" TO AVOID ALTERING STANDARD
BOLT FACES.

The .219 Gipson Wasp

Currently the favorite of the bench-rest shooters, this little cartridge is *very* accurate up to 250 yards. Pressures run rather high, and cases must be in good shape. They may be made from .219 Zipper, .25–35, or .30–30 empty cases. Developed as a vermin cartridge, principally by Vernor Gipson, most of the publicity given the Wasp has been due to the very small groups shot at short range from bench rest. Different barrelmakers and gunsmiths have varied some of the dimensions, but most of them stay close to the "official" ones shown on this drawing.

The barrel shank of the Gibbs Farquharson is rather unusual, but it seems all the various makes of Farquharsons had different shanks.

Stoeger Arms Corp., 507 Fifth Avenue, New York, New York. (Salts, general supplies.)

Metal Finishing Equipment (Manufacturers):
Felt Polishing Wheels: Eastern Felt Co., 80 Canal Street, Winchester Massachusetts.
Lea Mfg. Company, Waterbury, Connecticut.
Chicago Wheel & Mfg. Co., 1101 West Monroe Street, Chicago, Illinois.
Wire Wheels: Black & Decker Mfg. Co., 600 East Penn Avenue, Towson, Maryland.
Polishing & Buffing Compounds:
Lea Mfg. Company, Waterbury, Connecticut.
American Buff Company, 711 West Lake Street, Chicago 6, Illinois.
J. J. Siefen Co., 5657 Lauderdale Street, Detroit 9, Michigan.
M. E. Baker Co., 143 Sidney Street, Cambridge, Massachusetts.
Harrison & Co., Box 695, Groveland, Massachusetts.
Charles F. L'Hommedieu & Sons Company, 4521 Ogden Avenue, Chicago 23, Illinois.
Roberts Rouge Company, 904 Longbrook Avenue, Stratford, Connecticut.
Buckeye Products Co., 7020 Vine Street, Cincinnati 16, Ohio.
Matchless Metal Polish Co., 726 Bloomfield Avenue, Glen Ridge, New Jersey.

Degreasing Materials:
Oakite Products, Inc., 20 East Thames Street, New York 6, New York.
Monsanto Chemical Co., Merrimac Div. Everett Station, Boston 49, Massachusetts.

Blackening Processes (Manufacturers):
DuLite Chemical Corp., Middletown, Connecticut.

Years ago the Niedner Rifle Corporation used to consider the Farquharson the best single shot action of all, and turned out super-accurate rifles. Most of the old .22 Niedner Magnum rifles built on these actions would shoot along with the present Wasp rifles any day.

A few other Farquharson threads are as follows:

Jeffery (Small) Shank length $3\frac{1}{32}''$, Diameter .685″, Thread, V type, 20 per inch.

Westly-Richards (Medium) Length of shank, $1\frac{1}{16}''$, Diameter, 1″, Thread, V type, 14 per inch.

Bland (Large) Length of shank, $1\frac{1}{8}''$; Diameter, 1″, Thread, V type, 14 per inch.

Unmarked Belgian large actions: Length of shank, $\frac{7}{8}''$, Diameter, 1″, Thread, V type, 14 per inch.

The Enthone Co., 442 Elm Street, New Haven 2, Connecticut.

E. F. Houghton & Co., 303 West Lehigh Avenue, Philadelphia 33, Pennsylvania.

Heatbath Corporation, Springfield, Massachusetts.

Alrose Chemical Co., 756 McCarter Highway, Newark, New Jersey.

Ceramic Tanks:
 General Ceramics Co., Keasbey, New Jersey.
 U. S. Stoneware Company, Talmadge, Ohio.

Rust Removers:
 International Rustproof Corporation, 12515 Plover Avenue, Cleveland, Ohio.
 Oakite Products, Inc., 20 East Thames Street, New York 6, New York.
 Kelite Products, Inc., 909 East 60th Street, Los Angeles 1, California.

Acids (Check with local druggist—he may be able to supply):
 Nitric:
  Lasalco, Inc., 2818 LaSalle Street, St. Louis 4, Missouri.
  Central Scientific, 2000 West Irving Park Boulevard, Chicago, Illinois.
  Seldner & Enequist, Inc., Brooklyn 22, New York.
 Sulphuric:
  Central Scientific, 2000 West Irving Park Boulevard, Chicago, Illinois.
  General Chemical Co., 40 Rector Street, New York 6, New York.
  Phillips & Jacob, 622 Race Street, Philadelphia 6, Pennsylvania.

Pumice:
 Usually available at any drug store.

Chemicals:
 Ammonium Nitrate: Any feed and fertilizer store.
 Sodium Hydroxide: Household lye, available at any grocery, is about 94% sodium hydroxide.
  Manufacturers of Sodium Hydroxide:
   Merch & Co., Rahway, New Jersey. (Chemically pure.)
   Puro Chemicals, Inc., 1643 St. Clair Avenue, Cleveland 14, Ohio.
   Belke Mfg. Company, 947 North Cicero Avenue, Chicago, Illinois.
   Udylite Corp., Detroit 11, Michigan.
  (Sodium Hydroxide is also commonly called "caustic soda.")
 Sodium Nitrite:
  Croton Chemical Corp., 114 Liberty Street, New York 6, New York.
  Eaton-Clark Co., 1480 Franklin Street, Detroit 7, Michigan.
 Sodium Cyanide:
  American Cyanamid & Chemical Corp., 30 Rockefeller Plaza, New York 20, New York.

P. O. ACKLEY
and (looking through the window)
Fisher's Peak, a famous Colorado–New Mexico landmark.

P. O. Ackley, of Trinidad, Colorado, has risen to be amongst those at the top in the gunsmithing field. A well rounded education covering science and teaching at Syracuse University and Colorado A and M College, plus a natural inquisitiveness which does not allow him to accept unproved statements have helped Ackley to forge ahead in this, still to some, mysterious field of gunmaking and ballistics.

While operating his small business in Oregon before the war, Ackley built up such a fine reputation that with the coming of the war he was placed in charge of the small arms plant of the Ogden, Utah arsenal. After the war, he finally moved to Trinidad, Colorado, where his fame and business increased to such an extent that today he operates in a new, spacious factory and employs around thirty gunsmiths.

Ackley is perhaps best known for his barrels, which are shipped to gunsmiths all over the Americas, and for his modern cartridge designs, which range from the .17 Pee Wee through a whole hatful of improved calibers on up to his custom magnums. He does general gunsmithing, builds custom rifles, and manufactures scope mounts and safeties. Recently he brought out a newly designed bullet of great promise which will properly expand at any velocity and yet always hold together.

Ackley believes in "proving the pudding by the eating thereof" and after the war, while many gunsmiths were vigorously condemning certain military actions and praising others, he set to work with actual blow-up tests, carried out in a scientific way, to find out just how strong these various actions were. The results from these first tests were rather surprising as they proved the 6.5mm Jap Arisaka to be the strongest rifle in the world. This made it look as if some of the other experts were basing their assertions on visual evidence and prejudice alone. Today these blow-up tests still continue and only recently in Ackley's shop a Carcano lay in the testing rack waiting to be destroyed in the interest of further and much needed gun knowledge.

P. O. is a good story teller and has a great sense of humor. So when he starts in you just settle back and listen. After all, it isn't every day you hear a first-hand account of the time a Model 11 action slammed shut on Elmer Keith's thumb; or about the time another certain gunsmith sat down on a loaded revolver while he filed away on it with the hammer held back by his thumb—until the thumb slipped; or that day Vickery forgot that it was a loaded cartridge he was using to check headspace—and a moment later casually pulled the trigger.

Today, P. O. is a busy man but not in the type of work that brings him greatest pleasure—for he would be happier doing his own work, with his own hands, in a small shop.

The Chemical Corp., 93 Broad Street, Springfield, Massachusetts.
Harshaw Chemical Co., 1945 East 97th Street, Cleveland, Ohio.
(See your druggist on cyanides, also.)
Potassium Cyanide:
duPont, Wilmington, Delaware. (Contact nearest duPont office.)
General Chemical Co., 40 Rector Street, New York 6, New York.
American Cyanamid & Chemical Corp., 30 Rockefeller Plaza, New York 20, New York.

Bolt-Bending Jigs:
Don Lowery, 34 West Adams Street, Tucson, Arizona.
Maynard P. Buehler, 697 Vernon Street, Oakland 10, California.

Receiver Wrenches:
W. S. Vickerman, 208 South Ruby Street, Ellensburg, Washington. (Universal wrench.)

Barrel Vises:
Pacific Gun Sight Company, 353 Hayes Street, San Francisco 2, California.
W. S. Vickerman, 208 South Ruby Street, Ellensburg, Washington.

Magnifying Glasses:
Compass Instrument & Optical Co., 268 Fourth Avenue, New York 10, New York. (All types of ordinary glasses, including goose neck base type and bench binoculars.)

Special Polishing Wheels:
Jackson Buff Corp., Long Island City, New York. (Soft wheels for abrasive belt polishing.)

Engine Turning Tools:
C. R. Pedersen & Son, Ludington, Michigan.
Frank Mittermeier, 3577 East Tremont Avenue, Bronx 61, New York.

Scope Block Drill Jig:
Claude E. Roderick, Monett, Missouri.

Leather Goods:
Paul Showalter, Patagonia, Arizona. (Custom cases, holsters, cuffs, belts, slings and other accessories to order.)
Brauer Bros. Mfg. Co., 817 North 17th Street, St. Louis 6, Missouri. (Moose Brand—gun cases, holsters, police items.)
George Lawrence Co., Portland 4, Oregon. (Holsters, cases, belts, cartridge boxes.)

I. Rome & Sons, Worcester, Massachusetts. (Slings, other items.)

Schoellkopf Co., Dallas, Texas. (Sheepskin cases of all kinds.)

Croft Mfg. Co., Olean, New York. (Cowhide rifle cases, gloves.)

10X Mfg. Co., Des Moines 5, Iowa. (Cases, shooting coats.)

King Sport-Line Co., 7034 North Figueroa Street, Los Angeles 42, California. (Deluxe cases of all types.)

Kolpin Bros. Company, Berlin, Wisconsin. (Sheepskin cases.)

Castle Sporting Goods, Inc., 628 Wythe Avenue, Brooklyn 11, New York. (Sheepskin & plastic cases.)

Eubanks Leather Goods, 6th & Main Streets, Boise, Idaho.

Colorado Saddlery Co., 1527 18th Street, Denver, Colo. (Both furnish plain and fancy holsters and western leather goods.)

S. D. Myres Saddle Co., El Paso, Texas. (Belts & holsters of all types.)

Sweet & Co., Box 447, Clovis, New Mexico. (Scope lens covers.)

Al Freeland, 3737 14th Avenue, Rock Island, Illinois. (Shooting gloves, arm cuffs, slings.)

FEDERAL FIREARMS ACT

AN ACT

To Regulate Commerce in Firearms

Be it enacted by the Senate and House of Representatives of the United States of America in Congress assembled, that as used in this Act—

(1) The term "person" includes an individual, partnership, association or corporation.

(2) The term "interstate or foreign commerce" means commerce between any State, Territory or possession (including the Philippine Islands but not including the Canal Zone), or the District of Columbia, and any place outside thereof: or between points within the same State, Territory or possession (including the Philippine Islands but not including the Canal Zone), or the District of Columbia, but through any place outside thereof; or within any Territory or possession or the District of Columbia.

(3) The term "firearm" means any weapon, by whatever name known, which is designed to expel a projectile or projectiles by the action of an explosive and a firearm muffler or firearm silencer, or any part or parts of such weapon.

(4) The term "manufacturer" means any person engaged in the manufacture or importation of firearms, or ammunition or cartridge cases, primers, bullets, or propellent powder for purposes of sale or

distribution; and the term "licensed manufacturer" means any such person licensed under the provisions of this Act.

(5) The term "dealer" means any person engaged in the business of selling firearms or ammunition or cartridge cases, primers, bullets, or propellent powder, at wholesale or retail, or any person engaged in the business of repairing such firearms or of manufacturing or fitting special barrels, stocks, trigger mechanism, or breach mechanisms to firearms, and the term "licensed dealer" means any such person licensed under the provisions of this Act.

(6) The term "crime of violence" means murder, manslaughter, rape, mayhem, kidnapping, burglary, housebreaking; assault with intent to kill, commit rape, or rob; assault with a dangerous weapon, or assault with intent to commit any offense punishable by imprisonment for more than one year.

(7) The term "fugitive from justice" means any person who has fled from any State, Territory, the District of Columbia, or possession of the United States to avoid prosecution for a crime of violence or to avoid giving testimony in any criminal proceeding.

(8) The term "ammunition" shall include all pistol or revolver ammunition except a .22 caliber rimfire ammunition.

Section 2. (a) It shall be unlawful for any manufacturer or dealer, except a manufacturer or dealer having a license issued under the provisions of this Act, to transport, ship, or receive any firearm or ammunition in interstate or foreign commerce.

(b) It shall be unlawful for any person to receive any firearm or ammunition transported or shipped in interstate or foreign commerce in violation of subdivision (a) of this section, knowing or having reasonable cause to believe such firearms or ammunition to have been transported or shipped in violation of subdivision (a) of this section.

(c) It shall be unlawful for any licensed manufacturer or dealer to transport or ship any firearm in interstate or foreign commerce to any person other than a licensed manufacturer or dealer in any State the laws of which require that a license be obtained for the purchase of such firearm, unless such license is exhibited to such manufacturer or dealer by the prospective purchaser.

(d) It shall be unlawful for any person to ship, transport, or cause to be shipped or transported in interstate or foreign commerce any firearm or ammunition to any person knowing or having reasonable cause to believe that such person is under indictment or has been convicted in any court of the United States, the several States, Territories, possessions (including the Philippine Islands), or the District

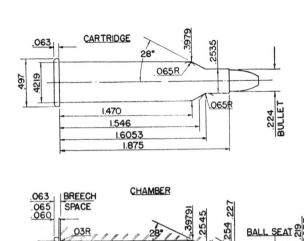

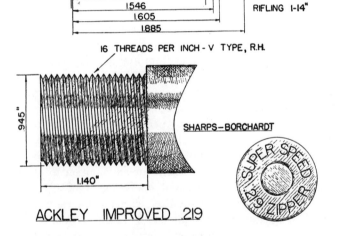

ACKLEY IMPROVED .219

The rather inefficient case design of the standard .219 Zipper has led to modification of the case, with Ackley's Improved version being the most popular. Standard cartridges are fired in the improved chamber, which allows them to blow out or fire-form to fit, and they come out something like the cartridge illustrated—you hope, and if Ackley chambered the rifle, they will.

Headspace is the same as for the standard cartridge and it will be noted that the cartridge and the chamber dimensions are identical in many instances, because the chamber itself governs the cartridge expansion.

Being a rimmed cartridge, the Improved Zipper is well adapted to strong single shot actions such as the heavy Winchester, the medium and large Farquharsons, and good Sharps-Borchardts.

of Columbia of a crime of violence or is a fugitive from justice.

(e) It shall be unlawful for any person who is under indictment or who has been convicted of a crime of violence or who is a fugitive from justice to ship, transport, or cause to be shipped or transported in interstate or foreign commerce any firearm or ammunition.

(f) It shall be unlawful for any person who has been convicted of a crime of violence or is a fugitive from justice to receive any firearm or ammunition which has been shipped or transported in interstate or foreign commerce, and the possession of a firearm or ammunition by any such person shall be presumptive evidence that such firearm or ammunition was shipped or transported or received, as the case may be, by such person in violation of this Act.

(g) It shall be unlawful for any person to transport or ship or cause to be transported or shipped in interstate or foreign commerce any stolen firearm or ammunition, knowing, or having reasonable cause to believe, same to have been stolen.

(h) It shall be unlawful for any person to receive, conceal, store, barter, sell or dispose of any firearm or ammunition or to pledge or accept as security for a loan any firearm or ammunition moving in or which is a part of interstate or foreign commerce, and which while so moving or constituting such part has been stolen, knowing, or having reasonable cause to believe the same to have been stolen.

(i) It shall be unlawful for any person to transport, ship, or knowingly receive in interstate or foreign commerce any firearm from which the manufacturer's serial number has been removed, obliterated, or altered, and the possession of any such firearm shall be presumptive evidence that such firearm was transported, shipped, or received, as the case may be, by the possessor in violation of this Act.

Section 3. (a) Any manufacturer or dealer desiring a license to transport, ship, or receive firearms or ammunition in interstate or foreign commerce shall make application to the Secretary of the Treasury, who shall prescribe by rules and regulations the information to be contained in such application. The applicant shall, if a manufacturer, pay a fee of $25 per annum, and, if a dealer, shall pay a fee of $1 per annum.

(b) Upon payment of the prescribed fee, the Secretary of the Treasury shall issue to such applicant a license which shall entitle the licensee to transport, ship, and receive firearms and ammunition in interstate and foreign commerce unless and until the license is suspended or revoked in accordance with the provisions of this Act: *Provided*, That no license shall be issued to any applicant within two years after the revocation of a previous license.

(c) Whenever any licensee is convicted of a violation of any of the provisions of this Act, it shall be the duty of the clerk of the court to notify the Secretary of the Treasury within 48 hours after such conviction and said Secretary shall revoke such license: *Provided*, That in the case of appeal from such conviction the licensee may furnish a bond in the amount of $1,000 and upon receipt of such bond acceptable to the Secretary of the Treasury he may permit the licensee to continue business during the period of the appeal, or should the licensee refuse or neglect to furnish such bond, the Secretary of the Treasury shall suspend such license until he is notified by the clerk of the court of last appeal as to the final disposition of the case.

(d) Licensed dealers shall maintain such permanent records of importation, shipment, and other disposal of firearms and ammunition as the Secretary of the Treasury shall prescribe.

Section 4. The provisions of this Act shall not apply with respect to the transportation, shipment, receipt, or importation of any firearm, or ammunition, sold or shipped to, or issued for the use of, (1) the United States or any department, independent establishment, or agency thereof; (2) any State, Territory, or possession, or the District of Columbia, or any department, independent establishment, agency, or any political subdivision thereof; (3) any duly commissioned officer or agent of the United States, a State, Territory, or possession, or the District of Columbia, or any political subdivision thereof; (4) or to any bank, public carrier, express, or armored-truck company organized and operating in good faith for the transportation of money and valuables; (5) or to any research laboratory designated by the Secretary of the Treasury; *Provided*, That such bank, public carriers, express, and armored-truck companies are granted exemption by the Secretary of the Treasury; nor to the transportation, shipment, or receipt of any antique or unserviceable firearms, or ammunition, possessed and held as curios or museum pieces: *Provided*, That nothing herein contained shall be construed to prevent shipments of firearms and ammunition to institutions, organizations, or persons to whom such firearms and ammunition may be lawfully delivered by the Secretary of War, nor to prevent the transportation of such firearms and ammunition so delivered by their lawful possessors while they are engaged in military training or in competitions.

Section 5. Any person violating any of the provisions of this Act or any rules and regulations promulgated hereunder, or who makes any statement in applying for the license or exemption provided for in this

Act, knowing such statement to be false, shall, upon conviction thereof, be fined not more than $2,000, or imprisoned for not more than five years, or both.

Section 6. This Act shall take effect thirty days after its enactment.

Section 7. The Secretary of the Treasury may prescribe such rules and regulations as he deems necessary to carry out the provisions of this Act.

Section 8. Should any section or subsection of this Act be declared unconstitutional, the remaining portion of the Act shall remain in full force and effect.

Section 9. This Act may be cited as the Federal Firearms Act.

Approved, June 30, 1938. (Public No. 785–75th Congress; Chapter 850–3rd Session)

(Note: The word fugitive is spelled "fugutive" in some instances, apparently a typographical error in original official printing)

Customs Rates and Regulations

On the importation of firearms and parts the government has set up certain rules and regulations as well as a sliding scale of duty to tax the importer. Only those of direct interest to gunsmiths are mentioned, and it will be necessary for anyone intending to go into the business of importing firearms or parts to contact his nearest Custom House for the latest procedures involved, as well as any possible changes in rates.

Where the items concerned are regular items of commerce, sold abroad in addition to overseas sales, the following percentages are figured on the wholesale or buying cost paid to the foreign supplier. However, if the item is made solely for export to the United States the percentages will not necessarily apply, and the Appraiser at the Custom House will set the duty.

On all shipments valued at more than $100.00, the government requires a bond from the consignee, and reserves the right to demand a bond on shipments of lesser value if it sees fit. This is to protect the government in case of damage claims or claims of fraud on either side. The bond is usually handled through a customs broker, who backs your deal with his own bond and responsibility for a small fee. He will also handle on the spot any details of paper work necessary. There are usually one or more brokers operating at each port of entry, and customs houses will advise you of names and addresses of licensed brokers in their vicinity.

To import firearms for resale an import license is required, which

.22/250

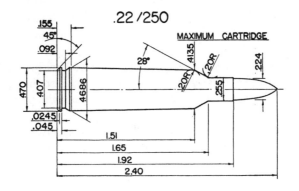

MAXIMUM CARTRIDGE

.155
45°
.092
28°
.4135
.20R
.20R
.224
.470
.407
.4686
.255
.0245
.045
1.51
1.65
1.92
2.40

MINIMUM CHAMBER

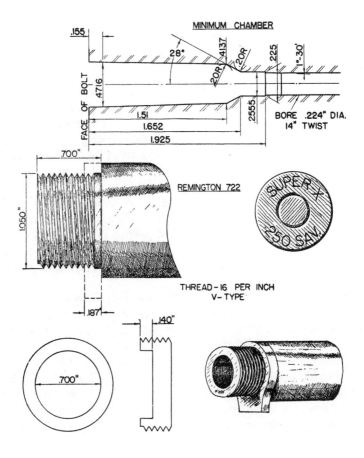

.155
28°
.4137
.20R
.20R
225
1°-30'
FACE OF BOLT
.4716
.2555
BORE .224" DIA.
14" TWIST
1.51
1.652
1.925

.700"
1.050"
REMINGTON 722
SUPER X
.250 SAV.

THREAD-16 PER INCH
V-TYPE

.187

.140"

.700"

must be secured through the United States State Department. The fee is high enough to make it uneconomic for small operators to go into importing.

Formerly a series of trade agreements covering "favored" and "unfavored" nations gave us double duties on imports from the latter

---

THE .22/250

Probably the most popular of the high velocity .22 wildcats. This cartridge is well balanced—easy to load to accuracy with almost any combination of components. Made by sizing down the necks of .250/3000 Savage cases, cartridge cases are easy to make, last a considerable number of reloadings, and do not develop dangerous pressures with any large-rifle powder. Barrel life is longer than with comparable wildcats or factory cartridges, and the use of graphite wads will just about guarantee an accurate life of over 5000 rounds with any good barrel steel.

This is the only .22 wildcat cartridge I personally would whole-heartedly recommend, particularly for a customer just taking up hand-loading. It is hard to go wrong in making up cartridges, he will not wear the barrel half out trying to find an accurate load, and any good barrelmaker can turn out a super-accurate job for it. Even variations in bore and groove diameters do not seem to greatly affect performance, although of course selection of bullets is influenced. Heavy barrels are not necessary for vermin rifles, for sporter-weight arms will deliver minute-of-angle accuracy.

This cartridge is really quite old, as Newton experimented with it almost forty years ago, but was not successful with the highly erosive powders of that time, and also due to the fact that all available .22 caliber bullets—and bullet design ideas—were much overweight and developed maximum pressures. Using bullets from 70 to 90 grains in weight, early experimenters could not obtain high velocities, naturally, so .22 center-fire development was stalled until Niedner and Shelhamer made up a hand press to turn out lightweight jacketed bullets for the .22 Niedner Magnum cartridges. Sisk and others began the manufacture of good bullets, in weights from 35 to 63 grains, and the .22 wildcat business became a popular pastime for rifle-minded gunsmiths. Today, everybody is in the act.

Present day powders and non-corrosive primers are equally responsible for the success of the .22 high velocity cartridges, however, for early primers were rough on barrel steel, and the combination of primer and powder made experimentation expensive. Even today, the Government FA 70 priming mixture is rough on small bores, as the chlorate compound causes a more concentrated salt deposit to invoke rust than it does in larger calibers.

The short-action Remington 722 can be used for .22/250 rifles, although hand-loaders will not care for it too much because the extraction system is rather arbitrary and will not permit the shooter to easily pick the fired case from the open action, as will Mauser-type extractors. With the Remington, the fired case leaves the receiver as soon as it is withdrawn far enough for the front end to clear the receiver ring. Headspace can be regulated somewhat by varying the thickness of the recoil shoulder-plate.

category, but now all nations are rated in the favored class and duties are constant for all nations.

The following list covers most items of interest:

Stock Blanks   Duty free, if in the rough. One side may be planed.
Rifle Parts   27½%
Shotgun Parts 27½%
Pistol Parts   105%
Rifle and Shotgun Fittings   27½% (Swivels, sights, buttplates, and the like.)

Rifles
Value less than $ 5.00	$0.75 each plus 22½%
Value $ 5.00 to $10.00	2.00 each plus 22½%
Value 10.00 to 25.00	3.00 each plus 22½%
Value 25.00 to 50.00	5.00 each plus 22½%
Value over $50.00 each,	25%

Combination Rifles and Shotguns   Value over $50.00 each, 32½%

Shotguns
Value less than $ 5.00	15%
Value $ 5.00 to $10.00	$1.00 plus 15%
Value 10.00 to 25.00	2.00 plus 15%
Value 25.00 to 50.00	3.00 plus 15%
Value over $50.00 each,	20%

Pistols & Revolvers $3.00 each plus 55%
Shotgun Barrels $1.00 each plus 15%
Rifle Barrels $2.00 each plus 25%

Sample items, not for resale, may be imported without the State Department license.

CHAPTER 5

Shop Practice

THIS chapter is concerned principally with taking care of the odds and ends of the shop proper—care of tools, making tools, filing out parts and other chores. The following chapter covers the little short-cuts, "tricks of the trade" and actual work on some of the commonest firearms which would technically come under the heading of shop practice.

First, we might as well go into the matter of sharpening tools. You need sharp chisels, saws, planes, drills and taps, because it is not only possible to do better work with sharp tools, but to do it easier.

Woodworking tools require practice in stoning, more than grinding, although you will need some skill to hollow-grind a straight edge across a plane blade. I hate the present-day carborundum stones, but we have to use them. Most wood cutting edges come hollow-ground, except on curved chisels, but not whetted. The bevel must be worked on to produce a razor-sharp even edge, so put a few drops of oil in the middle of the smooth or fine-cutting side of your whetstone and set the bevel on it, holding the bevel flat with the finger-tips of your left hand and the blade proper with your right (assuming you are right-handed). Your whetting motion is not back-and-forth, but an oval movement, with stiff wrists, keeping the bevel on the stone at all times, not rocking forward and back which will round off the bevel promoting a sharp edge in a hurry but one which will not last long. After a minute or so stop and wipe the oil from the blade and examine the edge, which should show a bright whetted even surface from $\frac{1}{32}''$ to $\frac{3}{64}''$ wide, and have a fine "wire" edge turned on the back side. If this narrow edge bevel tapers in width, you are putting too great pressure on one side or corner, and must whet again to straighten it up.

The wire edge is removed by placing the back of the blade flat on the stone and making a few circular passes, which straighten out the edge and may remove it entirely. If it is not removed, draw the edge across a bit of close-grained wood, through the corner to reach the end grain. Now, it is nice to have a white Washita oilstone and repeat the process to get that razor edge. Baker liked his tools *really* sharp, so gilded the lily by stropping. A razor strop is not so good—you want a fairly small piece of sole or saddle leather, smooth, backed by a block of wood. Two by six inches is sufficient area. Wipe on the leather the oily paste worked up on the stones while whetting, for a dressing. In stropping, the cutting edge of the tool is drawn away, always, in straight strokes, or rather, pulls. Just a few will fix an edge that really does the work. All plane bits and chisel edges should shave hair from your arm, for a test.

To use a plane, any type, first set the blade so that it is cutting an even depth, not deeper on one side than the other, and see that the bottom of the plane is as smooth and slick as polishing and use will make it. For leveling a board, plank or stock blank, keep the plane body parallel with the direction of the work. For removing wood in a small area or on a corner, keep the plane and cutting edge at an angle—whichever angle cuts best. Advising that it is best to plane with the grain is a platitude, but doing so usually is impossible, since gun stocks are chosen for figure, not straight grain. The block plane, designed for cutting across end grain, will not work well on hardwoods that way, but is extremely handy used in the regular manner. I do not use the standard block plane too much, but find a lot of use for the very small Stanley No. 100 plane as it is short and can be used to the very end in stock shaping, working around curves. It helps a great deal in getting the final contours faired into each other.

Straight chisels are sharpened in the same manner as plane blades and a lot oftener. You will use them to cut in all directions regarding the grain of wood and in all manner of holding and pressure. There will be one-hand work to some extent, but most chisel cutting will be done holding the handle in one hand and providing forward pressure with the fingers of the other hand. I believe a large rounded, rather bulbous handle is best. Sharpening the inside-bevel curved chisels and gouges is not the problem it used to be, for you can find a small mounted grinding wheel in the hand grinder accessories to fit every size. No, you do not use the hand grinder, except when necessary to cut the entire bevel back $\frac{1}{32}''$ or more to remove a nick or chipped corner. Use the little cylindrical grinding wheels fine cutting grades, finishing with white Arkansas type, mounted in the lathe chuck and running slow. All you have to do is apply a drop of oil now and then and hold the chisel bevel to the turning whetstone. Remove the wire edges on the flat stone and wood as suggested in the case of the flat chisels.

If a great deal of sawing on stock blanks is anticipated, you may find it economical in the long run to sharpen your own saws and for that job will require a saw vise and saw set. The saw vise is a long-jawed clamp affair costing from one to two dollars usually, and the saw set a tong tool for bending the teeth after sharpening, also a reasonably-priced item. The saw is clamped, teeth upwards, vise jaws from $\frac{1}{4}''$ to $\frac{3}{8}''$ from edge, and with a slim taper saw file (a small, sharp-edged triangular model) file the edges of alternate teeth, at the same angle as the original, then reverse the saw and file the teeth you missed from the other side, at their correct angle. From one to four fairly gentle strokes should bring the teeth to sharp points. A glance at your saw edge will give you the correct idea better than words. The saw set is used to restore, emphasize or increase the bend of alternate teeth to enable them to bite into wood easily, without the kerf, or saw cut in the wood, being too narrow to permit free movement of the "back" or blade itself. For hardwood, not much set is required. Setting a saw is much more of a job than filing it, for each tooth must be angled the same as all others on its side of the edge. After setting, check set by holding your steel scale against sides of teeth as a straight edge, or better, a piece of flat stock previously squared, to locate outstanding individual teeth. Mark them and use the set to line them up with their fellows.

Most general gun shops will not dull a saw in two year's use, anyway, and as every community, large or small, has some old codger who makes himself a few nickels sharpening lawnmowers and filing saws, it is cheaper to give the job to him, telling exactly what you want done, providing sample scraps of walnut for test cutting, and getting him interested enough to do a top-notch job.

That last point is the secret of getting good work done for you outside the shop, in any capacity; get the worker interested in the job.

In sawing, the idea is usually to cut square, or straight. Whenever possible, square the work, so that all corners are right angles, and draw a pencil line completely around it, as a guide line for the saw. The mitre box saw cuts square with its base—if it is a good one, you cannot make it do otherwise.

You do not sharpen files, you take care of them. There are industrial concerns which specialize in "sharpening" coarse files used in foundries, and large shops, but their sharpening consists of acid-cleaning files, which does restore rough edges for a short time. The process will not work on the gunsmith's files. When the gun file begins to dull from use, or inadvertent attempts at use on hardened or case-hardened steel, put it aside for use as steel stock to make scrapers, burnishers, little chisels, or even flat springs and gun parts in a pinch. During the war I made many parts and springs from file steel which worked very well. No other steel was available most of the time.

As Clyde Baker remarked, it is possible to write a book on filing alone. The gunsmith is in a peculiar profession—he must be a jack of all trades and master of most of them. The true gunsmith, in the original sense of the title, must be a better woodworker than the professional cabinetmaker, a better hand with solder and brazing than the tinsmith, a better machinist than the machine shop employee, and as good a filer as a tool and die sinker, which is getting very good indeed.

The average man rubs a file back and forth over his work and wonders why he clogs up the file and gets a rough finish. You can file that way with a coarse file and get some metal off, but the right way to use the tool is in one direction only, against the cutting edges, lifting the file clear of the work on the back stroke. Try to get your chest and head over the work, lifting your elbows so that both arms are away from the body. Keep your wrists almost stiff and attempt to move the file with arm movements from the shoulder, without swaying the body very much. This is all directed toward achieving a straight, parallel movement of the file across the surface to be filed, in order to file an even, square plane, avoiding the tendency to rock the file and remove more metal from each side or corner than in the center. Pressure to be exerted against the work varies, of course, with the cut of file and hardness of material to be filed. The correct pressure will produce a smooth surface, regardless of whether a smooth or coarse file is used. It takes a long time to learn to file correctly, and many men never learn to do a good job. Not practice, but experience will be the real teacher. You will learn on each job. The type of steel to be filed has a lot to do with each job. As previously mentioned, most modern gun steel is soft and tough, clogging files almost every stroke should you exert much pressure. A clogged file, of course, tears little grooves across the work which often take quite a bit of careful filing and polishing to remove. Hard steels can often be touched with fine-cut files—but abrasive cloth will cut anything.

Never make your filing job harder than necessary. Do not use a fine file when a coarser cut will do; do not try to file off a quantity of metal that can be removed by hacksaw or grinder. Rough it off down close to your limit line then finish with a file. Use small cast-iron or soft steel-jawed vises for not only holding work, but as guides in straight

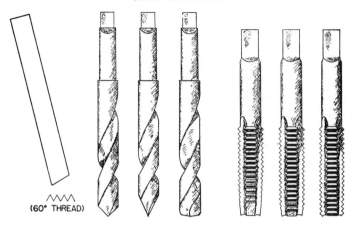

(60° THREAD)

TOOL POINTS

Shown at the left is a thread peening tool, as covered in the text, in slightly exaggerated working position to emphasize its purpose. In real use, it is canted more to the left.

The drills show standard pitch point for steel drilling; center, a pointed bit for special use on steel or general use on soft materials; and right, a bottoming drill.

Taps are, left to right, standard starting type, short lead starting or ordinary body tap, and bottoming tap.

filing, keeping the jaws square, clamping your work in them and filing right down into the jaws. You will not round many corners that way. Always make sure that the material being filed is held firmly in the vise. Very small irregular parts must sometimes be soldered to a larger bit of metal and the latter clamped, in order to work.

If you ever get the chance, go to a tool-making establishment and watch the die-sinkers at work. It is an education. You will see smooth surfaces filed in corners, curves, places where the file has very short movement.

Drills need to be kept sharp and in their stands. If you do not get the drill grinding attachment and must sharpen them by hand and eye, always drill a sample hole in a ¼″ piece of mild steel then try the drill bit in the hole with your fingers, and also the next largest size bit. If a larger size fits, you have uneven cutting lips. The correct drill should be a slip fit only—it should not wobble around. Occasionally you will meet up with a rifle receiver which is just a little too tough for the high-speed bits, but which can be drilled with a common carbon steel bit heated to cherry red and quenched in mercury. This makes it glass-hard and brittle, but with thinned cutting oil or straight lard oil it will cut with gentle, steady pressure on the drill-press feed.

Taps often require grinding for renewing dulled starting edges, and special shaping. Very long tapers need to be ground on starting taps for some deep holes in hard steels and occasionally you may need to grind the tap undersize its complete cutting length to get into the hole. More than once I have completely tapped a hole with three diameters of taps before getting the correct thread depth. Always use cutting oil, as used in machine shops, when tapping, and keep the hole clean, removing the tap every other turn at most, brushing off the tap and wiping the chips out of the hole. And, always drill your hole completely through the material wherever possible, as a safety measure in tapping. Blind holes, necessary in all barrel jobs and front receiver-ring locations, take a good deal more care than straight-through holes.

Handling a tap wrench requires care and concentration. Taps are of course very hard and brittle and must be turned on their axis—the least sideward movement or "springing" is liable to break it off in the hole. The tap wrench for small taps is either of two types, the old style being a straight bar of steel with adjustable fitting in center to clamp the square shank of tap, the newer version being a four-jaw chuck with a short body and a cross-bar handle. With either one, in tapping the handle is turned a very little—seldom over a one-eighth revolution at a time, and backed off a little to allow oil to reach the cutting edges for each movement. Whenever the tap begins to tighten in the hole, back it off very, very gently, and if it suddenly squeaks and will not budge either direction, stop and sweat—it is stuck. If you have an air hose, squirt air down the hole around the tap, flushing out what chips and dirty oil you can, put in more oil, blow it down well and try to get the tap back out. Should it refuse to move with the tap wrench, remove the wrench from the tap, put a bit of sheet lead around the tap down next to the hole, clamp on the parallel-jaw pliers, utter a short prayer, and attempt to turn it back. This usually works. When it does not, the tap breaks, leading us up to the problem of removing broken taps.

Except in shallow blind holes, this is not nearly the problem it is cracked up to be. If the tap is not smaller than the 6–48 size and breaks above, flush, or very slightly below the rim of the hole, it may be moved by setting the point of a prick punch against one flange next to the body of the tap and tapping the punch with the little hammer, driving the tap counter-clockwise of course. Should this fail and the tap chip off, keep chipping off, making slim taper punches and break-

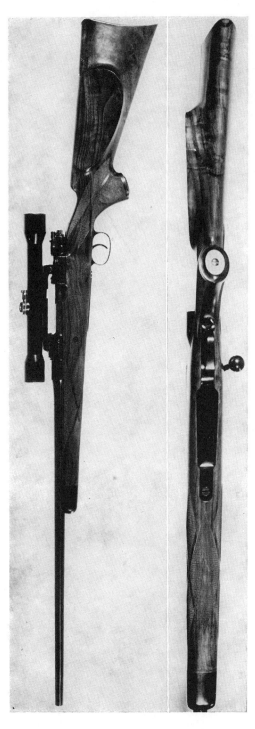

Custom .270 Winchester on military Mauser action. Barrel by Titus, stock by John Hearn, in good American walnut. Zeiss Zielvier lightweight scope in custom Tilden mount. Rifle weight is 8 lbs. 10 oz. Made for a very tall man, the butt is quite long. Barrel length, 23″.

In regard to the job above, Hearn writes: "When it comes to cheekpieces, I like them well sized and appreciable, else why have one at all? This one has considerable depth with a broad flare at the bottom and the face is slightly beveled-in to fit the contour of the shooter's cheek. This bevel cannot be too much however, because of the recoil of the rifle but I have checked the style of the above cheekpiece on my own rifle—a .35 Magnum which weighs but 7 pounds and 5 ounces—and it works out O K there."

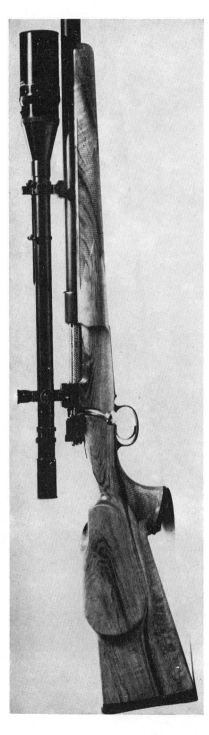

A .22–250 Bench Rest Pfeifer custom rifle for the South-Paw shooter who desires individual custom fitting. Action is FN Commercial Mauser, with firing mechanism speed-locked and an improved tool steel trigger installed.

Sighting equipment—2"—15X Target telescope with bases spaced 12" apart for a better point of balance and control. With this spacing .150 inches of movement per ¼ minute click for each 100 yards of range is obtained.

Pfeifer built this rifle for Mr. Marion E. Wiley of Laurel, Delaware, and custom stocked it with a very select close-grained piece of Oregon myrtle and fitted with an ebony pistol grip cap. A right-handed rolled cheekpiece individually made for this left-handed shooter. Notice groove in top forward portion of cheekpiece to allow removal of bolt.

ing the flanges and finally punching straight down on the center of the tap end. If the hole is clear through, you can drive the particles out, but keep freeing the work from the vise, and turning it upside down, shaking it, wiping holes, or blowing out with the air hose—anything to get the loose bits from the hole. You will seldom mess up the hole with the broken tap, as it is brittle and teeth break before tearing the partially-cut threads, but be careful with the punch, it will push the threads around if placed carelessly. Nickel steel is very good at holding its own against taps. I first learned this while once working on one of my own rifles, tapping an 8–40 thread in the thick top portion of a Remington Enfield receiver ring. The tap broke about $\frac{1}{8}''$ below surface and I, feeling very disgusted with myself, decided to just beat it on through, and figure on a larger-diameter screw and thread. I knocked it through with some effort and was surprised to find the threads not in the least damaged. In soft steel, such as .22 bolt action receivers, the threads would probably be hurt, but then I have never broken a tap in soft steel, and you probably will not either. Enfields, Springfields, Mausers and Winchester 54s and 70s will be the problem children.

In the blind holes, which should never be over $\frac{3}{16}''$ deep at most— $\frac{5}{32}''$ is sufficient on either 6–48 or 8–40 threads in my estimation— broken taps must be completely removed from the top and usually can be turned out with the punch method, or broken to bits and blown or shaken out. In all tapping, make sure the hole is right for the tap, never too small, and this especially applies to the blind hole. The No. 31 drill is correct for the 6–48 tap and the No. 29 for the 8–40. In soft steel, it is sometimes possible to use Nos. 32 and 30 respectively, for thin walled holes, such as in autoloading shotgun receivers, for instance.

Always, when tapping a blind hole, square the bottom of the hole after drilling it by using a drill bit ground almost straight across, to get a flat bottom. You may need three taps to properly thread the hole completely to the bottom, a short-tapered starting tap, a shorter-tapered one, and a bottoming tap ground flat on the bottom. Again, *always* mark the tap in some way—I wrap a strip of masking tape on it—so that you will know how much you have to go while tapping. Measure the depth of the hole against the end of the tap and mark the tap so you will know when to stop. Experience will develop your fingertips into pressure gages, but take few chances on "feeling" the tap bottom—it does not pay. Do not make small stop-collars to fit the taps.

When drilling a blind hole, it is a very good idea to mark the depth

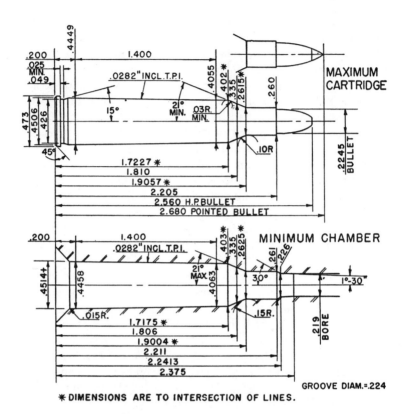

MAXIMUM
CARTRIDGE

.200
.025 MIN.
.049
.4449
1.400
.0282" INCL.T.P.I.
.4055
.402 *
.335
.2615
15°
21° MIN.
.03R. MIN.
.260
.473
.4506
.426
45°
.2245 BULLET
.10R
1.7227 *
1.810
1.9057 *
2.205
2.560 H.P.BULLET
2.680 POINTED BULLET

MINIMUM CHAMBER

.200
1.400
.0282" INCL.T.P.I.
.403 *
.335
.2625
.261
.226
.4514+
.4458
21° MAX.
.4063
30°
1°-30"
.015R.
.15R.
.219 BORE
1.7175 *
1.806
1.9004 *
2.211
2.2413
2.375

GROOVE DIAM.=.224

* DIMENSIONS ARE TO INTERSECTION OF LINES.

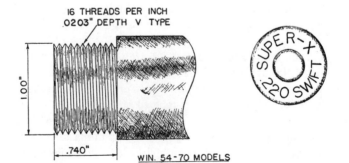

16 THREADS PER INCH
.0203" DEPTH V TYPE

1.00"

.740"

WIN. 54-70 MODELS

SUPER-X
.220 SWIFT

desired on the drill bit with tape as it is very embarrassing to drill through a barrel into the rifling. You may have to explain to the customer why he has to wait a couple of weeks until you can get him a new barrel. No one wants a barrel with a hole through it at right angles to the bore, however tightly plugged. (Actually such a hole appears not to affect accuracy at all, but causes a hard-to-keep-clean spot in the barrel. Many target shooters have fitted the old Colt-Marlin machine-gun heavy barrels to rifles for match shooting, plugging the gas-port in the bottom of the barrel. I recently removed a Stith telescope mount from a Winchester lever action rifle and found one of the front mounting holes drilled completely through the barrel. The rifle had never given trouble and was as accurate as any .30–30. In justice to the Stith company, I must add that they did not mount that telescope themselves.) The foregoing is inserted simply to point out that a barrel is not necessarily ruined by some blacksmith bearing down too hard on the drill. No gunsmith should ever do such a thing of course, and if he should, he should consider himself liable for the cost of a new barrel and all fitting charges on it.

THE .220 WINCHESTER SWIFT

The most highly publicized factory cartridge made, the Swift is still the fastest factory loaded sporting cartridge in the world at this writing. Muzzle velocity is rated at 4,140 FPS with the 48-grain bullet.

Intended for a vermin cartridge, the Swift has a spotted record as a big game rifle, due to its use by mediocre marksmen in the field. At ranges up to 200 yards, skilled hunters report excellent performance on deer, and at least one man I know of has killed several elk with the Swift, using handloaded ammunition. Used as intended, the cartridge is a very fine long range (400 yards) exterminator of crows, harmful hawks, woodchucks and other such targets. The loud report makes the rifle unpopular in densely settled farming communities, however.

The Swift is rather difficult to handload to maximum accuracy, probably because of the shoulder angle. Modern powders perform best in sharper-shouldered cases.

Reloaders find that the cases must be trimmed and sometimes have the necks reamed, as repeated firing causes the brass to flow forward and both lengthen and thicken the necks.

A high-pressure cartridge, the Swift has one of the strongest cases ever designed, being a semi-rimmed, thick base type. Originally, flashholes were small, approximately .060" in diameter, but now flashholes are larger, around .080", the same as other large rifle cartridges.

Good Mauser and Springfield actions, as well as 1917 Enfield and the Winchesters, are suitable for the Swift.

The final word on shop practice is—try and keep the joint clean as possible. Build shelves, drawers, put up pegs and hooks, and make racks to hold material and guns being worked on. Whether you keep the customers away from the shop area or not is up to you and the layout of the shop. Privacy is desirable at times, but it is impossible to keep the public completely away, and not too good business. The boys like to see you work. Some men are like myself, able to work and talk at the same time, and others are more single-tracked and cannot pay attention to the bench and conversation without the work suffering.

CHAPTER 6

Helpful Gunsmithing Knowledge

BEFORE you start reading this installment, you may as well know that it has no literary structure, no continuity (even less than preceding chapters) and probably poor grammar. It consists of bits of knowledge I garnered the hard way, and methods of doing many common gun jobs.

Dissassembling Guns. Naturally it is impossible to give detailed instructions on dismantling all small arms, and just a few principles need to be followed. The first is, never use much force. Every gun has a combination, like a puzzle (some really are puzzles, too!) and there is a system if you only study it a little. On bolt action rifles, especially large caliber arms, take out all the screws on the bottom of the stock, guard, forend, those under the guard—watch this, do not just remove the guard screws and pull at the stock. Some have hidden screws under triggerplates, and such places. If I remember correctly, the Savage Model 20 has five screws to get out before the stock is off. On fancy foreign rifles, watch out for Greener-type side safeties, checking to see if it interferes in the separation of the receiver assembly from the stock. You might even find cross-keys in forends on takedown bolt actions held in place by tiny screws.

Most shotguns are takedown type, the single and double barrel models having snap-on forends, removable by just pulling the tip downward against a spring, and barrels and receiver separating when the action is opened. Yet a good many old model guns and present-day high-priced shotguns have forends secured by plungers activated for removal by pressure on a button protruding from the tip, or flush catches placed on the bottom of the forend to be pressed, pushed or pulled.

If an unfamiliar double-barreled shotgun appears for action repairs, take off the buttplate and see if it has a stock screw; a few double guns do. On many of the sidelock type, the sideplate can be removed without removing the buttstock. Whenever it is necessary to snap the hammers or firing pins on a shotgun action, hold a block of wood over the face of the breech, for the pins to contact. The majority of concealed-hammer guns do not appreciate much dry-firing or snapping. Make a few dummies for trying them on triggerpulls or safety work, by cutting off live shells a half inch or so ahead of the brass base, removing shot and powder, firing the primer then replacing primer with a bit of fairly hard rubber or neoprene. Dead or dummy rounds for testing extraction and ejection, and feeding operations on repeating shotguns may be made from live shells by removing the shot wad, taking the shot and powder out, firing the primer, then making a wood filler for the shell, replacing the shot wad and crimp. You do not use fired shells because they are usually expanded oversize. I prefer dummies made as described over metal dummies, since they really approximate live ammunition.

Double guns are prone to have at least one very strong V or flat spring, usually working on the top lever, and these are hard to live with at times. The L. C. Smith always gave me trouble until I figured out how to hold things in line. The gun comes apart easily—but goes back together hard. It is necessary to remove the bottom or triggerplate to get at the safety and other interior parts, and as the bottom end of the top lever engages in this plate, when it is removed the stiff spring pushes the lever to one side, so that when you attempt to replace the plate, the hole and the lever no longer line up. As it is under great tension, the lever cannot be easily pried into position. I make little L-shaped tools for this job, usually just a piece of welding rod or stiff wire a little over $\frac{1}{16}''$ in diameter, with the leg of the "L" perhaps $\frac{1}{8}''$ long. Hold the action upside down in the vise, and with pliers compress the spring slightly to slip this part of the tool in place between the long leaf of the spring and side of cut in frame (bearing against end of lever and frame) to hold the lever over where it belongs. The long end of the "tool" is against the rear of the action, sticking straight out to the side. The stock is brought up against it, and just enough wood cut away to allow it to come to its proper position, with the tool carefully left in place. Now the triggerplate can be inserted and screwed in place, after which the tool is wiggled loose and out of the gun. The little hole does not matter, as the sidelock plate covers it of course, the sidelocks going on last.

On many of the cheaper shotguns, using coil springs and straight-line firing pins instead of the hammer system, study the action with the stock off before removing any springs. Many of the spring plungers,

or guides, have little holes through them. These are for helping to assemble, as the spring is meant to be compressed and a little pin inserted
through the hole to hold it in the shortened compressed condition for
removal and replacement. Often you will need to drill such holes yourself, to save a great deal of effort and time trying to push strong springs
into place.

The autoloading shotguns, at present all manufactured being the
Browning patent, are very simple to work on as the maker's directions

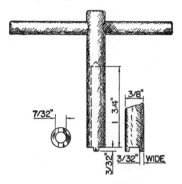

LEE-ENFIELD BOLT TOOL

Necessary for dismantling the bolt mechanism of the British Lee-Enfield
rifle. The bolt head is unscrewed with the fingers, the set screw removed
from the back end of the cocking piece, and the tool inserted in the front
end of the bolt and the firing pin unscrewed from the cocking piece from
the front. Hold the cocking piece firmly, as the mainspring is under tension
all the time during the disassembly job.

cover disassembly. Pump action shotguns are also usually quite easy
to takedown, although some of the obsolete Remingtons such as the
Model 10 are rather troublesome. On nearly all shotguns of this type
removal of the triggerguard will indicate what needs to be done.

Tearing down bolt action rifles is obviously simple, regardless of
type, and the same goes for disassembly of the bolt, with the possible
exception of the Mannlicher-Schoenauer, and Lee-Enfield. The Mannlicher bolt is broken down by pressing inward on the safety lever and
rotating the bolt nut, usually a quarter-turn only, and removing it.
Then the bolt head, with the locking lugs and extractor, is turned until
it disengages from the body of the bolt and the bolt head, firing pin
and mainspring are removed, from the front. The Lee-Enfield firing
pin and mainspring also remove from the front, but are unscrewed
from the cocking piece after the bolt head is unscrewed. The screw

head at the back of the cocking piece is a set screw only, and must be taken out first. It is necessary to make a special tool to take the firing pin out, a hollow tubular slotted screwdriver or wrench, as illustrated. A special tool is also needed to handle the Winchester 52 bolt, which is available from the Winchester Company, or used to be, anyway.

Pump or slide action rifles are almost always takedown models and the parts very accessible. Some of the older guns are not—the old Stevens Visible Loader is known in gun shops as the "Miserable Loader." I could write a book about that gun, too. With such rifles the only thing to do is study it carefully, take out one screw or pin at a time and try to get down a section at a time. Most trouble with pump guns is the feed system.

Lever action rifles are not at all hard to work on, although on most of them you have to take everything off to get at any one part. With Marlin, Savage or Winchester lever action repeating rifles the butt-stock is first removed to get at the action. The breechbolt of the Savage 99 can be removed without having to take out the lever and the Winchester 92 and 94 models are among the very few firearms which the layman can (and does) disassemble by what I call the "moron method"—taking out all the screws and shaking. Nothing complicated at all about either. The Winchester Model 71 and 95 require a little more thought to tear down completely, but offer no problem whatever to anyone who can think before and while using screwdrivers and punches.

Obsolete single shot rifles are usually lever action falling block types, and about the only generality applicable to all as regards stripping is—remove buttstock and forend and either completely remove or release tension on the mainspring. From there on, excepting the Sharps Borchardt, disassembly is rather obvious. This Sharps action, long obsolete and seldom seen, is still one of the best for custom varmint rifles and action work should be done only by men experienced in such work. Parker Ackley is one of the few who really understand everything about this action. If you can get hold of an old beat-down Sharps, you can play with it and probably teach yourself a lot.

I think I will just give up on the handgun instruction—besides the few American-made types, we now have in this country literally dozens of different foreign makes and types. I know of no military pistol which is difficult to tear down and reassemble, but some of the European commercial weapons are hard to figure out. The most sensible advice I can give is to get the two books on pistols previously mentioned—Smith's *The Book of Pistols and Revolvers* and Smith's

Small Arms of The World, The Stackpole Co., Harrisburg, Pa.

In disassembling any type of gun there are a few points to keep in mind. Remember how each part came out and the order of the parts in removal, for practically all firearms are assembled in reverse order, exactly. Keep a supply of containers—boxes or cans—to receive parts. I have a number of large tin cake pans, about 2″ deep, and for new and freshly-blued guns and parts, usually use cardboard boxes, or put a cloth in the bottom of the tin pan. These pans are also used filled with cleaning solvent to wash fouled-up guns.

Always use the right size screwdriver and punch for the screw or pin to be moved. When a screw is tight, put penetrating oil on every portion of it you can reach, set a screwdriver in the slot and tap the handle briskly a time or two and set the gun aside for as many hours as you can. If it is rusted in, a couple of days or a week is not too long and you may have to use heat from a torch to help move the rust around a little, using more penetrating oil as the receiver or main part cools—just a little heat—not enough to change color of the metal. A frozen pin may resist driving at first and if oil will not help you may as well resign yourself to spoiling the end of it and go ahead and beat it out by main strength. I find a small nail-set handy to start tight pins, as its end is less likely to skid over and mar a receiver. Replacement pins are not hard to make on a lathe and heat treatment is simple.

Cleaning. To the gunsmith, "cleaning" has a different meaning than to the layman. Cleaning the barrel is a minor point in the gun shop, and a clean-up job means disassembling the arm more or less completely—if you have an air compressor you can get the job done without taking off everything but what is left of the blue on the barrel. All separate parts, insides of receivers, barrel and magazines are washed in solvent, scrubbed with old nylon-bristled tooth-brushes to clean off the caked dirt, oil and rust (often necessary to use the power-driven wire brush on the grinder), pin and screw holes cleaned, everything dried completely and re-oiled. It is important to get the parts dried, for until all are bone-dry, you will not know they are clean, and also because if the solvent is still lurking in a few corners and holes when the gun is assembled, it will dry later and may leave spots open to attack by rust. The air hose greatly simplifies drying of course, and if not available, a rinse in clean solvent or even gasoline will allow quick evaporation. Gasoline is not to be recommended as a cleaning agent because of the fire hazard, but if you can step into the back yard a minute while using it, there is no great danger. After cleaning, be sure to oil thoroughly, getting into every crevice, opening, slot, groove and hole as well as on all smooth surfaces. The right way to oil a gun is to slop on all the oil you can then wipe off all you can. Here, the air hose is a very great help, as the jet of air will blow oil into any and all hard-to-reach spots, and blow off all but a thin film.

The cleaning angle can be a source of easy income to the gunsmith. I make a practice of charging $2.50 for complete cleanup and minor adjustment, on all types of weapons—pistols, revolvers, rifles and shotguns. The minor adjustment simply means knocking off objectionable burrs, setting springs right—no repair work such as adjusting triggerpulls or sights. The flat rate for all guns is a good advertising point, although of course some guns require a great deal more work than others. It averages out well, however. For every veteran Winchester M97 shotgun to be set aright you will get an easy job like a .22 autoloading rifle. Some guns will not come in until they are on the verge of retirement, but others will be in perfect condition, requiring only to have the old dirty oil washed off and replaced with clean. Such guns belong to careful people who take care of them and want to keep them in good condition.

Cleaning the stocks and forends and slide handles should be done dry, if possible, as either solvent or water may affect the seasoning and fit of the wood. In some cases it will be necessary to use water to remove dried mud, but the wood should be dried immediately, and unless the customer wants to pay extra for smoothing out a few dents and refinishing; just wipe the wood parts with linseed oil.

Barrel cleaning is usually a short process for the gunsmith since he can clamp the gun in the vise and work at it with several rods and brushes, employ powerful solvents and special cleaners. For cleaning shotgun barrels, all gauges, I have as a main rod an army .50 caliber machine-gun type, as well as the conventional wooden shotgun types. To get fouling, lead and rust out I simply put a .45 caliber brass brush in the rod and wind enough fine steel wool on the brush to fit the particular gauge of the gun being worked on. The .410 does not need much as the .45 brush works well alone. I find that the steel wool does a better job faster than the regular shotgun brushes and cleaners.

Rifle and pistol barrels are cleaned with both the proper size brush and one size larger, such as a .25 caliber brush for a .22, a .27 caliber for a .25 caliber rifle, and so on. Due to the advent of non-corrosive priming mixtures some twenty years ago, most .22 barrels are in good shape, excepting the very old guns. When confronted with an unusually bad barrel on an old rifle, rusted almost beyond use, I use one of the present-day rust removers on the brush. I think the bottle I have now is titled "Rust-Off." This mixture—and probably most of the others—seems to be nothing more than about an eight-to-one solution of water and sulphuric acid. It will take off blueing at a touch and must be handled with care. I do not approve too much of the use of acids on guns for any purpose but in the case of a badly-rusted barrel feel that scouring with a bronze bore brush dipped in acid solution is necessary, not so much for just getting the rust out as for killing the oxidation. To positively stop rust it is necessary to remove all the pitted surface down to clean metal. The rust-removing solutions eat all impurities, leaving pure steel or iron—and some of them are strong enough to pit smooth surfaces through this action. In any case, if a barrel is cleaned with an acid mixture it should be thoroughly washed out with water, preferably lukewarm, and very thoroughly dried before oiling. I neither use nor recommend this bore-cleaning system except on barrels in very bad shape, which would be replaced with new ones if the owner were not so hard up or just plain tight.

For the average barrel which is merely fouled up with lead, burned powder residue, and/or metal-fouling from jacketed bullets, the ordinary brass or bronze bristle brushes will work well, used with G. I. Bore Cleaner, the old Winchester Crystal Cleaner or other ammonia solution, Protectobore or Chloroil. Hoppe's No. 9 is excellent for cleaning arms using lead bullets and non-corrosive priming, but is not recommended for high-powered stuff, especially .30–06 issue ammunition. It will work, but you will spend a week cleaning one barrel. If you want to experiment a little, make up your own mixture of oil, powdered rouge and a wee bit of ammonia. For the G. I. chlorate primers, make an emulsion, using oil, water, rouge and ammonia. Shake it up each time you need it. Ammonia serves to dissolve lead and metal fouling, and can be omitted if an ordinary powder solvent is desired for just routine cleaning a gun after firing. Water must be introduced to the chlorate or salt-containing primer mixtures like the Frankfort Arsenal No. 70 or Western 8½ G. Oil will not dissolve salt, and salt is the great rusting agent. Ammonia solutions should not be left in the barrels for any length of time; G. I. Bore Cleaner and Chloroil can be left in the bores a week or ten days; Hoppe's, not over three or four days. I do not know about the others, not having used them in this manner. Protectobore is quite a good preparation for cleaning in general. The above references to leaving solutions in barrels for days refers principally to arms which are fired for one reason or another while being worked on, or your own rifles you may use on Sundays only. Sometimes you may test-fire or sight in a rifle or pistol and find that

.25/35 WINCHESTER

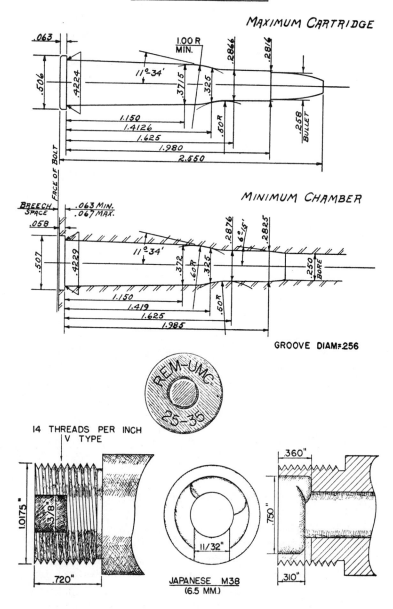

MAXIMUM CARTRIDGE

MINIMUM CHAMBER

GROOVE DIAM=.256

14 THREADS PER INCH
V TYPE

JAPANESE M38
(6.5 MM.)

further work is needed, so you must protect the barrel until the day you next get to the range.

In perfect barrels, soiled only with powder and primer residue, it is usually possible to clean them without the wire brushes by wiping them with patches soaked in solvent. Where corrosive primers have been used it is a good idea to use one of the new nylon bristle brushes. I have no use for the common "bristle" brush, made of hog hair. In all cases, solvents should be cleaned from the barrel before firing or oiling.

Oiling a thoroughly clean barrel is not the very simple operation it is usually considered, because if you are not careful, you will not get oil over the entire surface. Many a man who pampers his bore is puzzled by the rifling grooves developing dark corners. This is usually due to use of the standard-size cleaning patch for the caliber concerned, with a button-tip cleaning rod, also of the right caliber, resulting in

---

THE .25/35 WINCHESTER

This little deer cartridge has a good hunting reputation, in spite of its low muzzle velocity of 2,280 FPS with the 117-grain bullet. In the Winchester M94 rifles and carbines, the .25/35 is more accurate than the .30/30.

Years ago, this was one of the popular handloader's vermin cartridges, and many highly accurate single shot rifles were made up for it. Giving very little recoil even in the light Model 94 carbine, the .25/35 is an excellent caliber for a woman or young boy to use for deer, where ranges are short as up to 150 yards, the cartridge is an excellent killer. I have seen deer shot with it and noted the bullet's effect, which was considerably more than I expected from the low-velocity rating.

The Japanese Arisaka 38 barrel shank is shown, as these rifles are well suited for rebarreling to .25/35. The highly touted recessed barrel breech, which encloses the head of the bolt, is shown and contrary to many opinions, I fail to see any reason whatsoever why this system of breeching is any better than the Mauser or Springfield method. If anything, the rigidity of the barrel and receiver joint is decreased and in the case of an extreme pressure, the cartridge head can still flow to the left and gas blow back both inside the bolt and along the left receiver wall. The little support of the cartridge case between the bolt face and the breech of the barrel of this method over that of the Mauser is of practically no importance, since modern cartridge cases are solid at this portion of the base, and absolutely no holding strength is increased, because this is regulated by the bolt lugs engaging in the receiver recesses in the receiver ring in all large bolt actions of the Mauser family, of which the Japanese action is an offshoot.

One wartime Japanese rifle, with a cast action of soft steel, utilized a special type of barrel breech, in which the locking lug recesses for the bolt were machined, so that the bolt actually locked in the barrel. I have seen only one of these rifles, but have heard of others. Other cast actions had standard barrel systems, and would blow up on even light loads.

too tight a fit causing the oil to be squeezed from the patch when the rod is moved a few inches. I believe all oiling should be done with slotted-tips and small patches saturated in oil, passed at least three times through the bore. So far as proper oils are concerned, stick to "gun" oils: they are highly refined and tested for staying qualities. Any of the reputable brands are satisfactory—Hoppe's Gun Oil, Tri-Pak, Winchester Gun Oil, Nyoil, and such. I like Nyoil best, for absolutely no reason I can give. The combination oil-and-solvents like Marble's Powder Solvent Oil and Pacific Gun Oil are good, but the gunsmith should ignore the solvent feature and use them as light oils. Such preparations are ideal for the hunter or rifleman to use in the field at the end of a day's shooting, in inclement weather.

Automobile oil should never be used by a gunsmith, however highly advertised as "pure." I have scraped too much gummed auto oil out of actions to have any patience with the economy-minded few who think it is okay. Should any shop require so much oil as to make purchase of standard gun oils hard on the overhead, I suggest getting in touch with any of the large oil companies, for quantities of proper oil. The gun companies do not make their oil—they buy it; and you can too, specifying what you want. Very light oils, such as motion picture projector oil, are best for well-fitted actions as found on target revolvers and high-grade shotguns. These oils are usually more expensive than gun oils, due to refinement to produce great staying qualities. An oil which dries, gums or otherwise breaks down obviously is not so hot for a gun. Sperm oil is a natural, if you can get it—it is scarce today. I believe that the Tri-Pak Oil now on the market has a sperm base, which puts it up with any for quality. Do not ever use 3-In-1 Oil if you can help it. Keep some around—it is one of the best for heat blueing screwheads. This oil is advertised as having been improved and may be okay now, but in the past it was strictly undesirable in firearms.

Preserving a gun for any length of time, particularly in a humid climate, or one which has considerable variations in temperature, requires grease. I cannot bring myself to trust any oil for long periods of time. Properly greasing a bore is a chore, for it must be put in hot in order to spread over all surfaces and into all corners. Merely blobbing some grease on a patch and shoving it through the barrel is a fine way to promote a few rust streaks. Gun grease should be heated until it is the consistency of light automobile oil—say No. 10—and put into the barrel with a small patch. As the barrel will cool the grease instantly, it is well to warm the barrel slightly in order that the preservative may flow over all portions of the bore. Any gun grease advertised as such should be thoroughly satisfactory. G. I. cosmoline is a very heavy grease and must be heated for any use. Natural clear petroleum jelly or RIG (Rust Inhibiting Grease) are of lighter body and can be used cold. The purpose of greasing a barrel is to exclude all air from the naked steel, and the perfect way would be to fill the bore, chamber through muzzle, with solid grease or cosmoline. The next best thing is to coat the interior completely.

Patches, rags or other plugs should *never* be placed in the muzzle or chamber. However well oiled or greased, the pressure of insertion will thin the coat of preservative at that point in the barrel and eventually allow air, with its moisture content, to reach the steel and rust it.

Concerning the rods, I like Marble Pistol Rods and the one-piece Belding and Mull stainless steel rifle rods. With a lathe available it is of course easy to make rods from drill rod, but after fooling around a good many years, I think the smartest thing to do is get a set of B & M rods with all tips. All rods should be polished lengthwise with very fine worn abrasive cloth and then crocus cloth, to make them as slick as possible. A rough or soft-surfaced rod will pick up grit and cut the barrel. Hard rods will not allow any abrasive dust to imbed itself. I automatically wipe off any rod before inserting it into a barrel.

I consider the Mill-Rose bronze bore brushes best, although Gunslick and Marble brushes are very satisfactory. If you can swindle the nearest military installation out of a few .50 caliber machine gun brushes by all means do so, for they are very good on old .45 caliber barrels. Today short brushes are made for revolvers, the body of the brush passing into the cylinder well so that no bristles need to be reversed in pulling the brush out. Any rifle brush can be shortened by clipping it with the side-cutters, then twisting the cut end to keep the bristles in place.

The patch problem is always present. The gunsmith uses so many patches that the commercial ones cost too much in the long run, and government patches are not always available. The main thing is to get cloths and patches that have one side free of lint. I bought a batch of cotton flannel once, but have never used much of it because it leaves lint on the guns and gun parts. Always use cotton material, or scraps of linen, if any. Worn-out, well-washed cotton clothing of almost any sort is good.

In general cleaning, particularly in clearing dirty screw holes and removing the oily chips from freshly-tapped holes, I find great use for cleaning tissue. A small box of Kleenex will last me a week. Its absorbent qualities are very helpful. It does leave "lint," which is easily blown or brushed away.

Drilling. Drilling and tapping holes for mounting sights is one of the most frequent of gunsmithing jobs, and one which requires thought at all times. Nine out of ten holes go into curved surfaces, and it is not always easy to make the drill cut exactly where you want it to; you have to be careful, watch every step, stop and check, and stay on your toes.

In mounting sights, covered in a later chapter, I will go into the details, but now, for the generalities: The lay-out of the holes is all-important for proper location, and perfect center-punching all-important to proper starting of the drill. Your scriber or scratch-awl may mark the gun surface or it may not. Some very hard receivers resist scratching completely, and for these several treatments are possible—annealing, grinding away the hardened outer surface, or plating. You are not concerned with the blue at the hole area, as it will be both drilled away and covered with the sight or mount base, so it may be carefully polished off *at the approximate hole location only.* To get a perfect marking surface it is simplest to put on a drop of copper sulphate, which will plate the spot with copper in a minute or so. The copper is easily scribed. Thin case-hardening will sometimes allow center-punching while resisting the scribe, but if the punch fails, you are not set back very much. I favor annealing in just one spot—the thin right side wall on Springfield, Mauser and Enfield receiver bridges, or rear receiver rings—for mounting micrometer receiver sights. This I do with the welding torch, holding the actual welding flame to the spot involved until a $\frac{1}{8}''$ round red spot appears. By using the torch in this manner, only the spot touched by the blue flame core is softened. Annealed steel can be scribed, punched, drilled, and tapped easily.

Should the location of hole be in a part not suited to annealing, such as a front receiver ring, it is best to grind through the surface. My system is to locate the hole, take or make a little washer or plate $\frac{1}{32}''$ thick, with the hole the *body* size of screw to be fitted, put the washer or plate on a strip of masking tape, punch a hole through the tape to correspond with the hole in washer, then place this plate over the hole location and press the tape down. You now have a sort of grinding guide and can employ the dental engine or hand grinder with small stones to grind the hard gun surface away without straining your hand trying to hold the grinder in one position on exposed metal. Often you can cut the necessary few thousandths inch of hard surface away without disturbing your original scribe marking of the hole boundary

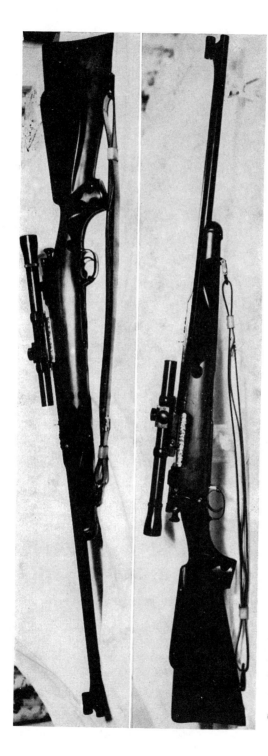

Custom Springfield, metalwork and barrel by W. A. Sukalle, stock by Thomas Shelhamer, engraving by Griebel and Hilton. This rifle has a ribbed barrel (integral) Mauser-type hinged floorplate and three-leaf express sight. Note the schnabel forend tip. Lyman Alaskan scope in Griffin & Howe mount.

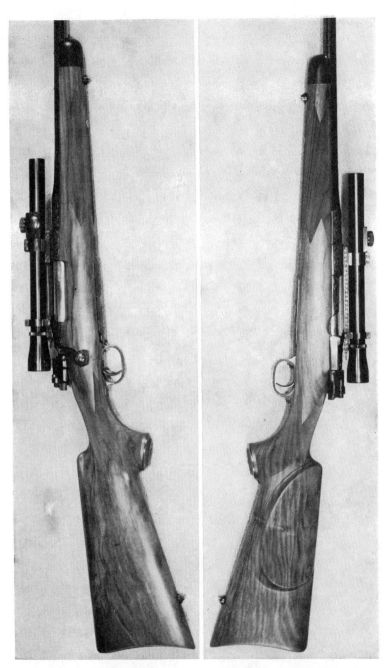

Custom .270, on military Mauser action, with hinged floorplate and considerable engraving. Barrel by Ackley, metalwork by author, stocked in French walnut by Shelhamer. Engraving by Cole Agee and Paul Showalter. Lyman Alaskan scope in Redfield mount. Weight of rifle, 8 lbs. 12 oz. Barrel length, 24″.

and you can center-punch the ground depression perfectly. In any case, it is not a great hardship to re-mark it, as you grind down, to keep center visible.

Soft steels and the nickel-steels used today usually scribe and center-punch easily. Winchester Model 70 receivers sometimes give trouble, evidently having spots of nickel in the places we gunsmiths need to puncture. I can remember having to grind on only one of them. Usually the steel is just very, very tough, not on the surface, but about $\frac{1}{32}''$ below. Just keep the drill sharp and you will get through. If the drill positively refuses to go completely through, get out the little grinding wheels and work down the center of the hole as far as it is started. Often just a little grinding will remove the hard spot of metal and allow the drill to proceed. Eddystone Enfields are somewhat the same, some being hard and tough, others just tough. "Work hardening," or hardening of metal under drill pressure often takes place on the mentioned rifles, so do not bear down on the drill unless it cuts.

A gunsmith I know used to spout what he claims is an old Norwegian proverb—"There is always a remedy for the sausage which is too long." I apply that reasoning to a great deal of gun work. You can always make a long part shorter, or a large part smaller or a little hole bigger. Reversing the system is difficult, you can see. So when the least possible doubt exists as to the centering of a hole, use a drill four or five numbers smaller than your intended tap size. By relocating the sight or mount base you can check by eye to see if this small hole in the gun is concentric with the larger hole in the base. If not, get out the needle file and make it so. If it is perfectly concentric, all you have to do is run the proper drill bit through and go ahead with the tapping. This method can be varied any way you find necessary—using a small, final and large size drill to complete the hole. Also, it is insurance against an incorrectly-sharpened bit cutting an oversize hole, which is important. The little extra time involved is nothing compared to the job facing you should the hole be rushed through and found in the wrong location. Drills like to skid over on a curved surface. I find it best to locate the center, use the automatic center-punch to put the center in the metal, punching it perhaps a half-dozen times. If a burr raises around the punch mark, file it off and make a final punch with a shallow, wide-tapered point. If, during the punching, the impression gets out of center, use the automatic punch held at an angle to move it back where it belongs. Always, make a starting center for your larger drills with a small one, something around a No. 45 or 50. A No. 31 bit does not always start true in a fairly deep punch mark.

Sometimes, in the hardened metals, you may run into trouble getting the drill through on the far side, due to that having a case (hardening) of its own. Grinding is impractical, so take a bit or bits (you need not go completely through with the smaller drills in checking, unless of course you find the hole going out of line) and put a long, tapered point on it—each lip $\frac{1}{8}''$ or $\frac{5}{32}''$ on a No. 31—and ram it through by main force on the drill press. You cannot cut that glass-hard steel, you must use the drill to break it away from the bottom area of the hole. Usually the smaller drills go through it easier than the larger, due to fact that the small point is exerting comparatively greater pressure on the steel. Marble's Nitro Solvent Oil works well as a lubricant in such cases. Ordinarily, no oil, or a drop of brown cutting oil serves. This inner hard "skin" can also sometimes be broken with a drift punch.

In drilling wood, I use the breast drill and drill press exclusively with metal-cutting bits, running them slowly. Holes should be carefully marked and punched, and it does not hurt a bit to run a smaller drill through first, checking as in steel drilling. Wood has grain and often steers a bit out of line in spite of your best drill-holding and clamping. A cockeyed hole can be straightened with a rat-tail file and then cleared to proper size.

I positively do not approve of drilling jigs for the average gun shops. Where one particular job is done constantly on one particular model gun, they are necessary and desirable, but for the shop doing general gunsmithing are not to be made up or used. In the first place, no jig is any good unless it and the work can be clamped together tightly and the two held rigid under the drill bit. The fixtures necessary to such arrangement would be costly, bulky, and take more time to set up than they would save in the long run. In the second, and more important, place, very few military rifles are uniform enough in dimensions to permit jig use, unless the jig is adjustable. Most of the sight and telescope mounting today involving difficult drilling is done on the Springfield, Enfield and Mauser rifles. And there is plenty of variation in receiver dimensions between different rifles in each design, due to production by from three to ten different manufacturing plants. A jig must fit perfectly, not just closely. A sight-mounting screw hole must be in the *right* place, not .005" up, down or sideways. Put 'em one at a time, line up the sight with the first hole in, with the first screw in, bore sight and level with each step—you cannot be too careful. Mounting a sight is no rush job. It would seem that simple jigs or drilling templates would be ideal for side mounting telescope installation, but nothing could be further from the truth. The sad details will be explained in Chapter 21.

The sad discovery that a hole *is* out of line, whether you had anything to do with it or not, may entail head-scratching or some of the language you remember from Army days. Winchester 70s and 54s have the receiver ring tapped at the factory for target telescope mounting blocks, and these holes are utilized by many of the telescope-mount makers for hunting scope bases. Quite often you will find that the holes in the rifle and the holes in the mount base will not quite get together. I have not yet figured out whether this is the fault of the riflemaker or the sightmaker, but am inclined to blame the latter. Sometimes the screws will pull in okay, but if not, the simplest remedy is to enlarge the countersink receiving the screwhead and file the screw body hole through the mount in the direction required. This method also works with receiver sights, although with them, turning down the screwhead slightly usually allows it to turn in straight. Sight and mount base screws should go into place against *no side tension.*

When a tapped hole is far out of line and the hole in the base cannot be moved to accommodate it, you still have three avenues open. First, if possible, see if the tapped hole can be pulled over with a file, enlarged somewhat, and the hole in base also enlarged, to line up for re-tapping for a larger diameter screw. If that street seems closed, you are faced with welding up the hole and relocating, drilling and tapping it in the right spot, not to mention polishing the weld down. If an original hole is *one-half or more of its diameter* off correct center, it may be possible to plug that hole with a bit of screw approximately the same hardness as the receiver, polish off the surface, then relocate, drill and tap. If the plug is harder or softer than the gun metal, the drill will tend to move over into the softer material.

Occasionally, a gun will come in with sight or base screws loose and if introduction of new screws of the same thread will not cure the trouble, you will need to enlarge the holes for the next size screw. For instance, 6–48 screws can be replaced by 8–40 ones, in many cases, or standard 6–48 NF screws can be replaced with Lyman 48 sight 6–48 Whitworth thread type.

Replacement of 1906 Springfield barrels occasionally is more than a vise and wrench proposition. The armory and factory barrels, thousands of which have been sold and are being sold as World War II surplus, are made to close tolerances in order that military armorers can fit them with proper headspace without use of chambering reamers. Such barrels are supposed to have not less than $\frac{1}{8}''$ or more than

$\frac{1}{4}''$ drawup, meaning that they should screw into the receiver freely until the index marks on the left side of the receiver and on the barrel are within from $\frac{1}{8}''$ to $\frac{1}{4}''$ of lining up. However, due both to rush of wartime manufacturing and fact that most Springfield receivers have seen some use—some have had four or five barrels in their time—about ten per cent of surplus barrels will wind in *almost* all the way without tightening sufficiently, perhaps $\frac{1}{16}''$ drawup. For such cases I simply line up the index marks and install a set-screw at bottom of barrel, in front of recoil shoulder, threading through receiver barrel ring into the threaded barrel shank just far enough to get a good grip. I use 8–40 or 10–32 screws usually. Of course, this method of holding a barrel can be employed on other rifles as well.

Keeping screws tight can be done by coating them with almost any sort of gumming material before insertion—better coat the hole too. About the best thing I have used is a viscous liquid called Glyptol, a General Electric preparation used for sealing purposes. Aircraft instruments and airtight equipment usually have Glyptol-dipped screws used in them. Linseed oil mixed with shellac can also be used on gun screws, or, if you really want it to stay put, dip the screw in iodine—it will rust in place.

Miscellaneous. Barrels occasionally loosen in solid-frame arms and come to the gunsmith for tightening. In some cases a thin steel shim can be placed between the shoulder on the barrel and the face of the receiver or frame, but usually any such method of taking up excess space will increase headspace. So it is best of all to move the threads around so they will seat properly and hold the barrel and the receiver in original relationship. Always work on the threads on the barrel, never on the inside of receiver. You will probably need to make a tool for each of the first four or five jobs encountered, to fit that particular type and size thread. Such tools are really dull little cold-chisels not over $\frac{5}{16}''$ wide, with edge beveled so that it fits into the thread when tool is held at approximately a 45° angle to barrel shank. By using this to peen the entire thread toward the rear, starting right at the back where the thread starts and working around and up to the shoulder, tapping the tool lightly with the heavy steel hammer it is possible to uniformly move the top portion of thread enough to make the barrel turn tightly into receiver. I picked up this idea from a British armorer and did not think too much of it until I gave it a good tryout. However, during the past year I have so tightened around a dozen barrels, ranging from Luger pistols to Winchester M95 rifles, and so far not a one has ever come back to the shop. All but one of these guns had had one or more of several methods tried previously to keep the barrels tight—threads of string laid in the metal threads, peening front of receiver, gummed linseed oil and shellac, and such. One of the old-fashioned methods of keeping barrels tight was to clean the steel threads and put a few drops of solder here and there. The solder runs in and over the threads and is nearly all dressed off with a sharp-cornered file, enough being left to just allow the barrel to be screwed back in position, using plenty of muscle on the wrench.

	Carbon Percentage
Auger, Wood	.60 to .70 (of 1%)
Axe	1.20
Ball Bearing	1.20
Bits, Mining	.80
Blades, Pocket Knives	.90
Blades, Reamers	1.20 to 1.22
Bushing, Spring	.80
Centers, Lathe	.80 to .90
Chisels, Cold	.85
Chisels, Chipping	.80 to .90
Chisels, Wood	.60 to .70
Dies, Envelope	1.15
Dies, Drop Forging	.85 to .90
Drills, Twist	1.20 to 1.22
Anvil Facing	.85 to .90
Screwdrivers	.60 to .70
Files	1.25 to 1.30
Machinist's Hammer	.90 to 1.00
Hatchet	1.15 to 1.22
Chuck Jaws	.85 to .90
Vise Jaws	.85 to .90
Paper Knife	1.05 to 1.10
Putty Knife	1.15 to 1.20
Spring, Common Flat	1.20 to 1.25
Taps	1.20 to 1.22
Saw, For Steel	1.60
Saw, For Wood	.85 to 1.00
Saw, Band	.68 to .75
Saw, Circular	.80 to .90

CHAPTER 7

Soldering and Brazing

THE art of joining metals together by heat through soldering, brazing and welding is well known in a general way, yet comparatively few become proficient in all these processes. Since all three enter the field of gunsmithing, the smith must know something of doing each, and know a good deal about *how* each should be done.

Soldering. Soldering, properly termed "soft soldering" is the process of uniting pieces of metal by means of an alloy having a relatively low melting point. The beginner's most common difficulty is making the solder "stick." Instead of flowing and taking hold on the metal it forms little balls which roll off. In a good job the solder is spread or flowed evenly over the work and when so applied has amazing holding strength. Brass, copper, zinc, tin, iron and steel are readily soldered with suitable alloys and fluxes and while the solder joint, due to greater softness, will not be as strong as the metals joined, it will resist any normal strain it is likely to receive and remain solid until removed by melting.

There are two principal methods of soft soldering; by using a heated soldering copper (generally called "iron"), to flow molten solder into the joint; and by "sweating." In sweating, a thin coat of solder alloy is applied to each of the surfaces to be joined, the surfaces are placed together and heated until the solder on each reaches melting point and forms a single bond. The sweated joint is used almost exclusively in gun work.

The first point in any solder, brazing or weld joint is making sure that the surfaces are clean, free of blueing, rust, oil—anything except raw metal. Polish with abrasive cloth and wash or wipe with alcohol, gasoline, or an acid solution made especially for soldering.

Your source of heat for a soldering copper is not too important—it can be a blowtorch, plumber's furnace, gas plate, coal or wood stove or welding torch. A gas burner seems the most convenient and easiest handled, so far as uniform heat is involved. The soldering copper itself should be large enough (one to two pounds) to hold heat a little while and sharp pointed, with smooth, clean, square sides. The point is "tinned" to convey solder to work, tinning being the term used to indicate a smooth coating of solder alloy. Mr. Baker recommended hollowing a small trough in a brick, to hold a small quantity of solder and flux. The soldering copper is heated until it will melt into this metal and coat the point. A soldering copper must not be overheated, as burned copper will not hold, handle or spread solder. Overheating can be observed—the tinned point takes on a dull, somewhat corroded appearance, the tin having burned into it. When this happens, file the point until clean again.

I prefer to tin a point by heating the copper and fluxing it and rubbing against bar solder until it is tinned. Flux is the substance used to prevent oxidation of the surfaces to be joined until the solder flows, and is vital to soldering and brazing. Flux makes the solder take hold and stay put, and can be any of a dozen types, as different metals and solders require different fluxes. Ordinary rosin, probably the world's oldest fluxing material, remains one of the best. Chunks of it can be broken down to powder and applied with wool swab or a brush, or prepared forms can be purchased. In much soldering, easiest to use is acid flux, using zinc chloride. This is easily made by dropping scraps of zinc (coverings of old flashlight batteries work fine) into a small wide-mouthed bottle of hydrochloric (muriatic) acid, which boils, fumes and heats slightly, until it dissolves all the zinc it will take. This acid flux is applied by a small bristle brush, such as a paste or mucilage applicator. Acid flux works best on the softer metals—copper, brass, soft steel, bismuth, gold, silver and alloys of these metals. Ammonium chloride (sal ammoniac) is best for gun steel and iron, and also works well on copper and brass. It can be purchased in powder form from most drugstores and is applied by brush.

Solder itself comes in all sorts of lead and tin and bismuth alloys. The "fifty-fifty" solder, half lead and half tin, is most common and will cover most of the gunsmith's needs. The following tables give alloy percentages and melting points of commercial solders:

SOLDERS

USE ZINC CHLORIDE FOR FLUX

Lead-Tin Alloys

Melting Point (Degrees F.)	619	563	529	504	464	428	374	365	392	421	450
Lead %	100	90	80	70	60	50	40	30	20	10	0
Tin %	0	10	20	30	40	50	60	70	80	90	100

Lead-Tin-Bismuth Alloys

Melting Point (Degrees F.)	205	214	257	262	293	298	322	358	360	453
Lead %	32.0	25.8	25	43	33.3	10.7	50	35.8	20	71
Tin %	15.5	19.8	15	14	33.3	23.1	33	52.1	60	9
Bismuth %	52.5	54.4	60	43	33.3	66.2	17	12.1	20	20

Copper-Zinc Alloys (Brass)

USE BORAX FOR FLUX

Melting Point (Degrees F.)	1983	1904	1823	1706	1652	1616	1508	1436	1292	1076	786
Copper %	100	90	80	70	60	50	40	30	20	10	0
Zinc %	0	10	20	30	40	50	60	70	80	90	100

By studying the tables you can prepare a solder to melt at any desired temperature. Some of the bismuth solders melt at boiling-water temperatures and would have very limited application in a gun shop. Softness, weakness and low melting points go together, but possibly you might someday have to use one of the very soft solders in repairing a gun whose blueing must not be affected. In my opinion 300° Fahrenheit should be the lowest melting point considered. That heat will not affect color or physical properties of the steel.

For ordinary soft soldering the parts or pieces are usually clamped or wired together in correct position and the proper flux is applied. Then the heated copper is used to convey a drop of solder to the joint and held to it until the solder flows into the joint. Wire solders are available with either rosin or acid core and, when used, the end of the wire of solder is held to the work and touched with hot copper to run it into the point desired.

Sweating has much more use in the gun shop than the iron method. Many gun processes involve this system—factories join the barrels of double-barreled shotguns together by sweating, forend lugs are often sweated on, also ventilated ribs. The gun shop will need to sweat on ramp front sights, swivel bands, in some cases sight bases, and many other odd jobs. For sweating a blowtorch or welding torch is necessary, scrapers for cleaning surfaces to be sweated, and a bit of woolen rag, or felt, for wiping excess solder from hot surfaces. Parts to be joined are clamped with soldering surface up, the spot well cleaned, heated, fluxed, and solder applied by any convenient method, such as rubbing a bit of bar solder on the hot surface or melting a few drops above the part with the torch. When a puddle of solder covers the right area, remove the torch flame and quickly wipe it with the cloth. This should remove all but a thin film of bright solder, leaving a smoothly tinned surface. If the metal has not been properly cleaned and fluxed, the solder will be spotty and you clean it up and start over. With both surfaces evenly tinned, the parts are joined together and clamped. The assembly is then heated with the torch and tension increased on the clamp as solder melts and continued while the joint cools.

It is theoretically possible to make good sweat joints on finished guns without spoiling the blueing, but I cannot do it. I either spoil the blueing and get a good soldering job, or am so careful about the finish I get a lousy sweat joint. There are at present two or three simple sweat-on ramp front sights for remodeled military rifles, some straight solder jobs, others employing a 6–48 screw which is tapped into the barrel for a very short distance. The screw is very handy for pulling down the ramp as the solder cools, but unfortunately, it may not pull down straight, canting the ramp slightly.

In the fitting of sweat-on ramps, barrel bands, or other parts visible on the exterior of the arm where blueing is not to be marred, the surface of the gun is, of course, cleaned bright only under the sweat-on part— put said part in place, mark around it with a lead pencil, and stay well inside your boundary in scraping blueing. Make the part to be attached really fit the gun barrel or receiver, paying attention to the edges in particular, for you do not want a shiny line of solder showing against the blue. Do not tin the complete matching surfaces; keep the solder in the middle, but flux all over. In fitting bands of any sort to barrels, let the barrel cool a bit and heat the band a little after they are tinned so that they will go together easily.

Once in a great while a target shooter will want the telescope mounting blocks on his rifle sweated-on, and this is a fine place to use the very soft solders. Tin the barrel under the blocks, bottoms of the blocks, tighten down the screws and lay a hot soldering copper on top of the block until the solder softens, then tighten the screws. (You will no doubt note that I have not mentioned how to keep solder out of screw holes: Truth is, I do not know a really good way. I try not to get any flux in the holes first, so that solder which does enter can be picked out cold. If it does get in, I heat the screw red hot and wind it in and out a time or two.) Putting a temporary flush-top screw in the hole while tinning would probably work okay, removing it after wiping, while solder is still hot.

After all the foregoing soldering dope, I have to come out and advise that there is not a wide use for it in the modern gun shop, due entirely to the almost universal use of the quick-process blacking now passing

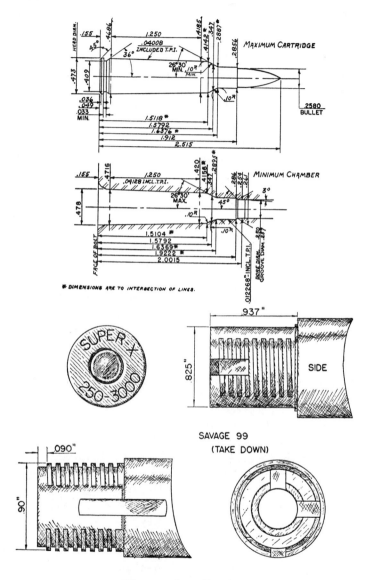

THE .250/3000 SAVAGE

Surprise—the famous 28-degree shoulder is not 28 degrees. It is 26½. Designed by Charles Newton, the .250/3000 was the first of our real high velocity popular cartridges. He just wanted a good .25 caliber cartridge for the 100-grain bullet, but Savage decided they needed a good advertising

for gun blueing. Most, if not all of the patent processes will attack lead in any form, dissolve aluminum alloys, and weaken or destroy any but the best-fluxed hard solder joints.

Brazing. Union of metals by means of a harder joint alloy than the lead soldering mixtures is done in the processes of brazing, silver soldering, or hard soldering. The heat required approaches welding temperatures, and the work is best done by use of the acetylene welding torch. You may figure on 1500° Fahrenheit for good application on brass or silver solder work, and as a rule, the commercial brass rod, wire or ribbon sold for the purpose will flow and adhere at that temperature. The correct brass rod should be used, rather than scraps you pick up, or odd bits of brass wire you run across. I carelessly got mixed up with some bronze rod once when brazing small tools, and now am convinced it pays to do things right!

Brazing naturally has a very limited use as applied directly to guns —brass does not blue worth a cent, so you seldom can use it on an exposed part. Its greatest value to the gunsmith is in sticking together the special tools and odd fixtures he must make from time to time. About the only exterior gun job I ever use brass on is putting "gold" front sight beads on for the open-sight boys.

---

slant so loaded an 87-grain bullet up to 3,000 FPS so they could call it the .250/3000. Velocities have not increased materially since the cartridge came out around 1912, although handloaders can boost performance somewhat, if using bolt action rifles.

Extremely accurate, the cartridge has little recoil and is a very satisfactory deer-killer. Both lever and bolt action rifles are available today, the Savage M99 model being ideal for boys and women who require light-weight hunting arms. Handloading shooters find the cartridge very flexible, accurate in almost any velocity range, and until the advent of the high-velocity .22 caliber craze, the .250/3000 was quite popular as a vermin cartridge, particularly in the West.

Shown is the barrel shank of the Savage 99 quick-takedown model, which I believe was made principally in the .22 Hi Power and .300 Savage calibers as well as in .250/3000. At bottom left is a bottom view of the barrel showing the machine cut provided for locking the barrel in proper location, through engagement of a lug on the steel forend base. The thread is 12 per inch. However, the most common form of takedown employed on the model 99s was a full-thread shank with enough tolerance in threading to permit screwing in and unscrewing by hand pressure, applied by removing the forend and using it as a handle, to engage the takedown catch lug on the barrel in a metal socket inside the forend provided for the purpose. This latter system is much stronger and less inclined to loosen than the quick-takedown joint.

To join brass to steel, or steel to steel with brass, the surfaces contacting the alloy must be cleaned chemically, with acid solution, or mechanically, with file. The acid solution (called "pickle" in the steel industry) is usually a weak, 20-to-1 water and sulphuric acid combination. Brazing requires a flux, as does solder, and while ordinary borax is the old standby, the modern prepared brazing fluxes are easier to apply and give uniform results. These may come in paste, powder or granule form, and are usually applied by heating the brass rod or wire until flux will adhere to the tip. The common method of brazing employs the same principles as welding—chamfering all exterior edges to form a V into which brass rod is introduced to join the separate sections. Gunsmiths can use this method for such hidden joints as brazing Enfield triggers together in the middle after shortening for use in sporter rifles when magazine is altered to streamline the action. Brass can be used in a sweating process, as in soft soldering, and this method has been widely used in the past to join broken parts in guns. In brass sweating, the surfaces to meet are cleaned, a thin layer of flux placed on each, and a ribbon of brass placed between them. This metal sandwich is then clamped or wired together and heat applied. The torch can be used, or the assembly can be placed in a clean coal or charcoal fire until the brass melts and joins the steel. For small parts, or where a close joint is desired, brazing spelter in the form of brass filings is applied, mixed with a powder flux, and the parts clamped while heating. Should I tell you to use a new, clean file to get those brass filings? They have to be *clean!* About all the brazing fluxes I have encountered leave a glass-hard scale around the joint and to remove this the acid "pickle" comes into its own. A few of the patent fluxes claim to be removable with hot water, but so far I have not been able to do so good with hot water. Very light brazing can be done with a blowtorch or one of the pressure nozzle arrangements for burning ordinary illuminating gas, but any bit of steel with the slightest bulk will require more heat. The red heat required to set brass to steel naturally limits brazing to non-hardened and non-case-hardened parts. Any such part as a bolt, breechblock, locking plate or receiver made of treated carbon steel must be re-heat treated after subjection to heat above 1000° Fahrenheit. And you do not want to get mixed up with a job like that.

One of the most useful brazing applications in gun work is the joining of two or more parts to form a special or altered extractor for bolt actions when a small-diameter cartridge head must be accommodated. If you will look at a Krag or Mauser-type extractor you appreciate at once what a job it would be to make one complete, and if the action is to be used for a .22 Hornet or .22/3000 Lovell cartridge, the extraction lip must naturally be extended to contact the extraction cut on the small case. The job can be done fairly easily by cutting off the original lip, and brazing on a section of annealed tool steel, then filing the new lip to fit the cartridge. This brazing of spring steel is possible because the brazing heat is just below that temperature required to anneal a tempered spring. Such a job is rather ticklish of course, particularly because an acetylene torch—either straight acetylene or oxyacetylene welding type—must be used, and the joint must be made at the lowest brazing heat—just enough to set the 50–50 spelter.

Silver Soldering. For joining spring steel, and most other brazing applications on firearms, I prefer silver solder, which is a mixture of silver and brazing alloy, in varying degrees of softness. Silver solder alloys are made to melt at temperatures from 900° to 2000° Fahrenheit so you have a rather wide range of heat tolerances. I have both ribbon and wire forms, melting at around 1200° Fahrenheit. Brazing fluxes can be used with silver alloys, but it is best to get a paste-form silver solder flux, made just for that purpose. The technique in using silver solder is the same as for brazing, but the lower melting points of the more common alloys makes it handle better for sweating joints. From now on I intend to use silver solder to attach the sweat-on ramp front sights for rifles. It is much more difficult to get an invisible joint line, due to the fact that the alloy cools so much faster than soft solder and complicates the squeezing-together-while-cooling business, but the ramp will stay on. I did one job which had an even line of bright silver showing against the blue of sight and barrel, and before I could apologize to the customer and tell him I would chemically color the silver so it would not show, he went happy about it—thought it added a fine bit of decoration to the gun! So maybe if you slip on the first job or two the gun owner will actually like the result. Seriously, though, on such jobs the solder should never show, and the best way to prevent it is to flux the barrel and bottom of ramp after they are clean (with most silver solder fluxes it is necessary to heat the flux on the work before introducing the solder) cut a strip of the ribbon silver solder not wider than three-quarters width of ramp, clamp ramp to barrel and heat. I have mounted several ramps on light rifle barrels without causing scale to form in the bore, but there is always a good chance for that sad circumstance, so I advise the purchase of ribbon silver solder with melting point around 1200° Fahrenheit, for the sole purpose of mounting ramps. Most modern barrel steels are heat-treated at some time or other in manufacture and are sufficiently inert as to resist warping at even red heat, but the formation of scale in the bore will injure it, since the interior dimensions are changed, to say nothing of the rough surface. So never get a barrel red hot. No need to, anyway. Talk to a couple of jewelers for real information on using silver solders, especially the soft types. They can also probably tell you where to get the hard-to-locate special fluxes you might think you need.

ALLOYS OF COPPER AND ZINC
Percentages in the solder

Copper										
100	90	80	70	60	50	40	30	20	10	0

Zinc										
0	10	20	30	40	50	60	70	80	90	100

Melting Point Fahr.										
1983	1904	1823	1706	1652	1616	1508	1436	1292	1076	786

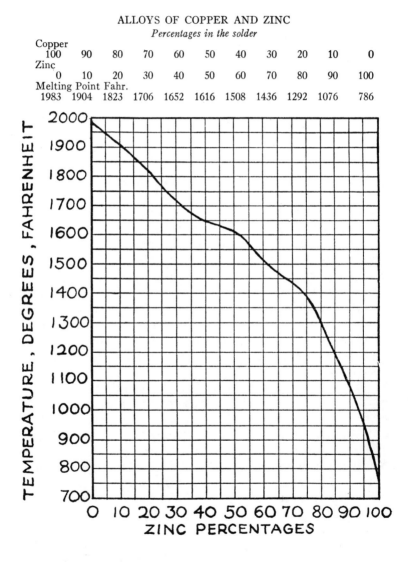

White Hard Solders. These are brazing alloys, similar to silver solder in appearance, but containing lead and tin to promote easy flowing and slightly lower melting points than regular brass spelter. "Gray Solder" is 50 parts zinc, 44 parts copper, 4 parts tin and 2 parts lead. Melting point is just above 1400° Fahrenheit. "White Solder" is 15 parts tin, 85 parts "Coppersmith's Spelter." (The coppersmith spelter is soft brass—three parts copper to one part zinc.) These and similar alloys see little use today, in or out of a gun shop, as either brass or silver solder is more available and about as easy to use.

Brass is of course an alloy of copper and zinc and the table of metal percentages opposite may be helpful in ordering spelter. To find out what mixture will give a desired melting point, lay a ruler parallel with the horizontal line at the temperature scale: where it bisects the heavy curved line, read up the vertical line to metal percentages.

Should you ever have to attach any sight blade or other part made of German silver, you must combine brass with nickel for a spelter, or joining alloy. Any approximate alloy with around 37 parts copper, 52 parts zinc and 11 parts nickel will do the job. Reducing the nickel and increasing the zinc will lower the melting point.

When mixing brazing or other metal alloys for soldering use, always melt the metal with highest melting point first, adding the lowest-melting metal last. When all are melted, stir thoroughly, then cover surface with powdered charcoal and raise heat at least 100° above highest melting point.

CHAPTER 8

Welding

IN WELDING, metals are joined by heating until the melting point is reached and the separate parts flow into each other. The technical term is autogenous fusing. The joint is usually strengthened by adding metal of sympathetic character or similar analysis in a molten state, so that the separate parts being joined and the added metal are fused into a homogeneous whole. There is no welded joint, in the sense of a soldered or brazed joint, but simply a "weld"—the place where the original separate pieces meet.

Three types of welding exist—forge welding, electric arc welding and gas welding. Forge welding is that practiced by the old-time blacksmith and gun shops, the separate metal parts or edges being forge heated until just at the melting point, or very slightly below it, and then joined and hammered on the anvil until they adhere to each other. Several heatings are usually required. Gun barrels were made in the old days by winding or bending a flat bar of mild iron around a round mandrel and forge welding it into a tube. Very little forge welding is done today, even in backwoods blacksmith shops. It not only requires a great deal of experience and effort, but is not as good as electric or gas welding, either for appearance or strength.

Arc welding is just what it sounds like—welding by an electric arc caused by short-circuiting electricity at the point of weld, one part being grounded, the other part, or the electro-welding rod, receiving current from a DC welding generator or converter. The heat generated by the arc will melt and fuse steel. In electro-welding by means of the arc principle, the electrode, or electric welding rod which provides the metal to be added into the joint is coated with a hard compound which not only acts as a flux but also helps to control the heat generated at the rod tip, since the rod is "hot"—connected to the electric current. As the tip of electrode touches the work, the arc is formed and both metals fuse, the tip of the rod melting off to form a "bead" in the joint area. Proper electric arc welding calls for peening, or hammering the weld while red hot, and also for pre-heating the work proper to at least 500° Fahrenheit for ordinary steels and as much as 900° for some tool and special steels. Electrodes are made in all varieties of steels— air hardening, water hardening, high speed tool, oil hardening, and such, as well as the common mild rods. Diameters come from $\frac{1}{16}''$ to $\frac{1}{4}''$. Discounting the considerable cost of the arc-welding setup, the method has little use for ordinary gun work, although many special desirable steels can be obtained for welding which are hard to duplicate with the gas system.

Electric welding (without the arc) is familiar to most men to some extent through the wide usage of spot-welding sheet and strip metals in metal fabrication of everything from saucepans to trucks. Spot welding is done in a clamp-type machine which holds two or more parts together while two electrodes create a concentrated spot of intense heat in a small area, fusing the parts together at just one spot, not over the entire surface. Electric welding proper is done by large electrodes contacting the entire surface to be welded.

No form of electric welding is of much value to the gunsmith in his work, although he may need to have some of his heavy jigs, fixtures and special wrenches electro-welded. Gas welding is not too well suited to heavy work, as the heat is slow to come up on bulky stock. Although somewhat skilled in gas welding, I know very little about electro welding and until recently was of the opinion that arc welding should be very useful in gun work, more so than gas, since special steels could be deposited where needed and the danger of "blow holes" or pits in the weld due to impurities or improperly regulated gas be greatly reduced. Also, arc welding can be done on hard steels without the heat spreading to anneal the material except near the actual weld.

However, before writing this I decided I had better find out a few things, and so talked to two master welders. One, a man who had little formal education and no technical training, is entirely self-taught through experience in all types of welding, and the other is a trade-school man, and expert in work through experience and practice. Both men are successful, own large shops and employ several men. Both gave me the same information and advice. And it was that I was right in my oxyacetylene techniques and handling of steels with the torch— and that electro welding was not suitable for hardly any of the jobs I thought it was. So we will get down to business and talk about really welding gun stuff.

Oxyacetylene Welding. Acetylene is plain carbide gas—the same that operates carbide lamps and lanterns. Under pressure, with oxygen, also under pressure, added, the mixture burns at temperatures right around 6300° Fahrenheit. The Balanced-pressure torch itself is an ingenious gadget which mixes oxygen and acetylene and regulates the flame.

Tanks, or bottles, of acetylene and oxygen are available in any town over 5,000 population in the country, I would say, and ordinarily are loaned to the user, the welder paying only for the gas and oxygen. Some concerns however require a deposit or a lease of some kind. When a tank is kept over 30 days, you usually have to pay demurrage of 2¢ a day. The tanks have tight (you hope) valves on top, opened by little round handles. The first thing you do is take these knobs off, lay them carefully on the shelf, and grab a couple of pieces of strap iron or steel ¼″ thick and six or eight inches long, cut a square hole in one end to fit the valve shank and put it on said shank. You can now turn your valves on and off.

Welding regulators are pressure gages, attached to the tanks, and the torch hoses are attached to regulators. Each regulator has a tank gage, capacity to 3,000 pounds on oxygen and 400 pounds on acetylene, a diaphragm regulation system with cross-bar handle, and a hose gage, graduated to show pressures up to 30 pounds on both tanks. This latter gage indicates the pressure in the hose and at the tip and is to govern you in supplying the proper pressure for the tip being used. (Heavy duty oxygen gages run much higher than 30 pound capacity, but you will not need one.)

The hose for oxygen is usually either green or black, and the acetylene hose red. And you will not connect them wrong, for the oxygen fittings have right-hand threads and the acetylene, left hand.

Anyone contemplating purchase of gun shop welding equipment should contact the Smith Welding Equipment Corp., 2619 Fourth St., S. E., Minneapolis 14, Minnesota, or the Johnson Welding Equipment Co., 2640 W. Van Buren St., Chicago 12, Illinois. The latter concern is a wholesale and retail welding supply house and handles practically everything in welding tools and material. The Smith Corporation are manufacturers.

I consider the Smith No. 2 Torch ideal for all gun work. I have altered many bolts with excellent results, and use it in making short actions, welding receivers and bolts together after shortening. This is the light aircraft type torch, and it is really light, which is an important factor. I have seen quite a few botched-up bolt jobs as a result of using the heavy, hard to control, standard torch. It is often necessary to keep a torch going fifteen minutes, and one hand can get very tired and shaky holding up several unnecessary pounds of metal. And you do not want to get shaky with a welding torch at the wrong time, which is usually just about at the finish of the job. I have six tips, and use only two of them ninety per cent of the time. The smallest is the Smith No. 21, which is really a large soldering tip, and works well for all general soldering as well as very light welding. The next size, which I use for bolt alterations and most work, is the No. 25. The larger sizes are Nos. 26, 27, 28 and 29, the latter capable of welding flat stock $\frac{1}{4}''$ thick, of any width. All of these are of the "a" type, producing long flames necessary on the type of welding needed in the gun shop. The No. 2 torch uses a $\frac{3}{16}''$ hose (inside diameter) rather than the standard $\frac{1}{4}''$, which adds to its handiness. Every welding manufacturer has his own set of rules for tip sizes, however, and you had best figure your tip size according to number drill size. The Smith No. 21 corresponds to a No. 71 drill and the No. 25 to a No. 58. Any of the welding companies will give the measurements of their tip apertures, although in their literature they usually list them by capacities, rating as to thickness of metal they will weld.

Besides tanks, regulators, torch and hose, you will require a few accessories—goggles, igniter for lighting the torch, tip cleaners and wrenches for tightening regulators and tips. All connections must necessarily be very tight. Except for the tanks, the cost of the whole outfit will not be over $75.00. It will pay for itself pretty quick. Invest a couple of dollars more in a welding handbook or instruction book, to read up on the methods used in welding various metals besides steel, too—you might need to know sometime.

For most gun welding the pressure is very low at the tip, scarcely over three pounds. The welding flame is regulated by the oxygen and acetylene valves on the torch body. The neutral flame is generally desired, that having the proper mixture of gas and oxygen to produce an inner cone which is sharp, clear, whitish and with well-defined edges. To light the torch, the acetylene valve is turned a little and the igniter snapped at the tip, lighting the gas, which burns with a very yellow, sooty carbide flame. The flame should burn lazily, just at the tip, not under visible pressure, and the oxygen valve turned slowly until the smoke and yellow color disappear. Both valves are regulated in turn until the neutral flame is achieved. The Smith No. 2 can be held and adjusted with one hand.

If oxygen pressure or quantity is excess, you will oxidize, or burn metal, blowing the weld full of tiny bubbles, visible through the goggles as sort of a foam on the molten metal. If an excess of acetylene is present, you have what is known as a carburizing flame, and are blowing carbon into the weld. This condition is sometimes desirable in heat-treating with the torch and in applying hard-surfacing rod to steel.

To insure a complete weld, it is necessary to first remove the edges of the material to allow the torch flame to properly fuse metal below the surface. You can call this chamfering, bevelling, scarfing or V-ing. In any case, you strive for a valley of some sort to add metal in, as the rod will not flow into a narrow seam or cut. I always try to fuse the metal of the two parts or elements together in the center without adding metal, and after joining, build up the joint with the most suitable material until the weld is complete, and of the desired dimension. The illustrations show rather clearly what is meant. The V or scarf should never be less than a 90° angle and about a 120° if possible.

When a bolt handle is altered for use with a low-mounting scope sight, the weld wants to be a weld all the way through, not just around the edges. I cannot think of anything more embarrassing than having the handle come off in the customer's hand, while the bolt stays in the receiver! This has never happened to one of my jobs, and I do not intend it ever shall, but I have actually seen such a thing occur twice, both on custom rifles whose bolt alterations looked perfect on the outside. You start a bolt weld at the center and after welding the point of bolt shank and base together, add metal down in this V, and melt it in a little at a time building up until the bolt has full body at the weld, with enough excess to permit grinding, filing and polishing to remove all scale and reach the desired dimension and shape in clear metal. Do not build up a great lump of metal around the joining location. The more you cook the weld the greater chance you take of covering a bit of scale, to be discovered later when filing. Preheating is very important to a solid weld—you just cannot make a weld hold if both parts are not hotter than cherry red at least ¼" from the edges, going to white and molten state at the junction. And you cannot expect to add rod and make it hold if the material is not molten at the spot, or each drop of steel added melted in.

High-carbon steels will throw off sparks as they heat up, the sparks being the carbon leaving, since it will not melt. It is necessary to good welding that the carbon content be very low at the weld. It is of course possible to put carbon back into the weld, or to harden the weld when suitable steel is used.

I use a 3.5% nickel-steel rod in most gun welding, which does not harden much, but is well suited for bolt and magazine alterations. For cocking pieces, bolt notches, hammers, and the likes, you can use water-hardening or oil-hardening rod; vanadium steel works well. In many instances you can plate a wearing surface with one of the hard-surfacing compounds made for the purpose, such as Stellite. I ran across a steel which is quite useful for hard contact and cam surfaces, this being the Arcaloy Oil Hardening Tool Steel Welding Electrode, coated for arc welder application. Its code color identification is blue.

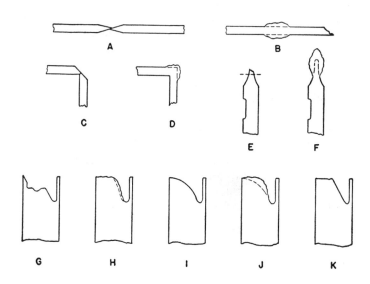

WELDS

A. Common tip weld. The tips are fused together then metal added until the full depth of the stock is reached.
B. Same weld, completed, dotted lines showing amount necessary to be filed or milled away from the weld.
C. Set up for corner weld. Fuse the edges together.
D. Corner weld completed, dotted lines show the final dimensions.
E. Broken firing pin tip. Grind it off at the dotted line.
F. Then anneal and build up by adding steel. Dotted lines show the final outline of the tip to be reached by cutting down excess welded metal.
G. Enfield bolt notch, more or less unaltered.
H. Same, welded partially up with nickel or soft steel.
I. The soft weld cleaned and cleared at edges.
J. Hard steel or surfacing metal laid over soft weld.
K. Finished notch of proper proportions shaped out of the hard portion of the weld.

This rod is oil-hardening when electro welded, but air-hardening when acetylene welded. The coating is knocked off before gas welding, of course. The welding deposit is very hard and tough—cannot be filed. However, on any spot reachable with the hand grinder, it is easily worked down. It applies best with a slightly carburizing flame.

Protection of gun parts during welding is an old bugaboo I hope to destroy. Welding was a great mystery to practically all gunsmiths until a very few years ago and they had all sorts of ideas about the damage welding heat would do to firearms. The business of altering a bolt handle had many weird ideas brought to the front, concerned with keeping the locking lugs unchanged in any way. Strange bits of plumbing were devised for running water through the bolt while welding, and all that sort of thing. (That I would like to see—cold water a fraction of an inch from over six thousand degrees of heat!) All that is necessary when welding a bolt notch or bolt handle is to wrap a 2″ strip of cloth perhaps 15″ long around the head, tie with string and dip it in water. A piece of old face towel is excellent. Should it be necessary to prolong the welding condition beyond five minutes, it is wise to dip the swathed end in water again, or whenever steam arises, indicating drying of cloth. At any time during or after the welding it is possible to pick up and hold the bolt by this cooled end in the bare fingers, which indicates to me that it does not get very hot. The body of the bolt will discolor from the heat perhaps 2″ from the bolt handle in extreme cases, but since you have to polish up the weld and reblue the bolt anyway, who cares? I have never had a bolt warp during a handle alteration, so do not consider it necessary to protect the body of the bolt proper from heat. As for softening a hard bolt, well, what are the best bolts made of? Nickel-steel, which is soft to start with. Of course, it may be necessary to harden the cocking notch if the bolt proves *too* soft, but as a rule, do not worry about cooking the base of the bolt tender. On the other hand, do not do it deliberately. I find it unnecessary to get any part of a bolt red hot except the stub or point to which handle is welded. I once altered the handle on a hard Mauser bolt without softening the notch, though I would not bet I could do it again.

For a rule of thumb on keeping parts cool, just pack the part with wet cloth or asbestos not closer than one inch to the weld.

The problem of keeping scale from forming, and removing scale after a weld job has bothered every gunsmith who ever had a weld look him in the face. Prevention of scale bothered me greatly until I took up the matter with my expert commercial-welder advisors. They stated emphatically that the best thing to do was not attempt to prevent the formation, saying that scale forming next to or on the opposite side of a weld was carbon and metal impurities cooking out of the molten steel. Prevention of scale therefore would keep these close to the welded material, not allowing a perfect alloying of metals and causing a somewhat weaker weld and one which might not finish properly as to color and texture. Meaning funny colors when blued and hard and soft spots in and about the weld.

On the other hand, scale is quite a nuisance to remove from the inside threads of a bolt, or any place else, for that matter. I usually scrape and polish it out, making hardened, pointed scrapers which break it from the steel in little flakes. The old U. S. Ordnance Department mixture for prevention of scale works very well, and you can make up a batch by using one pound of pulverized charred leather, one and one-half pounds of flour and two pounds of fine table salt. The leather can be scraps of sole leather from a shoemaker, placed in a pan over a slow fire until charred, then scraped and powdered. Keep dry, and mix up a little as you need it, using water to form a smooth stiff paste, then thin with more water to a thick varnish consistency and spread on the cold work with a brush, laying a thin coat. It is then dried on the work slowly over a slow heat. I think it is best to use this compound inside bolts, coating the bolt sleeve threads, before welding on a bolt handle. I cannot see how the weld can be affected by retaining the original analysis of the steel at this inner surface, well away from the actual weld. When scale forms, some of the bulk of the material is lost, and a bolt's inside diameter is increased slightly. In all probability no damage is ever done, and the bolt sleeve will not wobble around any, but it is a good idea not to change a dimension you do not have to.

When scale forms in a weld during the building up or adding of metal, it is visible as oxidation through the goggles, and must be cleaned before further addition of rod. In most cases it can be floated off to the edge of the weld and dashed away with a bit of welding rod, but once in awhile you cannot get rid of it that easily and must allow the weld to cool then file until clear, unpitted steel is presented for the second attempt. If scale is not cleaned off and metal built up on top of it, a very poor joint is made, with little or no strength, since the added metal is not fused to the previous layer. Some of the tool steel rods are sensitive to continued heating—they are made to be raised to their melting and fusing point just once, and if held in a molten state any length of time will deteriorate, as their analysis changes. With such material you must do the job properly in one continuous operation, or clean out all added metal and start over until you do the job in one pass. The common mild steel rods can take repeated heat if any care is observed, and the 3.5% nickel-steel I like can be cooked all day. This makes it ideal for bolt alterations since you can repair any mistakes as you go along—when a pit or flake of scale is revealed during finish filing it is easy to gouge it clean with a file point and weld over it. Often it is not necessary to add more steel, filing down until a shallow pit is cleared.

Only experience can teach you how to maneuver the torch and flame. Do not be frightened, for if you work only with similar types of good steel, on a few specific jobs, a little experience will teach a lot. The flame must nearly always be kept moving about over the area to be welded, not only to heat material evenly, but to prevent the tip from burning one spot, pitting it (melting a slight depression) and getting too hot and "popping." When a torch starts to pop and blow out, the tip is heated to the point of igniting the oxygen and acetylene mixture inside the tip. Molten metal and particles of scale or slag fly up and adhere to the tip nozzle, carrying heat. Keep a small piece of ⅔ sandpaper, tacked or glued to the bench and when the torch blows out during welding, rub the tip across it to clean the exterior. This will usually clear it sufficiently to allow completion of the job. It is necessary to keep the tip hole clean and round to obtain the correct flame and two forms of tip cleaners are available, one a sort of roughened, wavy pin which is pushed in and out a few times and the other a number drill of the correct size for that tip set in a metal handle to be inserted and turned with the fingers. For flat welding the torch tip is customarily held at approximately a 45° angle to the work and the rod lowered into the weld from the opposite side at about the same angle. However, for gun welding, no hard and fast rule can be observed, due to the irregular shapes involved.

While a couple of types of welding fluxes are on the market for use with steel, they are not necessary at all in gun welding, being intended for commercial welding on material not too clean or of indefinite analysis. Keep the rod and the gun metal clean to start with and you will have little trouble making good welds.

To give a little idea of the relation of heat to the more common metals look over the table of Physical Properties of Metals.

The meanings of weight, tensile strength and melting point need no explanation. Thermal conductivity is ability to transmit heat from point of reception throughout the mass of the metal affected. In other words, radiation or dissipation of heat. Copper is the standard used,

METAL	Weight Lb. per Cu. In.	Tensile Strength Lb. per Sq. In.	Melting Point Deg. F.	Relative Thermal Conductivity Copper = 1.00	Specific Heat	Coefficient of Linear Expansion	Approx. Expansion from 60° to Melting Point In. per Ft.
ALUMINUM							
Cast........	0.093	15,000	1210	0.524	0.22	0.0000123	11⁄64
Drawn......	0.098	24,000 to 40,000				0.0000136	12⁄64
BRASS							
Cast, Red...	0.3103	20,000	1740	0.251	0.09	0.00000957	12⁄64
Cast, Yellow.	0.2959	18,000		0.208			
Drawn......		40,000 to 78,000				0.00001052	14⁄64
BRONZE							
Manganese..		75,000 to 90,000	1692	0.735			
Phosphor....	0.32	50,000				0.00000986	12⁄64
Tobin.......		60,000 to 100,000					
COPPER							
Cast........		22,000	1980	1.00	0.095	0.0000094	14⁄64
Drawn......	0.3195	31,000					
IRON							
Gray cast....	0.2604	20,000	2190	0.124		0.00000556	9⁄64
White cast...		18,000	2000				
Wrought....	0.2779	55,000	2730	0.157	0.11	0.00000648	13⁄64
LEAD........	0.411	1,780	620	0.091	0.03	0.0000155	7⁄64
NICKEL......	0.312	76,000	2650	0.155	0.11	0.000007	14⁄64
STEEL							
Mild........	0.283	50,000 to 75,000	2690	0.118	0.117	0.0000063	12⁄64
Hard.......		65,000 to 80,000	2570		0.1175		
ZINC.........	0.2526	5,500	785	0.29	0.09	0.0000144	8⁄64

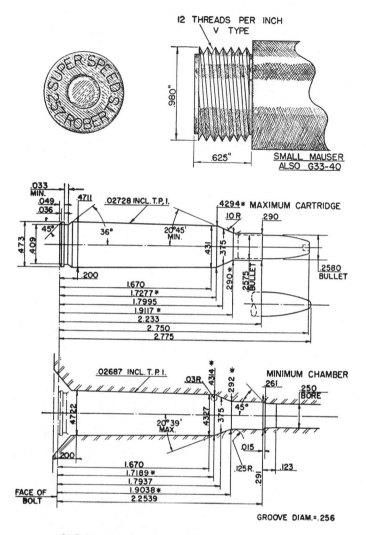

The .257 Remington Roberts

Developed by the late Mr. Ned Roberts, this cartridge had a difficult start, being called the .25 Roberts more or less officially, but being made by a number of custom gunsmiths who changed dimensions now and then to suit themselves. Remington became interested, changed it a little more, and brought it out as the .257 Remington Roberts. Winchester fell in line, calling their product the .257 Winchester Roberts, but managed to restrain themselves from there on out and followed Remington's dimensions.

Based on the 7mm Mauser cartridge, the .257 features an extractor cut

as it has a very high rate compared to other metals. Although its melting point is lower than that of steel, it is necessary to use as large a tip and expend as much heat as on steel (of the same bulk) for a proper copper weld. Specific heat is the unit of measure, being the number of calories taken up by one gram of metal during a temperature rise or fall of one degree Centigrade. A metal having a low melting point and relatively high specific heat may require as much heat to bring it to its point of fusion as a metal of high melting point and low specific heat, as in the case of aluminum compared to steel. (That is what makes welding aluminum so interesting—you must heat it above its melting point before it fuses!) The coefficient of expansion is the linear increase per unit length when the temperature of a body is raised one degree C. This is not of great concern to the gun welder in ordinary work, as he is not affected by the expansion and contraction of small work.

Expansion and contraction of welded work cannot be controlled mechanically, nor can warping by uneven contraction during cooling be prevented by use of jigs or clamps. If you must weld items like bolt bodies and receivers and they do warp, you must un-warp them through use of heat again. Warped metal can be heated and bent straight by force, or heated and the cooling controlled so that it is really warped back where it belongs. This is done by cooling the ex-

---

shallower than that of the .250/3000, .270 and .30–06 cases. The .257 case is strong at the head, but rather thin walled.

Factory .257 rifles are throated for the deep-seated factory bullet cartridges and accuracy is generally improved when the throat is reamed out sufficiently to permit cartridges loaded to 3″ or 3⅛″ overall length, even when the short loaded factory ammunition is used.

The .257 is a handloader's cartridge and the reloader can considerably improve the accuracy and the velocity over the factory loading as a general rule. The factory cartridge and rifle usually will not equal the .250/3000 Savage factory cartridge and rifle combination in accuracy.

The Mauser carbine action is ideally suited to the .257 cartridge and the Springfield action is excellent, although a short magazine block is required for dependable feeding.

With regard to small-receiver Mauser actions, particularly the 7mm actions made for and by Mexico, a word of caution is in order: fit every barrel to the individual receiver involved as tightly as possible, making the thread diameter maximum. With high-pressure cartridges bulged chambers are possible unless this is watched, since the barrel walls around the chamber are rather thin. Utilize the strength of the receiver through a tightly threaded shank to strengthen the barrel.

panded side faster than the contracted side. Or, on say a bolt warped in a curve, cooling the outside of the curve artificially and allowing the opposite side to cool naturally. Such cooling is done by laying the hot metal on a wet cloth, or on a cooled flat steel plate. A dull red heat is the highest needed, and often a lower temperature will serve. For straightening by bending, a bright red or cherry red may be needed on stock as heavy as a rifle bolt. An uneven distribution of metal will cause distortion through warping, but often can be prevented entirely or to a large extent through application of diminishing heat while cooling. Rifle bolts such as the Springfield with its safety lug, or the Mauser with its guide rib, nearly always develop a slight curve when cut in two and welded to make a short action. The opposite side naturally cools sooner than the other and the thicker side with more bulk just contracts slowly and pulls the tube into a curve, stretching the thinner side. If lessening heat is applied so that the entire surface cools at the same rate, the tendency to warp is greatly moderated.

In any bolt welding, especially concerning 1917 Enfield cocking notches or cams, contraction may cause surface cracks in the exterior of the metal adjoining the welded area. These are often almost microscopic and visible only after the bolt is polished and then only in bright sunlight. Never more than a very few thousandths deep, they may not affect in any way the safety or operation of the rifle, but should always be repaired. The best way I have found is to use the little thin carborundum cut-off wheels for the hand grinder, cutting a trough where each crack exists, then welding in nickel-steel and polishing it down. Such cracks are caused by the outer surface cooling much faster than the inner surface, generally due to heating the metal too fast with the torch, getting the surface much hotter than the complete thickness at that point.

MELTING POINTS OF METALS

Covering those in more-or-less common use today. These are laboratory figures and may differ slightly from actual working temperature encountered in working commercial metals, because of impurities in the metals.

Metal	Degrees Centigrade	Degrees Fahrenheit
Aluminum	659	1218
Antimony	630	1166
Barium	850	1562
Beryllium	1800	3272
Bismuth	271	520

Cadmium	321	610
Chromium	1510	2750
Copper	1083	1981
Gold	1063	1945
Iron	1520	2768
Lead	327	621
Magnesium	651	1204
Manganese	1225	2237
Mercury	−39	−38
Molybdenum	2500	4532
Nickel	1452	2646
Platinum	1755	3191
Selenium	217	423
Silver	961	1762
Tin	232	450
Tungsten	3000	5432
Uranium	2400	4352
Vanadium	1750	3182
Zinc	419	786

Other Elements

Calcium	810	1490
Phosphorus	44	111
Potassium	62	144
Silicon	1420	2588
Sodium	97	207
Sulphur	113	235

CHAPTER 9

Heat Treatment of Metals

TO REALLY understand hardening and tempering of steel you need to know something of the character, structure and manufacturing processes of steel itself. Steel is an alloy of refined iron and any one or several other substances—Carbon, Nickel, Vanadium, Chrome Manganese, Molybdenum, Tungsten, Silicon or such. Modern manufacturing methods cut down the impurities formerly found in most steel, and steel plant laboratories have stabilized production so that very uniform metal is produced. In the old days, every lot of steel was different, and had to be tested for each purpose intended, and the ultimate user had to learn how to handle each separate piece he bought.

The gunsmith is principally concerned with nickel and carbon steels because of the fact that practically all guns and gun parts are made of those steels. Winchester barrels for high-powered rifles are nickel-steel, and Winchester Model 54 and 70 receivers as well as 1917 Enfield and 1903 Springfield high-number actions are of nickel-steel. Such steels have from 3% to 5% nickel content, and a very low carbon content. They are not particularly hard, but are very tough, having great tensile strength and resiliency.

Carbon steel is used in practically all shotguns, pistols, revolvers and .22 rifles, the working parts having such composition as to take hardening and case-hardening, with the barrels, receivers, slides, and the like, being of mild, easily machined steel.

The carbon steels are handled in many ways, since it is possible to obtain almost any desired degree of hardness with them with a minimum of special equipment. Before going into details on treating steel, however, we better get a few things straight. First, the double meaning of the word "temper." To steel manufacturers it means the percentage of carbon in a particular lot of steel, regardless of whether the steel is annealed or hard. To the user of steel, or to the layman, "temper" means the hardness after heat-treating and finishing, and the resiliency, or "spring" of the steel. The latter condition can have no standard of measurement between different-sized parts or pieces.

The term *point* is used to denote carbon content, a point being *one one-hundredth* of one percent. Therefore a 100 point steel is 1% of carbon; 60 point is $\frac{6}{10}$ of 1%, and so on. The higher the percent of carbon, the easier it is "burned," or carbon cooked out of it. What the steelmaker would call razor temper or razor steel, is about 150 point, or 1½% carbon. Saw-file temper is 137.5 point. Such very high carbon steels are very difficult to work with, as the temper will burn out so easily when ground. Chisel temper is 100 point—1% carbon. For tools requiring a hard cutting edge and great body strength it is ideal. Properly tempered it is excellent for hammers and triggers or other parts subject to wear and strain, although harder than really necessary for such applications.

Set temper is 87.5 point, or ⅞ of 1% carbon. It is better for most gun parts than the harder higher-carbon steels. This type is used in stamping and pressing dies.

You can buy carbon tool steels almost to your own prescription, if necessary, and it is wise to use these known-analysis metals as much as possible. Drill rod, for instance, is 1.25 carbon—too much carbon for many applications, so it would pay to have lower carbon rods for such work as making screws and pins. Many tools can be used as a source of steel, if you know that they are made of and how to treat them. The following table, credited by Mr. Baker to Woodworth's *Hardening, Tempering & Annealing* gives a good idea of the carbon steels used in common tools. A flat type gun spring needs to be from 110 to 120 point carbon before tempering, so you can see where, *in an emergency*, you can find such steel in an old file, by annealing it, shaping and re-hardening.

CARBON STEELS USED IN COMMON TOOLS

	Carbon		Carbon
Augur, wood	0.60 to 0.70	Jaw, vise	0.85 to 0.90
Axe	1.20	Knife, belt	0.80 to 0.85
Ball bearing	1.20	Knife, paper	1.05 to 1.10
Barrel, gun	0.60 to 0.70	Knife, wood working	1.15 to 1.20
Bits, mining	0.80	Knife, putty	0.90 to 1.00
Blade, pocket knife	0.90	Magnet	1.23 to 1.25
Blade, reamer	1.20 to 1.22	Machinery, crucible	0.55 to 0.65
Bushing, spring	0.80	Mower, lawn	1.00
Centers, lathe	0.80 to 0.90	Plow, crucible	0.85 to 0.90
Chisels, cold	0.85	Punch, blacksmith	0.80 to 0.85

	Carbon		Carbon
Chisels, chipping	0.80 to 0.90	Rake	1.15 to 1.25
Chisels, wood working	0.60 to 0.70	Saws, circular	0.80 to 0.90
Dies, envelope	1.15	Saws, for steel	1.60
Dies, drop forging	0.85 to 0.90	Saws, cross cut	0.85 to 1.00
Drills, twist	1.20 to 1.22	Saws, band	0.68 to 0.75
Driver, screw	0.60 to 0.70	Skate	1.15
Edge, straight	1.05 to 1.12	Spring, common lock-	
Facing, anvil	0.85 to 0.90	ing	1.20 to 1.25
Files	1.25 to 1.30	Spring, railroad, or	
Hammer, blacksmith's	0.67 to 0.78	locomotive	0.90 to 1.10
Hammer, machinist's	0.90 to 1.00	Taps	1.20 to 1.22
Hatchet	1.15 to 1.22	Tools, blacksmiths'	0.60 to 0.70
Hoe	0.85 to 0.90	Tools, moulders'	1.25 to 1.30
Hooks, grass	0.60 to 0.70	Tools, bricklayers'	0.90 to 0.95
Jaw, chuck	0.85 to 0.90	Wrenches	0.80 to 0.90

Annealing. When steel is made the outer surfaces of the billet bars or shapes are usually hardened in the rolling and cooling processes. The machined tool steel you buy will be annealed so that it can be cut and formed, but should you use or encounter a hardened piece of steel, you will have to anneal it yourself to make it workable. Annealing is simply heating the steel slowly and allowing it to cool slowly, so that its hardness is removed. It is best never to heat steel more than just enough to anneal, trying a dull red first, and working up to bright cherry red if lower temperatures leave the steel hard. Do not get mixed up with tungsten alloy air-hardening steels—they harden automatically as they cool. Such steels can be annealed only by being held at a particular temperature for several hours in a special furnace, and cooled under control. This process comes under the word "normalizing" which covers specialized annealing.

Small parts and spring stock can usually be annealed by simply putting in a pan over a gas flame, or in a metal box and then the box heated red by welding torch. Light annealing can be done with the exposed flame of the torch, but it is not too good an idea. Steel to be annealed should not come in contact with actual flame. I have never had any trouble with just letting annealed small pieces of steel cool in open air, but for any part with bulk or mass, such as a revolver hammer, it is advisable to slow the cooling by burying the red-hot metal in lime, powdered charcoal or hot sand. Very small parts which require delayed cooling can be clamped between pieces of soft wood while hot

THE PFEIFER PLANT

A custom gun shop with *room*. Pfeifer's main shop room, which houses the rifling machines, turning lathes and barrel fitting equipment. Not visible are four rooms on the right—tool room, where tools and jigs are made; a metal-working room for welding and metal alterations; a blueing and metal finish room; and the stock department.

All of these side rooms have plenty of floor space to offer a healthy working area.

That box on top of the room at the back is an ingenious oven in which gunstock wood and blanks can be stored or cured. Both temperature and humidity can be closely controlled. A very, very worth while accessory for the custom gunstocker in any locality.

Short action 1903 Springfield, with Titus .22/250 24″ light barrel. Stocked in French Walnut by John Hearn. Hensoldt Duralyt 6X scope in modified Redfield mount. Metalwork by the author. Weight, complete as shown, 8 lbs. 4 oz. This is my own varmint rifle. The scope is mounted high and set back, but is perfectly satisfactory on this light-recoil arm. On a heavy-caliber rifle recoil would be uncomfortable unless the scope was set lower, or a high cheekpiece used.

and allowed to burn themselves in, slowing their cooling in the airtight pocket created in the wood.

Controlled annealing is practically impossible without a pyrometer (device for measuring heat at high degrees). By experiment you can learn a little about a particular type of steel, but you will never be able to depend on the uncontrolled method for uniform results. When a bit of steel is to be softened just enough to make it workable and not an iota more, you cannot do so well by guesswork and eyesight. For a lot of non-vital quickie jobs however you can flame anneal (either gas plate or torch) the material and after holding it at the desired heat a second or two—one of the shades of red—allow it to air-cool until black then quench in warm or hot soapsuds or heavy oil. All ordinary steels you will come in contact with will anneal at low temperatures, compared to welding heats, and if a welding torch is your source of heat you will have to take it gently. Over-annealing, or exposure to too much heat, not only plays hob with the structure of the steel, but shrinks the metal enough to change dimensions on even small parts.

The only absolutely reliable means of uniformly annealing and hardening steel parts is the heat treating furnace. Such furnaces are really ovens capable of being raised to high temperatures by gas, or electricity. Any gunsmith or gun shop contemplating the manufacture of some special part of tool for general sale, or the making of numerous parts for obsolete firearms should by all means install a furnace. If around TVA or in an area of low-rate electricity, the electric furnace is very eligible, but in most localities the cost of operating even the smallest sizes runs the light bill up. The gas fired furnace is the most popular variety, and is available in all sizes, up to great industrial ovens. The amount of insulation determines the heating capacity, so a unit capable of very high temperatures will be both larger and more expensive than one with the same inside dimensions but rated a few hundred degrees lower. Practically all the small commercial furnaces will go to 1800° Fahrenheit or slightly higher, and some are available with capacity to 2000°. The standard furnaces start with interior dimensions of around three inches heighth, width and depth, and go up a little at a time so that practically any desired size can be procured. I believe the very small ones would handle most gun-part work, but the real McCov is the size capable of taking shotgun receivers for case-hardening, which would mean it would have a minimum capacity of around 10″ x 6″ x 6″ inside. Such a unit, purchased from a manufacturer, will cost over two hundred dollars. Mostly over. The small units are priced from sixty to one hundred fifty dollars at the present time. All come equipped or with fittings for dial-reading pyrometers covering their heat ranges. A shop desiring a fair-sized gas furnace will do well to consult the smartest heating engineer in town to see if he cannot build one at a reasonable price. Small commercial furnaces for gun work are available from Mittermeier or Brownell. Write the Colloid Equipment Company, 50 Church Street, New York 7, New York for literature on the Huppert Furnaces—25 models are made.

Hardening. All steel has a "critical temperature"—a degree of heat at which the structural formation and/or analysis undergoes a change. Naturally, this temperature varies with different alloys. The steelmakers are no longer secretive about their products and usually with no more effort than reading their descriptive literature or possibly writing a letter, you can find out exactly how your type of tool steel behaves at what degree. Most of the ordinary medium and high carbon steels must be heated to between 1400° and 1650° Fahrenheit for hardening. This is quite a variation, so the practice of heating to "cherry red" and quenching does not always give the same result on different steels. Since nearly all carbon tool steels change color in the same way at almost the same temperatures, the hardening and tempering colors which appear while heating indicate the approximate temperature of the metal. The following chart gives a rather complete color range and can be used as a guide.

Hardening and Tempering Colors	*Degrees Fahrenheit*
Faint Yellow (flickering)	400
Faint Yellow	425
Pale Straw	450
Straw	456
Yellowish Brown	500
Light Purple	525
Purple	530
Deep Purple, or Blue	550
Polish Blue	575
Dark Blue	600
Blue-Green	625
Red-barely visible	900
Black Red	1000
Blood Red	1200
Cherry Red	1400
Salmon (Red turning to yellow)	1600
Lemon	1800
Very Light Yellow	2000
White	2200

It must be understood that judging by color can be affected by several factors: the light under which you are working—in sunlight the colors are not as easily defined: the type of heat employed—if an open flame is used, the colors will appear brighter than they really are: and last, individual eyesight. Few people judge colors the same, even when normal in color perception. Some men call "orange" what appears to be cherry red to others. Incidently, this oft-repeated "cherry red" is a bright, clear, glowing red, without any tinge of yellow. (What a color-blind gunsmith would go by, I have not even a guess! He would have to get a furnace and pyrometer.) The chart colors are approximate for medium-intensity lighting, such as indirect artificial or indirect natural sunlight.

The matter of hardening means just that—hardening soft or annealed steel—either as an end in itself, or in preparation for tempering to a prescribed tensile strength. Case-hardening means surface hardening only, and will be discussed later.

Carbon steels are hardened by being brought to their critical temperature and quenched, or quick-cooled, the abrupt change from hot to cold condition effecting the change in the steel. The heating may be done in many ways—furnace, flame, forge or by hot bath. The latter may be chemical solution or molten metal. This latter method is especially well suited to irregular parts with holes, varying thickness or mass, and such, since all parts heat uniformly to the desired temperature. With the flame or forge system often a thin portion of the part will get too hot while waiting for the balance to reach the proper heat. The lead bath is commonly used in *tempering*, employing pure, sulfer-free lead and the heat controlled by use of a pyrometer. The lead is brought to the desired heat and the steel springs or other parts, preheated to around 300° Fahrenheit are suspended in it by wires or hooks or racks. Because lead may plate or adhere to the steel, the latter may be dipped in a solution of potassium cyanide (one pound to one gallon of water) and allowed to dry before placing in the lead, without preheating. As pure lead vaporizes at around 1190° Fahrenheit and the vapor is poisonous, the molten lead when around 900° should be covered with a coat of powdered charcoal. The low temperature limitation will not permit the lead bath to be of much use in hardening steel, but for tempering springs and small parts, and for some annealing jobs, it can be very useful.

The gas or electric furnace is the best way of all to harden steels, and as it can be also used for tempering, annealing and normalizing, represents the one appliance usable in all forms of heat-treating.

The best liquid heating bath for *hardening* steels for the gunsmith to use is the barium chlorid bath, which permits temperatures as high as 2400° Fahrenheit. Tool steels requiring very high temperatures can be hardened, and for steels not requiring over 2000° Fahrenheit a mixture of three parts barium chlorid and one part potassium chlorid is easier handled.

With the steel heated to the correct hardening point, it must be quenched and I think probably every liquid known to mankind has been tried at one time or another. Legend has it that ancient Eastern smiths quenched their finest sword and knife blades by plunging them into living animals and sometimes human slaves. Equivalent to a heated oil bath, which is cheaper and more civilized.

Water—plain, rain, as brine, or in solution with most anything else that will dissolve, is a common primitive quench, but is not suited to all purposes. If water is used, it should preferably be at 75° Fahrenheit. The colder the quench, the harder the material, and greater the brittleness. Salt water, or brine, makes steel harder than plain water. The gunsmith does not want his steel very hard and brittle as a rule. He just wants it hard. Oils do not give as hard a quench as does water, but the variety of oils which can be used allows considerable leeway in attaining a desired degree of hardness on any particular item.

Raw linseed oil, or cottonseed oil, is good for hardening tools such as chisels, gouges and wood-cutting tools in general. Lard, sperm and whale oil are better for small gun parts, the sperm oil being especially suited to springs. Mineral oils work satisfactorily on heavier work, but the fish-oils are better for the gun shop. I have hardened many a bit of steel in ordinary SAE 10 motor oil, and found that it works best after being used awhile. There is no positive rule on quenching—occasionally you will meet a part which will not oil harden enough, but will be cured okay in water or brine.

All of the above dope on "hardening" actually covers *re*-hardening, or the treating of steel with suitable carbon content to obtain the hardness possible. The matter of making naturally soft steel harder is a little more complicated. The introduction of carbon into finished steel is rather out of the scope of the small shop, except for elaboration for the case-hardening processes. There are two or three patent compounds on the market which are capable of giving hardness to steel for an appreciable depth below the surface. "Kasenit No. 1" made by the Kasenit Company, New York 14, New York, is one of the oldest and best known; it is a carbon-rich powder. In use the steel is heated cherry red and dipped into the powder which sticks to it, melting on and forming a coat. The steel is again heated to bright red heat and quenched in clean cold water. The powder burns with a bright flame during this second heating, and evidently some carbon cooks into the steel. This system is as mentioned a case-hardening system, but capable of imparting quite a deep surface hardening. It works on everything from mild iron to tool steel. The process can be repeated on the same steel, with some increase in hardness.

Case-Hardening. Imparting carbon to the exterior of steel or iron in order to obtain a very hard outer surface is known as case-hardening, case-carburizing, or just carburizing. The technical term is "cementation," implying the binding of hardening substance to metal. The surface of the steel is changed to very high carbon hardened steel. The depth of hardness, called "skin" or "case" is only a few thousandths inch, seldom as much as .008″, usually only .005 or .006″. The carbonizing agent is almost always animal charcoal in some form or mixture. Bone dust is the most common, although charred horn, leather and hoofs have been used. Many other substances are mentioned in formulae, such as wood charcoal, salt, sodium carbonate, saltpetre, rosin, flour, hair, limestone, and ferrocyanide. You can get along fine by just getting some bone dust or meal from the nearest fertilizer dealer and charring it in a pan yourself, and supplying yourself with charred leather; buy a little hydro-carbonated bone.

Besides the piece of steel and the carbonizing agent, you must have a hardening box—to fit the furnace, if you have one. A hardening box should be cast-iron, pressed steel, or welded mild steel. I favor steel, as it is less liable to crack. The boxes or pots must have loose-fitting lids, to be cemented in place with fire-clay when the box is heated. If you did not buy the furnace, you must make one or use a forge to heat the box in and since it is sometimes necessary to hold steel at a high temperature six hours or so, the forge idea is not so good. (Once upon a time I was talked into doing a week of forging, making and hardening some tools. Since then I have very little interest in forges. Those hammers get heavy.)

For very fine grain case-hardening, use only charcoal, granulated raw bone, hydro-carbonated bone and charred leather for the first heat. Bring to cherry red heat (the box and all, with the work and carbonizing agents inside) and hold to that heat, around 1400° Fahrenheit, from two to four hours, depending on the size of the work. The bigger the piece, the longer the heat. Leave the box to cool slowly. This "cements" or forms a steel outer skin high in carbon content, with open grain. When the work is cool, unpack and heat the parts to

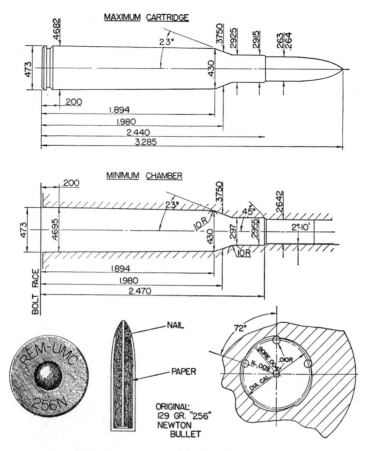

MAXIMUM CARTRIDGE

MINIMUM CHAMBER

ORIGINAL: 129 GR. "256" NEWTON BULLET

ACTIONS SUITABLE --- 1903 SPRINGFIELD, 1917 ENFIELD, 1898 MAUSER, WIN. 54 & 70, REMINGTON.

The .256 Newton

Here is one Newton cartridge which should not be allowed to die. The case is really a .30–06 necked to 6.5mm. Before the .270 Winchester came upon the scene, the .256 Newton held the spotlight as the high-velocity hunting cartridge to be desired.

In spite of extravagant claims by Newton, the .256 never reached the velocities claimed until duPont brought out their series of improved powders. Today, with modern propellants and components, the cartridge is really worth while. The .256 will better the performance of the .270 without developing the sharp recoil of the latter. By using a custom barrel of proper 6.5mm dimensions, the many excellent European 6.5mm bullets can be loaded for the .256.

There were never any real standards for Newton cartridges or chambers,

red in molten lead, then quench in oil as in hardening tool steel. Then repack in box, using only granulated wood charcoal and bring to a dull red heat. Remove from oven and dump the work instantly into clean luke-warm water. This treatment brings out a dense, tough, and very hard surface. Whenever quenching case-hardened material, the process should be very fast, so that air does not get a chance to contact the work. This means the box or pot should be opened and dumped right at the quenching tank.

The preceding method will produce no color, or dull colors. To case-harden without color, Mr. Baker advised to place a ½" layer of granulated raw bone in the box, then the parts to be treated, then another layer of raw bone, and so on until within an inch of the top of container. Then fill the box with old, used bone, seal and heat, at cherry red, three to four hours. Parts are quenched in clean, soft water, or if very small and thin, in quenching oil. This results in good even hardening and parts are clean steel gray.

Malleable iron is seldom encountered in guns today, even for butt-plates and pistol grip caps. It is case-hardened by packing with a mixture of one part granulated raw bone and three parts granulated charcoal (wood), heating at 1400° Fahrenheit, two to four hours and water-quenched.

Color case-hardening, as on some shotgun receivers and single-action revolver frames, is an uncertain business. In spite of good equipment and known formulae, failures are common. Charred bone is the principal ingredient in color hardening mixtures, and sometimes will do a good job by itself. Any material to be color hardened must be polished very bright, without buffing as buffing fills the pores of the steel and spoils the finish. Polish with fine abrasives and clean the parts by boiling in a lye solution or pickling, handling them with clean cotton gloves. Any trace of grease, even a fingerprint, will spoil the color. The work is packed in the box with the charred bone layers about ¾" thick. The box is held at 1400° for the usual two to four hours and the

---

so that existing arms or cartridges may not agree exactly with the figures given on the drawing regarding diameters at necks and shoulders.

Shown sectioned is one of the original Newton bullets designed for the .256, which gave very good performance on game. The core is pure lead, the jacket pure copper, with a band of paper between core and jacket to act as insulation for the bore-bearing area. The wire-point is really a sort of nail, with its head at base of bullet, and coming to a flat point at the bullet tip. This was to strengthen the bullet as well as to prevent battering the tip in rifle magazines.

work quenched in clean cool soft water. Too high heat will result in no color, although length of heating time has no particular effect over the required time for the size parts concerned. The quenching bath should have a wire mesh screen six or eight inches below the surface and from the bottom of the tank bring up a pipe connected with an air pump so that the water may be agitated while dumping; or the water may be paddled vigorously while dumping. It is the air bubbles in the agitated water that give the fine mottled finish so much desired and admired. When cool the work should be taken out and boiled in clean soft water, dried in sawdust and oiled or lacquered. I believe that different types of salts can be used to deepen colors, but only experimentation can tell, and I am not at present setup for the work. Color case-hardening is at best a very tricky proposition, and what might give good results on one gun frame might be a total failure on the next. Oil quenching will give dull, but lasting colors, though not hardening the surface very well. Color casing is primarily a decorative finish, to my notion, with the strength of metal secondary, and since I do not care much for the result, I would rather surface-harden without color, where necessary, then finish in a regular blue color, by a blueing process.

Cyanide Hardening. This is the business—when you really want a surface hardened. Some color-finishing can be done with cyanide, but the true value of this system is appreciated when it is desired to harden low-carbon punches or tool parts. Practically no equipment is required for such work—just heat the metal red, dip in powdered potassium cyanide, reheat to a slightly higher red, and quench in clear water or brine. For more hardness, or deeper case, the part may be heated, dipped, re-heated and re-dipped two or three times more before quenching. Such hardening is very applicable to soft gun hammers, sears, triggers, and large shotgun firing pins for double-barrel guns. Parts can be made, or tools, for that matter, of cold-rolled steel, and cyanide-hardened into excellent serviceability. The surface of the metal is both hard and tough, while the core remains normal for the steel involved. The best way I know to make good gun screws is to use cold-rolled round stock and cyanide-harden the finished screw.

Cyanide can be used to color steel without hardening, or will both color and harden. To accomplish the latter, parts are heated red in melted cyanide contained in cast-iron pot or crucible, then quenched in water, similar to case-hardening with animal charcoals. Mr. Baker states that the same process, using a mild steel pot, made by riveting and welding, will produce color without hardening, although the first

ACKLEY IMPROVED .257

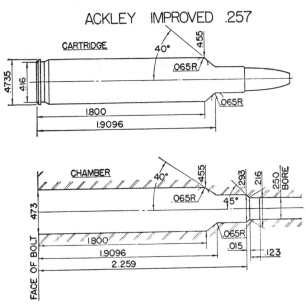

The Improved .257 is one that Mr. Ackley does recommend highly. The case is formed as with the above description, and when reloaded delivers very creditable velocities—the 87-grain bullet can be driven around 3,400 FPS; the 100-grain 3,250 FPS; and the long 125-grain hunting bullet from 2,950 to 3,000 FPS.

time the pot or box is used, the parts will have some hardness. The pot should be heated a half-hour before putting in the cyanide.

Warning. Potassium cyanide is one of the quickest, deadliest poisons known—you handle it carefully. Should it enter the body in any way, by mouth, eye, or cut, you die fast. Yet, very few people ever get in trouble with it accidentally, for only a few precautions need be observed. Do not leave any of it around—keep your cyanide in a well-marked container, whenever any is spilled or thrown around clean it up in a hurry. Do not contaminate any glass, jar, can or other receptacle with it which might under any circumstances come in contact with any person or animal. Most important, when using molten cyanide, have the parts to be immersed thoroughly dry, for if any moisture is brought to the cyanide it will spatter as would molten lead.

Mercury Hardening. The use of mercury as a hardening quench is limited to small drills and taps, in my estimation. (Principally because no normal man can afford to own enough mercury to handle large objects!) The drill—ordinary carbon steel type—is heated almost cherry red and quenched quickly in mercury. Taps are handled the same way. In some cases, it may be necessary to raise the heating temperature to bright cherry color, but the lowest heat which will accomplish the result is desirable, in order to preserve the sharp edges of the tools. Sharpening after hardening with the use of hard Arkansas stones is helpful, too. Hardening carbon steel bits with mercury enables them to cut steels at which most high-speed drills and taps balk.

Baker's Hardening "Kinks." For drilling glass, chilled iron, hardened steel, take a sharp new drill which has never been heated, make a solution of half water and half muriatic acid in which zinc has been dissolved to the saturation point. Heat drill to dull cherry red and quench in solution until cool. Use turpentine for drilling lubricant, or a coolant.

A short piece of cast-iron pipe, with ends threaded for solid caps, makes a good small hardening box. Weld a rod or handle of some sort to it, so it can be handled when hot, and make at least one cap with very short thread, or interrupted-screw thread system, so that it can be removed very quickly. For best results, both caps should be quick-removable, and notched for some sort of spanner or wrench, so that they may be taken off and contents of pipe pushed directly through it into the quench bath.

Yellow prussiate of potash is sometimes substituted for potassium cyanide with good results in hardening small parts. Also, a mixture of prussiate of potash, sal ammoniac and salt. Some mechanics use a mixture of prussiate of potash and black loam, mixed to a paste with water and spread on the work. When dry, heat to red heat and quench in salt water.

When hardening low grade steel by case-hardening, avoid the use of raw bone as the phosphorus it contains will make the steel brittle.

CHAPTER 10

Making and Fitting Sights and Accessories

SINCE Baker wrote on the manufacture and substitution of small parts two important factors affecting this point have cropped up in the gunsmithing field. The first is the rise of many specialist gunsmiths and accessory makers, whose business is furnishing the special ramp sights, barrel bands, swivels, and the like, which Baker and his contemporaries had to make for themselves. It is now possible to purchase most special items, thus doing away with the necessity of having drawers and racks full of special jigs, reamers and tools. The second factor is the high cost of living—it is not possible for any professional general gunsmith to make such items as swivels and ramp sights of the band type to fit and sell at a price he can get. A set of swivels costs from less than a dollar to four dollars, from the plain screw-in type to the elaborate quick-detachables. Would you like to make a pair of QDs for four bucks? Or a plain set for a dollar? Discounting all overhead, a skilled gunsmith should consider his labor worth not less than two dollars an hour. Who will pay six dollars for a plain barrel band it took the smith three hours to file out, fit, polish, blue and install? Unless he goes into production and makes a batch of them, using machine tools to streamline the work, he is much better off to buy such items from others who have gone into production and who make it their principal business. So do not hang your neck out too far for the customer who wants something different, unless he is willing to pay for the time involved, as well as for the headaches you will get figuring the job out to suit him!

Having got the above off my chest, and it being understood that we work on the lazy man's system of never making anything we can buy, we will go into some of the problems which if not everyday occurrences, crop up often enough to warrant comment. You will have enough trouble fitting ready-made accessories and parts which are supposed to require no fitting, anyway.

First, rifle ramp front sights: Actually, the sight and the ramp are practically always separate, but just saying "ramp front" seems sort of incomplete and the custom is to term the whole assembly as "sight." The band type is much to be preferred over the plain ramp, due to its ease of installation, strength and, to me personally, appearance. The band part, which encircles the barrel at muzzle, should be very thin, not over $\frac{1}{32}''$ for best appearance. The Pacific Gun Sight Company furnishes excellent band ramps, finish machined, but not polished or blued, on order, at reasonable prices, and these can be shaped up very well in an hour's time. It would be nice, of course, to have taper reamers to finish the inside of each band to the perfect diameter for the barrel it is intended for, but you will need a lot of reamers. You can fit bands accurately, however, by polishing the insides smooth by means of a mandrel with abrasive cloth around it, then driving and peening it on a "dummy" barrel. Get an old barrel, polish the outside mirror-smooth (after tapering it from .45″ to .70″, muzzle to point 15″ from muzzle). Measure the barrel of the rifle receiving the sight at the proper point then mark your dummy barrel $\frac{1}{8}''$ forward of the point at which it measures the same as the rifle barrel. Using wood blocks and soft-metal hammers, drive and worry the sight around on the dummy until it reaches the mark. It will then come within $\frac{1}{8}''$ of proper location on the rifle and, when finished, should give no great trouble when driven that distance. (All this is done, of course, on the assumption that your ramp is slightly smaller than the barrel it is to fit, which is the way to order it, to insure getting a true, close fit.) After the sight is the correct fit, it may be cleaned up on the outside, both front and back edges cut toward center in order to remove any chamfer which may have developed during inside polishing or fitting, and all marks of tools removed.

The front sight blade should be fitted at this time, then removed, and the ramp blued, then fitted. Even if the rifle itself is to be blued, the sight may be blued separately, because unless the band fits the barrel absolutely perfectly, blueing solution will work under it and show up some trouble. If any oil is present under the band, and the old style cold blue, or Baker's hot blue, is used, the oil will foul up the blueing at edges of band and ramp. However, if the sight is blued separately, there is always a good chance of scratching the barrel a bit in installing it, so it is six of one and half-a-dozen of the other.

The band ramps all are held in place with either a set screw in the top, under the sight blade, or a pin through the ramp engaging in a groove across top of barrel. The blades are held with small set screws, pins, or are of the drive-in dovetail type. Where the ramp is held with set-screw and blade is on top of screw, naturally being installed after sight is in place, the sight blade or dovetail must go into position quite easily. You do not want to do any pounding, driving or much filing after the ramp is fixed and finished. I squeeze dovetail sights into ramps by simply folding a small piece of thin sheet lead over sight and ramp (sight should go into right side of slot one-third its width easily, by hand) put the works in the vise and wind it up slowly. Since the vise presses side of ramp and side of sight, with no twisting action of ramp on barrel, the ramp cannot be pushed out of line. Should any driving be necessary, clamp the vertical portion of the ramp, back of the slot, in the vise, so that force of drive will be against sight only, not band and barrel.

If you must make a ramp sight, there are three systems usable. The ramp can be milled and bored out of a solid piece of stock—as are Pacific and Redfield ramps—this makes the nicest job. A flat strip of metal can be welded to a tube, and the sight machined out of this rough-fabricated blank. This can be as good as the solid type, if weld is perfect and the steels used are homogeneous so as to allow it to be all one color when blued. The last way is to fabricate the ramp without welding, and this is a good method for the smith who does not have welding equipment but who can use a lathe. The illustration shows all three types well enough to convey the principles of manufacture. With either of the first types, a milling machine is almost a necessity as doing the job with files means going into those hours of time you cannot afford to put in, unless business is awful bad.

When attaching ramps to barrels by screws, or using screws in ramps as in No. 3, the 6 x 48 thread is handiest to use. It is fine enough so that $\frac{1}{16}''$ depth of hole will give good holding strength. Holes must be of course, flat-bottomed and tapped to bottom. The sighting plane of the ramp can be lined with a 50-line checkering file, matted with a matting tool, sand-blasted, or hand-matted by rolling a small round file, #2 cut, over it. With either the No. 1 or No. 2 types, the barrel hole must be carefully cut to size—and do not forget that the barrel tapers slightly. If adjustable reamers are not at hand, you use a boring tool in the lathe, and with reasonable care, excellent fitting can be obtained. The "dummy" barrel is your real gage, and if the rifle involved in the particular job has any peculiarities in muzzle dimensions, you take time out to make an exact duplicate of it, for fitting. The making of a ramp is a lot of effort, but occasionally necessary. Today many sporting rifles are made for telescopic sight use only, but ramp front sights are installed solely for appearance. Also, (for me) to keep the rifle from skidding off a tree when I lean it against a handy oak or pine! For such jobs the honest, full-size commercial ramps are unnecessary, besides being in the field of view of the scope half the time. What is desirable is a small, low, neat ramp, narrow rear plane, with a small gold bead blade, no hood. I wish somebody would make such ramps, so I could buy some. As it is, the lowest Pacific band ramp, slenderized, or Sukalle's low sweaton ramp, for Mauser rifles, is the best.

I do not like the plain sweaton as front ramps for rifles. They are easy to make and cheap to buy, but hard to mount in the right place and keep on. Most of the recently made American ramps of this type have a 6 x 48 screw running down from the top into the barrel, and usually after blueing this screw is all that is holding the sight on. As mentioned elsewhere, practically all of the widely-used caustic blackening processes masquerading as "blueing" today will attack lead and solder. Most of the time—not always—your sweated joints have a very good chance of coming un-jointed in the blueing tank. If a cold blue, or old-fashioned hot blue is to be used, do not worry about the solder. Should you be required to mount sweaton ramps, I advise the use of two 6 x 48 screws, as shown in the illustration, placing the rear screw midway between front screw and rear tang of ramp. This screw should have its head diameter cut down and be countersunk to such depth as will allow the head to be filed down to the contour of the ramp face, which is then matted or lined or checkered when the sight is firmly mounted on the barrel. The best sweaton ramps available are those made and used by W. A. Sukalle. These are the hooded type, whereas most of the ramps advertised are not, and are quite wide, giving a much larger area for the joint. A holding screw is provided.

I still think the best way to keep a sweaton ramp on is with silver solder, not soft solder.

Hoods for ramp front sights are no problem to make. The front end should be knurled to provide a non-slipping finger surface for removal and replacement of the hood on the sight, but if no knurling tool is at hand, the end can be grooved on the lathe. The best ramps have small plungers set in the hood grooves, to engage in a small notch in the hood when in place, to prevent accidental removal in the gun case, scabbard, on in the brush. (Why a hood should be in place in the hunting field, I do not know, but a lot of people think it belongs on the sight at all

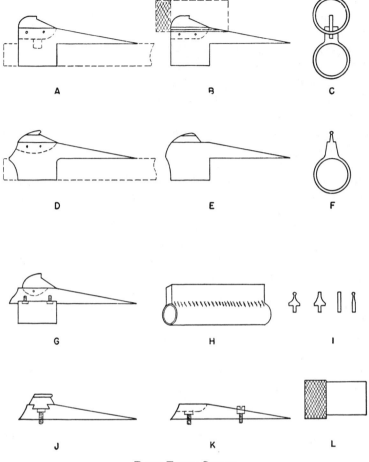

RAMP FRONT SIGHTS

A. Conventional band ramp, with locating set screw and pin held blade.
B. Same as "A," except slotted on the sides for a hood.
C. Muzzle view of band ramp with hood, showing relative position of the top of the blade to the hood diameter.
D. Somewhat streamlined ramp with bead blade held by pins.
E. Solid or one piece ramp with streamlined blade. Hard to make but good for saddle scabbard use.
F. End view of same, with bead. Blade is stronger than the bead.
G. A fabricated ramp, made of tubing and flat stock connected by screws.
H. Tubing, with bar welded on, to form blank for a band ramp.
I. The commonest forms of blades commercially available.
J. Ordinary sweat-and-screw attaching ramp, with dovetail blade sight.
K. Same type ramp, showing a second screw for holding, the protruding portion of the head of this screw to be filed off after fitting.
L. Hood for ramp, to show raised ring of knurling at the front.

times.) While hunting rifle sight should rarely be used with the hood, the hood must be made with relation to position of sight blade, therefore no set dimension for diameter can be followed. The top of blade or bead should just touch the center of aperture formed by the hood, in order to allow the proper sight picture when hood is used during shooting. Since the bottom of hood is cut away to fit ramp, allowance must be made for this loss of diameter in ramp hood, so figure on a hood diameter around $\frac{3}{64}''$ greater than *twice* the height of blade above top of ramp.

For a plain hood, where plungers are not to be used, that shown in Figure A is a practical type. Most hoods are slotted simply by milling or filing the metal through, which gives sharp edges to engage in V-grooves along the top sides of the ramp. This I do not like, because the sharp edges wear rapidly themselves if not hardened, and if hardened, cut the grooves in the ramp deeper and eventually the hood becomes loose and is knocked off easily. Mr. Baker's original system can hardly be improved upon—use the correct diameter tubing (from $\frac{7}{16}''$ to $\frac{5}{8}''$, outside diameter) saw a narrow slot across it with the length of cut on outside not greater than width of ramp; then hammer the portion back of cut flat, holding the hood on a mandrel turned to inside diameter of tubing, with flat filed on it, width of flat to be width of ramp *plus* depth of hood grooves in ramp. With the hood flattened on one side, except for the knurled end, which is to be left round, the center of flat is filed or milled away, to width of ramp *minus* depth of hood grooves. This method of hood forming is more work, but gives contact surfaces the full thickness of hood material. The edges should be rounded very slightly, notches cut for plungers if they are to be used, and the hood case-hardened without color, or given a spring temper if the tubing will take it. Notches for this type hood must be cut more-or-less square, and my idea is that a Starrett screw-slotting hacksaw blade is the ticket for the guy without a milling machine.

Naturally, all turning and knurling on the hood must be done before it is slotted. Probably the easiest hood stock to get is Shelby steel tubing, in $\frac{1}{16}''$ wall thickness. Put it on your mandrel and stick it in the lathe, to cut the body of the hood to $\frac{1}{32}''$ thickness, leaving a raised band for knurling or lining. I think the diameter of the raised portion should be governed by the depth of the knurling—that is, the bottom of knurl or line should be about at body diameter of the hood. In most cases this will mean a wall thickness around $\frac{3}{64}''$.

Pistol and Revolver Sights. The making of pistol and revolver fixed sights is a common job. I work in the West, and get a lot of jobs making

A Springfield rifle, after being restocked by Leonard Mews, one of America's best craftsmen. This stock is of California walnut which, as Mews states, "is as red as any cherry wood." The forend tip and grip cap are of African Blackwood, with red and white spacers .010" in thickness. The Whiteline buttplate was curved a bit to fit the shoulder better. Note that the comb-line of the raised cheekpiece is higher at rear than at front; this to ease recoil by allowing the stock to recoil away from the face. This stock was designed and made for I. J. Kitch, Loveland, Colorado. Details of the checkering pattern are shown on following page.

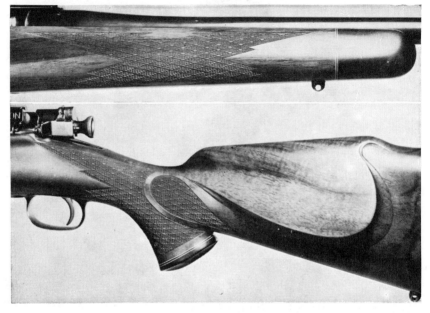

Above is an example of checkering done in the "French" or "skip" system —as done by Leonard Mews and the pattern shown is one of his favorites.

This particular job is 14½/29, on a 1 to 3 ratio. That is, three lines of 29 lines-per-inch to each 14½ line-per-inch spacing.

While at it, you might as well take note of the neat fillet worked in around this cheekpiece and the manner in which it is worked out into the comb of the stock.

"bead" front sights. The popularity of the .45 Colt pistol and its use in target shooting bring many of them to gun shops for installation of higher and wider sighting equipment. Some adjustable rear sights are available commercially, but many of the boys are hard-headed and want one-piece jobs they know cannot get out of adjustment. So you make 'em. The front sights are filed to shape, back matted if of the ramp type—whatever is ordered—I find it easier to work from the back of the sight forward, keeping the sight part of the main bit of flat stock it is being made of until it is almost completely shaped all over. The regular Colt fixed blade sight is held by a small stud on the bottom which goes through slide and is peened on inside. Do not try to put on your larger sights with this system—there is not enough holding area. I prefer to file the blade, making it into a low, rectangular shape, then, in the bottom of the new sight, drill a series of small holes, clear them to fit over this filed-down original sight, and silver solder the larger sight over it. If the correct milling cutter is at hand, it is simple to cut a slot to just fit over the old sight. This not only makes a good joint, but provides a fool-proof method of getting it in the right place. After the solder is cool, the sight can be polished clean and touched up where necessary with needle files.

For a decent-looking finished job, the whole slide should be reblued after sights are fitted, and it is wise to polish at least the top before fitting the sights. What little mess the solder job leaves on the front can be cleaned up easily by hand, by wrapping abrasive and crocus cloth around small files. If complete slide polishing is left until after sights are in place, polishing wheels are very likely to round off some of the edges you want sharp. No soldering is necessary on the rear sight on this pistol—just a good file job. The original rear sight can be built up by welding, or by slotting and a separate blade sweatedin to give a higher notch, but these methods, while saving the dovetail, give just about as much work as starting from scratch on a piece of $5/16''$ x $3/8''$ flat stock. You do not need that much metal, of course, but it pays to have plenty of height to start with. File the stock into a rough T-shape to start with: Make the original sight and narrow down your T arms to its dimension, then file each side separately to the angle of the dovetail, comparing often with the original. Note the very slight right-to-left taper in width of the bottom on the original, but make your sight square, until the dovetail base just begins to enter the slot in slide, from the right side. Then slightly taper your base, on the left side, so that it can barely be driven to center, from the *right*, tightening up as it goes. When you can tap it about two-thirds of the way in place with the rawhide mallet, stop working on the bottom and shape up the top. Height of sight and depth of notch is of course regulated by height of front sight. Individual shooters will specify their desire—whether deep, shallow, narrow, or wide. The average notch is approximately two-thirds as deep as it is wide, and wide enough to allow a clear line or space on each side of the front sight. It must of course have a thin wall at rear, so you must chamfer your front edges.

Give yourself leeway on these rear sights, making them high, and notches a little small—then give the customer his gun, smoke it black with a carbide lamp, and make him shoot it, so if the sights need any alterations you can make them before blueing the slide. If the gun is sent you from a distance or for other reason the owner cannot test the sights before the job is to be blued, *and he advises the original sights are okay for him,* I know of only one way you can approximate the correct height. This is to use your thin 12″ steel scale (rule) on the factory sights placing it on edge in the rear notch and on top of front blade, then, by means of little wedges, drill bits or pins placed between scale and slide just at rear of both front and rear sights, determine the difference at front and rear. If the front is three one-thousandths of an inch lower than the rear, you must figure on making your rear sight notch that distance higher than your front sight. It is a rule of thumb, but absolutely no standard for these guns can be set up, and anyone who thinks he can make them all the same has not been around much. In the first place, no two pistol shooters ever can agree on their .45 sight setting, and in the second place, the guns are not uniform as to fit of slide on receiver, which affects the position of parts when firing which in turn are affected by power of the load used, and other factors. For handgun front sights it is best to use $\frac{1}{8}$″ thick cold-rolled steel; $\frac{5}{16}$″ width of stock is sufficient for most height of sights. If the $\frac{1}{10}$″ width is desired, I prefer to use the $\frac{1}{8}$″ stock and narrow it to $\frac{1}{10}$″ at top, either a straight taper or cutting top portion square if desired.

Occasionally someone will wish to convert a fixed-sight revolver to a target-sighted type. For the rear a fixed blade can be sweated into a slot, or a small dovetail cut and rear sight filed out. The best way is to buy one of the commercial adjustable types and fit it. The Smith & Wesson target sight formerly used was quite easy to install, requiring only that two square notches be cut in the revolver frame, one along the top strap, the other at the rear. The King Gun Sight Company can furnish two or three models of adjustable rear sights.

The round blade factory fixed sights can be easily filed to shape for target use, as illustrated. When a barrel is cut off and another front sight installed, you have your choice of three methods: Sweat on a sight; mill a slot in the barrel and sweatin the blade; or fit a rib with screws and soft solder. The first is the easiest method and if silver solder is used, probably as strong as the others. However, the base of the blade should be large enough to provide good holding area. Leave the top of the sight flat and square while sweating in place so that clamps or vise can be used to squeeze it tight during the sweating and insure a good job. Such a joint will be amply strong for any filing or shaping needed after fitting.

I do not consider it necessary to harden sights, although some of the boys do beat them up. Generally speaking, the man who has special sights for his guns is the type who takes care of them and does not drop them on cement floors, like policemen or soldiers!

Muzzle Protectors. Rifles which are to be cleaned from the muzzle should be equipped with muzzle cleaning guides, which are merely adaptations of the old false muzzles of black powder target rifles. Their only purpose is to prevent the cleaning rod wearing away the rifling at the front end of the bore, and they are simply concentric-bored metal tubes which center the rod in the barrel and will not allow it to bear against the lands. Steel is naturally best, but I see no reason why bronze or brass would not last the average shooter a lifetime. A piece of metal between three and four inches long, and $\frac{1}{4}''$ greater in diameter or width, if square stock, is bored out to a slide fit over the muzzle of rifle for a depth of approximately one inch, then bored or drilled completely through with a hole very slightly under bore diameter of the rifle. It must be larger than rod diameter, in case you might feel like using brushes or patches during your cleaning.

The U. S. Rifle, M1, known to riflemen as the Garand, is a good example, for quite a few are in civilian hands and more will go out through the N. R. A. for training purposes. Your counterbore for the muzzle should be $\frac{33}{64}''$ and your rod-centering hole made with a Letter M drill, which is .295″. Bore diameter should be .300″ and you should keep under it. The M1 rifle which will be used almost entirely with corrosive issue ammunition and so will require cleaning after every firing must be cleaned from the muzzle, and care should be taken. I have seen many of these rifles with lands entirely worn away for an inch back of the crown, solely from use of cleaning equipment. And, believe it or not, a string pull-through cleaner is just as hard on a muzzle as a rough rod. String picks up grit and becomes a saw.

Cleaning guides for round-barrel rifles are easy to make, requiring only care to get the holes concentric, but for an octagonal barrel you will need a little more time. Such barrels are scarce today, but perhaps you might have to fix one up for an old timer. When an old barrel is cut off to renew the muzzle, if the cut off portion is between one and two inches long, it forms an ideal rod guide if bored out and sleeved to slightly less than bore diameter, or a usable one unsleeved. Simply solder or braze narrow flat strips of metal on the sides, projecting an inch from the bottom, so that they can slip over the end of barrel and position the guide. If you must work from scratch on an octagonal or hexagonal barrel, turn your piece of stock carefully, inside and out, inside diameter to be diameter of barrel across the flats, boring it straight through. Then take it to a machine shop and have the flats broached inside, to exact barrel dimensions, after which you must bore out one end until round, and fit a sleeve, drilling this sleeve to the desired guide size.

Breech Protectors. A gadget once enjoying limited popularity is the breech protector, or false bolt. The Japanese supplied these as regular cleaning equipment to their armed forces, making them of hard wood and (sometimes) lining with a metal tube. The purpose is to protect the rifling at the throat of the barrel, thus keeping the lead undamaged by rod wear, and of course is only for breech-cleaning arms. Single shot or lever action arms can be protected quite well by just using an empty cartridge case bored through at rear to desired size, or even larger. For bolt actions a dummy bolt is made, of hard wood or soft metal, turned to bolt dimensions and bored to take the cleaning rod. A small loose collar, with a stud, similar to the extractor collar on the bolt, should be fitted to hold the guide in receiver while cleaning, although you can do without it by holding the gadget with the free hand. This collar should be positioned for convenience in the action to be used—in Enfield, to lock in the bolt-handle recess, or in Springfield and Mauser, on the front of the bridge, passing through the bridge in the safety lug slot or guide-rib slot. The ideal guide of this type would have its front end machined in the shape of the cartridge case, to fit up into the chamber, but for any ordinary use, an empty case with the base drilled out will serve, seated ahead of the guide. These guides should fit the receiver fairly loosely, since they have a long bearing surface on the rod and would be very difficult to center absolutely perfectly with the bore. They may be bored to groove diameter of the caliber involved. If you can pick up an unserviceable bolt for the rifle, you are in luck, for all you need to do is bore out the firing-pin hole to correct diameter, make a plug to screw into the rear end, run bolt full of hot lead, then bore through for the guide hole.

Plungers. Occasionally there is need for a spring plunger as a friction holding device, either front or rear sights, or other points. These pictured are the common types, the round end being easiest used. The square-tenon end version is useful in holding caterpillar front sights—the longitudinal-dovetail type familiar on German sporters and popular in Mr. Baker's day. It has few applications, since the square end engages in a through-hole drilled for it, and must be depressed in usage by a punch or pin. It could be used on ramp front sights with the conventional dovetail, should anyone desire a removable blade or to be able to change heights of sights, by setting the plunger in the top of the ramp and drilling the engagement hole through the sight.

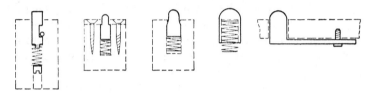

PLUNGERS

The use of plungers is quite limited in gunsmithing, but they occasionally come in handy on a custom sight or special telescope mount application.

Shown are five plunger principles, from right to left; first the flat spring type, mounted on one side of a thin wall and acting through a hole in that wall.

Next is the hollow plunger, with spring inside. These are used as pressure plungers inside or between parts, with or without the retaining method.

Center is the blind hole plunger, with the edges of the hole peened down to retain it in its seat.

On its left is the plunger held in position by a plate which is in turn held by screws.

At the left of the line is the pin held plunger, backed by a spring and a set-screw. The set-screw can of course be applied to any of the others to back the spring.

One use for the ball-end plunger is to tighten bolt handles in receivers, to prevent the "jump" prevalent when bolt parts have been poorly fitted. Writers have suggested installing these in the rear right receiver wall on such rifles as Springfields and Mausers but I hardly think they ever really did much of this, for on most of these rifles, particularly when they have been polished down and reblued, this wall thickness is too scant to allow anything like a $\frac{1}{16}''$ diameter plunger, which is the minimum size for such work. I believe it is better to follow the German method and make a little housing on the outside of the receiver, screwing or sweating it on, and holding the plunger mechanism. What you do for space for this item when a receiver sight is in place, I would not know! Personally, I would place the plunger in the bolt handle itself, to engage in a depression cut in the receiver wall. This would only be practicable on a standard full-size bolt shank, not an altered job, though come to think of it, I have seen quite a few altered bolts thick enough to do anything to. Such a plunger would not have too much effect, because of the necessarily short length of spring which could be used.

All plungers should be thoroughly hardened and polished. It is best to work from the bottom up, cutting the spring end, filing the pin notch, if any, measuring carefully before cutting off and rounding the contact end. The three ways of holding plungers are illustrated, the best of course being the through-hole with set-screw backing up spring; next, the pin; and last the peened-over end which is often the only method possible in a blind hole in heavy stock.

Swivels. At the beginning of this chapter I railed against the idea of making swivels, but I must confess I have made a good many detachable swivel *bases*, solely because at present I can find none of the type I like manufactured. I do it the hard way, using ½" cold-rolled steel rod, cutting down on the lathe to get the shank size. The hole for the swivel is bored after the shank is turned down, then the thread is cut—I do it by hand because I happen to have an adjustable die outfit which gives me a particular thread to fit a supply of ferrules I have—then cut off the stock and shape by file and saw. It takes all of ten minutes to do this and butt swivel bases could be made the same way, using the lathe to cut a very coarse deep thread to hold in the wood. Being somewhat bullheaded and figuring a wood screw ought to have a wood thread, I make mine in two pieces, cutting the head off a suitable wood screw, drilling a ³⁄₁₆" hole in the end of my ½" round stock, silver soldering the screw in place, drilling swivel hole and finishing as described for front swivel base. This is a little more work, but I like the finished product. Actually, a fast, deep machine-thread will hold very well, so thread yours on the lathe.

Barrel Bands. These can be divided into outside and inside types, and each subdivided into split and solid versions. The outside band is that which surrounds barrel and forend and sometimes handguard, seen on Krags as solid type and Springfield as split. For sporter use the outside band is nearly extinct. Inner barrel bands are fairly popular, these going around the barrel only and being held in the forearm

BARREL BANDS

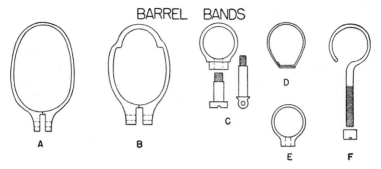

A. The standard military lower band, which is not much use on sporting arms unless it can be reshaped something like

B. The Springfield Sporter band. Very useful on low cost military conversion jobs where the original stock is retained in cut down form.

C. Tie down band, to hold the barrel firmly to the stock, can have either a plain screw, or a screw with the head shaped to double as a swivel base. This type of band now is in popular disfavor.

D. Fabricated band, made of thin strip stock and held at the bottom with a thin nut inside the band and a screw threaded up through it. The Schmidt band is this style. These are best in appearance on the gun.

E. Solid band, as above in use. Almost identical with "C," but lighter in construction.

F. Adjustable band, as furnished by Leroy Rice.

by a screw, bolt, or swivel base. Winchester makes wide use of an adjustable inner band on their target rifles. Con Schmidt advertises a very excellent fabricated band, and Terhaar a good solid type. If you must make one, the procedure is obvious—for a solid job you need either a block of steel sufficiently large enough to permit boring for barrel, thinning down on top and sides, with enough stock left at bottom for holding screw; or, you might find a bit of tubing and weld or silver solder a block on the bottom to take the screw. The split or fabricated type can be made by bending strip steel over a mandrel slightly smaller than the barrel at point band is to locate, putting a bar or block in the vise to pull band into correct shape. The block for screw is then filed to shape, not forgetting barrel contour, and fitted to band with four small screws, two on each side. Such a band should be not less than $\frac{1}{2}''$ wide. Solid bands can be narrow, and it is a good idea to make them narrow—they are just as strong for the purpose and easier to fit, besides looking neater. Bands should always be carefully reamed or filed to barrel taper, and should be thin, not over $\frac{1}{32}''$ thick, for best appearance. I do not believe they should ever be sweated in place, on the barrel.

Leroy Rice, the Krag sight man, makes a very simple, economical barrel band, as shown in the illustration. Its construction permits use on varying sized barrels—any of the military types—and its only fault is the large nut for the bottom. A smaller nut can be made, and a detachable swivel base with hollow, threaded shank can be used, screwing onto the shank of the band, which can project below its locking nut.

Sight Base Bands. Once in awhile you get a diehard open sight addict who wants a buckhorn sight put on a Mauser, Enfield or Springfield. It is not only poor engineering to file a dovetail in these barrels, it is a lot of wasted work and besides, the sight will not be high enough to work right, due to the taper of Enfields and Springfields ahead of chamber. Oh, I have seen it done, but I do not like the result. The best thing is to make a barrel base band for the sight, which is just a band around the barrel at the point of sight dovetail, with set-screw in bottom and dovetail for the open sight in top. There are commercial bands made in unfinished steel, but in this case the price—from $3 to $4.50 is too much for a simple lathe and file job. If you have the material—¼" thick Shelby steel tubing in ¾" inside diameter—you should make one in half an hour, unless you want to chamfer the sides and dress it up, in which case you may as well pay Pacific for one.

Better than a sight base band to hold an open or leaf type sight is the caterpillar or express type base, as seen on foreign rifles of better grades. This is a bar or block of metal profiled to fit the top of the barrel at the desired point and attached by means of sweating or small screws. Any required dovetail or sight-attaching screwhole can be placed in this base, which of course can be of a length suitable for correct operation of the standard manually-adjustable open rear sight with its sliding elevator.

Buttplates and Pistol Grip Caps. Standard rifle buttplates of present manufacture leave little to be desired. In steel, the Niedner plate is the best custom checkered plate, or should a fancy one be desired, write Emil Koshollek—he makes fancy types, checkered, engraved, and trap styles. Ditto pistol grip caps. For target rifles, either the Winchester Model 52 or Remington Model 37 are excellent. Frank Pachmayr and the Fray-Mershon outfit make very fine non-slip neoprene rifle buttplates as well as recoil pads for shotguns. I like these very well, for they are not as likely to slip on hard surfaces as the steel types and are easier on automobile interiors should the customer be in the habit of doing much car shooting—it is legal in some states. However, it must be admitted that they do not look as well as the

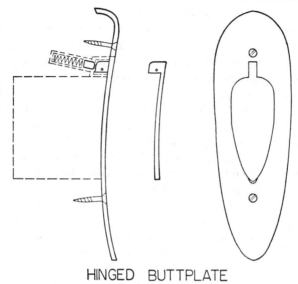

HINGED BUTTPLATE

Better, and perhaps more properly termed the "trap" plate. This illustrates the use of a plunger to hold the trap or gate open or shut. The trap is shown separately, and the angles on the hinge section are just about right. The plunger angle can of course be experimented with if you are not limited for space.

steel plates. No plastic or composition plate is worthy of comment.

Special plates are sometimes desired by target shooters, either in large, sharp-toothed standard style or Swiss type or home-designed schutzen meat-hook version. For the first, if a foundry is available, make a wooden pattern, checkering and all, have it cast in aluminum or light alloy, or if customer desires weight, in brass or bronze, then finish up by hand with files. The same method can be followed for the off-hand rifle plates, but an alternative is to take a bar of soft steel $\frac{5}{16}''$ thick $1\frac{1}{2}''$ wide (or wider if stock is thicker) and as long as necessary, bend it to the desired shape and fit it to a piece of the same steel size of butt, welding them together and filling in the open spaces to make a smooth appearance.

The making of a trap buttplate is a devilish job, and I am glad they are not so popular with American hunters. Stoeger, in New York, usually carries some of these, and it would be best to purchase one from him. If you have to do one, just study a Springfield or Enfield plate— the idea is simple, the execution is hard. Your sporter trap should run up and down, giving access to at least two spare cartridges, and preferably three. The hinge must be at the top, and the spring tension as strong as you can make it, because the length of the trap door gives good leverage for opening. Bevel the edges of door and plate so that the door can just close flush with the plate.

Pistol grip caps are available in steel, plastic, or any other substance you feel like using. Since strength is of little importance, any material which will hold its shape is okay. Horn is fair, ivory very poor—cracks soon and bad. Personally I like thin steel caps, slightly cupped for shaping, and checkered or engraved. You can get a sheet of material—Tenite or Bakelite metal, or fancy wood, such as ebony, snakewood or rosewood, and make your own. Stock need not be over $\frac{1}{4}$" thick, and pick out your own dimensions. The Germans used to make theirs too small, and we tend to make ours too large, looking at the matter from the deluxe sporter stock angle, but the customer is his own law. Show him large, small and medium and be guided by his desires. Oval in shape, a good average size is $1\frac{3}{8}$" x $1\frac{7}{8}$".

Trap grip caps are out of the picture in America today, due to fact that the only purpose for such traps is to hold extra front sights and we do not make quick-detachable front sights for sporters. Not if we can help it, that is. These were originated in Europe, for characters who wanted special luminous beads for night shooting. To make one simply duplicate the military-type trap found on the buttplates, on a smaller scale, holding the cap to grip with two screws, front and rear, rather than the customary single center screw. It is possible to make a trap cap from a Springfield rifle buttplate, but the cap is necessarily rather long.

Really fancy caps can be made by making wood models and casting them in bronze, silver or other metal and engraving them afterward.

Shotgun Sights. People are always losing the beads off the front ends of their scatterguns, or wanting bigger or smaller ones. The nicest factory bead is the Marble Bi-Color, but where it is not used, you can make sights easily, turning brass or aluminum rod to fit the barrel or rib hole, threading it if it is the threaded type—$\frac{2}{56}$ is the commonest thread—and fitting it. Pressed-in beads naturally must fit tightly and you may find it wise to make up a few little square reamers to clear up those battered-up holes. The ones furnished by the sight companies will often be too small. The beads are seated by vise pressure to best advantage, for if they are pounded in by soft metal hammer or wooden block, there is some tendency between blows to get it out of line and loosen it up. Screw-in beads are wound in easily by holding in a four-jaw pin vise—what little marring may occur is easy to polish off without bothering the barrel. Press down a bit of masking tape over the bead to protect the blue of rib or barrels and the crocus cloth cannot touch it. In extreme cases the bead may be slotted and turned in with a screwdriver, ending with the slot at right angle to line of sight so bead presents a round outline. If a square sight is desired, it is easy to make it high and file down until slot is removed after fitting.

Small ramp-type sights can be sweated to the barrel with soft solder very easily.

CHAPTER 11

Making, Fitting and Heat Treatment
of Parts

INTELLIGENCE and experience are both required when the matter of actually manufacturing a part for a gun is up for consideration. In the first place, one constant paradox confronts the smith; if he makes the part right—that is, duplicates exactly the original—it may not work! Barring springs, this is more the rule than the exception. The cause is usually the worn condition of the arm, for naturally old guns greatly outnumber new ones when it comes to busting innards. Should a new or well-kept recent model of good grade firearm break a small part it is simple to install a new factory replacement part. Such jobs require little more than a bit of smoothing up of the new part occasionally. But, even on older arms of models still manufactured, you have to use your head.

For instance a Winchester lever action carbine comes in with a broken firing pin: if you have a new one in the cigar box, it will work fine when installed, but if you do not have a new one and the customer cannot wait two weeks for one to arrive from the factory thereby putting it up to you to make it, use your head. Is the firing pin hole in the breech block enlarged? Yes. Has the owner's young son been playing Indian and snapping the hammer repeatedly, or have years of usage beaten down the back of the block, burring the edges of the firing pin hole? Probably. So when you make your pin, make the tip larger than standard, to better fit the hole in face of block, and make the body of the pin a few thousandths shorter than a new one, fitting it so that when the hammer falls the protrusion is not excessive and the pin is stopped in forward travel by the shoulder inside the block and its retaining pin rather than the cartridge primer, and so that the hammer will come to rest on the rear of the block when fired, not held out a fraction of an inch by the rear of the firing pin hanging out from the

146

beat down area of the block. Such made-to-requirements parts work better than if made to original specifications.

In all cases consider the job thoroughly, do not just go ahead and replace the item damaged or lost. If the owner disassembled his gun and lost a part, that is different, but sometimes guns shake pieces loose. Then you want to know why, so your part will not suffer the same fate. Firing pins and springs occasionally break of metal fatigue, but other parts seldom do, and in any event you want to try to correct the condition which caused the breakage, as well as the damage itself. When a shotgun firing pin breaks because it was brittle and not well supported when fired, you do not want to make one equally brittle and fragile.

A replacement part must enable the gun to operate correctly. Should a revolver require a new hand or cylinder locking bolt, it is not enough to make a new one, or install a factory part so that it will merely work. It must work in correctly with the timing of the action, both when gun is operated single action and double action.

With reference to the above, gunsmiths are going to have trouble for the next fifty years with Colt revolvers. The Colt firm has discontinued the Single Action Army model, and claim they have no parts available for it, as well as for six or eight other obsolete models. Because no one ever discards an old gun, these arms will come in for replacement parts in ever-increasing numbers as the years pass. Most of the parts are very difficult to make, but many will have to be made. A smart thing to do would be to get hold of models of these arms, such as the Single Action, Lightning, and Bisley, and keep them as patterns, copying the parts. One of the things to watch for, particularly on the Lightning, is worn pinholes, which allow parts to move out of place sufficiently far to impair operation even when new parts are available for use.

Springs. Broken springs probably outnumber all other damaged parts. Flat springs are subject to metal fatigue, if not of the very best steel and perfectly heat treated, and break in time under stress, if cramped or disturbed in their action in any way. Practically all of the old-time flat springs were tapered thickness types, regardless of application. In many instances it will be possible to replace such springs with flat, non-tapered springs made of commercial "clock spring" stock, which is spring steel sold in strips or rolls, usually by weight. It is available from most good hardware stores and all mill supply houses in thicknesses up to $\frac{1}{16}''$ and widths from $\frac{3}{16}''$ to $\frac{3}{4}''$. You will want nothing wider than $\frac{3}{8}''$ but as many thicknesses as you can get. Up to around $\frac{1}{32}''$ thickness you can bend it cold to a fairly short radius and maintain fair spring tension, but for sharp or full V-bends it must be heated, shaped and tempered again. It is very handy for the cheap revolvers, (even some factories use it for main-springs!) replacing triggersprings and in some cases mainsprings. Where carefully-regulated tension is demanded, the tapered spring is essential and this necessitates filing heavy clock spring stock to shape and retempering, or cutting a spring out of spring stock, but the Smith & Wesson straight mainspring should be of good steel carefully tapered and treated. Flat rifle mainsprings and shotgun action springs, flat or V type, require the best steel and shaping and tempering.

Two types of temper are employed, which I term soft and hard, again exemplified by the Colt and S & W revolver mainsprings. The Colt spring, while having good tension, can be bent, within slight limits: the S & W is hard tempered, and will not accept a bend or set under almost any pressure. Clock spring has the soft temper, which limits its use to fairly light tension jobs where the spring is not bent to any great degree.

The heat treatment of springs calls for experience and practice. With all the equipment in the world, you will not get good ones every time. I lacked confidence in my flat springs for years, breaking at least fifty percent of all I made over-abusing them in testing, since I had no furnace to control heat and never was sure what was happening. How-ever, of all those I made by open-flame heat only one ever weakened and came back to me.

"Working" heat, or the degree of heat a piece of spring steel stock must reach for forging or bending is 1480° to 1500° Fahrenheit, or a very few degrees higher for heavy, thick springs. With furnace and lead bath in use, the shaped spring, coated with chalk and alcohol is preheated to around 750° Fahrenheit then immersed in the molten lead and temperature raised to between 1400° and 1450°, for five or six minutes, to insure thorough, uniform heating. Steel will float on lead, so you will have to hold it down some way. The handiest way is to slot a bit of rod and press the base end of the spring into it. Keep your can or tank of quenching oil close, so that the hot spring can be transferred from lead bath to oil (lukewarm) quickly, keeping the spring on your rod and moving it around slowly in the oil until cool enough to touch.

The spring is now hardened and you must "temper" it by controlled annealing, to give it flexibility as well as strength. I find 700° Fahren-heit is a good all-around temperature for the tempering bath, either of commercial tempering salts or your own pot of potassium nitrate. Use a clean wire wheel on the spring and preheat in hot oil or water about 200° before putting it in the tempering tank. Fish it out after it has been in the salt from five to fifteen minutes, depending on size, and again quench in oil. Now buff it off and pray nothing went wrong.

Test it for "set"—if a V type, use the micrometer across the arms of the V, then compress in the vise from five to ten times, slightly more than the spring is compressed by the action of the gun, and then mike it again. It should set a little, but in no case over fifteen thousandths of an inch at tips when spring arms measure between 1¼" and 1½", much less when the V is short. If it breaks, that is tough. You start over, make a new one, heat in a lead bath not quite as hot as before—say 20° less, and finish as before. If it just bends and stays bent, there is hope of salvage—throw it back in the lead and heat it about 20° hotter and finish again. Should this give it the desired tension and apparent strength, give it a thorough test. Not only the closing in vise and opening, a couple of dozen times, but leave it in the closed or tensed condition half an hour or so, then measure. If it checks out then it is serviceable. Should it fail to hold tension strength, forget it and try again, making the new one from different stock.

Testing a flat spring calls for your own judgment. Lay it as it comes from the final oil bath on a flat surface—a piece of plate glass or a plane blade—see if it is straight, noting its contact, or marking degree of curvature. Place base end in the vise and carefully spring it with a block of wood held against the contact end. Do this until you are tired, remove it from the vise and lay it on the flat surface and see if you bent it appreciably; you know what to do from here on.

If you are poor and without the fancy heat-treating equipment, you must use what you have, which I trust runs to gas plate or forge, for heat source. This is where you learn the hard way and experience builds up. Your shaped spring is held by the base or rest end of the V type, heated over flame or coals until bright red, then quenched in oil. Polish it clean and smooth with fine abrasive cloth, and again heat. You are now attempting to guess the correct tempering heat and, going by color, you want a blueish-purple. I generally heat a spring hot enough to burn motor oil, then let a couple of dippings of oil burn off. Err on the far side if you must, getting too much heat rather than too little, for if you do not reach the correct temperature, the spring will not be soft enough to spring, but will break like glass when you test it. If too soft, you can re-harden and re-temper. I have made dozens of springs this way, and apparently re-heating and quenching does not matter a bit, so long as you do not get the steel hot enough to lose carbon. I have made a lot of very tough springs, too—magazine gate springs for Krags, lever springs for shotguns, and none have bounced so far. That one which failed was a S & W mainspring. If a spring lasts two hundred actionings without change it is usually good for long service.

Thin flat springs can be made over any open flame, quick-quenched in oil and immediately returned to the flame to burn off the oil. This is called "flashing." One flashing is sufficient for very thin flat springs, such as sear springs on old model revolvers, and two or three for springs up to .030″ thickness, as a rule. For the very thick strong springs, I find flat drill rod stock satisfactory, and overseas, during the war, I often made springs from old files, cooking a little carbon out of them while heating, and allowing them to cool to what I thought was around 1400° for quenching. Now, we should all be able to get spring steel stock. Swedish steel, and English steel (Swedish with a British accent) used to be considered best, but American steels are equal to either today. Swedish iron ore is the purest in the world, consequently steel made from it was very free of impurity and quite uniform. Steel is steel and refining is what makes or breaks it, and today I feel that our plants like Republic or Columbia are tops.

The cart got before the horse—heat treatment before shaping. However, all should agree that it is easier to accomplish the physical end of spring-making than the technical or brain end.

A ready-tempered spring to be altered can very occasionally be filed and polished with abrasive cloth to shape without softening. When the stock is hard, the best way to anneal thin pieces without affecting carbon content (assuming you do not have the furnace) is to lay between two slightly thicker pieces of flat steel stock and heat the assembly red, allowing for slow cooling. Should it be necessary to drill holes in the spring, this should be the next step, selecting the proper drill and holding the spring by a clamp flat on a block of soft metal—aluminum or copper, not lead—so your drill will cut a clean hole and not push through, cupping the spring at that point. The hole is your locating point for measurements in laying out the spring dimensions.

When flat springs have to be curved, length measurements are sometimes difficult, and I employ a transfer method. Just take soft, thin strap steel, the type which is used to strap packages is okay, and clip out a dummy model, fitting it into the gun, adjusting to proper curve, and other dimensions. Then take it out, flatten, and use as a pattern for the spring. It is no fun to make a good spring and then find it is just a hair too short when installed.

Filing thin flat stock is a problem of holding—this is where a good pair of smooth, steel false vise jaws come in handy. The tapered springs usually taper both in thickness and width and the first is to be considered first. Keep the stock parallel on the sides and you can clamp it quite well in the vise, flat side up, and enough clearing the top of jaws to permit filing the unnecessary metal away. The edges are then tapered to dimensions. Should the contact end of the spring need to be notched and bent to accommodate a stirrup dog on the gun hammer, as in the S & W mainspring, this is done next, cutting the notch first, full depth of the bend to be made, this tip is then again heated red and the desired bend made with round needle-nosed pliers, one jaw of which has been ground into a pin shape. Leave the stock a little thick at this point so you can touch up this contact point with small round files after forming. It is rather hard to bend both lips at the same time, so bend them separately, then clamp a bit of $\frac{1}{16}''$ flat stock, with edge filed and polished round, in the vise and gently peen these stirrup lips to perfect alignment with each other.

You can hog off excess steel any way you want to, but the final cutting and all polishing must be lengthwise of the spring. All cross scratches must be eliminated and the taper must be even, never having waves in it. V springs especially should be carefully polished on each side as rough surfaces prevent uniform heat reception and quenching.

When a very, very thin tapered flat spring must be made, as for a return spring on a set-trigger, use a strip of the thinnest clock spring, puncture one end, bend it over sufficiently to hold on the end of a hardwood block with tack or nail and with the vise press part of the exposed stock into the wood, or at least create a slight depression for it. Then wrap abrasive cloth around a file and polish the spring. The end over the depression will be forced into it, while the other portion will have nowhere to go and will be cut by the cloth to a greater extent. This is a crude method, but is the only way I have been able to obtain tapers on very thin steel. After polishing has removed enough metal, the spring is removed and cut to shape with strong scissors. Tempering of such springs is touchy and sufficient heat can be obtained from an alcohol lamp. Quenching oil is held close to the flame so that the spring will not cool in the air, and flashing off is done carefully, by wiping off about half the oil remaining from a dipping.

Wire Springs—Coil and Other Types. Springs made of tempered wire have supplanted flat springs to a large degree in modern arms. They are cheap to buy and last indefinitely, except when forced out of position and mangled, as happens with the hand springs of cheap revolvers. The compression coil spring is used in all sizes from the very tiny ones used in Colt revolver bolts to the magazine springs of repeating shotguns. About the only flat spring it has not supplanted is the magazine spring in the large bolt action rifles. It is cheaper to purchase a selection of coil springs from a mill supply house and keep a stock of the more commonly-used gun springs (.22 Colt Woodsman extractor springs, .45 pistol springs, mainsprings, for Springfield, Enfield and Mauser) than to get spring wire and attempt to wind springs as needed. Frankly, you cannot make a coil spring from spring wire which will have the tension of a factory-made spring of the same dimensions and wire size.

Except in very light sizes, coil springs are made hot and tempered. If you own a good furnace and have facilities for settingup hot oil baths you can experiment and probably learn how to make coil springs and it probably will not cost you over five dollars a spring, after you get going. As the factories do not charge over two bits for any springs, it is much more intelligent to purchase springs of known quality. A dozen each of all the compression springs under ¼″ outside diameter available from your supply house will take care of all the odd little replacement jobs which turn up—trigger springs, extractor and ejector springs on .22 rifles—for a long time. The cost is very low, averaging only two or three cents a spring. These are usually from two to three inches long, and you cut off what you need, with a pair of side-cutters you do not care much for, or a little chisel. Keep a few odd diameters of rod handy, so you can slip a spring over it for the chisel to bear against when cutting.

These over-the-counter springs are not suited to all gun applications, such as mainsprings in present-day shotguns, or for any heavy tension job, because they are not readily available in strengths suitable for heavy duty. Some powerful small diameter ones are perfectly adapted for extractor use, however. In fitting such springs care must be taken to get the right length as well as diameter, and the simplest way is to cut it a little long and keep trying it, trimming off a half-turn at a time, until the part it operates functions perfectly. Never mind how it operated with the original spring—if that had been perfect you would not be replacing it. Maybe your spring will be stronger or weaker, as needs be; I have found it necessary to use much stronger extractor springs on low-priced .22 bolt action rifles than were originally furnished. After the guns have seen some service and perhaps the chamber is not kept as it should be, extraction becomes a little harder and a tougher spring cures the complaint.

There are a few mild types of coil spring you can wind if you have to, such as weaker sear springs for military bolt actions, when the customer objects to heavy takeup, but steer very clear of most coil winding. If an odd size is needed, as for a foreign pistol, it is better to spend an hour checking on American guns of all types to find one which will do the job, rather than to make a mandrel the inner diameter of the spring and try to wind it.

Helical and V types of wire springs are a different story. These are found in modern low-priced arms, replacing flat springs in the original design. You can keep a few feet of spring wire on hand and shape with pliers nearly any of them. In fact, I think you can make better ones than the factories! At least it is possible to make it a size and tension which guarantees reliable functioning and add a curlicue here and there to hold it in position, which factories do not do and results in the springs getting out of place. When making a V or double V type wire spring such as a H & R triggerspring, the dimensions are sometimes hard to get exact and it is well to make a dummy out of soft wire, which is easily bent to shape and cut to length. Found correct, the spring can then be made right the first try.

Any spring has a job to do, and that job is important, not the spring. So long as the spring does its work and will keep on doing it, ask no more. You cannot go far wrong on fitting coil springs, for most of them go either in a hole or on a guide, and the wrong size will practically always be the wrong tension. If in doubt, err on the strong side.

I have seen funny things in the spring line—two or three short springs substituted for one long one (very wrong) small ones inside larger ones, and the like. During the war the Filipino guerillas had trouble with the Enfields they had, the ejector springs breaking nearly 100%. They had no metals nor tools to make new ones, so they cut little blocks of rubber from old rubber heels and discarded tires and placed them under the bolt stop spring and it worked very reliably. I have even torn down their rifles and found bits of rubber substituted for sear springs! I hope we never get that hard up.

Firing Pins. Broken firing pins rival spring difficulties in numbers. Every type of arm made can have firing pin trouble, and does. Whenever possible, use a factory replacement part, and charge a small fee for installing it. When the part has to be made, think over the price to charge—some of them are simple turning jobs, made in a few minutes on a lathe; others are complicated types requiring milling or much filing and hand work, fitting as well as heat treating.

The material best suited to the job may be drill rod, low-carbon tool steel, or cold-rolled. In a turning job, such as a pin for a Winchester Model 12 shotgun or 94 rifle, I cut the tip first, making it around $\frac{1}{16}''$ longer than necessary. After trying the rod through the block or bolt to see that the tip is a good fit in the hole and moves freely back and forth, the flat slots are filed in and pins tried in their holes in the block. With the tip clearance okay, the rod is pushed as far forward in the block as possible and marked flush with the back of the block, then cut off at the correct angle and the edges slightly chamfered. Last, the tip is shortened and rounded to the correct protrusion when forward and correctly retracted when back.

Most long firing pins are hardened to prevent excessive wear, and therefore are rather brittle at the tip. The majority of long pins will come in with the tip end missing, from $\frac{1}{8}''$ to $\frac{5}{16}''$, and where time is short the man with a welding outfit has a short cut to making it serviceable. Either good steel is built up a sufficient distance to permit turning to proper length, or a short length of round stock is welded to the stub and cut to length. The former is the best method, but in a few instances, such as the old-style Remington autoloading shotgun flat pin, the latter works out. One year, greatly rushed and with no factory parts available, I welded up thirty or forty firing pins, including six or eight of the Remingtons, all of which gave yeoman service and are still out, although I offered to replace each with factory pins when they became available. Most of the tips were drill rod, untreated in any way.

I have experimented with the buildup jobs a little, using both a tough nickel-steel which is left unhardened, and carbon steel surface-hardened by Kas-N-Ite. The untreated nickel-steel seems to stand wear quite well, and is of course absolutely unlikely to break. In the buildup welding process, the old pin is held upright in a vise and the end heated until the broken tip fuses and throws off carbon sparks before any metal is added. If the end is not normalized the weld will not hold perfectly. Usually only the first half-inch of pin gets hot enough to change structure, so that the pin and lever notches and rear end of pin are left hard and will resist battering as originally intended. With a blob of steel where the tip is to be after welding, some time and effort can be saved by grinding it roughly round and to shape, before placing in the lathe for finishing.

I also made plenty of long pins from drill rod and from a good medium-high carbon tool steel. Both of these are hard to turn, but the definite characteristics make reliable heat treatment possible in all cases. The drill rod is to be hardened and drawn almost exactly as in making a flat spring. You should be able to just mark a finished pin with a fine-cut file. The tool steel pins can be left untreated, but they will wear in time, and I like to surface or case-harden them a little, or else harden and temper.

Small firing pins, particularly shotgun pins, require careful treatment—they must be tough to resist hammer battering and in some guns, being pushed around by extractors as the gun is opened, not brittle. Even heat is the answer, and this is where your lead bath and pyrometer earn their keep. Treat your firing pins as if they were springs and you will have little trouble. When open flame heat is used, hold the pin by the tip in an old pair of pliers, so that the pliers draw some heat, otherwise the tip will heat first and get too hot while the heavier portion comes up.

In turning a pin, it is always easier to cut almost straight back, that is, the cutting tool is brought sufficiently close to center to rough out the pin point, then brought back to the desired shoulder, preferably in one cut. You cannot make repeated shallow cuts across a thin rod supported at one end only. Final cutting to size is done by lathe-filing and polishing by holding abrasive cloth against the pin in the lathe until tool marks are removed, then crocus cloth is used to polish. Not only the tip, but the entire bearing surface of a firing pin should be polished glass-smooth.

Flat, or odd-shaped pins which cannot be made on the lathe are laid out as flat gun parts and made accordingly, but are to be polished, fitted and heat-treated as round pins.

Last, we come to the dimensions of firing pin tips. Tip diameters are always good for an argument—some intelligent people claiming that they should all be .075″ for all center-fire rifles and large caliber band guns and .985″ for all shotguns. These are satisfactory average figures and you will never go far off the path if you stick to them, but I am strictly a cut-and-try workman and believe each job should be fitted according to its peculiarities, if any. If the rifle's firing pin hole is enlarged four thousandths, I think the firing pin should be made oversize enough to just fill it when protruded the proper distance, and so on. If the hole is too blasted big for reasonable consideration of oversize pin, bush the hole and make a legitimate size job of it. In any high-pressure caliber arm, I think an oversize firing pin tip—oversize considering the .075″ dimension—much more desirable than a small tip in a large hole. That is the thing to work by—fit of the pin in the hole

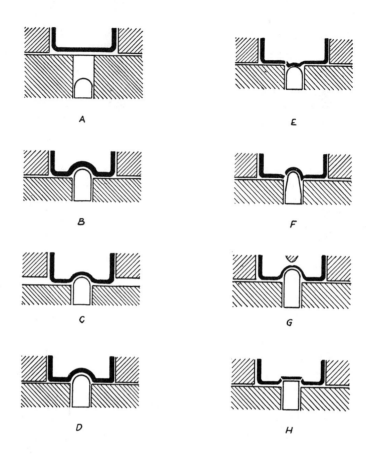

PRIMER AND FIRING PIN RELATIONSHIP

A. Primer seated deep. The normal firing pin travel does not indent it as deeply as is proper.

B. Normal pin and primer, except that the metal of the primer cup is heavy and spreads the force of the pin impact.

C. Primer not seated in pocket. Some of the firing pin energy will be expended pushing the whole primer deeper in the pocket, with the result that a cushioned impact fires the shell, igniting it improperly.

Shells fired with very light loads often extrude the primers to the rear somewhat, however this happens after ignition.

Lever action rifles with generous headspace usually produce empty cartridge cases with primers forced out of the pockets slightly.

D. Proper firing pin imprint in properly located primer.

E. Result of weak firing spring, or very light striker or pin. Pressure inside the primer has forced the pin back and stretched the primer metal at the edges of the initial imprint to the point of rupture.

at the face of the bolt or block. Some old shotguns have very large holes in their breeches, that you cannot sew a plaid patch over. Those gaping ⅛″ orifices can only be bushed, and as the guns are usually worth little, the owners do not care to go to that expense, so you either make a great big pin or turn down the job. The big pins are satisfactory if the boys do not insist on using high velocity loads.

Every ten years some experimenter suddenly gets worried about displacement of the primer cup during firing and tries to control ignition by new types of firing pin tips. The old Mann-Niedner firing pin, for single shot rifles, was installed from the front of the block, behind a bushing, and would retract only until tip was flush with the face of the block. All sorts of tip shapes have been tried. The original purpose of the pin was to control gas escape in the event of a punctured primer. Another type of pin which has been tried is a flat-end version of diameter just under primer diameter, so that when fired, practically all of the primer area is contacted, not just the portion over the anvil. Fired cases have flat, unindented primers, closely resembling unfired Remington primers. This type of pin must also be fitted with a stop so that it cannot retract past the face of the bolt or block and the mainspring employed must have slightly greater strength than for a standard pin in the same arm. I have had no experience with this system and know nothing of its good and bad features.

Protrusion of tip is another argued matter—although the argument is not loud. Shape of the tip has a very little to do with protrusion distance, a very small tip apparently requiring a thousandth of an inch or so greater length than a tip of larger striking area. Speaking of center-fire arms I hold that the diameter of the tip of the pin at the face of the bolt or block, when protruded, for large rifle primers should be .074″, plus or minus .004″, and protrusion .064″, plus or minus .002″. This would apply to the large caliber bolt actions, such as Mauser, Enfield, Springfield, Winchester, Mannlicher, and such. You will not have full control of this dimension, however, due to limita-

---

F. Small tip on firing pin, with the result that a high pressure load forces the primer cup metal back around the tip into the firing pin hole in the bolt or the block, with the possibility of rupture if the metal is stretched back far enough into the hole.

G. Excessive tip protrusion of pin, stretching the cup metal through drawing action in forcing it in further than necessary. If the inner wall of the cup meets the top of the primer anvil, it is liable to puncture at the center.

H. Sharp edged tip on the pin punches hole in the primer instead of imprinting it.

tions imposed by the firing pin hole in the bolt face. Going by the book —any book, including this one—and using the correct size tip through a hole twenty thousandths of an inch larger is poor business. Get your tip and hole sizes pretty close, within reason by use of an oversize pin, or by bushing the hole. For the small rifle primer, I believe that tip diameter of .062″ is probably best, plus or minus .002″ and protrusion .050″ plus or minus .001″, when pins are to be made for single shot rifles rebarreled to one of the high-pressured little cartridges such as the .22 Hornet, .218 Bee, or .22/3000 Lovell. When large bolt actions are adapted to the small primer cartridges, for best ignition it is wise to bush the firing pin hole and polish the pin down, if over .064″ in diameter and the hole is enlarged. If the pin is of that dimension or slightly smaller, and it is a good fit in the face of the bolt, simply shorten it approximately .050″ and use as is. I know of one .22 Hornet rifle, three .218 Bee and two .22/3000 R2s all made on military actions where this system was used and all perform perfectly, with no fault to be found with ignition and accuracy.

Revolver and non-inertia type pistol firing pins can be of the same diameter as the small rifle type. You may find some small caliber European-made pistols using smaller diameter pins, and in such cases, be guided by the firing pin hole, making your pin to fit. As for the inertia type firing pin found in the .45 Colt pistol, the Italian Beretta, and others, the diameter is obvious, but as for protrusion—figure it out yourself! Such firing pins are stopped in forward movement by the cartridge primer in most arms, the firing pin spring and shoulders not always limiting the motion. Where such pins are retained in slides by cross pins you of course have something to go by, and can make your initial protrusion approximately .050″. Only test can tell what is correct for some of the odd arms floating around today.

Tip shape is best explained by the drawing. The perfectly hemispherical type seems to work best on single shot rifles and revolvers, and is usable on every type of arm. However, on bolt action rifles, particularly those for very high pressure cartridges I believe the slightly flattened rounded tip is best. I have used this type on my own rifles and have never had a punctured or ruptured primer in my life. Many of the European countries have long used this type in military equipment, sometimes carrying it to extremes. Some Italian arms have firing pin tips almost perfectly square in profile—not good; cuts into primers.

Punctured primers are usually caused by either a too pointed tip, or a rough one. Due to use of corrosive primer compound, many military rifle pins have pitted tips, the pits having sharp edges which tear into the primer cup during firing. Often these pin tips may be polished smooth in the lathe without shortening beyond the minimum protrusion length.

Oversize pins and strikers can of course be polished down to desired size, but it is necessary to weld on and build up tips for the undersize numbers. For the Enfield rifle there is an easy way out—get a Remington 720 firing pin as it is considerably longer on the front end and can be shortened and turned down to any desired size of tip.

Specially-shaped pins must sometimes be made for foreign pistols, hollow types, with lugs here and there. In all cases, select stock large enough to encompass all projections then drill and polish the spring or guide hole first, to the desired depth. Make a mandrel to fit this hole and do the rest of your turning operations holding this mandrel in the lathe chuck and the pin blank on the mandrel, to insure the outside being turned concentric with the hole. Cocking cams or safety lugs or whatever other projecting points there are must be milled or filed out, after pin is rough-turned to size. Such pins must be made just as hard as you can without making them brittle, and due to the thin walls of the pin this is often a tough problem to figure out. Cyanide case-hardening may make the walls too brittle unless a close-fitting rod (that mandrel might do) is retained inside the pin during the hardening process.

Due to breech fitting, headspacing and takedown wear on shotguns, I am not going to stick my neck out on protrusion figures regarding their pins. That length which might be perfect on a Parker or Winchester 21 might be too short to fire on an old Blank Superstrong Deadly Double, put out by the long-defunct Jones Hardware and Plow Corporation! If you are making a pin for a double gun and as usual, only one is broken, look at the remaining one and copy its dimensions. If both pins are missing, use your own judgment, letting yourself be influenced by measuring every shotgun firing pin in the shop and taking an average. Shotgun firing pins should always be tested with factory loaded unaltered shells. Taking the shot out and firing the blank under the bench tells nothing. A fired shotgun primer should have a neat round, hemispherical detent, not over .003″ deeper than half the diameter of the tip at its largest exposed dimension.

The firing pins of most modern shotguns run between .075″ and .085″ in diameter, and protrustion .075″ to .085″. They have been getting smaller for the past sixty years, as the pressure of the ammunition went up. Winchester uses a very small pin tip in their model 24 double, but a larger size in the top-grade model 21.

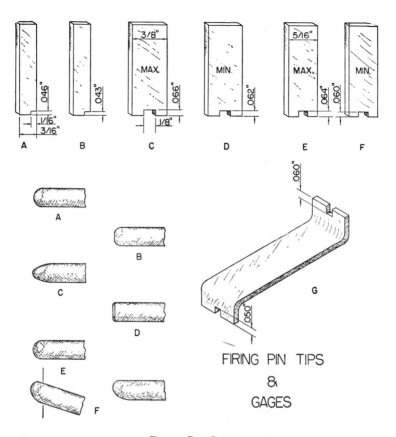

FIRING PIN TIPS & GAGES

Firing Pin Gages

Simple snap gages can be made of flat stock to serve in checking firing pin protrusion. Center-fire pin tips can definitely affect gun performance if incorrect.

A. Maximum gage for .22 rim-fire arms.
B. Minimum gage for .22 rim-fire arms.
C. Maximum gage for center-fire rifles using large primers.
D. Minimum gage for center-fire rifles using large primers.
E. Maximum gage for center-fire rifles using small primers.
F. Minimum gage for center-fire rifles using small primers.
G. Combination maximum and minimum gage for center-fire pistols and revolvers.

These are all "using" gages—pins protruding sufficiently to contact either minimum or maximum are satisfactory. Only when the pin is visibly less than minimum, or holds the base of the maximum gage away from the bolt face is the pin incorrect. They are *not* GO and NO-GO gages.

The .22 caliber rim-fire pins come in all shapes of tip, and varying protrustion distances, due to poor headspacing and wear. The high quality target rifles are in a class by themselves, and while the shooters never stop worrying whether or not they might get a little better ignition and accuracy with a sharper tip, or one with slightly greater contact area, or slightly less, you must either follow factory specifications or experiment, should the customer desire something different. I am not a .22 specialist and there is more I could know about tuning up Winchester 52s and Remington 37s. My own personal inclination is to make .22 pins approximately .050" in diameter, flat-ended, rounding the tip sufficiently to prevent cutting into the soft case heads. Location of the tip as regards the rim of the cartridge is very important —the outside edge of the pin should be in line with the outside edge of the cartridge rim. Most of the trouble with .22 arms misfiring is due to either striking inside the rim, in which the priming compound is contained, or an over-large pin distributing its falling force over too great an area on the case head, most of which is dead as regards ignition—reliable ignition, anyway.

The lower-priced sporting .22 arms may have any sort of tip—wedge, round, pointed, square, or any variation or combination of these. Due to the above-mentioned headspace variation, no gage can be made or dimension set for protrusion distance. If you make a pin extend .035" beyond the face of the bolt, and there is .010" of nice vacant space

---

FIRING PIN TIPS

A. The more-or-less standard hemispherical tip, satisfactory in all central firing arms.
B. The flattened tip rounded end type, used by many foreign countries. I like this for high-pressure cartridges.
C. The pointed tip. Very unsatisfactory as it punctures primers. Often caused by reshaping a tip to get rid of rust or pits.
D. The flat tip, with relieved edge. Not satisfactory, as only soft primer cups will take it without rupturing. Italy used this tip on a number of small arms.
E. The round tip, with end pitted from corrosive primers or other causes. Should be polished smooth, as the pitting causes primer metal under pressure to flow into the pits and therefore weaken, to occasionally break.
F. Two views of the angle striking single shot rifle pin tip. Generally speaking, it is rounded, with the bottom relieved somewhat. This shape gives a correct blow to the primer and has proven very satisfactory on the Stevens 44½ action in particular.

between the bolt face and the cartridge head if the cartridge is seated to full depth in chamber, just where are you when that pin falls? Short. The outside lubricant used on .22 cartridges builds up in the chamber and tends to hold the rim back against the bolt, but causes a cushion effect as the pin falls, so you have to figure this in also when fitting a pin. You cannot go by a clean chamber, for the customer will not clean it every other shot. I reluctantly stick my neck out to say you can make your .22 pins stick out .037″, plus or minus .002″, but I take no responsibility for all such pins working right.

It is best to make odd rim-fire pins just long enough to miss contact with the barrel or chamber edge. A few .22s are made so that large round pins are used, only a portion of the tip contacting the rim of the cartridge, and the barrel is recessed slightly to accept the remainder of the tip. Under no circumstances should the tip of the pin batter against the barrel. Every gunsmith has seen cheap .22 revolvers with chambers horribly burred from the hammer falling against an empty cylinder. You should be able to dry-fire, or snap, any .22 arm without any danger of breaking the pin or burring the chamber. If it is possible to insert a shim stock between the bolt or block and the barrel when the action is closed, use a strip of .006″ steel as a gage, passing between barrel and firing pin in the forward condition. However, no damage will be done if the pin is longer and consequently closer to the barrel, so long as it does not touch and has no cutting edges.

For other caliber rim-fire cartridges, should pins be made, be guided by the above information regarding the pin contacting the barrel, and attempt to gage the length by the thickness of the rim. Take a fired cartridge of the caliber involved, and carefully crush the rim together in the vise (at unindented portion of rim of course) and mike this rim, getting a fairly close measurement of thickness of the rim in collapsed condition. One-half of this measurement is your clearance between the firing pin in forward position and the edge of the chamber. This will give you a slightly long pin, which will probably work very satisfactorily, or it can be stoned shorter, should fired cases appear to have unnecessarily deep indentations.

Odd Gun Parts. By odd I mean all the different flat and round parts which cannot be classified individually—hammers, for instance. Once in awhile a gunsmith has to make a hammer, for an obsolete rifle, shotgun or revolver. For such jobs the best steel is a medium-low carbon tool steel, if you can find something around .75 carbon, and cyanide case-harden, or harder steel hardened and drawn. In some instances the broken parts can be sweated together and used as a template, or sweated to your steel stock and the new part milled to exact profile as the old. Such pains are seldom necessary, though. Paint your stock with Prussian blue or copper sulphate, drill the hole, square it out should it be for an old hammer shotgun taking a square axis pin, then fit the pin or make a dummy the exact size, lay the broken parts on the steel stock, locating with the pin and scribe around them very carefully. Clamp them to the steel if necessary to hold rigid while marking, then cut out the blank and file to shape.

To blank out odd shapes in flat stock, use the drill press, center-punching a series of holes completely around the outline of the part and drilling them out—saves a lot of sawing and filing. Make your replacement part a trifle larger than the original and fit it into the action, cutting and trying until it works perfectly, with reduced spring tension, so as not to mess up any safety or sear notches in the unhardened metal. When it will *just* work smoothly and is still close in all dimensions, you heat treat and then hard-fit the part, flat-polishing and stoning after hardening until it works smoothly.

You polish with abrasive cloth and crocus cloth by hand, and by buffing wheels and fine compounds on the motor buffer. For fine, closely fitted arms you will need to mark the part during this process, coating with copper sulphate and assembling in the gun. Movement of the action will cause high or rough spots to show up through the copper-plated surface, which is so thin it should not be completely obliterated however close the parts fit. Such spots are removed by careful hand work with hard Arkansas oilstones and crocus cloth. Under no condition try such short cuts as putting lapping compound in the action and working it repeatedly. This method works only when all the parts require smoothing at the same time, and is not at all to be recommended even then.

It is sometimes not only possible, but desirable to make replacement parts larger than the original in some dimension, in order to gain strength. Pistol and .22 rifle extractors often operate much more reliably if made as large as the action cuts allow. On the other hand, should you be called on to make a hammer for a Winchester single shot rifle, make it as light as you can and still get good ignition.

Perhaps the hardest of all parts to make, as a class, are lifters for .22 pump-action rifles. I have seen some which would require six or eight machine setups to copy even approximately. These parts, which when the slide-handle is pulled to the rear, lift a loaded cartridge from the tubular magazine up to the mouth of the chamber, are nearly always activated by cam action and must be very carefully fitted, in

6.5 MANNLICHER
(6.5 X 54 MM.)

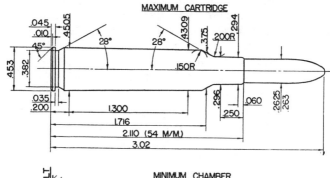

MAXIMUM CARTRIDGE

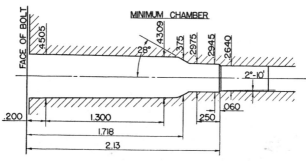

MINIMUM CHAMBER

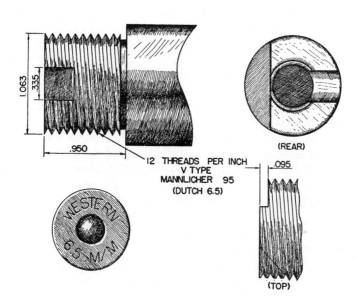

12 THREADS PER INCH
V TYPE
MANNLICHER 95
(DUTCH 6.5)

(REAR)

(TOP)

order to deliver the bullet to the barrel, not high, low or to one side of chamber. Whenever possible salvage the old part and try to use it; if worn, by welding on steel and reshaping by hand; if broken, by sweating the parts together in a brazed joint. This is one of the few applications of the old custom of brazing broken parts of which I approve. To cut a new part out of tool steel will in most cases be a more costly job than the owner will buy. Since the great majority of parts to be made will be for obsolete arms in poor to fair condition, customers sensibly do not care to spend over a couple of dollars on the gun.

In making any flat part, make it *flat* and make your holes the right size for the pin or screw it operates on or against. Old guns nearly always need new pins when new parts are installed, due to the old pin having been worn undersize. Avoid any tendency to "rock" stones or polishing mediums when smoothing a part in order to maintain even thickness and prevent rounded corners. When spring or cam or sear notches must be cut, leave the outline of the new part slightly large at that point, file in the notch, smooth it, and after hardening and polishing the sides of the part, stone this extra-deep notch edge down to correct depth, keeping your stone movement at right angles to notch the edge and doing no further cross-polishing. This will insure a sharp, square notch.

6.5MM MANNLICHER/SCHOENAUER

This is one of the most popular hunting cartridges in Europe, and has been used all over the world. The long bullets made abroad have great penetrative ability and though muzzle velocity is low, maintain velocity very well and so can be used to quite respectable ranges. No United States company makes the ammunition today, although formerly all companies loaded it. Barrels are rifled with fast twists, for the long heavy bullets, and recoil, while light, is noticeably heavier than with our .257, which has greater powder capacity.

During the past few years, the 6.5mm has become popular in Europe as a target caliber for free rifle competition, with superb match ammunition made for such use. The Swedish 'Norma' 6.5mm boattail match bullet is now available in this country, so perhaps we'll have a few rifles for it around before long.

The barrel shank shown is for the 6.5mm *rimmed* Dutch service cartridge, not the 6.5mm Mannlicher shown above. The Mannlicher rimless case is smaller than the Mauser series, and cannot very well be made from any American case. Incidently, the Dutch cartridge is practically identical in all measurements with the rimless case, except for the rim. The British at one time highly favored the Dutch Mannlicher M95 action for use on target rifles, they using long (30″ or 32″) .303 barrels. Barrels are very tightly threaded into receivers, incidentally.

Burnishing. For the final word on smooth finishes, use the burnisher. A steel burnisher is a tool used after lapping and stoning to close the surface of steel and make it as smooth as is humanly possible. Burnishers are available from Starrett or Brown & Sharp at very low prices—less than a dollar—or are easy to make, if you have an hour of free time. Take a discarded fine-cut file, not thinner than $\frac{1}{8}''$ (width is of no particular importance) break it off approximately $3''$ ahead of tang, ram a file handle on the tang, and carefully grind the teeth off on a motor grinder. Keep a can of cold water beside the grinder and dunk the tool in it just about every other second, for you must not burn the steel. A burnisher must be harder and smoother than glass. You may short-cut the job by not grinding the teeth off the sides of the file—in fact, it does not hurt a bit to leave them as an aid to holding the tool should you desire to use both hands on it for pressure. Only the edges are used for actually burnishing, these being rounded in both directions, the edges being stoned and polished with abrasive cloth until very smooth, then you really start smoothing them up. Use crocus cloth, hard slip stones, the buffing wheel and finally hone it on leather until you can press any part of the edge across a piece of polished brass or copper and make a smooth, shiny mark. In use the burnisher is simply rubbed across the finished gun part until its surface has an even, highly-polished appearance.

The preceding information on gun parts is rather sketchy, as it is difficult to give much instruction without referring to specific gun models and parts, and I prefer to cover these as we come to them, under chapters devoted to each particular type of arm.

A PROFESSIONAL GUNSTOCKER AT WORK

Above shows John Hearn checkering a stock in his shop. He writes "I work from both standing and sitting positions and find that a swivel-base machinist's vise is easier to adjust when directing the stroke than a carpenter's vise. I use Dem-Bart layout cutters and try to work either 20 or 24 lines to the inch. Smaller is too fine; larger, too coarse. I make my own deepeners and finishers. Work mostly with daylight through the windows seen in the background and use electric light occasionally to show up high or low spots.

"In the picture, I am pointing to the only layout line that I use to go over the grip, in checkering the pattern shown; there is another one on the other side of the grip and the two meet at the top. This line, when carried over the top of the grip, becomes the other side of the diamond for the pattern. The angle that these two lines make when they meet determines the shape of the diamond in the pattern.

"The checkering frame shown, crude as it may seem, has been in use for over four years now, and can be extended to handle full-length Mannlicher stocks."

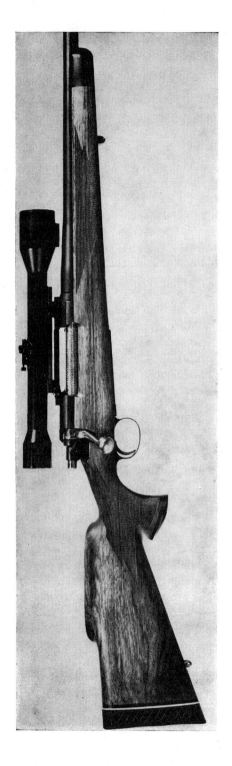

Joe Pfeifer's own hunting rifle, a .300 H & H Improved, built on remodeled 1917 action, with Zeiss 6X lightweight scope in custom mount. Note straightened bolt handle. The bell-bottomed grip is an innovation and a good one as it assists in holding the hand up on the grip and in position with less conscious effort on the part of the shooter. Stocked by Monte Kennedy in French walnut. The high cheekpiece is necessary with the high mounting required by the scope. The very fine Pfeifer-Cramer single-stage trigger is used, as well as all other mechanical refinements Joe could think of.

CHAPTER 12

Cartridge Information for the Gunsmith

Rifle Cartridges. On the American scene, the past twenty years have changed the cartridge situation very considerably. We not only have had cartridges like the .220 Swift and .257 Remington brought out by the factories, but a multitude of "wildcat" cartridges have been developed by individual experimenters through alteration of standard factory cartridge cases. Our gun powders have improved considerably and we now have specialized types suited to practically every capacity cartridge case and bullet weight available or desired. The great and growing popularity of the telescopic sight and interest in hand-loaded ammunition has boosted our standards of accuracy over 50%. Intelligent gun editors have educated the ordinary part-time hunter and shooter to the point where he demands results equal to those attained only by the master gun cranks and experimenters of a generation ago.

Today we can obtain higher velocities and better killing power in hunting loads because we have better powders and bullet designs, and at the same time less barrel trouble. Barrel steels are better than ever before and constant experiments are being made with newer alloys. Non-corrosive priming mixtures, powders without ingredients which damage steel, and bullet jackets which do not foul the barrel make the modern rifle require little care. Even our military cartridges cause little damage, requiring only that primer fouling be cleaned from the barrel and bolt face after the rifle or pistol has been used. The manufacture of metallic cartridge cases is beyond the scope of the individual gunsmith or experimenter, except in a very limited way, as you will deduce from the following data.

Naturally there is no sense to making any case you can buy, so there remains only those odd foreign rimmed and American obsolete cases for good arms in the hands of devoted shooters. It may be possible to purchase in the near future, rough-drawn brass cartridge cups of sizes necessary for these large rimmed cases. If not, you set up the lathe and turn such cases out of brass rod, necessarily copying the dimensions from an original case or sulphur cast of the rifle chamber. Where the original primer pocket and flash-hole dimensions are for obsolete primers, of course make these for modern primers, copying from new, unfired commercial cases. Turned cases are not as strong as drawn, or pressed, cases, but this is of little importance on the old guns, designed for black-powder pressures and where, by careful hand-loading, pressures will be kept under control.

For the large European rimmed cartridge rifles, you just cannot load to original ballistics, if the cases are to be used any number of times. The drawings throughout this book give the necessary operating procedure in turning cases from solid stock. Always, one case only should first be made up and tested, being reloaded and fired several times to check for base expansion, stretching and metal fatigue. Control of the latter is by annealing, and all turned cases should be annealed at least once, preferably all but the base being treated. Brass tends to work-harden very slightly, and anyway, the operations of turning and polishing may relieve or set up strains in the finished tube which should be normalized a little.

Factory cartridge cases are drawn from brass strips, the first stage being a disc stamped out, around $1\frac{1}{4}''$ diameter for a large rifle cartridge and $\frac{1}{8}''$ thick, which is pressed into a shallow cup. This cup is then passed through punch presses and progressively drawn out longer and thinner, being annealed between each draw. When the cup is formed into a closed tube of the proper size it is trimmed to length and goes through the heading machines, the rim being upset on the closed end, primer pocket punched, and manufacturer's markings stamped on the base. If of the rimless or semi-rimless type, an automatic lathe attachment cuts the extractor groove. Last comes the necking-down process for the bottle-neck case, it being forced into from one to five dies, each reducing the neck diameter a small amount, until the correct size is reached. The flash-hole is also punched during necking, as a rule. It is annealed between each sizing and after final sizing in order that the neck and shoulder will be soft enough not to split when the cartridge is fired. All these annealing operations require considerable equipment and skilled personnel, for the finished case must be of the correct grain structure to withstand the great pressures it will be subjected to in use.

When a cartridge is fired, the case expands to fill the chamber, then as pressure drops and the case cools, the brass contracts slightly, allowing it to be extracted. It does not return to its original dimensions, however. A case which is too soft will not contract well, and so causes difficult extraction. A case which is too hard will not expand correctly, and may break, or rupture, on firing.

The dies necessary to make cases naturally cost a great deal of money, so the factories are always very careful about putting out new cartridges. Wildcat cartridges like the .22/3000 Lovell and the .22/250 are no doubt used in far greater quantities than the comparable factory .218 Bee and .220 Swift, but the factories have not yet placed them in production. The .22/3000 cartridge is waning in popularity and probably will never be made commercially.

The .22 rim-fire cases are drawn the same way, although requiring little annealing once metal is blanked from the sheet or strip. Copper, brass and plated versions are made, the stronger cases being necessary for the high-velocity type loading. The case is drawn, first into a straight cup, then the head is swaged on and stamped and last, the priming mixture is inserted, usually in the form of a liquid drop, the case is then spun and centrifugal force places the mixture out in the rim. (The British have a better system, I think, at least on their high-velocity and match cartridges—they fill the complete head of the case with priming mixture, so that if a firing pin bats into the case anywhere you get ignition.)

The making of metal-jacketed bullets varies somewhat between the different types, although principles of manufacture are very similar. Full-patch, or completely jacketed bullets, of the military patterns, are drawn from cupped discs as are cartridge cases. The jacket material used by the factories is known as "gilding metal" and composition is of copper and zinc, percentages being between 90 and 95% copper, 5 to 10% zinc, to a little tin. Jackets must be thicker and harder for high-velocity rifles than for medium power calibers. A .30–30 bullet of early days would disintegrate in the air if fired from a souped-up .300 Magnum cartridge. Jackets and cores are made separately, the jackets being cupped from discs of gilding metal, drawn to correct thickness and approximate diameter, then the lead centers, either of swaged shape or cut from lengths of chilled lead wire the correct weight desired are inserted, and the assembly of jacket and core swaged and sized to final dimensions. Soft nose bullets have the jacket cut with the closed end at the base, exposing the lead; full patch types have the nose solid and base open. Where special points, such as the Winchester "Silvertip" or Remington "Bronze Point" are used, these tips are made separately and inserted along with the lead core in the final assembly pressing.

Some of our small independent bullet manufacturers use copper tubing for jacket material, cutting it into short lengths, swaging one end partially closed, inserting a slug of lead wire and swaging the point closed. Practically, all of such bullets do not give Grade A accuracy, although they give excellent results on game. Sisk, Speer and Morse all make bullets equal to similar soft-nosed factory types, however they all use solid-base jackets and know what they are doing.

Boat-tail, or tapered base bullets of the hunting type have disappeared almost completely, and remain commercially available only in the Western 180-grain Match type and Remington Taper-Heel 180-grain.

The boat-tail is vital to maximum accuracy in any caliber, especially at ranges beyond 600 yards. While the streamline has no beneficial effect until the speed of the bullet drops below 1500 feet per second, the reduced bearing surface on the barrel allows use of bullets long and heavy enough to balance well in flight and "buck the wind" better than a flat-based projectile. Because the reduced diameter of the bullet base allows a reverse funnel effect of powder gas on the barrel, the boat-tail does cause slightly greater erosion than a flat base bullet, against which the gas contacts only a flat, bore-filling surface. Much experimenting was done, all degrees of taper being tried before our government found that a 9° angle gave maximum ballistic results with minimum erosive effect.

Steel jackets, tried by practically all military services throughout the world, have never gone far in civilian life. At one time it was customary to use a nickel and copper alloy for jackets and these white bullets were erroneously known as "steel jackets." The true steel-jacketed bullet, if properly made, is very little harder on barrel steel than gilding metal types. The steel must be very thin, however, and plated on the outside with gilding metal or copper, and lead core must not be hard lead. We are coming to steel jackets, so get used to the idea. It has already been determined that in .280 and .30 caliber the very long, needle-pointed boat-tails necessary for extreme accuracy will strip their jackets if not of steel, the rifling simply tearing the jacket, rather than cutting into it and spinning the bullet. One extremely painstaking experimenter could not get even fair results with ordinary jacket material but with steel-jacketed bullets obtained groups at 600 yards any normal character would brag about if he did as well at 200 yards.

The loading of cartridges by the factories is of course done by machines, the finished case having the primer inserted and passing along on assembly line, mouth up, under powder measuring devices which drop the required amount in, then the bullet is inserted and, in most cases, crimped in, the mouth of the case being pressed into a rolled or pressed cannelure in the bullet at the proper point. The factories maintain far greater tolerance in powder charges than most hand-loaders. Western's hand-loaded match is really hand-loaded, the powder being dumped from the measure onto the pan of a powder scale, additional powder added if too light, removed if too great, the accurate charge being poured into the case and the match bullet seated in a regular hand-loader's tool.

I hope I can clear up the headspace business a little. No other gunsmith book I have seen yet has more than a vague paragraph or two, with a sketch showing rimless and rimmed cases, usually the .30–06 and .30–40 Krag as examples, which is confusing, because all rimless cartridges are not gaged the same as the .30–06. The .30–06, according to U. S. Arsenal drawings is gaged from the face of the bolt (i.e., base of gage) to the *upper corner* of the shoulder—not the middle. Complicating this conception for most people is the fact that the upper corner of the shoulder does not exist, either on the gage or in the rifle chamber! The gage is beveled, or indented, at the corner of the shoulder, in order that the chamber corner may be slightly rounded because it would be too hard on cases if it were sharp, and too difficult to make either cases or chambers that way. Most gunmen and gunsmiths believe that headspace is measured from *center* of shoulder to face of bolt, principally due to the fact that factory drawings of cartridges show measurements to this point, which actually indicates proper point of contact of cartridge shoulder slope and chamber shoulder cone.

Wildcat Cartridges. Every modern gunsmith must have at least an honest talking knowledge of the individually-developed special cartridges so popular today. At least three-quarters of the variants are poorly designed and of no value, however we cannot find out what a new idea will do until it is tried out. The great common factor of the wildcats is that they never seem to work as well for the customer as for the "inventors." Of all the dozens of .22 center-fire varmint cartridges thought up in the past twenty years only a few are worthy of recommendation.

I positively do not like the .22/3000 Lovell and its improved types for use in single shot rifles. A good action is okay, but I feel only three are safe—the Winchester highside, blued type, Sharps Borchardt and the Remington Hepburn. Yes, a lot of them have been made on Stevens

44½ and others, but—a *majority*, not *some*, of the loads developed for this rifle and recommended in print by people who should know better develop pressures that would strain a nickel-steel Springfield or a Winchester Model 70. A good many of these loads run over 50,000 pounds pressure, and quite a few around and over 60,000! A Canadian ballistic engineer made up a pressure gun for the cartridge, and some of the information he obtained is hair-curling.

The .218 Bee, while a factory-made cartridge, can be considered almost a wildcat. Pressures run considerably lower than the Lovell, and performance is very nearly as good, notwithstanding comments by Lovell devotees.

The .22 Chuckers, both rimless and rimmed types, developed by Leslie Lindahl, are very well-balanced medium high-velocity varmint cartridges and well worthy of bolt action rifles built for them. Similar cartridges are out, the most publicized being the Gipson Wasp. Great performance is claimed for it, velocities comparable to the much larger .220 Swift, and so forth. However, I will withhold comment to some extent. Whatever they say, you cannot get such velocities in a case of small capacity without running pressures up plenty. Too, according to most of the results I have seen, they got the velocities using HiVel powder for propellent, and accuracy checks were made with duPont 4320, which is a horse with a different collar. The cartridge undoubtedly has great promise, and by the time this sees print the Wasp may have settled down to become one of our ace wildcats.

Probably the finest of all wildcat .22s is the .22/250, made by necking the .250/3000 Savage case to .22 caliber, not changing shoulder angle, headspace, or length. This cartridge has kicked around for over thirty years, being experimented with to some slight degree by Charles Newton, Donaldson and, I believe, Niedner. Lack of suitable powders held development back until the early 1930s, when a number of men took up the cartridge. The man who really put it on the map was Jerry Gebby, who assembled fine rifles for it, and patented the name "Varminter." Practically every barrelmaker and fitter in the country cut in on the deal, stamping barrels .220/250 or .22/250. The cartridge is suited only to bolt actions of military size, either left full length or shortened around ¾″ to make a neater job. It is a high-pressure cartridge, though nearly all loads are well below critical points on even second-rate actions. It is accurate in any loading, with any available .224″ weight bullet, and pressures maintain a more even curve than other .22 cartridges. The Swift, for example, is tricky to load to accuracy, very slight variations of a good load combination giving erratic results. It is hard to go wrong on this .22/250—barrel life far exceeds most of the "hot" varmint cartridges, especially when colloidal graphite wads are used. A 49-grain bullet can be driven 3,800 feet per second (muzzle velocity) with safety, using three to five grains less powder than some of the recommended loads.

The Canadians have developed a rimmed cartridge of almost identical shape, capacity and general characteristics as the .22/250, based on the .303 British service case and called the .22/303. It can also be made from .30–40 Krag brass, and is of course suited to the very strongest single shot actions such as the Farquharson and Winchester highside thick walled types.

We have a multitude of "improved" Swifts, most of them no doubt actually improvements, as the factory cartridge leaves quite a bit to be desired in the way of accuracy. The Wilson "Arrow" is probably one of the very best. One of the most popular and best-balanced of the rim varmint .22s is the Ackley Improved Zipper, based on the .219 Zipper case. It is below the .22/250 in velocity, but suited to any single shot action safe for the .22/3000 Lovell.

Before leaving the .22s a word on the "K" business. Lysle Kilbourn several years ago had a bright idea for improving the .22 Hornet—he simply reamed out the chamber most of its length almost straight, so that regular Hornet cartridges, when fired, would expand to fill it and come out with a larger body diameter and a short sharp shoulder. When reloaded, the case of course holds more powder and velocity is increased enough to make things worth while. He later did the same thing to the .218 Bee, with similar results. The cartridges are known as K-Hornet, or Kilbourn Hornet and Kilbourn Bee. Others have adopted the system and sometimes credit by prefixing their case with a "K," which has come to mean a method of blowing out an existing rimmed case to greater capacity. I believe Mr. Kilbourn himself confines most of his work to low-cost rechambering jobs for shooters who want their Hornets and Bees pepped up a little, for which I honor him. Factory ammunition can be used in these chambers, should the owner get tired of hand-loading once in awhile.

Fire Forming. This is a term now in rather wide use, which is completely explained in principle by the foregoing paragraph, although it is used on rimless, semi-rimmed belted and rimmed cases alike. The rifle chamber is cut oversize so that when a standard case is fired, it will expand to the desired dimension.

It is possible to do a very radical forming job on a belted or rimmed case, but on a rimless or semi-rimless (.220 Swift) about all that is possible to do safely is to change the angle of the shoulder or to increase the diameter of the case at the shoulder, cutting down the body taper.

The Ackley Improved Zipper is a good example of changing a poorly-designed case to one which will burn powder right and give excellent velocity and accuracy.

.25 Calibers. None. A lot of the boys have played and are playing with .25 caliber rifles, trying to get high-velocity varmint rifles. They get velocities, all right, but seldom turn in a report of accuracy suitable for vermin hunting. The .25–06 was first worked out by Niedner many years ago, but never was as successful as his .25 Krag, of smaller capacity. The .250/3000 Savage cartridge is still the most accurate .25 caliber, and is likely to stay so for awhile, for reasons I will go into at the end of this spiel.

.270 Caliber. Ackley and others have tried to improve the .270 Winchester by blowing out the body of the case to gain greater "boiler room," but frankly, very, very little is gained. Roy Weatherby shortens, necks down and fire forms a large-capacity .270 Magnum cartridge and this case, together with the .270 Ackley Magnum, also made on the .300 H & H Belted Magnum case, are the only worth while large capacity cartridges in this caliber. However, as with the .25 caliber, it is difficult to beat the standard factory cartridge for accuracy, the .270 Winchester holding its own.

.30 Caliber. The best of the .30 caliber special cartridges for the average man is the .30 Ackley Short Magnum, made by shortening and blowing out the .300 H & H case. It approximates the .30 Newton, which was the best of all .30 caliber large cartridges. All standard bullets can be handled accurately at velocities two to three hundred feet per second more than the .30–06. The Weatherby .300 and Ackley .30 Long Magnum are good cases, but slightly hard to load to accuracy with any but the heavier bullets. For a long-range game rifle either is excellent. Pfeifer's improved .300 is also excellent, and easy to load.

General Comment. There are wildcat cartridges in the larger calibers, but since the advent of the .375 H & H in this country by Winchester, the .35 Whelens, .400 Whelens, .400 Niedners, and the like, have taken a decline in popularity. The first two are made from .30–06 unnecked cases; the last of the unnecked .30 Newton, all being necked down to the proper bullet size by the rifle maker or owner. The .400 Niedner was the most potent big game rifle ever built in this country, having considerable more power than the .375—on both ends.

What most of our experimenters take years to discover is that each caliber and bullet weight has a limitation, the condition being, for want of a better name, "bore capacity." Meaning that you do not necessarily get anywhere just by putting a little bullet in a big case in front of a lot of powder. The .257 Remington cartridge is an excellent example—it is just on the limit of the .25 caliber bore capacity. Hand-loaded over factory velocity, cartridges improve somewhat as regards accuracy, and in factory ammunition, accuracy is just not quite up to the smaller .250/3000. My personal belief is that if someone would "wildcat" the .257 and decrease the case capacity about a few grains, velocity would hold up and accuracy increase. I am not interested enough in .25 calibers to experiment. The .25 Krag, popular among the advanced gun cranks twenty-five and more years ago, was right around the .257 in capacity, and the powders used in those days made for good accuracy in the tapered case.

In the .22 cartridges three diameters of bullets and rifle bores are used—.223″ in Hornet and Bee and similar small type cases; .224″ in the higher velocity cartridges up through the .22/250; .220″ and .228″ in .22 Savage Hi-Power and larger wildcats. The relation of bore to cartridge capacity is brought out rather clearly—regardless of case size, when bullets over 55-grains in weight are used in .224″ diameters accuracy falls off as velocity is increased, and it is necessary to go to the .228″ bore for best performance with the heavier bullets.

The .25–06, made from the .30–06 necked down, with all sorts of shoulder angles and neck lengths, has received quite a bit of attention since the end of World War II. The universal mistake has been to try to make a super-varmint cartridge, using light bullets at high velocities with the result that the barrels are usually shot out by the time the rifle is sighted in. With hot hand-loads, the .25 calibers, even the .250/3000, are hard on barrel throats, erosion being evident after a couple of hundred rounds. Used with bullets not lighter than 117-grains, loaded to velocities not over 300 feet per second greater than the factory .257 cartridge, the .25–06 is a very fine game rifle caliber.

With present-day propellents and bullet jacket construction, each bore diameter has a definite limit for the velocity attainable, regardless of cartridge shape or capacity, as regards accuracy.

Shoulder Slopes and Body Tapers. About the time I was born, Charles Newton decided that a shoulder angle of 28° would do better than the 17° and 18° slopes then used for bottle-neck cases. The 28° shoulder really proved out during the late 1930s, after duPont and Hercules perfected modern smokeless powders as we now know them.

While some of the more responsible custom gun and cartridge men advocate a 30° shoulder, the Newton standard remains the best all-around rule. A sharper shoulder causes the case to burn some powders better, but increases pressures, and a longer, more tapered shoulder funnels pressure and burning gases into the throat of the barrel, increasing erosion. The boys who want to be different are always turning up with queer-looking cases—shoulders practically a right angle step, or a curved shoulder—but these usually drop by the wayside in a couple of months, when the rifle is burned out, or too many cases separate in the chamber, or otherwise become unusable.

As for body tapers, the trend has been lately to straighten the cases in order to lower base pressure. Chamber pressure is not always a measure of safety or danger, for it can be divided into two forces, that outward in all directions from the center of the case, against the inside of the case and consequently the barrel chamber, and that portion of it which is directly against the head of the case, forcing it back against the bolt or breechblock. This latter force is called "bolt thrust" and is actually the limiting factor in the strength of rifle actions, since the remaining pressure is against the barrel walls at the chamber and the modern heavy-breech barrel will withstand greater pressures than our actions.

The tapered case is a self-actuating wedge when fired, the burning gases not only forcing the bullet out the barrel, but tending to drive the case backward by expanding against the tapered chamber. Tapered cases are a little easier to extract because of this action and for that reason are suited to those actions with poor extraction leverage.

The wildcat cartridge is based entirely upon the hand-loading practice and for that reason, if no other, no cartridge which is hard on the brass cartridge case itself should be recommended. There are two or three fairly popular high-velocity cartridges which destroy over 15% of their cases during initial forming and firing, and close to that in each successive regular loading and firing. Few riflemen care to underwrite the expense and labor of constantly making cases. I personally would not own a special rifle, however fine its performance, if individual cartridge cases would not withstand ten re-loadings.

The preceding pages will no doubt affront quite a few "wildcatters" but the gunsmith should never recommend a cartridge other than one of proven value to the customer who desires to enter the hand-loading and special cartridge field. The characters who go in for the extreme experimental stuff will seldom ask advice anyway, for they usually know as much or more about their chosen item than the gunsmith! If a customer has just read a hot write-up in the *Rifleman* on the Joe Blow .249 Dynamiter and wants you to get him one made up, take him off in the corner and have a man-to-man talk with him and make sure he is willing to take all the responsibility should his projected $250 job not prove up to expectations. Make it plain you are not recommending anything you do not know about. For any special cartridge for an over-the-counter customer take several things into consideration besides the matter of special ammunition and loading equipment; can you get barrels correctly chambered from a reputable maker; what dimension barrel will best suit customer and cartridge; what sight or sights will enable customer to realize the capabilities of the rifle? You must disregard to some extent what the originator of the cartridge accomplished with Whoozis Powder No. 4—which has been off the market fifteen years—and a batch of bullets made by his friend before the war—and shot in a fifteen-pound bullgun from a bench rest at 100 yards. Will that cartridge perform well with modern components available today through commercial channels, in an eight-pound custom sporter? If not, the cartridge is of no practical value in the field.

Pistol Cartridges. Pistol and revolver cartridges are manufactured practically the same way as rifle cartridges, most if not all now being of the solid-head or solid-base type, in which the drawn cup is left heavy at the closed end so that the primer pocket is punched or cut in solid brass, the head of case being thick metal. Formerly most rimmed revolver cases and some rifle cases were of the folded-head construction, in which the case cup was drawn thin at bottom and the primer pocket pressed into it. Some call this the "balloon base" construction. These were of course much weaker cases and the advent of higher-pressured loadings required the solid construction in most calibers. Many revolver and pistol cases are cannelured or indented at a point which determines the depth of bullet seating. Lead bullets are crimped in—that is, the mouth of case is indented in the bullet in a groove made for it. Jacketed pistol cartridges have cases crimped in the smaller calibers, but in the larger calibers the bullets are simply seated friction-tight, for the mouth of the case governs headspace in some calibers, such as the .45 ACP. Lead bullets are swaged, made under pressure from lead alloy to insure uniform density and weight.

Shotgun Cartridges. During the past few years the American shotgun shell picture has changed somewhat. Formerly we had an immense number of loadings to select from, (over 4000 in 1925 including all makes, with duplications) many of them overlapping each other in purpose and effectiveness. The manufacturers got together and decided to simplify their lines, so today we have only a few standard loadings (about 160 total, all makes) to cover the various scatter-gun usages. The popularity of Skeet had a great deal to do with the modern shell construction, research bringing out several different types of wadding and case closure to eliminate the pattern damage caused by the old-style heavy front wad wandering around in the pattern as the shot charge left the barrel.

The first shot shells were of metallic construction, folded head construction, very similar to early revolver cartridges. These were replaced very shortly commercially by the paper shell, although the metallic cases were used for years by hand-loaders. It is very possible that brass shotgun casings will again be produced for sale, but no commercial ammunition will be loaded, due to the high cost. The paper shell is formed of a paper tube crimped into a brass, copper or aluminum base, with this metal base section strengthened by thick, heavy layers or sections of cardboard or fiber to approximate the construction of the solid-head type case. Two types of cartridge are made, the standard velocity shell with "low base" or narrow metal base cup and the high-pressure shell with "high base" or wide, strong base.

For obsolete arms, such as 8-gauge guns, it is possible to make brass or aluminum shot shell cartridges, turning out the cases on a lathe. These hand-made cases are loaded similar to standard factory shells as regards types of powder wads and spacing of wads, and shot is sealed by a thin cardboard disc held in the case and waterproofed by wax. Black powder is used almost entirely.

Proof Firing. Arms which receive repair work or alteration to chambers, or breech mechanisms, should be test-fired as a safety measure. Handguns and shotguns can be adequately tested by a dozen or so rounds of the heaviest factory loads furnished, although of course if tools are available it is wise to build up hand-loads about 10% above factory standards. For rifles, proof cartridges should always be loaded, taking a recommended maximum load and boosting it about three grains in powder charge.

The cartridge cases used should be new, unfired and unprimed, if available, so that flash-holes can be inspected before loading. Primer flash-holes, if oversize, will give visible signs of excessive pressure, and if undersize, or badly burred at edges, often give faulty ignition, occasional hang-fires being the extreme. In the large rifle cases flash-holes run from .080 to .0815", easily checked by number drills—a No. 46 drill should enter the hole, and a No. 45 should not. The .220 Swift alone had originally a flash-hole .060" in diameter. Proper diameter for the small-rifle primer, as in Hornet, Bee, and the like, and all pistol and revolver cartridges is .070″. The Swift now has an .080″ flash-hole. If new cases are not at hand, use once-fired cases, of the best brass you know of (it varies, from lot to lot, regardless of maker) clean them well, inside and out, full-length size, trim to correct length and load.

At least five proof loads should be fired, and the gun headspaced after each, to check for setback of breech mechanism. All locking recesses, face of bolt or block, and chamber should be absolutely clean and dry, as well as having a clean barrel for the first shot. If headspace gages are not available for the caliber involved, you must use loaded cartridges made up which on assortment or by intent are very slightly oversize—enough so that when they are inserted in the chamber and the *stripped* bolt or block, not under any spring tension, is closed, a definite resistance is felt. This make-shift system is sufficiently accurate to insure safety, if the operator has any sense of feel at all in his hands, and most gunsmiths have plenty. If the action slightly resists closing on the test cartridges before proof firing (do not force it on these of course) and falls shut on it after firing, you know something has changed and can check further to find out whether or not any damage has been done.

New actions practically always "set back" or stretch a trifle when first fired, and after the first two or three rounds settle down and hold their position from then on, so if a thousandth or two of an inch change occurs in proof firing such a gun, do not worry about it, but continue to fire and check until you are sure it is safe and normal in dimensions. Discs of shim stock can be placed over the back of the gage cartridges to measure stretching. Should the action continue to set back and headspace steadily increase—that is all, brother. Another action is in order. Any military action which is rebarreled, if it has been used at all, should show no set back whatsoever. In proof firing the arm should be artificially supported, for safety to the firer. You can tie it to a tree, put it in a heavy wooden box, or some such arrangement, and fire by a string from a point of cover. I prefer to lay guns across a wooden box place a heavy, canvas-covered sandbag across them, and use a string to pull the trigger.

Note: For further information on cartridges, see Appendix II.

CHAPTER 13

Rifle Barrels and Barrel Information

NO, WE are not going to go into barrelmaking as such. That is a profession all by itself and could take up several large volumes just in conversation. Even with war surplus machinery available, the investment necessary to equip a shop to make barrels would run from $10,000 up, and most of the independent barrelmakers have several times that amount tied up in equipment. The ordinary gunsmith must however fully understand barrel design, material and alteration. Practically all of our barrelmakers supply barrel blanks, which are barrel steel rifled tubes, to the individual gunshops who make a business of fitting custom barrels and building complete rifles to order. The gunshop turns the blank to the desired size, threads it for the action used, fits it, chambers it and finishes it, inside and out. Such operations are within the scope of any conscientious careful gunsmith who possesses a lathe of sufficient dimensions to handle the turning-down and threading jobs.

Barrel steel itself has improved considerably during the past decade. Nickel and molybdenum alloys have proved more wear and erosion resistant than the straight carbon-manganese alloys formerly used for high-power barrels, and countless variations of these are available. Graphitic tool steels are used for the very "hottest" cartridges in order to prolong barrel life. I am listing information furnished by the individual barrelmakers regarding their barrel dimensions, tolerances and material, with their comments on characteristics of special steels. The machinability of some modern steels plays an important part in barrel costs, incidentally. When a metal is very hard to cut clean, either in rifling or chambering, taking considerably more time in working and in keeping tools sharp, naturally the price goes up. Many small shops buy such special blanks and then turn out poor jobs in chambering these tough steels.

Mild carbon steel is used in pistols, .22 rim-fire rifle barrels, and other barrels intended for use with lead bullets. This soft steel pushes out of shape rapidly when used with jacketed bullets at medium and high velocities. The better class .22 target rifle barrels are usually made of a tougher metal, which of course would be any suitable high-power steel, but usually is similar to the alloy known as "Ordnance Steel," as it was developed by Army Ordnance for rifle and machine gun barrels just before World War I. I believe the Savage Arms Corporation uses this for all center-fire rifles. The general composition of such steel is:

Carbon...................... 0.45 to 0.55
Manganese.................... 1.00 to 1.30
Phosphorus (Maximum)......... .05
Sulphur (Maximum)............ .05
Silicon...................... .15 to .35

Normalized at 1650° Fahrenheit and annealed at 1600° Fahrenheit for two hours, then hardened by heating to 1550° Fahrenheit for one hour then quenched in oil.

Yield point 75,000 pounds per square inch
Tensile strength 110,000 pounds per square inch
Elongation 20%

Winchester and Remington now use nickel alloys for barrels in large calibers, and the Winchester Model 70 .220 Swift has a stainless steel barrel, of composition to resist erosion more than the regular nickel types. (Many a gunsmith has been greatly surprised when he did a re-modeling job on a M70 .220 and tried to reblue the barrel!) The stain-less steels now being used in barrels by some makers is not the original type of high-chrome content iron or soft steel, but is a harder alloy, very difficult to machine. I understand that in finishing, Winchester coats (electroplates) these barrels with iron, which allows a blue to "take." If this iron plating is polished off, the stainless, non-corrosive finish will not take any normal blue solution, the blueing being in the last analysis, a corrosive process. To color a stainless barrel two alternatives face the finisher; first, to paint the blasted thing with black enamel (do not shudder—it has been done, by factories, too); or at-tempt to plate it with copper and then turn the copper black. I say "attempt" because this stainless stuff does not like being plated very well, either.

Within the next ten years I believe we will see further advances in barrel development particularly regarding stainless and long-wearing steels. Parker Ackley is experimenting extensively with stainless alloys and told me he has located a blacking process which is very satisfactory.

Dimensions. External barrel dimensions are quite important, especially on sporter-weight arms for high-pressure special cartridges. So far as length is concerned, the accuracy is not increased by very long barrels. A .22 long rifle rim-fire cartridge bullet has received practically all the benefit it gets from the rifling by the time it has traveled eighteen inches, a .30–06 bullet in twenty-three inches. Longer barrels increase velocity slightly, in the case of some bullets do aid accuracy, and in any case a longer barrel makes a heavier rifle, easier for the expert rifleman to hold steadier. The long 28″ and 30″ heavy target barrels aid the shooter more than the cartridge, except in the large special calibers using slow-burning powders which develop better pressure curves in long barrels.

Diameters of barrels at the breech must be held to certain standards for safety, but through the body of the barrel its diameter can be governed by individual desire for lightness, graceful contour or recommended weight. My personal theory regarding barrels is that a feather-weight can be as accurate as a heavy "bull" type, although it may not shoot a group at all comparable. A properly made light barrel—normalized steel, not straightened during turning-down—properly bedded in a sporter stock, with or without barrel band, should be able to shoot as small a group as a heavy barrel of the same caliber, twist and chamber dimensions, *providing* all shots are fired at a state of uniform barrel temperature. In other words, the barrel is allowed to cool between shots. A heavy barrel is able to absorb heat, radiate it slowly and more or less evenly, and is stiff enough to resist the tendency to warp by the heat generated in fairly rapid firing.

I have had some experience with fine custom-built sporters, stocked by the finest stockmakers in America, the inletting usually being very close and tight. Almost without exception these rifles will put their first two or three shots, fired rapidly, very close together. Successive shots will spread out and enlarge a 200 yard group several inches—who cares?

In a hunting rifle the important thing is to get the first shot and maybe the follow-up, in the right place. If shooting is very deliberate, these light-barreled rifles are extremely accurate by target standards. For this reason I think most of our varmint hunters are kidding themselves by staggering up and down the hills with very heavy, long-barreled smallbore rifles. A prairie-dog exterminator might have need for a rifle which would hold its center of impact for fifteen or twenty

TOM SHELHAMER AND HIS CHECKERING SET-UP

Tom clamps the cradle in this position, generally, and keeps it at about this height—working both sitting and standing, according to how he feels. The electric bulb is moved about a bit to help him follow his lines easily, and to throw light (and shadow) where he wants it. After laying out the pattern he usually goes over it about six or seven times, using his own design and make of checkering tool, similar to that shown in the illustration in Chapter 3.

It takes Tom almost a day to do a simple pattern on both grip and fore-arm and up to two full days to work out an intricate one. His technique and movements are so simple they are hard to follow but his checkering is tops in today's gunstocking.

Drilling a barrel blank, at Roy Weatherby's shop.

rapid shots, but I have never been able to shoot a group on a live crow, hawk or jack-rabbit—shots just do not come that fast!

Safe Breech Diameters for High Pressure Cartridges. The following table is of practical value in determining barrel dimensions, and I have worked out several principles which I believe are easily applied for specific jobs. For instance, the walls of the barrel at the chamber, illustrated as the "cylinder section" should not be less than two-thirds as thick as the diameter of the body of the cartridge. Length of the cylinder is governed by the length of the cartridge case, the shoulder of cartridge regulating the shoulder of the barrel cylinder. I have seen a lot of barrels with short cylindrical sections, the body of the chamber extending beyond them into the smaller-diameter portion of the barrel. This I do not like. A thin-walled chamber is very likely to swell, or bulge, from continued firing of the more powerful cartridges. This used to happen to Krags. While increasing difficulty of extraction usually causes the rifle to be set aside as unserviceable before any danger of bursting exists, there have been instances of barrels bursting at the chamber. Enfield barrels should not be rechambered for the long, oversized Magnum cases such as the .300 Weatherby or comparable cartridges. Many such jobs have been done without later ill effects, but every once in awhile a chamber bulges or lets go. I know of two Enfield barrels splitting at the chamber when rechambered for the standard .300 H & H cartridge.

In the matter of barrel contour, several schools of thought exist. For appearance I think the slightly convex outline at the cylinder taper and the barrel body are nice. For rigidity and resistance to barrel vibration the straight-taper or concave curve outlines are probably more efficient. The Germans developed the step-down taper as a means of dampening vibration in light-weight barrels. We could do with a little experimentation on this line ourselves, however, the system must be carefully worked out for each caliber and each weight of bullet and loading, since the steps are placed at points to control a "wave" of vibration set up by a particular bullet-velocity combination. The necessary laboratory equipment for such experimentation is far beyond even our largest independent barrelmakers.

This matter of barrel vibration, popularly called "whip," has considerable to do with accuracy, though the latter is as much a matter of stock bedding as barrel contour. The passage of a bullet through a rifled bore causes a microscopic expansion of the barrel, thus setting up a vibration which actually bends the barrel in more than one direction during the bullet passage, similar to the action of a rubber hose when water is allowed to flow into one end suddenly under pressure. The hose flips around—so does a rifle barrel. In the illustration the curves are evident, and as the bullet leaves the barrel eventually, the position of the muzzle at departure often is out of relation to the normal line of bore and sight setting. Changes in ammunition often radically effect barrel vibration, and consequently sight setting. Barrel bands are quite often applied in an effort to dampen vibration and even the performance of light barrels, and in some cases, weights have been placed on muzzles to slow down the final whip.

The relation of bore diameter to barrel diameter also deserves mention. It is evident that a .22 or .25 caliber bore takes less metal out of a blank than a .270 or .30 bore. Consider for example the Winchester Model 70 in .22 Hornet and .30 caliber—external barrel diameter is the same, but the smaller bore of the .22 makes its barrel heavier. For a rule on establishing muzzle diameters for sporter barrels, double the bore diameter of the caliber involved. For "featherweight" or extremely light barrels, this can be cut down as much as 15%.

As for attempting to figure what a given diameter, contour and length barrel will actually weigh when finished, only a record of weights of similar barrels will guide you. The number of caliber-sporter weight combinations makes any possible table rather complicated. In .30–06 caliber, the Enfield 1917 barrel, cut to 24″ length, is excellent for a standard sporter barrel in that caliber, and weighs 3 pounds 8 ounces. The Springfield 1903 service barrel, 23.79″ long, is considered slightly thick in the middle for aesthetic perfection, and weighs 2 pounds 13 ounces. I like the Enfield outline myself, and consider its dimensions excellent for the small bore varmint cartridges under Magnum length, as the barrel bulk is sufficient to give good group accuracy.

Turning Down Barrels. The factories and arsenals forge and rough-turn barrels to approximate finished outside dimensions before boring, reaming and rifling but all the smaller makers I have been familiar with bore, heat-treat, ream and rifle blanks in full diameter—1⅛″ or 1¼″—then turn down the blank. The possibility of releasing strains in the metal during this process and causing the barrel to warp and bend out of shape is always present, though by no means the bugaboo most men unfamiliar with barrel work consider it. It is very true that often a lathe hand turns a heavy blank down to a slim, light-weight barrel and finds it bent when he takes it out of the lathe. Nine times out of ten this is the fault of the machinist, not the barrel. Modern alloy-steel normalized barrel blanks have little tendency to warp even

SPORTER BARRELS

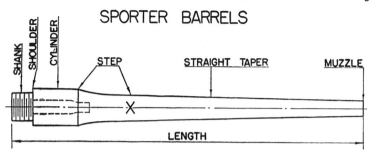

The following recommended dimensions cover the common calibers in sporting rifles—.22 caliber concerns only central-fire cartridges. The "step" or "X" dimension is the point at which the concave curve down from the cylinder ends, and the straight taper to the muzzle begins. The length of the cylinder depends upon the length of the cartridge case. It should contain the case to shoulder length, and the following lengths are recommended:

Minimum   1.125″
Maximum   2.250″

Weight Type	Caliber	Cylinder Diameter	Length to Step	Diameter at Step	Muzzle Diameter	Length
Minimum	.22	1.03″	2.5″	.625″	.40″	22″–24″
Light	.22	1.0625	2.5	.687	.50	24 –26
Standard	.22	1.125	3.0	.750	.55	24 –26
Minimum	.25	1.0625	2.5	.650	.45	21–23–24
Light	.25	1.0625	3.0	.750	.50	21–23–24
Standard	.25	1.125	3.0	.800	.60	24 –26
Minimum	.270	1.100	2.5	.750	.50	23 –24
Light	.270	1.100	3.0	.775	.55	24
Standard	.270	1.125	3.0	.800	.60	24
Minimum	.30	1.100	2.5	.775	.50	22 –24
Light	.30	1.100	3.0	.800	.57	22 –24
Standard	.30	1.125	3.0	.850	.625	24 –26
Heavy	.30	1.250	3.0	1.000	.650	26 –28
Standard	.35–375	1.250	3.0	1.000	.650	24 –26

when a large amount of metal is removed, if it is removed properly. Light cuts only can be taken, with a sharp cutting tool (rounded point) and as long a surface turned at each cut as the intended contour permits. The breech end of the barrel must of course be trued concentric with the bore if it is to be held directly in the chuck, and a muzzle plug made for the tailstock. Such plugs must be made of hardened steel, ground on centers, the end entering the muzzle as closely fitting the bore as it can and yet not bind.

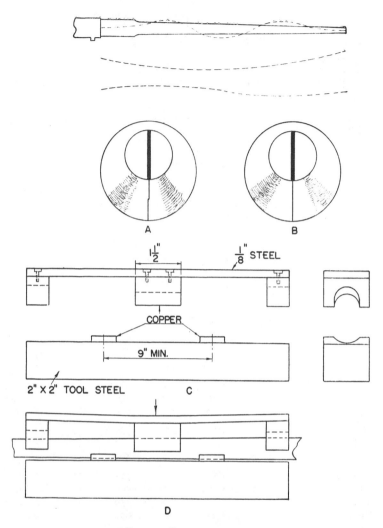

BARREL CHARACTERISTICS

At top we have a sketch of a high-power rifle barrel, with dotted lines indicating the vibration waves possibly affecting it when a bullet passes through the bore. The double curve shown in the sketch of the barrel is exaggerated for emphasis. Only with very long thin barrels is more than an S curve generated. Barrel whip is more likely to be per the two lower dotted line curves, and it must be remembered, that while the stock forend has a dampening effect, the barrel still can have a tendency to whip to either side slightly. The "whip" is not limited to vertical movement. It is because of the whip, which is slightly different with each weight of bullet in a given caliber at each velocity loaded, that some rifles change the point of impact

Handling the tailstock, or rather, not handling it, is where the boys manage to "spring" and bend barrels in turning them down. Pressure of the point of the lathe cutting tool naturally causes a constant slight bend in the material being turned and the friction of turning develops heat—heat causes the barrel blank to expand lengthwise, creating ever-greater pressure against the tailstock. If the tailstock is not adjusted several times during turning to compensate for the increased length of the barrel then the barrel is going to bow (as in bow and arrow) and come out somewhat warped or bent. Turn the blank down a little at a time, keep slacking off the tailstock and you will not have much trouble with the finished product not being straight.

Actually, I believe more trouble is encountered in turning down finished barrels to a lighter weight, as regards warping, due to these mainly being of military origin and probably undergoing forging in manufacture, heavy turning-down cutting, and arsenal straightening, necessary in their rough manufacturing methods, as compared to private makers. Once a barrel has been straightened it will always give trouble if altered in any way later.

Luckily, most military barrels are of such dimensions that actual turning is seldom necessary, usually only very, very light cuts if any, more often just filing, will remove rough surfaces and permit refinishing to commercial standards of appearance. On such jobs, the breech end may be chucked in any of several ways—chuck jaws directly against the barrel threads if no appreciable holding pressure is needed; a mandrel in the chamber and lathe-dog setup; or the muzzle end can be inserted through the chuck first and the cylinder section polished, then reversed so that this section is clamped in the chuck. This will

---

markedly with different loads, and why the handloader finds some loads which shoot either to the right or the left of others, regardless of elevation.

A. Represents view through the bore of a barrel at the shadow line. This is a crooked barrel, as the shadow of the line in the bore is broken. Generally, however, there will not be a sharp break as illustrated, but the line through the barrel will be curved at the crooked point or bend.

B. Appearance of the shadow line through a straight barrel.

C. A simply made barrel straightening jig, to be used with a heavy hammer in straightening a barrel. The copper contact faces protect the outer surface of the barrel.

D. Sketch of the jig, with the barrel in place. The top piece of a jig, with the large copper block in the center, is flexible and bends down to contact the barrel as shown, force being applied at the point indicated by the arrow.

protect the threads, of course and the muzzle plug is used as for a blank.

When the lathe tool is used, make your cuts with a very sharp round-edged cutter, and use plenty of oil. For filing, run the lathe fairly fast, and use sharp mill files, always passing the file across the barrel at right angles to it and never holding it in one place. If you are taking off a Parkerized surface, clean the file at each stroke, and in any case look at it after each two or three strokes to see that it is not clogged in anywhere. A tiny fragment of steel in a file may gouge a ring in the barrel you may spend five minutes removing with smoother files. No. 150 abrasive cloth, wrapped around the file, will take nearly as much metal off, without marking the surface.

Straightening Barrels. The first word on this is—do not do it unless you absolutely have to as a straightened barrel is necessarily bent straight, and the steel in it is under stress. When that barrel becomes heated from firing, it tends to return temporarily to its original state, so shoots in a different place. Actually, to a trained eye, very, very few barrels are perfectly straight. Any expert barrelmaker will tell you that a slightly bent barrel will shoot as well as a straight one, and hold its point of impact as well. You understand of course, that these "bent" barrels we talk about would appear perfectly straight to any eye except when checked by the shadow-line. They do not curve around so that you cannot see through them! Most barrelmakers therefore prefer to leave a barrel alone if it is just a little off-kilter, rather than straighten it and turn out a rifle which is very likely to change its point of impact during firing.

The real trouble with a barrel blank turning job is getting the initial turning cuts off without springing and for that reason it is wise to check for straightness six or eight times in reducing a heavy blank. Should the first few thousandths of metal removed cause the blank to spring badly, you must straighten it before further turning. Otherwise, you can carefully turn down the barrel straight on the outside, with the bore crooked. Such a barrel, if sawed in two at the bend would prove to have the bore off-center, leaving a greater amount of metal on one side than on the other. When such a barrel is fired, the uneven distribution of metal is heated and the barrel distorted because of the uneven tension developed. Should a barrel be turned straight on its exterior and the bore found sufficiently crooked to warrant straightening, it must be straightened and the outside turned concentric with bore.

The shadow-line is the simplest method available to checking straightness of barrels. You need either a clear window with a good

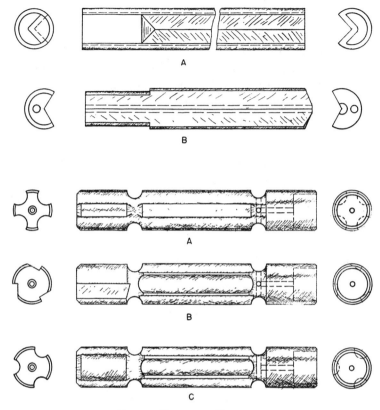

BARREL DRILL AND REAMERS

Drill

A. Tubular body of the drill or the bit extension, showing crimp to lock the bit in place
B. Bore drill bit, with sectional and end views to illustrate hole back through the body. The bit cuts only on one lip of the tip. The metal cut away passes back through the V-slot, helped by oil being forced through the hole in the bit coming down through the drill extension tube.

Reamers

A. Four flute roughing reamer. The flutes are carried through the rear pilot to provide clearance for shavings and chips to pass back. Tubular extensions, smaller than bore diameter, can be used, and oil forced through them and through the dispersal holes in the reamers as indicated.
B. Six flute finishing reamer, with three cutting edges on the bore riding front pilot. Three clearance flutes on the rear pilot are necessary for chip passage.
C. Burnishing reamer, six flute, with rounded edges on all. Three flutes provided on the front and the rear pilots. Oil for lubrication is delivered as for the reamers used for cutting.

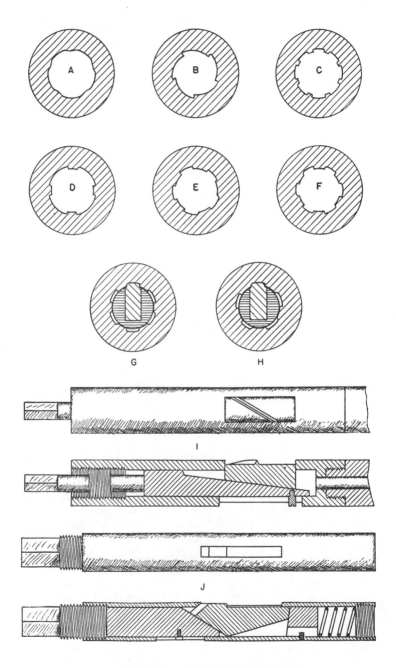

RIFLING - RIFLING CUTTERS

light through it, or a straight object, such as a pole or post, set a distance away in clear sunlight. A thin straight rod or heavy wire is placed across the window, if it is to be used. The barrel is held steady, preferably in V-blocks and the wire, rod or post viewed through the bore. It will cast a shadow, visible as a dark line down the barrel, straight if the barrel is straight, curved or even broken if the barrel is crooked. The illustrations give the idea, although exaggerated, of course. Most bent barrels show a very slight curve apparently for its entire length. The bore of course must be very clean, and must be turned so that it may be checked at all points of its circumference, in order to ascertain the exact location of bend, for you must bend it exactly opposite to straighten it. This is the hard part. The crooked blank must not only be forced straight, it must be forced beyond that point so that it will spring to a straight position when straightening tension is released.

Applying this force can be done either by clamp or hammer, the factories and large barrelmakers using a wheel-actuated machine known as an over-head clamp, which allows sighting through the bore while applying tension. The old method is to use two lead blocks, placing the barrel on them, outer curve of the "bend" up, and strike with a heavy lead hammer. This naturally requires considerable experience,

---

RIFLING AND RIFLING CUTTERS

A. Segmental rifling. Used by Newton to some extent.
B. Elliptical or leading edge rifling. Experimented with considerably in past years, but of little value with modern small arms.
C. Lead bullet rifling, of the type used by Pope, Schoyen and others in principle, utilizing many narrow lands.
D. Modern four groove rifling.
E. British five groove rifling, as seen in Enfield rifles.
F. Modern six groove rifling, used by most custom barrel men.
G. Illustration of rifling tool in the barrel with an even number of lands and grooves.
H. Illustration of rifling tool in the barrel with an odd number of lands and grooves, showing how one land is directly opposite a groove and so supports the rifling head directly. Theoretically, this is the best system, insuring a more evenly machined bore, but in practice, the even numbered groove barrel is just as perfect.
I. Top and sectional views of rifling head, of the old scrape cutter type. These are slow in action and best suited to the softer barrel steels.
J. Top and sectional views of a modern hook cutter rifling head.

Both types of head are adjusted by screw actuated wedges raising the cutters.

to develop the judgment necessary to estimate the force of blow needed for a particular type of bend.

A combination of the two methods is possible, by making clamp blocks as shown in the drawing and these blocks can be actuated by a large arbor press or by hammer. Make them of heavy steel, with copper, brass or bronze offsets. I do not believe they should be made with shorter contact area than shown—however, should jobs turn up requiring straightening out of a very short-radius bend, an extra set of inserts can be made for the blocks. It is not possible to use an ordinary machinist's vise for straightening—even if sufficient pressure is available without breaking it—as the jaws are not wide enough to properly support straightening clamps. I suppose steel false jaws could be worked out, to replace the removable steel vise jaws which would do the job, but I would hate to try to do a good straightening job in a vise. In fact I hate to try to do any straightening job anywhere.

Rifling. The inner machining of a gun bore to handle single projectiles has received exhaustive thought for about four centuries. Just about every type of groove, slot and other shape which can be introduced into a hole has been tried. Harry Pope developed the lead-bullet barrel to perfection as we know it, and anyone who wants to know something about the part rifling plays in bullet performance should read *The Bullet's Flight* by Dr. Mann.

Concerning modern bores, for jacketed bullets, some little experimentation is always going on, but in the main we have settled on the Mauser or Enfield system, using sharp-cornered lands and grooves. The four-groove barrel, with wide lands, seems to last longer than the six-groove type, although accuracy is perhaps a shade better with the latter.

The British developed four rifling systems, all of which have some merit. The Metford used rounded lands and grooves, and proved very successful with lead bullet, black powder military rifles, due to its ease of cleaning and consequent long life—black powder barrels never shot out, they rusted out. The Lancaster oval-bore was tried out by Charles Newton, but did not quite live up to expectations of accuracy. In this method, there are no lands nor grooves, the bore itself is elliptical, turning to give the desired twist. The Rigby system of flat, sharp cornered lands, with corners of grooves rounded, is a good one, and some of our barrelmakers use a form of this—the principle is to eliminate the sharp corners where fouling might accumulate or erosion get a toehold. The last British system is the two-groove barrel, used also by the U. S. in late 1903 and 1917 replacement barrels and wartime rifles.

This is actually a cross between the Lancaster oval-bore and standard multiple-groove and land type, there being only two wide opposing lands.

A further type of rifling, which I feel is due to be that used in the future, is the cloverleaf, or four-land type of rounded lands and grooves, similar to the Metford. The Japanese used rounded grooves in their rifles, but sharp lands. The cloverleaf bore should theoretically handle bullets at very high velocities without stripping jackets. Some of the ultra-power experimenters are trying them now, and perhaps in twenty or thirty years, we will all be shooting steel jacketed or heavy bronze jacketed bullets through them at 6000 fps!

The depth of grooves varies with caliber of course, and I will not set down any standards, but leave you to the decisions of the barrel-makers themselves, as given on the following pages. Bore diameter is naturally the diameter across the bore, or rifling, from land to land, groove diameter the diameter from groove to groove.

Width of lands compared to grooves varies somewhat, the six- and eight-groove barrels having quite narrow lands. Most six-groove barrels have lands approximately two-thirds as wide as their grooves. There is no set rule on this, and apparently no one has ever figured out just what relation land and groove area should be for all our modern calibers.

BARREL BLANK SPECIFICATIONS

J. R. Buhmiller

Caliber	Bore Dia.	Groove Dia.	Rifling Twist	No. Grooves
.22 L.R.	.217 –.2175	.2215–.2225	16″	6
.22 Hornet	.2175–.2185	.223 –.224	16″	6
.22/3000	.2175–.2185	.223 –.224	16″	6
.22/250	.2185–.2195	.2238–.2245	14″	6
.220 Swift	.2185–.2195	.2238–.2245	14″	6
.250/3000	.250 –.251	.2568–.2575	14″	6
.257	.250 –.251	.2568–.2575	10″	6
.270 Win.	.270 –.271	.2778–.2785	10″	6
.30–06	.300 –.301	.308 –.309	10″	6
.300 H & H	.300 –.301	.308 –.309	10″	6
.22 Cal.	Width of Lands,	.075 to .078		
.25		.085 to .088		
.270		.090 to .093		
.30		.105 to .107		

Steel used, Chrome Molybdenum SAE 4150 specification.

J. R. Buhmiller
Kalispell, Montana

Mr. Buhmiller has for a number of years made a business of supplying rifled barrel blanks to gunsmiths, for turning, fitting and chambering in their own shops.

His comments regarding .22 caliber barrels are quoted herewith:

"Regarding the .22 rim-fire, there are two schools of thought. One goes for the old standard groove diameter—.222″ to .223″; the other for a tighter barrel. I make barrels as nearly to customer's specifications as I can, where they indicate a preference. Personally I am strong for a bore diameter of around .2165″ and groove diameter around .2205″ but do not dare make such barrels for any customer unless so specified. My experience is that a tight barrel like that handles modern smokeless ammunition better than the larger groove diameters. Unless ordered differently, I usually fill orders with barrels with a groove diameter slightly under .222″ which is a sort of happy medium and more or less satisfies nearly all gunsmiths or shooters.

"Regarding the high-velocity .22s, there is a good deal of difference of opinion there too. Some men will specify a groove diameter of .2235″ for varmint rifles using .224″ bullets and prove their judgment by submitting very small groups fired at 200 yards. Others will specify groove diameter of .2248″ to .225″ 'Because of accuracy,' so I think very close specifications are not necessary in .22 wildcat barrels, although unless otherwise specified I try to keep mine within the limits listed.

"One good customer is always on my waiting list for any 'oversize' barrels I may have measuring up to .226″ in the grooves, as he says they are very satisfactory and some of his customers ask for deep grooves. In the Hornet caliber, it has been demonstrated that a barrel as tight as .222″ in the grooves will shoot well, but most experienced gunsmiths prefer them between .223″ and .2235″.

"Just why the twist should be 14″ in the high speed .22s and 16″ in the Hornet and Lovell is beyond me. I have made most of my own Swifts and .22/250s with 16″ twist and find them all that can be desired for bullets up to and including the 55-grain weight. Some well-known gunsmiths use the 14″ twist in Hornets, Swifts and .22/250. The advantage of the 14″ twist is that the 60-grain Wotkyns Morse 8-S bullet can be used for long ranges in windy weather."

Mr. Buhmiller does no barrel fitting or gunsmithing work at the present time. His business is completely devoted to the manufacture of barrel blanks. He is a shooter himself, and of course his comments are worth remembering as straight dope.

P. O. ACKLEY
Trinidad, Colorado

P. O. Ackley, Inc. is our largest custom gunmaker. With a large, well-equipped shop, Mr. Ackley produces almost everything desired, from barrel blanks to complete custom rifles. He also manufactures the Ackley quick-detachable scope mount, made on the Turner patent. Operating a small shop in Oregon before the war, he was in government service through the war years, in charge of the Small Arms Division at Ogden Arsenal. After the war he went to Cimarron, New Mexico and opened a gun and barrel shop, but then moved to the larger and less-isolated city of Trinidad, Colorado. Here he developed the large and progressive business now in existence. He attempted to run a GI training program, teaching gunsmithing in his own plant, but found he could not keep up the quality of the production, so ceased this line. However, the college at Trinidad instituted a course in gunsmithing, with Mr. Ackley as head of the staff.

The latest Ackley venture is into bullet-making, this being the controlled-expansion bullet featuring a solid copper base. The bullets are turned from solid stock in somewhat cylindrical form, with one end hollowed deeply. A lead slug is inserted in this hollow, then the assembly is swaged to bullet shape, with pointed lead nose. The rear section of the bullet is solid copper or rather, copper alloy, which cannot blow up at any range at any velocity now attainable, while the soft lead and thin-jacketed tip can expand readily. No matter what happens to the tip, the base remains a solid one-piece slug.

In addition to covering practically all phases of barrel work, several Ackley cartridge improvements have been made, principally in the reforming of standard cases to improve ballistic performance. Constantly striving for progress in rifle development, considerable experimentation has been done with stainless steel barrels to the end that Ackley can now furnish dependable stainless barrels, or blanks. To blue these barrels both for production and for customers, a system has been set up, using the PX formula furnished by the Heatbath Corporation. Mr. Ackley advises me that the setup required is more expensive and not practical for small shops, so that he will refinish stainless barrels for other gunshops or concerns.

The present stainless steel is Type 416, with some molybdenum. This machines quite well. Regarding barrel steels in general, Mr. Ackley advises the following:

"We have found it impossible to predict what any particular type of steel will amount to, after it has been made into a barrel. There seem to be a lot of factors which are more important than the material itself, and also, certain alloying elements are doubtless of value. I feel that the tensile strength and freedom from stresses are more important than the analysis itself.

"All of our experience with tool steel has been poor—we have never found any advantage in it in any way, unless graph-mo might wear very slightly longer. Then, graph-mo has the very bad characteristic of being very susceptible to rust. In fact, if government primers are fired in a graph-mo barrel, it takes days to get it cleaned, and if it is set away without being thoroughly protected, it is very apt to be ruined by rust. This tendency to rust is much greater than you might think. The steel seems to almost have an affinity for rust, which is hard to explain. So that characteristic lets graph-mo out entirely, and it is extremely hard to work, which is true of all tool steels. I can find nothing in their analyses to warrant their use as barrel steels over the regular alloy types.

"We always attempt to use a steel rather high in manganese, at least a steel with 1.25 manganese, for good machinability. Manganese also probably helps to get a more uniform heat treatment throughout the bar so that it will not be hard only on the outside. We have had batches of steel shipped to us which tested 340 Brinell on the surface but when tested in the center portions sometimes showed 100 points less. Manganese has a tendency to do away with this. Most likely molybdenum, nickel or similar alloying elements increase the wearing qualities slightly, but this increase might be so slight that such barrels would not live up to the advertising put out about them. I say this because I have made two barrels from the same bar of steel and chambered for the same or similar calibers, with one barrel going many thousands of rounds while the other shoots out in a relatively few rounds, and for all we could tell, the two bores were identical. Tests with stainless steel seem to indicate that this type might give longer wear. Chrome and nickel always seem to increase wearing qualities and of course are present in greater amounts in stainless steels.

"Our standard barrel steel is very similar to 4150 but has a higher content of manganese so that it is actually a high carbon, high manganese chrome moly steel. It has approximately 55 points carbon and 1.25 manganese. The Brinell is 280, but we are trying to get the same material heat-treated to 340 and if it turns out as we expect it to, we will standardize on it for the future. This will be a special steel, supplied by the Crucible Steel Company."

BARREL SPECIFICATIONS

P. O. ACKLEY

Caliber	Bore Dia.	Groove Dia.	Rifling Twist	Number of Grooves
.22 L.R.	.217	.223	16″	4 & 6
.22 Hornet	.219	.224	14″	4 & 6
.22/3000	.219	.224	14″	4 & 6
.219 Zipper	.219	.224	14″	4 & 6
.22/250	.219	.224	14″	4 & 6
.220 Swift	.219	.224	14″	4 & 6
.228 Ackley	.220	.226	10″	4 & 6
.250/3000	.250	.257	14″	4 & 6
.257	.250	.257	10″	4 & 6
6mm	.236	.242–.243	10″	4 & 6
6.5mm	.256	.263	10″	4 & 6
.270 Win.	.270	.277	10″	4 & 6
7mm	.276	.284	10″	4 & 6
.30–06	.300	.308	10″ & 12″	4 & 6
.300 H & H	.300	.308	10″ & 12″	4 & 6
.375 H & H	.368	.375	10″ & 12″	4 & 6

		6 Groove	4 Groove
.22 Cal.	Width of Lands	.028	.043
.25		.032	.049
.270		.035	.053
.30		.039	.059
.22 Cal.	Width of Grooves	.084	.129
.25		.096	.147
.270		.105	.159
.30		.117	.177

Either four or six groove barrels are furnished, as ordered, and to whatever twist is desired, besides the ordinary standards listed.

BLISS TITUS
Heber, Utah

Bliss Titus is one of the most skillful barrelmakers we have ever had. With a background of work in Springfield Armory and the Remington Plant, he went into private barrelmaking himself after World War II. His barrels are very smooth and beautifully rifled, and are rapidly gaining a reputation for above-average accuracy. I have used a considerable number of his barrels and have yet to find one which was not above expectations.

Mr. Titus concentrates on center-fire calibers and does little gunsmithing beyond bolt-altering, blueing and scope mounting.

In an effort to aid left-handers and lever action adherents who desired a better hunting cartridge, he came up with the .270 Savage, which betters both the .250/3000 and the .300 for medium game purposes. This is suited to the Model 99 Savage rifle for which he furnishes barrels. The cartridge closely approaches the .270 Winchester for performance, with such accuracy that a number of bolt-actions have been rebarreled for it.

His views on rifles and rifle barrels coincides quite closely with my own—Bliss states that he feels a rifle barrel should be made to fit the individual needs of the shooter, as concerns the purpose for which the rifle will be used and the environment it will be used in. A mountain hunter should have a light rifle, because he gets plenty tired just carrying himself around, let alone a couple of extra pounds of iron and wood. Bliss says that by his own experience, he is convinced that anyone doing woods and brush-country hunting needs the shortest barrel he can use with his caliber, and also a light rifle, in order to swing it fast on quick snap-shots. The man hunting in open or rolling country, or doing much of his climbing on horseback, can use a heavier, longer-barreled arm. The target man and vermin hunter can write his own ticket on barrels, as he presumably knows under what circumstances he will use it.

To quote directly from Mr. Titus. . . .

"I think that equal distribution of metal on the outside of a rifle barrel is almost as important as an even-cut straight bore inside. That is, the wall thickness should be equal and the taper constant, regardless of how small the muzzle diameter or the diameter of the breech end. At least, in doing this, we do almost all that can be done to smooth out barrel vibration which is one of the big reasons why some barrels will handle several bullet weights very well and others only one par-

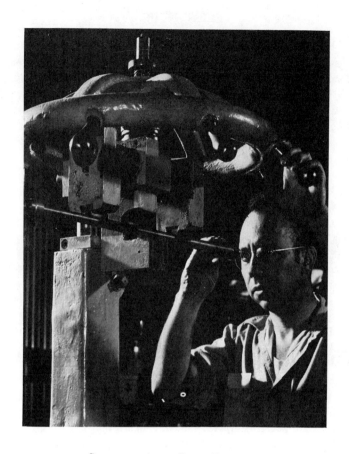

STRAIGHTENING A RIFLE BARREL

Joe Pfeifer, the California riflemaker, checking a preturned blank for straightness. The barrel jack, or overhead clamp, is commonly used for straightening barrels which warp when turned down. With modern steels and careful turning, it sees little use in good shops today.

RIFLING A BARREL

A Pratt & Whitney universal rifling machine, with a few improvements put on by Joe Pfeifer for use in their plant. This is the most commonly used machine of its type in this country, although the design is quite old now. For flexibility and high quality work no better is available.

ticular weight, scattering different weights all over, or shooting to a different point of impact, aside from velocity and weight reasons.

"Probably like most other gunsmiths, I think that the heavier the barrel up to a certain point the more consistently accurate it will be.

"I probably chose gunsmithing for the same reason many other gunsmiths did, because I liked it and loved to shoot. Right after the First World War a great many shooters bought Krag rifles through the N.R.A., including myself, with a couple of cases of ammunition for it. The first fall after receiving it, I went deer hunting along with three other fellows, all using the long Krags. In the heavily-timbered country we hunted in, we saw plenty of deer, but none of us took any home. We couldn't swing those long Krags fast enough to get a shot. As soon as we returned home, I took a hack-saw and cut my barrel to 24″, squared the muzzle in a lathe, and fitted a new front sight. I was crazy and had ruined my gun, according to my hunting companions. However, when tested, the 24″ barrel grouped as well as the old 30″ length did, of course. This was practically the start of my gun career, as I shortened probably a hundred or more of those long Krags thereafter.

"As things went on, I could see that to get very far in the advanced gunsmithing business a person must be a good toolmaker, so I got what machines I could and studied everything I could get on tool and die-making and gun work. I then learned the barrelmaking business in Rock Island Arsenal, but I would still say that toolmaking comes long before anyone should attempt barrelmaking."

BARREL SPECIFICATIONS

BLISS TITUS

Caliber	Bore Dia.	Groove Diameter	Rifling Twist	No. Grooves
.22 R.F.	.2175	.222 to .2235	16″ to 20″	6
.22 Hornet	.2175	.224 to .2245	14″	6
.22/250	.2175	.224 to .2245	14″	6
.220 Swift	.2175	.224 to .2245	14″	6
.22 Savage	.219	.226 to .2265	12″	6
.250/3000	.250	.257 to .2575	14″	6
.257	.250	.257 to .2575	10″ & 12″	6
.270	.270	.278 to .2785	10″ & 12″	6
.30–06	.300	.308 to .3085	10″ & 12″	6
.300 H & H	.300	.308 to .3085	10″ & 12″	6
.22 Cal.	Width of lands, .040		Width of grooves, .076 to .080	
.25	.046		.080 to .085	
.270	.051		.090 to 0.95	
.30	.057		.100	

Steels used: Carbon, and Chrome-Molybdenum-Manganese alloys.
            Maxel 3½—Slightly difficult to machine.
            Hy-Ten B. 3X—Machines and cuts very well.

Both these alloy steels are similar in analysis, and are heat-treated and normalized to relieve strains. They are drawn to approximately 285 Brinell, or 29 Rockwell C. Tensile strength is 137,000 pounds and yield point of 120,000 pounds. The Hy-Ten alloy is used in some military barrels.

Manganese makes a close-grained steel, but one slightly hard to cut smoothly. The alloys are used to make erosion-resistant bores.

PFEIFER RIFLE COMPANY, INC.
11252 Penrose St.
Roscoe, Calif.

Joseph Pfeifer has long been in the barrel business, but only within the past few years become nationally known. He now has a very excellent modern shop and a staff of competent workmen, with the most efficient operating system I have yet seen in any gun plant. Custom gun work is placed on a production-line basis as much as possible.

The Pfeifer line includes turned and unturned rifled blanks as well as finished custom barrel jobs and complete tailor-made rifles. Practically any caliber, .22 and larger, is made, including muzzle-loader and pistol blanks, and special twists can be made to order as well as eight-groove barrels.

Joe started young, and today is our youngest big-time barrelmaker, which is good on account of he will probably last awhile. His barrels are top quality, smooth and clean-cut, and are meeting with the approval of the new fraternity of bench-rest shooters. Meaning their accuracy is of the very highest rating. Over 100 different chambers are available, including some of the old black powder ones still retaining some popularity, such as the Sharps line, .38–55 and .45–70. As with Ackley, the Sharps-Borchardt action is a favorite of Pfeifer's, and he is able to do almost any conversion work possible with this action.

A skilled toolmaker, Mr. Pfeifer makes his own rifling heads and barrel tools, as well as custom single-stage trigger assemblies of the finest tool steel. He makes some of his own chambering reamers, but on the matter of these, works very close with Red Elliott, who furnishes most of the reamers used.

F. K. Elliott is our foremost reamer and chambering expert, his finishing reamers being practically perfect. Pfeifer thus can guarantee smooth, clean chambers in his barrels, with uniformity within each caliber. The hand-loader appreciates being able to use cartridge cases fired in his old barrel in his new one.

Chief stock man at Pfeifer's is D. J. Kennedy, one of the best in the West. He is expert at bedding a rifle for accuracy, being a shooter himself. A good supply of foreign and domestic wood, in as good qualities as can be had today, is kept on hand, and an electrically-controlled drying chamber is used to season doubtful blanks before using.

Of all the custom gun and barrelmaking firms at present in business, the Pfeifer Rifle Company appears most likely to take the place of the old Niedner Rifle Corporation as the ranking quality outfit for all phases of gunmaking. Pfeifer's rifles not only look right, but shoot right.

BARREL SPECIFICATIONS

PFEIFER RIFLE CO., INC.

Caliber	Bore Diameter	Groove Diameter	Recommended Rifling Twist	Number of Grooves
.22 L.R.	.217″	.2225″	16″	6
.22 Hornet	.217–218	.223 –2235	14	6
.218 Bee	.217–218	.223 –2235	14	6
.219 Zipper	.218	.2235–224	14	6
.22 Wasp	.218	.224	14–16	6
.22/250	.218	.224	14	6
.220 Swift	.218	.224	14	6
.250/3000	.250	.257	14	6
.257	.250	.257	10–12	6
.270 Win.	.270	.277	12–14	6
7mm	.276	.284	10	6
.30–06	.300	.308	12–14	6
.300 H & H	.300	.308	14	6
.35 Whelen	.350	.357	16	6
.375 H & H	.368	.376	14	6

.22 Cal.	Width of Grooves, .085″
.25	.097
.270	.105
7mm	.110
.30	.118
.35	.128
.375	.134

Steel used in center-fire barrels above—Oil hardening high carbon-manganese-molybdenum alloy.

W. A. SUKALLE
Phoenix, Arizona

Bill Sukalle has been making barrels for a considerable number of years and enjoys a solid reputation as an outstanding custom rifle-maker. Literally everything in the way of metal-working except engraving can be furnished. Custom jobs such as special triggerguards, safeties and scope mounts can be supplied, as well as barrels. Sukalle is the only American barrelmaker at present able to make barrels with integral top ribs.

His scope safeties for the Springfield action are the best designed I have seen, and his front sight ramps, previously mentioned, are among the handsomest. These items can be purchased by other gunsmiths. At the present time Sukalle cannot do special alteration work except on rifles being rebarreled in his shop.

BARREL SPECIFICATIONS
W. A. SUKALLE

Caliber	Bore Dia.	Groove Dia.	Rifling Twist	Number of Grooves
22 L.R.	.2175	.222	16″	6
.22 Hornet	.2175	.2235	16″	6
.218 Bee	.2175	.224	16″	6
.219 Zipper	.2175	.224	16″	6
.22/250	.2175	.224	14″	6
.220 Swift	.2175	.224	14″	6
.250/3000	.250	.257	14″	6
.257	.250	.257	10″	6
6.5mm	.256	.263	9″	6
.256 Newton	.256	.264	10″	6
.270 Winchester	.270	.278	10″ & 12″	6
7mm	.276	.284	10″	6
.280 Ross	.280	.289	10″	6
.30–06	.300	.308	10″ & 12″	6
.300 H & H	.300	.3085	10″ & 12″	6
.35 Whelen	.350	.3575	12″ & 14″	6
.375 H & H	.367	.3755	12″	6

.22 Caliber	Width of Grooves, .045	Width of Lands, .028
.25	.076	.055
.270	.094	.059
.30	.095	.062
.375	.112	.080

Steel used—Heat-treated Chrome-Molybdenum to 265 to 305 Brinell hardness.

STANDARD RIFLING DIMENSIONS

The following table gives common bore measurements for the cartridges listed, without tolerances. It is intended only for quick reference in identifying unmarked or doubtful firearms.

Caliber	Make	Bore Diameter	Groove Diameter	Twist of Rifling
.22 Short	All	.218	.223	20"
.22 Long Rifle	All	.218	.223	16"
.22 WRF	Winchester	.219	.226	14"
.22 WCF	Winchester	.218	.2235	16"
.22 Hornet	All	.218	.2235	16"
.218 Bee	All	.218	.224	16"
.219 Zipper	Winchester	.218	.224	16"
.22/250	Private	.218	.224	14"
.220 Swift	Winchester	.219	.224	14"
.22 Savage	Savage	.221	.226	12"
6mm Lee	Winchester	.236	.243	7½"
.25 Stevens R.F.	Stevens	.2495	.257	17"
.25–20 WCF	Winchester	.250	.257	14"
.25–20 S.S.	Winchester	.250	.257	14"
.25–35 WCF	Winchester	.250	.257	8"
.25–36 Marlin	Marlin	.250	.256	9"
.25 Remington	Remington	.250	.257	12"
.250/3000	Savage	.250	.257	14"
.257 Roberts	All	.250	.257	10"
6.5mm Mannlicher	Steyr	.256	.263	7½"
.256 Newton	Newton	.256	.264	10"
.270 Winchester	Winchester	.270	.278	10"
7mm Mauser	Mauser	.276	.285	8.66"
7mm Mauser	Private—USA	.276	.284	10"
.280 Ross	Ross	.280	.289	8.66"
.30 WCF (30–30)	Winchester	.300	.308	12"
.30 Remington	Remington	.300	.308	12"
.30 US (30–40)	Springfield Armory	.300	.3085	10"
.30–06	Springfield Armory	.300	.308	10"
.30 Newton	Newton	.300	.309	10"
.300 Savage	Savage	.300	.308	12"
.300 H & H	Winchester	.300	.308	10"
.303 British	British	.303	.312	10"
.303 Savage	Savage	.300	.308	12"
.32–20 WCF	Winchester	.300	.311	20"
.32–40	Winchester	.312	.320	16"
.32 RF	Stevens	.2985	.314	25"

Caliber	Make	Bore Diameter	Groove Diameter	Twist of Rifling
.32 Remington	Remington	.312	.319	14″
.32 Win. Special	Winchester	.315	.320	16″
.32 Win. S.L.	Winchester	.312	.321	10″
8mm Mauser	Mauser	.312	.324	9½″
.33 Winchester	Winchester	.330	.338	16″
.348 Winchester	Winchester	.340	.348	12″
.35 Winchester	Winchester	.350	.358	16″
.35 Remington	Remington	.349	.356	16″
.35 Win. S.L.	Winchester	.344	.351	12″
.351 Win. S.L.	Winchester	.345	.351	16″
.35 Whelen	Private	.350	.3575	14″
.35 Newton	Newton	.350	.359	12″
.375 H & H	Winchester	.368	.375	12″
.38–40 WCF	Winchester	.395	.400	36″
.38–40 WCF	Remington	.395	.400	20″
.38–55	Winchester	.370	.379	36″–20″
.38–56	Marlin	.370	.379	20″
.38–70 WCF	Winchester	.370	.380	24″
.38–72 WCF	Winchester	.370	.380	22″
.38–90 WCF	Winchester	.370	.380	26″
.40–50 Sharps	Winchester	.397	.404	18″
.40–60 Win.	Winchester	.397	.404	40″
.40–65 Win.	Winchester	.397	.403	20″
.40–70 Win.	Winchester	.397	.403	20″
.40–82 Win.	Winchester	.397	.403	28″
.40–90 Sharps	Winchester	.397	.403	18″
.40–110 Win.	Winchester	.397	.403	28″
.400 Whelen	Private	.400	.410	14″
.401 Win. S.L.	Winchester	.400	.408	14″
.405 Win.	Winchester	.405	.413	14″
.44–40 WCF	Winchester	.4225	.429	36″
.45–60 Win.	Winchester	.450	.457	20″
.45–70 U.S.	Springfield Armory	.450	.457	22″
.45–75 Win.	Winchester	.450	.457	20″
.45–90 Win.	Winchester	.450	.457	32″
.45–125 Win.	Winchester	.450	.457	36″
.45–3½″ Sharps	Sharps	.450	.458	18″
.50 Sharps	Sharps	.500	.509	36″
.50–95 Win.	Winchester	.500	.512	60″
.50–110 Win.	Winchester	.500	.512	54″
.50–70 U.S.	Springfield Armory	.500	.515	42″
.505 Gibbs	British	.495	.505	16″

Pistols & Revolvers

Caliber	Bore Diameter	Groove Diameter	Arm	Twist of Rifling
.22 L.R.	.2175	.2235	Colt	14" Left
.22 L.R.	.2175	.2235	S & W	15" Right
.25 ACP (6.35mm)	.2495	.2515	—	16" either
.30 Luger (7.65mm)	.300	.310	DWM	9.85" Right
.30 Mauser (7.63mm)	.300	.310	Mauser	8" Right
.32 ACP (7.65mm)	.300	.311	—	16" L (Colt)
.32–20	.300	.311	S & W	12" Right
.32–20	.300	.311	Colt	16" Left
.32 S & W	.300	.312	S & W	18¾" Right
.32 Colt	.300	.311	Colt	16" Left
.357 Magnum	.350	.357	S & W	18¾" Right
.38 Special	.350	.357	S & W	18¾" Right
.38 Special	.348	.354	Colt	16" Left
.38 S & W	.351	.361	S & W	18¾" Right
.38 ACP	.350	.356	Colt	16" Left
.380 ACP	.350	.356	Colt	16" Left
9mm	.348	.354	Luger	10.6" Right
.38–40	.395	.401	Colt	16" Left
.41	.395	.401	Colt	16" Left
.44–40	.4225	.427	Colt	16" Left
.44 Russian	.4225	.427	S & W	20" Right
.44 Special	.4225	.427	S & W	20" Right
.45 ACP	.445	.451	Colt	16" Left
.45 Colt	.445	.452	Colt	16" Left
.455 Webley	.450	.455	Colt	16" Left

CHAPTER 14

Chamber and Barrel Work

MEASUREMENT *of Barrels*. In the good old days, the Ordnance Department measured Springfield bores with the "Star Gage." This was an instrument made like a hollow rod, with another rod inside it, this second rod having projections which could expand to contact the groove and bore at any point, and a graduated scale on the handle which could indicate the diameter at any given point. The gage would record barrel interior measurements accurately, so the word "Star Gaged" came to mean a selected barrel, one which had been checked and found to pass required standards of uniformity. It showed up the tight and loose spots, caused by varying hardness of steel (the rifling cutter would cut deeper into a soft spot than a hard one). The star gage tool was very expensive to make and has never been commercially available, so the gunsmith must stick to the old lead slug method.

The general system used is to take a soft cast lead bullet, unsized, several thousandths of an inch larger than the bore diameter, and drive or push it through, from the breech to the muzzle. However, the best barrel men nearly always use a slug of soft lead, cast or cut from heavy lead wire, approximately bore diameter. This is inserted a short distance into the barrel, at either end, then a flat-ended rod is placed in the barrel on each side of it, one rod supported, the other struck with a hammer until the slug is upset and a complete, tight fit in the barrel. The supporting rod is then removed and the other used to push the slug through the rifling. If it moves under a steady tension all the way, the barrel is uniform in diameter. Should it suddenly require added force you have a tight spot, or if it moves easily at a certain point, a loose one. The bore should be carefully oiled before slugging with a very thin oil. Even if it is necessary to pound the rod through with a mallet, you can judge tight and loose spots quite well. The actual push rod should be as near the bore diameter as possible, very smooth and polished, flat-tipped, and with a strong rotating cross-handle you can bear against with both hands and all your weight.

Catch the slug as it falls free of the barrel in a padded box or by hand. It can be measured easily across the raised portion, if the barrel has an even number of lands and grooves, this representing the groove diameter. Bore diameter can be determined by carefully cutting away these projecting fins with a sharp knife and miking the body of the slug.

Measuring a barrel with an odd number of lands and grooves, such as the 1917, is a little harder. The slug will have a land opposite a groove, so cut away the edges of the raised portion of the slug (representing the barrel grooves) on one side until the micrometer can contact the body of the slug. You can now measure the slug across to the opposite groove, finding the bore diameter plus the depth of one groove. Now whittle off more of the slug until you can force it through the bore in any position, rotating it so that it eventually has no engagement with the rifling, but merely fills the bore. Measure it, finding the bore diameter, then subtract from the first measurement, which gives the depth of one groove. Double this, add it to the bore diameter and you have the groove diameter. A mathematician could probably figure out the desired information with a slide rule, but I can barely understand a micrometer, so I do things the hard way.

Measuring Chambers. The sulphur cast is still the standby for chamber measurement as melted sulphur, poured into a chamber, will cool without enough shrinkage to worry about. The chamber and barrel throat are thoroughly cleaned and oiled with a very thin film of light oil. Take a cork slightly larger than the bore diameter, push a piece of fairly stiff wire five or six inches long through it, hooking the end slightly so it will hold in the cork. With a rod push the cork through the barrel until it is from one-half to one inch in front of the chamber, with the wire extending past the breech end of the barrel, closely centered. Clamp the barrel breech up and pour in the cast compound. The Baker mixture was composed of the following:

Sulphur	2 ounces
Powdered lamp black	3 grains
Gun camphor dissolved in alcohol	2 drops

A simpler formula is—

Sulphur, by volume	10 parts
Ordinary powdered graphite	1 part

The cast material is to be heated very slowly, until it reaches a thin pouring consistency, when it is poured slowly and evenly into the chamber. Enough sulphur is poured, or added as the cast cools, to cause the chamber to be completely filled, over the breech. If the compound is heated too rapidly it will be too thick to pour well. When the barrel is cool, the cast is removed by a rod, pushing against the cork at its bottom end, and from now on it is to be handled by either the cork or the wire handle. Very accurate micrometer readings can be taken from sulphur casts, as they do not shrink more than .0005", miked the day of casting, or .001" after more time has passed.

Mittermeier can usually supply a prepared chamber cast material which is less critical than the home-mixed preparations, but a little practice will enable almost anyone to get satisfactory results with the above formulae.

Chamber casts will reveal peculiarities of individual chamber dimensions and diameters, and are of considerable value in identifying the proper cartridges for unknown guns, but are of little or no value concerning that most important of all chamber measurements—

Headspace. The term itself is rather ambiguous today, for the word comes from the old rim cartridge days, signifying the distance or space between the face of the bolt or the breechblock and head, or the base of the cartridge. The modern rimless bottle-neck cartridge is stopped in forward movement by the cone or the slope of the shoulder, so your "headspace" is actually "shoulder space," if you want to be technical about words.

Rimmed cartridges are headspaced from the forward point of the rim recess in the chamber to the face of the bolt or block. While rim thicknesses vary considerably in manufacture, the rimmed case is almost foolproof as regards safety in headspacing, for the rim prevents excess forward movement of the case in the chamber. Semi-rimless cases, such as the .220 Swift and the 6.5mm Japanese retain some of the safety of the rimmed case, but headspace should be governed on such cartridges by the shoulder, as in the true rimless case.

Rifles for Magnum belted cases are, theoretically, to be headspaced from the front of the belt recess to the face of the bolt, similar to rimmed cartridges, and most of the wildcat cartridges based on these cases employing the fire forming system depend on the belt acting as a rim, while the chamber itself may not touch the case between the belt and the neck. When new, or perfect used cases are used, with belts of original size and not mutilated or worn to any extent, the method is perfectly safe, but some people can beat up these belts until they are thoroughly out of shape and in no condition to be considered a governing factor in headspace control.

The true rimless case, such as .250/3000, .30–06 and 7.9mm Mauser, must be accurately and carefully headspaced from the face of the bolt to the upper corner of the shoulder, which is the point of measurement, and also the center of the shoulder slope. Most factory drawings of cartridges and chambers show a dimension from the base of the cartridge or the bolt face to the center of the shoulder, which is the contact point of the cartridge shoulder and the chamber shoulder.

A good many commercial rimless cartridges have been measured in the past by both methods, that is, from the base to the corner of the shoulder, and from the base to the center of the shoulder. This is of course the safest method as it allows better headspacing of undersized cartridge cases, which if smaller in diameter at the shoulder could move further forward in the chamber unless arrested by the chamber shoulder. The U. S. Arsenals formerly measured the .30–06 headspace from the base to the upper corner of the shoulder (which is recessed on gages, so that an actual physical corner does not exist) but they have changed over according to the following letter I received from the Winchester Repeating Arms Company:

"Generally speaking the headspace of all rimless cartridges is taken from the face of the bolt to a determined point of the angle of the shoulder between the neck and the body. This is true on the .250/3000, .257 and .270 to which you specifically refer. This is also true on the .30–06 as the Ordnance Department in 1946 adopted the commercial system of measurement and the latest drawings of the cartridge case give a dimension from the head of the shell to a point midway on the shoulder angle as well as the dimension to which you refer from the face of the bolt to the upper corner of the shoulder."

So, on a modern rimless case, actually two headspace measurements are considered, although gages of course will be marked for one. The .30–06 and .270 gages (identical) will no doubt continue to be stamped as in the past, but other caliber gages will carry the measurement from the base to the center of the shoulder, the shoulder of course being made the correct angle to insure support at the corner of the shoulder. With all the experimentation being done on changing shoulder angles, increasing body length and so forth, a lot of rifles are going to be headspaced with cartridges, the chambers being shaped to support some part of the existing cartridge shoulder only with cartridge cases altered and sized so that they will be held securely enough for fire forming. For such guns, special gages are only to be made up when a number of rifles are to be built.

CHAMBERING

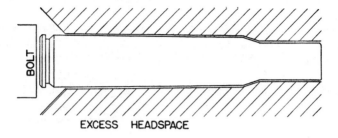

EXCESS HEADSPACE

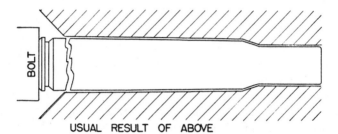

USUAL RESULT OF ABOVE

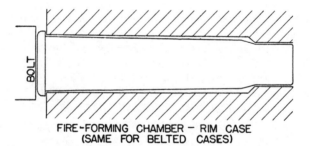

FIRE-FORMING CHAMBER — RIM CASE
(SAME FOR BELTED CASES)

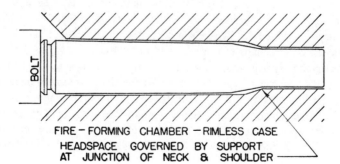

FIRE — FORMING CHAMBER — RIMLESS CASE
HEADSPACE GOVERNED BY SUPPORT
AT JUNCTION OF NECK & SHOULDER

CHAMBERING

Shown are our three types of chamber, the top two standard though incorrect, and the two types of fire-forming chamber. Top to bottom, we have . . .

Rimless chamber, with excess headspace. Incorrect, of course. The cartridge either under feeding impetus or firing-pin fall moves forward into the chamber, the base leaving the face of the bolt. The thin walls ahead of the base will expand and grip the chamber walls when the cartridge is fired, and the unsupported base will blow off and back against the bolt with great force, allowing quantities of gas to come back through and around the bolt.

Result of firing cartridge in above circumstance. The cartridge case expands and grips the walls of chamber ahead of the solid rear portion, and the latter, being unable to expand, is forced back by internal pressure and is broken from the remainder of the case. Gases are then free to pour back through the rupture and into the action of the arm, to possibly "blow it up." Cartridge cases will occasionally rupture at approximately this same point through repeated resizing and reloading, even though headspace is correct. Under these circumstances there is no danger to rifle or shooter, although such cases should not remain in use.

The fire-forming chamber, for rimmed cases. This is quite safe compared to the rimless forming chamber as headspace is normal and the gas seal of the case fully dependable. The only trouble is when chamber is too large at the shoulder and case is called upon to expand beyond its capabilities, in which case it splits at the shoulder and allows gas to escape around it. This ruins the case, but unless it happens many times in exactly the same place, will not injure the chamber. Belted cases are almost as good as rimmed for forming, as they headspace in the rear safely. P. O. Ackley and Russell Hightower have worked out a method for putting belts on government .30–06 cases which permits them to safely make very high-pressured cases through fire-forming after initial shaping to .22/250, .257 or similar cases.

Bottom is the rimless cartridge fire-forming chamber. A ticklish business, for the case must be supported by the neck only, at junction of neck and shoulder, that is, possibly aided by strong extractors in a few cases. Should the newly-reamed chamber be a trifle long, or the chamber neck be a bit oversize, or the case length be a bit short, the standard cartridge may go a mite deeper into the re-formed chamber than necessary, thus creating what amounts to an excessive and dangerous headspace condition with a result similar to that shown in the second sketch.

A condition similar to that shown in the two bottom sketches can also be brought about by excessive resizing of a fired case or case neck, pushing back the shoulder of the case until it seats improperly in the chamber of the gun. Where a rimless case is used, and reloaded with full charges, this condition should be guarded against.

Any shop fitting barrels for rimless cartridges should have go and no-go gages for all the calibers handled as standard items, but the general shop, not doing barrel work, needs only .22, .30–06 and 8mm Mauser (8 x 57) for checking odd rifles. A lot of the present-day sportsmen are aware of the importance of headspace and want their Springfields, Enfields and Mausers so checked before they use them.

I probably check at least 200 rifles a year, as a safety measure, and find that most Mausers run very close to maximum, or actually will swallow the no-go gage, even when the rifle is a unit—all original parts, numbers matching. Apparently the Germans believed in long headspace, and must have had field service gages somewhat greater than my European military maximum gage. Practically all Mausers made outside Germany have closer tolerance and I have never found a complete original rifle of this class which will take my maximum gage. On the German-made arms I pass as safe all that do no more than allow the bolt to barely close on the no-go, because if the Krauts could shoot their wicked military loads, we can shoot hunting ammunition. Besides, I have two military Mausers which I have tested thoroughly and found safe, even though one has quite a bit excess—more than I will pass on most customer's guns. The British 7.92mm gages for the cartridge we call 8 x 57mm, are 47.22mm minimum, 47.47mm maximum; in inches, 1.8590" and 1.8669". I also have German gages, one approximately .003" longer than the British maximum, and a set of Forster Brothers American gages.

Many small gunbuilders do not have a full supply of gages, and use cartridges to check headspace, which is, of course, a poor practice. I know of at least three .257 rifles which came to my attention during the past year which would accept only Remington-made cartridges, that were undersized compared to Western- or Winchester-made .257s. Obviously the barrelfitter had used a few old Remington cartridges for gages, as the chambers would not take the minimum .257 gage. It is possible to obtain a safe and satisfactory headspacing by means of cartridges, but a large number of cartridges are necessary, trying all four makes—Peters, Western, Remington and Winchester. If possible the cartridges should be tried in another rifle of the caliber concerned, to find those few which require a slight pressure to fit. And it is a very smart stunt to pull the bullets in a loading tool bullet puller or in a loading tool such as the Pacific or Universal, holding the bullet with pliers and pulling the case away from it with the regular shell holder. The body of the case and the neck should not be deformed in any way. The reason for pulling bullets is that a new barrel, until throated, will

offer considerable resistance to the bullet and therefore give an unre-
liable tension on the bolt handle when the cartridge is seated.

This is your standard—the pressure necessary to close the bolt on a
test cartridge. As a rule, two out of ten cartridges will offer slight resistance in a correctly headspaced rifle. If in chambering, you stop the
finishing reamer, try fifteen or twenty cartridges and if you find perhaps three which need a very little pressure on the bolt handle—that
is all. You do not ream any more, except perhaps the barrel throat or
lead. (Correct spelling of last word is "leed," and it is so pronounced,
not as "led.") All you do after this is polish and lap the chamber.

Twist of Rifling. Factory and the more-or-less standard twist information is contained in the tables in these pages, but some little
discussion is in order. Bullet shape, weight and velocity have a great
deal to do with barrel performance, and barrel twist can determine
performance of a particular type of bullet. Generally speaking, the
longer the bullet, the lower the velocity and the faster the turn of twist
required. Some of our most popular cartridges are used in barrels which
could be rifled with different twist to advantage; the .30–06 for instance, has a rifling with one turn in ten inches; most of the .30 caliber
Magnums will do better with fourteen inch twists. The most accurate
.30 caliber rifle I know of is a 34″ barreled .30 Newton bullgun, with a
14″ twist. It operates in one-half minute of angle, using 180-grain
bullets.

Our factories go to great pains in testing and experimentation, yet
this matter of rifling twist does not get much attention. On one very
popular caliber, the factory originating it—and they adopted it cold,
not taking it from any wildcatter—simply picked the twist of rifling
out of the air, with no testing whatsoever of different twists, and the
barrels made in that caliber today have the same twist, which gives
satisfactory results, but not quite as good as does a slower twist. Quite
awhile back—1911, I believe—a test man at Springfield Armory found
a batch of rifles which were definitely more accurate than the regular
run. He investigated, and found one rifling machine had a slipped
guide, and was cutting a twist of 11½″ instead of 10″. What happened?
You know—the machine was set back for 10″ twist and the 11½″
twist rifles disappeared.

A fast twist offers greater resistance to bullets and therefore wears
slightly faster than a slow twist. Complicating the matter is the number of different bullets available in most of our calibers. In the .22
center-fires we have heavy and light bullets, and factory twists must
be compromises, to handle both as best they can. In the .25 calibers

we have 87-, 100- and 117-grain bullets—a 14″ twist will handle the 87 and 100 fairly well, but will not stabilize the 117-grain. The .250/3000 Savage has a standard twist of one turn in 14″, the .257 one turn in 10″, so the .257 will better handle the heavy bullet, if it is not pushed too fast. Formerly a half-dozen or more bullet weights were available in factory .30–06 ammunition, but now only three seem to be on the market—the 150-, 180- and 220-grain weights, in different types. The 220-grain is perfectly adapted to the 10″ twist, but the others are over-stabilized somewhat. A couple of years ago I had a .30 caliber Newton barrel made with 12″ twist, intending to use only 150-grain bullets at high-velocity. I figured wrong, though, for it will not shoot well enough with the 150-grain bullets for really fine varmint work—but, it handles 173- and 180-grain bullets wonderfully well, so the next time I have a .30 caliber barrel made for myself, it will have a 14″ or maybe even a 16″ twist.

The rifling must spin a bullet fast enough to stabilize it through gyroscopic action, and not fast enough to over-stabilize it and cause it to "corkscrew" or wobble in flight. A bullet turned too slow to be stabilized loses its balance and keyholes, or turns end over end.

Barrel Fitting. All gunsmiths must or should do some barrel fitting, as a matter of general service in keeping factory-made arms in use. The arms manufacturers will no longer sell barrels for high-powered rifles, but require that the actions be sent them so they may properly fit and headspace the jobs. However, nearly all .22 rim-fire barrels and lever action rifle barrels are available and are easily fitted. These com-pletely finished barrels must of course fit the old receiver as they come, and usually do. Once in awhile you may find an old receiver which al-lows the new barrel to turn in easily and go past the index mark, or sight line, so that sights will not line up. If only a very little past, or just lining up without tension on the wrench, it is possible to set the barrel in tightly by removing it and carefully peening the shoulder of the new barrel, drawing the metal out so that it will offer greater bear-ing surface against the front of the receiver. Should the barrel go too far past for lining up by peening, the best thing to do is to make a washer of thin shim stock to go around the barrel shank between the shoulder and the receiver. The threads on the barrel shank can also be set back, as described in Chapter 6. If the barrel will not screw in to the index, you file the shoulder on the barrel back, cutting an even amount off all the way around. The work can be done on the lathe better, but take only a very, very little off at a time. Never file or cut the front of the receiver back—always work on the barrel. One of those

AN EFFICIENT BARREL VISE

A heavy barrel vise and adjustable clamp receiver wrench is used in all barrel fitting jobs by the Pfeifer Rifle Company.

This tool is of their own design—and generally takes them off and on again. Occasionally they strike a receiver that wants to stay put—whereupon the assembly is put in a lathe and a portion of the barrel turned out from where it bears against the receiver; then it goes back into this vise and that receiver comes off easily.

Jaws of soft metal are made for all popular barrel contours and it is seldom that a barrel is marred.

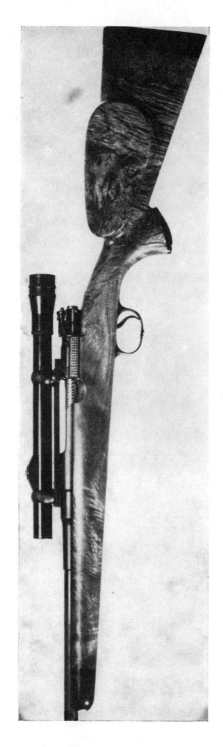

An F. N. Mauser action with trigger altered to meet shooter's grip and finger reach. This stock shows a fine piece of stump walnut with the figure so beautiful that the owner decided that he wanted no checkering on top of it. Can you blame him?

pin-in unthreaded barrels may fit loosely, due to a worn pin or pin-hole. The remedy is to set the barrel in tight against the receiver, clamp it there someway, drill out the receiver and the barrel together for a slightly larger pin and/or put in a sturdy set screw just for insurance.

Replacement of Springfield, Enfield and Mauser barrels is as described above, usually a very simple matter. Not so simple is the matter of holding and use of the wrench. Always clamp the barrel in the vise and turn the receiver. The receiver wrenches for bolt actions have been illustrated, with a barrel vise. Two or three commercial barrel vises are on the market, but it is possible to make your own, as shown in the drawing. It is also possible to use the regular style rigid-base machinist's bench type vise for barrel work, but such a vise, of the size and strength necessary for barrel removal and replacement would cost at least twice as much as a commercial barrel vise. Do not try to remove Mauser or Enfield barrels in your regular four or five inch bench vise, or you will be suddenly picking up pieces of vise from the floor.

The barrel vise or clamp *must* be mounted very rigidly, in cement, or on a very heavy, solid bench. Just as important as a strong, well mounted vise and well fitting wrench are the jaws. These may be of very good grooved hardwood, to be powdered with rosin before fitting to the barrel, or, better, of lead or Babbitt metal, cast to the contour of the barrel involved. The job is to hold the barrel tight enough to prevent it turning when you bear down on the wrench. Jaws should be smooth for fitting finished barrels without marring them, but can be of scored steel for removal of unwanted, unusable military barrels, which are usually set in very tightly. You can cast lead jaws by taking an old barrel and making a mold of clay, or even wood, laying the barrel across the mold and pouring molten metal to half diameter of barrel. A barrel should be clamped as close to the receiver as conveniently possible, to minimize twisting action.

When the barrel just will not unwind, the welding torch can sometimes be applied, the receiver ring over the threads being given a fast heating to expand it slightly. Only a little heat is necessary—not enough to change the color of the metal—but it should be fast, so that the receiver gets the benefit and not the barrel shank. A blowtorch can be used, but it spreads a lot of heat around and does not concentrate it as does the acetylene tip. The heat job is recommended only for extreme cases of course, and for best results two men are needed, one to handle the torch, the other to move the receiver wrench in place and apply pressure the instant the heat is cut off. Should even this

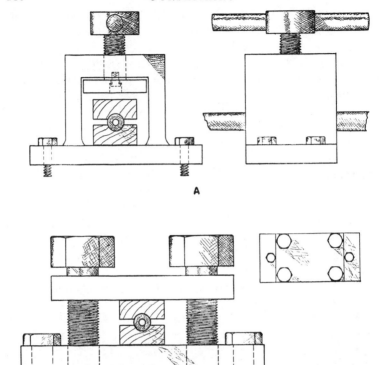

BARREL VISES

A. Welded body vise, with hand screw contact plate, as shown. Make of 1″ stock and attach to strong base.
B. Clamp type vise, adjusted by two large machine screws at least—better with four as shown. It is slower but stronger than "A."

method fail to loosen a stubborn barrel, the only thing left to do is cut the barrel off at the front of the receiver, and bore out the shank on the lathe.

Setting new barrels in bolt action receivers is simply the reverse of removing the old one, naturally, and as a rule is much easier, the principal trouble being keeping the barrel clear of marks from the blocks. Hardwood blocks are almost the only type which will not mar a finished barrel. The ideal fit is to have the barrel thread into the receiver so that it can barely be started by hand but turned easily by a wrench until within $\frac{3}{16}''$ to $\frac{3}{8}''$ of lining up, if going by the index marks on the barrel and the receiver, or approximately one-tenth turn otherwise. It should then tighten until all your strength is required on the receiver wrench, using a 30″ length of pipe for extension handle, to bring the shoulder of the barrel against the receiver ring tightly. The shoulder should seat firmly against the receiver all the way around. This is particularly true of .22 rim-fire match rifles, or any target arm, for that matter. It can be spotted by painting the shoulder with copper sulphate and turning in until the shoulder bears against the receiver lightly, then removed for inspection, the spots showing wear being reduced slightly. As a rule, the barrel shoulders will be more accurately machined than the front of the receivers, on large caliber rifles, so clear the front of the action before fitting the barrel.

Inspection of barrel and chamber interiors reveals unpleasant defects sometimes. In checking any barrel, it of course must be thoroughly clean—a good idea is to dip your final patch in alcohol, which will cut the oil film out of those microscopic corners. Springfield Armory made quite a few barrels around 1938 or 1939 which developed cracks in the chambers, visible as faint lines, parallel to the chamber axis in most cases. Tool marks in barrels are today unfortunately very common and very evident, and nothing much can be done about them, except to hope that the barrelmaker will stone his rifling cutter edges and quit using that rough carborundum wheel! Scoring marks are something else and can hurt the performance of the arm. A rough rod driven or pushed straight through a bore may cut gouges and beat up the rifling, causing it to pick up metal fouling rapidly. A carelessly-handled chambering reamer may get nicked, clog up and tear a ring in the chamber, which can be plenty serious, as it will make extraction difficult.

Any rough barrel will of course foul more easily than a smooth one, as jacket material will be scraped off by tool marks. I think the smartest thing to do with any rough new barrel is to shoot it a couple of hundred times with low-velocity lead bullet handloads. This is a lazy way of lapping, but it helps a lot, especially on center-fire .22s and the .25 calibers.

Lapping. Actually doing a full-scale lapping job on a finished barrel may not be as brilliant an idea as it sounds. The process must necessarily enlarge both the bore and the land diameters as much as twice the depth of the deepest tool mark removed, which obviously would not be desirable in all cases. When a barrel blank is purposely bored

RECEIVER WRENCHES

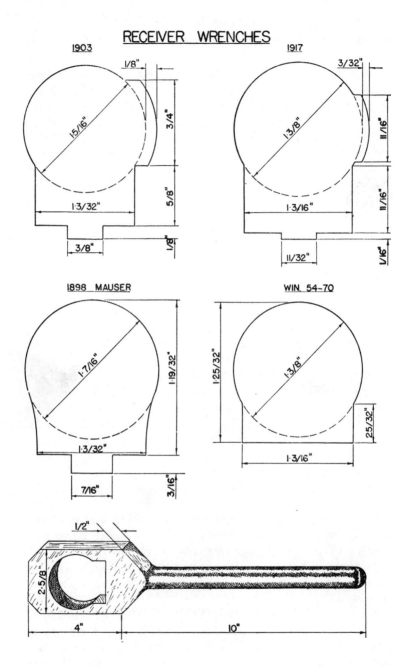

1903

1/8"

1.5/16"

3/4"

5/8"

1.3/32"

3/8"

1/8"

1917

3/32"

1.3/8"

11/16"

11/16"

1.3/16"

11/32"

1/16"

1898 MAUSER

1.7/16"

1.19/32"

1.3/32"

7/16"

3/16"

WIN. 54-70

1.3/8"

1.25/32"

25/32"

1.3/16"

1/2"

2.5/8"

4"

10"

and rifled undersize, then lapped to correct dimensions, you have something. Such barrels are the finest available, as the smooth bore surface offers less resistance to the passage of the bullet, accumulates little metal fouling and because there are few recesses for corrosion and rust to work in, really last longer.

Lapping itself is the process whereby two items are rubbed against each other, with a cutting compound in between them to smooth the surfaces. In metal lapping, it is best to use a soft metal and a hard metal, the softer material being called the "lap," and the principle is that the cutting or polishing substance will penetrate and adhere to the surface of the lap and wear away the hard surface faster than the soft. Lead, copper, bronze, and even cast-iron are used as laps for steel, but for barrel work the lead lap is almost the only kind used. Occasionally, a copper or bronze lap is used to enlarge a bore only, not affecting grooves. Such laps are simply cylinders of metal turned to a push fit in the bore, threaded into the end of a free-turning rod.

The lead lap for both bore and groove lapping is made right in the barrel—a steel rod slightly smaller than bore diameter is used, one end being turned down and notched both lengthwise and crosswise for a distance of $2\frac{1}{4}''$, as illustrated, the other end being set in a strong cross-handle with a ball bearing, so that the rod can turn freely and follow the twist of rifling when pushed through the barrel. Buy a "thrust" bearing, which will not resist turning when forward and back force is applied. This will insure a smoothly-turning rod which is essential. The barrel is cleaned, mechanically and chemically of all fouling and foreign matter, a film of thin oil applied—"cutting" oil

---

RECEIVER WRENCHES

I have not attempted to show complete wrenches, but give you the dimensions for making each type. A boring tool in the lathe makes it possible to cut the receiver ring diameter dimension easily. If you wish, you may allow enough distance over the dimensions given to permit a thin aluminum or brass liner for the wrench opening.

These wrenches are the front engaging type, that is, they go on the receivers from the barrel end.

The small ring Mauser size is not given on the drawing. It is very similar to the '98 except that the diameter of the receiver opening is a shade under $1\frac{5}{16}''$.

At the bottom is a sketch of a finished wrench, with the handle welded on, and minimum measurements added. The handle serves as a base for the heavy duty detachable handle, which is a three foot section of pipe large enough to slip over the integral wrench handle.

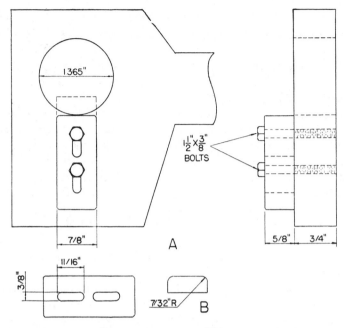

REMINGTON 721–722 WRENCH

On the present Remington action, the recoil lug is not integral with the receiver and so cannot be used as a base for exerting force against to unscrew the barrel and the receiver. The receiver is perfectly round, and the best wrench design for it I have seen is that of Bill Sukalle, the principle of which is shown.

The wrench has a perfectly round hole to fit the tubular receiver, entering upon it from the rear, and a sliding dog to engage the front end of the magazine box recess milled in the bottom of the receiver. This dog is on the rear of the wrench when on the receiver, of course. The dog has slotted holes so that it can be dropped below the edge of the receiver hole to slide under the solid rear portion of the receiver (on bottom) then be raised to engage quite closely in the front of the magazine recess.

A. Represents the complete wrench, face and side views.
B. The sliding dog part, with top portion—that shown as raised portion by dotted lines in figure "A"—being rounded on corners to $\frac{7}{32}''$ radius, to conform to the shape of the front of the magazine cut in the receiver.

In use, the wrench is slid over the receiver, then the dog is raised to position and locked in place by the two $\frac{3}{8}''$ screws, and the receiver screwed on or off the barrel. Handle detail is as on other wrenches.

I believe this is the most practical style of wrench for this model receiver, for I have been told that use of a strap wrench style tool or straight round clamp tool squeezes the receiver tight on the barrel and makes for difficult use.

is fine—a cotton string wrapped tightly around the front end of the rod in the rear cannelure, the tip fluxed and the rod pushed through the barrel from the breech end until the tip is within an inch of the muzzle. Heat the first three inches of the barrel at the muzzle well—until it will scorch cloth, then pour it full of molten lead, this reaching from the string-wrapped point on the rod to the muzzle, around three inches or slightly more. When cool, push the molded lead tip half an inch out of the muzzle so that you may trim off the button on the end and cut a slight chamfer or shoulder all the way around the end.

Now your lap is made for that barrel. It is no good for any other, and not much good for that one if it is ever completely removed from the barrel during the first six or eight passes. Coat it thoroughly with light oil and very carefully push it out through the barrel until from one to one and one-half inches of the lap are visible at the muzzle, and oil that portion. You can now apply your cutting compound—emery flour, crocus or rouge powder, rottenstone—whatever is desired. Only a little powder is used at first, and much oil.

Flour of emery cuts steel quite fast and is used for the initial lapping of rough bores; crocus and rottenstone are polishing mediums and remove almost no metal unless overworked considerably more than in ordinary usage.

The number of times a lap is to be passed through a bore is of course governed by the condition of bore, but one lap may be coated two or three times—only with the same compound—moved perhaps ten times with each coating.

The lap should push through the bore with steady tension. When it moves freely at a particular point, you have a loose spot, and must lap the remaining tight sections with short strokes, in an effort to enlarge them to the same diameter. Do this by making three or four short passes at tight points, then a full pass to check progress.

When you think the barrel has the same "feel" at all points, remove the lap, clean the barrel with solvent, wipe out all traces of the cutting compound and slug it for measurement. When found undersize, you tear the old lap off the rod, cast a new one, and take up where you left off. You also make new laps for the polishing compounds used to give the final inner finish. Naturally, if a barrel is to be lapped a few thousandths of an inch larger, you will have to make two or three cutting laps, as the first will lose its effectiveness as soon as it cuts its limit.

You cannot lap a rusted or eroded barrel to a larger caliber—that is a re-cutting job, which is in the rifling department. For polishing up a rough rifling job, or an undersize one, lapping is the final word, and the final word in lapping is ordinary tooth powder, or calcium phosphate. This will turn the bore into a mirror.

Lapping finished barrels is annoying, because of the care which must be used to protect finish and sights, but it is often necessary. The amount of heat needed at the muzzle will often loosen a soft-soldered front sight, so you have to worry about replacing it sometimes. Never lap from the muzzle, but always from the breech end. If the lap accidentally pops out of the muzzle, *stop* right there and cast another one.

Cutting and Crowning Barrels. The simplest and best way to do these allied operations is to use the lathe. There is more stupid nonsense in gun books about them than any other simple job. Crowning is represented as being a highly technical, painstaking and skilled hand effort. It is plain hard work when done by hand, but by lathe is about a sixty-second pleasant interlude. The "crown" is just the raised area on the muzzle end of a gun barrel after recessing it slightly at the bore, and is a protection against the exposed ends of lands and grooves getting marred, peened or otherwise malformed should the muzzle be struck against a hard object, or vice versa. The rifling must be absolutely true at the end of the barrel for maximum accuracy, of course, and should be protected. The crown can be of any of the types illustrated, but the radius or rounded type is most popular and in general the best-looking.

The lathe can be used to cut barrels, either by a cut-off tool or assisted by a hacksaw used against the turning barrel, and naturally will true the end, making it absolutely square with the axis of the bore —providing the bore is concentric with the outside, which it should be! I have simply ground and stoned a cutter, as illustrated, so that by drawing it straight towards the barrel it cuts the rounded profile desired. For trueing and smoothing the cone at the bore I use one of these perfectly round grinding stones provided for the hand grinder, in a medium grit. If I could get one in a very fine grit for the last polishing, everything would be perfect. As it is, I just hold abrasive cloth against the rounded surface with my finger. Since the finger is too large to press the cutting cloth in the bore far enough to round off edges of rifling, the system is safe. You do not want to make a gradual curve into the lands—they should have a definite angle. By using first coarse, then fine cloth, finishing with crocus, and holding crocus cloth over the ball, the entire crown gets a mirror finish. The whole job takes less time than reading about it.

On those jobs where the size of the barrel or other consideration the lathe cannot be used, you must cut the barrel by a hacksaw in the

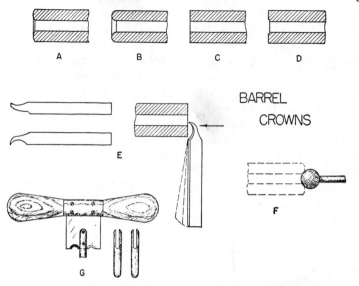

BARREL CROWNS

A. The correct crown, shown in sectioned form. The curve of the crown forms a distinct corner at the junction with the bore.

B. Incorrect crown, curved too much inward, allowing the lands to taper off too gradually at muzzle.

C. Flat muzzle. Okay for test or target rifles which can be protected. Any blow or object disturbing the ends of the lands will affect accuracy.

D. Correct target crown, in the form of a countersink.

E. Lathe cutting tool shaped for barrel crowning, side and top views, and set up for job, the dotted lines representing angles at which the tool can be adjusted to cut any desired crown, the arrow indicating straight line movement of the tool by means of the lathe carriage.

F. Finishing touches, by means of a round brass ball coated with abrasive powder and oil, or a round ball mounted stone from hand grinder accessories.

G. The old hand crowning tool. Removable separate pilots can be used for similar calibers, such as .25 and .270, or .30 and .32, but three separate blades are necessary for all calibers.

vise, file it true, or square with the bore, and crown it by hand. Here is where the old-fashioned crowning "balls" can be used. I use the round grinding stone to really recess the bore, however, wrapping it with abrasive cloth for the polishing and finishing, and filing the outside curve or shoulder using the breast drill to turn it. If you like to make tools and have time, you can make up a crowning cutter as pictured. These are more-or-less limited in the size of the barrel they will cut, but they do a good job of preliminary shaping. The muzzle crowning ball itself should be twice the diameter of the bore, and preferably made of brass or bronze, perfectly smooth on its lower hemisphere. It is used as a lap, being coated with oil and cutting compound, finishing with crocus powder or rouge. The frame of the drill is rotated so that the ball not only feeds fresh oil and cutting material while in motion, but will tend to keep centering itself and cut a true bevel.

Chambering. Cutting a good chamber breaks down to about 60% due to good finishing reamer, 30% to method of using the reamer, and 10% ordinary good sense.

For years, the best reamers were those made by Red Elliott (F. K. Elliott, Ramona, California) who never comes even close to catching up with his orders. His reamers are ultra-precision jobs, made to exact specifications from accurate drawings, and a sample check chamber is cut with each one made before it is shipped out. The steel used at present and in the past is a special tool steel imported from England, which is exceptionally hard and dense. Mr. Elliott considers reamers made from this steel to be capable of cutting from 100 to 150 chambers before requiring re-sharpening. However, because of import troubles, future reamers may be made of American steel, probably the "Star-Zenith" brand made by the Carpenter Steel Company, which is very, very near the English type for strength and hardness. Elliott reamers are perfectly ground and are honed uniformly sharp on all flutes by a honing jig of his own design.

We now have the H. & M. Tool Company reamers, which are also of excellent quality. They are of the Carpenter "Star-Zenith" steel, well-finished and accurate. I am using .30–06 target barrels at present, chambered with an H. & M. reamer, the chambers being practically perfect. Bliss Titus uses many reamers by this company and I have yet to see a poor chamber in one of his barrels.

Finishing reamers are always six-fluted and always cut for the body and neck of the cartridge case. Usually a short leed, or bullet seat, is also cut, but quite a few barrel men prefer to cut the throat separately, using a throating reamer to match a barrel to a particular bullet to give or to allow for long-loaded special cartridges. Roughing reamers may be six-flute, four-flute, or single-edged. The single-edge half-round reamer is easy to make, being turned from good steel on the lathe to dimensions desired, then the section to be used for cutting is milled or otherwise cut to exactly one-half diameter. The single cutting edge is relieved back of the edge, of course. Roughing reamers are solely to hog out excess metal, so that the finishing reamer will not have to do all the work and so will last longer. They cut undersize in all dimensions, naturally. While the finishing reamer and throating reamer must have straight flutes, the roughing reamer may really be anything, even a large twist drill bit ground to shape. In fact, many a gunsmith uses nothing but finishing reamers, and step-drills the chamber instead of roughing it out. Step-drilling means just running in drill bits of different diameters to get most of the metal out of the proposed chamber, and it is possible to do a complete chambering job with a finishing reamer, although this is a slow proposition.

The actual process of chambering differs with arms of different construction. Shotguns, handguns and some rifles require the barrel separate from the receiver for chambering. For most bolt action rifles, particularly those for completely rimless cartridges, it is best to chamber with the receiver and the barrel assembled. Chambers can be roughed out in separate barrels, but finishing requires the assembled arm.

Every known method of handling the chambering reamer (finisher) from brace and bit to drill press has been tried, with most men settling on use of a large lathe eventually. The barrel, with or without receiver attached, is chucked in the lathe, and the reamer forced in with the tailstock, being held from turning by a lathe dog. The reamer is usually not chucked, but is held by the tailstock center which enters the center (cone depression) in the end of the reamer shank. Shank extensions are used most of the time.

This system is considered quite reliable in the matter of over-cutting (reamers like to cut oversize) since the reamer is centered by the bore itself and the barrel and the tailstock can be aligned. It is possible to further reduce the chance of over-cutting by use of the hand only to hold and force the reamer into the barrel, without employing the tailstock at all. This requires a good right arm and a good leather glove! The lathe runs in back-gear, slow.

Stop collars, or just grease pencil marks on the reamer, are used to regulate depth of the chamber until the final cutting is being made. At this time the chamber is of course checked by headspace gages in the regular manner, and the chamber deepened by cut-and-try until the desired headspace is achieved.

A military method, of cutting final headspace only, utilizes a special dummy bolt, through which the chambering reamer passes, its forward movement being limited by adjustable stop collars. This rig can be "set" by closing the bolt section in a similar rifle of known correct headspace, and the reamer moved forward to the limit of the chamber, and then locked that it may move no further forward. The rig is then used to chamber other like rifles, since it will not cut an excess chamber with a normal bolt. This system is suited only to finish-chambering on military rifles. The reamer is turned by hand and the barrel clamped immovably during the job. The whole idea is theoretically incorrect, since the reamer is centered in the receiver, rather than the barrel, and just what makes you think the barrel and receiver are always perfectly concentric? Very often they are not.

It is always best to keep a finger or part of the hand on the shank of the reamer while reaming to prevent chips catching on the flute edges and scoring the chamber. With a little experience it is possible to feel the vibration or drag caused by this condition. How often the reamer must be withdrawn from the chamber, wiped clean, and the chamber cleaned and oiled, is determined by the steel of the barrel. As a rule, the softer the steel, the more often the reamer and chamber must be cleared—sometimes after each couple of turns—because the soft metal comes off in shavings which can clog the reamer, while the harder steels come off more or less in scrapings, which flow away from the cutting edges.

Ordinary cutting oil, lard oil, or thin mineral oil can be used, as for any industrial reaming application. Use plenty. An air compressor, to blow chips down the barrel out of the chamber and off the reamer by means of a high pressure hose nozzle, is highly useful.

The final stages of chambering—the last few ten-thousandths of an inch—are best done by hand alone. It does not take much pressure or very many turns to take out three or four tenths. A topnotch finishing reamer will cut a clean, smooth chamber, but if the reamer has been kicking around with a few other tools and picked up a few tiny burrs and nicks, you are going to have to touch up the chamber to get it smooth and so insure good extraction.

Polishing Chambers. All types of guns turn up with chamber trouble, the chambers usually pitted, scored, or badly machined. On the older .22 rim-fire rifles pitting is common, causing difficult extraction, ruptured cases, stuck empties and the like. Frequently—in fact, practically all the time—the only cure is a new barrel or a setting-back and rechambering job on the old one. Where only light pitting is found in any chamber, polishing will often cure the complaint. Naturally the chamber cannot be enlarged to any appreciable extent, but often just a little lapping will be necessary. Revolvers sometimes turn up with roughened chambers due to firing of old style short ammunition in past years, and considerable lapping can be done to these without affecting the accuracy. Shotguns give little chamber trouble, only needing polishing up every once in awhile, to clean out light rust. The chambers are so big they are easy to clean and oil, so I guess the boys can take care of the obvious as few bad ones turn up. The center-fire bottleneck cartridge rifles are the headaches, rough chambering causing nine-tenths of the extraction difficulties experienced with the high pressure arms. Longitudinal scratches in any chamber seldom cause much trouble, but the slightest "ring" means hard extraction.

Lapping. Lapping a chamber requires a bit of judgment, but not much equipment. The rimmed cases of course have no interior shoulder to govern headspace, and the rim of the case forms an automatic stop for the lap, since you use cases for laps. Take fired cases which will enter the chamber freely, if possible, otherwise new ones; braze or solder a rod into the primer pocket to act as a shank to be checked in the breast drill, coat with oil and lapping compound, insert the case into the chamber and start turning. Keep the cutting mixture away from the inside edge of the cartridge rim. The lap is not pushed into the chamber firmly and spun around, but is to be turned at an even speed and moved in and out for a third of its length constantly.

The rimless rifle calibers headspace on their shoulders and of course if a case is coated with grinding powder and turned in one, with forward pressure, the shoulder is going to move forward and increase headspace. (This is one of the best ways to correct a rifle with insufficient headspace!) So you oil your lap-case and carefully place the powder *not* on the corner of the shoulder. By removing the lap, cleaning it and the chamber every four or five turns, you can eliminate most of the danger of increasing headspace. Usually not much lapping with emery flour is needed, the crocus or rouge being used to polish the chamber walls. These will not remove enough metal to worry about, even though you get tired turning the drill handle. I have never been able to measure an increase in headspace caused by rouge, which I use most. From brass-polishing army days I have a small block of jeweler's rouge which I keep for chamber lapping, as it is so convenient to use. Just oil the case, rub the block of rouge over it, and use it.

Frequently it is not necessary to remove all the scoring, tool marks and rings from a bad chamber in order to cure extraction troubles. A good polishing job will do wonders, even if some defects are left. I once did a lap job on a rifle chamber which had a large and fairly deep tear in it just back of the shoulder. The owner said he had great difficulty extracting fired cases and thought that if it were lapped he would be okay. I worked the drill-lap for an hour and then gave up, polished it and gave it back, saying I could not do anything without enlarging the chamber too much and that he should send it to the barrelmaker for a rechambering job. He did not and is still shooting it, happy with no extraction trouble whatever, in spite of the fact the chamber is technically out of order!

Removing Obstructions. Odd things get stuck in guns. My latest surprise was finding a penny jammed 'way back in an autoloading shotgun action. Most obstructions are barrel jobs, but the ruptured cartridge case hung up in the chamber is still with us. Occasionally a handloader will get his cases mixed up and just neck size when he should full-length size. When the cartridge is loaded into the chamber, it does not quite make it and often hangs up. I have done this myself a few times. Usually the cartridge can be forced out by a cleaning rod from the muzzle without danger, even if you have to beat rather strenuously on the end of the rod. The bullet is forced down into the cartridge case against the powder, but the powder is not sensitive to gradual force. The absolutely safe way to remove jammed loaded ammunition from chambers is to use the barrel clearing drill to cut a hole down through the bullet, after which the powder is shaken out, and force applied to the cartridge.

When a fired cartridge case sticks in a chamber it is usually easily removed by the rod, without involving much force. The barrel is held perpendicular, muzzle up, and the rod lowered until it enters the empty case, then raised a few inches and allowed to fall of its own weight. For field use, an emergency case knockerouter can be made of a four-inch length of drill rod, polished very smooth, chamfered at each end, and if possible, plated with nickel or chromium in order not to rust in the pocket. Diameter is naturally determined by the caliber involved, as the short rod must be a free sliding fit in the bore. In use, the barrel is held up with the muzzle up, the knockout rod inserted most of its length, held between two fingers so that perhaps one-half inch is above the fingers, then hit smartly with the heel of the other hand, driving the tool down through the barrel and against the obstruction— sometimes it works!

Ruptured cases, occurring when a brittle case parts during firing or is stretched too far in a rifle with excess headspace, are not too great a problem to remove. The head of course is gone, and you may find from one-third to two-thirds of the front end still in the gun. The Marble-type expanding broken-cartridge extractor often removes it instantly, but if not available, other methods remain. It is not often necessary to completely cut through the case in order to collapse it—prying the rear edges free of the chamber walls quite often allows enough holding area to reach with the long-nosed pliers. This failing, a large-ended round file can often be turned in the case by hand until it locks in the brass and then can be tapped out from the muzzle. *Do not turn the file into the chamber walls!* The same holds true of the use of taps as case removers.

When I run into a genuine stuck case, I use a V riffler and file it, cutting a groove the length of the case, but not entirely through it, so as not to touch the chamber walls. The grooved case is broken at the cut, using a little tool shaped exactly like a screwdriver without any sharp edges, but quite thin at its point. This tool is not used to pry with, but is forced straight along the chamber wall between it and the case, at one side of the file mark.

Removing an unwilling case from a rifle chamber is very easy, compared with getting it out of a reloading die. When a case is forced into a full length die and the rim torn off in the tool, brothers, it is stuck! I have used everything from prayer to chambering reamers on such jobs and you will too. The boys always have the expanding plug inside, which cannot be removed through the top of the die and allow beating the case out with a punch, so the first thing to do is get out the expander and decapping pin. The simplest method is to drill a large enough hole in the base of the cartridge case to allow removal of the expander, then by using a large sharp-edged rod punch from the top against the shoulder remaining inside the base. If this fails, you put the die in the lathe and cut as much of the case out as you can without touching die walls, then proceed as for a rifle chamber deal. Roughing reamers, as used in chambering, help a lot, as they are enough undersize to prevent damage to the die and yet large enough to remove most of the brass.

An extreme method, which I use on my own dies but hesitate to recommend, is to cut the hole as outlined, removing expander and decapping pin shaft, then solder or braze a plug over the hole. It is then easy to drop a punch rod in from the top and knock the case out. One tool steel die I use for reforming large rifle cases has had this done at least ten times and shows no ill effects whatever from the heat necessary in brazing, but possibly some case-hardened dies might be damaged.

Barrel obstructions can be and are anything from bullets to twigs or weed stems. Rags and stuck cleaning patches are as common as any particular items found in gun interiors. Sometimes a stuck patch can be as much trouble to remove as a bullet; ordinarily, a thorough soaking in oil and a flat-ended, bore-filling rod will drive it out, but once in a great while you may have to braze a wood screw on the end of a rod and pick the cloth out a shred at a time. Such a home-made worm is useful to keep handy, anyway.

Extreme cases may call for heating the barrel, after the cloth plug has been allowed to soak up all the oil it will take. You do not burn the patch out or anything like that, just heat the barrel enough to get it too hot to touch with the bare hand, in order to expand it slightly and thin the oil enough to make it penetrate every portion of the plug. In the old days, gunsmiths sometimes heated a rod red hot and dropped it down the barrel against the patch. I cannot see how this could really hurt anything, but our modern rifles have such small bores that a rod would cool so quickly it would not do much good.

Lead bullets are easy to cut out, by a protected drill, made as follows. Braze a considerably smaller-than-bore diameter drill to a length of rod, and slip a brass or copper tube or sleeve over the drill itself, leaving about one-half inch of the tip free. The sleeve is not only to protect the barrel from the drill bit, but to act as a centering guide. With the rod in the breast or hand drill, the bit will quickly eat through the lead up to the edge of the sleeve. If only one or two bullets are wedged in the barrel, it may not be necessary to shorten the sleeve very much. However, not over one inch of exposed drill should be used. By cutting from both ends, this gives practically two inches of cutting distance, which is sufficient in the majority of cases. The drilled bullets can sometimes be pulled out with a worm, but usually can be driven with flat-ended driving rod without great difficulty. Jacketed bullets are handled in the same manner, but if of the full-jacketed pointed type, drilling must be from the base only.

Before settling down to a couple of hours on the job, pour some light oil in from each end and see if you cannot drive the bullet out—often you can. In pistol barrels you drive from the muzzle end always, and in rifles, as a rule, toward the muzzle. Naturally, if the bullet is just a very few inches from the breech, you drive it backwards.

In driving stubborn barrel obstructions, which can be forced without damage to the barrel, it is best to start with a rod not longer than two inches more than the distance from the obstruction to the end of the barrel from which you are driving. In other words, do not have much rod projecting from the barrel, as it will spring when struck and damage the rifling. Progressively longer rods can be used, or short lengths introduced, as the driving proceeds.

AN OPENED-UP ENFIELD ACTION

The above and the following illustration show a Model 1917 Enfield action, made by Winchester, after it has been modified and opened out sufficiently to handle the .375 H. & H. Magnum, instead of the .30'06 cartridge for which it was originally made.

The British gunmakers are now using this Model 1917 Enfield action entirely for rifles taking their popular big game cartridges, whereas they formerly used the military Mauser and the Magnum Mauser actions for this purpose. However, there are some of the biggest British cartridges which nothing but a Magnum Mauser action, now no longer obtainable, will accommodate.

The alteration shown here was done by Harold G. Rowe, Three Rivers, Michigan, who specializes in this kind of work.

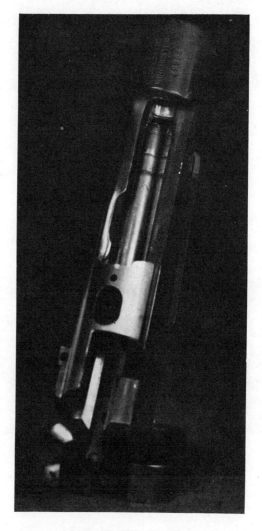

A .375 H. & H. Enfield

The 1917 Enfield action after alteration to take the .375 and similar length cartridges. Note where the receiver has been ground away just ahead of the bullet's nose.

The Model 1898 Mauser action, in standard or military lengths, may be opened-up in a similar manner.

CHAPTER 15

Rifle Action Work

THE word "action" concerning small arms is used as a noun today, to indicate that portion of it handling the feeding, firing and extraction operations—in the case of bolt action rifles, everything except stock, barrel and sights.

The gunsmith of today may be called upon to do anything from cleaning up an action to completely remodeling it. Old single shot actions are popular in some parts of the country for smallbore target arms—the Ballard is about the best—and for varmint calibers, the Winchester highwall and Sharps Borchardt being the best for such high-pressure cartridges as the Lovell and Zipper. The Stevens comes in between, and is not very well suited to either rim-fire or center-fire use at present, although the camming action of the breechblock in the 44 action makes for good accuracy in the .22 long rifle cartridge. The 44½ action is all right for center-fire cartridges consistently below the 40,000 pound pressure class, which considerably limits its use.

Single Shot Action Alterations. As mentioned, the Ballard is—or was, a very few years ago—quite popular for .22 target rifles. Since most Ballards are for old center-fire black-powder cartridges, they must be converted to handle the rim-fire, necessitating welding of the breechblock and cutting a new firing pin hole, as well as altering the firing pin or making a new one. This is not as great a job as would be expected, since the Ballard breechblock is not solid, but composed of two pieces, joined together down the middle. Disassembly readily illustrates what needs to be done. Stronger mainsprings are often desired, and can be made as any other flat type, except that Ballard springs require a lot of shaping to insure full efficiency. In the great majority of conversions, no change is made in the hammer, as it is quite light and falls fast enough to give speedy ignition. The action must breech up quite tightly—but not so tight as to fire a cartridge when the block is closed! Which has happened—and it is quite often advisable to make new pins and screws and link to take the excess movement out of an old action. The extractor can be altered to handle smaller cases than intended by welding on metal and re-shaping. The shape of the Ballard receiver or frame does not allow much freedom of design in the stock, but a satisfactory pistol grip can be attached separately, either to the receiver itself or to the tang of the lever, which can of course be altered to almost any curve or length desired.

Winchester single shots come in several styles, or rather, modifications. The takedown type is of course not too well suited for rebuilding into a super-accurate gun because of the inherent lack of rigidity in the takedown type of construction. The lowside wall action is not suited to any high-pressure cartridge, although many Hornets have been built on them—I had one myself once, before I knew better.

Three types of highside wall are fairly common—the case-hardened action, the thin-walled, and the thick side wall—some of the latter being of very fine steel and able to hold any standard cartridge, even the .30–06. Some actions had coil springs, most of them had flat springs and practically all had heavy, slow-moving hammers. The hammer is usually the first item considered in altering, being skeletonized to decrease weight and increase speed. The simplest way of lightening it is to drill a batch of holes in it.

The lower tang of the receiver may, if of the non-pistol grip variety, be bent downward enough to achieve a close curve for the modern type of target or varmint-rifle stock. The tang can be bent cold, but I think it is better to heat it a dull red and bend by using a piece of pipe or tubing slipped over the end and hand pressure applied. Hammer marks are sometimes annoying to remove. Longer tang screws must be made, and for a truly rigid buttstock fitting a block of steel is made to fit between the upper and lower tangs, drilled for the tang screw and threaded for a stock bolt which is installed as on the modern single barrel shotguns.

The Stevens 44½ action is the only Stevens suitable for any center-fire cartridge and is subject to the same general remodeling or altering as the Winchester.

The Sharps Borchardt remodeling requires some careful work on the firing pin, as in the original form the pin remains forward after firing at times and consequently obstructs opening the action. It is necessary to weld the slots in the breechblock, changing their dimension so that the firing pin is retracted at the very first movement of the lever. When this is properly done, the action gives little trouble. Winchester firing pins can be spring-loaded, and Stevens pins are retracted by the lever before the block moves.

For modern cartridges most Winchester and Sharps blocks must be altered for smaller-diameter firing pin tips. This can be done by bushing or by welding. The bushing system is the better, as when a block is welded its dimension may be decreased quite a bit after polishing down. I do not believe the bushing should ever be more than two-thirds the diameter of the cartridge base. If it is necessary or desirable to make a large bushing, put a heavy shoulder on it, so that the threads will not take all the beating from the cartridge thrust. Since a bushing must be shallow, make the thread as fine as possible, and, while sweating it in will not really make things any stronger, it will make things stay put. I have seen several loose bushings. The bushing is made as a blank plug, of course, and machined or filed off flush with the block face.

Drilling the firing pin hole is where a lot of the boys slip. It is not always proper to have it in the middle of the bushing, where it would appear to belong. Most old actions, after going through the loosening up of use and tightening of remodeling, end up with the block higher or lower than as originally designed. Naturally this can be governed to some extent by barrel fitting, but it is best to make each bushing job an original undertaking. Fit the bushed block to the barrel, so that the action will close with slight tension on three out of four cartridges or cases. Take a long section of drill rod and machine one end to just pass through a cartridge case flash-hole, shaping the tip in a cone. It is to be a full-length center punch. An unprimed case is chambered, the action closed and the punch rod is inserted in the barrel, its tip entering the flash-hole and resting against the bushing. One tap with a light hammer and you have the correct location for the firing pin hole.

Remove the block and drill the hole, parallel to the main hole behind the bushing. Simplest way to get it parallel is to make or find a short rod or pin the size of the firing pin body and insert it in the rear of the block. This can be levelled vertically for the drill press table or chucked in the lathe for lathe drilling. The tip hole must be parallel to the body of the pin, but not necessarily concentric with it—four times out of five it will not be. Do not worry about it. Make the firing pin with off-center tip, easily done by file or by chucking the pin in a three-jaw chuck with shims against two jaws. I have fixed two or three fancy single shot jobs in my time which had always given firing pin trouble, by making new pins a little wopper-jawed on the tip. Stevens pins strike the primer at a very pronounced upward angle, sort of skidding into the primer on the way up. For such rifles, or others with angled firing pins, the tip is not to be rounded, but is to be relieved slightly on its bottom edge, as illustrated. Even on such guns it is possible to make a firing pin which lands in the middle of the primer rather than out on the edge somewhere, as is too frequently seen.

Should a breechblock be badly pitted on its face, or otherwise in bad condition, it may be better to weld than to bush the hole. Take a large drill bit—$\frac{1}{2}''$ in diameter and not over $\frac{3}{16}''$ deep. This is filled by welding rod, and here is a good place to apply arc-welding. Have it welded with an oil-hardening electrode, which can be machined, then heat-treated to maximum strength and wearing quality. So far as the face of the block is concerned, I think welding is better than bushing, but the danger of the sides and back of the block scaling and shrinking slightly is always present. When this occurs, the block usually moves up, if of the "camming" variety. Barrel can be set back to locate block properly, unless a new barrel is being fitted, when of course the trouble is easily corrected.

Single shot actions are like a lot of things—men swear either by them or at them. My own secret thought is that anything you can do with a single shot, you can do better with a bolt action. It is possible to save from three to five inches in overall length of rifle by using a single shot action, but since 99% of the single shot boys want long, heavy barrels, why bring that up? For offhand shooting they can be built to balance perfectly, but there is precious little offhand target work these days open to such rifles.

The Niedner Rifle Corporation, in the two decades preceding World War II, probably made more fine single shot custom rifles than all the other outfits of that period combined. They considered the British-made Farquharson the best of all actions; stating that rifles built on them were always very accurate, while it was always a toss-up on American actions. Rifles on Winchester and Stevens actions sometimes had climbing tendencies, tending to string shots up and down—not always, but sometimes. Several theories were developed, the most reasonable being Tom Shelhamer's—that our actions had considerable locking or lug area below the face of the barrel, that is, the breechblock was supported below the line of cartridge thrust so that pressure against the block was not straight to the rear, but tended to pivot the block in the action causing an infinitesimal movement of the rifle barrel upward. Varying cartridge pressure of course varied the movement and resulted in the up and down group business. It is a known fact that ammunition must be very carefully hand-loaded for good results in single shot rifles.

Reconditioning. Placing either an old or modern action in good condition may call for nothing more than a good cleaning and a little flat-polishing, or it may necessitate the making of new pins, screws and parts. When a hole in a part is worn egg-shaped it may be cleared to a larger diameter and a larger pin or screw made, or the hole may be bushed. In a non-critical part, such as a lifter or link, the hole can sometimes be welded up and re-located. New firing pins can be made of course, or the old ones rebuilt. Notches, sear faces and the like can be cleaned up. In hammer arms the safety notch will often be broken out. It may be possible to use the hand grinder and one of its little cutting discs to cut another notch further up the hammer. If such a notch location is not advisable, the hammer must be built up by welding at the broken point, filed to shape, the new notch cut, fitted, polished, heat-treated and finished. Or a new hammer must be built up by welding at the broken point, filed to shape, the new notch cut, fitted, polished, heat-treated and finished. Or a new hammer made from scratch.

The worst thing to contend with in old actions is sloppiness due to wear of the softer parts and sometimes the receiver or frame slots and surfaces. This can often be remedied by building up metal on the moving parts. Cam angles and spring tensions can also be experimented with to good result.

Trigger Pulls. We had to get to this sometime. First factor is a set of weights. Get a two-foot length of rod—$\frac{3}{11}$", $\frac{1}{4}$"—whatever is handy, and bend as shown in the illustration. Shape up some sort of bottom plug or support for the weights, so that the rod will for convenience sake come out at $\frac{1}{4}$ or $\frac{1}{2}$ pound even. My bare weight rod complete weighs four ounces, and with weights I can weigh any pull from four ounces to eight pounds, by ounces. Make and mark your weights, of scrap lead, cast in an individual pie tin or other improvised mould, $\frac{1}{4}$, $\frac{1}{2}$, $\frac{3}{4}$, 1, 2, and 3 pounds, the last two weights preferably being 2 and 3 pounds minus the weight of the rod, so that when in use, you have an even number to work from. One- and two-ounce weights can be clipped out of sheet lead. Easiest way I know of to cast weights is to get a postal scale, put the mould pan or tin on it, adjust to zero and pour in molten lead to slightly over the desired weight. You must allow for the weight of metal to be removed in the slot for the rod.

Using a trigger weight is harder than making it—many men can snatch off a four pound pull with a three pound weight. The arm is to be held vertically, muzzle up, cocked, and the trigger weight, resting on floor or bench, is to have the trigger arm placed against the trigger with no tension whatever. Then the gun is raised vertically, lifting the weight with the center of the trigger straight up. *It must be raised very gradually.* For absolutely accurate weighing, rest the trigger weights on a yielding surface, such as a pillow or thick block of sponge rubber, so that the trigger receives the weight tension very slowly, as the gun is lifted *very* slowly.

Adjusting a pull may involve several operations. Flat-polishing all metal parts is the first, so that there will be decreased drag on moving sears, triggers, hammers and/or cocking pieces. Pins and screws must be polished round and fit their holes, which should also be round, for best results! Sear contact faces or notches must be clean and square, with sharp edges. Speaking generally, on the hammers, in hammer arms, the angle of sear or trigger notch-face can be governed by the pivot hole—that of hammer screw or pin; lay a straight edge across the hammer, bisecting the hole and see that your notch is in line with the straight edge. The sear contact face should be angled so that it meets this surface squarely. When the trigger is pulled, the hammer should not be cammed back before release and when cocked, the hammer should exert no camming force on the trigger or sear, anyway.

Stoning a notch to shape is a very trying job, for anyone, regardless of experience. Not one skilled man in a thousand can move a hard Arkansas or "slip" stone without rocking it slightly, so provide against rounding the edge. One way is to take one of the cheap iron vises, grind or otherwise relieve the jaws $\frac{1}{16}''$ back from the inner edges, clamp your part with notch flush or slightly above the edges, set at proper angle of course, and then stone it right across vise jaws, which will get the main benefit of the "rocking" of the stone. You still endeavor to move your stone straight across the sear, however; the vise is not a cure-all. Another way is to line up two pieces of $\frac{1}{16}''$ or $\frac{3}{32}''$ flat stock with the notch edges and stone across them.

Bolt action cocking pieces and sears are very easy to work with, but in the final analysis, as in every other type of arm, the short, creepless, "breaking-glass" letoff is attained by cutting down the engagement surface. You can work over the humps on the military triggers till the cows come home, but eventually you will have to cut down the sear top or the bottom of the cocking piece. A least 50% of the military arms—Enfield, Mauser and Springfield—have poorly-fitting bolt, bolt sleeve, and firing pin assemblies, meaning that they are loose in the receiver and wobble up and down when the sear is moved up and down. On these, it is often very dangerous to put a very good final pull, because the cocking piece does not maintain a uniform position. The bolt has less to do with it than the sleeve and cocking piece, so by

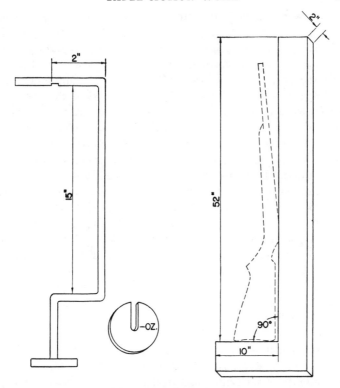

MEASURING ACCESSORIES

Shown above and to the left is a trigger weight rod and weight. The rod dimensions are okay for nearly all rifles and shotguns, and an effort should be made to make this rod come out an even weight, such as four ounces or eight ounces by itself. Lead weights, in the slotted disc form can then be made up in quarter-pound steps to handle any trigger you might get in.

At the right is a wooden pitch check form, preferably made of 2" stock. Mount it on the wall, in an upright position, with the bottom approximately two feet from the floor, as it is easier to use that way.

tightening the latter two so that when cocked and the trigger is moved they do not move until completely released, a very safe final pull can be achieved, however light.

The top edge of the Mauser type sear face describes an arc when rotated downward by the trigger movement and in many arms the angle of sear face and cocking piece face is such that the sear cams the cocking piece and firing pin assembly back when moved. In this case a light pull is difficult because of the tension of the compressed mainspring. The only thing to do is to change the angle of either the sear face or the cocking piece face so that the latter maintains its position while the sear is disengaging. This is a ticklish stone job, calling for the protecting-vise-jaw system, and changing the angle a little at a time, trying the part several times until the desired result is attained. Smoothing up the actual contact faces is easy, since they are quite large flat surfaces. Removal of metal from the top of the sear or the bottom of the cocking piece is the final operation. The sear has a narrow top and should be ground or stoned with a slight angle upward toward the rear. Enfield and Mauser cocking pieces are flat on the bottom and can be stoned easily—some can be filed.

The simplest way to cut down a Springfield cocking piece, or firing pin assembly, to be technical, is to take a short section of ½" round stock, lay it on your large flat stone, set the cocking piece edge on the stone with the firing pin across the round stock, which is now a roller, and move it back and forth. The roller is of sufficient diameter to relieve the bottom of cocking piece as the latter is cut down, and it is almost impossible to cut unequally or at a slant. A few passes with crocus cloth wrapped around a file will polish the surfaces very well, without rounding the edges.

The double-pull, or military takeup trigger, worries a lot of the boys and they want it eliminated. This is a safety feature, and removing the takeup on either Mauser, Enfield or Springfield definitely increases the possibility of accidental discharge. I do not wish to give the impression that the job should not be done, but let us be honest about it. In the hands of any man of normal intelligence a quick pull will not mean any more liability to gun accident than any other—but there are a heck of a lot of guys playing with guns who seem to be considerably below normal intelligence; so, before you give the guy the good pull, look him over and listen to him awhile.

Removing the takeup can be done in any one of a half-dozen different ways. First, you *do not* cut down the sear until the gun fires as soon as the trigger is touched—leave the sear face alone except for final adjustment. Work on the trigger. The little lip on the front which contacts the bottom of the sear and prevents forward movement is the easiest place to start. A drop of brass can be put on it and filed down to the right point; or steel welded on to make this tip longer, then drilled and tapped for a 6–48 screw, to gain an adjustable pull; or a sheet-metal clamp made to obstruct forward trigger movement. The whole idea is to hold the trigger back to approximately the second-pull or letoff point, camming down the sear of course. The same result can be gained by making a slotted plate and placing it between the trigger-guard and stock, held at the rear by the stock bolt. The slot is cut so that it will not permit the trigger itself to contact the front end of the slot in the guard. In some rifles it is possible to place a small screw in the cocking piece runway in the receiver going through to push down the sear. This permits adjusting the pull without disassembling the rifle, and can be done to almost any Mauser. Springfields and Enfields do not have any part of the sear projecting beyond the rear face under the receiver to afford screw contact. They can of course have a bit of steel attached for the purpose.

Arresting unnecessary rearward movement of such triggers after let-off can be done by installing a screw or a pin in the trigger to contact the triggerguard; in guard to contact trigger; or in the front end of the sear, through the sear spring, to bear against the receiver in Mausers and Springfields. A brass or steel plate between guard and stock is the simplest and neatest, requiring no labor to speak of, aside from in-letting a place for it. On these plates, if it is not desired to make it long enough to reach and be held by the rear guard screw, it can be held by a small wood screw.

Tightening up the sleeve and cocking piece is absolutely necessary if any free movement is present. Pins and plungers can be set in the bottom of the sleeve where it rests against the bolt runway, but the better method is to weld on steel and shape the sleeve for a tight fit. Sometimes it is possible to bend or beat in the sleeve edges to hold the cocking piece rigid when in the cocked position, but it may be neces-sary to build a little metal on that item too. The sleeve does not have to be hardened, but do not soften any more cocking pieces than neces-sary. Many of these are not hardened—if so, do not worry about them if they show no undue wear. If they are getting pushed out of shape, clean up the contact surface, case-harden deeply and polish. Some Springfield sears, triggers and cocking pieces are of chrome-vanadium steel, and are not hard, but resist wear very well. These are stamped "CV" so can be easily identified. Mauser cocking pieces should be case-hardened whenever welded on or cut so much that the original heat-treated surface is cut away.

Sear springs have quite a bit to do with pulls, and in most cases it is better to shorten the original spring rather than to replace it with one of less tension. On these no-takeup alterations, a positive sear re-turn is necessary to obtain the complete contact surface allowed and

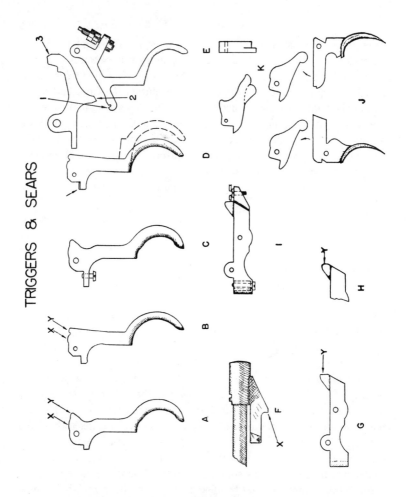

TRIGGERS & SEARS

TRIGGERS AND SEARS

Here we have triggers and sears of the four main bolt action rifles, plus the common two lever double set triggers:

A. The Springfield 1903 trigger: "x," the front "hump" controls the take up, or first pull; "y," the rear hump, controls the final pull, in length and creep. (The 1917 Enfield trigger is almost identical.)

B. The military Mauser trigger—"x" and "y" value same as for the Springfield.

C. 1903 Trigger with stop lip extended (by welding on steel) and drilled and tapped for a screw which holds trigger back, sear down and makes possible the single stage pull. This method can be used on the Enfield and Mauser also, but only with safety on *any* rifle with a tight bolt assembly and tight in the receiver.

maintain a uniform trigger pull, so springs should not be altered.

Should the second or final pull on a military rifle of Mauser type be too light or the edge of the sear or the cocking piece rounded, the top of the trigger can be worked down to allow the sear to move higher in the receiver. It may be necessary to cut down both humps to gain this end, although the front cam governs the position of the sear when at rest. The rear cam, or hump, governs the letoff, and removing metal from it decreases the engagement of the sear and the cocking piece for the second pull. Stoning the front cam increases the pull and decreases the takeup. You can alter pulls to quite an extent by working on the double stage triggers, but practically never can obtain a very good pull by this alone.

On any arm a checkered trigger is not only a nice-looking feature but a practical one. Some few triggers are case-hardened and the finger

---

D. Mauser '98 trigger with lip built up by brazing metal on the top, to serve the same end as above, except of course not adjustable as is the set screw. Can be used on Springfield and Enfield also.

E. Winchester M70 sear and trigger assemblies: The spring, set screw and lock nut affair on the back end of the trigger is the trigger stop only. It cannot regulate weight of the pull. Point 1 must be cut down to lighten the pull; Point 2, the sear nose, should not be touched—It should be polished smooth, to a fairly sharp edge. Point 3, the sear face, should be polished smooth.

F. Headless cocking piece for 1903, to show the straight face on the cocking piece "x." This face must be polished glass smooth, and the bottom edge must be straight and sharp.

G. 1903 sear, to show the rear face "y." This sear face must be sharp and square at the top edge, and the face angled slightly forward. It may be slightly curved in profile, instead of angled, but the straight sharp edge at the top must be preserved.

H. 1903 sear with top edge incorrectly rounded—Too much curve and rounded edge at the top.

I. 1903 sear altered for adjustable triggerpull: Pin or screw in sear spring recess acts as a trigger stop: the bit of metal sweated on the rear of the sear is tapped for a thin headed screw, and the small hole drilled through the sear well in the receiver to allow a small screwdriver to adjust this screw up and down, to increase and decrease sear engagement with the cocking piece.

J. The ordinary German double set triggers, showing movement of each against the kickoff, or sear lever.

K. Handmade sear lever, designed to give maximum sear leverage and shaped to contact both triggers efficiently. The left leg or contact lug should be made to engage the front trigger without any preliminary takeup to the latter.

curve must be annealed before it can be filed. Protect the cams or sear faces or other hardened portions with wet cloth or asbestos, heat the lower section red with the torch and let it cool slowly. The commercial checkering files are hopeless for trigger work, as they are much too wide. For triggers and other small metal parts—buttons, catches, and the like—use the 50-line-per-inch file. Break a section of the file about 3″ from the end. Now, if you care to spend half an hour on the grinder, grind it away until you have just three lines of checkering teeth on a narrow strip of steel. If you are lazy, anneal the piece of file, first protecting the teeth with the scale-prevention compound, then saw a narrow strip from it, to gain your three-line checkering file. Reharden it, set one end in a handle and you are able to file inside quite sharp curves. Cut all your grooves almost full depth from one side before starting the cross lines.

Enfield Actions. It would easily be possible to write a couple of chapters each on Enfields, Springfields and Mausers, but we can cover the main points pretty well without going into great detail. The Enfield is holding down more space in gunshops at present than the others.

The receiver bridge must be altered radically to suit either the sights and scope mounts commercially available, or the owner's eye, or both. The finest method of remodeling the bridge is to use a shaper to cut off the ears and roughly round the top, then cut to the desired curvature by a surface grinder, running the wheel parallel with the action and moving the action back and forth and turning it to round the receiver. The next best system is the milling machine, and finish with files. The strong-arm method is still popular, in which you take your little hacksaw, put the best all-hard blade you can buy in it and saw the ears off, cut whatever corners you can, use the grinder as far as possible, then start filing to fill the prescription.

All sorts of variations can be used to meet sight and customer requirements. The illustration covers a few of the commonest applications. Redfield now provides a scope mount with base flat on the rear end so that it is possible to mill a step in front of the bridge and fit the base easily. The entire top of the bridge can of course be cut down to this dimension, but that is a lot of unnecessary labor and I think the appearance is injured. The old story that you can round off the top of an Enfield bridge the same as the receiver ring and then use any sight or mount provided for the Remington 30 rifle is not always true. In most cases you will have to cut the top of the bridge down approximately $\frac{3}{32}$″ to achieve correct fitting of Remington 30 accessories. Because nine-tenths of the Enfields out are to be hunting arms, the clip slots are not needed, and the front of the bridge can be streamlined by cutting back to eliminate the slots.

The rear of the bridge can be improved considerably by removing most of the metal on the left side. However, do not take it all away right behind the rear edge of the bridge, where the primary or extraction cam of the bolt contacts. Some men cut off the rear end of the bolt stop spring, eliminating its rest—the "button"—and cut the left side of the receiver down right behind the hinge pin housing, creating a longer tang effect and a Mauser-appearing bolt stop. This works okay, but looks rather odd from the rear, as you see the exposed housing. Skillful welding can close up this slot and dress up the appearance, but more about the welding a little later.

Remington-made Enfields seem to be quite uniform in material, none of them being very difficult to work on. They all have solid top bridges. Winchester-made Enfields are also no great problem, but all have that large oblong recess in the top of the bridge, under the issue sight spring. Eddystones are very unpredictable, but as a rule you can expect the worst. They are usually hard as well as tough, and rough on tools. It will often be necessary to anneal the sides for drilling and tapping. When you are trying to put holes in the receiver ring, where you cannot anneal, they sometimes call for considerable patience. Some Eddystones have the recess in the receiver, and some do not; above and below a certain serial number, which I have never learned. Remingtons and Winchester rifles are sometimes very tough to drill around the receiver bridge but seldom if ever compare with the Eddystone.

That recess in the top of the bridge is an unsightly hole and hard to eliminate. Just fitting a piece of steel in it and peening the edges does not work very well. If it can be very closely fitted and sweated to the bottom of the hole, it will hold well enough. However, the plugs always show. Welding the hole full of nickel steel is not so good either. The amount of heat necessary will, in 50% of the jobs, warp the receiver enough to prevent movement of the bolt in its runway, so you have to worry about straightening it. Also, the heat causes the thin bottom of the hole to bulge downward, into the bolt runway. This bulge can of course be filed to clear the bolt without much effort. Incidentally, this brings up one easy method of tightening bolts—a very large punch or rod can be used in the recess to depress the bottom into the runway enough to prevent undesirable upward movement of the bolt when in place and action cocked. It is possible, however, to close the hole and achieve a perfect finish. A plug must be made to fit the hole, after the receiver has been roughed to shape but before the final filing and smoothing takes place. Chamfer the edges of the plug and the hole to form a wide V, then weld up this V with nickel steel. The welding must be done fast, with a strong flame and very little pre-heating, in order to avoid heating the lower portion of receiver to the point of warpage.

The heat will not affect the strength of the action, and here is a good place to emphasize the fact that on any Mauser type bolt action the strength, as regards cartridge pressure and safety, is in the receiver ring and the bolt head. The receiver, from the receiver ring back, and the bolt, from approximately one inch back of the face, could be made of lead without affecting the primary, or holding strength of the action. On a rifle designed for extreme accuracy, the action should be as strong and rigid as possible, in order that minute tensions created in stock bedding be resisted, but so far as safety is concerned, it does not hurt to soften any part of the action behind the receiver ring.

The bolt stop of the Enfield can be and should be improved. The spring is almost always unnecessarily stiff, making bolt removal difficult; grind or file it thinner, from the inner side, to weaken it enough to permit functioning with just one hand, or rather, thumb. An added refinement is checkering or lining the top or whole front end. The ejector is a poor design, in that it is one-piece, spring and ejector proper combined. Whenever possible, replace with the Remington 30 type, which employs a little coil spring attaching to the ejector through a small hole. Broken Enfield ejectors can be modified to this type, as illustrated.

Altering bolts to cock on the opening or upward movement of the handle is much more of a job than it is usually considered. The only proper and reliable method is to weld up the cocking notch, shaping it similar to that of the Springfield, according to the dimensions given in the drawing. Quite a few of the newer gunsmiths have "discovered" that they can make Enfields cock on the opening stroke by just cutting back the face of the cocking piece far enough so that it engages the sear on the primary opening movement of the bolt. This gives a very short firing pin fall and necessitates a very strong mainspring to obtain even fair ignition. I consider this a very poor system, as I have experimented with firing pin falls on the Enfield action from $5/16''$ up, and even with a light-weight firing pin and a spring so strong it required an extra man and a special tool to install and I failed to get satisfactory uniform ignition on commercial primers with any fall less than $3/8''$.

No, there just is not any easy short-cut to the job. Two types of welding alteration are possible, the first and my own preference using the Remington 30S or 720 firing pin, mainspring and cocking piece.

I believe only the 720 parts are now available, so you must use them, shortening the firing pin tip to the proper length. The firing pin is not a necessity, nor is the spring, but the pin is skeletonized and the spring quite strong—desirable factors in lock time. The first step in altering is the choice of welding material—you either use a tool steel which can be shaped and hardened after welding; or nickel-steel or other good steel. The notch is cleaned by filing off the Parkerizing then welded up, leaving a narrow opening next to the bolt. Make and use a template as pictured for shaping the notch, after boring out the inside of the bolt up to the threads to clear it to original diameter and filing or machining the excess metal off the exterior. If the weld is to be hardened, it is cut exactly to size now, but if of the softer steel, is cut $\frac{1}{32}''$ oversize on the cam side of the notch and across the rear of the bolt on the welded-up surface. This is then coated with hard-surfacing material which is then ground and stoned to the correct dimension. I prefer to use this latter method myself, as the very hard surface obtained takes a wear-proof glass-smooth polish and permits easy cocking. Several times in the past when using the hardening system on welded-up notches I have found microscopic surface cracks in the bolt body below the weld, caused by the hardening process. These take a re-welding to build the bolt up and refinish it—no very easy job. The commonest method is to just build the notch with any carbon steel rod and case-harden the finished notch. This works fine for awhile, then one day the owner tries to open his bolt and needs three hands and a vise to do it. The case wears or breaks through under continued use. The system is okay for ten-shots-a-year deer hunters, but not for the heavy shooter.

Shaping the notch requires care, for you are creating a safety feature. On the Enfield sear is a front pin which contacts the bolt body and prevents sear movement except when the bolt is closed or opened by the original system. This pin must be shortened when the bolt is altered, so that it no longer will limit sear movement. As in the Springfield, the new Enfield notch itself must prevent accidental discharge, or any discharge, before the bolt is fully closed, by presenting the cam side of the notch to the cocking nose or cam of the cocking piece and preventing free forward movement of the firing pin. In effect, if the bolt handle is not fully down when the cocking piece is relieved, the latter contacts the edge of the notch and expends most of its force in closing the bolt, before traveling far enough forward to fire the gun.

It is therefore evident that cutting a notch unnecessarily wide, or on an unnecessarily sharp angle, presents the possibility of the rifle being able to fire without the bolt being fully closed. Since the Enfield is satisfactorily locked and correctly headspaced before the bolt is completely turned, I may appear to be overcautious, but I believe it best to get the bolt handle down where it belongs before the gun goes off!

Make the notch come to a fairly sharp point at the forward end, with perhaps a $\frac{1}{32}''$ radius. At all points on the cam surface the notch should be in line with the radius of the bolt so that the nose of the cocking piece will have a full contact surface to cam against. It must not be so wide at the top that the cocking piece does not have a square surface to rest against when cocked and the bolt is in the open position. A very shallow, smooth notch should be made for the nose to rest in, to prevent accidental displacement and slipping back into the notch. Notches can be shaped best with files and the hand grinder, as it is difficult to make a milling machine cut the curving cam surface.

The cocking piece nose must be narrowed to fit the notch. When in the forward position, no part of it should bear against the notch, but should have a definite tolerance—about $\frac{1}{64}''$ on the cam side and the front. The length of the firing pin and protrusion of the tip is regulated at this time. If the cocking piece nose comes to rest against the bolt notch after falling, eventually the firing pin is going to break at the point where it keys into the cocking piece.

Both the bolt sleeve, or plug in correct nomenclature, and the rear tip of the firing pin must be shortened when the bolt is altered—a very brief lathe job, or not much work by hand. You should not have to do anything to the safety, but sometimes the Remington 720 cocking piece must be relieved slightly on the bottom rear section in order not to bother the depressed sear when cocking the action. This in no way cuts down the safety of the arm. Should the safety be burred or badly rounded off on its contact edge, it can be filed to clear metal and fuller contact area without changing any function. If the customer objects too strenuously to the large size and shape of the thumb-piece, you can remodel it a little; cut the wide top off, round the shorter shank and with the checkering file line it horizontally. Weaken the spring, cutting a half-turn of it off at a time until the safety can be operated fairly easily and yet snap to the full "off" position when thrown forward. It may be necessary to cut back the inner contact face so that the cocking piece will be cammed back just enough to free it from pressure against the sear. The short safety does not give much leverage so is difficult to manipulate against strong tension.

The bolt handle itself can be made to look a little better, by cutting

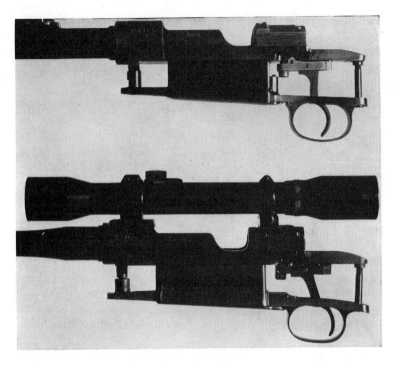

MAUSER GUARD CHANGE

Above, the standard '98 receiver and guard assembly, and below it, a Mauser receiver with Springfield guard and special trigger. Trigger is shaped to position the finger curve in rear of loop.

The Springfield guard has a better appearance than the Mauser: the loop is smaller and better shaped, the floorplate covers the bottom of box and inletting at sides of box, there are no lock screws, and the box is of course long enough to allow use of .30–06 and .270 cartridges without alteration, although the feed lip in the Mauser receiver must be cut forward a trifle.

Fitting to the Mauser receiver is quite easy, entailing only cutting down the top of the front guard-screw housing, filing the sides of the top portion of rear box wall of the magazine so that it enters the receiver opening, and drilling or filing the guard screw holes to slightly larger diameter. The Mauser guard screws must have their heads turned down to fit the countersinks in the Springfield guard. It is not absolutely necessary to bend down the receiver tang to provide the angled screw position of the Springfield. For an easier stocking job, the rear tang of the Springfield guard can be cut shorter, rounded off just behind the rear guard screw. This permits more leeway in shaping the pistol grip inner curve.

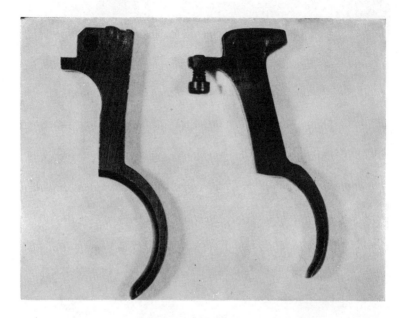

MAUSER TRIGGERS

At left is the standard Mauser '98 trigger, and at the right is a hand-made replacement trigger which is angled to place the finger curve about $\frac{5}{16}''$ further to the rear. It also has an adjustment screw to govern the sear and cocking piece engagement, to provide a single-stage pull.

Such a change has real possibilities. It enables the shooter to position his trigger to the spot on his trigger finger that *he* prefers to use, without shifting his hand about on the grip of the stock. The user of a Wundhammer bulge on his pistol grip can obtain perfect co-ordination of trigger, finger and grip by means of such an alteration.

it off and welding on a new one, shaped and raked back in the manner of the Winchester 70. The base of the handle, with its hole for the safety plunger to lock it down when safety is in use, must either not be disturbed at all, or the new handle drilled to accomodate the plunger.

Cutting down the magazine box capacity to slenderize the Enfield profile is obviously a simple hacksaw and file job, the metal to be removed from the bottom, of course. Do not try to change the angle of the triggerguard, but cut the ends up first, until your guard moves up far enough then trim off flush with the bottom of the guard. The trigger is now too long, and if the sight of the military trigger is not too displeasing, cut out the $\frac{3}{16}''$ or $\frac{1}{4}''$ you have to eliminate, in the middle of the shank and weld or braze it together again. It is not too great a job to make an entirely new trigger by hand to specific dimensions. Also, in the majority of cases, a 1903 Springfield trigger is just right; the knurled National Match style is excellent.

Straightening an Enfield guard is for me one of the hardest welding jobs to do perfectly. Metal must be built up right to the original surface at the front of the floorplate opening, without pitting the metal or melting out the catch notch, or scaling it to the point of allowing the floorplate to be loose. Several systems of cutting the guard can be used, as illustrated, none much better than the others. A simple welding jig can be constructed to insure a straight-line job, with the screw holes the correct distance apart—$7\frac{15}{16}''$, center to center. Simplest jig is to set $\frac{1}{4}''$ pins at that distance in a large fire brick, with a couple of side pins to keep the guard itself in line. The short tip is easy to line up by eye. A complete set of pins could be easily set in a steel plate, but make provision for holding the guard parts above the plate itself, in order not to dissipate heat. The front guard screw of the Enfield enters the action at 90°, so presumably the shape of the guard has no bearing on the length, or distance between the holes. Actually, when the magazine is to be left full size and the guard altered, it may be shortened, or the distance between the holes decreased about $\frac{1}{64}''$. If the rifle is to be custom stocked, you need not worry about having to file the front tang of the guard narrower after welding in order to obtain clean, sharp edges, but if any of the ready-made stocks or semi-inletted blanks are to be used, be careful while welding, as you need to leave the tang as wide as possible. The finger loop of the guard can be reshaped cold with a mallet and filed narrower, to good effect.

Loose floorplates can sometimes be tightened satisfactorily by peening or beating down the catch lip at the front end. Otherwise, you work on the back end, either extending the catch stem on the plate, as il-

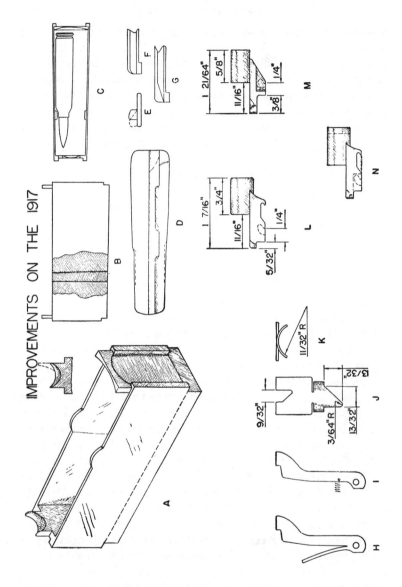

IMPROVEMENTS ON THE 1917 ENFIELD

A. The magazine box, dotted line showing the amount which can be removed and still permit five round capacity with .30–06 ammunition. Above is the front feed lip, with the dotted lines indicating the amount of build up necessary to insure smooth loading with soft nose ammunition.

lustrated, or building up the nose of the catch itself. The hinged floorplate is the real deluxe deal—lot of work, about twenty buck's worth, but well worth it on a topgrade gun. The familiar Mauser hinged floorplate systems are to me extremely homely. You have either a protruding lever along the bottom of the floorplate or a straightup in front of finger loop, with all the beauty of line of a bulldog's chin. Strange to say, I like my own style better, it requiring no welding and milling of the triggerguard loop and having an unobtrusive button release inside the top of the loop bow. The spring system took me a long time to figure out—it is so simple!—and it works.

To hinge an Enfield floorplate it is necessary to weld or braze a short upright on the top of the guard at the rear, to which the spring is attached. On the Springfield guard, the spring is attached to the check back of the magazine box with a 6–48 screw. The Mauser magazine is treated the same, but it is necessary to cut away the original catch and spring housing. On all three actions the floorplates are altered the same way, and the catch enters the guard loop in the same manner. The

---

B. Cut away view of the magazine, showing the cartridge guides, or bullet protectors, which are to be sweated to the sides of the box.

C. Top view of the box, with the cartridge guides illustrating the stopping forward movement of the cartridge in the magazine.

D. The follower, the dotted lines at the front indicating the metal which may have to be removed if bullet guides are used. Often this is not necessary. The rear of the plate indicates the direction of grinding or filing to permit the bolt closing over the follower after being altered as shown in

E. Rear end of the follower shaped per the dotted lines to permit camming down when the bolt is moved forward. The metal is welded on at the back end to the left of the rib and shaped as shown.

F. Side view of the rear end of the follower, unaltered.

G. Ditto, altered.

H. Military ejector, with integral spring, that breaks.

I. Ejector, broken or otherwise, altered by a little grinding and drilling of one small hole to accept a short coil spring, which will not break.

J & K. Side and end views of a template to be used in altering bolts to cock on the opening movement. The top cut is for the nose of the cocking piece.

L. The standard 1917 cocking piece.

M. The Remington 30S cocking piece, designed for the altered bolt.

N. The 1917 cocking piece, the dotted lines showing the necessary cutting and welding to bring it to the dimensions of the 30S. The vertical dotted line at the rear indicates the amount of shortening possible, if desired, or use with the Remington firing pin.

catch is made of $\frac{1}{8}''$ x $\frac{1}{4}''$ cold-rolled steel, one end filed round and bent to form the finger release, the other shaped to engage the notch in the floorplate stud. The spring, made of ordinary clock-spring stock, is held to the top of the catch with either one or two 6–48 screws. One is enough, as the catch cannot turn and get out of line. The notch in the floorplate stud is not straight, or parallel to the line of the plate at its top edge, but rather angles slightly upward to the rear. If made straight, the floorplate will not be held tightly against the guard by the catch, as the latter moves in an arc and necessarily must clear the rear edge of the notch before moving to full engagement. Considerable adjustment is possible by bending the spring, but the notch must of course be filed after the catch is made, in order to insure a correct fit. The finger release end of the catch is last rounded very slightly and checkered. Regulate its length and that of its slot so that it is flush with the guard as floorplate is released. In use the catch is pressed upward and backward, to open floorplate, and of course automatically engages when plate is closed.

Enfield magazine followers may be ground or filed to allow bolt to cam them down when magazine is empty. Make your cut slightly curved from about $\frac{1}{32}''$ above bottom rear edge to the top of the follower rib approximately $\frac{1}{2}''$ forward, as illustrated. A feeding guide, to prevent jamming and mutilation of soft-pointed hunting bullets against the edge of the chamber, can be made by building up the right lip of the magazine box feed shoulder. Weld, or put on brass if customer wants a fast and economical job on this lip, until it can be filed and finished to leave a wall almost $\frac{1}{16}''$ wide right up through the receiver opening. Clear the top so that it will not interfere with the bolt and try cartridges, to make sure that it steers the left-side ones into the chamber.

Springfield Actions. The principal '03 job necessary is altering the bolt for low scope installation. Basically, all bolt handle jobs are very similar, differing only in the styling—thickness of shank, shape of knob and curvature. The drawing tells most of the story. I find it best to saw off the handle close to bolt, grind to clear for welding, turn it on its side and weld at the lower angle. The knob itself must stay somewhere near its original location, and it is easiest to gage this by measuring from the straight side of the cocking notch, placing the inner edge of the knob from $1''$ to $1\frac{1}{4}''$ out from a straight line based on the side of notch. The size of scope eyepiece involved has some bearing on the position of the knob when open, as it must be possible to grasp the bolt firmly when opened, without the ocular cell taking up too much room.

The handle can be raked back—turning it on its side takes care of that detail—or made straight down. Only the French point bolt handles forward; looks like Hell and works the same way.

Three general styles of handle are illustrated: the detail x may apply to any style, and is governed by the amount of metal added in welding close to the bolt; the dimension A applies to any alteration and regulates closeness of the knob to the stock when the bolt is closed; dimension B is governed by the lowness of the scope mounting, and C by the size of the ocular cell. Do not bother too much about setting up hard and fast dimensions for these, unless you plan to concentrate on bolt alterations, but cut each bolt job to clear the scope and by $\frac{1}{32}''$ at least. On windage-adjustable mounts such as Tilden or Redfield, make allowance for movement of the scope to the right.

The thickness of the shank at point y determines the strength of the handle, and here you are torn between desire to make a slim, streamlined job, and a heavier, stronger handle and its necessarily deeper cut in receiver and stock. If a perfect weld is achieved, the shank at this point can be cut to $\frac{3}{16}''$ in thickness, but it is better to have it at least $\frac{1}{4}''$ to make sure. Quite a few men make extremely heavy, clumsy-looking alterations, unnecessarily bulky. A bolt handle is approximately $2\frac{1}{2}''$ long; well, take a bar of any steel at all, $\frac{1}{4}'' \times \frac{3}{8}'' \times 3''$, around the edges, put $\frac{1}{2}''$ of it in the vise and try to bend the remainder with your thumb and forefinger. When you can do it, let me know, and I will come watch—then I will make heavy bolt handles.

On the opposite side, I have seen a few handles made too thin, with sharp angles at point x, which, if poorly welded, were a very good bet to come off at the wrong moment.

After the alteration, when the bolt is cleaned and polished, the scale and debris cleaned out of the threads at the rear and the front end dried from the wet cloth or asbestos used to protect lugs while welding, and it moves freely under the mounted scope in the action, you are ready to fit it into the receiver. A notch must be cut in it, and in the stock, to accommodate the new position of the bolt handle when the bolt is closed. The shank in the cross-section at points x and y may be either rounded or square at bottom, and a notch cut to accept it in the side of the receiver. The hand grinder really pays for itself here, as some receivers are tough filing, and the angle of the notch may prevent very long strokes. Cut the notch or recess a little at a time, trying the fully assembled bolt until the safety will just turn to the fully-locked position. Relieve the notch at the rear edge, so that the bolt handle will have some freedom when closed on loaded cartridges and also that it is

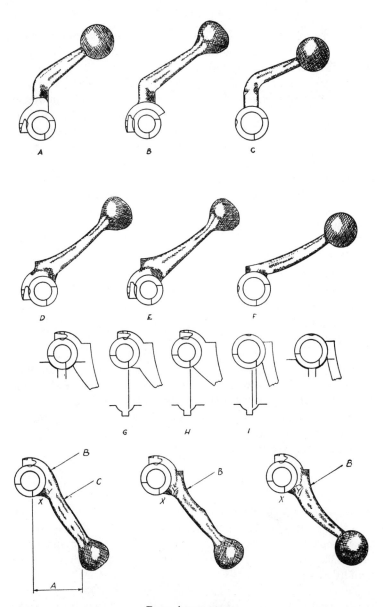

Bolt Alteration

The alteration of a bolt for a low mounting telescopic sight can be made difficult or easy and the altered bolt can be a distinct improvement in appearance over the unaltered version, or not. I much prefer the welded bolt alteration to the forged alteration.

not firmly held forward by the notch at any time. The recessed handle, if square in section, becomes a secondary safety lug and as such must not be under any tension. Be careful not to make the notch too deep,

---

A, B & C represent rear views of the 1903 Springfield, Winchester Model 54 and Mauser '98 bolts.

D. Springfield bolt altered for fairly high bolt position, knob altered to pear shape.

E. Winchester 54 bolt altered for normal low scope mounting.

F. Mauser bolt altered for very low scope mounting.

G. Here we begin to get into the fine points. When the bolt is altered as shown, a notch for the handle must be cut in the receiver; the depth of this notch is important—if shallow, it can hold the bolt partly open; if too deep, the bolt may "jump" when the firing pin falls. At the left is a drawing of the Springfield bolt in the receiver runway, showing how the edge of the bolt notch lines up with right wall of the sear well. "G"—with line to show the lineup of these points, for the normal bolt root.

H. Same as "G" except that on this '03 bolt, the weld of the root has been brought close to the edge of the notch, necessitating a very deep notch in the receiver tang edge for the handle to seat properly.

I. The '98 Mauser set up, showing that the bolt notch does not line up with the sear well, but sets approximately $\frac{1}{16}''$ above lining up. At right, drawing represents Mauser bolt in the receiver well, with relative positions of the well and the cocking notch shown. (The 1905 Mauser employs a slightly different cocking piece than the '98 and on it the notch edge and sear well wall do line up, as with the Springfield.)

In cutting the handle notch in the receiver tang on either the Mauser or the Springfield, be governed by two things—firing pin protrusion and safety operation. As a rule, cut the notch just deep enough so that when the bolt is turned down, the original military safety can be turned to the fully locked position. With the Winchester 54, no notch is necessary, as the lug on the bolt root is the new root location and the factory notch for it takes care of the matter.

Down at the bottom of the page we have examples of alteration stylings, all of which look in reality better than the pictures. The principles to be followed are indicated, as follows:

At left, a Springfield bolt with streamlined handle. "A" is the distance of the knob from the edge of the cocking notch, to regulate the position of the handle and the knob on the assembled rifle—$1''$ to $1\frac{1}{8}''$ is a satisfactory dimension for "A." "B" represents the dimension on all alterations for the clearance of the scope ocular cell, and "C" the point on the handle most likely to contact the scope through play in the bolt during manipulation.

Center shows a conventional alteration, cut to fit the job, and at right is a deeply curved handle to accommodate a very low scope.

"X" is the distance from the notch to the body of the bolt, and "Y" is the amount of the metal at the root, determining the strength of the job, as the hardest part of the welding job is at this point.

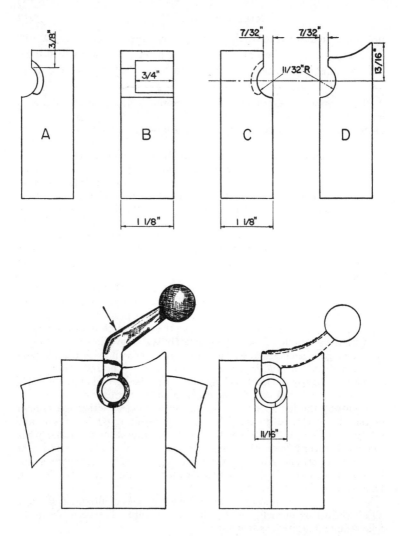

1903 Bolt Bending Jig

Don Lowery, of Tucson, Arizona, worked out this jig, which works very well indeed. It is much simpler to make than the Mauser jig, and the bolt handles forged for scope use with it do not require the receiver tang to be cut or notched. As with the Mauser jig, the vertical dimension is dependent upon the size of the vise employed—1⅛″ cold rolled square stock is large enough for the blocks. With either this or the Mauser jig, no protection whatever is necessary for the locking lugs on the bolt. The blocks absorb excess heat, and it is possible to hold on to the front 3″ or 4″ with the bare hand during the entire job, if necessary and you have three hands!

so that the bolt turns down too far, or it will "jump" when fired or snapped.

The modern low scope mounting requires a special safety, of which many are on the market. For Springfields, the Buehler is excellent, except on extremely low mountings, when the Sukalle or Eads must be used. Buehler also makes the nicest one for the 54 Winchester. For Mausers, the F.N., Tilden, and Ackley are good for very low mounted scopes, and the Buehler on those jobs with sufficient clearance to permit its use. The F.N. is left hand type only; Ackley makes both right and left hand models; and Tilden is right hand only.

Alteration of bolt handles by bending is possible for the Springfield action, although a welding torch is required to furnish heat. The illustrated jigs are quite practical. The bolt is clamped at the root of the handle, as pictured, heat from the torch applied until the handle becomes cherry red, then the handle is hammered down to meet the curve of the jig. The two halves of the jig must bottom on the crossbar of the vise, or on an anvil, being held together on the bolt by clamps.

The Mauser jig is used in exactly the same manner. However, the altered Mauser bolt is lowered so much at the root it is necessary to notch the edge of the receiver, as mentioned for the welding alteration. The Springfield bolt can have sufficient strength if made to clear the receiver, as if unaltered. Winchester 54 bolts cannot be altered by bending.

Receiver runways in any action can be polished *slightly*. Do not try to take out all the toolmarks, or your bolt will be too loose and for the same reason you cannot machine down a bolt very far—hand polishing and machine buffing give the best results. When the action is to be re-

---

A. Front view of the left hand block, showing the cut to take the extraction cam on the top of the bolt.

B. Inside view of the left hand block, showing the depth of the cut for the cam.

C. Rear view of the left hand block, showing dimensions.

D. Rear view, or profile of the right hand block.

At the bottom left, the bolt clamped in the vise, with an arrow showing the direction of the hammering after heating to cherry red. Bottom right, the handle forged to shape, with dotted lines indicating the final shape. This shape necessitates a rather deep cut in the side of the stock, but accommodates the largest and the lowest mounting telescopic sights.

The jigs must be a close but not tight fit on the bolt, and should not hold the bolt any tighter clamped than unclamped. It is possible to injure the bolt if the jig is either too loose or too tight.

barreled, the lugs can be well polished, but otherwise take it easy on them, for no metal can be removed without increasing headspace.

For the rebarreling jobs, and for complete rifles with minimum headspace, it is a very good idea to spot in the lugs. Clear and polish the lug recesses or "seats" in the receiver as best you can, not rounding any edges appreciably, polish the backs of lugs until bright with crocus cloth, then coat recess shoulders with lampblack or Prussian blue and turn the bolt into them, with a fired cartridge in the chamber. High spots on the backs of the lugs will be marked and can be stoned down. The idea is to get the full area of the backs of the lugs in contact with their locking shoulders in the receiver recess. Usually very little metal needs removing, especially on used Springfields which have taken their initial "setback" long ago.

Firing pin holes you know about, as previously covered. Strikers are actually firing pins and tips treated as such. The three-piece Springfield firing pin and striker combination has always been criticized because of the sponginess of the fall, due to loose fit between striker, striker collar, and firing pin proper. Do away with it by making a little steel shim to fit between the end of the pin and the base of the striker, so thick that you have a devil of a time assembling the parts.

The back end of the firing pin, the head, or cocking piece, can be altered if desired, to the headless type but do not just drill a hole through the thick section for a pin and chop off the finger knob—the pins just are not strong enough, and will shear in time. Go ahead and pin it, and cut it off, then with a shallow-pointed large drill bevel or countersink the pin ends very slightly and on the lathe turn a V at the junction of the pin shaft and the cocking piece, then light the welding torch and really tie it together. You probably had to anneal the cocking piece in the first place, in order to drill and cut it. The headless cocking piece is a nice item on a target or varmint rifle, but really is undesirable on a general sporter or hunting rifle. It is nice to be able to cock the rifle without opening the bolt at times.

The cutoff housing must of course be filed to the shape desired, and about all you need to know is—do not file through into the axis pin hole. With a section of rod measure its depth, or rather, length, and mark it with a scratch on the outside. Sight down from the top with the pin itself halfway in the hole and you will have a pretty good idea of its size and how much metal is wrapped around that hole and where you can remove some.

The foregoing applies to the genuine Springfield and Rock Island Model 1903 rifles. The first of the Remington-made World War II 1903 rifles were practically duplicates of the nickel-steel Rock Islands, excepting for the poor fit of the floorplates and the safeties. Later Remingtons, the 1903A3 and A4, were made of different steel, carburized in the Mauser manner. These can be considered as being case-hardened all over, very deeply. Receivers and bolts resist filing, and must be reshaped by grinding or polishing equipment. Because of the crude machine work and difficult material, it is hard to make much of a rifle from one of these models. Toolmarks are very deep on both bolt and receiver, and even when polished well, the hard surface resists blueing much more than other models.

Mausers. One of our minor post-war industries is the rebuilding of souvenir Mauser rifles into sporting arms. The rebuilding may be any degree of change from a mere substitution of a Bishop stock blank for a military stock to a complete custom rifle using only the Mauser receiver and bolt, replacing other parts entirely. There are two main classes of military Mauser actions, the standard 1898 pattern, which takes in the Models 12, 24, 28, and 35, of German, Czech and Belgian manufacture, as well as the Polish Radom, a few of which have a slightly longer receiver ring, but are otherwise identical, and the 1898 Carbine action, which has the smaller-diameter receiver ring. The Czech Vz 33 and German G33/40 are the most common examples of this action. The 1905 action is the '98 with a longer firing pin, cocking piece and stronger mainspring.

After 1941 Germany became sloppier and sloppier in manufacturing and the rifles became poorer and poorer. Actions made in 1941 and in earlier years are usually quite well machined and of excellent material, most of them being of Swedish steel and expertly heat-treated. Later actions were less carefully machined and the '43, 44 and 45 receivers and bolts were often made of poor grades of steel, from German scrap, and sometimes not heat-treated at all. As in the last 1903 actions, a good bit of metal must often be removed to present a smooth finish and Mauser bolts are loose enough as it is, without making them undersize to eliminate the toolmarks. Not all of the later actions were poor— some of the manufacturers kept their standards fairly high. Those guns made outside Germany, by forced labor, are the poorest. Sauer & Sohn, one of the largest German plants, made a very sad production model of the '98, called the VG-1, of which only a few have turned up in the U. S.

I prefer the Czech and Polish Mausers over the German. They actually seem to be of a steel very similar in working qualities to the nickel-steel used in the high-number Springfields. It cuts, drills, taps and welds very well, something which cannot be said for the German materiel. Original specifications for the Mauser action call for carburization of the wearing surfaces, meaning they were deeply case-hardened inside. All variations of the treatment are found, however. Some actions are deeply hardened on all portions, others have just the receiver ring treated, some have a light case all over, and some few have no hardening apparent, although heat-treated. Bolts are usually quite hard, or hardened. Czech, Polish, 1918-vintage German, and a few Belgian Mausers have straight bolt handles, projecting straight out from the stock. Later German production of the '98 action have bent-down handles, and all of the small-ring actions have curved handle shanks. These latter have knobs flattened on the underside, sometimes checkered, and the G33/40 has its knob hollowed on the underside.

Beyond polishing down undesirable toolmarks, little needs to be done to the Mauser receiver. The triggerguard is another matter. The guard screw lock screws should be retained, I believe. For a very high-class appearance it might be advisable to weld up their head recesses and re-cut the guard screw countersink, but for a high-class rifle, why keep the Mauser guard at all? The Springfield 1903 triggerguard can be fitted to the Mauser '98 action with very little effort, and it really does look good. The magazine lip at the top must be filed to enter the Mauser receiver, and very occasionally it may be necessary to change the angle of the rear guard screw hole. One way is to heat the Mauser receiver tang and bend it down $\frac{1}{32}''$ or so; making bend $\frac{3}{4}''$ from end, to not affect the seating of the bolt sleeve in the runway.

When substitution of guards is not practicable, the Mauser can be improved a good bit by grinding and filing the finger bow loop. Older guards had a swivel hole in front—as a pin hole for a Mauser type hinged floorplate, or have front edge of loop filed back to include this hole and eliminate it. The loop is then thinned and narrowed all over, to make a graceful appearance. Nothing much can be done with the floorplate, other than polishing it. The stamped, or fabricated guards of course cannot be much improved. About the only thing to say of them is that they are a heck of a lot better than *our* stamped types.

If the Mauser action is rebarreled to .270 or .30–06, and the original guard retained, the magazine box must be filed at each end, in order to accommodate the longer cartridges. Actually, the unaltered magazine will handle commercial ammunition in .30–06 and all but one loading of the .270. For use with Government .30–06 cartridges the box must be lengthened to approximately 90mm. File the back wall of the box $\frac{1}{32}''$ or thereabouts, then start on the front end, filing it until you can move issue cartridges through it at any angle they might take when loaded in the magazine. The feed lip, or shoulder, of the receiver of course must be then made even with the box so that cartridges will ride smoothly into the chamber. Mausers as a rule feed hunting ammunition quite well, seldom having difficulty with blunt, soft-pointed bullets.

Older Mauser followers were so constructed as to depress and allow the bolt to cam them down when the magazine was empty. Later arms had a step machined in the left rear corner of the follower which allowed it to rise into the bolt runway and block the bolt when the last cartridge was fired. This is considered a valuable military feature, since it prevents an excited soldier from working an empty rifle, but is not so popular on sporting arms, the owners of which like to be able to manipulate the bolt at will on an empty rifle. The remedy is of course welding up this step and cutting a slight bevel on the corner of the follower rib. Do not plan on just grinding the back end of the follower at an angle and expect it to feed perfectly—it may, or it may not!

Bolt handle alteration on the Mauser is very similar to the Springfield alteration, except that a definite step should be left at the top, and that the straight side of the cocking notch is *not* even with the sear well except on the 1905. So as you cut the handle recess in the receiver, watch this notch and sear-well relationship and when the former comes within $\frac{1}{16}''$ of lining up, begin to try the assembled bolt, working the original safety until it will fully lock, turning completely over to the right side. Check the firing pin too, by measuring the movement of the cocking piece when snapped in the gun against the movement when released in the withdrawn bolt. Allow the bolt to turn down just far enough to insure full tip protrusion, which in turn means that the cocking piece has completed its forward movement. The cam side of the cocking piece nose may come to rest against the cocking cam of the bolt, but should not expand its full force there, or, as in the Enfield, the firing pin may break.

Bolt welding of Mausers is in itself no more difficult than any other type, however, the varying alloys encountered may require differing treatment. Some handles apparently are quite high in carbon content and consequently require high-temperature preheating. Such handles resist addition of metal except at intense heat and therefore you use plenty of heat. Whenever the bolt shank and stub throw off a lot of sparks and visibly scale in the torch flame when approaching bright red, you have one of these painstaking jobs—and take pains, or the weld will have no strength.

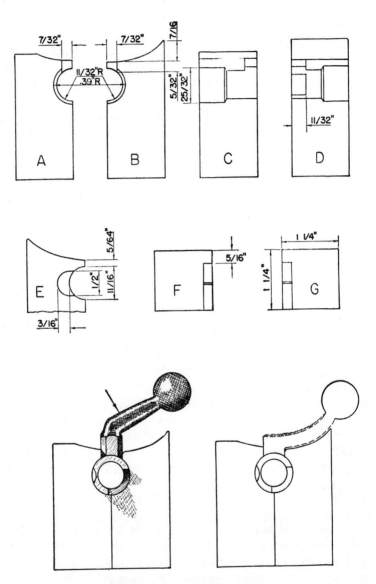

MAUSER BOLT BENDING JIG

This gadget is something of a time saver in bolt altering, but of course does not allow the freedom of design and shaping possible with the alteration by welding. You can make the jig yourself, and ordinary cold rolled steel stock will last so long you will want a new one for a change before you wear it out. Tool steel is very little better.

A short cut, of sorts, is possible with the straight type of shank, in that it is possible to arrange a low-bolt alteration without completely cutting off the handle. First, heat the center of the shank red and with a wrench or pipe bend it upward, raising the knob approximately $\frac{1}{4}''$ from its original position. Viewed from the rear, the handle now has a fairly graceful upward sweep. The next step is to saw or file a "V" $\frac{1}{8}''$ deep at the bolt root, or stub, on the underside inner edge of the stub, $\frac{1}{16}''$ or slightly more from the body of the bolt. Then make a saw-cut $\frac{1}{8}''$ deep on the top side, about $\frac{3}{16}''$ from the body of bolt. Make a V cut in the rear edge of the bolt, joining the two cuts already made, and if desired, you can make a shallow joining cut at the front edge. Now you heat the cut area to a bright red and bend the bolt down to the correct point, also bending it slightly back, gaining the rake-back effect. After cooling, grind the top side of the shank to approximately the correct low profile position, clean any scale from the cuts and weld them up. The job is polished and finished as in the standard alteration,

---

The jig is designed to support the body of the bolt and the root of the handle while the handle is heated by an acetylene torch and forged into the new shape by hammer.

A. Rear view of the left hand block, showing dimensions and styling of shaping.

B. Rear view of the right hand block, showing measurements which must be followed to achieve the correct curve.

C. Side, or rather, inside view of the left hand block, showing dimension of boring to accommodate the enlarged bolt base.

D. Inside view of the right hand block, showing the depth of the cut necessary to protect the safety lug on the bolt.

E. Front view of the right hand block, showing the cut to protect the safety lug.

F. Top view of the block, showing dimension of the lip, which is desirable on both blocks to prevent unnecessary pressure on the body of bolt when clamped in the vise.

G. Top view of the block, showing the recommended stock dimensions.

No vertical dimension is given, since this is regulated by your vise. The blocks must bottom on the screw housing of the vise, and project just enough above the jaws to permit use of the jig.

At the bottom left is shown the jig assembled on a Mauser bolt, with the arrow indicating the direction of the hammer blows. After the handle is cherry red, begin hammering at the root first, and continue until the bottom meets the top of the right hand block. At the right is shown the forged bolt handle, ground down, with dotted lines indicating the final shaping to be done by a file. This shape is very similar to that of the postwar FN Mauser low bolt, and it is necessary to notch the receiver tang so that the bolt may be fully closed.

but, aside from the one extra heating, requires less time and effort, as you need not setup and align the separate cutoff piece and make a complete welding. No jigs, bricks or supports of any kind are necessary.

The bent-down handles are often rather difficult to alter, as some manufacturers really put a crimp in them, making it necessary to grind considerable metal off the shank preliminary to welding, so that it is necessary to add or buildup quite a bit of metal in order to have a substantial shank. Shanks may be turned on their side and welded, or retained in their original position and simply welded on lower down, the top edge being set low enough to permit scope use after being dressed.

Scope safeties for Mausers are installed as for the Springfield, except that adjusting them is a little easier. If the Mauser cocking piece rides too far forward when cocked, so that the safety requires considerable strength to operate, simply grind, file or stone the forward top edge of the cocking piece back until the safety works smoothly. It should be required to only cam the cocking piece away from the sear—a very short distance is sufficient. Of course it should hold securely and to that end make sure that when in the engaged position a flat face is presented to the edge of the cocking piece, which should also be flat, and polished. If either of these contact surfaces are angled, the tension of the mainspring tends to disengage the safety through camming action.

General. Winchester Model 54s require the same type of bolt alteration for telescopic sight use as the Springfield and Mauser, and are treated the same way. Bolts are of nickel-steel and except that no notch for the bolt handle is cut in the receiver, the weld is quite easy. Due to the pear-shaped knob, the altered handles have a very good appearance, very similar to that of the Model 70.

For either Mauser or Springfield, the thickness of the shank at its junction with the knob prevents a very good appearance, so use the file to thin it down after the alteration. Otherwise, the shank may have so little taper it presents a straight, stiff appearance. Personally, I do not like perfectly round knobs, preferring the pear or semi-acorn type. Diameter of the knob need not be so great, either; $1\frac{1}{16}''$, or even $\frac{5}{8}''$, on a streamlined alteration is sufficient.

Length of the bolt handle may be kept at the standard for general use, the standard being the original length for the rifle involved, but on a rifle intended for use against dangerous game, such generally being of heavy caliber or high-pressure loading, I would recommend making the bolt handle longer by $\frac{3}{16}''$ to $\frac{3}{8}''$. This extra length would not only create extra leverage for cartridge extraction, it would also

Above is shown a war-relic of First World War after it has been cleaned up and altered a bit by Harold G. Rowe, Three Rivers, Michigan. This action came from an Oberndorf 1916 straight-bolt rifle that had been stored down a cellar for years and which was so badly rusted up that Hal got it for $5.00.

The bolt was first set down properly; the locking-screw holes welded out; sling-swivel hole in forward part of guard then welded out and the guard streamlined. Then the matting done; bolt knob checkered; receiver ring and frame matted properly until all lettering and pit markings had vanished and the body of the bolt then "frosted" neatly.

All parts polished by hand, to preserve edges and corners. Averages about 16 hours time, in all, to do a proper job such as shown above. Costs $20.00, delivered in either blue or white.

There are any number of old, rusted war-relics lying around that can be treated in the above manner and made to look like a new, custom-built job throughout.

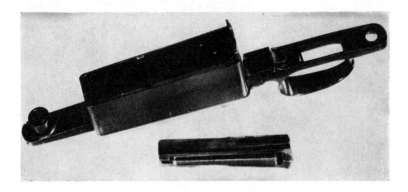

MAGAZINE IMPROVEMENT

Springfield 1903 triggerguard altered for use with .257 cartridge and Mauser action. Note the cartridge guide visible in top of magazine box. These little vertical plates (one on each side) contact cartridge shoulders and prevent forward movement under recoil.

The Mauser follower is narrowed very slightly at the front so that it will move freely between the guides.

offer a more prominent knob for manipulation under trying conditions. For the target shooter, a longer bolt handle with its greater opening and extraction leverage makes rapid fire work a little easier.

Cartridge guides can be installed in sporting arms to prevent mutilation of soft-pointed bullets. These guides are merely metal supports at the sides of the magazines which contact the shoulders or cartridges and prevent the bullets from being forced forward against the front wall of the magazine box through recoil as the rifle is fired. The best method is to solder thin, half-round strips of metal to the inside walls of the box just ahead of the point reached by the shoulder of the cartridge. I have used these on several guns. Credit for the idea, I believe, goes to Fred Barnes, the bulletmaker. A commercial bullet-point-protector, a bent strip of spring steel, is available for most rifles at present. With either method, it is necessary to either notch the sides of the magazine follower at the point where the cartridge stop shoulder contacts it, or narrow down the follower from that point forward.

There are many other rifles which could be mentioned here, however, only a few merit attention. The Japanese guns can be altered for scope use, but why? The same goes for the assorted Mannlichers, although most of them require fairly high mounted scopes, no matter what you do. The Mannlicher-Shoenauers can be rebuilt into American type sporters, by cutting off the clip slots and setting the handle about $\frac{3}{16}''$ lower. In converting the 6.5mm to .257, which seems to be a popular idea, it is necessary to make a new magazine cartridge stop, or radically alter the old one, and set a block in the bottom of the magazine to support the bullets and insure good feeding. For a scope safety, the only way I know of to make a good one for this rifle is to alter to curve the original, cutting the thumb-piece off and welding a new one, curved and thinner, on at a lower angle. No commercial ones are available.

Set-triggers, sworn by or at, are common on European sporting rifles. Unwanted Mauser set-triggerguards can be replaced with standard military guards and triggers, unless of course they are on short or magnum actions. To replace set-triggers on either of the latter you will have to remove the set-trigger housing, make a block to take its place in the guard, slot it for a regular trigger and install same. Many German and Austrian-made sporters have their pistol grips set so far back on the stock that it is difficult to reach either the front trigger, or a standard military trigger if substituted. For such arms it is best to make a trigger out of flat stock, angling its shank backward so that the finger curve is positioned far back in the loop of the guard.

Adjustment of set-triggers has apparently received little attention since the days of the International Matches, even abroad. Practically all have poorly-fitting trigger levers, or sear kickoffs. This, the part which replaces the trigger in the sear and pulls the sear·down when kicked by the set-trigger mechanism, must be very carefully made. On the Mauser set-trigger—that type used by the Mauser factory on its former commercial sporting rifles—it is possible to shape the bottom tip of the trigger lever so that a very good pull is obtained when using the trigger unset. A lip must be fashioned on the bottom edge of the lever to contact the front trigger cam when the trigger is in forward position. This permits a short pull for firing when the trigger is not used set. Sear engagement is cut down, if necessary, to give a fair pull, without too much creep—most set-trigger arms have the sear faces reduced anyway.

The most important facts relating to any type of set-trigger mechanism are the hardness of its parts and the fit of its pins. In a set-trigger you have pocket-watch parts doing punch-press work, and the steel must be the very best. Pins of course must not be a sloppy fit in their holes.

Several types of special triggers have come up in the recent past, the best known, possibly, being the Mashburn. This, like the Micro-movement trigger made by Allen Timney, is a sear-release type, in which the special sear is held in place by the trigger nose or a special part, being freed when the trigger is pulled, allowing the cocking piece to force the sear downward. The Winchester Model 70 employs the sear-release trigger in a different form. All of these give quick trigger pulls, without takeup or creep and with little movement of the trigger itself. The creepless letoff is obtained by having very little engagement of working parts and while theoretically not as safe as it should be, actually is quite practical since parts are of the finest tool steel well hardened and carefully adjusted.

Speedlocks for large bolt actions—Springfield, Mauser and Enfield—can be made by shortening the length of the cocking notch and adjusting the length of the firing pin cocking piece assembly to match. Sedgely used to make quite a few speedlock Springfields, but they never created a great deal of interest. For any of the actions mentioned, when the length of the notch is diminished and cocking cam angle therefore eased, the cocking piece is naturally limited in forward travel and the firing pin must be lengthened by the amount the bolt notch is decreased. Such actions cock easily, with standard springs, but should be fitted with extra strong springs to insure ignition.

TABLE OF BARREL-SHANK AND RECEIVER DIAMETERS

Receiver	Shank Diameter	Receiver Diameter
Mauser, Standard	1.100″	1.42″
Mauser, Small Ring	.980″	1.35″
1917 or 1914 (Enfield)	1.125″	1.375″
1903 Springfield	1.040″	1.35″
Winchester Models 54 & 70	1.00″	1.35″
Remington Models 721 & 722	1.05″	1.35″
Krag-Jorgensen (U.S.)	.980″	1.29″

There have been made some small ring Mauser receivers threaded for the standard barrel shank of 1.100″ diameter. Also, the military rifles, particularly Mausers, will vary slightly either way in receiver diameter from the dimension given, due to manufacturing and finishing methods.

The receiver diameter of course governs the maximum barrel diameter at cylinder, or just ahead of receiver. Therefore either the Enfield or standard Mauser can allow more barrel stock at this point than the other actions.

CHAPTER 16

Pistol and Revolver Work

THE gunsmith's cross—good guns are easy to work on, but good ones seldom need work. It is the cheap revolver that puts the gray hairs and thick spectacles on the gunsmith, and the non-pedigreed foreign junk.

Might as well dispose of the foreign stuff first. Nearly all German, Austrian and Italian handguns are quite well made and safe, so you need have no conscience trouble in repairing them. Spanish and Belgian arms need serious thought. All Spanish pistols and revolvers are not pot-metal junk. There are at least two makes of Spanish revolvers which compare in quality with Colt, or Smith & Wesson, but since they are equally high priced are very scarce in the U. S. In fact, I have never seen one in this country.

The common Spanish import is made in Eibar, Spain, a home-shop gunmaking town, which turns out an endless variety of very low grade autoloading pistols and revolvers. Not all of these have Spanish names or legends, having instead stamping in French and English. However, in some out-of-the-way spot you can almost always find "Made in Spain" and Spanish proofmarks. Excepting the "Astra" or Star brand, these can be given a blanket condemnation as not only poor mechanically, but actually unsafe to fire. The larger military type Astra pistols are safe enough with standard ammunition if in good condition. Most Spanish revolvers are copies of S & W outwardly, but employ a modified Colt lock system. Not all are of poor metal, so when one comes in for repair, inspect it closely before taking the owner into the corner and breaking the news gently that his pet is strictly NG and he should take it apart and then throw the pieces in different rivers. I ran into a Smith & Wesson copy which was exact in all parts, and made of good steel throughout, all parts being forged and machined, not cast and polished.

The usual trouble with revolvers is old age. Holes enlarge, parts wear, springs take a set, and so on. The hardest job is rebuilding a cylinder ratchet which has been worn down to the point where even the best-shaped hand nose will not revolve it in perfect timing. The teeth of the ratchet must be very carefully built up by welding, then cleared and re-cut. A milling cutter of the correct radius is naturally the best method of reshaping the teeth, but it is possible to do a satisfactory job with the hand grinder fitted with one of the little carborundum cutoff discs. Sometimes a faulty ratchet can be made serviceable by simply deepening with the relief cuts and emphasizing the teeth. The "hand" or part which engages the ratchet and turns it must be adjusted to the job so that each chamber will be brought exactly in line with the barrel. And the cylinder lock, called "bolt" by Colt, often requires adjustment, either elimination of burrs, or the making of an entire new bolt to obtain a larger locking surface to engage worn cylinder notches. This is all much harder to do than it reads.

Hand springs on the little pocket, suicide and burglar guns—H & R, Iver Johnson, and a host of obsolete similar arms, are always giving trouble. Earlier models used small flat springs stuck in a cut in the hand itself, which break, and later ones use wire helical springs, which get out of place and jimmy up the rest of the action. For the latter I have evolved my own system—make a spring wire, with ends bent to loop around convenient edges of the parts to hold them in place. Next time you take one of these guns apart look at the hand and you will be able to figure out just what that particular gun should require. Triggersprings often break and must be replaced, either with flat or looped-wire V types. Pins nearly always are very soft and burr, wear and bend easily. Mainsprings are easily replaced by lock-spring material, as they are straight flat types, not the tapered flat style. Looseness of cylinders is almost impossible to eliminate, but satisfactory timing can be achieved by working on the hand and cylinder stop.

The worst thing about these cheap revolvers is their general makeup —you can fix one thing and two days later it is back in the shop for an entirely different ailment, which the owner does not understand, and thinks you did not fix it right in the first place. I make it understood that no work is guaranteed on such guns except as specifically applied to the part or function repaired. The hardest job on most of the guns is putting them back together, as usually the triggerguard must be sprung into position in the frame, with the trigger, sear, and other attachments loose inside, to be pinned afterward. To hold sears in place in their cut in the rear of the guard while assembling you may employ either the old matchstick system or the modern assembly pin plan!

A short pin is desired, to hold the sear in place, which is pushed through the hole in the frame by the true pin. The only requirement is that it be of approximately full hole diameter and shorter than the width of the guard.

Colt Revolvers. The many Colt models in use are an ever-growing headache, as new parts are available only for the modern line. The old Army single action, famed in song, story and cinema, will be with us from now on, and will continue to break springs, bolts and, once in a while, a hammer. The cylinder locking bolt is the bottleneck. It has two prongs at the rear, which are spring temper, the stop portion is hardened, and the shape is hard to work out. The part is not difficult to make, either by hand or with the milling machine, but adjusting it and then hardening and tempering—not so easy. Aside from losing screws and breaking cylinder stop bolts, the single action is not too hard to repair. Replacement barrels can be made without much trouble by any of the rifle barrelmakers, although they will want quite a fee. Firing pins sometimes break, but as they are simply an insertion in the hammer, a new one can be easily turned and fitted. The Dem-Bart Company features a floating firing pin assembly for these guns. The heavy fall of the hammer annoys some shooters, and the hammer can be lightened a good bit without harming ignition. It can also have the tang welded up, for reshaping into the lower, and wider Bisley style.

The original Colt double action, or Lightning, model, is a thorough troublemaker. The cylinder locking bolt and the trigger must be adjusted perfectly, or the cylinder will not revolve properly. A camming stud on the trigger activates the bolt, and if the stud and the cam edge of the bolt do not coordinate, the bolt is not moved sufficiently far to the rear to clear the heads of the cartridges when the cylinder is loaded. This cam end of the bolt is also a spring in itself, which adds to complications. The frame itself is rather soft, and the holes in which trigger pin and bolt pin (part of the bolt) move, tend to push out of shape, which disturbs the timing of the action. The sear, hand and hammer mechanism do not give so much trouble, although sometimes the hammer notch must be worked on in order to obtain both single and double action functioning. The Lightning is a great gun to hang on the wall over the fireplace, so advise its retirement, rather than repair, if you do not have two or three free days to spare on it!

Another old Colt is the .38 double action Army—the side-wheeler—whose cylinder turns in the opposite direction to other Colts. While practically a modern design, no replacement parts are available. My experience has been that the main complaint on this model is that the ratchet wears to the point of uselessness, requiring a complete re-shaping job.

The few obsolete autoloading pistols—.38 Navy and .38 Pocket model—are not too bad to work on, providing no major part is missing or broken. Firing pins, extractors, ejectors, springs, and the like, can be made, providing enough of the original remains to give an idea of what its shape and dimensions should be for proper functioning.

The modern Colt arms are of course familiar to every gunman, and replacement parts are available. In these guns, for general repair work it is best to use factory parts, wherever possible. When a standard arm is to be remodeled into a target gun, then of course it may be de sirable to make special replacement parts.

Colt's revolver lock mechanism is vaguely reminiscent of an old Rube Goldberg cartoon, but it usually works. Because the V-type mainspring gives its greatest tension at the start of the tension, or compression, therefore causing the hammer tension in manual cocking to be heaviest at the beginning of the movement and easing as the hammer comes to full cock, the Colt is preferred over the Smith & Wesson by most target shooters. The S & W straight mainspring requires increasing strength to bring the hammer to full cock. Some adjustment of hammer tension on the Colt is possible by weakening the V mainspring, either by bending together slightly, or spreading the V to gain greater tension. A lot of the boys have broken these springs by ramming a screwdriver into the V to open it out. If you must stretch one of these, put one "leg" of the spring into the corner of the vise clamping it $3/16''$ or $1/4''$ above the V bend, then, with the fingers, pull the other leg outward. Safest way of all is to anneal the bend, adjust, and retemper.

Safety levers hardly ever give trouble, and ratchets do not wear excessively. Once in awhile it may be necessary to fit a new hand, or polish up a rebound lever. The latter controls trigger return, through tension of the lower leg of the mainspring. Firing pins break fairly often, and while easy to make, use a factory one if such is handy. It is practically impossible to duplicate the Colt firing pin rivet at the price it sells for, so buy it too. A pin can be used to replace it of course, if necessary. If made, both firing pin and its retaining pin should be hardened and drawn just enough to eliminate brittleness. These parts take considerable of a beating.

Again, the bolt is the wrongdoer in most cases of Colt offtiming. In old or worn guns, a new bolt may function perfectly double action, but be off in single action timing. The simplest corrective for this is to

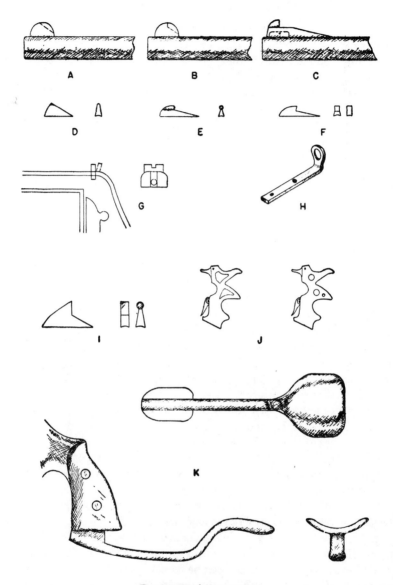

REVOLVER ALTERATIONS

A. Showing how standard fixed front sight can be reshaped to semi ramp form.

B. Ditto, showing how target sight can be cut from standard.

C. Ramp front sight, attached to barrel or to remains of original front sight by means of pins. Can be sweated on.

limit its movement inside the action, not cut down the bolt engagement stud. Often a tiny pin set in the frame will cure the trouble, or metal can be added to the bolt itself at the front of the hump at the pivot hole. Study of the action with sideplate removed will give a clear picture of the bolt's movement.

While mentioning sideplates, it is always customary to remind the reader to remove the screws with the correct sized screwdriver and then tap the frame with a block of wood until the tight plate loosens up. Save time also by removing the screws and then snapping the gun a few times.

Loose crane joints are easily tightened if you have a good lead hammer and know where to wallop. I believe in having the gun apart at the time, using the hammer with discretion on the crane housing in the frame and closing the opening slightly in order to take up the slack. Oversized ejector pin holes in the crane are cured by either bushing or making an oversize pin.

Adjusting the sighting of a fixed sight model revolver is often a rather hard job. When the customer comes in and says his Official Police or whatever he has shoots six inches to the left at twenty yards, you must resist the temptation to tell him to aim six inches to the right to compensate. If he will not hold still for an adjustable target type rear sight, you must work over the gun as is. One method of lateral sight movement is turning the barrel either in or out slightly, which cants the front sight, bringing the top to the desired point. While this presents a somewhat odd appearance, the practice has some merit, in

---

D. Plain tapered semi-ramp front sight, for quick draw work.

E. Bead front sight, for soldering to barrel.

F. Undercut target front, with ramp, for same attachment to either revolver or pistol.

G. Rear sight blade locations, the blade being made separate and installed in a cut in the top of the frame to accommodate it.

H. Peep rear sight for handguns. The hole must be quite large—around $\frac{1}{4}''$. The front screw hole in the base is for attaching to the revolver frame or pistol slide, the rear hole being slotted slightly so that the sight can be pivoted to one side or the other for windage correction.

I. Large and high front sights, for use with peep rear.

J. Two methods of lightening revolver hammers.

K. Wrist support for revolver, side, bottom and end views. These are to be adjusted so that when arm is held in normal sighting position, the support plate contacts the underside of the forearm just behind the wrist and relieves some of the holding strain. Adapted for heavy revolvers in slow fire shooting.

that no changes need be made in the frame of the arm. Filing the rear sight notch in top of frame to one side allows a slight adjustment, but may not be desirable, as it naturally results in a wide notch. Moving the front sight is possible although it is sweated into a milled cut in the barrel. Removing the sight, milling the slot wider on one side, fitting a new sight with the top in the right place, then reblueing the barrel, amounts to a good deal of work and expense. I have thought of a way to move the front sight profile, but have never tried it. Just cut the sight thinner on the "far" side (away from point of impact) then attach a small plate with pins, screws or soft solder on the opposite side. This is to bring the blade to its original thickness, or to the desired width. If solder is used, the plate should overlap the rear edge of the blade, so that when blued, an even surface will be presented to the eye when aiming.

If the revolver shoots high, the original blade may be removed and a higher one installed. If low, the factory blade can be filed down. Simplest in the long run is probably sight correction by widening the rear sight notch and milling a thin cut across the top of the frame for installation of a rear sight blade, with a notch of correct lateral and vertical dimensions cut after installation. Start with a small, narrow notch, letting the owner of the gun shoot it and widening and deepening the notch to his orders.

Trigger pull adjustment on the Colt revolver depends very slightly on the mainspring tension and principally upon the trigger-hammer engagement. Very careful, guided stoning and honing is necessary first to smooth the surfaces of the notches, then to shallow them to reduce the engagement. At the start just polish them, clean up the action, oil, reassemble and try the pull. Trigger weights are used as for the rifle. A short weight rod can be made for convenience in handling. Never reduce the sear engagement on any gun of any type until you have tried all other means of trigger adjustment. Polishing often helps a great deal, and in many cases, a plain, ordinary clean-up job and re-oiling does the work, all by itself.

Colt hammers can be skeletonized, as illustrated, but get a real drill to make the holes. My belief is that it is best not to anneal these in order to cut them, as the heat-treatment necessary to obtain the tensile strength and wearing qualities is extremely difficult to do. Once a hole is cut in the hammer, it can be elaborated by the hand grinder. Moving the point of the hammer, to obtain a short action, is a major operation, involving all the action parts and their functions. Leave such work to the handgun specialists such as King and Buchanon. I have re-timed several makes of short actions, and see no particular merit in them.

Smith & Wesson Revolvers. The S & W lock mechanism is simpler than that of the Colt and the parts are somewhat better finished. The commonest fault found is the extractor rod loosening, unscrewing slightly and preventing the cylinder being swung out for loading—all it needs is to be screwed back tight again. Turning it tight with a pair of pliers usually makes it stay organized, but if not, linseed oil may be applied to the threads before tightening, in order to hold it. Timing the S & W is governed almost entirely by the point of the hand. Prewar Smiths were very closely fitted—so closely that often they come to the shop with the action frozen, from dried oil and lack of use. Firing pins are of the same type as the Colt and are treated the same way in replacement, held by a flush pin.

Regulation of triggerpull is handled principally through manipulation of the trigger return spring. This very stiff spring creates most of the tension on the trigger, whether the arm is cocked or not. I weighed the last S & W triggerpull job I did—a new gun, pull very crisp, weight 4 pounds 1 ounce. With the mainspring removed, and holding the hammer out of engagement, the trigger would lift 3 pounds 3 ounces without moving! With a 2¾ pound pull ordered, it was obviously necessary to weaken the trigger return spring. I have found it impractical to substitute weaker springs. It is best to shorten the original spring, slipping about a third of a turn off at a time and trying the pull thus obtained. With the great majority of Smith & Wesson revolvers, no stoning of the notches is necessary to reduce a heavy pull. The very slight engagement and releasing friction has very little to do with the pull, as compared with the trigger spring. Should a gun have creep, naturally the notches must be cleared to smooth surfaces and sharp edges. Mainspring tension is subject to some adjustment of the screw through the front strap of the grip, but in the main, this screw should be turned in almost all the way. The flat mainspring can of course be thinned to make the gun cock easier, but ignition may be affected if much change is made.

Sight adjustment of the fixed sight Smith & Wesson is much more difficult than on the Colt, as the front sight is forged integral with the barrel, hence cannot be removed and relocated. Turning the barrel slightly is not possible of course, due to the ejector pin housing and any real correction must be made by installation of a rear sight blade. The old-style S & W target or adjustable rear sight could be mounted fairly easily on almost any Smith or Colt by milling or filing the slot in the top strap to accept it, but the present target sight is more work to fit.

38 S&W SPECIAL

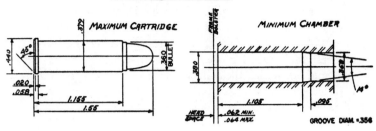

357 S&W MAGNUM

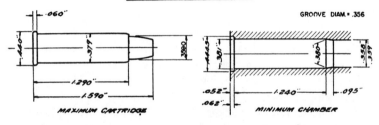

9 MM. '08 LUGER

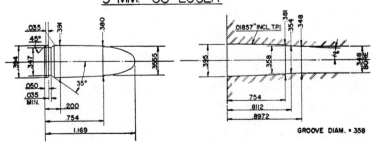

Military Pistols. The U. S. Browning-designed Colt .45 caliber semi-automatic pistol Model 1911 is now the most popular center-fire pistol in the United States. Used not only by U. S. forces but also by all Mexican services, and in some other foreign nations in limited quantities, great numbers have been made by Colt, Remington, Ithaca and two or three wartime contracting firms. The finest models are considerably more accurate than the standard arms, and quite a business exists in converting the latter into comparable match guns. Design of the pistol and military manufacturing tolerances do not make for maximum accuracy possible, and several parts must be altered or replaced for best results. Adjustable sights of course are desirable, but some target men prefer fixed sights to special dimensions. Usually these are much higher and larger than the issue, not only for better perception, but to raise the sight line farther from the top of the slide in order to minimize heat waves or mirage and their effect upon definition.

Sights can be made, but there are several manufacturers of good .45 sights—every issue of *The American Rifleman* seems to carry a new advertisement. The real accuracy job starts at the front end of the

---

.38 SPECIAL, .357 MAGNUM & 9MM LUGER

The .38 Special, originated by Smith & Wesson, is today the most widely-used revolver cartridge in the U. S. A. Almost all police departments require their men to carry this caliber in a service pistol. It is also our most popular center-fire target cartridge and as such is loaded by both factories and individuals with super-accurate match components.

The .357 Magnum, also a Smith & Wesson development, is a super-power .38 Special, the chamber allowing use of all .38 Special cartridges as well as the longer .357. Do not attempt to rechamber standard .38 Special revolvers for the Magnum case. The chamber pressure of the .357 load is high enough to blow out cylinder walls in many models of handguns. Only the S. & W. Heavy Duty, or the similar Outdoorsman revolvers will permit rechambering for .357 and the Smith & Wesson people are very much against even this.

The 9mm Luger is world-famous, both as cartridge and pistol, and probably more different pistols and sub-machine guns have been made in this caliber than in any other single caliber. The cartridge has been used by a great many nations as a military service standard and is still in wide use. It is a well-balanced unit, giving maximum velocity and energy with minimum recoil. As will be noted from the drawings, bore diameter compares with our .38 Special dimensions. Due to innumerable manufacturing plants of both arms and ammunition, there are many slight variations in case and chamber measurements but none which will prevent interchangeability.

pistol and works back, as the secret of making a .45 shoot is getting the barrel tight in the slide and the frame when locked. The barrel bushing must fit the barrel closely when the slide is forward, yet allow for the vertical movement of the barrel in the unlocking stage. First of all, the barrel should be turned down very slightly either to a true cylinder or with a taper turned on it, the taper being from .002″ to .004″, beginning ⅛″ from the muzzle and extending from 1½″ to 1¾″ back, the large end being to the front, and the smaller diameter to rear. Modifications of the principle are also used—the barrel being turned down from .002″ to .005″ straight from a point 5⁄16″ or ⅜″ back of the muzzle for a distance of approximately 2½″ and the bushing bored out so that only a narrow band supports the barrel. As for the bushing itself, it can be enlarged and an inner bushing inserted, threaded and sweated, or replaced. I think that it is by far the best idea to buy an old-style Colt Super .38 bushing and very carefully bore and polish it until your barrel will just fit.

The barrel may have steel added by welding to its underside, at the link housing, in order to better support the link. The link itself should be used as a pattern for a new one, made of tool steel and oversize enough to force the barrel locking lugs tightly into the lug recesses in the slide when the gun is locked, ready to fire. Holes in the link must be slightly farther apart than in the original and should fit their respective pins—link pin and slide stop—very closely. Case or surface-harden this link deeply—it must resist wear and yet not be brittle, so do not harden it all the way through. A good way to get correct dimensions easily is to make a dummy link of brass or bronze first, then copy it on the flat steel stock. Still another trick is to build back the metal lip on the rear of the barrel, filing it until it contacts the slide face when a cartridge is in the chamber. This gives a uniform headspace as well as tension on the barrel forward, which is supposed to be good for something or other. I have never thought too much of the idea, personally, but several dyed-in-the-wool .45 owners think it very fine.

Tightening the slide is quite easy and simple. *Do not* put the bottom edge of the slide in the vise and give it the works as you are likely to spend the next four hours opening it up again. The slides are fairly soft and bend easily. First of all, polish the grooves and guide rails in the slide and on the frame, then close-in the slide so that it will just move freely back and forth, with no side play or "wiggle." A block of hardwood makes a good anvil and a rawhide hammer will do the work as well as a lead hammer and not mark the slide at all. Be careful at the rear edges of the slide and where the slide stop cut is located, for at these points the metal is easier bent than at the remaining portions.

Little is done to the frame, or receiver, other than polishing of the inside surface and cuts. The hammer is not to be touched, beyond polish, except possibly remodeling the tang for easier cocking—broadening and checkering. The trigger runways should be smooth, and the trigger should slide smoothly forward and back, but should not have any vertical play. This can be eliminated to a large extent by bending the trigger loop either up or down—easily done by clamping about ½″ from the rear in the vise and pressing the balance with the fingers. The rear face of the trigger loop, which contacts the sear, is polished. In fact, you flat-polish everything but the top of the disconnector. Sear and hammer contacts are adjusted as for any similar triggerpull job, but only on a tightly fitting sear and hammer combination can a very light pull be reliable in use. It may be necessary to make new hammer and sear pins, should the holes have too great tolerance. The jar of the falling slide will trip a too-slight sear engagement, so it is best to keep the pull above 3¼ pounds in all cases. Some of the match shooters keep extra hammers which are fitted to their guns, giving various weights of triggerpull.

In an accurate .45 pistol, or Super .38, when the slide is forward, the exposed portion of the barrel at the ejection port will not move at all when pressed down or sideways.

The little lip on the grip safety can be enlarged by welding to reach the rear of the trigger and adjusted by filing and stoning so that when the pistol is held and fired with a normal hold it will act as a trigger stop. The tang of the grip safety can be lengthened so that the hammer tang cannot reach the web of the hand, for protection of large-handed men.

Other Colt pistols are all commercial weapons so they need no rebuilding. The Super .38 is almost a duplicate of the .45 except for barrel parts and slide face. Overseas, during the war, I and other military armorers converted many of them to .45 caliber, so that issue ammunition could be used. The slide face had to be filed wider, to accommodate the .45 cartridge base, and a new barrel bushing used. The .25 and .32 pocket pistols need only routine repair work occasionally—usually putting in a new part does the job. The .22 Woodsman is highly popular and quite a few owners want them fixed up, pulls lightened, barrels heavier, and all that. In my opinion this is one of the hardest guns to put a really good pull on, because of the weird helical trigger spring and the connection system. Actual sear and hammer notch contact is treated as in any other similar lock system. The extractor is the weak part of the Woodsman, or has been. The new model has a better extractor and housing system.

Two other Browning pistols are now quite numerous—the Polish Model 35 Radom and the Belgian Model 35 GP, both for the 9mm Luger cartridge. A very few of the Belgian guns have been made for the 9mm long Browning and the 7.63mm Mauser pistol cartridge. These two pistols could be classed as the son and grandson of the 1911 (Colt) .45. The Polish pistol is one of the strongest ever made, so far as cartridge pressure is concerned, and is a very rugged arm. The barrel link is not used, nor is the barrel bushing, and the guns are quite accurate as they come, in spite of generally rough manufacturing standards. The barrel is cammed out of engagement with the slide by contact with a fixed stud or crossbar in the receiver. Any attempt to improve the barrel fit would involve changing the dimensions of the camming surfaces on the barrel stud itself. The trigger system is of the round-spur type, due to the fact that the gun was designed for cavalry use with one hand (remember the famous Polish Cavalry) and hammer styled so that the gun could be cocked by rubbing hammer across the thigh. The hammer release on the slide, which when pressed cams the firing pin forward, then trips the cocked hammer, was for the same reason, so that hammer could be lowered safely under any conditions without requiring both hands. It is quite reliable. The Radom is easy to work on, but due to lack of new parts, any damaged part must be repaired.

The Belgian gun, best known for its double-row magazine with thirteen-round capacity, is more modern than the Radom model. An entirely new trigger system is employed, incorporating a lever in the bottom of the slide to connect the trigger and the sear. Hammer and sear engagement is flush with the top of the receiver, so it is easy to observe and check and despite the extra connections, it is possible to put excellent trigger pulls on the guns. The locking system is the same as on the Radom, and the gun has the round-spur hammer. Unlike either Radom or Colt, there is no grip-safety, and the upper tang of the frame is rather short, so that the hammer spur will bite the web of any fair-sized hand. The round spur can be reshaped by grinding the lower portion away, up to the aperture, to a somewhat similar profile to American hammers, which save most hands from getting hurt. The original Belgian pistol had a tangent adjustable rear sight and a safety bar on the trigger, which prevented the gun being snapped or fired when the magazine was withdrawn. Later guns made under German "supervision" had fixed sights very much like those of the Army .45 and some

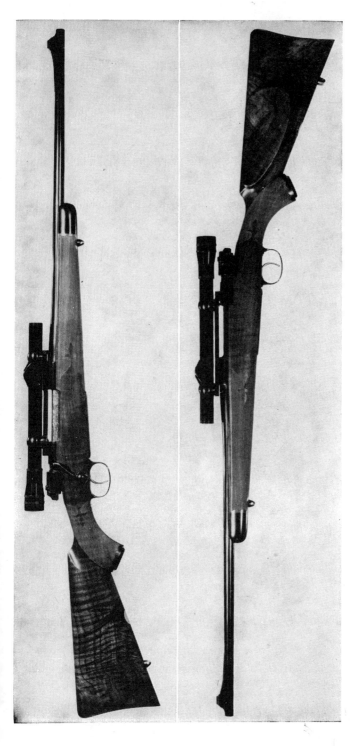

A .257 Roberts Stocked by Bob Owen

Here is another .257 Roberts on a Mauser action; barrel made by Ed Warner of Port Clinton, Ohio, from a Buhmiller blank, on which Ed did a beautiful job of chambering and general shaping. This rifle was made for Mr. Curtis Thompson, of Limestone, Maine.

This gunstock is a rare piece of American walnut that was at least 30 years old when acquired, and was grown in Ohio, a state that at one period shipped thousands of fine stock blanks all over the country. Strange to say, this piece of wood had all of the fine characteristics of fine French or Circassian walnut; the blank was formerly owned by Hon. Vic Donahey, once governor of Ohio.

Custom .22/250 on 1917 action, by P. O. Ackley. Note the fiddleback figure in the American walnut stock, and the contrasting wood forend tip. Also note the lines of the stock. I consider this the best-looking rifle I have ever seen on the Enfield action. Hensoldt Dialytan scope in Tilden mounts.

of them did not have the magazine safety feature. Germany modified the Radom also, to the extent of eliminating the takedown catch on some guns—this is in the location of the manual safety on the Colt—substituting a notch on the hammer nose which engages the slide to hold it to the rear for removal of the slide lock. The only safety on the Radom is the grip safety, and the Belgian gun has the manual safety and also a half-cock notch on hammer.

The Luger is still with us, and likely to be around for a long time, even if new guns are never made again. Fortunately, the M '08 pistol seldom breaks parts, and if it does, quite a few private individuals have spare parts for sale. The firing pin tip is the weak point of the arm, and when these break off, they can be rebuilt by welding. Except for the Italian Glisenti, which we will not mention otherwise, I think the Luger is probably the hardest pistol to put a good triggerpull on as about six parts are involved in releasing the striker or firing pin, and the pull can be affected by any or all. The dimensions and fit of the triggerplate, or sideplate, itself have quite a bit to do with the pull, and often if several plates are available they can be switched around to provide a satisfactory result without alteration of parts. The trigger lever, the L-shaped connecting bar between the trigger and the trigger bar (sear) will regulate the length of the takeup and the final pull. It can be bent to some degree, for adjustment, or can be copied on tool steel flat stock to obtain a thicker lower arm, which will take up more space in the slot in the trigger and therefore eliminate some free movement. This lower arm can be made shorter, with the end rounded, and give good results. The sear face of the trigger bar and its contact face on the firing pin should also be polished of course, to cut down creep. Replacement of the mainspring (recoil spring) can be rather trying if you do not first catch a turn of the wire under the hook of the recoil spring lever and then hold the spring and turn the lever until it winds the spring down, compressing it to a length readily insertable in the frame.

If you must remove a Luger barrel, be sure to make a block of aluminum or brass to fit tightly between the receiver walls close to the breech, so that your wrench cannot spring the walls together. Remove as you would a rifle barrel, clamping the barrel in blocks of hardwood and applying a wrench to the receiver ring or the barrel housing.

Walther's contribution to the souvenir hunter was the P 38, the double action autoloader. Well-made P 38s are quite accurate, but some of the production models are very loosely fitted, and I have not been able to figure out any way to fix them up short of welding up the grooves in barrel and then recutting them. Weakest points of the gun are the hammer release on the slide and the sears—both break. The hammer release does not retract the firing pin, then trip the hammer as does the Radom, but just blocks the firing pin and drops the hammer against it. The release (I refuse to call it a safety, although that is what it is intended for and so marked!) has a good many weakening machine cuts and recesses in it and the part which blocks the firing pin can break and allow the hammer to fire a cartridge, when the hammer is released on a loaded gun.

Although entirely different in design, the sear and hammer connection is comparable to that of a double action revolver and can be worked on in the same way. The milled face of the sear does not extend all the way across the part, which makes stoning it very difficult. You will need the newest and sharpest-edged hard Arkansas slip stone you can find to work on this notch. The trigger connecting bar can be worked on to eliminate some of the slack in the pull, but as a rule, these pistols have excellent single action pulls except for creep and weight, which can be eliminated by working on the hammer and sear. The locking block, which locks the slide, the barrel and the frame for firing, can be omitted in assembling the pistol, and some guns may come in without this vital part. The Germans took great delight in throwing away Luger sideplates and P 38 blocks, so gun-ignorant Americans brought home quite a few unusable souvenir arms.

Italian Beretta Model 1934s are a pleasure to work on—the only thing that ever breaks is the hammer, and that only when someone drops the gun on a cement floor. Trigger pulls can be lightened to quite a degree by cutting the hammer notch shallower, but it is difficult to get less than a 4 pound pull because the sear is part of the mainspring guide, therefore it is under great tension and so resists being pulled out of engagement with the hammer notch. The notch cannot be cut too low or the sear will engage the safety notch when released. The pivot plate, which connects trigger and sear, often has too wide a notch for the sear stud, allowing some unnecessary takeup. A new plate is easy to make, or the slot on the original can be welded shut and recut. Firing pin tips on most Berettas are practically flat, and it does not hurt to round the edges very slightly. The barrels are pinned into the frame by the safety, and should they become too loose to be contacted and held uniformly by slide pressure when the gun is loaded and cocked, the stud can be built up and filed to just permit the safety to function, in order to tighten the barrel fit.

Almost any pistol or revolver is considerably improved by having its action parts and pins polished, or "honed." Honing in that instance means smoothing the flat parts by rubbing them on a razor hone—the very fine whetstone used for straight razors. This insures smooth flats, with square edges, which is theoretically at least, the perfect method. Practically speaking, you can lay a sheet of crocus cloth on a piece of plate glass and polish your parts to equal functioning ease. Please note the beginning of the paragraph—*almost* any pistol or revolver—not all, handguns can be improved by easing the movement of their parts. Honing or polishing will not help much on a loosely-fitted action, where parts are free to slide hither and thither—such arms need parts fitted or replaced, before any real "improvements" can be introduced. It may even be necessary to install washers or fillets of steel shim stock to keep parts properly placed.

Excepting triggerpull jobs, you will seldom run into exactly the same problems on any given model handgun, therefore considerable thought must be expended on such repair work. Be sure you find the correct cause of trouble, before tearing into the job to fix the gun. The cylinder seems to drag—is it due to the cylinder lock riding high? Or is it a burred hand hanging on a ratchet, or a bent ejector rod, or a crane knocked out of line? Or has the gun at some time or other been washed in gasoline and improperly oiled afterward, so that hidden parts have rusted? You may save time in the long run by first disassembling the guns, cleaning up and reassembling, then oiling properly; often you will find out what causes the trouble without guesswork. If you are a whiz at diagnosis, take up medicine and be a doctor—you will make more money and keep your hands cleaner and the hours are not much worse either.

Special Work. Most special work on handguns will be done for a class of shooter which can be labeled the "in-betweens"—the men who are fairly well bitten by the gun bug, who shoot better than the poor marksmen and poorer than the experts. They are the ones who go for trick sights, special actions and fancy stocks, always seeking a short cut to high scores. Do not discourage them by advising the purchase of ammunition for practice rather than the newest gadget—eventually they will realize it themselves. Keep them happy by doing your best to satisfy their wants.

Custom stocks, or grips, will usually be quite well worked out before the customer brings the job to the shop. Standard blocks, or the gun butt itself, will be taped so with blocks or wood or built to desired shape with plastic wood or other material, so that usually the gunsmith has only the job of duplicating the result in good wood. It is a very

.38 COLT SUPER AUTOMATIC

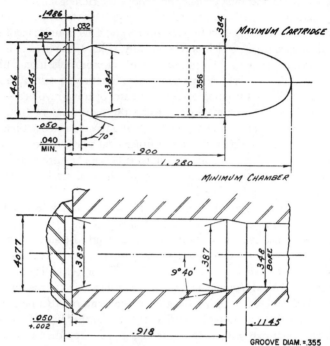

MAXIMUM CARTRIDGE

MINIMUM CHAMBER

GROOVE DIAM. = .355

45 ACP

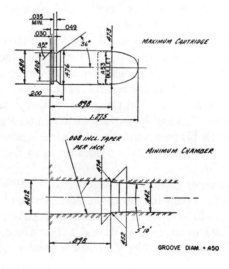

MAXIMUM CARTRIDGE

MINIMUM CHAMBER

GROOVE DIAM. = .450

excellent idea to make a set of stocks in soft pine first, checkering roughly, for trial use before the final good set is finished. Most men make the mistake of making their own stocks a trifle too large, and not thoroughly testing them. A revolver or pistol stock which may feel perfect in slow fire target work often proves unwieldy in rapid fire, due to bulk. Because weight is no factor and practically no strain is exerted on the stock, pistol and revolver stocks can be made of any kind of wood hard and dense enough to take and keep sharp checkering. The small blanks necessary are inexpensive in even the finest imported woods, so there is really no reason to use just any piece of walnut you have around. Hard maple is very excellent, though rather hard to work.

Checkering on handguns should be coarse and sharp—not finer than an 18-line, and 16-line is best. Where stocks are inletted to completely enclose the frame of the butt, a router bit for the drill-press saves a lot of time. As in any stock work, the inletting is completed on the square blank, before any outside shaping is done. If a router is used, your blanks must be squared and smoothed on both sides, so that the bit will cut an even depth. Factory screw escutcheons can be utilized, from old stocks, or ornamental ones made of aluminum, brass, silver or even plastic.

Wide hammer spurs are quite simple to make. Just make a large

---

The .38 and .45 Automatic Colt Pistol Cartridges

These two cartridges are considerably different: the .38 is semi-rimmed, and headspaces on the rim, or flange of cartridge base; the .45 is truly rimless, and headspaces on the front end of cartridge case. The sharp shoulder shown in the .45 chamber is quite pronounced, well illustrating the point of headspace.

This term "headspace" can be a bit of an understatement as the cartridges also "position" or "chamber" on the points mentioned.

The .38 ACP and .38 Super ACP are identical except for power of loading. The Super cartridge is one of the most powerful pistol cartridges ever developed and has a considerable edge over the .45 in velocity, energy, and range. With the expanding-type bullets formerly available, the .38 Super was an effective caliber against small and medium game in the hands of an expert shot, however at present only the full metal jacketed bullet is loaded by the factories.

The .45 ACP is world-famous as a service pistol and submachine gun cartridge, being used by many nations besides the United States. I do not believe there is any appreciable difference in chambering for the Colt pistol and for the Thompson or Reising submachine guns, other than manufacturing tolerances.

plaster of wet asbestos, molding it about the hammer's lower portions up to and over the pivot hole, and around the firing pin, then weld additional steel to the spur. (It is a good idea, too, to first grind away the original checkering on the spur.) After the welding is cool, the tang can be filed to the desired dimensions and checkered.

Occasionally detectives or policemen will want their service arms altered for fast action—front of the guards cut away, sights cut down or angled forward, butts rounded and other changes. One style of such alteration, originated by the FBI, should be called to the attention of such officials who have not been made aware of it. This is a modification of the cut guard, in which only the right front half of the guard loop is cut away, to expedite the forefinger reaching the trigger. (Left front half for left-handed men.) The rounded service front sight is made into a ramp type by filing from its bottom rear to the highest point. The slanting flat surface thus gained may be fine-matted or sand blasted, but is not to be checkered or lined.

The above manner of altering the guard loop makes the trigger almost as accessible as by completely removing it forward of the tip of the trigger, without losing any safety. With a cut loop, the trigger can of course be accidentally caught on the edge of the holster or the pocket when sheathing the gun, and in addition, the unsupported half-loop is easily bent up, to block the trigger action. Hammer spurs can be ground off easily, to make the gun snag proof, but I believe it is a good idea to cut a few grooves or checker the remainder, just back of the firing pin, so that the hammer may be cocked manually, starting it back double action, then bringing it to full-cock with the thumb without slipping. When it is not desirable to soften the hammer for checkering, a fairly satisfactory and neat substitute is cutting fine grooves across it with the hand grinder, using the little cutoff discs.

Some special alterations for handicapped men may turn up—large peep and front sights for failing eyes, or wrist supports for heavy guns. The peep sights must be very large, with about $\frac{1}{4}''$ apertures, and can be made of flat steel stock bent, shaped and drilled properly. It is usually necessary to cut a flat on the top of the revolver strap or pistol slide for them. Use a large, fine-thread screw at the front for hold-down purposes, and a smaller at the rear, with slightly larger hole in the sight leaf so that the sight can be pivoted enough for windage adjustment. Elevation can be worked out by installation of additional screws threaded through the sight leaf, but bearing against the top of the gun. The sketch illustrates better than words this type of sight. Front sights for use with such peep rears must be very high—start at

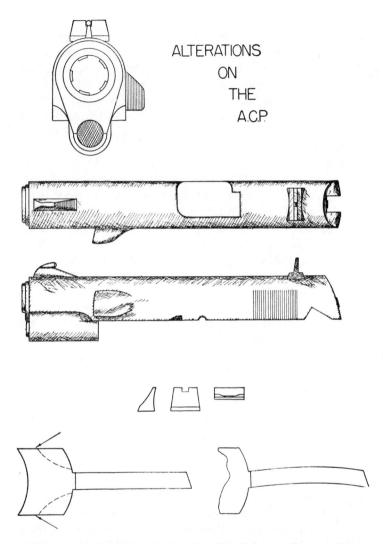

ALTERATIONS
ON
THE
A.C.P.

Which can also be used on pistols other than Colt manufacture, of course. At top is a frontal view of pistol showing the cocking lug welded on the side of the slide, for use of the one handed shooter, as mentioned in the text. Below are top and side views, showing the lug, and plinking sights made, with side, rear and top view of the target rear sight below the slide.

The trigger of the Colt pistol is sometimes quite a sloppy fit, having play up, down and sideways. The arrows point to portions which may be built up slightly by welding on metal to obtain a smooth slide fit, and at right the loop of the trigger is shown bent, to take up excess space in the grooves inside the frame, and to also cut down undesirable movement.

$\frac{9}{16}''$ above the barrel, and then cut them down to suit by shooting tests.

The drawing shows special pistol alteration and sights made for Anthony Lerua, Sr., to his order. Mr. Lerua has only his right hand, and likes to shoot pistols as well as revolvers. Since it is possible to load a magazine and insert it into a gun with only one hand, but rather difficult to hold the gun and pull back the slide to load the barrel ready to fire, the cocking studs or lugs were welded on the left side of the slides. In use, the pistol, with a loaded magazine, is held with the right hand and the stud placed against any convenient resistance—the edge of the shooting table, post, or heel of shoe, and forced forward. The slide is held by the stud and the pistol moved far enough to cock and load. On the Colt arms this operation is perfectly safe, and the idea is passed on to one-handed pistol shooters in the hope that it may be a way out for complete safe operation without help from others. I used the nickel steel welding rod on the .45 and .38 slides, and mild steel on the .380, all turning out well. The nickel-steel welded better and blued as well, no warpage was encountered and no objectionable scale resulted. I did not attempt to protect any portion of the slides, fearing unequal cooling of the metal might cause warping. Care must be taken to avoid melting through the slide at the thin portion over the groove, but otherwise, plain, careful welding will cause no trouble. The studs are not built up—that would require too much heat—but are basically a section of round stock cut at an angle and lap-welded all the way around, with welding rod added. Cut and shape this stud well before attaching to the slide, cutting the front angle and grooving this face. After attaching, the welds are naturally smoothed and the stud contoured into the slide, the face being touched up with needle or die-sinker's files. I thought of attaching these studs with screws or rivets, but felt that the thin walls of the slides might not hold well enough, besides not being as neat as a weld. On .22 pistols it might be possible to attach a stud with screws very easily, but a large stud would be needed. In steel, the added weight might interfere with functioning of the arm, so it might be wise to make the stud of dural, or other light alloy.

CHAPTER 17

Shotguns and Shotgun Work

THE repair and alteration of shotguns provides a large proportion of the general gunsmith's work, and in many sections of the country, nearly all of it. Scatterguns range from the ridiculous to the sublime, covering the simplest and poorest examples of the gunmaker to the highest possible type of craftsmanship. Modern arms—made, say after 1915—of the American production type seldom offer any great problem in repairing as new factory parts, or serviceable used parts for now obsolete models can usually be located. Older guns may require handmade replacement parts.

A good many of the cheap shotguns made and sold prior to World War I were "hardware store" jobs, made by now defunct plants for hardware jobbing concerns and marked with whatever name desired by the buyer. For these, few parts are available, and because the guns were of poor material, they are constantly coming into gunshops for repairs, which present quite a problem to the gunsmith, as usually everything is worn to the limit and a great deal of work should be done to put the gun into dependable serviceable condition. This may mean as much as twenty dollars or more, and the owners of such shotguns seldom can stand the tariff. The gun of course is often not worth the price of repair. Parts of such "orphan" arms are usually made of low-carbon steel, with a thin cyanide case-hardening. The hard surface is so thin it disappears at points of wear and holes pull out of shape, firing pins batter up, pins bend, notches wear out and the actions become very loose. Flat or V springs in this class of shotgun do not break too often, as they were not made of good enough material in the first place! They are usually simple in style, and easy to copy, but often are merely set from long usage and can be reshaped and re-tempered to good effect.

Low priced models made by the reputable manufacturers are sometimes little better than the orphan guns, but as a rule material is better and the more complicated parts can be purchased. In repairing the low cost gun, it must be remembered always that repair charges should be kept low in proportion. You do not make a hammer by hand for a ten-dollar single-barrel and charge the guy seven bucks, when you can order one from the factory for a dollar and charge another dollar to install it. When you can not order one, that is different.

Very often one of the more difficult parts to replace, such as lifters and slide levers on repeating shotguns, can be fixed by welding on steel to build up worn points, or attaching broken segments by welding or brazing. Single and double gun extractors, and forend metal parts, also can be repaired as well as replaced. Pump or trombone action guns sometimes wear all the action parts loose, thereby requiring replacement or repair of several parts in addition to the particular one which rendered the arm unserviceable at this particular time.

SPECIFIC MODELS AND TYPES

Remington

This firm today makes only autoloading and pump type shotguns, although probably they will resume the manufacture of their over-under double eventually, if demand should warrant it. The autoloader now being made is the Model 11–48, which has not been on the market long enough for me to have acquired any knowledge of its performance. So far, it seems very good. The gun is light and balances much like the pump action 31. It has no friction-ring assembly to be adjusted by changing the components around, as does the old model, but instead a marked ring at the same location is turned to the proper setting for light or heavy loads. The recoil spring is carefully balanced, and if a compensating choke device is installed on the barrel, a special weaker spring must be ordered from the Remington factory. Do not attempt to weaken the standard spring, to make a gun function after attaching any compensator.

The 11–48 is very easy to disassemble—a pin-punch and hammer will allow removal of trigger assembly—pins are held by spring plungers instead of lock-screws, and the operating handle can be pulled out of the bolt easily. Hunters can dismantle this shotgun in the field just with a nail and a stick or stone for a hammer, and no doubt will. The link is in two pieces, halves really, and the rear ends of both must go into the recess in the action spring follower. Or else! Should a layman remove the bolt from the receiver, then attempt to replace it without removing the triggerplate assembly so that he can see what he's doing, he is very liable to not get the link seated properly. It is doubtful that he could ever fire the gun so mis-assembled, but possible that he could damage parts by attempting to function the action by hand if of the heavy-handed brotherhood.

Model 11

Gunsmiths will be mainly called upon to work upon the old Model 11, of which many thousands are in use. This was made on license from Browning, to the original Browning design, and the guns are very similar to the Belgian-made autoloaders bearing Browning's name. Principal troubles are with wood—not metal—for both forends and stocks are easily cracked. The forends cannot be in too bad shape, however well repaired, as they serve to keep the barrel and receiver assemblies connected, holding them together against the tension of the recoil spring. If the forend is weakened by splitting or becoming oil-soaked next to metal parts, it will not serve its purpose as spacer and will allow the metal parts to undergo unnecessary punishment when the gun is fired.

Mechanically the system of the action is very good, breakage of parts usually being restricted to firing pins, extractors and mainsprings. Hammers are subjected to hard service and rapidly wear their pivot holes off center. Apparently this can go to an extreme point without affecting the operation of the shotgun, but it is a pertinent matter to bring to the customer's attention. A few parts are seldom broken in service, but not infrequently are messed up by the owner demonstrating some unskilled labor in tearing the action down and trying to put it together again. These are carrier springs, trigger springs, friction rings, and screwheads. He breaks the springs, loses the friction ring and some of the small locking screws to hold the triggerplate pin and large screws in place, and burrs up the tang screw, sometimes to the point of making it almost impossible to remove or replace. The gunsmith should therefore make an effort to stock the above mentioned parts. Excepting the friction ring, all are interchangeable between Model 11 and Sportsman models of all gauges. The old type milled flat type firing pin can be repaired when the tip is broken by welding on another tip, or replaced by the present round type pin, using the adapter furnished by Remington.

Failure of proper functioning in the Remington autoloading shotguns is more often due to improper adjustment of the friction assembly and lack of proper care on the owner's part than to any defect or fault of the gun. A diagram is given of the correct friction assemblies, as a ready reference chart. Often a well meaning shooter will oil every-thing heavily, which in the case of self-loading arms is detrimental to operation and life of the gun. The magazine tube, on which the friction parts do their work, should be quite smooth, but not polished. Burrs should be removed with a fine file and the whole tube smoothed by a light rubbing lengthwise with medium-coarse emery cloth. Tubes should be oiled with gun oil, then wiped clean with a lint-free cloth.

This type of repeating shotgun seems to pick up more dirt, grit and general foreign matter inside the action than does a vacuum cleaner. The accumulation of muck inside the receiver and over the operating parts naturally absorbs as much oil as is present and forms a thick sludge or even a hard mass at points it can find room to build up in. It is therefore wise not to use any more oil than is necessary to ease friction between moving parts and assemblies. The action spring as-sembly which returns the breechblock to the battery (firing position) seems always to get either too much or too little lubrication. If too much, the oil gets through the tube and around it, to the detriment of the stock wood at that location. If too little, of course the spring may weaken by rusting, and the follower, which communicates tension to the breechbolt (or block) and the locking block through the link, also slow up. This condition naturally leads to functional failures such as failure to load and eject correctly.

Taking up some of the specific troubles which may crop up, the fol-lowing may be encountered:

Failure to Feed Properly. (Shell not moving from magazine to correct position in carrier.) Possibly this is due to a bent or dented magazine type, blocking passage of the follower in the tube but more likely it is due to rust, dirt or other matter in the tube, or a broken or badly set spring. The carrier may not reach its proper position to receive the shell, so check the shell stop, carrier latch and locking block latch spring, also the friction ring adjustment, to see that it is correct for the load being used at the time of failure.

Maximing. (Firing more than one shot at a single pull of trigger.) This is often due to foreign matter blocking the movement of the safety sear assembly. If the safety sear spring is out of commission, the gun may double if the muzzle is pointed up, but seem okay when the barrel is held in a horizontal plane. Worn safety sear, hammer, or trigger notches may slip from engagement or jar off when the barrel and bolt assemblies slam forward. This is not common, however. The trigger, at the center of the curve, should require $\frac{1}{16}''$ movement to fire the arm, and the weight of the triggerpull should not be less than $4\frac{1}{2}$

RECEIVER

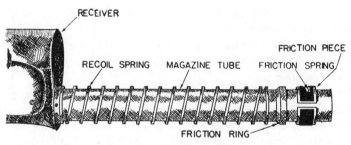

FRICTION PIECE

RECOIL SPRING   MAGAZINE TUBE   FRICTION SPRING

FRICTION RING

POSITION 1 — HEAVY LOADS

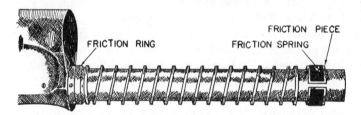

FRICTION PIECE

FRICTION RING   FRICTION SPRING

POSITION 2 — LIGHT LOADS

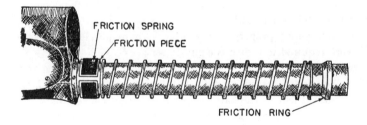

FRICTION SPRING

FRICTION PIECE

FRICTION RING

POSITION 3 — WITH CUTTS COMPENSATOR

RECOIL ADJUSTMENTS - REMINGTON MII AND SPORTSMAN

pounds nor over 6 pounds if you adjust it for a fussy customer. Many scattergunners want heavier pulls, as they may hunt in cold weather wearing gloves or with a cold-numbed bare trigger finger which cannot be sensitive enough for a light pull.

Action does not stay open. The bolt should remain open, in the rear position when the magazine is exhausted and the last shot fired, unless released purposely. Failure to stay to the rear can be due to a number of defects: Foreign matter under the front end of the latch; a broken carrier latch or latch spring; a worn carrier dog; or a defective retaining notch of the link shoulder or operating slide. Again, check the friction ring assembly.

Carrier does not function. Can be due to a broken carrier dog, carrier latch, dirt or foreign matter blocking full movement, or worn or broken operating slide.

Hammer will not cock. Can be broken or worn notches in the hammer, trigger or safety sear, or a broken trigger spring. Also, of course, to the presence of a foreign object preventing correct functioning of any of these parts—I found a piece of button doing it once. Worn or broken notches seldom cause this trouble, as in practically all cases the gun will double or Maxim before wear reaches the point of allowing the hammer to follow the bolt forward without firing.

Failure to lock. (Bolt does not lock to barrel extension.) Due to a jammed or broken locking block latch spring, burrs or foreign matter in the locking recess in the barrel extension, or grit, burrs or other defects in the receiver at this point.

Failure to close properly. The breechbolt should slam forward positively when released and if it does not do so, the trouble will usually be found in the action spring assembly—either the spring rusted or broken, or the link not engaged in the recess in the action spring follower. The same condition can be found if the carrier is damaged, or the carrier latch is jammed, or the locking block latch or its spring are not functioning properly. Very often a thorough cleaning is the only work required to return the gun to service.

Timing. This should be considered somewhat when correcting triggers or the condition of firing fully automatic, and can be regulated only by adjustment of the hammer, sear and trigger assemblies. Try to pull the trigger when the action is cocked and the bolt is held partially open. You should not be able to release the hammer until the bolt is $\frac{1}{8}''$ *or less* from the full forward position, determined by the position of the bolt handle, or, properly named, the retracting slide handle.

Headspace. Other than making the simple headspace gages as illustrated and checking guns, there is little you personally can do to correct excess headspace. A new breechbolt must be fitted, and the factory does this themselves, requiring that the gun be shipped to them. Insufficient headspace could of course be corrected quite easily, by making a rim reamer or counterbore, or even by careful—very careful—use of the boring tool in the lathe, but I have never run into a case of insufficient headspace on any of these guns, so I have never done the job myself. Excess headspace is to be suspected if the gun begins to break extractors, or if fired shells show bulging and deformation of the base just in front of the rim. Do not be unduly alarmed by a very slight bulge next to the rim, which is customary and not dangerous at all. In fact, there is little real danger in shooting a Browning-type autoloader which does have excess headspace, so far as concerns the shooter. However, the gun will not last long, being subjected to far greater battering than usual, and normally it will cease to function before becoming physically dangerous to fire.

Carrier fails to return. (To lower position when action is closed.) Usually due to a jammed or broken carrier latch, but it can be a broken, set, or damaged carrier spring. Removal, disassembly and cleaning of the carrier, spring and catch, usually corrects the trouble.

Failure to eject empty shells during firing. Because of a broken or worn ejector, broken extractor, incorrect setting of the friction ring assembly or interference with its action on the magazine tube. Can also be due to a damaged chamber in the barrel—rusted and pitted, or badly scored so that the chamber walls will not readily release the fired shell.

Safety does not operate. If loose in its recess, probably due to a broken leg on the trigger spring, which gives tension on the ball bearing acting as a detent to retain the safety in either on or off position. If difficult to move either on or off, it may be due to burrs in the slots in the body of the safety or a damaged web on the rear of the trigger, or just plain dirt tying up things.

Safety sear does not release trigger. (When gun is cocked and hammer will not release, with all principal springs in good condition.) Almost always due to a jammed safety sear spring follower. The safety sear itself can be worn off-angle, but I have never encountered one which would not release through wear.

Double feeding. (Two shells pass from magazine to action on one functioning of action.) May be due to failure of the shell stop, carrier latch, or carrier dog. (The carrier dog, if you are in doubt, is the spring loaded cam catch on the rear of the carrier.)

Jamming of trigger mechanism. Can be due to a jammed safety, foreign matter in the safety sear assembly and the hammer notch. Sometimes it is caused by bits of the fiber buffer fastened into the rear of the receiver to cushion the rearward stop of the breechbolt. This buffer disintegrates under service, and pieces are liable to be found anywhere in the action. Its value is debatable, in view of the fact that the Browning design does not provide for it at all, and Browning-made autoloaders of this type do not have it. Remington claims it is desirable, making for better operation and longer life of the arm. Many Remington guns have had it go to pieces and continue in service without any apparent battering of either the receiver or the breechbolt, although I have heard of cases where the rear wall of the receiver was cracked because the fiber cushion was not replaced when it was destroyed. It is riveted in, and because of the length of the receiver, is quite difficult to replace unless you make up special tools for the job. I am diagraming the special punches and bushing required. The bushing can be made of brass for ease of machining, for it serves only to guide the steel punches. New rivets and fiber buffers can be bought from Remington. The first two punches are of course for seating the buffer and rivet—sometimes the original rivet can be reshaped to serviceability—and the third for actually riveting after the buffer is in place. Drill out the old rivet if it cannot be used.

There is an alternate system, used by many gunsmiths, requiring two tools to be made, both easy. Braze a drill bit to a 10″ rod, and do the same with a tap, both of course of proper diameters to drill into the factory rivet hole and tap it. A screw of the same thread—should be as fine as possible—with a very thin head is used to attach the cushion or buffer, the screw head being countersunk as much as possible below the surface of the buffer. The head can be as large in diameter as $1\frac{1}{32}″$, to maintain strength in holding. No centering bushing is necessary, as the original rivet hole acts as a center, and only care in drilling and tapping must be observed. You *do not* want to pull a hole clear through the back end of the receiver! Measure the receiver inside and out, to get an idea of how much stock is in the rear wall, and mark your elongated drill and tap accordingly, allowing for sufficient depth without penetration.

Barrel assembly. Except for bore defects, and occasional loosening of the barrel from its extension, both corrected by previously described cleaning, polishing and thread tightening methods, the only real job which can crop up on an autoloader barrel is replacing the brazed-on barrel lug, which sometimes comes off. This can be a nasty job, for the mass of metal involved requires sufficient heat to cause scale in the bore unless great care is observed; and the scale prevention compound may help. I have successfully replaced these lugs with both brass and silver solder and believe the silver solder is to be recommended, using an alloy with a melting point around 1200° to 1300° Fahrenheit. This is a sweat joint, naturally, and must be practically perfect to hold against the beating it takes. Remington makes the sighting ribs integral with the barrels, and may make some of the lugs integral—they should be—

Ackley's plant. The largest and most complete private gun plant in the country, located at Trinidad, Colorado.

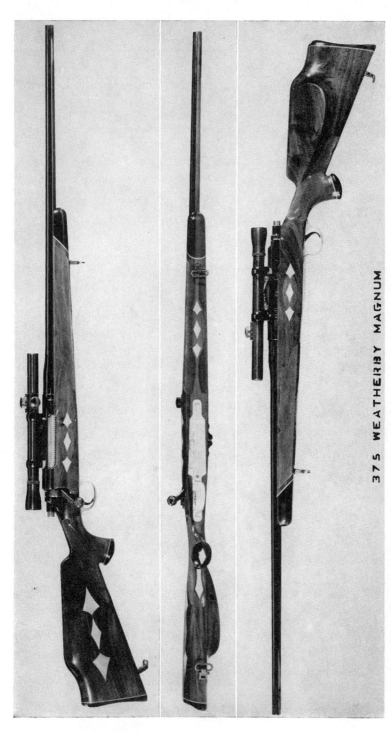

375 WEATHERBY MAGNUM

A .375 Weatherby Magnum, on 1917 action, highly decorated. Triggerguard and floorplate are engraved and gold-plated. Stock of rare imported wood, with white inlays.

but on older guns they were sweated on with brass.

General. Care should be taken in oiling autoloaders to use a light gun oil, such as Nyeoil, sparingly. If the gun is to be used in low temperatures, apply oil only to points in the action showing friction wear. If graphite is to be used—and it should be used only when the gun may be subjected to very cold weather—the moving parts should be cleaned in solvent and thoroughly dried before a light sprinkling of powdered graphite is applied. Oil and graphite are never to be used together for cold weather lubrication. This advice can be applied to almost any type of repeating arm. It must be remembered that all types are very prone to break flat springs in cold weather, and customers should be so advised and offered extra springs, if available and they wish to be well prepared.

Remington Pump Actions

The present Remington pump gun, Model 31, gives little trouble. The triggerguard assembly, including hammer, trigger, sear and safety assemblies, is quite difficult to break down to reach some of the parts, but other than that, the action is quite simple as regarding diagnosis and correction of particular problems. The trigger is quite a long part and foreign matter at any point can put it out of commission by blocking movement. The safety is very similar to that on the autoloaders and subject to the same troubles and corrections prescribed. Feeding from the magazine, and failure to do so properly, are also as covered for the autoloading Remington 11, and are applicable to other tubular magazine shotguns. Both right and left-hand cartridge stops must function properly for correct feeding, and these should be checked first, if there is no apparent damage to the magazine tube or any of the magazine parts.

The Model 31 seldom breaks firing pins, but once in awhile it does require a new extractor. The carrier gives trouble only when foreign matter blocks its action, or some heavy handed character bends it out of shape with a tire iron or similar tool. Most trouble comes in the triggerguard or triggerplate assembly, by foreign matter displacing the springs or blocking movement of the parts. Loose barrels can be corrected very quickly by movement of the barrel adjusting bushing.

Among the individual troubles which can decommission the M31 we have:

Headspace. Evidenced by excessive recoil and expanded shell bases, as in the M11, and possibly broken or blown off extractors. It is rather easily corrected in most instances, by movement of the barrel adjustment bushing. If the standard bushing will not move the barrel to its proper relationship with the breech bolt, a special or larger bushing can be procured from the factory. Headspace should not exceed .0605″ in 12 gauge.

Action does not lock. (Breechbolt failing to lock.) Can be due to burrs on the locking lugs, breechblock, or slide, or caused by foreign matter on the face of the block, in the lug recess in the top of the receiver, or the extractor grooves in the receiver. Occasionally it is due to the condition of the rear of the barrel, or its position.

Fails to extract or eject. Due to worn, broken or burred extractors, or broken, set, or missing extractor springs, or the same condition in the ejector and ejector springs. It possibly can be due to the chamber, should it be very rough.

Hammer slips. (Action fails to stay cocked when functioned.) May be due to the condition of the sear notch in the hammer, or on the nose of the sear (front leg of the trigger), a broken or incorrectly assembled trigger spring, action bar lock, or a blocked or improperly assembled hammer link. Dirt, hardened lubricant, or other foreign matter in the hammer notch or in the trigger assembly can also cause this condition intermittently.

Action slide bar sticks. Usually due to a burred or battered lug on the rear end of the bar, bent bar, or a dented opening in the receiver. Foreign matter in the receiver or on the breechbolt can also delay its action, making it stiff in operation.

Slide lock failure. (Action bar lock not functioning.) The lock may be bent, burred or broken, or the spring broken, or the lock spring housing can be assembled incorrectly. The mainspring follower can be out of place, the hammer link displaced, or most common, the nose of the lock may be worn away. The contacting lug on the rear of the slide can also be worn, of course.

Double Feeding. (Two shells passing from the magazine into the receiver at one time.) Usually due to dirt in the shell stop seating grooves in the receiver but can be caused by bent or broken right-hand shell stop.

Magazine fails to retain shells. Usually due to failure of the left-hand shell stop or the stop-plunger-spring.

Shells stick in magazine. Same as other guns with tubular magazines —a corroded, bent, broken or set spring, dented tube, or foreign matter in the tube. A good cleaning often takes care of the trouble.

Safety sticks. Can be due to foreign matter in the trigger web recess, a rusted spring and ball, or an improperly placed spring.

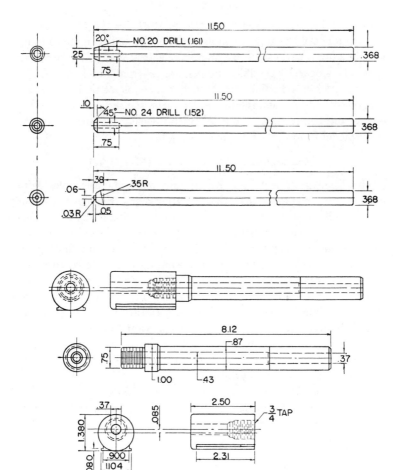

REMINGTON M11 BUFFER RIVETING
TOOLS

To replace the cushion or buffer in Remington autoloader shotguns
(Model 11) the illustrated tool set can be made up. The three punches
shown at top of drawing do the work, with the bottom parts forming a guide
or jig through which they are passed in order to locate correctly. The top
two tools are rivet cutting and setting punches, with the third being the
riveting punch. The holder at the bottom can be made of brass, if desirable.
It approximates the breechblock of the gun and slides in the same guide
ways in the receiver.

General. Few parts need be carried in stock for the M31 unless a large number of the guns are in local use or the shop can afford to invest in a large parts stock. Extractors, ejectors, and action bar locks should be stocked if possible, and perhaps a hammer and trigger.

Remington has modified the Model 31 a couple of times since first bringing it out, and in ordering major parts, the serial number of the gun should be given. The slide lock detail is slightly different on the skeet model from that on the standard gun.

Remington Over and Under (Model 32)

This Remington model is quite carefully made and assembled, with much closer tolerances than the repeating arms. Foreign matter or gummed oil in the action can cause the gun to misfire, or fail in any particular mechanical functioning. Most of these guns were made with selective single trigger, and the trigger mechanism sometimes gives trouble. I believe all these trigger assemblies were riveted together, and as very careful work, plus experience, is necessary to adjust or repair them, it is a good idea to return them to the factory to have the work done. Special fixtures and jigs are necessary to proper assembly and disassembly, although, of course, if you want to you can tear anything apart by force. These guns seldom break firing pins, or any springs. There are no flat springs used, and only rust or foreign matter will affect the coil types in the gun.

Some of the ailments possibly affecting the Model 32:

Failure to eject. All models have automatic ejection, and failure to eject can be due to worn or broken ejector sear or sears, a burred or blocked ejector (on sliding guides, breech portion) or a damaged cam end, at front.

Failure to cock. May be broken or damaged cocking rod or rods, a damaged sear, a damaged or missing sear spring or a broken cocking lever.

Failure to fire. (Trigger will not release.) Usually due to breakage, wear or foreign matter in the trigger assembly. It can also be caused by failure of the safety, and, of course, by foreign matter blocking movement of the sear or of the hammer.

Failure to fire. (Trigger releases, but gun misfires.) May also be due to blocking of the hammer, but usually it is caused by foreign matter interfering with movement of the firing pin or rust weakened firing springs.

Safety failure. If the safety fails to prevent discharge of the arm when set, check the trigger mechanism. It may be necessary to build on metal at some point. Should safety merely be difficult to move, check the safety detent, spring, and slide adjusting screw, for rust, dirt or gummed oil. Cleaning usually clears up the trouble.

Loose hinge. (Gun does not breech tightly when closed.) Send to the factory quick. Yes, you can press the hinge pin out and make new ones, and all that, but in this case it is smarter, easier, and probably cheaper in the long run to let Remington do this job.

Forend troubles. The forend catch can be repaired without much difficulty, to tighten loose forends. The forend iron itself will not give trouble under any normal usage, but should it be badly damaged, it is another job to pass on to the factory for fitting.

General. The M32 models require only careful lubrication, with the very best non-gumming light oils, and cleaning, to stay in action. I would not advise any parts be kept in stock for them, unless you do considerable work for skeet or trap organizations.

Obsolete Remington Pump Shotguns

The obsolete Remington pump guns are a genuine headache— Models 10, 17 and 29 are all very sad shotguns. A few factory parts— never the ones you need—are still available, but generally you have to make new ones or repair old ones. Carriers are simple on the 17, but complicated on the 10 and 29, having several cams which must be right if correct timing and feeding is to be achieved. If a good carrier is at hand for a model, a damaged or broken one can be repaired by welding and reshaping, but otherwise you are in for a good bit of experimenting as you work. The lug on the rear of the action bar, or slide, which engages the breechblock often is worn enough to make operation difficult, or even impossible. This is encountered on the 10 and 29 only, and of course can be repaired by welding on metal and shaping as required. Too, on the Model 10, the ejector frequently breaks, and new ones must be made. This is a flat spring about 3″ long, the rear section being slightly dovetail in cross section, to slide into a dovetail recess milled for it in top of the receiver, inside. It curves downward, approximately $\frac{9}{16}$″ at the front tip from the receiver top wall when the breechblock is to the rear. When the block is brought forward, it forces the ejector up into the recess in top of the receiver, and as the block moves to the rear, the spring of the part brings it down, to contact the empty shell and force it out of the receiver through the ejection port at the bottom of the gun. These ejectors must, therefore, be made of the finest spring steel. The action has a spring loaded firing pin, or striker, not having a hammer of any type. Defects in feeding and safety operation are similar to those on the 31 and may be corrected by the same methods.

Winchester Shotguns

Probably the most common single model of repeating shotgun coming in for repair will be the Winchester 1897, called the 97—not because it is a poor design, or anything like that, but because so blasted many of them have been sold and used constantly for the past half-century! This old gun, with its exposed hammer, was still being made and well received in 1947 and I do not know whether it is definitely discontinued at this time.

As the action is quite exposed, it picks up dirt readily, but it is easily cleaned and it will function reliably with less care than any other repeater. Breakage of parts is most common in the ejectors, firing pins, and extractors, in that order. Forends also crack easily, but in most instances can remain serviceable even when cracked. Because of the age of many M97s, bad barrels and chambers may be frequently seen, due to use before non-corrosive ammunition was on the market. The guns were made in solid frame style as well as the more familiar takedown, and several modifications of slide bars and handles have been made. When ordering handles, give the factory the serial number of the gun for which it is intended.

The most common troubles with the Model 97:

Action does not lock. Can be due to foreign matter on the face of the bolt, in the extractor cuts in the barrel, on the locking shoulder of the bolt, on the carrier, or a worn slide bar cam lug. This latter is fairly common on very old guns, and can easily be built up with the welding torch. Use a tough steel to build with, as it should be left natural, not hardened. A case-hardened lug will wear out of shape if of soft steel originally, and a thoroughly hardened one is not only liable to breakage, but will punish the carrier unduly.

Shell is not ejected. (After gun is fired.) Either a broken ejector, a badly set extractor spring, or the user is not bringing the slide handle fully to the rear position. In this arm, ejection is manual, depending upon the operator bringing the slide positively to the full rear position.

Shell is not extracted. (After gun is fired.) Can be a broken extractor, a jammed or missing extractor spring, or a very rough chamber.

Double feeding from magazine. Practically always due to foreign material blocking movement of the shell stops or shell stop springs can be rusted or set to a point of occasional malfunction.

Shells stick in magazine. Same as for other tubular magazines—a dented tube, a rusted follower, a bad spring, or dirt in tube. Check for homemade plugs, used to limit magazine capacity to two shells per Federal law, as such plugs are liable to be of any material and any shape, whether or not suitable for the purpose.

Slide disengages from breech bolt. May be a worn lug on the slide bar, or a worn slide hook. (Action slide hook.) Sometimes the entire action may be so loose that parts disengage. New and oversize hooks are easily made and usually will correct the trouble by themselves.

Slide sticks. The bar may be bent, the bar cam may be worn or burred, or there may be dirt gravel, or other foreign matter in the carrier runways, or burrs or gummed lubricant on the breechbolt runways and guides.

Hammer fails to cock properly. Can be due to dirt in the hammer and sear assemblies, a broken sear spring, a set sear spring, foreign matter blocking the trigger movement, or just worn notches in the hammer and a blunted nose on the sear.

Hammer falls as action is closed. This can mean accidental discharge, and is usually caused by one of the above conditions. Usually a clean up job and retouching of the sear nose and the hammer notch will fix the gun. (Make sure the customer is releasing the trigger as he works the slide—in this model, if the trigger is held back the hammer is free to fall or follow the bolt forward.)

Firing pin does not retract. Can be a rough tip on the pin sticking in fired primers, or due to a broken or missing lock spring, broken firing pin, or dirt or gummed oil inside the breech bolt.

Slide lock fails to lock. Possibly due to a broken lock or spring, or foreign matter under the lock. Burrs on the lock or slide bar can cause intermittent failures.

Loose Breech. (Takedown joint.) Can be corrected by movement of the barrel adjustment bushing, or by use of a new oversize bushing if the standard bushing will not take up all the slack. Winchester furnishes several sizes.

Headspace. Seldom gives trouble, even when excessive and may be corrected through adjustment of the receiver extension.

General. The action slide hook screw head serves as a cam lug to move the shell guide to clear the ejection port as the bolt is brought to the rear and therefore this screw head must not be battered or worn to too great a degree. It must remain seated to full depth, in order to retain engagement with the action slide hook on the opposite side of the bolt. The Model 97 uses the cam principle extensively, and naturally is sensitive to burrs and foreign matter on the cam surfaces. The carrier often is helped considerably by a thorough cleaning and polishing of the cam shoulders and runways. There is no safety on the gun, aside from the inertia lock, manually released by the action slide lock, except the safety notch on the hammer. This notch can break out, of course, but it seldom does, and can be deepened to become again serviceable if it should do so, without the necessity of buying a new hammer. The trigger has a spring of its own, and, operating only as a lever to force the sear out of engagement with the hammer, also has a stop screw limiting rearward movement. These parts almost never fail or give trouble.

Some of the magazine assembly screws are constantly being lost, these being the magazine plug screws and the magazine band bushing screws. These should be carried in stock, along with ejectors, firing pins, and extractors and it is not a bad idea to keep a couple of stocks on hand. A spanner wrench should be made for removal of the action slide sleeve screw cap, so that slide handles can be replaced.

Model 12

This hammerless slide action gun is one of the sturdiest repeating shotguns made, its only weakness being a tendency to break firing pins. It is slightly stiffer in action than some of the competing pump guns, but a quick polishing job on the breechbolt works wonders sometimes. Not so open as the 97, it acquires less dirt in the action and is very reliable, however, the following conditions may be found:

Firing pin does not retract. Can be a broken pin, but also may be a burred or jammed retractor, or a jammed retractor spring.

Breechbolt does not lock. Almost always due to foreign matter lodged in the locking recess in the top of the receiver, but can be due to a burred action slide cam lug.

Hammer does not cock, or slips out of engagement. Probably due to burrs or foreign matter in the sear notch in the hammer, a damaged sear nose, or may be due to a broken trigger spring.

Slide sticks. Possibly caused by a bent bar, or foreign matter in the lug runway in the bolt. A damaged bar lug also will cause difficult operation.

Slide goes too far forward. Nearly always due to the retaining lug on the magazine tube under the handle, against which the action slide spring acts, breaking loose from the tube and it must be brazed or silver soldered back in place.

Slide lock functions improperly. Can be due to improper assembly of the hammer and the lock in the triggerguard, with relation to the lock spring; also, to a broken or bent slide lock spring, or burrs on the action slide bar.

Safety sticks. Probably due to dirt or caked oil in slots of the safety, or a damaged plunger spring and a burred plunger can also make for hard operation.

Shell sticks in magazine. If the tube, follower and spring are in good shape, check the receiver extension, to see that the magazine tube opening is not obstructed by the lip in the extension. This occurs most often with 16 gauge guns.

Double feeding. Check the shell cutoff for damage, and clean its recess in the receiver wall.

Loose breech. Same system as on the Model 97—can be corrected by barrel bushing adjustment or replacement. Winchester makes six sizes, which can handle any degree of looseness. Be careful in ordering these—No. 1 or No. 2 will tighten up very shaky guns!

General. The Model 12 is easier on ejectors and extractors than most repeaters. The gun is very simple to clean, it being possible to remove all action parts from the receiver in less than a minute. Stocks give little trouble, being strongly supported, and the triggerguard assembly mechanism is easily disassembled for cleaning and repair. The takedown system is identical in principle with that of the 97 and the Model 12 loses as many magazine plug screws and bushing screws as the 97. These should be stocked, together with firing pins for all gauges.

Winchester Model 42

For this little .410 slide action shotgun the Model 12 action system was used, although modified considerably. A sideplate is used, making a two piece receiver shell, which also makes for easy takedown and cleaning of the receiver. Stampings are used to form the carrier and action slide lock. The M42 is very sturdy and has no particular weak point. Firing pins, ejectors and extractors seldom give trouble, and about all that goes wrong is a misplaced spring now and then, or foreign matter interfering with the safety or action slide lock.

The Model 21 Double Barrel

This is Winchester's pride and joy in the scattergun line, and is a good quality arm. More modern in design than comparable doubles, it avoids breakdown troubles by extensive use of coil springs and good modern steels. The double trigger setup is similar to that on conventional doubles in the standard version, but the gun is also available with double triggers and selective ejection, and with selective single trigger mechanism, with either selective or non-selective ejectors. Winchester will sell all components of the various assemblies, so that worn parts can be replaced in the small shop. Sears are of very good steel, and also the hammers, so that notches seldom wear to the point of unserviceability. Firing pins are attached to or part of the hammers so that there is little danger of breakage. I have never heard of a broken pin in a Model 21.

Most functional failures in this model are caused by one or more parts being prevented from normal movement by foreign matter or gummed lubricant. It is of course possible for burrs to develop on some parts, and wear to reduce dimensions on others, but I know of no individual weak point in the Winchester M21. The majority of complaints received will concern safety operation, the trigger mechanism, and the ejection assemblies. The forend catch also can bring a gun into the shop, to cure a loose forend. The spring, or properly named, forend retainer, is treated no differently than on a cheap mail order double of the same type—lengthen the end of it until the forend iron snaps smartly in place. The 21 is and has been made almost to individual order, and almost any combination and alteration possible to a double barreled shotgun can be had from the factory so that there may be considerable variation between guns brought to you. Major parts are of course basically the same, although even the frame or receivers of the selective and non-selective ejection models differ. Non-selective guns cannot be converted to selective.

The Winchester Model 24

This is the low priced, or competitive double in the line, and notable chiefly for the amount of strength required to open and close the gun. Composed principally of coil springs and stamped metal parts, the action does not give a great deal of trouble. Sear notches and cocking lever notches wear, but are easily filed again to proper shapes. The extractor levers are also likely to wear, more because the arm requires such force to open it and therefore it is treated roughly, than from normal wear use. Very occasionally a cocking slide will break or chip at the edges, requiring installation of a new one. The 24 has no hammers, using the spring loaded firing pins only, and while the pins seldom break, they do manage to get bent. Safety and trigger relationship sometimes gets wopperjawed, to the end that the safety may fail, but inspection of the action with the buttstock off will show what is wrong and common sense will indicate the remedy.

The hardest job on a Model 24 is taking the action apart and putting it back together. Most of the work I can remember doing on this model is assembling it after the owner had torn it apart, usually from curiosity, and polishing jobs in an effort to ease the action. At least half a dozen times I have had the Model 24 brought to me in a paper bag, thoroughly disassembled. The layman can get the gun apart, but usually has to have a gunsmith get it together again. The job which floors the gunowner is getting in the firing pins and their springs. The rear ends of the firing pins are spring guides over which the firing pin springs, in this case acting as mainsprings, operate. The springs must be assembled and compressed on the guides before placing the assembly in the frame. Clamp the forward section of the pin (not the tip) in the vise, take a short section of tubing which will pass over the guide and abut the end of the spring, notch the end of this tube and use it to compress the spring to the point you are able to insert a short pin through the small hole in the guide and retain the spring in the compressed position. This little pin is left holding the spring until the action is completely assembled.

Triggers that wear at their pivot holes and become sloppy may be repaired by welding up the hole and re-drilling, although new triggers cost less than a dollar each. The safety is a simple minded affair and no parts are prone to breakage, although dirt or rust or gummed oil can affect the safety slide spring and cause difficult or even faulty operation. In the event it will not prevent firing when in the "on" position, the safety tangs on triggers can be built up to dimensions such that the safety will be positive.

The Model 37 Single Barrel

This little gun is so simple and so well made of good materials that nothing much ever goes wrong with it. The extractor is about the only part which ever shows wear or is affected by it. The forearm catch is a plunger affair which seldom allows any looseness to develop and seems to automatically take care of wear.

The forend iron is a stamping and may be bent hither and thither, if desired. Although the M37 has an exposed hammer, it is not a hammer type action, and employs a straight line firing pin, with the hammer attached to form a cocking lever and its lower portion is conventionally notched to act against the trigger in cocking and firing. Quite good trigger pulls can be put on this model.

Obsolete Winchester Shotguns

The Model 1893 slide action fortunately did not last long, so that few are in existence—or at least in use. Very similar in outward appearance to the solid frame Model 97, the 93 was a poor design and practically anything can and did go wrong with it. I believe that the main trouble was that the cam surfaces were not sufficiently well worked out, so that ordinary wear soon caused malfunctions. No parts are available and very few 97 parts can be used. The gun is subject to the troubles of the 97, only more so, and as a rule the same remedies apply. Winchester disowned this model a long time ago.

The Model 20 single barrel was a conventional light gun with nothing wrong with it except that it cost more to make than the M37 which replaced it. Principal trouble is with the hammer notches wearing and the firing pins breaking. This is a coil spring gun, and an excellent single. Almost all parts are available.

The Model 01 Lever Action Shotgun—the "cornsheller"—had some devotees who praised the type highly, but generally speaking, this 10 gauge repeater was never popular. Nearly all parts are still available. I know nothing about the gun—only worked on one and that was just to clean it up—but oldtimers tell me that the trigger springs, firing pin tips and firing pin retractors were prone to breakage, and foreign matter would gum up the carriers sometimes.

Model 11 Selfloading Shotgun

Winchester designed this after disagreeing with John Browning in a deal for his autoloading patent, and it is about the sorriest and most complicated autoloader ever made. Disassembly of the magazine tube parts is more of a job by itself than actually repairing anything on it! The weakest point is the bolt stop, which is constantly breaking and fairly often a bolt itself will break off a section at the rear. Getting the carrier out of the receiver is a bit puzzling, unless you know the combination, this being that it is two piece, not one as it appears, and you spring the forward legs together down out of the receiver, bringing a screw into view. Removal of this screw allows the two halves to be removed separately. I have never found an easy way to take down the magazine assembly. You make wrenches, sleeves and vise jaws, get in at the back end with a small punch and fiddle around getting the little sleeve there unscrewed. After this holding sleeve is out, you can get the spring and follower out, among other parts. There is no trouble getting the action parts out of the receiver.

16 GAUGE (2 3/4")

MAXIMUM SHELL

INCL. TAPER .005" PER INCH

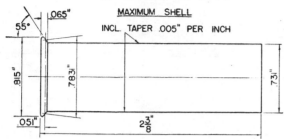

MINIMUM CHAMBER

INCL. TAPER .005" PER INCH

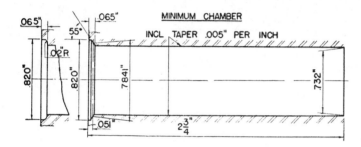

12 GAUGE (2 3/4")

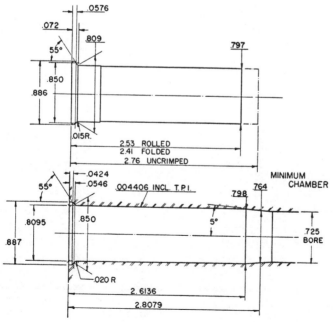

410 GAUGE (3")

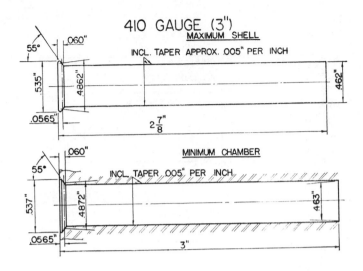

MAXIMUM SHELL
INCL. TAPER APPROX. .005" PER INCH

55° .060"
.535" .4862" .462"
.0565" $2\frac{7}{8}$"

MINIMUM CHAMBER
INCL. TAPER .005" PER INCH

55° .060"
.537" .4872" .463"
.0565" 3"

20 GAUGE (2·3/4")

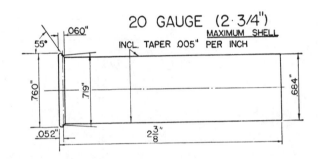

MAXIMUM SHELL
INCL. TAPER .005" PER INCH

55° .060"
.760" .719" .684"
.052" $2\frac{3}{8}$"

MINIMUM CHAMBER
INCL. TAPER .005" PER INCH

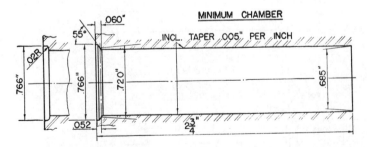

55° .060"
.02R .766" .766" .720" .685"
.052 $2\frac{3}{4}$"

SHOTGUN CHAMBERS

.410 Bore, 20, 16 & 12 Gauge

Little comment is necessary on these, beyond pointing out that there is variation in rim countersinks in chambers, as indicated, and that modern shells are considerably shorter than modern chambers. This is due to the

Firing pins and extractors last pretty well, and as coil springs were used, there is little spring trouble. The M11 was made before the advent of the high-velocity shotgun shell, and has no provision for taking up the greater recoil of the new shells. I .think this is probably the reason for bolt and bolt stop fractures now occurring fairly frequently. To give the gun its due, it was well made and quite reliable in its day. My father had one for many years and had no trouble whatever.

Some factory parts are still available. Cartridge stops sometimes fail, through wear, and can be built up by welding. The action must be timed rather accurately, this being controlled principally by the bolt stop, and I have cured several guns of malfunctioning by smoothing up or building up the bolt stop lug.

The Model 40 Autoloading Shotgun

In the 1930s Winchester again tried to develop a good autoloader, and again failed. The Model 40 was not only a poor gun, but was expensive to make, which undoubtedly influenced the maker to drop rather than perfect the model. A very nice looking arm, the action combined some features of the M11 with some Browning ideas. Principal troubles were with the sear mechanism and I have seen one broken breechbolt. Winchester will sell a few parts for the Model 40, but for anything important, they request you to send the gun to them, and after they get it, they send you a new Model 12 pump gun and tell you to forget about the autoloader! Which is a good deal.

Stevens Shotguns

The Stevens slide action was, I believe, an early Browning design basically, although many modifications have been made, and as many model numbers assigned. Although there are definite differences between them, Models 520, 521, 620, 620A and 621 are the same action, insofar as functioning and repair is concerned, and the same guns, under assorted names, have been and are being sold by mail order houses. The 520 and 521 have a tang safety, similar to that on double

---

new style of top crimp. I went out and measured new Winchester shells and found they were 2⅜″ long (marked 2¾″, of course).

For longer shells, chambers are lengthened in accordance with the dimensions of the shorter chamber—the same breech and end diameters are retained, which decreases the taper slightly.

Short shells may be used in long chambers without in any way damaging the gun.

barrel guns, while the 620 line uses a cross bolt safety behind the trigger as in the Remington design. The metal used in the guns is rather soft and receivers, barrel heads and action parts can all wear out of shape and burr up easily.

Some of the troubles of the Stevens slide actions are:

Loose breech. In this design, the barrel head (Winchester's "receiver extension") is milled with six parallel vertical ribs, or lugs, which slide into corresponding recesses in the receiver. A sleeve with two protruding lugs, called the magazine nut, is threaded on the magazine tube and moves forward and back to engage in the barrel head and lock the barrel and receiver assemblies together, or take them apart. For takedown, it is screwed forward out of engagement with the barrel head and the barrel and magazine assemblies slid straight down out of the receiver. The magazine nut will not correct a loose joint; it is necessary to lessen the tolerance between barrel head and its seat in the receiver. Peening the lugs on the barrel head is only a temporary measure, and the only real way a tight fit can be obtained is to make a new barrel head or return the whole gun to the factory that they may fit one which will be tight. Stevens will not sell a barrel head for fitting outside the factory, considering it an integral part of the barrel.

Sliding breech fails to lock. Can be due to foreign matter on the face of the slide, in the extractor grooves in the barrel head, or in the locking recess in the top of the receiver. Burrs on the edges of the locking block may also cause the condition, although rarely.

Hammer does not cock, or slips. Probably due to worn hooks on the hammer or sear, a missing or broken sear or trigger springs, or a jammed mainspring.

Slide handle sticks. The bar may be bent, the magazine tube dented, or burrs or foreign material in the slots in the receiver or the barrel head.

Firing pin fails to retract. May be a broken pin, burrs on the firing pin, or dirt in the locking block slot.

Slide does not come all the way to rear. Can be a broken hammer, a jammed mainspring, or on the Model 620A, a cracked stock displacing the receiver tang. Also, of course, foreign matter blocking the action parts.

Slide lock fails. The lock may be bent or burred, or burrs on the rear of the slide bar, but probably the slide lock spring or the release spring is out of place, broken, or missing. This is a rather frail helical wire spring, easily rendered *hors de combat.*

Safety jams or fails. On the 520 models can be a broken or jammed

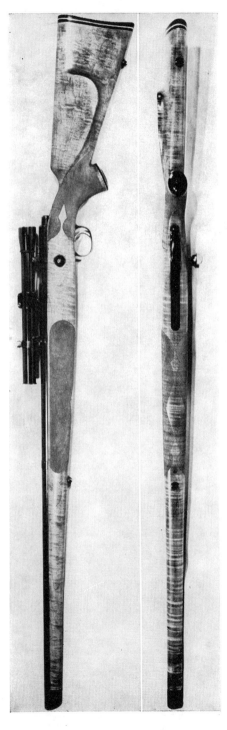

A .22 Rim-Fire Job

Shown above is Leonard Mews' "old sparrow rifle" as it is known around Appleton, Wisconsin.

This is an assembly of a Winchester 69 A action, to which had originally been fitted a Winchester 52 barrel, later replaced by a .22 Titherington barrel fitted with George Turner's original type mount to which he fitted a 4X Noske scope. A Springfield guard was reworked and adapted for use with this 69 action and its magazine.

Stock is of curly Wisconsin maple, from a blank given Mews by Al Linden some years back. Checkering is 24 lines to the inch, copied from an old Linden pattern. The inletted and whiskered stock was given a light "Suigi" torch browning to bring out the figure and darken it slightly and the job was then oil finished.

This stock, from the grip forward, has swells and bulges in the proper places, and is in full Mannlicher-Schoenauer style. Sometimes such swelled lines look better than the stiff, severely straight lines, but they should not be overdone.

This rifle is muzzle heavy, weighs 8¼ pounds, has a 26½ inch barrel, was built to Leonard Mews' personal specifications and is a deadly offhand rifle. According to the owner it is also hell on sparrows and starlings.

Cutting down a recoil pad after fitting to buttstock. The sanding disk, rubber-backed, cuts the neoprene pad smoothly. Wood is protected by masking tape. This unit is a 1750 RPM ⅓ HP motor, with a 7″ disk.

spring plunger or spring, or dirt in mechanism and on 620 models, foreign matter, rust, gummed oil or even burrs on the trigger web or in the safety slot.

Fails to extract fired shells. As on other repeaters, due to worn, broken or blocked extractor or springs, or a bad chamber.

Fails to eject fired shells. Worn or jammed ejector or extractor spring.

Double feeding. Can be bent, broken or jammed shell stop—most likely is loose shell stop screw.

Shells stick in magazine. As in other tubular magazines, check tube and spring. Can be foreign matter under shell stop.

Stevens Single Barrel Shotguns

Parts are available for most of the obsolete Stevens singles of the breakopen type and main troubles are broken mainsprings and trigger springs. Hammer notches wear and break out, and forend springs need stretching. Extractors wear and break, but to no great extent. Firing pins break more often than other parts, but are easily made. Late models have coil springs.

Stevens Double Barrels

Parts are available for the hammerless models, and a few for the old Model 215 hammer gun. Safeties, triggers, cocking levers and sears cause most repair jobs on the hammerless guns. The safeties break quite often, and new ones must be bought. The triggers wear loose, sometimes having so much play they lose engagement with the sears or firing pins. Small washers help this condition considerably. The notches on the firing pins and sears wear rapidly, but can be filed to re-engage properly. Cocking levers burr up and make difficult cocking, and, of course, firing pin tips break off frequently. Extractors as a rule do not cause much trouble. Most, if not all, of the Stevens doubles, have stock bolts securing the stock to the receiver. As in any shotgun, foreign matter in the action or around the hinge joint can make for improper functioning.

Stevens Bolt Action Shotguns

The low priced 20 gauge and .410 shotguns of the bolt action design are very simply made and repairs usually obvious. The clip or box magazines will sometimes not feed properly, but little goes wrong with these guns beyond an occasional broken firing pin or extractor. The tubular magazine .410 bore sometimes has lifter trouble and will not feed correctly, and it may be necessary to bend or otherwise alter parts to achieve smooth feeding into the chamber. Notches on the firing pins and the sear noses will wear to the point of causing failure to cock, but parts can be built up or new ones installed to correct this.

Savage Shotguns

Savage has long owned the Stevens company and at present the Savage plant is the same as Stevens, both being located at Chicopee Falls, Massachusetts in the same organization. Some models of guns are identical except for name, although shotguns have been kept individual.

The Savage Autoloading Shotgun

This is a Browning design, and so similar to the Remington Model 11 that all remarks made concerning the Remington will apply to this make as well, excepting that parts will not interchange readily between the two guns. The Savage gun operates at almost minimum headspace. The recoil system is basically the same as that on the Remington, but adjustment is slightly different. The Remington friction ring has an inside bevel on one side, outside bevel on the other, while the Savage has only an inside bevel on one side. The Remington has a stop ring around the magazine tube at the receiver, while the Savage has no ring, the recoil spring contacting the face of receiver directly. The lightweight models have duralumin receivers.

Savage Over and Unders

Models 420 and 430 were formerly built, being the same except that barrel matting, checkering and recoil pad was provided on the 430. It is doubtful if they will be made in the future, as there is little market for a medium priced arm of this type. All springs used were coil type, not likely to break, but trigger and safety mechanisms are liable to both breakage and jamming. The optional single trigger is susceptible to wear, gummed oil, and dirt, and any one or a combination of these are able to put the gun out of service. The extractors and firing pins do not appear to give much trouble.

Obsolete Savage Shotguns

The models 21 and 28 Savage pump action shotguns were quite decent guns, but never seemed to get very popular. These were concealed hammer right side ejecting arms, similar in general appearance to the Winchester M12, except that they had tang safeties, located as

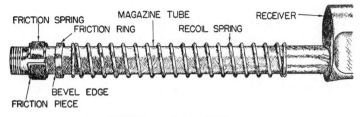

FRICTION SPRING   MAGAZINE TUBE   RECEIVER
      FRICTION RING   RECOIL SPRING

BEVEL EDGE
FRICTION PIECE

POSITION I- HEAVY LOADS

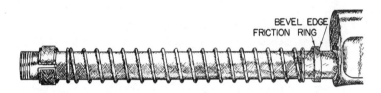

BEVEL EDGE
FRICTION RING

POSITION 2 — LIGHT LOADS

RECOIL ADJUSTMENTS — SAVAGE SHOTGUN M720

on double guns. In general, troubles and repairs are in line with the comments made on the Winchester 12 and Remington 31.

Browning Shotguns

The only Browning guns sold as Brownings in this country have been the autoloader and the over and under doubles. The autoloader is like the Remington M11, with the addition of a magazine cutoff, and remarks regarding the Remington apply to the Browning. The fiber buffer cushion in the receiver is not used by Browning.

The over and under Browning is a very finely made shotgun, with hand finished parts. Selective single trigger is standard on all, as are automatic selective ejectors. The close fitting of parts makes the model sensitive to foreign matter and poor grades of oil, it being quite easy to put the gun out of commission by allowing it to get dirty or oiling with improper lubricants. Rust can affect the firing pins and ejector hammers, although this is seen very infrequently. Perhaps the only real complaint to be encountered will be that the action is hard to close. This is almost invariably due to burrs on the receiver, caused by careless handling while the gun is apart, and usually the dented portions with their resulting burrs can be forced back into proper position by using a smooth ended punch and applying a light hammer—just a little long distance peening. The trigger mechanism can be worked on to correct doubling, to some extent, but if new parts are needed, you might as well send the gun to the factory in St. Louis. If they will sell you the part you want, you will have to do so much work fitting and adjusting that you will not make anything on the job!

Parker Shotguns

The Parker shotgun was formerly made by Remington. Only one hammerless model has been made for many years, although many grades of the same model are available. Considered a good quality double barrel, the boxlock design is good though old. The V-type mainsprings are less liable to breakage than on other similar guns, and the firing pins not likely to break at all. They are integral with, or permanently attached to the hammers. The very best material was used throughout and what little trouble develops is usually in triggers or safety, as on all doubles. The latest modification of the Parker employed sears which can break, and also firing pins liable to tip breakage.

Fox Shotguns

The Fox name is owned by Savage, who make the present Fox double in the Stevens plant. There have been some doubles marked with the Fox name sold at low prices which have been identical with the late model Stevens double gun. However, the "Sterlingworth" and better grades of Fox brand guns have been very fine. So far as design is considered, in the mechanical sense, I am inclined to believe that the Fox is just about the best double made—anyway, I have heard fewer complaints about the Fox line and do not believe I have ever had to really repair one. The ejector sears look frail, but do not break or apparently wear. The triggers are very well made and the safety works unless blocked by foreign matter. Firing pins do not break and hammers apparently seldom wear out notches. The firing pins are actually hammer noses, as on the Parker or Winchester 21. Trigger pulls and ejectors sometimes need smoothing up, but that is about all the weak points.

Ithaca Shotguns

Ithaca's double barrel is furnished in all grades, but it is basically one action. The lowest price version is sold as the Western Arms Corporation "Durable Double," but all others bear the Ithaca name. All sorts of trigger variation, cocking indicators, and such may be found on the more expensive guns, but the inside of all them is pretty much the same. The action is quite good, coil springs being used extensively, and only the safety is liable to breakage or jamming. Cocking hooks or levers in the older guns may wear somewhat, and the ejector mechanism tie up through wear, breakage or burring of the ejector kicker sear or its spring.

Ithaca Model 37 Slide Action

This shotgun superficially resembles the Remington M31 in exterior appearance, although bottom ejecting. With the Ithaca parts list, the word "slide" means the breechblock slide, which moves in the receiver under the block. The M37 is quite popular, competing with the Remington 31 and Winchester 12 on equal terms. A lightweight model is made, and the regular model is available in special grades, with custom alterations.

The following troubles may be encountered:

Breechblock does not lock. Can be due to burrs on the locking lugs of the breechblock or slide, or foreign matter in the locking recess in the receiver, or on the face of the block or in the extractor cuts in the rear of the barrel.

Firing pin fails to retract. May be due to a broken pin, a jammed spring, or foreign matter in the firing pin hole.

Slide handle sticks. Can be due to a broken slide pin, a broken slide, or burrs or dirt on the slide.

Hammer fails to cock or slips. Probably worn notches or foreign material under the trigger or trigger spring. The nose of the sear may be worn, the trigger spring broken, or the action bar lock damaged.

Slide stop fails. (Action bar lock.) Can be caused by worn nose on the stop, a displaced or broken spring, or foreign matter in the slot in the trigger plate.

Double feeding. Can be a worn right-hand cartridge stop, or dirt in the cartridge stop recess in the receiver wall.

Safety sticks. As on Remington, can be dirt, or a damaged plunger or spring.

Fails to extract. Can be due to worn or broken extractors or springs, or jammed extractor springs.

Fails to eject. On this shotgun the carrier acts as ejector, the empty shells coming out the bottom of the receiver. If the gun fails to eject, the carrier may be bent or foreign matter may be interfering with its movement.

Fails to fire. (When all parts of firing mechanism—firing pin, hammer and springs are all right.) Check for foreign matter or any defect preventing movement of the breechblock slide or the action bar (slide handle) to the full forward position. The Ithaca mechanism will release—trigger can be pulled and the hammer will fall—when the slide or slide handle is within $\frac{5}{16}''$ of the full forward position, but the hammer will contact the slide and not fire the shell.

General. Feeding and magazine troubles are seldom encountered with the Ithaca, but should you have a gun with a dented tube brought in, the repair is obvious. The design of the gun keeps out more dust and foreign matter than other pump guns acquire.

Marlin Shotguns

Marlin has made some very poor slide action shotguns in the past, parts for a few of which are still available, but I would advise that little repair work be done on them as most of these early guns are actually unsafe to fire with modern ammunition. Gun editors of my acquaintance advise me that they receive many letters telling of blowups and accidents with obsolete Marlin repeaters. The Models 28, 31, 43, 44, 53 and 63 are reasonably safe with modern low-velocity shells, but are prone to break the flat springs on ejectors, safety latches, and other parts. The forend slide bar wears its lug down, which can be repaired, but the carrier also seems to wear, and although also repairable, it is a rather difficult job. The dozen or so other models, from the 1898 to the 30G and 42 are less safe. The numerous flat springs break or are blocked by foreign matter, parts burr up and wear badly, and so on. All of the Marlins are likely to develop excess headspace.

A few .410 bore shotguns were made by Marlin on their lever action rifle frame, and these are very excellent guns. Repair work is exactly as on the Marlin 1894 rifle.

Marlin Over and Under Shotguns

The Model 90 was made in prewar years in all gauges, even .410 bore, and is quite good for a low cost arm of this type. It is stiff in opening and closing, and an hour or so spent smoothing up the action helps considerably. The sear, safety, and extractor levers are the weak points, not particularly subject to breakage, but they wear and burr enough to affect proper functioning.

L. C. Smith Shotguns

The Hunter Arms Company was purchased by Marlin, so that L. C. Smith doubles are now made by Marlin. Of the better grade double guns coming in for repair, L. C. Smiths probably outnumber all the others combined. The side lock construction makes for a very weak stock at the breech, so that cracked stocks are more the rule than the exception. Also, oil from the locks causes the wooden stock tangs to deteriorate.

The most common mechanical failure by far is broken firing pins. They are easily made on the lathe, and do not bother trying to stock a few factory pins, unless for the current gun, because older guns used a number of sizes and types. The lock seldom gives trouble as the springs and sears are of the best steel, but occasionally a lock will loosen from the frame or the stock wood will swell or splinter to the point of interference with the lock action. Triggers on old and heavily used guns may become loose and fail to properly contact the sears. The top lever spring is the only spring liable to breakage, and do not try to make it— buy one from the factory. It is immensely strong for its size, and making such a spring is extremely difficult, even with proper steel and a lead bath for tempering. I have made them, but only when unable to wait for delivery from the factory. The safeties do not give much trouble as a rule, although the whole gun is rather sensitive to foreign matter and gummed lubricants. Rather good trigger pulls can be put on the L. C. Smith guns, and the single triggers available can be fairly easily adjusted.

Miscellaneous Shotguns

Savage Combination, Model 219. This single barrel model, with interchangeable rifle and shotgun barrels, is principally victim to broken firing pins and loose forends. Rifle extractors sometimes break or jam, usually due to the owner strongarming the gun improperly. Excellent trigger pulls can be put on this model.

Lefever Shotguns. Older guns are always likely to break the flat springs used and also are subject to safety and trigger trouble.

Stevens Over and Under Rifle-Shotgun .22/410. Chief trouble is with the rear sights and the selector button screws falling out of the gun and getting lost. Selector button screws, springs, and plungers should be carried in stock. Factory sights, or the Lyman aperture receiver sight made for this model, should also be kept on hand. The front sights for this model can be used on revolvers.

Iver Johnson Shotguns. On double barrel guns, the firing pin tips break, the safety block wears, burrs and sometimes bends out of engagement and the cocking rods will burr or wear so that the hammer slips in cocking. On single barrels, broken firing pins, broken trigger springs, worn ejector levers and worn ejector lever pins cause trouble. Also, the extractor stop pin sometimes wears to the point of causing the extractor to stick.

Harrington & Richardson Shotguns. These break firing pins, the trigger and mainsprings; extractor actuating parts sometimes burr or wear to affect functioning. Hammer notches also wear, but can easily be re-shaped and loose forends are common, but easily corrected.

General Shotgun Repair and Alteration Work

The most often repeated shotgun job will be installation of recoil pads. New guns, old guns, all types—someone is always deciding he needs a recoil pad, either to subdue the recoil or to change stock dimension. As much as 1⅛″ in length can be grained by the addition of some makes of pads, even after the butt is squared and I have put many pads on .410 bores just for that reason. Quite often a parent will get a light .410 or 20 gauge for a growing boy and have the stock shortened 1″ or 1½″, which deduction can be corrected after the kid grows by addition of a thick pad.

Use no pads except the neoprene types now available—the old fashioned rubber pads were affected by oil, heat and general treatment which the neoprene ignores entirely.

The perfect pad attaching job entails fitting to the butt and then cutting the pad to correct dimensions and proportions on the stock, cutting right down to the surface of the wood, through the finish. You refinish the whole buttstock, with the pad on for a good job. There are a few experienced workmen who can retouch and match a finish fairly closely, but never perfectly. Not a great deal more time is involved in refinishing the stock, except when a high grade gun with a fine oil finish is involved.

The customer is the first consideration—does he want the butt shorter, longer, same length, or more or less pitch? If he says it is fine the way it is, do not jump right into the job—several factors are involved. Number one, see how he handles the gun, so that you can tell whether he knows anything or not. The old timer may be right, but chances are that the stock should be ¼″ longer than he thinks it should. The novice may keep his head too far back and point the gun too straight to the front, thus making any stock too long!

Number two, the well-known trigger-finger-to-elbow rule applies roughly only to men of normal build. Stout, thin, short necked, long necked, and heavily muscled men can not go by it. And there is the occasional ape armed individual to whom no rules apply. The stout or thickset man probably will do better with a slightly shorter stock; the thin man can use a slightly longer stock; the short neck will be better off with a Monte Carlo or high straight comb, and the long neck probably will shoot better with a stock having considerably greater than present standard drop at the heel, in spite of the added recoil effect of this styling.

Number three, consider the clothing. A man may bring his duck gun in for a pad in the middle of July (it probably will be the night before the season opens, but there are a few duck hunters who can and do think) wearing his summer uniform, this being anything from a T-shirt to a business suit. If you fit the stock so that it is perfectly comfortable to him then, it will not be so good when he tries to catch a fast crossing shot attired in two suits of Bean's underwear, a wool shirt, a thick sweater and a heavy hunting coat. Allow from ¼″ to ⅜″ for clothing in such cases, making the stock that much shorter.

Number four, consider the purpose for which the gun is principally intended. If the customer will use it for every type of shooting—upland, waterfowl, rabbits and perhaps occasionally for a session at the traps or skeet range, the standard factory pitch will be satisfactory. Purely for trap or skeet, the buttplate should have 1″ less pitch, and if considerable quail and pheasant shooting is the main interest involved, about ¾″ less pitch than normal, for most effective performance. Trap shotguns should have the straight type stock, (no pistol grip) with fairly high comb, and butt should be from ½″ to 1″ longer than standard, or the sporting shotgun. The customer will have to determine for himself the correct length of his trap gun through test, and the easiest way is to use one of the leather-lace-on boots over the butt, trying the gun with different thickness pads inside the boot to vary the length and so find the most efficient length for that individual.

"Normal" pitch I define as 2¼″, this being an average of the factory standards as used on standard field grade sporting shotguns, taking in the Remington 11, Winchester 12, L. C. Smith Double, Ithaca 37, Remington 31 and Remington 11–48, all with 30″ barrels. Remember to figure from the 30″ barrel basis—a gun with 3″ pitch having 30″ barrel does *not* have the same pitch in reality as does a gun with 26″ barrel registering 3″ pitch in actual measurement. The checking gadget is just a 2″ x 8″ or 10″ plank, with right angle cutaway as shown. This is less subject to breakage and false figures than the extended leg square generally used.

Butt length, also called "pull," is measured from the center of the trigger to the center of the rear edge of the buttplate or pad. For guns with two triggers, measure from a point approximately in the middle of the two triggers. Most men will be fitted between 13½″ and 14½″, going by ¼″ steps at a time in checking them, if possible. Clothing has the greatest interference in perfect fitting as the shotgun may fit and handle easily in warm weather, when light clothing is worn, and feel like a fence post the next winter, when heavy clothing slows movement and cold tightens muscles.

The following table gives approximate butt-stock measurements for men of normal physical makeup:

Height of Man	Butt Length
5' to 5'4"	13½"
5'4" to 5'8"	14"
5'8" to 6'	14½"
6' to 6'4"	14¾"
6'4" to 6'8"	15"

Fitting the Pad

Assuming the correct overall length of stock and the proper pitch is determined, the stock must be cut off or squared at the correct angle. This is harder than it sounds, for most modern stocks are kiln dried to the point where the surface wood fibers are very brittle, and splinter out slightly as the saw passes through, on the far side. Use of a sharp and rapidly moving band saw will eliminate this somewhat, but it is extremely difficult to cut absolutely square and straight with a band saw—and you want to cut it straight, because as little as .002" off a plane face will show up in the finished job.

I believe that a sharp mitre box saw handled carefully is most efficient. Naturally it is easier to handle the buttstock only, so remove it from the gun to cut it, after setting the mitre box to cut at the desired angle to produce the wanted pitch. Use of masking tape on the bottom side of the stock helps somewhat in preventing splintering out at the cut, and manipulation of the saw, lifting the handle on the rearward stroke, so that the bottom edge of cut is made by this movement also helps. To be absolutely sure of not splintering, I sometimes make half the cut on top (with the stock held flat on the mitre box bed) which does not splinter or tear at the edges of the kerf, or cut, then remove the saw and with a sharp chisel make a cut extending the inner edge of the kerf about ⅟₁₆" deep and perhaps ⁵⁄₁₆" long, on the unsawed portion. The saw is again used, cutting to the end of these cuts, when the process is repeated, and so on until the stock is within ⅟₁₆" of being cut through. This last thin portion is cut with the chisel.

After cutting the stock off, it must be clamped in the vise vertically, butt up, and filed with sharp mill file until it checks out smooth and square both ways with a straightedge. Wet the exposed wood on the cut and raise the grain twice, filing smooth again. Now check the hard inner face of the recoil pad and square it, using files and an ordinary hand scraper with a straightedge. Next, if the stock involved is attached by the stock bolt to the receiver, assemble to the receiver—once on, you do not want to remove the pad. Place the pad in correct position on the stock, allowing for the length at toe, mark the top screw (at heel) by using a drift punch just the size to pass through the hole in the pad (hard section) tapping it with a hammer, then using a center punch to make a depression to start the drill bit at the correct location. Use the proper drill for the screws provided—usually a No. 31 or ⅛″ is right—and set in the screw. It is not a bad idea to tap the hole in the wood by winding in one of the screws before attaching the pad. With the pad attached by one screw, the second hole is marked with the pad centered over the stock in the same way and the first screw then backed off enough to allow the pad to be rotated away from position so that the second hole can be drilled. Now is a good time to coat the end of stock with heavy linseed oil—boiled oil mixed with drier and exposed to the air until it reaches the consistency of molasses. The pad is then screwed firmly into place. Do not get too strong and strip the screw holes. With the holes previously threaded by running in the screws, this is easy to avoid, as they go in quite readily, tightening up only as they reach their limit of movement, which is felt on the screwdriver handle.

Use a breast drill for the holes, so that you can control direction—straight in—and fairly long shanked screwdrivers, of the round shank type. The long shank springs a trifle and you are far less likely to strip out the hole.

If you do strip a hole, or find that new holes are not quite in line with the old buttplate screw holes, just run a ¼″ or ⁵⁄₁₆″ drill bit in, cut off a piece of birch dowel to fit, coat it with glue and drive it in, cutting flush with the buttface. The new hole is then drilled in this dowel.

A very common shortcut to close fitting of pads and buttplates is to slightly hollow the surface of the buttface with a gouge, leaving only the edges to be filed to order. This can be done if the saw cuts badly out of square, to save filing time, but be sure to leave wood around each screw hole location at the same height as the edges. Otherwise the center of the pad will pull down into the hollow and slightly gap the edges.

With the pad attached to the buttstock, the problem of cutting it to size comes up. If the stock is to be refinished, you start right in on the cutting disc, grinding away the protruding edges of the pad and fairing it in with lines of the stock. Grind the pad to the surface of the wood first, then start on the stock about 4″ in front of the pad, taking a light pass over the disc so that finish and surface cuts away at the joint. If you have been careful, the wood and the pad will meet in a perfect line, and the pad will not protrude beyond the lines of the stock. A good many present day factory stocks are slightly thicker ½″ to 1″ ahead of the original buttplate, so that often you will cut wood ahead of the joint before touching the joint itself.

Unless the disc is turning very fast, the wood and the hard portion of the recoil pad will cut clean, while the softer portion of pad will be from 1/64″ to 1/32″ larger all around. This is of course due to the more resilient material "giving" to the pressure exerted, and is neither preventable nor objectionable. A high speed disc will cut the softer cushion as clean as the hard base and the wood, and makes a better job.

On such jobs, where the entire buttstock is to be refinished, it is best to remove the original finish with varnish remover before even cutting the stock. After cutting and shaping, a good mill file is best for smoothing up the disc marks, followed by fine sandpaper. The grain is then raised twice and cut down, and the desired finish applied. Marks of stains, oils and varnishes on the pads are easily removed by rubbing with a cloth dipped in solvent, gasoline, or alcohol.

When the stock is not to be refinished, try to protect the wood as much as possible, wrapping with not over two thicknesses of masking tape, the rear edge of which should be 1/8″ ahead of the joint between the wood and the pad. The pad is ground to shape until about 1/32″ over the size of the stock at the joint, then you start fairing the pad into the stock lines, bringing the cutting disc into light contact with the tape-protected stock, and passing back across the pad. The tape will wear away, and with care you will cut the pad to within less than .010″ of the stock on the disc, without scratching the stock. Now remove the old tape and put on a single band around the stock, the rear edge about 1/16″ ahead of the joint, and with a fine mill file cut across the tape and into the exposed edge of the recoil pad. All you can file is the hard plate of the pad, but in 15 or 20 minutes you can make an excellent-appearing job. Rub the joint and the black plate with thick linseed oil and the job is finished.

On battered old guns, or those which have the stocks finished in plain oil, just cut the stock and the pad together, and match the finish as closely as you can. You will need burnt umber (in oil), linseed oil, raw sienna, burnt sienna, white shellac, orange shellac, spar varnish and wax to use in all the combinations you can think up to match assorted stock colors and finishes. Winchester stains their stocks, so that if the surface is removed anywhere, you have the natural color of the wood to alter. Most factory finishes today are types of spar varnish, over stain and filler.

Occasionally a customer will want his stock shortened, but will not want a recoil pad. In the case of butts which are fatter in front of the plate than at it, this can be embarrassing. You can cut the stock to whatever curvature is required, using the hollowing-out system to expedite filing, but the original plate just is not wide enough. So when you are asked to do such a job, get out the calipers and check the stock thickness. If you do not have a plain plate of suitable dimensions which can be altered to fit, sell the guy a recoil pad or one of the rifle butt-plates put out by Pachmayr or Mershon, which are fitted exactly the same as recoil pads.

The man who wants a stock lengthened, without use of a recoil pad, will probably be better satisfied if you add on layers of colored plastic or red fiber than if you attempt to lengthen it by a walnut filler. I have done both kinds of jobs, and only once have I ever been able to match a walnut stock with a piece of walnut which did not look a mess. That one time both pieces of wood were the same color, the same type grain and I got a perfect joint between the two pieces of wood and refinished the whole stock. To fit a lengthening block, or spacers, you must of course have the stock end perfectly squared, as for the pad.

Shotgun Barrel Work

At present there are numerous choke-control devices for use on single barrel shotguns, most with muzzle brake or recoil compensating features built into them. Installation is similar for all of them, either the end of gun barrel is threaded to receive a fitting, or a similar fitting or sleeve is silver-soldered to the muzzle. The threaded types, such as Weaver and PolyChoke, require that the proper rize of sleeve or choke be chosen for the size barrel involved. There is considerable variation between diameters of shotgun barrels, in the same gauges, so that a choke which will fit one make will be too large or too small for another brand of gun. The chokemakers of course furnish a selection of sizes to accommodate various barrels.

Weaver Choke—PolyChoke. These two devices require that the muzzle of the gun be trued on the lathe, the outer surface turned off for a short distance, and threaded. The thread is 40 per inch, V type. Be-

CORRECT SHOTGUN CHAMBERING

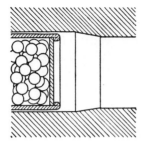 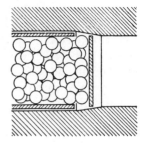

INCORRECT — SHELL TOO LONG FOR CHAMBER

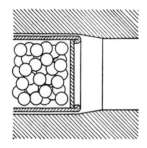 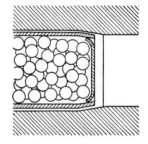

RIFLE — CORRECT NECK CHAMBERING

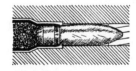

INCORRECT

cause of the variation in barrel diameters, it is wise to mike each barrel and order the device accordingly, unless you can carry a selection of sizes in each gauge. The factories furnish enough sizes to take care of practically all barrels. With the Weaver, the body of the choke screws directly on the barrel, and no pains are taken to make it line up in any particular manner, as the front sight is installed after the job is completed, by drilling for it in the top of the choke. With the Poly, you must line up the front sight in mounting.

Cutts. The Cutts Compensator is very well known and quite easy to install. A sleeve is furnished, threaded on the outside, and of proper diameter for the barrel involved, which is to be silver soldered on the barrel at the muzzle. It is necessary to turn the barrel down to

---

Neck Chambering

With the shotgun, the chamber must be made longer than the shell, for the length of the shell is considered in its fired condition. The crimp has to unroll as the shell is fired, and the chamber must have sufficient length to accommodate it. At the top is shown the correct chambering, with the unfired shell in the chamber at the left, and the firing shell at the right, at the time the wad leaves the opened shell mouth.

A short chamber will permit the entrance of a long shell, unfired, as shown, with the result that the forcing cone in the barrel constricts the opening of the shell, per the right hand sketch, thus raising pressures, causing deformed shot, and blown patterns.

Modern post war shell construction has been toward the no-top-wad, or frangible top wad style, with the result that the shells have become much shorter than they were formerly. The $2\frac{3}{4}''$ shell now is approximately $2\frac{3}{8}''$ overall in the unfired condition, and does not reach $2\frac{3}{4}''$ even when fired, in some styles of manufacture.

At the bottom, we have rifle characteristics. In the correct drawing, note that the chamber is longer than the cartridge. This is done so that the variation in cartridge lengths, and stretching of necks under several firings of the same case by reloaders will not be detrimental to performance of the arm.

Under "Incorrect" at the left we have the funnel throat, with too great clearance ahead of the cartridge mouth. Powder gases will rapidly erode the throat of the rifle.

At the right is the short chamber, with the neck of the cartridge forced up into the throat of the barrel. The case does not have room to expand and release the bullet, so pressures are forced sharply upward, and the mouth of the case is as shown at the extreme right. This is distinctly bad—accuracy suffers, and possibly dangerous pressures are created. Handloaders often cause this condition by not trimming, or shortening the cases, which, when used several times, lengthen out considerably.

receive this sleeve, cutting a shoulder far enough back so that the muzzle will be flush with the end of the sleeve when in place. The sleeve should be an easy slide fit. The barrel is cut to the desired length before this is done, the barrel proper not to be shorter than 22″, for best results. A set of mandrels to fit standard 12, 16 and 20 gauge chambers will have to be made up, so that you can turn barrels on your lathe.

After the barrel is shortened, and it must be shortened at least enough to eliminate all of the original choke, you clamp it in the vise, muzzle up. Screw the compensator body on the sleeve as tight as you can by hand, then slip the sleeve on the barrel. Turn the assembled sleeve and body together until the front sight (on the compensator body) is approximately $\frac{1}{10}$ of one turn ahead of lining up with the top of the barrel or the rib. Mark with a continuous pencil line across the sleeve and the barrel, parallel with the barrel axis, for an index line. Now remove the sleeve and, being careful not to wipe off the pencil mark, unscrew the body and set it aside. With Silflo, Easyflow, or other silver solder paste flux, coat the inside of the sleeve and pass it down over the barrel section so as to coat it also. Examine to make sure the flux is over all surfaces, then place the sleeve in position on the muzzle, lining up the penciled index marks. Hold in position with one hand and with the other wipe away all the flux which has squeezed out on the bottom of the sleeve at the barrel shoulder and also the pencil marks. With wire-form silver solder—$\frac{1}{16}$″ diameter or square— form an incomplete circle, to fit in the groove appearing between the outer edge of the barrel and the inner edge of the sleeve and lay it in this groove. The sleeve has a slight bevel to aid this and the wire circle should be complete except for an opening of approximately $\frac{3}{16}$″. Wipe any flux off the top and the inner edge of the muzzle, being careful not to turn the sleeve on the barrel. You now light up the welding torch, using around a No. 26 or 27 size tip (Smith type) and with about five pounds pressure on both acetylene and oxygen feed dials, give the sleeve only a fast heating, concentrating the flame on the heavier bottom section first and working around the whole sleeve. Do not ever play the torch on the barrel anywhere. Usually the sleeve is a dull red when the ring of silver solder suddenly begins to melt and disappear downward to form the sweat joint. With the commercial wire solders available, it is seldom necessary to heat any hotter, although a fairly bright red on the sleeve will do no damage. The silver will show through the small holes in the body of the sleeve and will disappear except as a plating at the muzzle, over the bevel. Heat is applied only for about 30 seconds as a rule, at least this has been my experience.

As soon as the solder flows into position, switch off and hang up the torch. Take the barrel from the vise, wait about eight seconds more, then dunk the hot muzzle with attached compensator sleeve in a small can of ordinary cutting oil, to blue the sleeve. Remove and wipe with a cloth (woolen is best) and redunk it a couple of times, then set it aside to cool. When cool, clean the barrel thoroughly, using a wad of steel wool to clean the muzzle under the sleeve. There should be no scale, but if any does exist, it should be removed. The barrel will not be injured by scale, in this case. It may be necessary to use a wire brush to clean the threads on the sleeve, with the blued shoulder section protected by tape.

Clamp the barrel in the vise, using soft wooden blocks hollowed to fit it so as to prevent deformation, and screw on the compensator body. Using a strip of $\frac{1}{16}''$ by $\frac{3}{8}''$ flat drill rod with rounded edges passed through the slots in body for a wrench, you should be able to turn the body on very tightly, just managing to bring the front sight into proper alignment. If you cannot make it turn far enough to line up, remove the body and clean off the rear face. The simplest way I know of to do this is to place a sheet of medium abrasive cloth on a flat hard surface —the drill press table used to serve me—and, holding the compensator body firmly in one hand, with the rear face pressed against the cloth, make two or three passes across the cloth. This will remove enough metal to make an appreciable difference in fitting the compensator but if the compensator turns past the sight alignment, the lathe must be used as sufficient metal must be removed from either the shoulder of the sleeve or the back end of the compensator body to permit screwing around the major portion of another full turn, so it will tighten up at the correct point to align the front sight.

After the compensator is mounted in correct position, the retaining set-screw is set to hold it in place. A recess for the point of the screw must be drilled in the sleeve, using the drilled and tapped hole in the body as a guide. The screws furnished are a trifle long, and should be shortened to obtain a flush fitting.

The most trouble with the Cutts is with the owner getting wrench-happy attaching the choke tubes. The wrench furnished is to be used to remove the tubes, not install them. Screwed in with ordinary hand pressure, a few shots will tighten them so that the wrench is necessary to remove and change them. If the wrench is used to screw them in tightly, firing will make them so tight that often so much strength must be used in removal that the compensator body turns on the sleeve, bringing the front sight out of alignment and tearing the set-screw in its seat—gumming up the set-screw recess so that it is difficult to again really tighten the body. Usually, however, the recess can be drilled slightly deeper, or pointed more, and a longer screw installed, to control this difficulty.

Cutts Compensators should be mounted exactly parallel with the bore axis. Should the shotgun pattern high, low, or to one side, correction must be made by alteration of the front sight, the stock, or bending the barrel.

PowerPac. The Pachmayr PowerPac compensating choke attachment is mounted in almost identical manner to the Cutts, the only real difference being that for some types of guns the barrel sleeve is bored at a slight angle and is marked on the top and the bottom for installation on the barrel in that position. Mr. Pachmayr is attempting to correct the tendency to pattern high of some slide action shotguns when equipped with choke devices. It is therefore necessary to have the proper choke assembly for the particular type of shotgun involved, rather than having one choke on hand which will apply to any shotgun of the proper gauge.

Off-Shooting

The matter of shotguns shooting high, low or to one side after installation of a patent choke attachment receives unnecessary attention sometimes, and often adverse comment regarding the choke and the gunsmith who installed it. Nine times out of ten, the owner never patterned the gun until after the choke was installed, and does not realize that if it patterns off center, it may have done the same with the original choke in the barrel. If he could have advised the gunsmith of the gun's tendency to shoot off, the matter possibly could have been corrected in the installation of the choke device.

It is actually difficult to mount a choke device improperly, and as the various devices are all made very uniformly, any defugalty arising after the installation is usually due to the gun itself. Shotgun barrels are easily bent, and any gunsmith who has mounted very many chokes is used to finding numerous sprung barrels. The barrel may look okay, but put it in the lathe and watch the wobble!—and maybe you want to straighten it and maybe you do not. The barrel may have been bent purposely at the factory in order to make it pattern correctly originally, and perhaps it will be okay as it is, with the patent choke installed. Perhaps the original choke in the barrel was off center and required that the barrel be out of true, and when the barrel was shortened and the choke removed, the pattern through the choke device would be incorrect. I do not know any way to tell if the barrel is okay except to mount the choke and try out the gun. The proof of the pudding is in the eating and the proof of a gun is in its shooting.

This brings up another problem which is hard to solve on paper. The rear sight on a shotgun is actually the position of the shooter's cheek on the stock, and two men will seldom get a true picture of the performance of the same gun if they use it as they do in the field. The customer should pattern his gun himself, but the gunsmith should emphasize very definitely that he should make a visible aiming point on the target paper and shoot at it just as he would use the gun in the field or on the trap or skeet range, pointing the shotgun fast and shooting fast. He must not aim at the mark as he would a rifle and hold the gun more firmly than usual, because if he does, such shooting will check the gun's patterning ability but is worthless for finding out the practical *position* of the pattern. A gun can be overshooting in reality, yet under the above circumstances, pattern perfectly to point of aim. The guy could center his pattern target, but miss his birds.

The method of handling a shotgun, the pitch of the buttplate, and the dimensions of the buttstock can all affect the position of the pattern as much as the barrel or choke device itself. A gun which undershoots slightly can often be made satisfactory by merely increasing the pitch of the buttplate, and of course the opposite also is true. The height of the comb also affects the height of the pattern through the position of the shooter's cheek when it arrests the upward movement of the butt as the gun is pointed. Shooting to right or left is sometimes due to straightness of the buttstock in that the cheek does not position properly in fast gun-handling. A man used to shooting a gun stocked with some cast-off is usually a lost ball in high weeds when he tries to use the same type of gun with a straight stock, and the man used to a straight stock will have plenty of trouble when he tries a cast-off stock. Remember, a shotgun is *pointed*, rather than aimed, and fast. And the trigger is not squeezed, it is pulled. Any factor interfering with the positioning of the gun as it is thrown to the shoulder and the trigger pulled will cause some deviation from the desired pattern position. The fact that most shotgun shooters uniformly pull the gun down and to the right very slightly when they pull the trigger is generally overlooked, probably because nobody, including me, can think of any way to do anything about it.

Mechanical alteration to cure misplaced patterns, aside from stock alteration, is an old and fairly simple process. The only two methods I am personally familiar with are those of bending the barrel and altering the muzzle of the barrel.

In bending the barrel several methods of protecting against making it out of round are common, these being to fill it full of fine sand, moist earth packed solidly, or water. The ends are of course plugged tightly. I question whether any barrel can be plugged tightly enough to prevent movement of the filling material under tension unless a very strong U clamp is used to hold both plugs. To accomplish the actual bending of the barrel, which is of course very little—almost imperceptible to the naked eye—any method which will not mar the finish of the barrel is satisfactory. One primitive method which does very well is to use a patch of damp sand with a protecting cloth over it, place a grooved block at points to support each end of the barrel—these can be under the cloth—and placing the barrel in the desired position, just bearing down on the center of the barrel with both hands placed close together. The barrel is sprung slightly by a series of rhythmic weight applications.

Barrels can be sprung by clamping the breech section in a barrel vise with long supporting grooved protecting jaws and using a long copper rod of approximately bore diameter inserted from the muzzle and forced in the direction of the desired bend. The barrel is of course bent in the direction it is desired to move the pattern.

Once in a great while it will be necessary to straighten a barrel bent accidentally and the above method is to be recommended. I remember one job on a rather good grade of slide action trap gun which had had its barrel run over by an automobile. The barrel was bent at least 30° out of straight, but the accident had occurred on fairly soft ground, so that the barrel was not flattened appreciably. I clamped the barrel back of the bend, heated the bend dull red with the welding torch and pulled it reasonably straight with a round bar thrust down the muzzle, then cold-straightened it until it appeared okay. The bore was sized by use of dent-removing plugs, the ventilated rib soldered back where it had broken free of the barrel, and the gun handed back to the owner for test. He never brought it back, so I presume he is satisfied with the performance. There was no sign that the barrel had ever been damaged or worked on save for a slight heat-marking of the blue at the position of the bend. It would not be possible to straighten a badly-bent barrel cold without producing a slight bulge on the outside of the bend, as the stretched metal at that point would be forced upon itself and the barrel would be weakened and possibly cracked at the inside of the bend.

The other method of correcting an off-shooting shotgun is in little

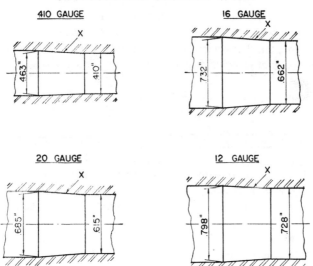

SHOTGUN THROATING

Here are shown approximate chamber and bore diameters, with length of throat as X, on account of it is more-or-less the unknown quantity. Everyone who makes shotgun barrels makes his own rules, so, as a rule for us, figure the throat, or forcing cone, as from $\frac{7}{16}''$ to $1\frac{1}{16}''$. I personally favor long cones, but shotgun experts advise that the short throat sometimes is best.

favor today. It consists of removing metal from the inside of the bore at the muzzle, in the direction desired to move the pattern. Metal must be filed, ground, or honed all the way back to the choke. The pattern is not really shifted, but is enlarged in the desired direction. Pattern density suffers considerably, and the method is not to be recommended.

High and low front sights give a small measure of pattern correction. The shotgun back sights, those small beads placed in the middle of the barrel, have no real effect on pattern placement, although they often make the shooter pay more attention to his front sight alignment on the target.

Alteration of Existing Choke

Formerly a common job, today there are few calls to change the choke in a barrel. In a good grade shotgun you can seldom increase the choke, but to decrease it is fairly simple. The choke mouth—toward or at the muzzle of the gun—is reamed or polished to greater diameter.

The front edge of the choke bevel may be anywhere from the edge of the muzzle to a point 1″ back. An expansion reamer, very sharp, is best for the job, but many a gunsmith turns out satisfactory work by using a mandrel wrapped with fine abrasive cloth, turned in the lathe or the drill press.

An exact degree of choke is difficult to achieve. No test can be made except by patterning the gun, of course, and even the tiniest amount of metal removed will make a difference. Very fine English made-to-order shotguns almost always show reamer marks at the choke, and custom-made American guns also, because the makers start their checking with considerably more choke than called for, reaming and shooting test patterns until the best pattern with the specified size of shot is found. They claim that to polish out the reamer marks would change the pattern.

The only means of achieving greater choke on a good gun is to equip it with a choke device, such as the PolyChoke, or in the case of a double, a new set of barrels!

Some cheap single barrel shotguns have the choke swaged into the muzzle end of the barrel. In other words, the barrel is made cylinder and the front end forced into a die to squeeze it down to full or modified choke. You can do the same thing, if you can locate a powerful press large enough to do the job. The barrel should be oiled and the tapered die forced over the outside of the muzzle. A simpler way, probably, is to rebuild an ordinary one hand pipecutter, removing the cutting wheel and replacing it with a hardened steel roller, as wide as possible. By applying it to the muzzle and increasing pressure as it is revolved around the barrel, the latter can be decreased in diameter sufficiently to gain any desired degree of choke. This same gadget is useful in dent-removing, for a finish tool to iron the outside of barrel perfectly smooth, after the dent is removed from the inside, and while the plug is in the barrel.

Shotgunners are always having pattern trouble, if they are of the serious type who do pattern their guns, one reason being that most duck and goose hunters want full choke guns, for greater range, but use the larger shot sizes. The factories use small shot in determining pattern and choke figures, from 7 to 8½, and a great many shotguns which give full choke patterns with such small shot will give badly blown patterns with 4s or 5s, while many a modified choke barrel will give fine full choke patterns with these larger shot sizes. So you may get some choke-opening-up to do yet, as the boys get wise.

Leading. Practically all standard barrels will lead to some extent when high velocity shells are used, and while it is no great undertaking to remove lead, the job gets tiresome. The gunsmith can polish a barrel and remove much of its tendency to metal foul. The lead lap is not practical since the shotgun barrel usually has several different diameters, shoulders and bevels in its length, so a wooden or metal mandrel should be used, with crocus cloth wrapped around it, should the barrel show toolmarks, or, if apparently smooth, with a plain cotton cloth saturated with oil and the finest lapping compound you have on hand. The lap rod is inserted from the breech and marked so that the lap will not reach into the muzzle end of the choke boring. It is pulled and pushed straight back and forth and should never be turned in the barrel. If the gun leads badly in the choke, that too should be lapped. Whatever little change you make in the choke cannot be as great as that caused by lead building up in it, to deform shot and blow patterns. Besides cloth, any sensible type of lap tip is of course usable, the best probably being pieces of sole leather placed on a bolt or mandrel and turned to a round cylinder slightly greater than bore diameter on the lathe, or shaped on the sander.

The use of copperized shot greatly reduces leading.

Sights

The front sight on a shotgun is definitely used as an aiming point by many shooters, while just as many really do not use it in the sense of a sight at all, but only as a means of knowing the muzzle distance and aiding them in control of the gun in fast swinging, as on crossing shots in dove hunting. These are the boys who claim they only need a bit of white paint or a strip of adhesive tape around the muzzle. They are right, for they have developed to a high degree the art of pointing a shotgun. But for the man who looks at his front sight before and when shooting, different sights may have beneficial values. As previously mentioned, my favorite among the patent shotgun sights is the Marble Bi-Color, for its strength. It will withstand treatment which will destroy a plain ivory or bone bead, and be as visible under nearly all conditions. In sunlight, the "gold" top reflects light and is highly evident against any background. You must remember that it is higher than most factory bead sights, therefore there is a chance that the shooter will undershoot when it is installed. This seldom happens, but the tendency is there.

All of the commercially available shotgun sights have their places, and if you mount many choke devices, you will soon accumulate a variety, in the ends of barrels you have cut off. Many of these will be in perfect condition and can be removed without marring by use of a pin vise to grip and unscrew them. If it is of the unthreaded, pressed-in type, you can of course drill a hole in the opposite side of the barrel, across from the sight, and punch it out with a long thin drift. Remington front sights on ribbed barrels are held in with a little cross pin.

Quite often the customer loses the pressed-in sight out of his barrel, and wants it replaced. The easiest way is to sell the guy the idea he needs a Marble Bi-Color, then ream out the hole and tap it for that sight. If he will not hold still for that and wants a duplicate of his old sight you turn one up on the lathe to his description, using brass or aluminum. The latter metal seems to be quite popular these days and is easily worked. There is no objection nor very much more labor involved in making the bead of soft steel. You cannot just turn out a bead with a shank to fit the hole in the barrel and push it in—if the original did not stay put, why should yours? It is necessary to rivet the shank in the barrel wall, which is not as hard as it sounds. Use a round needle file to enlarge the bottom of the hole, or inside edge, working through the top, of course, and it does not matter much if you also bevel the top edge slightly in the process. The shank of the bead must be turned to a close push fit through the hole and be around $\frac{1}{32}''$ longer than the barrel thickness, so that its tip will protrude inside the barrel slightly. Make a tiny shallow, cone shaped countersink in the end of the shank, and when this is done and the bead cut off slightly above its top, you are ready to install it. Some sort of anvil is necessary, to fit inside the muzzle, which can be the end of a $\frac{1}{2}''$ diameter section of drill rod rounded, polished, and hardened, or, if you want to be fancy, make up a rod with a round ball on the end. This is clamped solidly in the vise, the muzzle of the gun is placed over it so that the bottom of the bead shank contacts the rounded portion, and the bead is pounded on the top with a steel hammer until the bottom spreads into the slight countersink you made in the barrel. With the bead tight in the hole, you place a bit of adhesive tape with a tiny hole over the sight and on the barrel, to protect its finish, and file the top of the bead to the desired height and shape. The bottom end must be polished flush with the inner surface of the barrel, and the very best method I have found is use of the hand grinder with one of the little abrasive bands mounted on the rubber mandrels furnished for these tools.

Beads can of course be soldered to barrels easily, but the small area of contact makes for a weak joint. Should the customer want an individual sight, such as a small ramp, or short section of rib, soft soldering is thoroughly practical.

Dent Removal

It is no great job to remove a dent from a shotgun barrel, but a good workman should be able to also remove all evidence of his work. The dent must be forced out from the inside by means of drive or expanding plugs. You might as well go ahead and either make up or buy an expanding type for at least 12 and 20 gauge, because while solid drive plugs are easy to make, one which is made to close tolerance to fit one particular barrel probably will not fit any others you get in for a year or two. A large plug can be turned down to fit a smaller diameter barrel, but then it will not be much good on the next job, which invariably calls for a larger plug. An undersize plug can be made to work fairly well by tinning one side and building up enough lead there to make a tight fit in the barrel. This is a makeshift system, for emergency use, and is not recommended.

Very deep dents will require a long tapered solid plug for partial raising, so that the expanding plug can be inserted. For outside pounding on the dented area in cooperation with the plug, I have found the rawhide mallet better than either lead or composition-face hammers.

Expanding dent removing plug assemblies are now commercially available, one being that made by Alex J. Thill. However, any plug depending upon a turn screw for expansion force has some tendency to turn in the barrel, so should you decide to invent your own, put a holding rod on the far end which can be clamped in a vise or otherwise held to retain the plug in the desired position. The wedge drive plug described by Clyde Baker is one of the simplest and most practical you can make. A shaper or milling machine is necessary to cut the tongue-

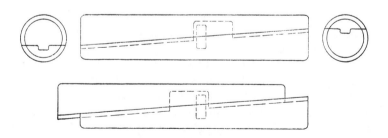

DENT REMOVING PLUG

The wedge action shotgun dent remover, as per Clyde Baker, and as covered in the text. Make for 12 gauge at least.

and-groove sliding faces, unless you have a lot of time to spend filing. The illustration shows construction very well. Two pieces of good steel are machined with angle faces, one with tongue, or rib, the other with matching groove, and fitted together, off center longitudinally—meaning the ends overlap—sweated together and turned to the desired diameter for the gauge involved, less .010". The stop pin should be installed to prevent spreading to greater than average bore diameter, plus .010", and should be very strong. This type of plug is used with two opposing rods, one being a drive rod, the other serving as an anvil.

Shotgun barrels are soft, and while your plugs should be of good hardened tool steel if possible, almost any type of steel which will take a case-hardening will do. All surfaces of all types of plugs should be polished and buffed as smooth as possible. The barrel is always cleaned thoroughly with steel wool, to remove any leading, and is oiled lightly with thin oil, before the plugs are introduced.

Dented or Bent Muzzles

Almost always found on double barrel shotguns, because of the thin barrel walls of such guns, muzzles may be bent out of round or deeply dented inward from the gun falling or being struck against some hard surface. As a rule these can be fixed fast and painlessly. Simply grab the nearest piece of round stock—steel, brass or copper—small enough to enter the barrel without a great deal of clearance, turn it smooth or file the end to eliminate any sharp edges, clamp it horizontally in the vise with about an inch protruding, slip the end of the barrel over it, dent up, and iron it out with the rawhide mallet.

Resoldering Ribs

This can be very intriguing. A complete job will mean refinishing the entire barrel or set of barrels, if not the whole shotgun while a partial job, such as tying down a rib which has come unhitched for a short distance, is just work.

For a complete job, such as fitting a ventilated rib to a single barrel gun or a solid rib to a double, you will need to gather some equipment and solid metal rods, preferably copper, of a diameter just small enough to slip through the barrels, should be inserted in order to insure a good sweat joint. They are necessary to hold the barrel or barrels at proper heat and should be heated to 500° F. before insertion. The blueing tank gas burners are excellent for the heating job. Tin the top of the barrel, or the V of double barrels, and the underside of the rib and place it in position, supporting it with little brass wedges if necessary (for doubles) put a small round rod—$\frac{5}{16}''$ is okay—the length of the rib, on top of it, and tie the rod and the rib down with wire, using one strand and wrapping it spirally down the barrel. If necessary, small wedges can be used to tighten the wire and force the rib close to the barrel. Slide the hot barrel rods in place and put the whole works on the fire, rib up, and when things get fairly warm—say around 400° F.—turn on the welding torch and heat up the rod on top of the rib, heating the rib at the same time. When the solder sticks, you are finished with that part of the job, and must clean everything off, scraping any visible solder from the edges of the rib and the barrels at the joint. On most doubles it will be necessary to use two small rods, one on the bottom as well as the one on the top of the rib. Barrels must be polished and blued after complete fitting of the rib.

Partial rib attachments are usually very easy, involving ribs which have torn loose at the muzzle, or ventilated types which have been dented enough to pull one of the holding studs away from the barrel. The hardest part of the job is cleaning the contact surfaces so they will again join. In most cases it is not necessary to add any solder, as enough remains from the original job to form a satisfactory joint. Since care must be taken not to pull or bend the rib away from the barrel, thin scrapers must be used to clean the parted pieces, and because you do not want to mar the blue, acid flux can be used only with great care. Use a pair of the smallest tweezers you can get, the eyebrow variety, with a tiny bit of cloth or cotton dipped in the acid to touch the exposed sweat joint faces. With the solder remaining on the rib and the barrel clean, use a short section of small rod on top of the rib and C clamps placed to hold rod and rib to the barrel. The welding torch is used to apply heat. When just an inch or so of rib is loose, a heated soldering copper will do.

Raising or lowering a rib, to change the pattern by changing the sighting plane, is possible on double guns with the original rib in many cases. The full job of raising a rib on a double barrel, or any single barrel, will entail making an entire new rib of the proper dimensions, for if the original is lifted any appreciable degree, there will be a gap between the rib and the barrel or barrels at the muzzle end. It is raised only at the muzzle end, of course, for any gun. Lowering a rib can be done on any gun with sweated on means of attachment. It is removed from the barrel or barrels, metal cut from the bottom or the sides and resoldered in place.

Cross firing. In double barrel guns there is occasionally the complaint of cross shooting, meaning that the right barrel patterns too

SHOTGUN HEADSPACE GAGES

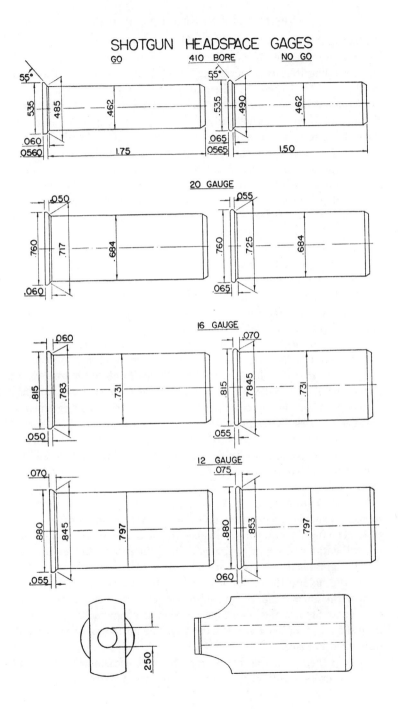

GO   410 BORE   NO GO

20 GAUGE

16 GAUGE

12 GAUGE

far to the left and vice versa. This is corrected by partial or complete separation of the barrels, wedges placed between them at the muzzle and slightly behind, and resoldering. A new top rib may have to be made, but the bottom filler piece usually will do all right even though it will be forced inward somewhat at the muzzle. If the original rib is retained, the amount of solder required to hold it in the raised position will be visible, and can only be painted black. A full corrective job is out of the scope of the small gunshop and should not be undertaken on a high grade gun. Barrels separated completely and then realigned probably will not breech up properly, so if the gun cross fires at close range—under 30 yards—send it back to the factory.

Cross firing at longer ranges can be corrected by partial separation and rejoining. Wrap a wet cloth around the barrel 10″ to 12″ from the muzzle on the back, and with the welding torch at low pressure, heat the upper and lower ribs from the cloth to the muzzle. Have a small wedge made which you can tap in between the barrels at the muzzle when the solder is soft. It is possible, through the use of wire wrappings and supporting rods on the ribs, to do the job completely in one pass—softening the solder, spreading the barrels at the muzzle, and getting the ribs to sweat together tightly in the new position when cooling. Getting the barrels spread the right distance is something else. Bore sighting does not mean too much, because the barrels are actually slightly bent apart, and sighting accurately down a curve is something I have not yet worked out. A wedge or shim sufficient to spread the barrels approximately .03″ will correct a gun shooting about 15″ off at 40 yards, figuring 28″ barrels—however, only trial can tell on any individual gun.

SHOTGUN HEADSPACE GAGES

These may come in handy on repeating shotguns . . . The flange angle (on the front of the rim) is slightly exaggerated to show that it exists, and it is necessary to make the gages this way, for the front end of the countersink in a shotgun chamber can be anywhere between 55° and 90°. If the gages are made with a 90° angle at the front of the rim, they may not seat in all chambers and therefore give an insufficient headspace check.

The rim angles and proportions are approximately the same for all gages. It is necessary to cut the sides of the gage heads down, as shown in the bottom drawing, in order not to be affected by extractors or ejectors. A hole should be drilled in the head so that in case a firing pin is snapped when the gage is in place, the pin will not be damaged. The hole can be filled with rubber to relieve the shock of the pin fall.

Shotgun Statistics

Shotgun bore diameters vary somewhat between different makers and grades of guns, but the general average is of the sizes listed below. The .410 bore is just as it is written—.41″—and is not a "gauge" as are the larger types.

Gauge	Bore Diameter, inches.
10	.775
12	.729
16	.662
20	.615
28	.550
.410 Bore	.410

Shot sizes are fairly well standardized in the U. S. A. now, only chilled shot in the American Standard sizes being loaded. However, loading companies experiment constantly to find the most effective patterns with various component combinations, so that loads of specific ammunition lots may have shot slightly larger or smaller than standard measurements. These are referred to as "large sixes" or "small fives," whatever the size they are closest to. Foreign shot sizes are not the same as American; for instance, take the #7 shot—the American #7 is 320 per ounce; British, 350 per ounce; French, 262 per ounce, and German, 230. The American standards are as follows:

Shot No.	Diameter	Number to Ounce
12	.05″	2385
11	.06	1380
10	.07	843
9	.08	616
8	.09	435
7½	.09½	365
7	.10	320
6	.11	237
5	.12	177
4	.13	143
3	.14	109
2	.15	93
1	.16	73
Air Rifle	.17½	55
BB	.18	50

Buckshot Sizes

We used to have two buckshot set ups, the "Eastern" and "Western," each with its own size standards. I believe that the "Eastern" won out and that it is used by all ammunition firms today. The sizes are as follows:

No.	Diameter	Number to Pound
4	.24″	340
3	.25	300
2	.27	235
1	.30	175
o	.32	142
oo	.33	130
ooo	.36	103

No. ooo Buck was formerly .34″ in diameter and ran from 115 to 122 per pound.

Round Ball Sizes

Not many people shoot round balls in their shotguns, but the muzzle loader fanciers use these to quite an extent, in rifles and revolvers. Other sizes than those listed are made up for their specific use, notably for .44 caliber cap and ball revolvers.

Size	Diameter	Number to Pound
.410	.380	84–85
.28	.515	45
.20	.545 to .570	25–28
.16	.605 to .610	20–21
.12	.650 to .660	16–17
.10	.707	13½

COMPARISON OF METRIC AND BRITISH UNITS

WEIGHT

1 gram = 15.432 grains	1 grain = .0648 gram
1 gram = .035274 oz. (av.)	1 oz. (av.) = 28.35 grams
1 kilo = 2.2046 lb. (av.)	1 lb. (av.) = .45359 kilo
1 kilo = .019684 cwt.	1 cwt. = 50.802 kilos
1 tonne = .98421 ton	1 ton = 1.016 tonnes

LENGTH

1 mm. = .039371 in.	1 in. = 25.4 mm.
1 metre = 3.2808 ft.	1 ft. = .3048 metre
1 metre = 1.0936 yds.	1 yd. = .9144 metre

AREA

1 sq. cm. = .155 sq. in.	1 sq. in. = 6.4516 sq. cm.
1 sq. m. = 10.764 sq. ft.	1 sq. ft. = .092903 sq. m.

VOLUME

1 c.c. = .061 cu. in.	1 cu. in. = 16.387 c.c.
1 cu. m. = 35.3148 cu. ft.	1 cu. ft. = .028317 cu. m.
1 litre = 1.7598 pints	1 pint = .568 litre

PRESSURE

1 atmos. = 14.7 lb./sq. in.	1 atmos. = 1.03 kg./sq. cm.
1 atmos. = .00656 ton/sq. in.	1 lb./sq. in. = .068 atmos.
1 kg./sq. cm. = .968 atmos.	1 lb./sq. in. = .070309 kg./sq. cm.
1 kg./sq. cm. = 14.223 lb./sq. in.	1 ton/sq. in. = 152 atmos.
1 kg./sq. cm. = .0063493 ton/sq. in.	1 ton/sq. in. = 157.49 kg./sq. cm.

ENERGY

1 m.-kg. = 7.2331 foot-lb.	1 foot-lb. = .13825 m.-kg.
1 m.-tonne = 3.2291 foot-tons	1 foot-ton = .30969 m.-tonne

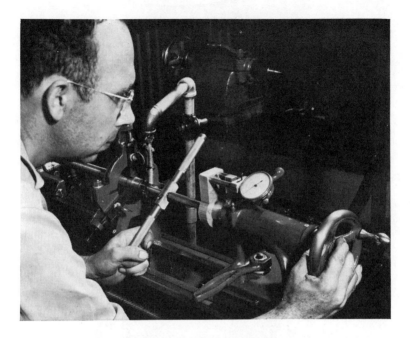

REAMING-OUT A CHAMBER

Pfeifer's precision chambering set-up. The barrel is being turned in the lathe, with steady-rest supporting and holding barrel true on the cylinder. The reamer is held from turning by the tap-wrench and feeding force supplied by the tailstock. Note the dial indicator attached to tailstock feed which allows careful regulation of reamer depth.

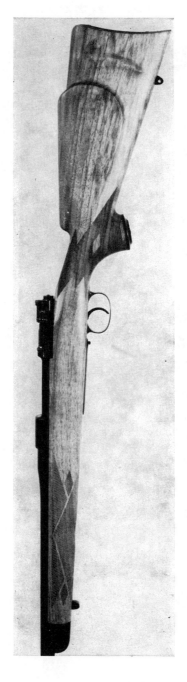

An FN Mauser stocked by Shelhamer. (Tom says that this cheekpiece is the customer's specifications, not his!) Note the open diamond left in the grip checkering pattern, with matching diamonds in reverse put into the forearm pattern. This is a nice grained piece of wood, with the grain running just right through the grip.

BRITISH SHOTGUN SPECIFICATIONS

Description	Minimum Diameter of Card Wadding	Usual Lengths of Case
Bore	Inch	Inches
4	.950	4
8	.847	$3\frac{1}{4}$, $3\frac{1}{2}$, $3\frac{3}{4}$, 4, $4\frac{1}{4}$
10	.786	$2\frac{5}{8}$, $2\frac{7}{8}$, 3, $3\frac{1}{4}$
12	.740	$2\frac{1}{2}$, $2\frac{3}{4}$, 3, $3\frac{1}{4}$
14	.704	$2\frac{1}{2}$
16	.673	$2\frac{1}{2}$, $2\frac{3}{4}$, 3
20	.625	$2\frac{1}{2}$, $2\frac{3}{4}$, 3
24	.588	$2\frac{1}{2}$
28	.558	$2\frac{1}{2}$
32	.510	$2\frac{1}{2}$
.410	.410	2, $2\frac{1}{2}$, 3
.360	.360	$1\frac{3}{4}$

NOTE. The $2\frac{1}{2}''$ case is actually $2\frac{9}{16}''$ long in 12, 16 and 20 bore sizes. In other calibers the nominal length is also the real.
BORE DENOMINATIONS. Shotgun calibers are designated by the number of spherical lead balls to the pound of a diameter to fit the bore. Thus the diameter of an 8 bore is the same as that of a 2 oz. ball of lead, of a 12 bore as that of a $1\frac{1}{3}$ oz. ball of lead.

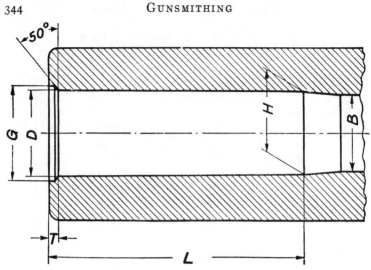

GERMAN SHOTGUN CHAMBER DIMENSIONS

Gauge	L Length		T Depth of rim counter-bore		H Diameter of chamber at base		D Diameter of chamber at mouth		G Diameter of rim counter-bore		B Bore diameter	
	min.	max.	min.	max.	min.	max.	min.	max.	min.	max.	min.	max.
4	82.60	82.70	3.25	3.30	26.30	26.40	27.35	27.45	30.55	30.65	23.40	23.80
8	82.60	82.70	2.90	2.95	23.20	23.30	23.65	23.75	26.35	26.45	20.80	21.20
10	65.10	65.30	1.90	1.95	21.50	21.60	21.85	21.95	23.75	23.85	19.30	19.70
12	65.10	65.30	1.90	1.95	20.30	20.40	20.65	20.75	22.55	22.65	18.20	18.60
14	65.10	65.30	1.75	1.80	19.35	19.45	19.70	19.80	21.55	21.65	17.20	17.60
16	65.10	65.30	1.60	1.65	18.60	18.70	18.90	19.00	20.75	20.85	16.80	17.20
20	65.10	65.30	1.55	1.60	17.40	17.50	17.75	17.85	19.50	19.60	15.70	16.10
24	63.60	63.80	1.55	1.60	16.50	16.60	16.80	16.90	18.55	18.65	14.70	15.10
28	63.60	63.80	1.55	1.60	15.60	15.70	15.90	16.00	17.50	17.60	13.80	14.20
32	63.60	63.80	1.55	1.60	14.30	14.40	14.60	14.70	16.20	16.30	12.70	13.10
36 410	50.90	51.10	1.55	1.60	11.80	11.90	12.05	12.15	13.70	13.80	10.20	10.60

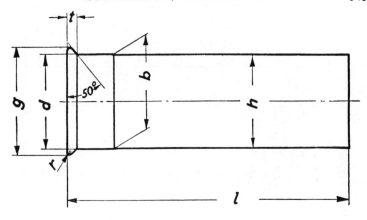

DIMENSIONS OF GERMAN PAPER TUBE SHOTGUN SHELLS

Gauge	*l* Overall Length		*h* Body diameter of shell		*b* Diameter of shell base		*d* Diameter of base at rim		*g* Rim diameter		*t* Rim thickness		*r* Radius of rim
	max.	min.	max.	min.	max.	min.	max.	min.	max.	min.	max.	min.	
4	82.50	82.00	26.25	26.00	26.60	26.45	27.30	27.15	30.45	30.20	3.20	3.05	0.80
8	82.50	82.00	23.15	22.90	23.35	23.20	23.60	23.45	26.25	26.00	2.85	2.70	0.50
10	65.00	64.50	21.45	21.20	21.60	21.45	21.80	21.65	23.65	23.45	1.85	1.75	0.50
12	65.00	64.50	20.20	19.95	20.35	20.25	20.60	20.50	22.45	22.25	1.85	1.75	0.50
14	65.00	64.50	19.30	19.05	19.45	19.35	19.65	19.55	21.45	21.25	1.70	1.60	0.50
16	65.00	64.50	18.55	18.30	18.70	18.60	18.85	18.75	20.65	20.45	1.55	1.45	0.50
20	65.00	64.50	17.35	17.10	17.50	17.40	17.70	17.60	19.40	19.25	1.50	1.40	0.50
24	63.50	63.00	16.45	16.20	16.55	16.45	16.75	16.65	18.45	18.30	1.50	1.40	0.50
28	63.50	63.00	15.55	15.30	15.65	15.55	15.85	15.75	17.40	17.25	1.50	1.40	0.50
32	63.50	63.00	14.25	14.00	14.35	14.25	14.55	14.45	16.10	15.95	1.50	1.40	0.40
36													
410	50.80	50.30	11.75	11.55	11.85	11.75	12.00	11.90	13.60	13.45	1.50	1.40	0.35

COMPARISON OF AMERICAN AND FOREIGN SHOT SIZES

English	American – Eastern Buck-shot	American – Western Buck-shot	Belgian	Canadian	Dutch	French	German	Italian	Italian	Spanish – Linares English type	Spanish – Barcelona Figueroa type	Spanish – Sevilla Maka type	Swedish	Turkish	Turkish
L G	000	2	—	—	—	—	II	—	—	—	—	—	—	—	—
MG (mould)	00	3	—	—	—	C.1	—	—	—	—	—	—	—	—	—
S G	0	4	—	—	—	—	III	—	—	—	—	—	—	—	—
Special S G	1	5 or 6	—	S G	—	C.2	IV	—	—	—	—	—	—	—	—
S S G	2	7	—	—	—	C.3	V	—	—	—	—	—	—	18/A	—
S S S G	3 or 4	8 or 9	—	—	—	C.4	—	—	—	—	—	—	—	17/A	—
S S S S G	FF		—	AAAA or 12 Seal	—	C.4 bis	VI	—	—	—	—	—	—	16/A	—
S S S S S G or A A A A	TT		—	AA	—	—	000000	—	7/0	7/0	—	—	11	15/A	—
A A A	T		—	A	—	5/0	00000	—	6/0	6/0	—	—	4/0	14/A or 13/A	4/0

COMPARISON OF AMERICAN AND FOREIGN SHOT SIZES (Continued)

English	American	Belgian	Canadian	Dutch	French	German	Italian	Italian	Spanish: Linares English type	Spanish: Barcelona Figueroa type	Spanish: Sevilla Mata type	Swedish	Turkish	Turkish
AA	BBB	—	BBB	—	4/0	0000	5/0	—	—	—	—	10	3/0	12/A
A or BBBB	BB	5/0	BB	—	2/0	00	3/0	—	4/0	—	—	9	0	11/A
BBB	B	4/0	B	00	0	0	2/0 or 1/0	—	3/0	—	—	8	1	10/A
BB	1	3/0	1	0	1	1	1	—	—	1	—	7	2	9/A
B	2	2/0	2	1	—	1	1	00	2/0	—	—	—	—	8/A
1	3	0	3	3	2	2	2	0 or 1	1	4	—	6	3	7/A
2	—	2	—	4 or 5	3	3	3	2	—	5	4	5	4	6/A
3	4	3	4	G.6	4	4	—	3	2	—	5	4	5	5/A
4	5	4	5	—	5	5	4	4	4	6	6	3	6	4/A
4½	—	—	—	—	—	—	—	—	—	—	—	—	—	—
5	6	5	6	K.6	—	6	5	5	—	7	7	2	7	3/A
5½ (m.g.)	—	—	—	—	—	—	6	—	—	—	—	—	—	—
6	—	6	7	—	6	7	—	6	5	8	—	1	8	2/A
6½	7	6½	7½	—	—	—	—	—	6	—	—	—	—	—
7	7½	7	8	7	7	8	7	7	7	—	9	0	9	1/A
8	8	8	9	8	8	9	8	8	8	—	10	—	10	1/0
9	9	9	10	9	9	10	9	9	9	11	11	00	11	2/0
10	10	10	—	10	10	—	—	—	10	—	—	000	—	—
11	11	11	—	11	11	11	—	11	—	—	12	—	12	3/0
12	12	12	—	12	12	12	—	14	—	—	—	—	13	—
Dust	—	—	—	—	—	—	—	—	—	—	—	—	—	—

CHAPTER 18

Twenty-two Rim Fire Arms

THIS will have to include rifles, revolvers and pistols, and we will go down the line in that order, although naturally some ailments are common to all.

One .22 barrel defect, seldom seen, is a peened muzzle. Meaning a barrel with rifling peened or burred at the crown. One or two lands with ends peened inward at the muzzle will cause the barrel to shoot far out of line. When a barrel appears straight, yet still will not line up with the sights in shooting until the line of sight is obviously at an angle to the bore, check the muzzle with a magnifying glass and see if a land or two has not been damaged. To clear the trouble up, chuck the barrel in the lathe and cut the crown back $\frac{1}{16}''$.

Disregarding the very old barrels, which are pitted and worn to the point where no repair work will amount to much, most barrel complaints center in the chambers, as the soft steel commonly used for .22 rim-fire barrels is easily scratched, torn or burred. Not many modern .22s are subject to damage by snapping, or dry-firing, but older rifles will come in with the rim cut and the chamber proper battered from snapping. Metal is pushed over into the chamber recess which forms a burr to obstruct passage of either cartridge or fired case. You do not use a chambering reamer to clear it, for the displaced metal may be work-hardened sufficiently to resist the reamer enough to cause it to cut the opposite chamber wall, thus enlarging the chamber. In fact, a .22 chambering reamer does more harm than good in the general gun shop and its uses are extremely limited.

The very best possible method of correcting such burred chambers is use of a special ironing punch with the tip shaped to fit the chamber closely, and the shoulder to exactly fit the rim-cut, should the barrel be of the type with countersunk rim. A small flat is filed or ground on the punch. This principle of course means that the metal will be pushed back into its original rounded edge location, with no loss of chamber

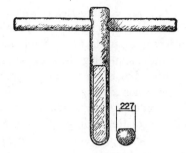

THE .22 CALIBER TOOL

For ironing out chambers damaged by careless snapping of long firing pin guns extruding metal into the chamber. You slide it into the chamber and then turn it, the idea being to push the misplaced metal back where it belongs.

surface. The punch is not driven forcibly into the chamber but is slid into it—the flat permitting it to pass the burred or peened-in area— then turned back and forth to force the metal into position. Because of the variations in .22 chamber diameters, the special punch or tool will probably have to be made to fit several different rifles. After accumulating three or four thusly, you will probaly be able to take care of most any such job coming in. The tool of course should be hardened, highly polished.

The preceding system is the hard way—the easy way is to just carefully file the burr away so that the chamber is clear. A slow-speed grinder with one of the small, fine mounted stones can be used also and in practically all cases such a rough job will be entirely satisfactory.

Longitudinal scratches in the chamber are seldom injurious to feeding and extraction, and as a matter of fact, are almost unpreventable, due to carelessly-handled ammunition carrying sand or grit into the chamber. I can suggest no remedy for this condition, for to polish or lap the scratches out would be to enlarge the chamber diameter, which is to be avoided at all costs.

Frequently a shooter will, due to defective cartridge or breeching, have stuck or ruptured cases in the chamber, which he removed with whatever was handy—rattail file or knife point or such tool—and gouged or tore the chamber walls sufficiently to really cause faulty extraction. The only cure is a new chamber, achieved by either cutting off the barrel ahead of the chamber, rethreading or turning it to fit the action, and rechambering; or drilling out the chamber to its full depth, threading in a steel plug, and rechambering this plug; or installation of a new barrel. The latter is to be considered on some of the low-cost rifles for which replacement barrels are available quite cheaply from the factory. Fitting, and chambering the plug, in that method, calls for very careful centering, but is routine lathe work otherwise.

On the obsolete lever action .22 single shots, the extractor lips sometimes wear, loosen, or erode, causing trouble at their cuts in the barrel face. Once in a while one of them will get blocked or bent, so that it punishes the chamber. Examination of the parts and fired cases usually makes the repair necessary obvious.

Some modern production-line repeating .22 rifles are carelessly machined in the extractor cuts in the barrel breech. Oversize extractor recesses allow cartridges when fired to expand at the unsupported areas, occasionally to rupture there. Theoretically, the only proper method of correction is to set the barrel back, and reface and rechamber to close tolerance. Actually, it is possible to correct the difficulty in practically all cases by installation of a hand-made extractor of such proportions to fill the barrel recess properly, and supporting it with a strong extractor spring.

Extraction Troubles. Dirt or foreign matter causes as much or more trouble with .22 rifles as does broken or jammed extractors or worn ejectors. Because of its lubricated ammunition, the .22 is messy—grease and powder fouling forming a sludge which works over all the breech parts and which combines with dirt and grit blowing through the air to make a hard mass in any recess it can reach. The extractor cuts in the rear of the barrel form natural pockets for it, and it can build up to the point of causing extraction failure through holding the extractor lip out of full engagement with the cartridge rim. It will also build up in the extractor slot in the bolt or the breechblock, to the same effect, and possibly back of the extractor to interfere with the action of the extractor spring.

Broken and worn extractors are obvious, but occasionally a worn extractor will still give worthwhile service by having a new spring installed, and the extractor itself touched up with a file to engage a trifle more. Jammed coil springs behind extractors in bolt action rifles are common. Some are apparently bent out of shape in the original installation, so that only a small portion of the spring really functions. Watch for those which fit their holes tightly—a coil spring expands slightly in diameter when compressed, and tolerance must be made accordingly.

Ejection Troubles. Most ejection failure has an easily-recognized cause, such as the ejector being worn, broken, or blocked from correct functioning. There are a few types of rifle in which ejection is manually-controlled, by movement of the slide, lever, or bolt, and positive ejection effected only by rather smart action by the shooter. An overly careful and slow or easy movement of the mechanism may not cause the ejector to function properly. In many of the more modern repeaters, the ejector works in close relationship with the extractor, and either defection in functioning or incorrect lip dimension of the latter can affect ejection.

On a number of modern low-priced .22 bolt actions, both extractors and ejectors are retained in the bolt by pins which are not of the best material. Should either of the parts be giving trouble, for no apparent reason, it may be found that the axis pin is bent or burred.

Firing Pins. Practically every style of tip imaginable has been tried on the .22 rim-fire, with the illustrated two types being more-or-less standardized on as best. The tip must be large enough to insure contact with a sufficiently large enough area of the priming compound to ignite it, small enough not to dissipate mainspring force over too large a portion of the cartridge head, and positioned to strike neither too far out on the rim, nor too far inside the edge, and not be sufficiently sharp or rough to cut into the case metal at all. It must protrude far enough to wallop the rim and not far enough to touch the chamber or rear of barrel—outside of that, it is not important!

The large drawing shows correct and incorrect breeching and firing pin detail, which will be of value in comparison with rifles having difficulties at this point.

Excepting for breakage of pins, there is little trouble with firing pins themselves. Oversize firing pin holes in the face of the bolt or the block are responsible for much .22 ignition trouble. This can usually be corrected only by making a new firing pin which is oversize at some point of its length so that is guided in its slot or hole, and perhaps with the tip shaped out of line in order to contact the cartridge rim at the proper location for ignition. Bent retaining pins, jammed retraction springs, and the like, can of course affect firing pin action also. On old guns with excessive protrusion of firing pin, the pin tip is sometimes worn or burred from dry-firing, because the tip contacts the rear of the barrel if no cartridge is chambered. Pins with old-style rounded or hemispherical tips often can be replaced with modern flat-tip, rounded-edge types having less protrusion and achieve equal or better ignition.

Springs. All types of springs are found in the various .22 rifles—coil, flat, helical, with modifications of each. A great many can be replaced from coil spring assortments sold by mill supply houses; helical

.22 TROUBLES

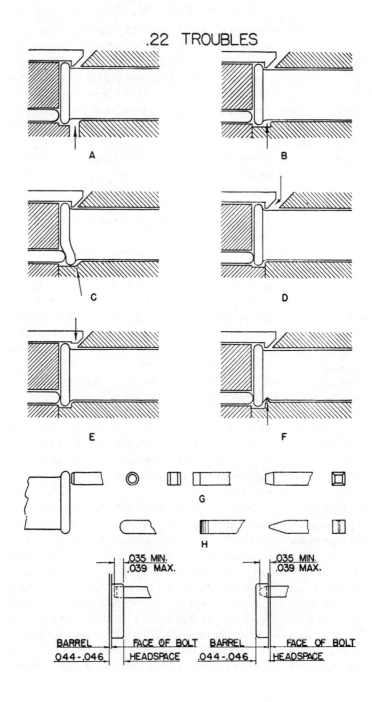

BARREL   FACE OF BOLT   BARREL   FACE OF BOLT
.044-.046   HEADSPACE   .044-.046   HEADSPACE

and grasshopper springs can be made from spring wire; and flat springs made from clock spring or flat spring stock. The long coil springs used in tubular magazines are subject to set, or loss of expansion through being kept in a compressed state, but this can often be corrected for a time by just removing the spring and stretching it by hand. Some of the .22 autoloaders with tubular magazines in the butt stock will not feed properly unless the spring is at its best. Since any .22 tubular magazine spring will fit practically all tubular magazines, keep a couple on hand. The longest ones I believe are made for the Marlin Model 39. You can always shorten the spring for a shorter magazine, being sure to use as long a spring as the full loading capacity of magazine permits.

The cartridge guide spring of the Marlin Model 81 is always getting jammed up or broken, so as to cause improper feeding. This is a flat spring, lying between the receiver and the barrel shank, with its protruding end shaped in a shallow V which acts as a guide for the bullet as the cartridge feeds out of the magazine and forward to the chamber.

.22 TROUBLES

The little .22 rifle is liable to numerous ignition ailments, a few of which are illustrated.

A. The bolt is not up to the barrel, whether held by foreign matter from moving forward, or just plain excess headspace. The arrow indicates the space which should not be there. The cartridge may not fire at all, and if it does, may rupture under the pin.

B. Here she is breeched up okay, but the rim countersink is cut too deep and will not support the rim when the pin falls.

C. It fell, and the rim pushed forward—maybe it ignited all right and maybe it did not.

D. Here we have the extractor cut too deep, leaving the cartridge case unsupported at the open space, which of course means the probability of its rupturing when fired.

E. Nothing wrong except that the lip is broken off the extractor.

F. Here nothing is wrong except that the firing pin has too great protrusion and snapping empty has burred the countersink, raising a ridge of metal as indicated by the arrow. This makes for difficult extraction as well as ruptured cases.

G. Satisfactory .22 firing pin tips; left—the flat, rounded edge type, showing the correct location with regard to the rim; center—the wedge type; and right—the square end type. All of these are satisfactory.

H. Left—the rounded, hemispherical tip, not satisfactory for rim-fire cartridges; center—the rounded wedge type, better, but not as good as those shown in "G"; and right—the wedge point, too sharp for good use.

At the bottom we have drawings showing headspace and maximum pin protrusion of both the round edged flat tip and the square end tapered type.

The barrel must be removed from the receiver in order to replace this spring, which is not too difficult as the shank is not threaded, but straight, and held in the receiver by a transverse pin. Just drive the pin out, then, with the receiver clamped tightly, use a ten-inch section of ½" drill rod with a smooth, flat front end, placed through the receiver and used as a punch against the face of the barrel to drive it from the receiver; they are not set at all tight and can be removed by hand sometimes. Keep a stock of the springs on hand. These springs are not hard to make, but no such spring is as cheap to make as it is to buy from the factory.

Trigger springs on the low-priced bolt action rifles are sometimes placed out of commission by interference from the wooden stock. Slots in the wood are undersize, or off center, or splinters protrude from the cuts to touch triggers or springs. No general comment can be made on triggers and trigger mechanisms themselves because of the many different systems used. It is difficult to lighten pulls, or put good trigger-pulls on most of the guns, because of the stiff springs necessary to provide positive cocking. Any of the pulls can be improved over the factory standard, by cleaning up contact faces and polishing all points of friction. On some of the Savage and Stevens arms, trigger springs can be weakened somewhat without making the rifles dangerous or undependable in cocking.

Takedown Joints. (Slide Action, Lever Action and Autoloading Rifles.) On .22 repeaters of the action takedown type, such as the pump guns, Marlin 39 and Remington 24 and 241, and Winchester '03 and 63, continual use of the takedown feature often causes the joints to loosen. On the Browning-patent Remington autoloaders, this can be controlled by adjustment of the barrel takeup lock, but on the others the meeting and inter-fitting parts of the joint must be worked on. This is almost always a peening job, to move metal so that sliding parts may be a closer fit in their recesses or grooves. The takedown screw itself is seldom of help in making a joint rigid. Sometimes grooves or lug recesses can be closed slightly by vise pressure, but as a rule the opposing male parts must be stretched, widened, or thickened to gain the desired fit.

Takedown Rifles with One-Piece Stocks. There is no particular trouble with the takedown screw in the joint of such arms, but occasionally the socket or screw lug will get the threads crossed or peened-in by improper centering of the screw. This is of course fixed by running in a tap, or tapping out for a larger screw. The real difficulty arising from the takedown joint of these bolt action and low-price autoloaders comes when mounting sights on the rifles. The receiver and barrel assembly is seldom supported solidly by the inletting of the stock at the point of takedown, so that tightening the takedown screw actually bends the barrel assembly down in the middle. Many a man has mounted a telescopic sight on such a rifle, being entirely correct in fitting and boresighting, only to find that when he puts the stock back on and tightens the screw, the rifle will shoot several inches high at fifty feet, and that point of impact can be radically lowered and raised by movement of the takedown screw.

It is obvious that the owner will experience difficulty in maintaining any particular sight-setting, even with metallic sights, should he be in the custom of carrying the rifle taken down and only assembling it in the field. Elimination of the trouble is by providing a solid bearing for the barrel assembly at the takedown, either by inletting a block of wood, or by channeling out the barrel groove forward of the joint so that the barrel will be free to move down as the takedown screw is tightened.

Cartridge Feeding Malfunctions. The tubular-magazine .22 bolt action and under-barrel magazine autoloaders give considerable trouble as regards feeding of ammunition to the chamber. The slide actions are quite reliable in this respect, although the older Winchesters and Marlins are likely to jam or feed improperly through foreign matter preventing proper carrier functioning, or a bent, broken or blocked cartridge stop or cutoff. Carriers in old guns are also likely to be bent, or have cams worn.

The bolt actions give trouble through bent or misshapen cartridge guide springs or improperly camming carriers, (called lifters, also) or through the magazine tube being forced from proper position. Lifter springs also get out of position. The cartridge guide springs for the Stevens-Savage autoloaders should be carried in stock, for quick replacement.

In the clip, or box-magazine rifles, feed troubles almost always center in the magazine itself or in the magazine guides. If cartridges pop out of the magazine too soon, or when the bolt is moved only a short distance forward, it is usually possible to correct the difficulty by carefully bending in the lips of the magazine a trifle. Once in a while a rifle gets out of the factory with incorrectly fitted magazine guides or stops, or a magazine retaining slot is incorrectly located, so that the top cartridge, when magazine is loaded, is not held in proper position for the bolt to move it into the chamber. It is possible to alter the magazine guiding and retaining parts to position the magazine correctly, but if the

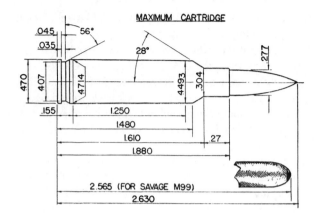

MAXIMUM CARTRIDGE

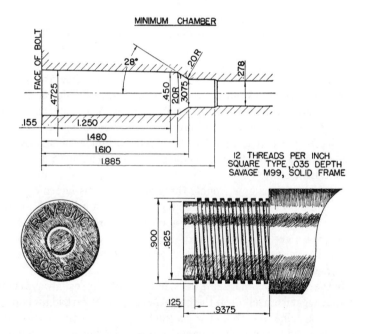

MINIMUM CHAMBER

12 THREADS PER INCH
SQUARE TYPE .035 DEPTH
SAVAGE M99, SOLID FRAME

.270 Titus Savage

This is perhaps the only wildcat cartridge brought out by the demand of regular hunters, instead of experimentalists in the handloading game.

The .270 Winchester received so much favorable comment that lever action addicts began to envy it and ask if they could not obtain a similar cartridge for their rifles. As the Savage 99 rifle is very strong, Bliss Titus decided there was no reason why the .300 Savage case could not be necked

magazine itself is at fault, this should not be done—a new magazine should be obtained. New magazines for Winchester, Stevens and Remington rifles should be kept in stock.

.22 Target Rifles

Work on top-grade .22 target rifles is a highly-specialized branch of gunsmithing, dependent on wide experience with just a few rifles, such as the Winchester 52, Remington 37, the Ballard and Martini single shot actions, and possibly the Stevens Ideal action, plus the ability to shoot these rifles as well as the expert or master class of .22 riflemen. I do not know half a dozen men in the country whom I would class as good gunsmiths on these rifles—and I am not one of them either!

It is necessary for the gunsmith to be an expert shot if he works on these rifles, for there is little repair work done on them, but a great deal of "tuning up," or improving the shooting ability of the rifle. Very little can be determined from rest shooting, and the rifle must be tested, prone, with sling, to really check its performance.

.22 Headspace. On the .22 rifle headspace, or breechspace, there should be .043″ minimum to .046″ maximum in new guns. Excess headspace, beyond .046″ leads to poor accuracy, poor ignition and once in a while, ruptured case rims. Minimum headspace is permissible on target rifles only, for with the .043″ space there is no leeway for off-standard thick cartridge rims. A combination of minimum headspace and over-maximum cartridge base can mean accidental firing of the rifle when the bolt or the breech is closed. The target boys expect things like this at times, and watch where they point the rifle when closing the bolt.

For target rifles, headspace should be .043″ minimum to .045″ maximum, with .044″ the desired medium. Many .22 match rifles are chambered to this headspace. Some target rifles have the face of the bolt counterbored for the cartridge head to the full depth of the rim (approximately .044″) and the bolt contacts the breech end of the barrel. However, others do not have the bolt face cut to full depth—the

---

down to .270, so went ahead and made up barrels for the 99 to handle this cartridge.

With 100- and 130-grain bullets, the cartridge is exceptionally accurate, and ballistics are surprisingly close to those of the much larger .270 Winchester. Performance is superior to both the .250/3000 and .300 Savage. There is an excellent chance that the .270 Titus will eventually be adopted by one or more of the factories, though the name will probably be changed to the ".277" or something else equally exotic.

Remington Model 513T bolt is counterbored to a depth of .031" to .037" and a space exists between the bolt face (outside of counterbore) and the barrel breech when a cartridge is chambered. By slamming the bolt shut forcefully on a cartridge, particularly if the latter is self-loaded from the magazine, it is possible to fire the cartridge. As the bolt is in no way locked at this time, such an accident is definitely undesirable. There is no real danger in this case, but it is hard on the nerves and on the fingers holding the bolt! The Winchester 75 can be fired in this manner also, but only by extremely fast and hard bolt manipulation.

Formerly there were numerous headspacing jobs done on Winchester Model 52 rifles, but complaints have died down during the past ten years to a large extent. Probably the factory began using harder steel in the bolt, for practically all the trouble was excess headspace developed through bolt wear and was corrected by means of shims placed between the bolt body and the bolt handle, the locking lug being on the handle. A lot of characters thought they wanted the minimum headspace, so they fixed their bolts up to the point where quite often the rifle would fire unintentionally when the bolt was closed on a live cartridge. This idea has gone out of style pretty well. It is true, however, that this model rifle will not shoot its best when headspace is much above minimum.

The trigger mechanism of the 52 is not what it could be, but aside from careful stoning and adjustment of spring tensions, there is not much that can be done for the present trigger, except, of course, replace it with one of the special triggers made, such as the Womack, or Thomas as I believe it is generally known now.

Standard-barrel 52s now have a split barrel band on the forend, which on many rifles makes them very sensitive to sling tension and shooting position. Should a shooter complain about his rifle failing to maintain point of impact, particularly showing a difference in group position between different bulls on the same target fired in one series of shots, it is well to try the rifle out with the band removed. If this corrects the trouble, cut the top portions of the band, those which contact the barrel, away, and leave only the lower portion, holding the front swivel, which is replaced.

Old model 52s sometimes cracked across the left wall of the receiver, either at the breech cut or at the safety cut. This of course raises hob with accuracy, and is not always obvious to the naked eye. Application of penetrating oil or solvent shows up cracks quickly. Winchester replaces cracked receivers of this type without charge. The receiver used

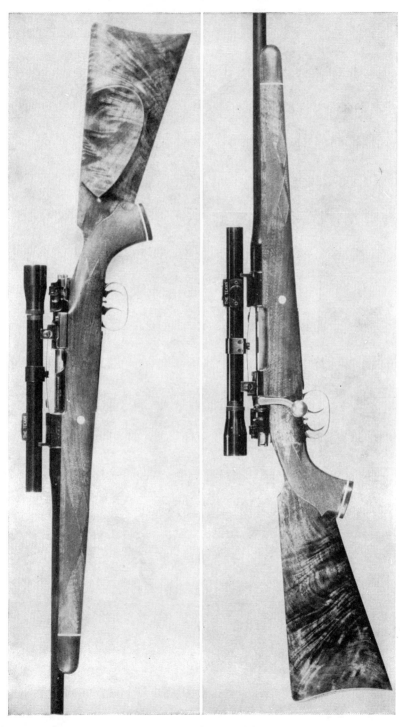

A Mauser action, restocked with a splendid piece of French walnut and fitted with a cheekpiece of peculiar design and placement—just where and what the customer wanted.

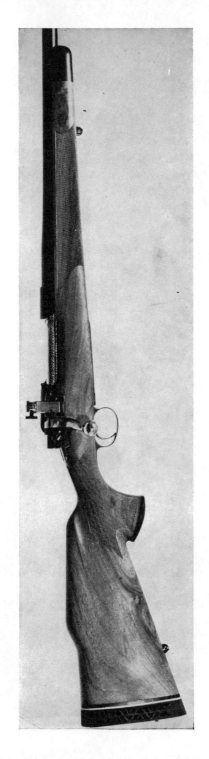

A .375 H & H Magnum Pfeifer-built big game rifle, equipped with Lyman Receiver sights and Dahl Ramp. Model 1917 Enfield action. Built for Howard Hill, world's champion archer, for a recent African Expedition where several large species of African game were successfully bagged with this rifle.

for the past ten years is not subject to any trouble I know of.

If the shooter complains of habitually getting a shot out at 7 o'clock every so often, for no apparent reason, it may be a good idea to lengthen the butt about ¼". Just take off the plate, put in a piece of sole leather and put the plate back on and get him to try again for a while.

Remington 37. About the only mechanical troubles I am acquainted with on this rifle are failure of magazines to feed properly, trigger pull not uniform, and breakage of the rear-sight mounting base. The magazines are not important, as very few target men use magazines, although examination and a little file work will usually cure them. The trigger pull on the 37 is ordinarily very good, the mechanism being very well designed and made. Lack of uniform pull can usually be corrected by dismantling the trigger mechanism, washing it in solvent, polishing parts which show friction wear, rewashing, drying, oiling with light oil and reassembling. The dovetail rear sight mounting bar is hardened and brittle enough to break through accidentally striking the rifle against some hard object, or dropping the rifle—just get a new one from the factory.

Martini. The British-made small Martini action used to be seen quite often on .22 target arms, but is now passing out of the picture. It is sensitive to firing pins—accuracy being affected by any factor concerning either the firing pin or the mainspring, and the assorted pins and screws must be kept tight. Any wear on them also affects accuracy.

Stevens. The Model 417 Walnut Hill was the last complete Stevens single shot target rifle made, and was quite popular with left-handed shooters and those who did considerable off-hand shooting. I had one myself for a couple of years, and was familiar with other shooters who used them. I broke one mainspring plunger, which was the only broken part I know of on this model gun. The principal trouble is keeping a good trigger pull. It is not difficult to achieve a good pull, but the metal of the hammer and the trigger will not keep it long. The mainspring is very strong, to maintain good ignition with the short hammer fall provided, so that the contact edges of the hammer notch and the trigger prong take quite a beating.

Stock Bedding of .22 Bolt Action Rifles. This is *the* problem. Individual barrels have as much non-uniformity in suitable bedding as they do in ammunition choice. The type of bedding which makes one rifle shoot its best may make a duplicate rifle shoot all over. There are three basic types of bedding, each divisible into two or more variations, and these are: fixed, floating, and contact.

*See Appendix I, page 713.

In *fixed* bedding, the barrel is tied down to the forend by an inadjustable band. This is not advisable for any target arm, and the method is not used today, except on some single shots. Tension on the sling is transmitted through the forend and the barrel band to the barrel, and affects the point of impact.

The *floating* barrel can be either full-floating, or semi-floating; the first meaning that the barrel does not contact the barrel groove in the forend at all, at any point forward of the receiver. It is not affected by sling tension or the shooter's position, but accuracy is dependent entirely upon the quality of the barrel steel. If the barrel has no stresses or strains in it and is very well made, the rifle will be highly accurate. If not, the rifle may change its point of impact as the barrel warms up. Never full-float a barrel which has been straightened during manufacture. This would apply of course to any barrels you might fit yourself from target blanks.

Semi-floating means either of two systems; either the barrel can be contacting the barrel channel in the forend very slightly at all points, with the forend exerting no pressure upward on the barrel, or the barrel can be full-floating with an adjustable barrel band or other support adjusted so as to resist any movement of the barrel in any direction. This is done sometimes to dampen barrel whip, and often will cure a barrel which tosses occasional flyers.

Contact bedding means that the barrel is in contact with the forearm and receives some upward pressure from the forend. Full contact means that the barrel contacts the forearm the full length of the barrel channel. Tip contact means contact at only the last three inches or less of the forearm tip. This latter is in most cases the method productive of best accuracy, although the rifle is somewhat sensitive to sling tension. The tip contact is of course to dampen barrel vibration, or whip.

Many variations of contact bedding can be worked up. The point support method, in which the barrel is supported by a movable V-block, or opposing angle plungers or studs, is the most common. The latest idea is the electric bedding gadget worked out by Edwards Brown of the N.R.A. and now manufactured by Al Freeland. It both places pressure on the barrel and checks the barrel position. Freeland also makes a spring-tension barrel band which can be used to achieve contact bedding. It is usually necessary to experiment with springs of different tensions or strengths before achieving accuracy.

Occasionally a barrel which checks accurate on the straightness test will not hold a tight-enough group, regardless of bedding. Before discarding the barrel, try it with muzzle weights in place, for it is entirely possible that the barrel will be highly accurate if the whip at the muzzle is dampened. The weight should be as close to the muzzle as possible, and need not be extremely heavy. A ⅜″ square bar of lead, bent in a circle and held around the barrel in front of the front sight by a hose clamp will permit a test. The permanent weight, if one is found desirable, should be of machined steel, made like a collar or thick washer, with three equally spaced set-screws to hold it in place. It can be removable, or can be left on the gun, and of course can be notched should it interfere with sights. The latter is unlikely, because of the height of present target sights.

Forend Bedding on Single Shot Rifles: With two-piece stock construction, as on Stevens, Ballard and standard Martini, the barrel is of course tight against the forend and firmly attached to it, since it supports the wood. Sling tension is of course a strong factor in causing such guns to shoot out of group, high or low, and not much can be done about it. However, quite surprising results in grouping ability are sometimes achieved by moving the position of the barrel band or the forearm screw, or both, either forward or back. The very heavy custom barrels

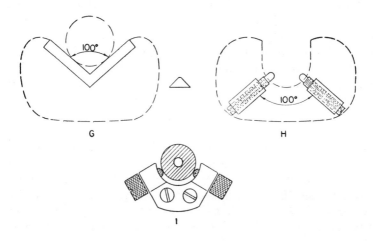

BEDDING CONTROLS

G. V-rest of metal inlaid in the stock forend, with a cross-section of metal shown at the side—theoretically the best.
H. Adjustable barrel support points, in the form of round tipped screws threading through ferrules or sleeves inlet into the stock as shown.
I. Sam Yasho's rest, available commercially, on the same idea as "H," but easier to install. Cut the forend off square and screw on the gadget.

used on this type of rifle by the seasoned target rifleman will resist sling tension and consequently the rifles are by no means inferior to bolt actions. One British-made Martini action .22 match rifle employed a full-length stock, the stock having sufficient width to support the forend when the action was inletted through it. This was to allow the barrel to be free of tension, of course, but the rifle did not show any radical improvement over the standard Martini with the two-piece stock.

Buttstocks. The factory target stocks furnished today are made very full-proportioned purposely, so that individuals may reshape to their own dimensions if necessary. A full-faced man will find the standard Remington 37 or Winchester 52 Marksman stocks too high-combed for comfort, even with telescopic sights. Metallic sights of telescopic height must be used for best positioning and the comb of the stock must be relieved for the cheek. This is best done by cutting on the side, to form a sort of recessed cheekpiece. Rasps, files and chisels can be used, but the easiest and fastest method of making a smooth reduction is to use the motorized sanding disc—believe it or not, you can make a better job faster.

All of the target rifle stocks are designed for prone shooting, and for the large number of smallbore shooters who take up gallery position shooting in the winter, somebody should do something. The stocks are from ⅜″ to 1″ too long for good offhand work, and the only practical correction is two different buttplates. The stock should be cut off at the desired point with consideration given to the buttplate to be used for offhand—it should be the standard type, not Swiss or Schuetzen—and threaded metal bushing installed in the wood to receive the bolt thread buttplate screws. Then, there should be a thicker buttplate for prone work which could be switched in half a minute with a screwdriver. The rear wood surface of the butt could be protected by a thin plate. No elaborate slot-and-key adjustable affair as used to be furnished for free rifles would be necessary. Some gunsmith can pick up a few bucks, I believe, if he would put out these buttplate sets, having available about three thicknesses of prone plate to suit different pulls. Cast of aluminum, a plate 1″ thick is not heavy enough to bother any prone shooter on a heavy rifle.

.22 Revolvers

The mechanism of the .22 revolver is naturally very similar to that of the larger-caliber models, and subject to the same troubles in regard to timing. The only specific ailment of the .22 revolver is a too long firing pin. The better grades of target arms today seldom have much trouble on this point, but older guns come in with edges of the chambers peened and battered from firing pin tips. Nearly always the tips are soft enough to be filed to proper proportions and then polished.

In the days when .22 target revolvers were widely used, shooters and some gunsmiths tried to facilitate rapid-fire shooting by weakening the mainsprings, which made the guns cock easier in single action use. This made ignition doubtful in some instances, so the boys sharpened the firing pins slightly in order to concentrate the force of the hammer fall in a smaller area. Occasionally cases would puncture or rupture at the rim close by the firing pin indent when fired. There was no danger to the shooter, but fairly often the cartridge would expand or blow back around a puncture to tie up the functioning of the cylinder.

.22 Autoloading Pistols. In discussing several models of .22 pistols made by Colt and High Standard we have to be concerned with several matters. The Colt Ace .22 is no longer made, now being replaced by the Service Ace Attachment which is furnished for the .45 and Super .38 pistols. The original Ace gave trouble principally with firing pins, the holes in the faces of slides sometimes being oversize enough to permit the pin tips to move away from proper location on the cartridge rim. Correction of this is making a new pin of such proportions just back of the tip to guide it properly, the tip of course being shaped to contact the cartridge rim at the proper point.

The Service Ace, or as it is now known, the 22/45 Conversion Unit, gives little trouble once installed and adjusted on the frame of the large-caliber automatic. On commercial pistols these fit quite well, usually with only a little smoothing up of friction points. Ejector points sometimes have to be stoned slightly. On military .45 frames, fairly often considerable work must be done to insure full functioning of the conversion units, and on some very rough and crude-machined frames, perfect semi-automatic functioning cannot be expected. Formerly the Super .38 barrels were smaller in diameter than the .45 (outside diameter, of course) so that the barrel bushing would not fit over the .22 barrel of the unit. For such guns, Colt will furnish a .45 bushing. Present .38 and .45 barrels have the same outside diameter and use the same bushing.

The floating chamber of the conversion unit gums up rapidly in some guns, due to the ammunition used should the latter be excessively lubricated. This condition causes malfunctions through failure to extract fully and failure to move the slide far enough to the rear to pick up cartridges from the magazine. The remedy is removal of the barrel and just cleaning the chamber mechanism thoroughly.

Older .22 Colt Woodsman pistols were prone to extractor breakage, particularly when high-velocity ammunition was used, but the present models have much stronger and better protected extractors. Trigger pulls are rather hard to adjust to perfect target pulls because of the strong helical trigger spring. Weakening this spring should not be done except as a last resort. The hammer notches can be touched up to give excellent sporting pulls, but if cut down to give trigger pulls less than three pounds in weight may jar off when the slide slams forward.

The new Woodsman line is better designed, but the steel is soft. Hammers and sears can be easily filed, which means they will wear quite fast. It is to be recommended that the notches be cut to the desired pull, stoned, and cyanide-case-hardened to withstand wear. They should not be hardened thoroughly for this would make them very liable to breakage. Colt will no doubt improve the quality of these parts in the future.

High-Standard .22 pistols are much easier to work on than the Colts except for stop lug defugalties. Trigger pulls are easy to adjust through sear and hammer notches, and remain dependable for considerable periods of time. Extractors were likely to wear on the earlier models. Also, firing pins were not stopped positively, so that repeated dry-firing would cause a peened detent on the breech of the barrel at the cartridge rim counterbore. This is not found in the present guns.

Three types of takedown catch assembly have been used, and the latest method sometimes causes trouble through the owner attempting to disassemble the pistol, and mistakenly removing the takedown lever before removing the slide from the frame. When this is done, the stop lug is released inside the frame and its spring plunger forces it up to firmly prevent movement of the slide. I have had a number of pistols brought to me in this condition. Sometimes the stop lug can be relocated through use of pins and pointed picks sufficiently to allow the takedown lever to be inserted in its seat, but a couple of times I have not been able to do this. Not being able to figure out how to disassemble the pistol for proper assembly without tearing the slide off by main strength and consequently breaking the lug, I sent these to the High Standard factory and let them worry about damaging the frame and slide.

Occasionally the slide lock on the target models fails to function, which is usually easily corrected by deepening the bend of its actuating spring, or making a stronger spring.

The target rear sight elevation system is not so good, the blade of the sight rocking up and down to give elevation adjustment, with a small prong on the axis pin engaging in shallow detents on the wings of the sight to retain adjustment. If free enough to move at all, the blade usually will slip down during firing. Cutting the detents in left sight wing deeper usually cures this defect.

The two-stage trigger annoys some shooters, and on the High Standards it can be changed to single-stage quite easily, by making a new sear bar with a rear notch or lip so located as to provide only the single pull.

High Standard stock screws are soft and easily stripped, as well as lost by amateur stockmakers, so keep a few of these in stock.

All the .22 autoloading pistols require good magazines for perfect functioning. Keep Woodsman and High Standard magazines in stock. When a customer comes in saying his pistol jams, or will not feed— slap in a new magazine and try it. Often it will turn the trick. A little experience and experiment with magazine lips will tell you a lot. If too close together, they will bind on the cartridge and fail to release it, if spread too far, the body of the cartridge is released too soon, and usually the bullet goes up out of line and hits the top edge of chamber. And a good cleanup job often is all the "repairs" a balky .22 pistol needs.

CHAPTER 19

Browning, Blueing and Blacking of Metal

DOING a good job of finishing firearms is neither art nor science. It requires care, some experience, and a little luck, not to mention plain work! A few years ago the processes of blueing and browning were rather uncomplicated, involving only a few principles of metal rusting and plating. Today we have alloy steels which require special treatments, as well as several comparatively new blacking systems, generally advertised as "blues."

Originally guns were rusted brown by various processes and the act was known as "browning," the finish as "browne." Eventually some smith discovered that if he cleaned off the rust a little sooner, the finish would be black or blue, instead of brown. Due to custom, after the blue finish almost completely supplanted the brown, the processes were still called "browning" although either a brown or blue finish could be meant. This sorry custom has been carried to extremes, even some modern writers in attempting to be erudite continue it, so that it is possible to read formulae and directions for using them without knowing whether the resulting finish will be brown or blue!

In the Dunlap vocabulary, there is going to be less confusion. When I say "blue" or "blueing," I mean that is the color intended; if "browne" or "browning" is mentioned, that means the eventual finish will be brown; black means black.

BASIC PRINCIPLES

There are a few points applicable to almost all processes and all finishes with all metals.

The first is cleanliness: The metal to be finished must be clean and the containers of the solution to be used and the solution itself must not be contaminated by any substance which will affect the action of the process upon the metal. The accessories used must be clean— cloths, brushes, racks, gloves and swabs.

The second point is care: Care in mixing formulae correctly; care in

366

timing all operations properly; care in heating and regulation of atmospheric conditions, and care in handling the metal at all times, from start to finish of the job.

The third point to be observed is not physical, but mental. Experience serves, of course, but many a bad job can be prevented if a little head work is done in advance. This usually means thinking over the process to be used with the metal it is to be used on. For instance, an old formula which may have worked beautifully on muzzleloaders and proven satisfactory on present day .22 rifles may be a hopeless failure on hard, tough military rifle steels. A regular modern hot salt quick blueing bath may do a perfect finish on a Remington-made 1917 action at 290° F. and fail on an Eddystone-made 1917 action at 300° F. even if left in the tank much longer.

PREPARATION OF STEEL FOR FINISHING

The final appearance of a blued, blacked or browned arm depends to a considerable degree upon the preparation of the steel before the coloring process is used. Of course, the two are interdependent—a well prepared gun with a poor blue job will not look well, but the best process will not help a poorly polished surface.

There are three classifications of finishes: *poor*, for any reason; *ordinary*, done with modern power polishing equipment and quick hot bath processes; and *good*, done with a good finish applied to a hand polished arm. The poor finishes are usually due to laziness, inexperience or inferior solution ingredients.

Stripping

Stripping is the term used for the procedure of removing any existing finish from metal and today means doing this by either acid bath or electro deplating tank. The latter is not necessary except for plated firearms.

When a completely new arm is built up, with all parts in the white, meaning naked steel with no finish of any kind in its past, stripping is of course unnecessary. Nor is stripping absolutely necessary to prepare a gun for refinishing—all traces of the original finish may be polished off mechanically.

However, acid stripping is to be highly recommended as the first step in preparing to blue or black a firearm. The acid not only saves a great deal of polishing time, but actually saves metal in corners and sharp curves through eliminating heavy polishing and buffing necessary to clean these locations. Also, the surface of the steel will take almost any type of finishing process much better, through the etching action of acid. Degrease the parts—washing in solvent is sufficient, although hot soda water or detergent solutions can be used—and apply a 25% solution of hydrochloric acid for from one to two minutes. For some of the military finishes, a one minute bath in a 50% solution is not harmful. A bath, or immersion treatment in a tank is best, but satisfactory results can be obtained by applying the acid solution with a cloth swab. If a tank is used, glass is recommended, but steel is satisfactory. When steel tanks are used, of course only put the solution in when needed, and as soon as the stripping is completed, return to a crock or glass container and wash out the tank with clean water.

After stripping, the parts should be washed in clean water, dried, and polished as required.

Deplating

I am not attempting to give information on plating, for the equipment to do satisfactory gunplating is not suited to the average gunshop—even large ones. It is expensive to set up, costly to maintain, and in general, not worth the bother. Commercial plating establishments can do your plating at reasonable cost, and there is at least one of these in every city of any size in the country, so make contact with one or more and arrange for them to plate whatever arms you send them.

There is, however, a real reason for a deplating setup in the gun shop. Plated arms are almost entirely pistols and revolvers, so that only a small tank is required. The gunsmith himself, in his own shop, should strip old plating from guns to be replated, in order to be able to do the polishing himself. If stripping and polishing is left to the commercial platers, they are very likely to almost ruin the arm through over polishing. Besides, they charge money to polish and buff. Also, plated arms which are to be refinished in blue or black must have all the old plating removed, and mechanical cleaning by polishing seldom will accomplish this. The deplating tank also will serve other purposes, as the reverse current used will remove not only plating from steel, but almost everything else—grease, old blueing, dirt, and rust.

As illustrated, the small deplating unit employs an automobile battery—or two of them in series—to provide the electric current. The wires should be insulated cables, with copper rods or heavy wires to contact cathode and anode in the tank. Copper will last about a year in ordinary use.

A glass tank or jar of around three gallons minimum capacity is

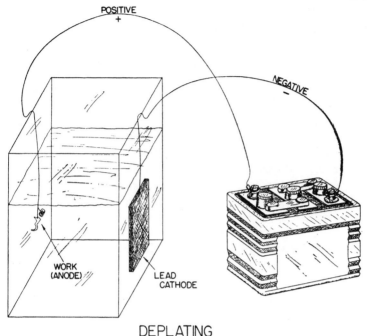

POSITIVE
+

NEGATIVE
−

WORK
(ANODE)

LEAD
CATHODE

DEPLATING

Using the sulphuric acid solution, the illustrated set up is satisfactory. Glass tank is shown. Parts to be deplated form the anode. A single auto battery is enough to provide current.

needed, preferably square. The solution used is one gallon of commercial sulphuric acid with one quart of distilled water. The acid is poured into the tank first, and the water added slowly. A lead sheet or weight, of sufficient external area to equal or surpass that of the gun parts, is used as the cathode, connected to the minus battery post. The anode is the metal to be deplated. Gun parts must be wired tightly to the anode, connected to the plus battery post. They may be hung on copper wires which are wound about them well enough to make good contact, and these wires connected to the anode. Stripping time is from five to ten minutes.

This solution will deplate nickel, chrome and cadmium, but not silver or gold.

Sulphuric acid is hygroscopic, meaning that it absorbs water from the atmosphere, so your solution actually increases in quantity. By using a deep tank, a considerable increase in volume can be permitted, but as the solution is weakened by the extra water taken in, more sulphuric acid must be added from time to time. Otherwise, deplating time will be longer and results poorer. The lead cathode can be used over and over.

Ordinary Polishing

The average preparation job today is done with little or no hand work, all emphasis being upon power driven abrasive, polishing and buffing wheels. The more different motors and wheels the gunsmith can set up, the faster he can work. Time is now the most valuable item on any cost sheet. Use of double shafted electric motors with felt wheels on each end is the most practical solution to the polishing problem in the general gunshop, with a similar setup for buffing wheels.

Three such motors, giving four felt wheels and two polishing buffs, provide satisfactory equipment. Of the felt wheels, one can be medium hard, one medium, and two soft. These are charged with abrasive compound—Brownell's Polish-O-Ray is the most convenient to use— in grits from coarse down to fine. The medium hard wheel, charged with coarse or medium abrasive, cuts metal almost the way a fine carborundum grinding stone will, and is used only sparingly on rough surfaces, such as the Parkerized military arms. The real polishing is done with the softer wheels charged with finer cutting compounds. The cloth polishing wheels, made of stitched muslin as a rule, are charged with polishing (buffing) preparations and used to give a high polish to the metal. It must be remembered always that the polish of the finished arm depends upon the polish given the metal before the blueing or blacking process is applied.

Lea Compounds, made by the Lea Manufacturing Company, are a complete line of polishing and buffing agents, available in many grades of grit and types suited to different metals. For gun work, use the types listed for carbon steel. Grade C, which is about 200 grit, is most useful for all around polishing. Learok is a buffing composition which gives a high polish, or finishing polish. The Lea compounds are entirely greaseless and do very good work, but they are hard to handle and store. When the containers are opened, the exposed material is apt to rapidly harden. The company makes a cap (Humidicap) which is supposed to exclude air from opened tubles, but does not always do so, therefore, it is better to use an airtight glass jar for each tube.

Ordinary light duty double shaft electric motors will not last long under constant polishing use. Those ball bearing enclosed motors made for grinders are better, and best of all are the large (½ HP up) special purpose grinder motors which extended endbells, such as made by

Baldor, Black & Decker and other firms. These are expensive, costing from $75 up apiece, and a shop specializing in blueing may be better off in the long run by setting up a series of polishing heads operated by a single large motor, placed either overhead or under a bench. The standard electric motor, with ventilated endbells, has a built in fan principle which sucks dust, lint, grinding compound and general debris into the motor—which is not good and is why such motors should be protected in some manner when used for polishing.

Over polishing is the curse of 90% of present day blue jobs—the boys bear down against the wheels to shine everything up and of course round off corners, blur outlines badly and in general make the metal parts of the rifle or the pistol look like a half used all day sucker. Refinished military rifle barrels often are prepared only on the wheels, with the result that a glance along them reveals swells, bulges, rings—anything except clean lines.

Polishing barrels is not quite so handily done as are other parts, and very often they are polished incorrectly, even when barrel shape and lines are okay. Barrels—and practically all other gun parts as well, especially receivers and triggerguards—should be polished *lengthwise*, not crosswise. Of course, preliminary cleaning-up can be done in the easiest manner, but final polishing and buffing should be in line with the bore. Study-out ahead the positioning of the wheels and the work. Naturally, running a barrel back and forth parallel to the turning wheel is not so easy. A final hand-working-over with crocus cloth helps a lot.

Standards of workmanship have gone down considerably during the past 20 years, particularly on blueing. A good many of the present gunsmith generation put out the shiny, high buff blue commonly seen today. This may be a tribute to their polishing equipment, but cheapens the appearance of any arm. A far better finish is achieved by polishing to good lustre, then wire brushing the metal, using a rotary wire wheel with .005″ wire. This aids greatly in producing the truly fine "satin blue" of the good custom gunmaker. This good finish was greatly appreciated by gun connoisseurs of the '20s and early '30s, who patronized Niedner, Hoffman, Owen and such top gunsmiths, and who would have wrapped a rifle around the head of anyone who attempted to foist upon them any gun with a shiny "niter job," as they were derisively called in those days.

A lathe can be a great help to good blueing, as barrels can be cleaned up with a light cut—almost a scrape—which helps military barrels immensely, and also the lathe can be used as a jig for draw filing or

270 WINCHESTER

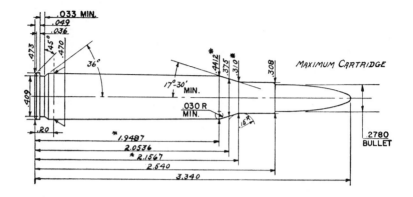

MAXIMUM CARTRIDGE

ACTIONS SUITABLE:

WINCHESTER 54, 70; SPRINGFIELD 1903
WITH NUMBER OVER 800,000; ENFIELD,
MAUSER.

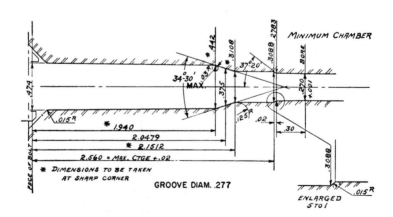

MINIMUM CHAMBER

GROOVE DIAM. .277

ENLARGED
5 TO 1

This highly popular hunting caliber is one of the finest American cartridges ever developed. The body of the cartridge is identical with the .30–06 U. S., however the overall length of the case is slightly greater and because of this, it is not wise for reloaders to make .270 cases by sizing down .30–06s.

hand scraping if desired. In draw filing, a file of the vixen type can be used for the preliminary work, and short sections of coarse mill file for finishing. Filing of course is only necessary to clear off toolmarks, rust pits and unsymmetrical bulges.

The polishing of curved parts is comparatively easy with power equipment, and the polishing of flat parts rather difficult—to do a good job, I mean, and not wear away metal at the edges or over screw or pin holes. However, there is a way to do fairly good flat polishing by power, although the apparatus must be made up. This is a belt sander, using 1½" or 2" belts of abrasive cloth, styled after a bandsaw. The Niedner Rifle Corporation made such a machine and although they did not use it much for polishing work to be blued, having it for polishing shop tools principally, the gadget could be used to great advantage by the blueing specialist. The belt is run around two or more pulleys, or drums, one of which is powered. The secret of success is a backing plate to the underside of the belt which is polished glass smooth so

---

The short neck permits gas cutting of the chamber neck if any number of such cartridges are fired.

On the development of the .270, two schools of thought exist—one believing that it was based on the .256 Newton (for some reason) and the other that it developed naturally from the .30–06. The latter line is somewhat correct. Winchester many years ago developed the .270 as a military cartridge in experimental work, dropped it, and a few years later brought it out as a sporting cartridge. I have seen some of the early military ammunition made right after World War I.

The .270 is at its best with the 130-grain bullet for all around hunting, loaded by Winchester to muzzle velocity of 3,120 FPS. The comparable .30–06 150-grain loading is 2,960 FPS. The better sectional density of the .270 makes it hold its velocity better up through 450 yards, after which the light bullet loses some of its ambition.

The cartridge has been used successfully by skilled hunters, on every variety of large game on this continent but the amateur going after Kodiak bear had better get a .375.

With factory hunting ammunition, the .270 is slightly more accurate up to and including 300 yards than the .30–06 with factory hunting ammunition. The .270 is one cartridge that the handloader can scarcely improve in velocity without getting into trouble. The factories load it up to the limit themselves, and reach excellent accuracy with 130- and 150-grain bullets. The factory 100-grain load is too hot for some rifles, and will not deliver good accuracy in other rifles. The custom 12" twist of rifling is better than the factory standard 10" twist in this caliber.

Many Western shooters use the .270 for an all around rifle, the 100-grain bullet loading for vermin, the 130 for deer and the 150-grain slug for elk and bear.

that the belt will slide freely over it even when pressure is exerted against the cutting side thus forcing the belt against the backing plate.

The belt should run just as fast as you can make it and retain control of the work. This is actually somewhat of a grinding operation and the faster the abrasive moves, the better the finish it delivers. Coarse, medium and fine belts can be made up for their appropriate uses. Provide some sort of guards—wooden ones are fine—so that when the belt breaks the free ends will not reach out and snatch you bald headed. The description explains the principles of this type of machine. Incidentally, with the backing plate removed, the same affair will do quite a bit of work in the stock department as a sander, using very coarse belts. The unsupported belt will evenly sand outside curves.

A commercial tool of this order, called the Mead Bandsander, is available from Brownell, but it is rather small and no long backing plate is provided. One could no doubt be rigged up without a lot of work, and save time at least in constructing a metal belt sanding device as outlined above.

A flexible shaft tool, or indeed, a flexible shaft attachment for any electric motor, with chuck in the free end of $\frac{1}{4}''$ capacity, is another very useful blueing accessory. Small felt hobs and wheels, mounted on $\frac{1}{4}''$ and even $\frac{1}{8}''$ shafts are available from Brownell and others, which can be charged with polishing compounds as are large wheels: (Hobs are small cylinders and balls of felt with built in mandrels.) These are almost a necessity for polishing within triggerguards, in the small radius curves on receivers and revolver cylinders. They save time, effort, and do a better job than the larger wheels.

Brownell Industries, Inc. of Montezuma, Iowa, has for sale practically everything in the blueing department except the location of the shop and Frank Mittermeier usually has the hard-to-locate items such as fine wire brushes and wheels.

Hand Polishing

Polishing a gun for blueing or reblueing can be done by hand without nearly as much time or labor as would be supposed by those who have never tried it—about five hours are required for a large bolt action rifle, to do all parts well. A hand polished arm of course looks better than a power polished one, since corners and angles can be maintained, with no loss of outline. A rather surprising fact is that an excellent final finish can be obtained on metal polished by hand to a decent degree of smoothness while metal polished by power to the same apparent finish before blueing will not turn out as well. A higher polish by wheels is required for the same finished blue appearance than for the same appearance when preparation is by hand and if you do not believe me, try it and see.

All the equipment necessary to do a hand polish job is your set of files, five or six feet of 1″ or 1½″ grit abrasive cloth, six or eight feet each of #240 and #320 strip and a couple of sheets of crocus cloth.

As for power polishing, the metal parts must be free of oil before starting the job. Solvent combines with the free grit or cloth to form a sticky, gluey mess. Water or alcohol should be used to clean the hands and work when they become fouled up with the cloth.

Use your files to smooth up the receiver and the barrel, clearing out toolmarks, dents and such defects. The #180 cloth is then used, more to show up the condition of the metal surface and to clean off light barrel toolmarks than to really polish. With the metal parts held in vises or special holders, use strips of the cloth around the curved surfaces in the old shoe shining routine, both on the barrels and the curved portions of the receivers. Depressions in the metal are revealed instantly to the eye.

· Following the cross polishing, you flat polish, with strips of cloth wrapped around mill files or blocks of wood, moving them lengthwise of the metal, along the bore and bolt axis, turning to cover the curves. This will reveal lateral depressions and marks of original machining. The process is alternated—cross and longwise movement of the cloth until all traces of the original finish, if any, and pits and tool marks are removed, after which only lengthwise polishing is done. Examine to make sure no portions are rounded at edges or ends undesirably (if so, reshape at such points with files) go over all parts again with worn #320 cloth, then do the same with crocus cloth. The crocus may be used in both directions, finishing lengthwise.

Final wiping and examination in good sunlight should reveal no scratches or polishing marks from the cloth and the steel should have a rather greasy looking dull sheen. If it is okay, wire brush, with rotary power driven brush, having steel wire bristles preferably finer than .005″, give a quick pickle or degrease and begin the blueing process.

There are a few places, as inside triggerguard loops, in the small curved depressions in bolt sleeves, and so on, where the power driven felt hobs will do a better job than hand work. Bolt action triggerguards proper—tangs and floorplates—are very easy to hand polish and should be so treated.

Arms with large flat surfaces, such as lever and pump action rifles, autoloading pistols and repeating shotguns are quite easy to hand polish, and also revolvers. Sheet abrasive cloth can be torn into wide strips and large blocks used to back them in working on flat surfaces.

The newest development in metal finishing preparatory to blueing is grinding. This is applicable to barrels only in the case of most guns, but does a beautiful job. Roy Weatherby, the California custom gunmaker, adopted this system some years ago. The barrels are externally ground full length, and in spite of the crossgrinding, have an excellent surface and texture on which the blue takes very well and leaves a nice finish.

Degreasing

Nearly all finishing processes require that the metal be absolutely free of any trace of oil or grease. Some of the blacking systems are so caustic they cut small amounts of oil and so are not critical on this point. However, all of the cold and hot blue methods require uncontaminated steel to take properly which means that the metal parts must be cleaned and kept clean during blueing and that parts must be handled by metal hooks or jigs, or with clean cotton gloves.

Formerly the old hot bath degreasing solution was clean water with about 1½ or 2 tablespoonfuls of lye or caustic soda per gallon, and the metal parts were boiled in the tank for about five minutes. The solution naturally was not too pleasant on the skin or clothing.

By far the best hot water cleaner is Oakite, made by Oakite Products, Inc. This is one of the oldest detergents, or grease cutting cleaning compounds, we have. It emulsifies or absorbs grease and will not hurt hands or clothing as it does not contain lye or irritating agents. The household variety is sold in grocery, paint and hardware stores, the 10½ ounce package now costing about 15¢. Four ounces should be used to each gallon of water. There are special industrial varieties of Oakite, which are cheap in quantity, and go further in use. The P. O. Ackley Company uses Oakite and recommends it, and since Ackley blues more rifles in a week than most other gunshops in a year, the advice is worthwhile.

Tanks and heating them

Nearly all the blueing and blacking, and some of the browning processes call for immersion of the metal parts at some time or other, either in the actual blueing solution or in the neutralization of chemical agents used in the process.

Stainless steel is the ideal tank material. These should be welded up, of fairly heavy gage sheet, about .050″ thick. Two of them will be sufficient—one for blueing solutions, one for acid solutions for stripping old finishes and for etching solutions of weaker action for pickling, if necessary. The degreasing tank can be of mild iron or steel.

If stainless steel is not available or too hard on the budget, all tanks may be made of black iron strip, called "hot rolled," to a size most economical for your shop. Inside measurements for the minimum most useful size are 38″ long, 5″ wide and 5″ deep. Remember, the bigger the tank, the more solution you will need. Smaller tanks, 15″ by 7″ by 5″ should be made for pistol and small parts blueing, since it is obviously a waste of solution and heat to use the large tank for small parts. Three tanks of each size should be made up and the acid tank can be both narrower and shallower.

Handles should be attached to each end, and small bars or rods of metal welded or wedged across the tank on the inside close to the bottom, to prevent the metal parts to be blued from contacting the tank bottom. Do not attempt a blueing job with new tanks—break them in by acid-cleaning, and boiling a weak blueing solution for half an hour at least.

Heat for the tanks is seldom a problem today, as gas is available throughout the country, either from city mains or from tanks. Butane, propane and similar manufactured gases are available to the rural shop. Kerosene burners, from kerosene stoves, can be hooked up in a close spaced row to do the job. W. F. Vickery, in his book *Advanced Gunsmithing* mentions the possibility of using electric heating elements in the tanks. I have never known of any shop using electric heat in this manner, but the idea is excellent. Such a set up would be very clean and neat, using insulated tanks supported on any table by a few bricks. Gunsmiths in the TVA or other low rate electricity areas may be overlooking a good bet by not trying out electric heated blueing tanks.

Gas is by far the most common heat used, and burners for blueing are easily arranged. Long burners are available commercially for the specific purpose; you can make them of pipe, or salvage a few old ordinary round burners from scrapped stoves or hot plates, hook them in a line and support in an angle-iron stand or on a metal table. A wooden table with a metal top can be used as well or better. Consult your local gas company or distributor for information regarding your burner, should you make up one, for burner apertures and flame adjustments are not the same for all gases, particularly for manufactured gases. The "bottled" or tank gas uses smaller apertures and burns with a shorter, hotter flame than natural gas.

A few plumber's tools are required to make your own long burners, which are best, and if you are smart you will let a plumber make up the outfit to your specifications. He will know the legal standards for gas installations in your area, has the equipment and knowledge to make all joints gas tight, and can adjust the burners to their most efficient settings in a jiffy. I favor two parallel burners, each made of a 38″ length of ¾″ pipe with holes drilled ⅜″ apart in a straight line for the individual gas flames, preferably with the gas entering each pipe burner at the center. This of course is for one tank only, with the two pipe burners spaced about 2½″ apart. The tank is centered over the two. Three such burner units should be enough for the ordinary shop, and can be arranged with regard to the space available in the blueing room. If sufficient space allows the burners and their tanks to be placed end-to-end, this is perhaps the most easily managed setup. If space is limited, one burner may be placed behind another, but never, unless forced to, put three tanks side-by-side against a wall, thus requiring that work be lifted across one tank to reach another.

Only two burners will be used at the same time in most processes, one for degreasing, one for blueing, but the extra one may be useful in experimenting. Quite often a combination of two processes gives an excellent finish, such as combining the first steps of Baker's hot blue with a blacking process. No heat is ever used with an acid solution.

Place the burners between 40″ and 45″ from the floor, making the tanks almost breast high so that you will not wear out your spine bending over to handle the work. This makes emptying of tanks slightly straining if you are strong minded and strong backed and do not provide *iron* faucets on the tank ends so that almost all the contents can be drained without lifting the tank at all. When draining tanks, use stoneware crocks for corrosive liquids, or make large buckets out of old wooden pickle kegs. Small new barrels can be purchased cheaply. Ordinary buckets are okay to catch unwanted material, but do not use the bucket for anything else.

An ordinary deep fat thermometer can be used to check temperatures of hot liquids, but it is wiser to buy one of Brownell's thermometers, which will last longer. None of them is graduated fine enough for extremely critical work, however.

The blueing or blacking tank should be cleaned and neutralized (by acid wash) when a solution is changed. If the same formula or mixture is to be used, washing with plain water is sufficient.

Covers should be provided for the tanks, both for keeping dust and dirt out when they are not in use and for speeding the heating when the burners are lighted for a job. Covers should be mild iron or steel, and be ventilated with small holes scattered over the surface.

Collect dark glass bottles, stoneware crocks, Pyrex glass containers and dishes in which to keep blueing ingredients and acids. The Pyrex loaf cake baking dish is very useful for a small pickling or etching solution tank to handle small parts.

A table with a top of some neutral material not affected by any of the finishing substances is necessary close to the blueing tanks. A table surfaced with one of the acid and burn proof materials used on laboratory tables—or the saloon bar—is better than a metal or a wooden top which requires constant cleaning. It should be at least 48″ long and 30″ wide, and on it you place assorted racks, wooden V-blocks to hold barrels, and oil cans, rods and brushes.

Steel wire to make the innumerable small hooks and parts holders, supporting racks to fit into the tanks, and cups made of steel screen to hold screws and pins in the tanks will be needed, and places to keep them as well. Surgical cotton, gauze or cheesecloth, cotton flannel and whatever other swab material is called for by the process involved, will be needed, in addition to long tweezers, birch dowels, rubber corks and muzzle plugs and probably a few other items you will discover yourself needing as you go along.

The above just about covers the equipment needed for blueing, blacking or browning, regardless of formula. The only possible addition might be a sweat box to aid the rusting action of some of the slow cold blue formulae. This can be easily made, by any gunsmith. A reasonably tight box, with close fitting cover, is constructed of wood, with the inside drilled in every appropriate spot to accept wooden or hard-rubber pegs which are used to support the gun parts by their ends or through holes. A can of water is placed in the box and also a fitting to take an electric light bulb. The bulb supplies heat to accentuate the rust provoking damp atmosphere. Cloth of any type can be tacked to the box so that it will fold over the lid and is wetted down to cut down evaporation inside the box. The light bulb must not be so large as to create enough heat to dry the parts and should be shielded away from the metal parts. If placed beside or under the can of water it will do its job. The bulb is not absolutely required. It is best to fill the can with boiling water to which a little salt is added, just before closing up the box.

BROWNING

The brown finish is seldom used today except by the few gunsmiths specializing on restoring antique arms, but information should be given on the methods and formulae usable. I personally see no objection to a brown finish on any gun, modern or otherwise, and believe it has some merits over the blue finish for some purposes.

A man living in a very damp climate should be better off with the brown finish, of the plain or rough type, since rust will not mar the finish as it will the blue coloring, which is very thin. The polished, shiny or lacquered browns are as easily scratched and show pitting as badly as does a high lustre blue.

The brown finishes work best on comparatively soft steels, although it is possible to obtain a close grain surface on the hard alloy steels, so long as they are not case-hardened or carburized. A "brown" is just a controlled rust, after all, and anything from salt water to iodine will cause rust and can be used. However, a good brown finish entails a rusting agent of known action characteristics which produces an even fine rust coating, called close grained. The rust pits of a good browning solution or mixture are microscopic and very little different from those of our popular blue and black finishes, so that the finished metal has a sheen similar to a good polish.

Not a great deal of equipment is needed for browning. Some of the formulae call for practically none, a few for the regular tanks needed for most blueing processes. The rotary wire brush, with steel bristles, can be used, but the old hand brush does as well, and steel wool in the medium grades, is a great help in carding, or removing the oxidized metal or loose rust between treatments and in finishing.

Clean cotton cloths or swabs must be used to apply the browning material, and plugs of acid free woods (dry birch or maple) made to plug the barrel at the muzzle and the breech. These plugs protect the barrel against rusting and also can be used as handles to hold the work. Nearly all the good browning formulae call for the mixture or solution to be swabbed or rubbed on the metal, so there is no great danger of rusting the inside of an action to any extent.

All surfaces to be browned must be thoroughly clean and free of all grease, including fingerprints, and the cleaning is easiest done in the regular tank, with Oakite solution. The best finish will be obtained by polishing and buffing the arm and all parts to be browned to a high lustre, as for a bright blue finish, then wire brushing, followed by a one minute bath in a 25% hydrochloric acid solution, then the degreasing bath. The Oakite solution has great wetting power and is ideal for a pre-browning cleanser. A weaker acid solution, 5%, is well worth keeping on hand as it is strong enough to do final cleaning on all metals but will not hurt the skin if any is inadvertently spilled.

Use distilled water in all solutions and all formulae calling for water. The old timers did not have it, so they used rain water in an attempt to keep away from well water possibly contaminated by undesirable elements. Distilled water can be aerated if desired by pouring from one container to another—and use clean containers, rinsed with more distilled water!

In mixing acid solutions, do it outdoors and use the water for the base ingredient—put the acid into the water, slowly. Only with sulphuric acid do you reverse this procedure.

The oldest and greatest defect in the browning system is "after rust," which means just what it says—rusting after the finish is completed through continuing action of the browning solution or mixture. Some of the old browning processes required heavy lacquering over the finish to exclude air from the surface of the metal and thereby prevent after rust. Light lacquering was popular on damascus and twist steel shotgun barrels not only for this practical reason but because it gave a high sheen to them. Lacquered finishes are easily scratched and practically worthless in the field. For guns in collections, they are highly worthwhile, showing the arms to best advantage and protecting against any form of rust to a very considerable extent.

Neutralization, or killing the rusting action of the process is generally done by boiling in pure water or by pouring scalding water over the heated metal parts, so that it will evaporate almost instantly. Raw linseed oil or beeswax, or both, is then rubbed on the metal, by hand or leather pad until the finish feels dry. If lacquering is considered, no oil is applied, and the barrels in particular must be dry and clean before application of the finish lacquer.

Acetone-based lacquers are best, and application is best with a spraygun. Alcohol-based lacquers or varnishes are less durable. My private idea is that a modification of ordinary marine spar varnish, sprayed on, would do all right, but I have never tried it. Generally, a perfectly clear coating is desired, although it is possible to color a lacquer or varnish to deepen the color of the browning.

Rusting is accentuated by an evaporative atmospheric condition so that the sweat box is useful as in cold blueing. For browning, no elaborate box need be made—any kind of old box large enough can be used, with a can of water inside and wet burlap sacks thrown over it.

Browning Formulae

1. *Salt*. Plain table salt, in a 10% solution, will do a browning job, causing a coarse rust to form in from four to ten hours, depending

ACKLEY .270 MAGNUM

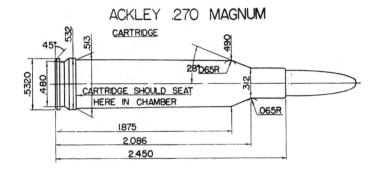

CARTRIDGE

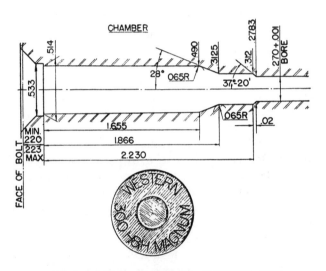

CHAMBER

ACTIONS SUITABLE: MAUSER '98, SPINGFIELD 1903, 1917 ENFIELD, WINCHESTER 54 & 70.

P. O. Ackley has designed a series of high-intensity cartridges based on the .300 H & H belted case, which are suited to standard large military actions without excessive alteration. Overall length is practically the same as that of the .30–06 cartridge.

Available in .25, .270, .30 and .35 caliber, the Ackley Magnums have the same case body dimensions and shoulder angle, only the neck diameter being different. It is therefore possible to rebore any to a larger caliber, excepting of course the .35 Magnum, so that a shot out barrel in .25 or .270 can be made into a .270 or .30 at low cost. A 7mm, or .276 Magnum is also made.

These cartridges are quite practical for the man who wants something a bit more powerful than factory standard cartridges. For the 1903 Springfield

upon the humidity of the environment. After a thorough, even coat has formed, it is carded or scratched off, almost to the point of removing it. The salt water solution is again swabbed or brushed on, and the process repeated from eight to twelve times, although the scratchings, after the first one, remove only loose rust and do not appreciably disturb the surface of the metal. The carding job can be eased by boiling or scalding the parts with plain hot water before beginning the carding at each stage. After the final cleaning, the metal is boiled or scalded well, then oiled and waxed, or lacquered. The final finish of a plain salt rust brown is a rather muddy brown, which looks much better than it sounds after waxing.

Appearance can be improved and after rusting cut down considerably by subjecting the metal, after the final rusting and cleaning, to a touch of copper plating. This entails only a half hour soaking in a very weak—Angier says .2%—copper sulphate solution. The color is shaded into a deeper brown, with something of a purplish cast, and looks very well.

Browning with salt is slow, cheap, and not too much work.

2. *Salammoniac Brown.* Browning with salammoniac, or ammonium chloride, was supposed to be very common in our early days, and many of the Pennsylvania riflemakers used it. A very weak lukewarm solution must be used, about .5% (half of one percent) and only about five passes are required as a rule. The solution is applied by swab. After the final cleaning the barrel is oiled and heated until it will "brown paper," probably around 300° F. What kind of oil the old-timers used, I do not know—probably anything from bear oil up. Linseed oil was earlier called "hard oil" in some parts of the South. Animal and sperm oils were the principal lubricants, but we do not know too much about early vegetable oil uses in gunshops.

Salammoniac rusting is about the same as ordinary salt in its action, although much faster. Additional passes with it will produce almost a

---

and 1917 Enfield rifles, the only alteration to the action is cutting the face of the bolt so that it will fit the Magnum cartridge base.

The .270 Magnum shown in the drawing is an excellent high-velocity long range vermin cartridge, as well as a game caliber. Velocity with the 130-grain bullet is rated at 3,500 FPS.

Hunters who wish to use the heavier 7mm bullets can obtain the 7mm Magnum which gives the 160-grain bullet 3,200 FPS.

The Ackley Magnums are handloaded cartridges, made from shortened .300 or .375 H & H Magnum cartridge cases.

black finish, and if the solution is boiled and the metal parts boiled in it, three passes will give a dull black finish with is very durable.

3. *Antigallic Brown.* This formula, credited to the U. S. Bureau of Standards by Angier, is another which can be made to produce either a brown or a blue black. The mixture, which is a paste, is not heated, but the gun parts should be warmed before application. Heat them until you can barely hold in the hand without acute discomfort. The mixture when applied shows no immediate action and the treated parts must be left in a warm place to dry and rust—it helps if the parts can be artificially heated very slightly. If the mixture does not dry evenly and fairly rapidly, undesirable and spotty pitting may occur. The colors showing, in order of coatings or treatments are: light blue, purple, gray, and brown. From six to eight passes are necessary, and all carding of rust must be done dry. The finish is with linseed oil after final cleaning by scalding with water. This produces the brown finish.

If the parts are boiled after each carding of rust, and the mixture then applied to the hot and dry barrel, a blue finish will result in four or five passes, and a black will appear if the process is continued.

The mixture is composed as follows:

Antimony Trichloride	4 parts
Ferric Chloride Crystals	4 parts
Gallic Acid	2 parts
Distilled Water	1 part

4. *Formulae for Browning Twist and Laminated Shotguns.*

Stelle & Harrison give the following "recipes" for mixtures suited to brown old style shotguns. All are the swab-on type, and the same procedure as with others listed is used—coat, let rust, card, repeat until satisfied with finish, neutralize and finish with oil, wax or lacquer.

a.	Sweet Spirits of Nitre	½ oz.
	Tincture of Steel	¼ oz.
	Corrosive Sublimate	½ oz.
	Nitrate of Silver	4 grains
	Chalk	"small lump"
	Water	1 pint
	Aqua Fortis	60 drops
b.	Sweet Spirits of Nitre	1 oz.
	Tincture of Steel	½ oz.
	Blue Vitriol	¼ oz.
	Nitric Acid	6 drops
	Corrosive Sublimate	14 grains
	Water	1 pint

With these formulae an excellent even rust is produced, of fine grain texture. To show up the twists or laminations of the iron-and-steel barrels, after the last carding dip them in a very weak hydrochloric acid solution for two or three minutes. The solution would be 1 ounce of acid to approximately 4 gallons of water and can be weaker.

BLUEING

Cold Solutions

No type of gunmetal finish can approach a good cold blue for fine appearance—for me, that is. They take time and work, so are seldom used today, for the expense involved because of the time element would be prohibitive for the average man.

Similar to the browning processes they replaced in years past, the cold processes depend entirely on successive passes and retreatments until the desired color is achieved. They are all rusting processes. Power driven steel wire wheels are desirable to remove the loose rust caused by each coating, though hand brushes and steel wool can be used for large parts and should be on small ones.

The following is a British Armourer's solution which requires a tank large enough to contain the gun parts, for they are boiled between coatings to limit the rusting action of each application. The solution is practically foolproof, although some varieties of steel will demand more coatings than others to achieve the blue finish. The first color will be gray, which deepens to a black, then becomes blue-black or blue. This finish is extremely durable and rust resistant. The solution is swabbed on with lint-free cotton cloth and a new swab must be made for each application.

I have used this process and consider it excellent. It produces a good blue color on hard Luger pistol frames, which many of our hot blues and blacks do not. The formula and working directions are given as in the old British manual:

"The following quantity is sufficient for 50 rifles:

Water, Rain or Soft (distilled, to you)	12 oz.
Blue Stone (Copper Sulphate)	$\frac{1}{16}$ oz.
Nitric Acid	$1\frac{1}{4}$ oz.
Tincture of Steel (Tincture of Ferric Chloride is as close as you will get)	$3\frac{1}{2}$ oz.
Spirits of Wine (Ethyl Alcohol)	2 oz.
Spirits of Nitre	3 oz.

"The above mentioned ingredients will be mixed in the order shown, directly they are received. They must not be kept in separate bottles as danger of fire is likely to arise from the nitric acid if it is spilt before being mixed with the other ingredients.

"They should be measured by fluid measure, as follows: 60 minims equals one dram; 8 drams equals 1 ounce; and 20 ounces equals 1 pint.

Process

"For the first coat only, take 2 ounces of the mixture and add ¼ ounce of nitric acid.

First Day

"Boil metal components for one half hour in strong soda water— 1½ pounds of soda to one gallon of water, to remove the grease, then wipe down with clean wet cloth to remove soda and wipe out barrels. When components are cold, coat them with the mixture, rubbing in well the first coat. Stand in a dry place for three or four hours, coat again with the mixture and stand in the drying room for the night. (Note that a dry place is specified, instead of a damp one, as with most other blueing solutions of this type.)

Second Day

"Boil components in clean water for 20 minutes and when cold, scratch off. Coat cold with the mixture and stand in dry place for three or four hours, then coat cold and stand in the drying room for the night.

Third Day

"Repeat as for second day.

Fourth Day

"Boil in clean water for 20 minutes. When cold, scratch off and oil."

It may be necessary to use the solution for seven or eight days for some steels, but the color can be seen at all times when the rust is removed between coatings, so is easily checked. Use rotary steel wire wheels for carding rust, with hand brush and steel wool to clean out corners. As the solution is not introduced into the barrel, the bore will not rust if it is wiped out before and after each boiling. No oil can be used. Rubber or wooden bore plugs can be used, but are not really necessary. Since the parts are placed in a dry room overnight, there is no tendency for the bore to rust even if the steel is not protected.

Old American Acid Blue

After browning went out of style, the American general gunsmith needed a simple solution, of ingredients easily obtainable, and found that a ferrous acid solution would create a rust which would produce a rather good cold blue. Only one boiling tank was necessary, and the solution would blue almost any steel, though at its best on the mild steels. With care and experience, beautiful finishes were obtained with these acid blues.

There were and are numerous variations in formulae, some with added ingredients which may or may not be worthy, but basically the old cold blue solution was nitric acid with iron dissolved in it, with or without hydrochloric acid in quantities up to equal the nitric. The following solution is simple and cheap to try and will give very excellent durable finishes on all unhardened steels. Tempered or heat treated parts, such as bolt action rifle receivers and bolts will require more applications than barrels, triggerguards, floorplates, and the like.

Here is the formula:

Nitric Acid	4 oz.
Hydrochloric Acid	3 oz.
Iron (Clean Nails)	½ lb.
Water (Distilled)	1 quart

The acids are mixed together, *outdoors*, in a glazed stone crock, then the nails are added. After the nails have been dissolved, add the water and put into colored glass bottles with glass stoppers. The solution will keep practically indefinitely if sealed up and kept in a fairly dark place.

In use, the metal parts are degreased, by boiling in soda water, lye solution, Oakite or Houghto-Clean, then when cool the solution is swabbed on and parts are placed in a damp room or sweat box for six or eight hours. When the heavy coat of rust has formed, scratch it off and boil in hot water for from five to seven minutes. The boiling can be done before the scratching and after it as well, to produce a fine grain final finish. After the barrel is cleaned and cool again, recoat with the solution. The process is repeated for six or seven days, or until the correct color is reached, then the metal is brushed clean, boiled for 10 minutes and oiled. Linseed oil is generally used, although a petroleum based polarized (water displacing) oil is better. Cotton cloths and swabs must be used.

Quick Acid Blue

This formula I have not tried, but it is reported very effective. It is the only cold acid blue I have heard of which requires less than 24 hours to complete!

Hydrochloric Acid	4 oz.
Nitric Acid	½ oz.
Ferric Chloride	1 lb.
Copper Sulphate	½ oz.
Distilled Water	1 gallon

The solution is made up, mixed outdoors, in a tank. The parts are degreased and immersed in the solution for 15 minutes, then dried for four hours, again placed in the tank for 15 minutes and dried for eight to ten hours. After this drying, the rust is carded off with steel wool and dry burlap, and the metal rubbed with mineral oil. Presumably, the rust formed is very light, and also, additional treatments could be given. Bores must be protected by plugs, or barrels carefully wiped out after each immersion in the tank.

The Niedner Cold Blue

Through the courtesy of Tom Shelhamer, who managed the Niedner Rifle Corporation during the days of its greatness, I am able to give the details of their blueing process. The finish on Niedner custom rifles was unequalled, being a deep, dark lustrous blue which would resist almost anything except a file. It withstood much greater wear and resisted rust far better than any of the present hot bath blues. I have one Niedner rifle which is about 12 years old at present, has had considerable handling and use, and the finish is as good as the day it left Dowagiac. It is not necessary to wipe off every fingerprint, keep everything oiled and so forth, as with most blues.

Similar to the preceding acid blue formula, the proportions are slightly different and probably the method of treatment was responsible for the magnificent results obtained at Niedner's. The process is given as stated by Mr. Shelhamer, and the amount of labor involved will not set well with present day rush bluers. Only a conscientious gunsmith and a firearms connoisseur can appreciate the true value of a fine rifle blued in this manner.

Nitric Acid	2½ oz.
Hydrochloric Acid	2 oz.
Wire Nails	1 oz.
Distilled Water	30 oz.

This is one-eighth of the full formula, which was developed originally by Zischang, well known gunsmith of two generations past.

The acids are mixed in a crock or large glass container outdoors, the nails dissolved in them, then the water added. It is stored in dark glass bottles, preferably glass stoppered. The method worked out in application by Mr. Shelhamer at Niedner's was somewhat unusual, and the result of much experimenting. The atmosphere in southern Michigan is slightly on the humid side, so for use in dry climates an artificially damp room or box may be necessary to aid the rusting action.

The Niedner system of blueing did not employ all the commonly used methods of polishing, which may have had an effect on the finish, also. Mr. Shelhamer states that they used Aloxite cloth, down to 320 grit, and while they had various sized rubber drums with belts of the same cloth, practically all polishing was done by hand. No buffing wheel or buffing compound of any kind was ever used. They thus prevented rounded corners, as well as "saucers" over screw holes in flat surfaces. After the 320 grit polishing, the metal was wire brushed, with an *oily* wheel, which blended the abrasive marks and showed up any scratches so that these could be polished out. The work was put in holders so that it could be handled without being touched by the bare hand, barrels were plugged by tapered plugs made from birch or maple dowels and degreased by boiling in Houghto-Clean for one hour, followed by rinsing in clean hot water.

The barrels were wiped out after degreasing and clean plugs inserted. As the metal must not be touched by hand, a vise with leather jaws lined with clean paper was used to hold while cleaning and driving in fresh plugs.

The blueing solution was swabbed on, using a pair of long nosed pliers to hold a wad of long fibered sterilized cotton. The barrel was wiped out also with cotton during the process, and it is emphasized that only the best long fibered cotton is suitable. (The barrels were not wiped with the solution, but only with cotton wet with plain water, and then with dry cotton. The solution is to be kept out of the bore.)

Niedner left the solution on the metal only about three hours, and allowed two coats per working day. The first coat takes little effect, for the trace of alkaline cleaner more or less killed it, so a second coat was applied over the first after only one hour.

After the application was on the steel three hours, it (metal) was boiled in clean water, the barrels placed in the vise, wet plugs removed and dry plugs driven in. The parts were carded clean on a fine wire wheel kept absolutely free of oil. Hand brushes were used a great deal.

The brushes should have wire diameter of .003″, not over .004″. Boiling loosens the oxide (rust) and it cards or scratches off very easily, while sticking very tightly if the work is not boiled. It also darkens the color, so makes possible the judging of the color during the progress of the work.

When cool, recoat and repeat. The solution was not left on overnight at Niedner's, the parts being left clean and recoated in the morning. Small parts—screws, triggerguards and sights—will be finished in seven or eight coats, or passes, barrels and tempered parts requiring from 10 to 12 passes.

The bore must be very carefully protected—dried out and fresh or dry plugs put in after each pass, because it cannot be oiled.

Should an occasional part resist blueing, or take improperly, polish it and start over. An excessive number of coats or passes will do little good, for with this solution there is a limit to the number of passes possible, after which the color begins to leave and the surface of the metal to pit.

Constant care against oil contaminating the metal during blueing is absolutely necessary and clean paper, in small sheets, should be kept handy, to use in handling pieces of metal or parts. Also, in this connection, it is wise to have a few pairs of cotton fleece gloves on hand, such as are used in plating plants. Once in my checkered career I worked in a tin mill, and we had to have such gloves to handle the steel sheets and finished tin plate with. In fact, if I remember correctly, we were required to have a new pair of "dry" gloves at the beginning of each eight hour shift.

During the boiling off process between coatings, should a trace of oil appear on the water, try to sweep it off with a piece of paper, or scoop it off and if this fails, and the finish is spotted, you clean off the steel by polishing it again and start over.

A large number of special holders are desirable, Niedner having about 75, consisting of barrel butts to hold receivers, split rods with sliding rings to act as tongs and fixed to hold pins, sight dovetail sections and other parts, and strips or bars of cold rolled steel drilled and tapped to take all varieties of gun screws.

This system of blueing entails a lot of patience and time, and considerable work of course. Experience in your own locality is necessary, as more time between passes, or artificial damp room may be necessary in dry climates. If you can obtain the beautiful satiny finish possible about the fifth time you try, you will not curse so much. Afterward, no other finish will seem very good.

HOT BLUEING

The hot blue processes followed the cold blues in popular use, although never displacing them, as they were capable of completing a finish in less than a day. Some of them would do the blueing itself in half an hour. Some good jobs were done, but a great many very poor ones, with more shades of lavender and purple than you would find in an interior decorator's color guide.

Clyde Baker publicized a formula which has come to be known by his name, as Baker's Basic Solution. The formula is as follows:

Sodium Nitrate	¼ oz.
Potassium Nitrate	¼ oz.
Bichloride of Mercury	½ oz.
Potassium Chlorate	½ oz.
Distilled Water	10 oz.
Spirits of Nitre	½ oz.

The ingredients are mixed in the order listed, but must not be ground together. The first four are mixed, then put into the water, which should be warm, and after dissolving, the spirits of nitre can be added. The solution does as well without the latter, however, as with it.

As Mr. Baker stated, it is a basic solution, to be altered if necessary to finish some types of steel. For hard steels, the potassiums may be increased 5%. Considerable experimentation is necessary with any of the hot blues before good results can be guaranteed. The water used is very important—rainwater or distilled water will nearly always greatly improve results.

The above solution should be mixed and immediately placed in colored glass containers with glass stoppers. It is not necessary to mix this formula outdoors.

To blue with this solution, one hot water tank is necessary. (Excluding degreasing or cleaning tank.) Pour two ounces of the formula into a small glass jar which is half submerged in the tank, so that the solution will reach boiling heat when the tank of clean water is raised to a bubbling boil, as it must be. Make a couple of swabs from small clean dowels and clean cotton cloth or gauze, and place the swab ends in the jar of solution. The metal parts must be thoroughly degreased. Baker recommends etching the metal with a nitric acid solution—½ ounce nitric acid to 6½ ounces distilled water—as a final cleaning and to insure the blue taking hold on the steel.

Boil the cleaned metal parts in the tank until they are as hot as the water will make them—a heavy rifle barrel may take 20 minutes—lift out with hooks or wooden pegs and coat it with the blueing solution, using the swab as fast as you can and rapidly cover the entire surface. The metal should be hot enough to dry the solution as fast as it is applied and leave a faint bluish-gray coating. As soon as the solution is dry all over, put the part back in the tank and boil for another two or three minutes. Rust will form all over if the solution is correct for the metal and the metal properly cleaned originally, and on removal of the metal from the tank a second time use steel wool and fine (.003″) wire hand brushes to remove the rust. This procedure is repeated from four to eight times, in most cases, before the desired deep blue finish is reached. Successive applications of the solutions and repeated boilings and cardings depend somewhat on the method of handling.

Speed is essential with this system of blueing, for the heat of the metal at the time the solution is applied is important. Parts must not be allowed to cool at all before the swabs get in their work. The swabs must be kept in the solution container until the very instant they are needed, in order that they too will be hot.

If, when the solution is first applied, rust appears before the part is returned to the water, the solution is not correct for that steel. Try diluting it, or replacement with another mixture having different ratios of the same ingredients. If spots on the metal refuse to react to the solution, they are undoubtedly contaminated by grease or oil, and the part must be again cleaned.

Finished hot parts may be burnished after removal of the final coat of rust by rubbing with fine steel wool, plain at first, and later with linseed oil on the wool. Coat the parts with linseed oil and then allow them to cool. When they can be handled comfortably with the bare hands, clean off the linseed oil and oil with light gun oil or other mineral rust preventive.

This system of blueing is in little use today, although quite fast. It is not a pleasant or easy job to blue a gun in this manner. From one to two hours of fast, hot and sometimes hard work is required. Once the job is begun, it must be carried through to the end.

The method is well suited to shotguns and any arms with soldered joints or accessories, and is quite fast and easy on steel telescopic sight tubes, to mention one item.

HEAT BLUEING

Three distinct types of heat blueing are used in gun work. First is the temper blue, achieved by heating steel in either open flame or oven until it reaches the blue in the color scale of heating. This is not often used in this country by either gunsmith or manufacturer except for small pins and screws, but is still used to some extent abroad particularly for finishing springs such as extractors and bolt stop springs on various breeds of Mausers.

Second is the heat blue reached by heating steel and quenching in oil. It is varied by repeated dipping in oil and burning off the oil. This last often provides an excellent blue for small parts, particularly pins and screws, but with some types of oil a false finish is developed which will flake off easily, being really only burned oil residue. Several quenches are useful to know, and often they can be combined to good result, dipping the hot part from one to another. The following are commonly used:

> Marble's Nitro-Solvent Oil
> Linseed Oil, mixed with Hoppe's No. 9 Solvent
> 3-In-1 Oil
> Motor Oil (SAE 20) mixed with Linseed Oil.

The steel must be between 700° and 1000° F. at quenching, to blue decently. The harder the steel, the higher the heat.

Third is the type of blue used by Colt and Smith & Wesson extensively in the past, this being a variation of the temper blue adapted to all gun parts, whether large or small. Large ovens are used, in which bone-and-oil mixtures, or commercial preparations such as Carbonia (made by the American Gas Furnace Company) are placed, along with a quantity of polished, cleaned gun parts. Temperatures run from 600° to 800° F. the gun parts remaining in the oven from one to three hours, depending upon bulk. Moving racks are used to hang the parts in or from, and these rotate constantly so that the blueing mixture, which is in powder form, is constantly contacting the metal surfaces. This process is well adapted to small parts such as sights, swivels, barrel bands and scope mounts, when large quantities must be finished.

PHOSPHATIZING

About 1910 it was discovered that by changing the surface of steel to a semi-neutral phosphate, considerable resistance to ordinary rust was gained and much military equipment has since been finished in this manner. The first process to gain wide use in this country was the "Parkerize" and our military small arms were Parkerized until about 1940, when similar but more modern finishes replaced it to a large extent. Bonderizing is a finish similar to Parkerizing, but with finer grain finish, and is widely used on automobile body parts as a rust preventive before priming and enameling. Both are patented processes produced by the Parker Rust Proof Company, Detroit, Michigan. A dull, non-reflecting surface is produced by either, dead-black on mild or carbon steel, gray, green, or blue-black on high nickel alloys or tool steels. As the chemical solution eats into the surface of steel, the process is necessarily limited in application to firearms. Only exterior surfaces should be so finished, and a fairly difficult protecting job done on close tolerance moving parts.

According to Angier, the first recorded experiments in this line were by the British Colonel W. A. Ross, with further developments by Coslett, Richards, and Parker. While patents and licenses cover advertising and development work on the processes, the original patents have expired and the original formulae can be used. Working instructions in detail are not available and I can only give general comments.

Basically, the phosphate finish is produced by boiling iron or steel parts in a phosphoric acid solution for several hours. Sand blasting before treatment aids in producing a dark color, which is the reason many military rifles are exceedingly rough.

The first Coslett formula consisted of the following:

Phosphoric Acid, density 1.5	365 grains
Iron Filings	91 grains
Distilled Water, add to above to total 1 quart.	

Degreased parts are boiled in the solution from one-half to three hours, to produce a gray-black color, which is darkened somewhat when dried and oiled. Boiling is stopped when the solution is reduced to one-seventh of original volume. Parts must be neutralized immediately upon removal from the tank, by boiling in plain water.

The Richards formula is slightly different, but of the same idea:

Phosphoric Acid, density 1.5	61 grains
Manganese Dioxide	37 grains
Distilled Water, add to above to total 1 quart	

Known commercially abroad as "Fermangan" this is practically the same as Parkerizing. The degreased metal parts are boiled in the solution from one-half to one and one-half hours, or until solution is reduced to one-third of original volume, or until parts are desired color. The solution must be kept at a bubbling boil. Water can be added from time to time, in order to provide sufficient volume to keep the parts covered, in which case the finish is watched for color. The chemicals do not leave the solution, excepting the small portion which adheres to the steel parts in the form of manganese and phosphate, and chemicals can be added to maintain the strength of the solution. This produces a black finish as a rule on all but tool and heat treated steels, which sometimes come out a dark gray.

The original Parkerizing process uses a similar formula, being as follows:

Phosphoric Acid	365 grains
Manganese Dioxide	22 grains
Water, add to above to make 1 quart	

Iron filings can be substituted for the manganese dioxide. The parts are boiled in this solution from two to four hours, rinsed in cold water, then in hot water, then dried in sawdust, after which they are heated dry to a temperature at which water dropped on is immediately thrown off, then dipped in linseed oil. The oil is drained off and parts heated slightly again to dry the oil.

Pentrate is a somewhat similar process, but giving a fine grain finish. It is more of a hot black bath finish than a phosphate, but as used on military small arms, has a somewhat similar appearance. It is patented by the Heatbath Company. A great many arms were so finished during the past war.

The phosphate processes are not suited to the gunshop, although the Du-Lite product, "Phosteel" has great promise. It is fast, requires no special equipment, and is safe to use, although it should be used only as a preliminary step and the metal later finished by blacking or blueing. The finishes resist rust, do not reflect sunlight badly, and look okay. Gunsmiths would be wise to check up on auto fender and body shops in the larger cities, for they very often have Bonderizing or other equipment in regular use and sometimes can be persuaded to treat firearms for a nominal charge. Bore plugs of neoprene should be made to protect barrel bores.

BLACKING

Contrary to general opinion, black finishing steel by use of a single hot bath chemical solution is not very new—some processes have been known and used since 1910. World War II gave the system considerable impetus, as a great deal of improvement work on the various formulae and chemicals produced stable mixtures and standardized procedures. The black oxidizing of steel at low temperature was first patented in 1901, but little development work was done until World

War I, after which interest again languished for a good many years. Around 1936 prepared salts and chemical mixtures became available commercially to gunsmiths and rapidly became popular. After the second war, these preparations swept the business and almost totally eliminated the older methods of blueing, because of the facts that they were cheap and time saving.

Although advertised as blues, and capable of producing a satisfactory gun blue on alloy steels, these chemical finishes are really blacks, and are known industrially as black oxides. Ordinary steels come out black, not blue. All have a slight etching action on steel, and many industrial users take advantage of this to remove microscopic burrs from machined parts.

Du-Lite

Du-Lite Black Oxide is one of the best known industrial finishes, and one of the best on firearms. Unpolished steel takes a dull, dead-black color, but polished steels, particularly the mild alloys used in rifles, come out a rather good blue-black.

Du-Lite salts are fused, coming in cake form, making them easy to handle as well as giving a more uniform material than is possible with mechanically mixed powders. The makers advise that for most steels, including mild alloys, their bath processes satisfactorily at from 295° to 305° F. Tool steels and special alloys may require 315° F. Depending upon the bulk of the metal as well as its alloy, blacking time may be from five to 30 minutes in the bath.

The steps in blacking by this system are:

1. Metal is cleaned in hot bath—Oakite, Du-Lite #29, or other solutions.
2. After cleaning, the metal is rinsed off in hot plain water.
3. The work is submerged in the Du-Lite hot bath, mixed according to factory directions.
4. After blacked or blued to taste, metal is rinsed in cold water.
5. The work is dried and oiled, or immersed in a water displacing oil for five minutes. The Du-Lite Company furnishes two such polarized oils, "Proctoil" which leaves a heavy coat of oil on the metal, and "Kwikseal" which leaves a light oil film.

Du-Lite penetrates the surface of the steel and causes microscopic pitting (as do all rust blues of course) which retains oil very well. The process is much used by aircraft enginemakers on their bearings for this reason. On firearms, the finish is more rust resistant than some of the similar blacks.

Houghton

The E. F. Houghton Company has for several years catered to gunsmiths with their prepared blacking salts, sold as Houghto-Black No. 15. This is used with "Houghto-Black D" which activates the solution. The solution is not too good on hard alloy steels, even when temperature of the bath is raised over 300° F. Normal operating temperature is around 295° F. although most gun steels blue at 290°. If the heat is raised much above 295° F. excessive loss of solution through boiling results. A gentle rolling boil is best.

The average blueing tank, long enough to take a bolt action receiver with 28″ barrel, will require from four and one-half to five gallons of solution, which means 45 to 50 pounds of Houghto-Black and from 22 to 25 ounces of the activating compound. This will blue from 10 to 15 rifles. Ten to 20 minutes is sufficient for most gun parts, although alloy receivers and bolts may require up to 35 minutes. The salts are added to the water—cold water—slowly, and the solution heated to 240° F. at which time the Houghto-Black D activating agent is added. Considerable heat is generated when the initial addition of the salts to the water is made, and care must be used to avoid dumping too much at a time which may cause the partially mixed solution to erupt and spray you with highly uncomfortable active alkaline chemicals. Rubber gloves, aprons, and good goggles should be worn at this time. The blueing room should be well ventilated, also.

The solution operates at just above its boiling temperature, so that there is a constant small loss of both water and salts. Water can be added any time the tank is not at full heat by means of a long handled metal dipper. This is filled with warm or hot water and the bottom of the dipper lowered into the solution, then tipped and drawn rapidly down the length of the tank, thus mixing the water into the bath.

A batch of solution should be allowed to boil down a bit from the original quantity and then kept at that point by adding water as needed to restore the amount in the tank. After six or eight guns have been finished, about 10% of the original amount of salts used should be added to restrengthen it. This addition can be done only once, and when the solution again begins to fail, it must be dumped and a new batch made up. When a bath begins to take much more time than usual to produce a finish, or begins to be critical about harder steels, it is time to get rid of it.

There has been some development recently in this product for gun finishing, and the using procedures may be changed somewhat. The salts are sold by Brownell as Houghto-Blue at present.

Mixed Blacking Formulae

No. 1. If you want to mix your own salts, here is a tested formula. It is not critical regarding either metal or temperature and operates at approximately 290° F. Cleaning and tank setup can be per the Houghton process.

Sodium Hydroxide	65 parts
Potassium Nitrate	25 parts
Sodium Nitrite	10 parts

I believe Sodium Nitrate can be used instead of Sodium Nitrite but will cause a critical solution—one which will take well on some arms and poorly on others. Approximately 10 pounds of the mixed salts are used to one gallon of cold water, in mixing the solution. A few ounces of manganese dioxide can be used as a catalytic agent, or activator, if the metal is reluctant to take the color.

In well ventilated shops, having exhaust fans to pull fumes out of the room, a *careful* operator can add four to six ounces of sodium cyanide, which will greatly reduce or eliminate the tendency of the solution to eat solder. It is therefore possible to refinish double barreled shotguns with this formula. However, the cyanide is dangerous to handle and should only be used with great care in ventilated rooms or outdoors. Keep the sleeves rolled down, wear neoprene or rubber gloves and apron, and if possible, get an old army gas mask, take off the canister and clamp on a length of hose long enough to reach outside, so you can breathe fresh air while the cyanide is mixing with the blacking solution.

Cyanide is one of the deadliest poisons I know, fatal in even the tiniest amount in either cuts or mouth. Cyanide gas is quick-acting itself, and *military gas masks are not proof against it.* When using cyanide in any form, use the greatest care at all times.

No. 2. Here is one so simple it is worth anyone's trial. For this I am indebted to Don Lowery, one of my competitors here in Tucson, Arizona. This is very possibly the most practical of all blacking processes, in that it is almost foolproof; the ingredients can be obtained at low cost in nearly any town; and the finish is more durable than any other I have seen. In appearance and wear resistance it greatly resembles the finish used by Germany on military small arms prior to 1942.

Lye	2 parts
Ammonium Nitrate	1 part
Water	see below

White Ammonium Nitrate Fertilizer, 33% type

The household lye you get at any grocery store. If you want to be technical, buy sodium hydroxide (ordinary lye is approximtely 94% sodium hydroxide). The ammonium nitrate you get at seed and feed stores—it is used by gardeners as a soil and plant conditioner.

> Solution:—5 pounds lye,
> 2½ pounds ammonium nitrate,
> per gallon of water

Working temperature is between 285° and 295° F. If you do not have a thermometer, heat until a metal part raised to the temperature of the bath will sizzle cold water slightly when removed and dipped into a pan or tank. This solution lasts almost indefinitely, or at least for between 35 and 50 blacking jobs. Add a pound of lye every 12 or 15 jobs, and water of course as necessary. From 15 to 40 minutes in the bath are required, depending upon the bulk and hardness of the steel involved.

The only unpleasant part of using this formula is that in mixing in the ammonium nitrate, a considerable amount of gas ammonia is given off. Considerable ventilation is therefore necessary to a finishing room, or the setup made under a leanto or in a shed which can be opened up on one side.

Lye is no problem to handle. In this formula, as in others using sodium hydroxide, the principal purpose is not to aid in coloring the metal but to raise the boiling point of the solution and thereby prevent excessive loss by boiling away of the other ingredients. In this mixture the ammonium nitrate apparently stays in the tank, and only water and a little lye are lost through boiling.

The black produced by this ammonium-nitrate-lye process is unbelievably durable. A finished part will take a wire brush test without damage which would totally remove almost all other finishes.

To use this solution, the metal parts are degreased either by Oakite solution or washing with plain dry cleaning solvent, dried, and placed in the tank. After blacking, they are rinsed in water, either cold or warm, and dried and oiled in the regular manner.

Blacking—General

All of the blacking processes attack lead and destroy soft solders, except when sodium cyanide is added as mentioned under the No. 1 formula. Depending upon the hardness of the solder, a sweated joint will withstand from 10 to 14 minutes in the solutions before suffering,

7 M/M MAUSER

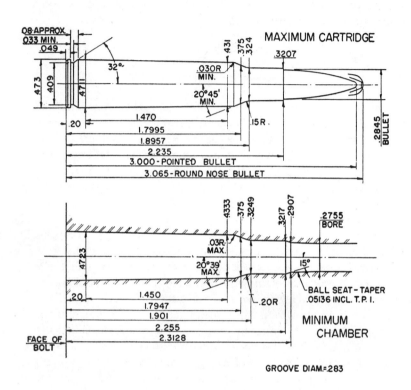

MAXIMUM CARTRIDGE

.08 APPROX
.033 MIN.
.049
.473
.409
.471
32°
.431
.375
.324
.3207
.030R MIN.
20°45' MIN.
.20
1.470
1.7995
1.8957
2.235
3.000 - POINTED BULLET
3.065 - ROUND NOSE BULLET
.15 R
.2845 BULLET

.4333
.375
.3249
.3217
.2907
.2755 BORE
.03R MAX.
20°39' MAX.
15°
BALL SEAT - TAPER
.05136 INCL. T. P. I.
.4723
.20
1.450
1.7947
1.901
2.255
2.3128
.20R
FACE OF BOLT

MINIMUM CHAMBER

GROOVE DIAM.= .283

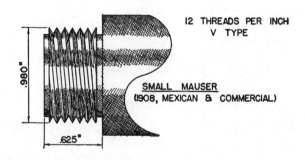

12 THREADS PER INCH
V TYPE

.980"

.625"

SMALL MAUSER
(1908, MEXICAN & COMMERCIAL)

so remember this when blueing rifle barrels with sweated on ramp front sights.

The processes do not attack aluminum alloys—they devour them! *Rapidly.* Under no circumstances place an accessory made of aluminum or dural in a steel blacking solution. It will be dissolved quickly.

Silver, copper and brass are not affected at all by the solutions.

The principal common trouble with both blacking and hot blueing solutions is loss by "drag out," or undrained solution remaining on and in gun parts when they are removed from the solutions and placed in the rinsing tank. This also contaminates the rinse water, though not to a damaging extent during a single blueing or blacking job.

It is not economical to use distilled water for rinsing, naturally, but an effort should be made to obtain rain or soft water for this purpose.

The blacking processes, if working properly, do not cause rust to appear on the metal being treated. If rust does collect, it is a sign that the solution is too weak.

Blacking solution dries to a white powder and if not thoroughly rinsed or blown out with air pressure from close places such as under barrel bands or band sights, the drying solution will work out to the air and build up a white, caked deposit, known as "bloom." This can be removed with slight pressure from wooden scrapers, sometimes

---

THE 7MM MAUSER (7 X 57)

Official military cartridge of Mexico and a number of other nations, the 7mm has enjoyed popularity as a hunting caliber all over the world.

In Europe and Africa it has been used for decades as a game cartridge and is still considered an excellent "small buck" caliber, used with expanding bullets. Bell, the famed African hunter, killed over 800 elephants with the 7mm, using 175-grain full metal jacketed bullets practically always for head shots.

Until the 1920s the 7mm was widely used by ballistic and firearms engineers in the development of small arms. With the 175-grain round-nose bullet they could get around 2,350 FPS at less than 40,000 lbs. pressure. The designers built the guns to operate the 7mm, then adapted the designs to other calibers.

American factories provide excellent 7mm hunting ammunition (not for elephants, though!) and the Western 139-grain high-velocity bullet is quite popular in the western United States. Winchester's 150-grain pointed-expanding is perhaps the best all-around bullet for the American hunter in 7mm, although the handloader can do a lot with such a flexible cartridge.

Both Remington and Winchester have in the past made their best models of rifles available in this caliber, as it has been quite popular in Latin America as well as in the United States.

rubbed away with oily cloth, or just scratched away with fingernails.

The addition of a couple of tablespoons of ordinary hydrated lime to most blacking solutions serves to prevent the mixture from hardening in the tank when not in use and so greatly simplifies pre-heating of the solution. The lime should be well stirred in, with the solution warm and, of course, empty of gun parts.

Finishing Non-Ferrous Metals

The coloring of silver, nickel, brass and copper in the gunshop concerns mainly sights, or other small parts. Aluminum alloys can be colored only by black paints or enamels, for the commercial anodyzing processes are highly complicated and require special equipment. The following are recommended:

Silver

To Blacken: Use swab to rub on silver nitrate solution until black, wash and dry.

Copper

To Blacken: Dip in pure nitric acid, then heat to dull red. Let cool, wash and dry. The Savage M99 rifles often have front sights made completely of copper, which often require refinishing.

To Blue: Immerse the metal in the following solution until the desired color is reached, then wash and dry:

Liver of Sulphur	1 oz.
Chlorate of Soda	1 oz.
Distilled Water	500 oz.

To make Bright Red: Immerse the metal in the following solution until the desired color is reached, remove and wash, dry in sawdust, then lacquer or varnish:

Sulphide of Antimony	2 drams
Pearlash	1 oz.
Water	1 pint

Brass

To Blacken: Mix in a glass container the following:

Potassium Sulfide	1 oz.
Ammonium Hydrosulphide	2¼ oz.
Water	1 gallon

Dip polished, cleaned parts until deep black in color, wash and dry.

To make Brass Blue-Black: Heat the following solution to approximately 180° F. and immerse the metal for one minute, or more or less as desired concerning color:

Copper Carbonate	1 lb.
Ammonium Hydroxide	1 quart
Water (Distilled)	3 quarts

To antique-finish Brass: Mix the following solution and immerse the metal in the cold solution for one or two minutes, drain well and let dry 24 hours, wash and rub with linseed oil:

Wine Vinegar	1 quart
Copper Sulphate	233 grains
Iodized Salt	470 grains
Sal Ammoniac	470 grains
Hydrated Copper Carbonate (Mountain Green)	1000 grains
Ammonia	470 grains

Nickel

To Blacken: Immerse until black in the following solution, then wash and dry, (use rubber gloves):

Nickel-Ammonium Sulphate	525 grains
Potassium Sulphocyanide	3 oz.
Copper Carbonate	2 oz.
Water (Distilled)	1 gallon

CHAPTER 20

Fitting Commercial Metallic Sights

INSTALLATION of metallic sights is too often passed over as being "elementary" and too simple a job to warrant much notice. This is far from the truth, and many a gunsmith spends years learning, the hard way, the little things involved in sight mounting.

Bore sighting is often the only means of alignment the gunsmith has on a particular sight job, and he must do the best he can. Bore sighting is a makeshift at best and should be considered only as an approximation, to install sights in the correct physical locations and to save ammunition when the arm is really sighted in later on a range. Any character who thinks he can adjust sights to a specified setting without actually firing on a target is kidding himself more than his customers. Barrel whip, forearm tension and the ammunition used, or to be used, all affect actual sight alignment in relation to bore alignment on center-fire rifles, and the type of ammunition used and the method of holding and gripping a handgun affect sight setting on pistols and revolvers. Thumb pressure alone can change a point of impact on a target handgun.

Having mounted a great many hunting telescopic sights as well as all types of metallic sight combinations, and having sighted-in a considerable percentage of these on big game rifles at ranges of 200 and 300 yards, I consider myself qualified to advise on bore sighting. My advice is—do not ever stick your neck out to state that a bore sighted arm will shoot within four feet of the desired point of impact, unless you have targeted the gun! I have mounted sight combinations which required only one-quarter minute change to put the customer himself dead on at 200 yards, and, with exactly the same sight combination, on the same type and caliber of arm, with the same bore sighting method, on the next job be off as much as fifteen minutes of angle.

The preceding paragraphs are intended to do one thing—make you think. A little experience on the range with different jobs will aid greatly in sight mounting. Model 54 and 70 Winchester rifles tend to shoot slightly higher and often a trifle to the left, as compared with other large caliber bolt action rifles, particularly if the forearm stud screw is very tight. Floating or semi-floating barrels, or barrels supported with light forearm pressure, as a rule shoot to a reasonably uniform point of impact in relation to bore alignment. The .257 caliber rifles tend to shoot high, regardless of the type of bedding or weight of the barrel. With .22 light rifles, remember the comments made in Chapter 18 regarding bedding and the takedown screw. Consider the caliber and the bullet weight involved—if the customer intends to use 220-grain bullets in his .30–06, do not align the sights as for the 150-grain load, or he will be unhappy over shooting about two feet low when he tries out the rifle!

Set up some sort of bore sighting target, a heavy vertical line with one heavy horizontal crossing line and a lighter crossing 1½" above the first (center to center) is excellent. If it can be 100 yards away, fine; if it is fifteen or twenty feet in the shop, okay too—You can get along. But *get used to your own setup*—for each type of job you do for quite awhile, check the bore sight picture vs sight alignment *after* the gun has been actually sighted in correctly by firing, and write down a note on the matter, giving approximate measurement in fractions of inches on your bore sighting target. This is of course the distance between the mark seen through the bore and the point on the vertical line cut by the line of sights. About 10% less than the distance between the line of sight and the bore axis will do for a start, at close range. Write down any pertinent information on each job—type of bedding, sights, caliber and such.

With handguns, about all you can do is note the type of ammunition and caliber. Midrange or light handloads will not shoot the same as full or service loads, particularly with the .45 pistol. No gunsmith can do much of a job in aligning sights on handguns, because of the many individual factors involved on the owner's part—does he hold the stock tight or loosely, does he hold a line of white between front sight and bull. Where does he hold his thumb, and similar differences. What is one man's sight picture will not necessarily work for anyone else, in the pistol game.

No one knows better than I that one man cannot sight in a rifle for another man perfectly, but it is possible in the great majority of cases to do so within one minute of angle, which small adjustment is usually within the capabilities of any man with normal intelligence.

It will sometimes be found that a specified sight will be unsuitable, such as a readymade ramp for the 1903 Springfield being too high for a particular 1903 rifle. Substitution of a lower ramp made for the 1917 Enfield will be the remedy. Some of the commercial ramps made are rather low so they require proportionally higher blades. The toughest deal is when a receiver sight does not go low enough and requires a very high handmade front, which usually does not aid the appearance of the arm. In all cases it is naturally best to have both front and rear sights as low as possible when the rifle is sighted for pointblank range, meaning 100 yards in this country. When the rear sight must be elevated considerably from its lowest position to sight the rifle at short range, install a lower front blade or bead.

Do not be a makeshift smith, or go alteration happy, but do not close your eyes to sound solutions of sight problems made possible by shifting around customary sight combinations and applications. If you have not the particular sight for a job as decreed by the sight manufacturer's literature, use your head and see if another sight can be made to fit correctly. If you have a Redfield 70 receiver sight with target knobs for a Mauser, and a Redfield 70 receiver sight with hunter knobs for a Springfield, and the customer wants a Mauser sight with hunter knobs, there is no law against your interchanging slides or knobs, providing you tighten all the screws correctly afterward. No gunsmith can be expected to carry on hand all the sights made for all guns, but the good shop will have a representative stock of front and rear sights by the best makers for the most popular types and models of guns in his locality.

DOVETAIL SLOT SIGHTS

The cross dovetail slot is widely used in this country to retain both front and rear sights in rifle barrels. Widths of the dovetail front sights for military rifles such as Mauser, Enfield and Springfield 1903 are arbitrary, and uniform only for the model rifle involved. Commercial sporting rifles have now, I believe, a $\frac{3}{8}''$ dovetail as standard, in all makes. This is the $\frac{3}{8}''$ bottom width, with .090'' depth. A modification of this of the same width and dovetail angle, but with .075'' height, had been used on a few center-fire rifles up to World War II. The old Stevens sights were $\frac{5}{32}''$ wide at the bottom of the dovetail, and .085'' in depth, so any aged Stevens rifles should be checked before attempting to fit new sights. Lyman lists a third dovetail dimension with a dovetail base width of $1\frac{9}{64}''$ and height of .090''. The Lyman catalog is very valuable for the chart it contains which gives proper height of front sights for almost all rifles likely to be encountered.

Today, with sight and slot sizes standardized, things should run smoothly, and someday perhaps will. The bug in the gunsmith's pie is sloppy workmanship by both sight manufacturers and gunmakers. Dovetails are cut crooked, undersize, oversize, too deep, not deep enough, and so on—a perfect fitting of a factory sight in a factory slot is the exception, not the rule. Probably the most common defect is poor machining of the male dovetail on the sights, in leaving rounded, poorly angled sides which do not fill up the barrel slots. This of course results in the joint not being as tight as it could be and the barrel slots are usually milled with full dimensioned sharp corners. There is not a great deal to be done in such cases. When the gunsmith slots a barrel for a particular sight he can of course allow for any irregularity in the latter.

The preceding dimension given as "depth" and "height" of dovetails refers to the thickness of the male dovetail portion only, and to the depth of the slot in the barrel. Practically all sights have a shelf or projecting platform at this point, and quite often these are improperly located, either high or low. If high, the sight when driven in position will show light between barrel and shelf. With the sight and the barrel dovetails permitting, the bottom of the sight dovetail can be filed off to compensate, but if both are of the correct size, to do so will reduce the width of the sight dovetail and so make for a loose joint. If low, the bottom of the shelf can be filed enough to permit the sight to position correctly.

Tightening a loose sight in a slot can be done in several ways, the best of which is by peening down the edges of the barrel slot. This can be done either directly by a steel hammer, or by a hammer and a large driftpunch. To prevent undesired damage to the slot, take an old sight and make it into a dovetail blank, using just the portion to fill the slot and place it in the slot when peening. Peening makes for a neater finished job than tightening by shims or a centerpunch.

To tighten by a centerpunch, which is possible sometimes when the sight is just a little loose, use a manual punch and hammer to make deep marks from left to right across the slot, in a double line, the deeper impressions being to the left. The punch extrudes a little metal up around each detent, which serves to bottom the sight.

With the adjustable open rear sight, it is often possible to drill and tap the sight through the dovetail for one of the little 6 x 48 "blank" screws furnished by the factories in rifles which are produced, drilled and tapped for standard receiver sights. The screw of course acts as a set-screw against the bottom slot, which should have a depression cut

GUNSMITHING

for the screw end. These screws have heads rounded more or less, and if of a length to go slightly below the top of sight when tightened, can be kept tight by using a hollowed punch to peen the edges of hole over the top of the screw. Do not get too strong on this peening job, or you will loosen the joint.

Cutting Dovetail Slots. Standard size sight slot milling cutters are now available, so the gunsmith with a milling machine can save a little effort, if nothing else, in slotting barrels for standard sights. As these cutters are usually made right, more often than not the sight will not fit perfectly! Undersize cutters are now sold by Brownell.

To cut a slot by hand is not difficult and, taking into consideration setup time, probably quicker than the milling machine. The tools needed are a 12″ mill file, an 8″ pillar file, an American Swiss 8″ triangular file #1 cut, a diesinker's triangular file, #2 cut, and a straight-edge. A bar of ground flat stock, ¼″ x 1″ x 12″ is ideal for the latter.

The rifle is leveled horizontally in the vise, by the level against a correct flat surface on the rifle. If you cannot find a place from which to orient the rifle, go by eye, checking against either the front or the rear existing sight. When a barrel is to be shortened and the front sight moved back, the job is simple—mark the barrel and the slot for the new sight position before cutting off the barrel. Use of two straight-edges laid in the slots will serve to line them up easily.

With the rifle leveled approximately correct and the portion under the proposed slot clamped in the vise, use the mill file to cut a straight slot across the barrel to almost the full depth—around .085″. This will be approximately 3⁄16″ wide, and is widened with a pillar file until it is as wide as the *top or narrow* part of the dovetail of the sight. Do not waste time measuring it—take an old sight (better have several different makes, to correspond with your new one) file the edges of the dovetail off, making it just a straight little bar, and use this for a snap gage in checking the slot.

When the slot is approximately the correct width and almost full depth it is time to check for cant, with the straightedge. If the rifle is leveled, the straightedge will show to any eye instantly whether or not the slot is true. It is simple to keep the slot at right angles to the barrel while filing, as the mill file or straightedge held against one side of slot will make obvious any error.

If the slot is correct, it is deepened to the proper size for the depth of the dovetail involved. If canted, the highside is filed with the narrow pillar file until it is correct when rechecked. The large triangular file, with one side ground smooth for several inches back from the tip, giving a 45° angle instead of 60°, is now used to widen the slot at the bottom, cutting the dovetail. The smooth side of course is down, sliding over the bottom of the slot and when by eye it appears to be reaching the correct dimensions, you use another old sight, this one with one of the dovetail sides filed a trifle, to make it undersize. By pushing and driving it into the slot and examining the walls of same, you will see where to clear out metal with the diesinker's file. When the slot will accept the old try sight all the way without a great deal of driving, you try and file the slot using the new sight for a model. The new sight should slide in smoothly by hand halfway across, and drive the rest of the way with a rawhide mallet.

Sights and slots are tapered very slightly, the right ends being wider. Therefore all dovetail sights should go in from right to left. Do not attempt to file a tapered slot from the start—the finishing touches with the fine file will take care of this point. Actually, the fitting of a dovetail sight takes less time than reading about it—from five to ten minutes is par for the course.

Keep one of the old barrels you will acquire which has a good factory slot in it and use it for a check gage on new sights which you buy. Try with the fingers all new front sights and slot blanks, sorting out the undersized and oversized ones, as a help in future fitting.

Fitting Dovetail Sights to Ramps. A number of factory and cheap commercial front sight ramps use standard dovetail sights, rather than plain blades. There is no real difference in fitting these than in fitting directly to a barrel slot, except that more care must be exercised. Except on the Winchester 54 and 70 with ramps integral with the barrel, no force can be applied against the sight unless the ramp itself is supported. I almost always file the slot in the ramp until it will accept the sight a little over half way without application of force, then squeeze the sight into place with the vise, having one jaw against the sight, the other against the opposite side of the ramp.

When installing a ramp of the dovetail blade type on a barrel, always fit the sight to the ramp before placing the ramp on the barrel. When the sight can be brought to correct position and is tight, drive it out and go ahead with fitting the ramp, sweating it, screwing it down if necessary, and blueing. The blade goes on last.

RAMP FRONT SIGHTS

The ramp front sight is today almost universal in use on metallic sighted hunting rifles. Its wide popularity has brought a half dozen readymade sight units on the market, some of the band type, others

.30 W.C F (30-30)

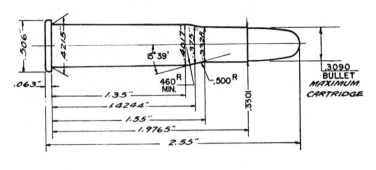

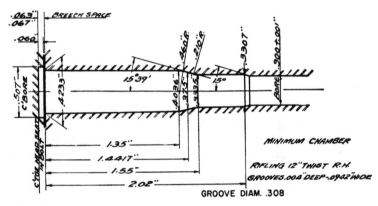

MINIMUM CHAMBER

RIFLING 12" TWIST R.H.
GROOVES .004" DEEP x .0942" WIDE

GROOVE DIAM. .308

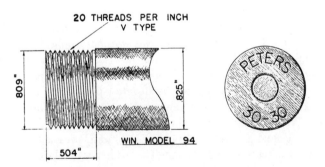

20 THREADS PER INCH
V TYPE

WIN. MODEL 94

This was the first bottle-necked "smallbore" hunting cartridge to achieve wide popularity. The designation originally meant ".30 caliber-30 grains of powder," in accordance with the custom of the time in nomenclature. Rifles of all types have been chambered for the cartridge—single shot, bolt action,

plain ramps. In the band type, which are easiest to fit, we have King, Redfield, Dahl and Terhaar sights available, all of excellent quality and appearance. In the plain sweaton ramps, with concealed barrel screw, we have Sukalle and Flaig sights, plus a number of others. Sukalle's is the best in appearance, having a hood and using Redfield type blades, not dovetails.

The band ramps are furnished with bands of diameters appropriate for most of our bolt action hunting rifles, but unfortunately there is not enough call for odd sizes to make it worthwhile for the manufacturers to make diameters smaller than .55″ or larger than .65″. While there is little demand for extra large diameters, every so often someone wants to cut a Krag to 18″ or something like that, and there is an ever increasing demand for small diameter ramps because of the growing popularity of lightweight rifles, with muzzle diameters from .45″ to .50″. So you may have to make a few ramps after all. The Pacific ramp, furnished unfinished to gunsmiths, allows considerable leeway in dimensions and a few should be carried in stock. Right after the war no commercial sights of this type were available, but as the shop had about two-dozen Pacific ramps in the rough, I did quite a bit of finishing and alteration on them. If they were not big enough, I sawed open the band, spread it out, welded in metal and then finished it up. If too large for a job, I would saw a slot, clamp the band together and weld it up again.

Most ramp work is merely a matter of minutes, except making a ramp from solid stock, as mentioned in a previous chapter. The band types all are made, or fitted by the gunsmith, to the correct taper and diameter of the barrel each is intended for, so that only a few taps with a mallet locates them properly on the barrel. Getting them exactly upright is sometimes rather difficult so far as it concerns the customer, but no great effort for the gunsmith physically.

With the set-screw universally used to hold these sights removed,

---

lever action—and are on the market today. Highly publicized, this is perhaps the most controversial cartridge we have. It is popular all over the United States as a deer cartridge, though experts condemn the rifles made for it. In a bolt action rifle, the .30–30 is very accurate, however, and though ballistics now class the cartridge as a medium-power one, it is thoroughly adequate for game of the deer class up to 200 yards. For a comparison, the .30–30 at 200 yards about equals the .30–06 at around 325 yards, using the same weight of bullet in each.

The cartridge is quite low-pressured and this, combined with the rimmed construction, makes for utmost safety in rebarreling and chambering.

and minus blade, a substitute blade is made, of any strip of metal of proper thickness six or eight inches long, and stuck in the slot, so that it projects high above the barrel. With the receiver level, any deviation from the vertical plane is clearly evident, and the ramp can be turned until it lines up correctly. Remove the high check blade and scribe the barrel carefully through the screw hole. If the ramp is very tight on the barrel and might perhaps suffer damage in removal, centerpunch through the hole in the ramp at the center of the scribed hole and make the countersink very carefully. It must be perfectly centered in order to hold the sight in the correct location. Coat the screw with your thickened linseed oil or other screw holding compound and wind it in as tight as you can. The blade is then installed, and with the ramp, the job is complete. Pins holding the blades should be pushed in with the vise, as mentioned for installing dovetail sights in ramps. Loose pins occur sometimes and a fast, though not good remedy, is to bend the pin slightly. The only right way is to make a pin which is a tight fit, cut it a little short (a trifle less than the thickness of the ramp) round the ends, put it in place and peen the hole at each end over it, using a small roundend punch.

OPEN REAR SIGHTS

Open rear sights, located on the barrel, are often of the dovetail type, but quite often a customer will want such a sight installed on a rifle not made for the standard type sight—military rifles in particular. The Mausers come with open military sights which are usually satisfactory to the hunter, and the same is true of most Krags, but Enfields and Springfields fare not so well. The previously discussed sight bands are rather unsightly, although easy to make. With a lathe, a milling machine with a sight dovetail cutter and a couple of feet of Shelby steel tubing it is possible to turn out a year or two's supply in half a day.

Much to be preferred over the band is the fixed base on the barrel, with a slot or a screw for attaching the open sight. These are much neater in appearance, support the adjustable type open sight better and there is less chance of the elevator slipping than when a band is employed. The same type base can be utilized to hold two or three folding leaves or an additional support for long telescopic sights.

In the case of telescopic sighted rifles, auxiliary metallic sights are often desired, usually a ramp front and an unobstrusive rear which does not interfere with scope use or removal. Open type sights can be installed on the front ends of Redfield, Buehler, Ackley, and other scope mounts with some metal of the base reaching to or beyond the front edge of the rifle receiver ring. These are usually just notched plates with the retaining screw holes slotted to allow movement of the sight sufficient for sighting in the rifle for short range. An open rear sight must be eight inches or more from the eye to provide any kind of definition. The installation is governed considerably by the position of the telescope tube, which limits the height of the rear sight above the scope mount base. On standard factory rifles, perhaps the best solution to the auxiliary sight problem is the installation of a folding leaf rear in the rear sight slot in the barrel. On custom rifles, the fixed base method can be used to install a folding leaf sight, as covered in the preceding paragraph.

APERTURE REAR SIGHTS—RIFLE

The micrometer adjusting receiver sight is now popular on almost all types of hunting rifles, as well as universal on target arms. There are several makers, some of whom produce three or four types. Lyman and Redfield can provide sights for almost any rifle mentionable, and Pacific, Vaver, Marble-Goss and Firearms International cover the most popular models.

To install any of them on rifles which require drilling and tapping necessitates first of all the level and a clamp. The small parallel jaw toolmaker's clamp is very useful in mounting receiver sights on large bolt actions, as one jaw will go into the bolt runway or extractor slot in the receiver and the top of the sight base. The sight must be held in some manner firmly against the receiver, adjusted to correct position as checked by the level, and one of the screw holes scribed. With slide type sights such as the Lyman or Redfield, the slide is removed from the base and a small block of metal—an old target scope block is satisfactory—placed in the slide slot in the sight base, for the clamp jaw to contact. The level is used against the bottom of the receiver and the top of the sight.

Positioning of the sight base against the receiver must also be done with the features of the receiver itself kept in mind, as well as to level the sight; the slide must not be over the clip slot, if any, and the windage knob on the slide must not interfere with operation of the magazine cutoff on the 1903 rifle. In this connection, using the Redfield Series 70 sight with target knobs on the 1903, there is no fore-and-aft leeway whatever and the upper front corner of the cutoff thumb piece must be ground off a little. With the Lyman 48 rightside mounting types care must be taken to set the base slightly ahead of the back edge of the receiver wall so that the little screw holding the takedown spring of the sight will not contact the bolt handle when the latter is operated. I believe that Lyman has just changed this particular feature of their sights, substituting an inside coil spring for the exterior flat type and doing away with the screw. New sights therefore will give no trouble at this point.

When the sight base is located in the proper spot and leveled so that the aperture will move straight up and down in a vertical plane, one of the screw holes—either one—is scribed through the hole in the sight base, and the base removed from the rifle. With a prickpunch make a mark in the exact center of the scribed hole, which is then deepened and cratered with the automatic centerpunch. Should the receiver be so hard that you cannot scribe it, polish off the blueing or other finish at the approximate location of both holes and apply a drop of copper sulphate, which will plate the exposed metal with a thin copper coating. This is easily scribed after the sight is located.

Should your punch fail to mark the surface correctly—often you can centerpunch with ease where you cannot make a scribe mark at all—use the washer-grinder method to grind away the metal inside the scribed circle. This system was described previously, as a means of protecting all but the exposed area from the grinder, through use of a washer or small plate with a hole in it which is placed over the proposed screw hole and held with tape while the hand grinder is used to grind the gun metal through the hole. If, after removing the surface metal from the hole, the remaining metal is too hard for a punch, or of course, a drill, that spot must be annealed. A wet cloth is wrapped around the receiver, leaving only the metal around the scribed hole exposed, and the welding torch is used to heat the hole area to dull red. If allowed to cool slowly, the metal is usually annealed sufficiently to permit punching and drilling.

Perhaps a better method of annealing for screw holes, and certainly a less bothersome one is to use an automobile battery. Two insulated wires—heavy single strand wire—are hooked to the terminals, one of the free ends skinned clean and turned into a hook which can be hung on the vise easily, and the other free end taped heavily with rubber tape as a handle, with about one-half inch of clean wire protruding. This end is touched against the center of the desired hole location to form a hot arc which anneals the metal at that point only. By this method, only the metal in the immediate area of the contact is softened, and there is no possible chance of discoloring the finish elsewhere as sometimes occurs with the torch on very hard receivers re-

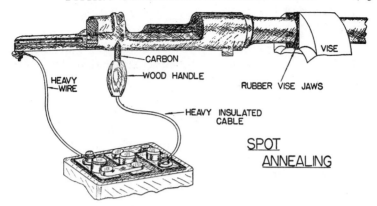

HEAVY WIRE

CARBON

WOOD HANDLE

VISE

RUBBER VISE JAWS

HEAVY INSULATED CABLE

SPOT ANNEALING

Using an auto battery is okay for annealing case-hardened receivers. One wire must be firmly attached to the receiver—a small bolt and nut through the tang screw hole or clamped against a flat surface anywhere is satisfactory. The other contact should be a heavy insulated cable, with a wood or rubber handle close to the tip, which is attached to a small pointed carbon. (The local motion picture projector operator will give you all you need—he throws them away when they get short, and you want short ones.) Intense heat is generated, which is why you need insulated cable and a protecting handle on the contact end. The system is recommended only for surfaces with a thin case-hardened skin, to prepare them for drilling and tapping.

quiring considerable heat or several attempts are made to anneal.

With the center of the hole punched, the receiver is to be clamped or otherwise supported on the drill press table—here is where the Palmgren angle vise comes in handy—and leveled both ways, so that the drill bit will enter the receiver at right angles to the face of the base. When mounting the Lyman 48 it is particularly important to get the holes in squarely, as the long mounting screw exaggerates the effect of an off-angle hole and the base will not pull down tight to the receiver at all points. The drill therefore moves parallel to the bottom of the receiver and at 90° longitudinal axis of the receiver.

It is important to drill and tap the holes correctly so that either screw will hold the base firmly and tightly to the receiver at all points. If the screws are angled improperly, they are under side tension when tightened, and tend to work loose.

The first drill used, assuming the sight screws are 6 x 48 thread, should be a No. 35 or 36—anything between a 33 and 40 will do, though, and the hole drilled in the receiver. Check the border of this hole against the scribed hole visible around it, and if the two are not concentric, make them so with a round diesinker or needle file. Then, with the receiver again leveled the No. 31 drill bit is run through.

As these holes are all completely through the receiver walls, only a single starting tap is required, being run far enough through to thread the complete hole full depth. Use a drop of cutting oil on the tap, to make for easier cutting and a tighter hole.

Attach the base with one screw through this tapped hole, tightening it down firmly. Now, try larger drill bits through the other hole in the sight base, taking the one which is the tightest fit, yet turns freely —it will probably be a No. 27 or 28. It should be sharp and have more of a point than for standard drilling. Put this bit in the drill chuck and again clamp the receiver, with the mounted sight base in the proper leveled position under the bit. Bring this large drill down through the screw hole in the sight base until it cuts a depression approximately $\frac{1}{8}''$ in diameter. Now remove the sight base and run your small drill through the receiver, centering and starting it easily in the crater created by the No. 27 or other large point. Again attach the base with the first screw and check through the second screw hole to see if it and the hole in the receiver are concentric. Ninety-nine times out of a hundred it will be, but do not take chances. Run the No. 31 drill through, tap the hole, check the screws to see if they protrude into the receiver on the inside, and cut each off to the proper length. Wipe out the receiver holes and with alcohol or solvent to remove all traces of oil from the holes and the attaching screws. Now put a little thickened linseed oil or Glyptol on each screw and in each hole and attach the base, making each screw as tight as you can without damaging the slot, clean up the inside of the receiver, assemble the sight, and the job is done.

A considerable timesaver in keeping steel chips from the drilling and tapping out of the receiver is to place a wad of Kleenex or other tissue inside the receiver ring and the bridge. When you pull it out after completing the drilling and tapping, nearly all the particles of steel come with it.

Shortening the attaching screws when they are too long can usually be done only by the grinder, as nearly all are hardened. To save fingers and grind screws evenly, make a plate of metal about $3''$ long and $\frac{3}{16}''$ thick, width can be from $\frac{3}{8}''$ to $\frac{3}{4}''$, and drill two holes in it, with deep countersinks for screw heads, one hole to accept and hold 6 x 48 screws and the other 8 x 40 screws. Should you require additional holes for other screw sizes, they can be made in the same bit of metal. In use, a screw is placed in its hole, most of the shank protruding of course, and by holding the bar in one hand and holding the screw in its hole and against the grinding wheel with a screwdriver in the other, the screw can be shortened with ease in a few seconds. The screwdriver serves to turn the screw while it is against the grinder and so cuts the end evenly. This works best against the side of a medium-coarse stone. Do not touch the screw for a few minutes after shortening—it will be hot! I have collected many a blister through impatience, but there is no reason for you to be stupid too.

Your sight attaching screwdrivers should receive considerable care, and it would be wise to make one tip to fit Lyman and Redfield screws, and keep it just for sight jobs. Even the case-hardened and heat-treated screws are easy to disfigure. It is also a good idea to keep extra screws on hand, and to use old ones throughout the mounting jobs, substituting the new ones for the final attachment.

The preceding paragraphs are intended principally to instruct in the installation of receiver sights on the Enfield, Mauser and Springfield rifles, but the same general theory is to be followed on all types of rifles and adjustable receiver sights. There are a few inexpensive sights made for .22 rifles in which the attaching screws do not enter the receiver at right angles to the vertical axis of the receiver, but approximately 15° above. The directions furnished with such sights specifically call attention to this point. A very few sights use screws smaller than 6 x 48, such as 5 x 40 or ⅛ x 40, or 3 x 48.

There are a few large rifles and a considerable number of .22 bolt action and autoloading rifles with round receivers having no discernable point to accomodate a level. Going by the takedown screw studs, trigger assemblies, and the like, is not too good, but aids somewhat. The best method is to use the eye, holding the sight with a clamp or tape on the completely assembled rifle and moving it until it appears to be square with the front sight. Dovetail front sights can be removed and a straightedge laid in the slot, against which the sight arm of the receiver sight can be compared in an attempt to make the two appear parallel.

Mounting closely machined micrometer receiver sights on ex-military rifles is often a trying job, for the receivers are not uniform. While the sight bases will locate properly and usually remain tight, there are often slight gaps between the base and the receiver wall. On a top-notch job, the sight should be mounted correctly first, then, with the receiver coated with Prussian blue or other spotting material, the sight is fitted to the exact receiver contour by careful filing. The rifle receiver wall can also of course be smoothed up, should it have deep toolmarks or ridges which cause a poor fit between the receiver and the sight base. With the 1917 Enfield rifle, the receiver bridge must be completely remodeled anyway, to accomodate any of the better sights, so it can be cut to fit the desired sight in the first place.

Installing receiver sights of the micrometer or plain elevation slide type on flat walled receivers such as lever actions and the better .22 autoloaders is very simple, as you need not bother about leveling. The side of the receiver is flat and the underside of the sight base is flat to match, so if anything is wrong, it is not your fault. I have never seen a base machined so incorrectly it threw the sight off or canted it, but should one come up, a few minutes with a file can square it.

Bolt Sleeve Sights. These are a horrible holdover from the '20s and rather unpopular today. The Lyman model cocking piece sight furnished for the Mannlicher-Schoenauer rifles is worthwhile, since no other decent aperture sight is available for this particular type of rifle. Due to tolerances between cocking pieces, sleeves, bolts and receivers, these cocking pieces and bolt sleeve sights have never been considered as accurate as the standard type, and also there has been criticism that they were too close to the eye on rifles of heavy recoil.

Marble-Goss now have an improved model of bolt sleeve sight for the 1903 Springfield, with strong builtin spring plungers to maintain uniform sight and bolt position. This may be practical for target or field. The sight is quite sturdy and well made, and easily mounted.

Auxiliary Aperture Rear Sights. On custom big game rifles having as main sighting equipment the telescopic sight, auxiliary peep rear sights of some type or another are often desired for emergency use. A few scope mount makers are now incorporating such sights in their mounts, so that when the scope is removed, metallic sights are instantly available.

I usually provide some sort of peep rear on custom jobs of the best grades by utilizing the existing folding leaf rear sights. A peep disc is made to fit in the usual notch-plate slot in the sight leaf, and the base cut to fit either the rear of the scope mount base or the receiver bridge behind the mount base. On the 1917 Enfield receiver, the bridge is of such length that it may be dovetailed to accept the standard folding sight base. These sights are zeroed for windage and readily adjustable, but the peep usually has enough elevation movement to allow for sighting and adjustment up to 400 yards by means of a small screwdriver. The bases can be either sweated or screwed to the scope mount, whichever is most convenient. The leaf must fold down out of the way of the scope tube, when the scope is mounted.

CHAPTER 21

The Mounting of Telescopic Sights

TARGET TELESCOPES

FOR the past decade or more, all target telescopic sights have utilized the same dimensioned mounting base, this being a dovetail in cross-section, approximately .475″ at the top, dovetailed inward 45° below, to a depth of approximately .185″ minimum. On the right side of the block, at the top, a milled cut is made in the edge of the dovetail, to a depth of approximately .060″ using an end mill .310″ diameter with relieved center so that the cut is deeper at the edges than at the center. The raised central portion forms additional support for the hollowed end set-screws used to attach the target mounts. Excepting a minimum of 1.20″ for the rear and .910″ for the front, there is no set length for the bases. Total height is of course governed by the barrel contour and the size of the telescope objective cell, and the scopemakers furnish all heights required for the various combinations of barrels and scopes.

Formerly, an odd size dovetail block, narrower than the above standard, was used by the Malcolm telescope people, but during the 1930s they also made their mounts to use the standard blocks if so ordered. This company was purchased a few years ago by P. O. Ackley, however no postwar scopes have yet appeared. Malcolm scopes required bases mounted 7.5″ apart, center to center. Also, the earlier Lyman scopes and others featured a pointed set-screw in the left side of the dovetail block instead of the milled cut described above. Present mounts will not hold firmly on such old blocks, nor will the old mounts hold well on present blocks, unless the latter are drilled to accommodate the screw point.

Our modern blocks, whether made by Lyman, Fecker, Unertl or others, are interchangeable insofar as the make of telescope is concerned. All are furnished hardened, and unnecessary strain is needed to keep these hard screws tight on the hardened block. I prefer to anneal my scope blocks, which allows the screw to bite into the block very slightly. I do quite a bit of shooting with heavy calibered rifles using target telescopic sights, and my screws never loosen while firing and I have never yet had to replace a block because it was burred or battered from the locking screw. This is my personal opinion on hard and soft blocks and you are under no obligation to accept it as gospel!

The present quarter-minute clicking rear telescopic sight mount is so made that it moves in one-quarter minute-of-angle change when the mounting blocks are 7.2″ apart, center to center; this is approximately 7¾₆″ on the fractional scale. Should it be necessary because of rifle construction to place the blocks 6″ apart, center to center, the value of the mount adjustment is .30″ per click per 100 yards instead of .25″ as with the 7.2″ the value of adjustment decreases; blocks spaced 14.4″ apart, center to center, would give one-eighth minute of angle adjustment with the standard quarter-minute mount, for example.

Excepting those made by Fecker, all blocks are solid and full proportioned in cross-section. Fecker blocks have their tops relieved by a longitudinal rounded groove, which is a holdover from the days before high target sights were made and which permits a slight lowering of the supplementing iron sight line. This weakens the walls of the dovetail considerably, and while in normal usage Fecker blocks are as good as any, I have seen five or six broken at the thin web behind the milled cut for the mount locking screw by heavyhanded gentry who bore down too hard on the screw.

Mounting the Blocks. The mounting of target scope blocks is one of the hardest gunshop jobs to do absolutely right, and one of the easiest to do in just any old fashion. The blocks should be perfectly level with each other, level with the rifle, and be parallel. This is hard to do, particularly to achieve the last condition, on account of the blocks not being made any too accurately. Check the next half dozen or so rifles which have blocks mounted that you run into, and see for yourself. A steel straightedge against the edges of both blocks very often reveals interesting angles.

Use of drilling jigs is very limited and I would not advise making any. The scope blocks themselves serve as foolproof hole spacers. It is not, however, a bad idea to make a marking template to aid in spacing the blocks, when the blocks to be used are the most common dimensions of 1.25″ rear and .91″ front lengths and the standard distance of 7.2″ is in order. This template is just a strip of metal 7½″

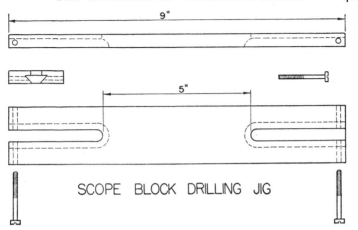

SCOPE   BLOCK   DRILLING   JIG

This is a simple affair which is practically foolproof. The clamp action on the blocks nullifies irregularities of individual blocks, and permits whatever spacing is most desirable, should the standard 7.2″ between centers not be possible or required.

It is just a bit of flat stock, approximately ¼″ x 1″ by 9″, or longer if wanted, dovetailed and split as shown, with clamping screws for holding the blocks tightly at the desired spacing. You use the holes in the blocks themselves for drill guides, marking the holes with a No. 27 or 28, then drilling with No. 32 and then 31. The jig is clamped on the barrel and of course leveled properly.

long, with a No. 27 hole close to one end and a very small hole—just enough to allow the point of your scribe—in the other, the distance between holes being 6⅚₂″. This is the approximate distance between the *front* screw hole of the *rear* block, and the *rear* screw hole of the *front* block. The rear block is always mounted first, and with its front hole only drilled and tapped, your template is held to the barrel with a short 6 x 48 screw through the No. 27 hole, and the scribe used through the front hole to mark a line across the top of the barrel about ⅛″ long. The template should not be screwed down so tightly as to prevent the slight pivoting necessary. The short line scribed on the barrel thusly gives the longitudinal location of the front block, as it is to be centered through the rear hole of the block.

If you insist on a jig, the only practical type is the type illustrated, having a dovetail slot slip over the tops of the individual scope blocks. You do not take a bar of metal and bore holes in it here and there. The tops of the scope blocks are supposed to be parallel, or close to it, so that if they are of the proper height, the dovetailed bar slipped over the tops will be reasonably parallel to the bore. This jig's principal advantage is simplifying the leveling of the blocks. The slotting of the top naturally permits variations in spacing of the blocks as well as for any differences in the blocks themselves. As the dovetail is machined to close tolerance in order to prevent any possibility of the blocks tipping when in it, only a slight clamping action is necessary, and the two clamp screws shown are sufficient.

Many factory bolt action rifles are now turned out with the receiver ring drilled and tapped for the rear scope block, however, it is theoretically best to have both blocks on the rifle barrel, instead of one on the receiver and one on the barrel. With a rigid mounting, there is some justification for the theory, since the receiver and the barrel do not undergo the same vibrations when a cartridge is fired, but with the flexible target mounts there is no true defect in the mounting blocks on the receivers and the barrels. Naturally, though, it is more practical in most cases to mount both blocks on the barrel, since the receiver-mounted block demands a higher front block and necessitates the entire scope being mounted as much as $\frac{1}{8}''$ higher than the barrel-mounted rear block. The distance, of course, is dependent upon the relation of the barrel diameter at the cylinder to the receiving ring. It is always desirable to keep any scope sight line as close to the barrel as possible.

A surface plate is nice for layingout scope mountings, but the vise, the leather jaws for it, a pair of parallel clamps and your little level are sufficient to do just as accurate a job, faster.

Clamp the protected barrel between the approximate block locations, level the rifle through use of the toolmaker's level against the bottom of the receiver, or other leveling point, if any. Clamp the rear block on the barrel, preferably butting against the receiver ring, level the block then scribe, punch and drill the front screw hole. Use the same small-drill-first system as for mounting metallic rear sights, to insure perfect centering on the scribed outline, drilling to a depth between $\frac{1}{8}''$ and $\frac{3}{16}''$, depending upon the barrel wall thickness and tap with starting, standard and bottoming taps.

Be very careful in tapping, not because of possible tap breakage, which is not common, but to insure a straight-tapped hole. With the starting and standard taps, avoid any tendency to bottom the tap, for many barrels are so soft that you can pull the threads out of the hole with the tap. Relieve the lip of the bottoming tap's first thread-cutting edges only, and it will cut to the bottom itself. A bottoming drill is used to clear the bottom of the hole *before* any tapping is done.

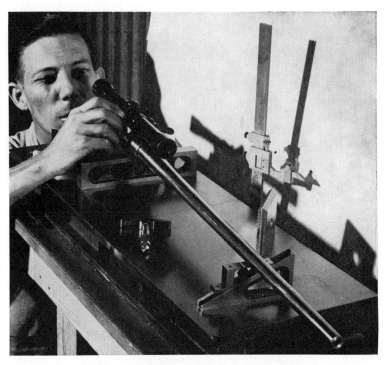

MOUNTING A SCOPE—WITH THE PROPER TOOLS

Items such as large surface plates, parallels and such as shown above cost bucks, but are worth while for the large shops doing a great deal of scope and sight mounting. The plate is, of course, kept level so that set-up time is cut down greatly.

However, if you cannot afford either the pictured tools or the room to set them up and keep them organized, do not be downhearted. A vise with leather jaws, a small level and a couple of clamps will turn out just as good a job. In fact, a lot of the time something is out of kilter on either receiver or mount base, and even with a technically perfect set-up such as shown you must fudge a little somewhere to achieve a perfect mounting. Meaning crosshairs standing plumb and in the middle when sighted in.

Drilling set-up in author's shop, showing support arm bolted to table of drill press with adjustable rest to allow leveling of rifle barrel-receiver assemblies for drilling in the mounting of sights and scopes.

The support of course rises and lowers with the table, being rigidly attached to it, while the adjustable plate allows adjustment for individual jobs regardless of how clamped in the drill vise.

The wood plate over bottom table or base of press allows mounts, sights or other parts to be laid on it without any possibility of marring.

It is wise to use an old scope block mounting screw which has been been found slightly undersize, for holding the block in the new hole and for holding your marking template.

Using the template, or marking by scale if your prefer, find the distance for the front block's rear hole. This block is clamped and leveled with the rear block and the rifle receiver, and the hole scribed. Your previous scribe mark on the barrel will transect this scribed circle and make centering the punch easy. The hole is drilled to a depth of from $\frac{1}{8}''$ to $\frac{5}{32}''$, bottomed clear, and tapped.

With both blocks held by one screw each, attempt to make them parallel by holding a straightedge along one side and tightening them down. Do the best you can in case the blocks themselves are not parallel-edged. Get them reasonably tight, scribe through the remaining two holes in the blocks, remove and centerpunch the approximate centers. Replace the blocks and with a No. 26 or 27 drill—whichever is the closest fit in the block holes—drill through the blocks into the barrel enough to make a crater approximately $\frac{1}{8}''$ in diameter. Again remove the blocks and drill and tap the holes with proper No. 31 drills and 6 x 48 taps.

In all drilling, the rifle must be leveled under the drill press so that the holes will be at 90° to the top of the blocks.

Clean all holes, remove all traces of tapping oil with alcohol or solvent, and run the new mounting screws into the holes, checking against the blocks to determine the correct lengths, shortening if too long. The perfect mounting will have the screw ends within $\frac{1}{64}''$ of the bottom of the hole. With the holes and the screws clean dry, apply your holding compound—gummed linseed oil, Glyptol, or your own secret formula—and attach the blocks.

All leveling and clamping is done with the blocks in the correct position of course, with the holding-screw cut to the right.

All target scope mounting blocks are mounted in the above manner. Rifles of the bullpup type require very high blocks, from $1''$ to $1\frac{1}{2}''$ in height, and it is advisable to anneal the blocks so that each can be drilled for an additional screw, making three holding screws in each block. These high blocks can be made in the shop of solid stock, or of standard blocks sweated to sub-bases to bring them to the required height.

Do not attempt to rush a block-mounting job. An improperly located hole is a headache almost impossible to cure. Remember you cannot move the blocks back and forth to drill a new set of holes without affecting the distance between them unless both blocks are moved exactly the same distance. The only remedy I know of for a wrongly located block is to obtain an extra long block without holes or with holes spaced so that they will not cover the incorrect holes in the barrel. By "wrong-located" I mean blocks mounted offcenter, not spaced incorrectly. Make or buy four long dummy screws in 6 x 48 thread, from two to three inches long. By screwing these in the barrel holes you can easily see if any of the holes are drilled or tapped at an angle, and so correct by judicious, appropriate side pressure on a sharp tap. Unless the holes and therefore the block holding screws are parallel, unequal tension will always be trying to loosen the screws.

Loose scope block screws are more often due to wear and strain in the tapped holes than to undersize screws. Should the screws fail to remain tight, the best remedy is to make slightly oversize 6 x 48 screws with an adjustable die. As a last resort, the hole can be enlarged and tapped for an 8–40 screw. Offcenter holes can sometimes be corrected by pulling the hole into the correct position with a small grinding stone in the hand grinder, clearing with No. 29 drill, and tapping with an 8–40 tap. However, it is extremely difficult to obtain perfect centering by this method, although approximate and satisfactory location can be achieved.

The dovetail rib is not much used today, although the Hill hunting scope mount base is a perfect example of rib use. The dovetail rib is nothing more than a very long scope block, profiled to fit whatever barrel or receiver contour is involved, and of course takes both front and rear mounts.

I have never felt it necessary to sweat scope blocks to a rifle, although the job would be easy, using one of the low melting point bismuth solders. The screws are of course used to locate the blocks. Any barrel so thin-walled as to restrict use of screws has no business with a scope on it!

HUNTING TELESCOPES

Knowledge of scope disassembly is vital to the present day gunsmith, since nearly all mounts require dismantling of the scope to some extent in order to place the mount rings or brackets on the telescope tube. Many of the straight tube type, such as Alaskan, Texan, Leupold and Stith require only the removal of the ocular cell, or eyepiece. The shorter eye relief scopes with enlarged objective cells require removal of the adjustment turrets as well, and the German scopes have the focusing ring to contend with.

This is not a treatise on optical constructions, but merely the common external work done by the average gunsmith in fitting mounts to scopes. Considerable care is required in handling scopes. Place a clean cloth or paper on the bench when a scope is to be taken down to any extent. Remove the eyepiece—all I know of unscrew readily—and set it, open end down, on a piece of clean paper. Have the mount rings ready to spread and slip on quickly, then do whatever is required next.

Weaver K-4 & K-6. Removal of the eyepiece and its locking ring is easily done. Loosen each adjusting screw 2½ turns, then with the screwdriver which fits the slots, remove first the two side screws in the adjustment housing or turret, then the central remaining one, and lift off the whole housing, with the adjusting screws or knobs and all. Slide on the mount rings quickly, remove the wedge or rod you have them spread with, and replace the adjustment housing, placing the central screw first and tightening it almost all the way before putting in the two side screws, and screw on the locking ring and eyepiece. Then spread the mount rings enough to move them to their proper positions without scratching the scope tube. Turn the adjustments back to their original setting.

The Weaver company places a scratch on the tube at the front edge of the adjustment housing, which indicates the approximate correct setting to eliminate parallax at 200 yards. Should parallax be found, it is only necessary to loosen the three housing screws and tap the housing forward or back until the scope is optically correct.

Unertl 4X Hawk and 6X Condor. The procedure for the Weaver scopes is essentially the same for the Unertls in principle. However, it is not necessary to loosen the adjustments before removal of the housings. Elevation and windage screws have individual housings, each held by one duralumin screw. File a screwdriver blade to fit the slots in these, polish it, and wire brush it to remove all sharp edges, for the soft screws are easily marked. No guide marks for repositioning of the housings are made, and there is no objection I know of to your making your own prior to removal from the tube. A common sewing needle will do, for the dural tube is soft and easily scribed.

For adjustment on the range, remember to loosen both screws before attempting to move either housing forward or back. Should it not be possible to correct parallax by this means, or if it is desired to focus the scope to very short range, it may be necessary to change the position of the objective lens. By movement of the housing you can determine which way to move it—if the glass is close to the desired setting with the reticule as far forward as it will go, you obviously want to move the objective lens back, to shorten the distance between them, and vice versa. Use pieces of automobile inner tube, from 4″ to 8″ square and, holding the scope in one hand, grasp the objective retaining ring at the front of the scope with the rubber in the other hand and unscrew. Wash the pieces of rubber before using, and keep in a dustproof container when not in use. Removal of the retaining ring permits the objective lens to slide out the front end of the scope. Catch it in a clean cotton cloth or tissue paper, and set it where it will not be disturbed or get dusty.

Looking down the open scope tube you will see a supporting ring at the lens location, which is slotted on each side. Make a wide "screwdriver" to fit this slot and turn the ring forward or back, whichever is required for adjustment. Do not forget that half a turn means a considerable adjustment in focal length on these scopes. Replace the lens and its retaining ring. Try not to touch the lens with the fingers, holding by the edges if necessary to hold at all in the bare hand. Scope manufacturers get very irate about people taking their scopes apart, but sometimes it has to be done.

Hensoldt. The Germanmade Hensoldt line is again available commercially in this country and as these are among the best scopes made, will continue to enjoy some popularity. The lightweight models with mounting rails are best mounted with special Tilden mounts, or by special adapting clamps, (Schmidt) to the Redfield. The Griffin & Howe special side mount can also be used, of course.

Under no circumstances ever remove the dovetail rib or rail from the bottom of the scope tube. It serves to strengthen the tube and maintain optical alignment of the instrument. The short rail on the objective end of the scope can and should be removed. I do this by clamping the dovetail itself in the vise, objective end up, and saw down to remove most of it from the main tube section, then with a mill file cut the balance down flush with the curve of the tube end, or rather, objective bell. Hold the scope in one hand and file with the other—do not try to clamp the scope tube in a vise! All this advice I have given you applies to the Zeiss lightweight type scope as well as the Hensoldt.

To disassemble the Hensoldt, unscrew the eyepiece, then slide one finger into the scope tube until it contacts the focusing ring nut; with screwdriver unscrew the focusing ring screw from the outside which, when completely removed, allows the nut to be removed by the fingertip holding it, therefore permitting the focusing ring to be slid back off the tube. To remove the adjusting turret, first unscrew the slotted cap in the top of the adjusting screw, then remove the inner screw revealed after the cap is taken off, and last, the two small screws holding the turret itself to the tube. Now lift the whole works from the scope. Replace in reverse order, of course.

In spite of the focusing ring, most Hensoldts seem to have a little builtin parallax. Adjustment of the objective lens is difficult, and correction is usually made by moving the crosshairs or post forward or back inside the reticule ring. This is an optical job, and gunsmiths should keep their fingers off.

Zeiss. The Zeiss scopes are perhaps the best in the world for mechanical construction, although Hensoldt and Unertl are equal optically. The focusing ring device has not been used by Zeiss for many years now, which means more leeway in mounting than with Hensoldts. Only the ocular cell, or eyepiece, and the adjustment turret must be removed to mount rings on the tube, and the operation is almost identical with that described for the Hensoldt. As in American scopes, changes have been made from time to time, so that all Zeiss or Hensoldt scopes are not exactly the same, even in the same models. Earlier scopes sometimes had the reticule attached to the turret, leaving the reticule cell inside the tube when the adjustment turret is removed. As with Hensoldt, dovetail rails must not be removed from lightweight scope tubes. In the Zeiss featherweights, a screw goes up through the rail from the bottom to lock part of the reticule cell inner housing.

Hunting Scopes—General. The American straight-tube scopes, such as Lyman Alaskan, Texan, Weaver K 2–5, and others, offer little trouble in mounting. It is seldom necessary to remove the adjustment housings, and if so, only a screwdriver or a small Allen wrench is required, to eject the holding screws and permit the housings to be lifted clear of the tube.

I know practically nothing about the new Lyman Challenger, except that it is ostensibly sealed against the weather and is not supposed to be taken apart outside the Lyman plant. The scope tube is slightly over 1″ in diameter so it requires different rings than the 1″ diameter Weavers and Unertls. Splitring or bracket type mounts are made by Redfield, Griffin & Howe, and others, so that the scope can be mounted without disassembling in any way.

The large Maxwell Smith scopes are patterned after the Hensoldt idea, and can be handled the same way.

The following tube diameters are considered more or less as standard, although some of the foreign scopes, particularly the lightweights, may be slightly under or over:

¾″	Weaver 330, 440, J 2–5, J–4, J–6, & G Series
⅞″ (22mm)	Lyman Alaskan, Texan, Leupold, Zeiss Zielklein, Stith, G–88, Vectra, Noske, Hensoldt Zielklein, and others.
1″	Weaver K 2–5, K–4, K–6; Unertl Falcon, Hawk, and Condor.
26mm	Lyman Challenger
26½mm	Hensoldt Dialytan, Zieljagd, Ziel-Dialyt, most Ajack scopes, Zeiss Zielvier, Zielsechs, Zielacht.
30mm	Zeiss Zielmulti, Ajack 10 x 50.

The matter of recoil can limit scope selection somewhat. Rifles developing 20 pounds of free recoil will injure all but the very strongest mechanical scope construction. All of the above scopes, excepting the ¾″ Weavers will safely take reasonable recoil, as from a .30–06, .270 or .300 H & H rifle the total weight of which, including scope, is not under 8½ pounds. However, for very light high-intensity rifles, such as the Remington 721 and .300 H & H, many of the scopes will not take it. For such rifles developing powerful recoil, the scopes to be used in the 2 power class are Stith Bear-Cub, Lyman Alaskan, and Leupold. In the 4 power class, Zeiss Zielvier, Hensoldt Dialytan, and Lyman Challenger can be used.

Defective Scopes. Defective scopes do turn up, mainly due to faulty assembly or poor factory workmanship, which is usually revealed after mounting when the rifle is fired a few times. Do not render a few defective yourself, however, by careless dismantling or poor storage. Remember that cemented lenses are sensitive to heat—do not park a good scope in the show window where a hot sun will shine on it for several hours each day. You are likely to suddenly find a few spots in the objective.

One little known defect in scopes which sometimes drives unknowing gunsmiths to drink their cleaning alcohol is the canted objective lens. Sometimes other lenses may not be mounted exactly correctly, either— I have seen four or five of the highest priced scopes with this ailment. Of course, if it is a new scope, and you discover it in time, shoot it back to the maker, who will be glad to fix it up. If you do not find out, or for other reasons cannot return it, you will have to compensate in the mounting.

A canted objective is one which is not at exact right angles to the axis of the scope tube. It causes an offcenter line of sight, angling away in one direction. Naturally, the scope will not boresight correctly, or even close, with any normal mount, no matter how you level and sight.

The scope tube itself will be at an angle to the bore of the rifle when correctly mounted. The mount must be canted, angled, or otherwise put in an abnormal position to permit correct use of such scopes.

The most extreme case I am familiar with is that of a local shooter, who, a few years ago, picked up second or third hand a scope of reputable make and a Stith mount to fit it and his particular rifle and brought the three to me to assemble. After putting the mount on the scope and trying both on the rifle, I realized something was radically wrong. So I put in one screw on each end, and weird as it looked, sent the customer out to shoot the rifle on the range. He came back, saying it lined up right, so I put in the remaining screws—four in the receiver, I remember correctly—and handed him the gun. He now gleefully allows gunwise strangers to examine the outfit, and they are aghast as they note the scope tube fully $\frac{3}{16}''$ out of line with the barrel in its short length and view the pronounced downgrade effect. Then he innocently says it shoots okay, and allows them to shoot it and prove it for themselves. The crosshairs are exactly in the middle of the field of view, and the rifle is sighted in on the button at 200 yards. The practicality of the job is perfect, but the appearance makes people go off talking to themselves!

Such scopes do not reveal anything at all wrong until boresighted with rifles and mounts. Any defect in the curvature of an objective lens also alters the line of sight from the axis of the scope. Years ago foreign scopes were made with offcenter objectives purposely, and the objective cell could be rotated to change the point of impact and therefore adjust the scope.

HUNTING SCOPE MOUNTS

American gunsmithing ingenuity for the past twenty years has in large part been devoted to design, experiment and production of hunting telescopic sight mounts, with the result that we have over a dozen makes now available.

European gunmakers and smiths always considered the telescopic sight an accessory to the rifle, and while very fine scopes were made, the mounts provided were, as a rule, more detrimental than helpful. Styling their rifles for use with open metallic sights, the scopes usually were mounted very high—so high as to permit use of the metallic sights with the scope mounted. This, of course, made practical use of the telescopic sight difficult, and the mountmakers, anticipating the customer's eventual disgust, provided for quick removal of the scope from the rifle, to allow easier use of metallic sights. The mounts were

.300 SAVAGE

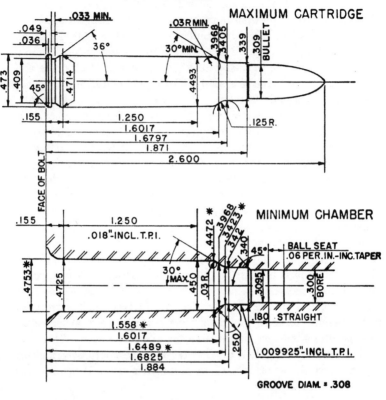

MAXIMUM CARTRIDGE

MINIMUM CHAMBER

BALL SEAT
.06 PER. IN.-INC. TAPER

GROOVE DIAM. = .308

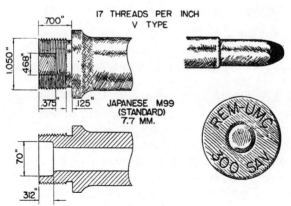

17 THREADS PER INCH
V TYPE

JAPANESE M99
(STANDARD)
7.7 MM.

high, heavy, and practically never returned to the correct positioning when the scope was removed and replaced in the field. Last, but not least, most foreign scopes were made with the elevation adjustment only contained internally, so the mounts had to be adjustable for windage. There is nothing wrong with this idea, except that the fur-riners would not pivot the front section of the mount, and generally depended upon bending the scope tube by side pressure in the rear mount for windage adjustment!

American riflemen very soon discarded the European concept of the scope sighted rifle, and gradually the present idea was evolved, to the end that the telescopic sight, if it is to be used at all, is a part of the rifle in the same sense that metallic sights are a part of the arm. Ameri-can gunsmiths now design scope rifles with the thought that the tele-scopic sight is to be used either at all times, or at all times when the scope is physically usable. In other words, the scope is not an ac-cessory, but becomes a major part of a rifle when mounted.

So our mounts are made to provide the most efficient use of tele-scopic sights. In order to keep buttstock proportions—drop, comb and cheekpiece—as close as possible to the iron sight standard, which for balance, fit and appearance is desirable, the telescopic sight is mounted as close to the rifle receiver as possible. In the case of some mounts and scopes, the scope sight line is less than ½″ higher than the metallic sight sight line on the same rifle. The mounts are made to attach to the

THE .300 SAVAGE

This cartridge was developed several years back to give the left handers and lever action adherents a cartridge comparable to the .30–06. Ballistics are practically the same as the 1906 cartridge, but the .30–06 has improved considerably since the .300 Savage came out, so that there is now a gap be-tween the two in performance.

The .300 Savage has been considered seriously as a military cartridge, since its short length is well suited to automatic weapons.

Literally every type of sporting rifle has been chambered for the caliber, bolt, lever, autoloading and slide—(yes, Remington made a few slide action .300s once). The cartridge is at its best with the 150-grain bullet at 2,660 FPS.

The Savage Model 99 rifle, in this caliber, makes a very light and handy rough country hunting rifle. The .300 Savage cartridge will do anything the modern .30–06 will, providing you are 100 yards closer, therefore at ranges of 225 yards or less is a thoroughly competent caliber.

The Japanese Model 99 action is well suited to rebarreling for the .300 Savage cartridge, which will feed well through its magazine without any alteration.

common rifles without requiring any alteration to the receivers other than drilling holes for screws and/or pins. Mounts with windage adjustment provide pivoting movement in holding parts, so that the telescope itself is never under strain.

Most Americanmade mounts provide for reasonably quick removal of the scope from the rifle, although in most cases this results from manufacturing and attaching problems, rather than being a deliberate effort to provide the shooter with a quick choice of metallic or telescopic sights in the field, as were the foreign mounts.

There are three types of mount construction—the quick-detachable, the detachable, and the fixed. The first is exemplified by the Ackley-Turner, Stith Mastermount, Kesselring and others. Detachable mounts are Redfield, Griffin & Howe, Tilden and such; and fixed mounts, the Weaver U & Q types, and custom one piece mounts.

In the three types, we have two styles—top mounting and side mounting, referring of course to the point on the receiver or the barrel against which the mount base is held when attached. The side mount is seldom desirable, except on jobs where metallic sights are occasionally used, since it leaves the top of the receiver clean. The top mount is stronger and less likely to loosen than the side mount, but, except for the Kesselring Q-D type, leaves bases on the top of the receiver when removed, which calls for special metallic sights should emergency sights be desired on the rifle.

Handling of Rings, or Mount-Clamping Bands upon the Scopes. The most accurate mounting job possible can lose its appeal to the customer if the gunsmith scratches the scope tube in placing the mount rings on it. All the bands are split on one side at least, and made so that they will clamp the tube without the split ends meeting. Practically all have some spring to them, although the Tilden rings are the only ones I am familiar with which are spring-tempered. The split can be spread $\frac{1}{8}''$ without damage to the ring, although it is not usually necessary to open this much. I have used wooden wedges, aluminum, brass and steel plates, coins, and ordinary screwdrivers for the job, but the best and most sensible thing to do is to obtain two bits of soft metal— aluminum or dural—polish them to a thickness of approximately $\frac{3}{32}''$, with one edge deep rounded so that it can be forced into the rings in the closed position. They can be from $1''$ to $1\frac{1}{2}''$ square, with rounded corners. The ring clamping screws should be removed entirely before attempting to spread the rings, and it is wise to take a smooth bar of steel, around $\frac{1}{4}''$ square, and scrape the inside of the rings also. This will tend to eliminate any burrs which might scratch the tube.

It does not hurt to use it an angle on the inside of the rings, either, to create a microscopic bevel through burnishing pressure. And for real insurance, take a small square stone and make a pass or two through the ring with one corner in the split, to cut the sharp edges down a little.

Often rings can be spread without damage by a smooth screwdriver edge inserted up through the bottom of the split, from the inside of the ring, so that the holding wedges can be introduced without strain. The foolproof method of spreading rings, possible where the clamp-screw holes are drilled and tapped completely through the ring over the split, is to remove the screws completely, place a thin metal plate in the split and force it and the other unthreaded part of ring back, thereby spreading the ring, by putting the screw through in reverse.

Place the rings on the tube with the fingers, to the approximate locations, then remove the wedges so that the rings will close on the scope and not move around to cause possible scratching, while you are reassembling the scope. Be sure to read the manufacturer's directions and do not get the rings turned around. The final position of the rings determines the correct eye relief setting for the customer, so it is best not to tighten them until he is at hand to try the rifle with the mounted scope. Spread the rings again of course, so that the scope can be moved freely within the rings without damage. You can set the reticule upright easily when the rifle is still leveled in the vise, but do not be surprised when the customer wants it turned a little this way or that. I have come to the conclusion that about 70% of our riflemen cant a rifle slightly, myself included. Do not worry about it, or you will spend half your time arguing with the trade. Tell 'em about it and let them decide for themselves. After all, if they see things the same way every shot, no damage will be done. The slight amount of cant usually found will not be enough to throw shooting off enough to matter anyway at the average hunting ranges of 350 yards or less.

In tightening ring clamp screws, do not get too strong. It is possible to damage many of our scopes through excessive pressure on the rings as the thin tubes can be cramped slightly. Wind in each screw until it tightens up, then give each a quarter turn at a time until stiff resistance is encountered, then stop. Should they not be tightened enough, the scope will slip under recoil and very likely the tube will be scratched.

SIDE MOUNTS

The Noske side mount was the first Americanmade scope mount worth using, and the present Noske model is perhaps the best of its type available. It is made of steel, is quite strong, and returns very reliably when scope is removed and replaced. In spite of being made of steel, the weight is small. I consider this the best side mount available. The old Niedner mount was perhaps a little better, but much heavier, and is not available today, anyway. Noske makes his mounts for the 22mm diameter scope only, and at present is not furnishing mounts except with his scopes. No doubt later he will be caught up enough to sell mounts separately.

Griffin & Howe. The G & H side mount is lever tightening, has a steel base and a mount bracket of aluminum alloy. These are very well finished mounts, furnished for practically every diameter of scope tube in existence, and for foreign scopes with dovetail mounting rib on the tube. The scope rings are detachable from the main arm of the bracket, so that it is fairly easy to install them on any scope tube. Standard single split rings are furnished for most scopes, and a double split set of rings for the Lyman Challenger scope, so that they may be installed upon that scope without disassembling it in any way. The G & H mount is fairly popular with the dilettant set of sportsmen, but is not considered strong or rigid enough for the dyed-in-the-wool shooter.

Echo. The Echo side mount is also of the dural-bracket, steel base construction. The clamping system is different than any other, depending upon screw-activated steel tongues engaging milled cuts in the steel base. The bracket is one piece, and the rings are not removable. The base mounts in the same manner as Noske, G & H and Jaeger, using three screws and two taper pins. The Echo is one of the most difficult mounts to attach correctly, as the base cannot be clamped to the receiver very easily for liningup. As a side mount, the Echo is not bad. Theoretically, the attaching system is not the best, as foreign matter can easily prevent the correct fit between the bracket and the base, but in practice the mount is satisfactory. At least the few I have mounted have stood put and the owners claim they can take the scopes off and put them back in the same place. Which is *the* test. All American scope diameters can be accommodated.

Jaeger. Jaeger mounts are well made and possibly next to the Noske in strength, although light alloy is used for the bracket. They employ the sliding dovetail engagement of bracket and base, as in Noske and G & H, and are available with either one or two locking levers. The dovetail is not split, and the clamping action is by grooved plates (activated by locking levers) against milled cuts in the base. The mounts are made for American and some German scope diameters.

Mounting Side Mounts. The side mounted scope has a problem all its own—inertia of the scope itself acts against the recoil of the rifle to cause a twisting action of the mount base against the receiver, which tends to loosen the mount screws. Because of this, it has become standard practice to install taper pins through the mount base and the rifle receiver, the idea being that the pins make a rigid joint and prevent any possible fore-and-aft movement of the base on the rifle and so take the punishment of the recoil, while the screws do their own job of holding the base tightly against the receiver.

The taper pins as a rule create a problem in cutting off and finishing, in the case of a mounting job upon a finished rifle, as the ends must be cut flush with the base and the inner face of the receiver wall, which is hard to do without disturbing the blueing. I do not believe that taper pins are absolutely necessary in all cases. One substitute system I have used a few times replaces them with screws. After the base is installed and held with the three main screws, a No. 29 drill is run through the taper pin holes in the base and through the receiver wall. This hole, through both base and wall, is tapped for a headless 8 x 40 screw threaded all the way, which replaces the pin. One of the main reasons for the side mount bases loosening is the use of 10–32 holding screws, which are too coarse to hold in the thin receiver walls of some rifles. The 10 diameter is desirable, but we need more than 32 threads per inch. About 40 would be right, but unfortunately there is no 10–40 thread.

The first step in attaching a side mounted scope to a rifle is to install the bracket on the scope. Then, with the rifle clamped and the receiver leveled, the scope, bracket and base can be assembled and clamped on the receiver for preliminary viewing. Eye relief can be figured approximately, and the base marked at the most appropriate spot on the receiver, which is the desired location. By using a level or square on the scope base you can determine if the base and the receiver contours are correct—if not, make 'em so. Locate, punch, drill and tap the center hole only, and attach the base and as the holes are completely through the receiver wall, only the 10–32 starting tap is necessary. The drill used is the No. 21. For thin receiver walls not too hard, such as polished down nickel-steel 1903 Springfields, use the No. 22 drill.

With the central screw hole made and the mount and scope assembled to the rifle, the hard part begins. You boresight to the very best of your ability and experience and mark either of the end holes through the base. After drilling and tapping this hole, the mount is attached by two screws and you head for the rifle range with a short prayer that the point of impact and the point of sight through the scope are somewhere

30 US (30/40-KRAG-JORGENSEN)

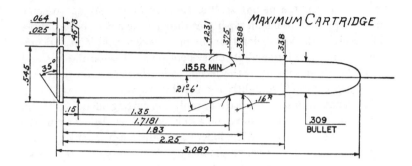

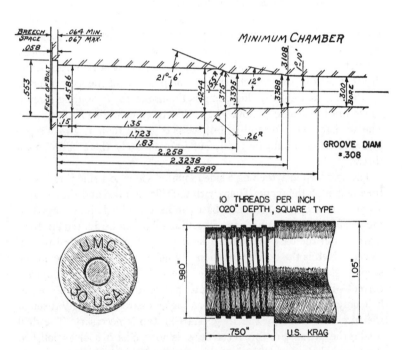

Since Winchester dropped their M95 rifle, no arm has been made for this cartridge, however, thousands of Krag rifles are in use, and likely to remain in service for many years to come. I think I have seen only two broken parts in Krag rifles, which is a testimonial to their sturdiness.

Present ballistics are similar to those of the .300 Savage, in fact, Winchester lists the same muzzle velocity of 2,660 FPS for the 150-grain bullet in both Krag and .300 Savage cartridges.

in the neighborhood of each other. At least, so close together that the necessary adjustment to sight the rifle perfectly will not take the sight reticule far enough from the center of the scope field to be noticeably objectionable. Windage adjustment can very often be aided by filing or milling the underside of the mount base so that it will point the scope to one side or the other, as desired. Elevation is the problem—should you find the scope too high or low for internal adjustment, remove the end mount screw, and loosening the center one very slightly, pivot the scope and mount on the rifle to the approximate correct location, as shown by boresighting on the range. Holding the scope and mount in the correct position, mark the remaining screw hole through the base.

Drill and tap this third hole and again head for the range, with the scope and mount this time held by the center and the new end screws. You should have no difficulty sightingin the rifle now, keeping the reticule centered in the scope. Back in the shop, check the first end screw hole location against the hole and countersink in the mount base over it. Usually, the best thing to do is to grind or turn the head of the mounting screw slightly, so that it will go into the slightly non-concentric hole easily. It is possible in most cases to screw it in without great difficulty as it is, since the hole location is never more than a few thousandths off, but because unequal strain on the screw head sides tends to loosen it, clear the head so it is free in the countersink. Keep the scope mounted while you wind in this last screw and find a friend to look through the scope at some aiming point while you do it, to see if the mount pulls in any direction. If it does, find out where the tension is and relieve whatever point causes movement—it may be a high spot on the receiver, incidentally. Should the mount screw up tightly, check your screw lengths, remove and cut them off, clean the holes and set in again with your holding compound.

Gunsmiths will have an increasing number of rebarreling jobs on Krags in years to come, and I hope they will keep in mind that the limit of the rifle action is under 45,000 pounds in pressure strength. Rebarrel for the .30–30, .30–40 or .25–35 cartridges. Some "improved" versions of the Krag case have come out, but do not attempt to ream out a standard Krag issue barrel to increase the chamber capacity. With a heavy breech custom barrel this can be done to a limited extent. In the days when the Krag was in wide use as a target arm, hot handloads would sometimes swell the barrel and chamber, expanding the rather thin walls to the point of causing difficult extraction.

P. O. Ackley will rebarrel the strongest Krag actions for his Improved Zipper cartridge, but the rifle is not at all well adapted for telescopic sight use, which limits its suitability for vermin rifle application.

Now for the taper pins. Drill the receiver through the two pin holes in the mount base and ream with the recommended reamer until the pins project about $\frac{1}{32}''$ through the receiver wall. Clean the holes and the pins with alcohol or solvent and set the pins in the holes—an arbor press is handiest for the job, although a strong vise can be employed. The hammer is of course, the last resort, and if you have to drive the pins with a hammer, do it with one good blow on each. Repeated hammering tends to loosen the pins in the holes. With any means, the inner receiver wall must be supported at the pin location. A short section of old .22 rifle barrel, milled or filed to fit into the receiver wall, centered of course over the end of the pin, makes a good anvil. After the pins are set, saw them off on the outside, if they are sawable, and grind flush with the base. Some pins are hardened all the way and can only be ground down. Small narrow grinding wheels will reach into the receiver and cut the ends flush with the receiver wall. A popular method in the past was to employ thickheaded attaching screws and use a surface grinder to cut the heads and pins down and make a clean face across the base, with no screw heads, slots or pins visible except as round dots after blueing. This does look nice, only it complicates things to beat the devil when any of those slotless screws loosen up! This infrequently does happen, and the idea is worthwhile on the best of jobs.

The described manner of mounting, laborious as it sounds, is the only method by which you know the job is going to be right before you even start. To go straight ahead and make a complete job of it without test firing the rifle is to fly in the face of the gods, as the saying goes. You may be right, and you may not, and if you are not, times are going to get tough when the customer finds the crosshairs or the tip of the post away down in one corner, or so high further adjustment is not possible. The cut-and-try business is slow, but it is close to foolproof.

Drilling for the side mount must be done with regard for leveling of the receiver under the drill, and the same principle of using a smaller drill than tap size first as previously described should be followed. Quite often it is necessary to spot anneal for the screw holes, which is done by acetylene torch or hot arc. It is possible to drill for side mounts horizontally, in the lathe, providing you have a milling attachment for the lathe. The milling attachment adjustments can be controlled very closely, and the rifle receivers clamped in almost any position firmly.

Weaver Side Mounts. The general gunsmith mounts many of the little Weaver low priced scopes on .22 rifles, using the pressed steel N mount. These are easy to handle on some rifles and hard on others. Only a few models are made, each presumed to be usable on a number

MOUNTING A LYMAN 48 REAR SIGHT

Sight-mounting layout, with minimum of equipment. The rifle is held by barrel in vise, protected by leather, and leveled by using the Starrett level on bottom of receiver. When rifle position is satisfactory, the vise is set up to hold it firmly, then the sight base is clamped against receiver as shown.

The clamp jaw against the sight is covered with masking tape to prevent any marring of the finish. The base is then moved against the contour of receiver until top is level, when clamp is set tightly and a thin scriber used through one of the mounting-screw holes to outline correctly the location of the hole. Removal of the base and careful center-punching in the exact center of the scribed hole allows drilling at the proper spot.

In the illustration, an old target scope mounting block is placed in the dovetail slot of the Lyman 48 base for the clamp to bear against.

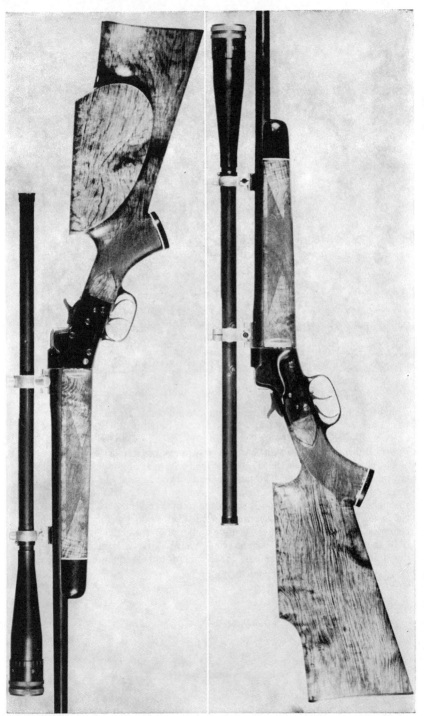

An old Remington Hepburn action after being rebarreled and stocked for scope sight use as a varmint rifle.

of rifles and often it will be discovered that a specified mount will hold the scope too far to one side or the other on a particular rifle. You put it in the vise and straighten or bend it until it centers the scope over the bore. Unless it is an offset deal, of course.

With the scope in the mount brackets, hold the assembly to the rifle while boresighting to get the approximate location, then clamp or hold it otherwise, while you scribe one of the four holes. Drill and tap this hole—8 x 40 thread, using a No. 28 or 29 drill bit, and attach the scope with the one screw. Move the mount until it boresights correctly, then scribe another hole and make this hole. Do it one hole at a time— should anything cause one hole to go off, you can compensate on the others. It is good insurance to assemble the rifle after two holes have been drilled and tapped and the scope held by these, and fire a test group.

You may be unpleasantly surprised to find your careful boresighting has doublecrossed you. If so, and the rifle shoots far high or low, remove one screw and pivot the mount very slightly to the correct position and fire another couple of shots, holding the scope in position with the one screw and shims or clamps. When it is correct, scribe another hole. Drill and tap this, and attach the scope with this screw and the preceding one and again test fire. It should be right on the button, and leaves only one hole to be drilled and tapped, and one in the mount to be pulled by file slightly up or down to permit the first incorrectly located screw to enter properly. It is work, but you do not have to worry about the job bouncing back.

Should the scope point offside, remove the scope from the brackets, and the mount from the rifle. Clamp an 18″ or 20″ length of ¾″ round stock or heavy tubing in the mount brackets, and the base of the mount in the vise, and twist. *Do not* try to bend the mount on the rifle with the scope—the tubes bend as easily as the mounts. I keep a length of ¾″ cold rolled steel on the bench all the time and it sees plenty of use for these jobs.

Every so often a peasant walks in with a Weaver mounted away off on his .22, usually due to the guy that mounted it not paying any attention to the fit of the stock, which bends the barrel out of line when the rifle was assembled after the mounting and sent out without any testing. Clearing the forend enough to relieve the barrel may fix things up, but sometimes the whole mount is off at an angle to the line of the bore, in which case bending the mount will help. Occasionally it will be necessary to pull the holes in the mount up or down to change the angle of the mounting. Do this by holding the mount with one or two screws loose enough to allow correct positioning, scribe the amount to be filed from the other holes and file this away and set in the screws for test firing. If satisfactory, remove the mount and in the now oblong holes, weld in a drop of metal to take up the undesirable space. This is of course filed down and the hole cleared to proper fit for the screw head.

Use sharp 8–40 taps on these soft .22 rifles, in order to get clean, good threads as the metal is none too strong.

Weaver U & Q Side Mounts. These extruded dural mounts are one piece affairs similar to the steel N mounts, but of course are of very much better appearance. The U holds the 1″ diameter scopes, the Q the ¾″ diameters, and they are identical otherwise. The attaching screws are 8–40, four in number. These should always be inspected for burrs on the heads, in order to prevent scratching of the mounts during installation.

These mounts cannot be bent, and adjustment for lateral liningup is by filing the underside of the base off at one end or the other, to change the angle at which the scope is held over the bore axis. Few of them can be leveled with clamps and bubble, and the eye must be the mainstay. Holding the assembled scope and mount on the receiver, boresighting, and scribing is essentially the same as with the N mount, and the mounting procedure almost the same. The only real differences are that you must work on large rifles of hard metal, and as a rule, with larger scopes having more parallax at short range to gum up the boresighting somewhat.

With the U side mount, it is possible to mount the K 2–5 scope on Springfield and Mauser rifles ahead of the bolt handle, thus avoiding bolt alteration and scope safety work. Many hardup customers will take advantage of this if advised of the possibility. On some 1903 rifles, the gas escape port is so large as to interfere with one of the screw holes. Move the mount back enough to clear it if possible. I suppose three screws would hold all right in a pinch, but I would equip the customer with a screwdriver on such jobs! Incidentally, the 1903 rifle is easy to locate this U mount on, as the index mark for the barrel set on the left-hand side of the receiver ring is the correct center line for your row of holes.

The Weaver U mount is the neatest and almost the only one available for the Krag rifle. The U2 should be used, offset to the left enough to allow ejection of the fired cartridge cases. Krags usually have a thin case hardening which can be punched but not drilled. Cut this away with the hand grinder at the hole locations. The rear mount screw may interfere with the magazine cutoff, and drilling its hole must be done very carefully, or the drill will skate down when its point contacts the far wall of the cutoff axis pin hole. The screw can be cut very short so as not to interfere with the cutoff functioning—it will not hold any better if longer.

A few years ago when autoloading rifles were legal for hunting in my state, I mounted a few Weaver K 4s and K 2-5s on Remington Model 8 and 81 rifles. The sad discovery was made that there was not enough of the web cut away between the mount rings to permit the adjustment housing to be turned to bring the reticule upright. Filing the web helped this, but it was found that the windage screw portion of the turret obstructed loading, so we turned the scope a quarter turn to the. left and made the elevation screw act for windage and the windage screw act for elevation.

Weaver Detachable Side Mounts. These mounts employ a base, attached the same as the U mount, and a bracket with two large coin slotted screws which engage in holes in the base to permit reasonably fast detachment and attachment.

TOP HUNTING MOUNTS

I cannot cover all mounts but will endeavor to touch upon the most popular ones. The principles of mounting are of course very similar, if not the same with all, and the gunsmith will have no difficulty with unfamiliar mounts, particularly as the manufacturers almost always put out detailed instructions with each.

Tilden. This is my favorite, though it is not as easy to install as most top mounts. A bridge type mount, meaning with two separate bases which hold the scope so as to bridge the gap between receiver bridge and ring, it is extremely strong and tightly fitted. The bases are hardened and cannot be filed to fit an off standard rifle receiver. The Tilden mounts can be furnished for ¾", ⅞", 1" and 26½mm diameter scopes, for nearly all bolt actions and the Model 99 Savage rifles. Also for the foreign dovetail mounting rail scopes, on special order. For these, it is best to send the rifle and the scope to Tilden for the mounting job, as quite often the dovetail dimensions vary from scope to scope.

In mounting the Tilden, the front base goes on the rifle first. With the standard Mauser, Springfield, or Enfield base, the lip on the base fits the rear of the receiver ring—in other words, it laps over the back end, not the front. Level the base with the bottom of the receiver, scribe the rear hole, punch, drill and tap it, going completely through the receiver, of course. Attach it with one screw and scribe the front hole. This is a blind hole and should be around $\frac{5}{32}''$ deep and there is no objection to its contacting the threaded portion of the barrel. Drill and tap this hole, to the bottom, clean the holes and the screws, and set the base on firmly.

The rear Tilden base is not hard to install, although almost impossible to level with instruments. However, the front base serves as a guide in alignment, and it is quite easy to move the rear until its top is parallel with that of the front, gaged by eye. With a parallel or a C clamp, hold it in the correct location until one hole can be scribed, then drill and tap this hole, going through the bridge. Holding the base to the receiver firmly with the one screw, spot the second hole with a No. 27 or 28 drill through the base, which is thick enough to serve as a jig, then drill with No. 31 drill and tap. The Tilden mounts with 6 x 48 screws.

The Tilden rear mount base for the Springfield rifle attaches with two angle screws, one on each side going into the thick portion of the bridge below the top. Locating the holes is not much more difficult than for the top locations, but care must be observed in drilling that the holes do not move down out of alignment with the holes in the base. As the holes go straight toward the axis of the receiver, only the outside receiver contour can affect the drill direction and often a touch with the hand grinder will allow straight drilling. The angle vise is almost a necessity to achieve such drilling jobs.

On the Tilden mounts, the screw heads in the rings are toward the right, and the lettering on the rear base toward the left. The scope attaches by setting the front ring lug in the front base at 90° to the left, then with the front ring engaged, the scope is turned to the right one-quarter turn and lifted over the low "wings" on the rear base and moved until it is between the adjusting and the holding screws, then it is lowered and the rear ring engaged and held by the opposing screws, which also allow windage adjustment of the scope. These windage holding screws are very strong and tight, being lapped in place just enough to move under strong persuasion. Occasionally, it may be necessary to grind the tip of one screw pin shank down slightly, making a bevel at the point, when the scope is moved far to one side or the other and one screw consequently is so far down in the mount that its end contacts the receiver through the mount base.

Although Tilden mounts are not supposed to be interchangeable insofar as rings and bases are concerned, each front set being individually fitted, very often rings and mounts can be changed around. This is necessary when for some reason or other a rifle shoots exceptionally high or low and therefore, with standard mount, the reticule is objectionally high or low. If high, some relief can be had by grinding the bottom of the rear base, in order to lower the rear ring, however, on many models, space is definitely limited. Tilden can of course furnish several heights each in front and rear rings, which can combine to form a correct mounting for any job, providing you know what you need—which you will not until you have put on a standard model and shot the rifle. The rear rings are all interchangeable with all rear bases, incidentally.

Tilden mounts place the telescope as low as it can be and still allow the bolt to function. With the Unertl scopes and other with large eyepieces, it is necessary on Mauser rifles to flatten the top of the bolt sleeve. Weight is very low, from 2 to 3½ ounces depending on the model, of course. Extension bases are furnished for some rifles, which give better support to long scopes, as the rings are spaced further apart.

Redfield. The Redfield Senior mount is very similar to the Tilden, which it preceded. The principles of attachment and adjustment are identical, although the Tilden rear base system and adjusting screws are much stronger. Redfield's Senior mount has not been made for several years, although not officially discontinued.

The Junior mount has become widely known, and perhaps more widely used than any other single model of mount. Of the single base construction, it is perhaps the easiest mount made to attach, which no doubt accounts somewhat for its popularity in gunshops. Both rings attach to the single base, which is held by 6–48 screws. (The model made for the U. S. M1903A4 Sniper Rifle is attached by two 8–40 screws.) Nearly all commercial models are held by two front and one rear screw.

To mount, the base is leveled with the rifle receiver, the rear hole in the receiver *ring* is scribed, punched, drilled and tapped, and the mount attached by this screw. Using the mount for a drill jig, a No. 27 drill is used to spot the rear hole in the mount, in the receiver bridge. Remove the mount, drill and tap this hole, and attach the mount by the two screws now accommodated. Spot front hole in the receiver ring with the No. 27 drill bit, remove the base and drill the hole for the screw, using the 31 drill of course, to an approximate depth of ⁵⁄₃₂″. Clear it to the bottom and tap all the way.

As in the Tilden mount, the screw heads in the ring are to the right, but to attach the scope, the front ring lug is engaged in the seat provided for it at the front of the base, holding the scope at 90° to the right. Then, with the right adjusting screw removed, the scope is pivoted one quarter turn to the left, bringing the ring up against the left adjusting screw. The right screw is then replaced. These screws are hollowed end or cupped, and engage in the matching cuts in the rear scope ring to hold it down and move it and the scope to the right or the left as one screw is loosened and the other tightened.

The Redfield Junior mount is made for literally every rifle which has a place on top to put it, and for ¾″, ⅞″ and 1″ rings. In addition, a few private makers furnish odd sized rings for it to fit foreign scopes. They are particularly suited to low cost Enfield remodeling jobs, as any long mount model which will reach across the magazine opening can be easily altered to fit an Enfield receiver profile job. The quickest, easiest and cheapest way is to cut a flat step at the rear end of the mount, then cut a matching flat across the receiver bridge under the mount, to a depth sufficient to bring the mount level with the receiver in both directions. In this way you can make a neat scope mounting on most of the home remodeled Enfields floating around without having to machine or file the whole bridge to correct the contour for a standard mount, with the prospect of reblueing the receiver staring you in the face as well.

Nearly all Redfield Junior bases and front rings are interchangeable, which means you can switch different sized rings back and forth between mounts, to accommodate different scope diameters. Three different mounts, each with different ring diameters, gives you nine possible scope-rifle combinations.

The weak point of the mount is the adjusting screws and with a 10–32 threaded portion, there is enough strength to bend and break the heads off as the pressure of the rear ring is against the edge of the head which is twice the diameter of the threaded shank. In other words, the screw will break itself or at least bend, if much effort is exerted in tightening. Keep a few replacement screws on hand. Also, as neither base nor rings are heat treated, wear is rapid, and continual dismounting and remounting of the scope and ring assembly from the rifle will result in a loose fit of the front lug. Judicious peening can temporarily repair it— but only temporarily.

Buehler. The Buehler mount is copied from the Redfield Junior in principle, with a new wrinkle in the ring design. The base is on the same order, but longer, providing the front lug seat ahead of the receiver ring and giving the mount a long wheelbase. The base is mounted exactly as is the Redfield, in all respects, however, the rings are entirely different. The front ring is split on the bottom, and has its clamp screw (one) through the base engaging lug. The screw head goes on the right. The rear ring has no clamp screw at all, and is also split on the bottom.

All clamping action on the scope tube is a by product of the action of the holding adjusting screws, positioned the same as the Redfield's. Both rings are rounded in outline, and quite nice in appearance. The rear ring has cuts machined into its bottom to accept the cup end adjusting screws. It is advertised that both rings are lined with a microscopic thin coating of rubber, to aid in holding the scope securely without great pressure. The rear ring has no sides, and cannot be put on wrong.

To attach the scope to the rifle, loosen the screw visible at the right side of the front end of the base ahead of the lug recess, engage the lug, holding the scope 90° to the right, and bring it around one quarter turn to the left until the rear ring is in position to engage the rear mount screws. (As with Redfield, first remove the righthand adjusting screw.) Replace the right screw, tighten the front base screw, then tighten the rear adjusting screws but do not attempt to tighten them excessively. The screws are slightly stronger than on the Redfield, but still on the same off-center-tension idea.

Mashburn-Williams. Both of these mounts utilize the single base, and mount in the same manner as the Redfield. The Williams is of light alloy, not steel. Care must be used in mounting, since it cannot be reblued should the finish be damaged. The ring assembly is different and there is no windage adjustment.

Hill-Lehman. The Hill mount base is a dovetail rib, which mounts in the previously described manner. The rings slide on the rib from either end, with holding screws to engage detents in the rib at desired points. The Lehman mounts employ single dovetail blocks, which are individually mounted as are target scope blocks, or as Tilden bases. They must be exactly parallel. The rings are of light alloy in the form of round bands, with the scope tube opening bored offcenter, leaving enough stock at the bottom for the dovetail cut, clamping, and holding screws. There is no windage adjustment in either of these mounts, and they are available for American scope diameters. They are well adapted to mounting scopes upon foreign rifle-shotgun combination guns and single shot rifles, as well as modern arms.

Ackley-Turner—King-Pike. These Q-D mounts are top mounting two base types, using 6–48 screws, and mounted in the same manner as the Tilden. It is quite easy to level both the front and the rear on most rifles, and care must be observed only in the spacing of the front and the rear. In the case of standard receivers, the construction of the bases prevents incorrect spacing. The only difficulty I can remember with the King-Pike is that the attaching screws were very soft, and dis-

.30-1906 U.S. (.30-06)

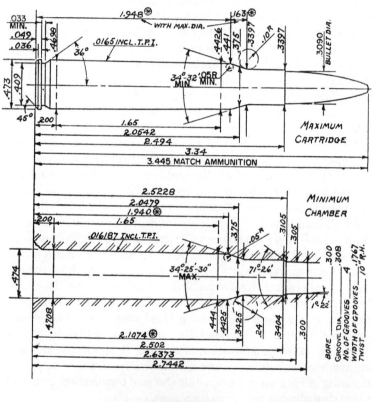

MAXIMUM CARTRIDGE

MINIMUM CHAMBER

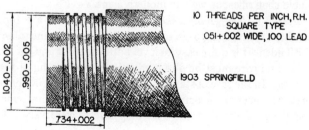

10 THREADS PER INCH, R.H.
SQUARE TYPE
.051+.002 WIDE, .100 LEAD

1903 SPRINGFIELD

figured easily when tightened. Some file work is occasionally necessary to make the springloaded holding plunger work correctly. The Ackley mount is very simple and well made, easily mounted and adjusted. The V-block principle insures exact return to position of the scope when removed and then replaced.

Kesselring. This Q-D mount is not at present available to gunsmiths, but no doubt will be by the time this is read. Some time ago, Mr. Kesselring showed me half a dozen of them, mounted on different types of rifles, and I was greatly impressed with its possibilities.

The mount is instantly detachable and leaves no bases on the rifle when removed. Aside from the accepted use for rifles, I can see that it would be ideal for shotguns. The shotgun scope has a place, but must be readily detachable without affecting the use of the gun without the scope. The early Weaver shotgun scope failed, I think, principally because the only mounts for it were heavy, cumbersome and nondetachable without strong screwdrivers. Shotgunners did not want holes drilled all over the tops of their guns to put on a semi-permanent sight not suitable for all types of shooting.

THE .30 SPRINGFIELD (.30–06)

Dimensions of both cartridge and chamber are the latest standards, and it is unlikely that there will be any further changes in the future.

The M1 service rifle uses a chamber slightly larger in diameter at the rear (.471 dimension) to facilitate extraction. The bolt action chamber is per the dimensions given.

The cartridge case drawing gives military specification dimensions, not commercial. Commercial cases may vary slightly—I have found some cases thicker at the base and thinner in the side walls than military cases. Handloaders find the military cases somewhat stronger for repeated reloading, but they must reshape or ream the primer pockets on the fired cases to eliminate effects of the arsenal crimp around the military primer.

We have developed the cartridge in all directions in this country and have found it quite flexible. Handloaders get accuracy with lead bullets at low velocity, use 110-grain jacketed bullets at around 3,300 FPS for vermin shooting, and precision match bullets for target work. Hunters have a choice of 150-, 180- or 220-grain factory loaded hunting ammunition, with a wide choice of bullet types.

The .30–06 is still a U.S. military rifle and light machine gun cartridge, and it is used by other nations to a limited extent—Mexico for one, has long used machine guns in .30–06 caliber, and loads excellent military ammunition for them.

The Kesselring mount requires two small holes drilled in the right side of the receiver, one at the receiver ring and one at the bridge, or at the approximate locations on non bolt actions. These holes are not tapped. On the left side of the receiver, a hole is drilled approximately midway between the preceding holes on the opposite side, and a small, unobtrusive stud set in. It can be threaded in, or riveted in—that is all that there is on the gun.

The scope is held in two rings, split at one point, the bottoms of which are profiled to fit the top of the arm involved. These are connected on the bottom left side by a single spring steel rod, which has on it a little lever and cam. On the bottom right side of each ring, inside the curve for the receiver, is a small stud. To mount the scope, the two studs in the rings are engaged in the corresponding holes in the receiver and the rings set down on the receiver, while the spring steel bar goes over the stud in the left side of the gun. The cam lever is brought to bear on the stud and turned, causing the bar to bend and exert downward tension on the mount, holding it firmly to the receiver. The mounting is quite strong and reliable.

Weaver. The Weaver U and Q fixed top mounts are rather difficult to mount correctly, as the screw holes go into the receiver at angles instead of straight down from the top. I have never found any way to level or line up these mounts other than by eye. Put the rings on the scope and set them on the rifle with the clamp screws loose. Wind a couple of turns of adhesive or masking tape around the scope and the receiver to hold them in place. Then, with the rifle leveled, get behind the scope and action and try to set the scope and mounts directly on top, boresighting at the same time. No windage adjustment whatever is possible in the mounts once they are attached. The tape will serve to hold the assembly while you push it from side to side until satisfied with the location. Scribe one hole for the front ring and one for the rear, but drill and tap only the one at the rear. Tie down the scope and rings with this one screw and again boresight.

You can now check the sight picture—bore vs scope—and can cure some windage error by moving the front unattached base slightly to one side of the other. It may make the mounting look a little cock-eyed, but according to my rules the sight picture is more important, and most of the customers agree. Line up to your satisfaction and see if the previously scribed hole is still okay, for your own amusement—go by your fresh location, of course, and drill and tap for one more screw. Holding the scope by one screw in each ring, again check for bore sight correction. If everything is in line, scribe and drill the two remaining holes and attach the scope permanently. If it is found that one of the holes has pulled off for any reason and the scope is out of line laterally, remove one of the first two screws, move the mount to correct location and scribe for the opposing screw in that mount. Holding the scope with that screw and the screw or screws in the other ring, it should lineup. Should the first screw involved now be enough out of line to fail to enter through the mount hole, file the hole in the mount base to clear the screw when it pulls down.

Weaver screws often have little burrs on the sides, where the slot has been cut. Break or grind these off, or they will cut visible gouges in the alloy mount bases as they are screwed in. Use ordinary camera "flat" enamel to touch up alloy mounts when the finish is damaged. The top mounts can usually be filed on the bottoms to give a little leeway in adjusting elevation. The 6–48 thread is used on Weaver top mounts.

Weaver Detachable Mounts. These mount in the same manner as scope blocks or Tilden bases, and the bases being flat on top, are easy to level with the rifle receivers. Each base has two holding screws, 6–48 thread. The front and the rear rings are identical, being dove-tailed to the slide on the bases, with large coin slotted screws, the shanks of which enter the ring and pass through it, engaging in a groove across the top of the bases. These Weaver rings are split at one side and have two screws to give clamping action on the scope tubes. Made for the Weaver scopes, the diameters furnished are ¾″ and 1″. The principle of the mount is very sound. I would like them better if they were made of steel. Bases are available for all suitable arms and the mounts permit ready interchangeability of bases, so that one scope with rings can be used on more than one rifle, providing the bases are mounted on each gun. Weight is less than five ounces.

Stith Mounts. Some of the Stith models are top mounting, and some are combination side-and-top attaching. The Mastermount is basically a Q D top mount, although a side plate is furnished to permit attachment to factory drilled rifles with receivers drilled at the side for receiver sights, such as the Winchester 70. A beautiful piece of machinery, the only possible objection to this mount is the weight, which is over 11 ounces.

It is mounted by level as closely as possible, and presents no new problems in attaching. Both windage and elevation adjustment of the scope is possible in this mount, and the principle of the V-block is used to insure a scope returning to the exact position when removed and replaced. Instead of straight edges, however, the V is represented by opposing steel cones, against which the scope tube rests, held by downward spring tension as in the Ackley-Turner mount.

The standard Stith mount furnished for the Savage 99 is top mounting and requires no drilling of the receiver. I consider this mount the best possible mount for this model rifle, especially for a saddle gun. It is available with or without windage adjustment, for all American scope diameters.

Stith's regular line of attach-it-yourself mounts employs the rear sight dovetail on the barrel to hold the front mount base, and uses the receiver sight holes in the side of the receiver to hold the rear base. The rear rings are more or less standard type, split, with threaded hole to attach to the rear base, and front rings are long sunshade hoods. These keep the sun off the objective, but make cleaning difficult. Allen head 6x48 screws are used for attaching and clamping, which is a good idea, as they can be tightened more than the standard slotted type.

Unfortunately, this side and top combination of mounts allows inertia of the scope, working against recoil, to keep pulling at the rear base screws and loosens them. I never had much trouble with them, having Glyptol to put on screws before I tightened them until the little wrenches twisted, but the laymen who put them on themselves are always having them loosening in the field.

The Stith custom mounts—those which the Stith firm build to accommodate any variety of scope and rifle sent them—with windage built in if desired, give no trouble whatever on this point.

Stith and Tilden are the best finished mounts I have encountered and both are very well made and carefully machined.

CLEANING SCOPES

Optical glass is quite soft, comparatively speaking, and easily scratched by unskilled cleaning. The worst possible way to clean a lens —meaning of course only the exterior surfaces—is to take a clean cloth and start rubbing. Any dust or grit on the glass will be scraped across it and cause minute scratches, eventually causing the lens to appear dull and cutting down the optical qualities. Use of lens tissue is not too good, either, in the hands of the layman, for there is also the tendency to use pressure on it against the lens. Cleaning by liquid is the best method, but requires care. Scope lenses are of the compound type, meaning made of two or even three pieces of glass cemented together, usually with balsam gum and almost any solvent will dissolve this cement if it reaches the edges of the lens. It is therefore obvious that no cleaning liquid can be poured on the lenses, as it would run down the edges under the retaining rings. I have found plain good alcohol—Ethyl or grain—to be best, applying with either a cotton swab or bit of Kleenex. Sufficient alcohol is used to wash the lens without permitting any surplus to accumulate at the edges. As the alcohol dries very rapidly, there is little danger of injury to the lens. The alcohol cuts any grease or fingerprints from the surface, loose dust is picked up by the swab, and after the lens is dry any lint can be blown away or wiped with lens tissue—or a good grade of toilet paper!

CHAPTER 22

Wood for Gunstocks

THE different types of hand and shoulder firearms can influence the choice of wood to be used in stocking. The one piece rifle stock requires a blank not less than 30″ long, as a rule, and one having certain grain characteristics. It must have tensile strength combined with a grain structure which will resist warping after the stock is shaped. Short buttstocks, such as on single shot rifles and double barreled shotguns, need little strength and can be made of very fancy wood having cross-grains, since the stock is not required to support the entire rifle or shotgun, particularly when stock bolts are used. Pistol and revolver stocks of course can be made of almost any wood, hard or soft, as no strength is required of the wood. Checkering should be quite coarse, which allows the use of softer woods. So, keep an open mind on the matter of stock material as a blank which is superbly suited to one type of arm may be unfit for another.

The firearm itself demands little from its stock—a non-warping, well bedded support in the case of the bolt action; the human element bringing in the matters of weight and appearance. All too often the personal desires of either owner or stockmaker are allowed to overweigh the requirements of the rifle although necessary functional qualities should never be sacrificed to appearance.

Wood itself is becoming something of a problem, due to our own habit and tradition. Because the shoulder weapon was originally developed in Southern Europe and worked its way North, walnut became the standard stock wood, since it was obtainable in Italy, France, Spain and Austria, as well as in Germany and England. Strong, easily worked, and of good appearance, it has held top preference through the years. When the English and German gunsmiths in American colonial days began work here, to develop the Pennsylvania rifle (generally known as the "Kentucky" rifle) they naturally tried out native woods. The American black walnut wood of the Eastern area was—and is—considerably coarser than the European walnut, so maple, apple and cherry were used extensively, all of these having denser grain than Pennsylvania walnut.

However, walnut was used from the start for military muskets and rifles, and of course for lower-priced arms of all types. Arms factories standardized on it when the breechloader came into use, as it was not only generally popular, but readily available in quantities and not critical as to climate or seasoning. Sportsmen probably do not realize it, but walnut was formerly one of our most widely used American hardwoods, not only for furniture, doors and small items but also for building timbers. I am not so old, but I can remember my father cutting walnut for fence-posts and firewood! The past two wars have used immense amounts of walnut in rifle and carbine stocks also, so that our walnut prospects are not too good. There will be no shortage of plain wood for many years, but the better grades are very scarce even now.

Therefore, it behooves us to open our eyes to the existence of suitable gunstock woods other than walnut.

The firearm has its requirements as to strength. We will consider stock woods from the point of the rifle, which in the case of a large center-fire cartridge means a wood strong enough to stand recoil. This means it must have both strength and hardness. For arms of negligible recoil, this is a minor point. In other words, Junior, you can make a .22 stock out of white pine and get away with it, but for a .30–06 you need a wood comparable to reasonably hard walnut.

From the user's standpoint, weight is a vital factor in sporting arms. There are many tropical woods of limited availability in this country which are strong and excellent in appearance, but so heavy as to be undesirable except on vermin rifles where weight is considered unimportant.

So we are stuck slightly on the standard set by walnut: stock woods to be popular must come somewhere close to the weight and strength of either American or European walnut. As there is quite a variation in weights and colors of both woods, we do have considerable leeway, however, in our choice of wood.

On the walnut business, we now have a joker in the deck. I understand there has been a court ruling to the effect that European type wood grown in this country can be advertised and sold as European walnut, even Circassian, as it is reasoned that this variety of tree first appeared in Europe in the Circassian region. It is the same idea as a Missouri farmer selling pure bred Swiss cattle, even though the critters are thirty generations away from the Alps.

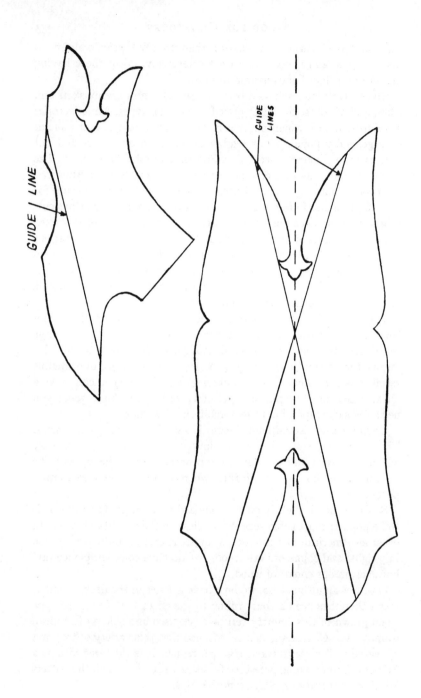

A John Hearn Job

This gunstock was made from California mesquite wood and all the dimensions and drawings to be followed were furnished by the customer. This gentleman is five feet tall and weighs one hundred and ten pounds, hence careful consideration had to be given to the length of pull and comb height of the stock. The rifle is fitted with the new, large Bausch and Lomb scope. By experiment, it was found that a 12½ inch pull was best and this high, double comb also fitted in quite well with this scope.

This checkering pattern is continuous over the top of the grip and under the one-piece forearm. Notice how nicely the grain of this splendid piece of mesquite shows through on both grip and forearm patterns.

In the laying out of these two patterns, Mr. Hearn writes: "This pattern carried over the top of the pistol grip. This is the most difficult job in all checkering, as making a straight line go across and over a rounded piece of wood and form the same size and shape diamonds on both sides is a trick that takes time in the laying out. However, a fill-in pattern is easier in one respect than one which uses the diamond lines for borders, because in this latter case the guide lines must come out at the same place to make both sides of the stock identical at this important point where it is so easily seen.

"As in any one-piece forearm pattern, I work from the two angle guide lines and make sure that these are correct before I begin. Then, six or seven passes later, the diamonds are completely pointed. Pure linseed oil is then applied to bring up the grain and soak the wood where the checkering has been done."

On the page opposite are shown details of the lines and angles of starting guide lines of these two patterns.

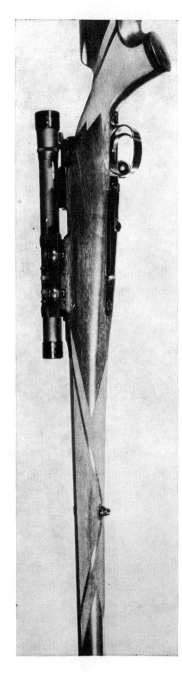

A John Hearn Job and Checkering

A .270 caliber Mauser with full-length Mannlicher stock. Metal work done by Philip R. Crouthamel, 308 Wycombe Ave., Lansdowne, Pennsylvania.

Mr. Hearn writes: "The customer wanted extreme light weight and I got it down to 7 pounds, 6 ounces, with scope, with a 22 inch barrel.

"The checkering pattern is centered around the sling swivel screw in the forearm and is of a total length of 13½ inches. The idea is to fill the long empty space that results in this style stock and still not have a solid pattern. The guide lines are laid out through the stud hole. For surest results on this pattern, or any pattern that uses the diamond shape as the border guide, do not cut out the outside edges until you have worked the pattern over to the desired line.

"The pistol grip meets the curved edge of the rear tang in the same pattern as the forearm. The narrow strips are difficult to cut with a checkering tool, so I use a diamond or wedge shaped carving chisel for this work."

Sketches showing details and layout of these grip and forearm patterns are shown in reduced size on opposite page.

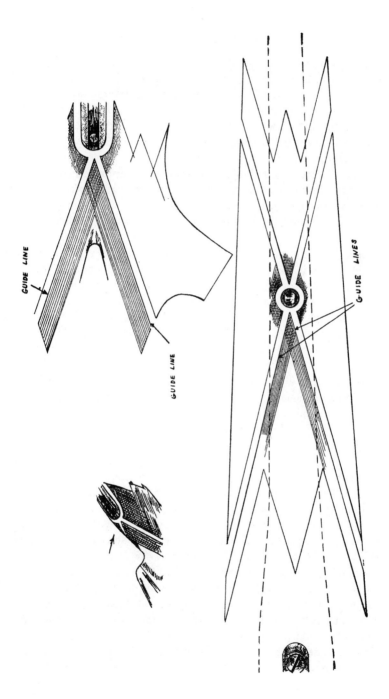

GUIDE LINE

GUIDE LINE

GUIDE LINES

European Walnut (*Juglans Regia*)

European walnut trees produce what we call the "English" walnut when we buy them at the stores for Christmas. Originally Chinese, the tree spread west throughout Europe and the character of the wood is determined by the soil in which the tree grows. Minerals in the soil, the amount of rainfall in the region, the climate and the changes in the climate all affect the texture, color and strength of the wood produced. The tree which survives in adverse environment, growing with scant moisture in rocky soil, has a close grained structure of good tensile strength. Chemicals and minerals feeding the roots give color. The tree which grows rapidly in a favorable environment with plenty of rain and rich soil produces a coarse, light wood, usually of plain brown color.

Good European walnut, regardless of the country or region in which it was grown, is the best stock wood obtainable, for strength, texture and lightness. Not all European wood is top grade, as can be determined by examining a few souvenir Mauser stocks, but as a rule the wood shipped to this country has been of quite good quality. Foreign stockmakers of course have the jump on us in selection, but we do get very good blanks at times, especially of the fiddleback grain figuring, which we like and they consider inferior to the crotch figure.

As mentioned above, all European walnut is basically the same, but due to generations of trees growing in different locales variations in grain figure and coloring have developed in each of the areas. While the majority of plain or straight grained walnut appears greatly similar throughout the continent, the figured wood produced may have qualities peculiar to the particular growing region. Here in America, with our somewhat Teutonic trait of attempting to pigeonhole everything in a particular category, we have rather arbitrarily decided that English grown walnut is a rather dark tan in color, with close grain and neat if not gaudy figure; French, a lighter color with dark streaks; German, plain and light; Italian, fancy and light and Circassian, out of this world. Through seeing choice examples of each type of wood we come to believe that each country produces a different wood, which is not so. There are differences in fancy blanks, but little differences in the plain wood, which are not always discernible. Some smart Frenchman could cut a tree on the north side of the Pyrenees and get stock blanks he could peddle as being whatever he wanted to call them— some could be rated "Circassian," some "French" and some "English" —and it would take a laboratory wood expert to call him a liar.

Complicating the European walnut situation, we now have our own home grown trees, which produce the "English" nuts for commercial use. These are almost entirely raised in California, so we have California grown wood, which is similar to European wood, being identical in origin. Except for the prevailing California custom of irrigating things, this wood would be very good, however, the trees grow too fast, and wood of good texture is seldom seen.

Taking up the individual woods mentioned:

Circassian. Walnut grown in Circassia (part of Russia) and in the Balkans in general was the favorite wood of past custom gunmakers both here and abroad, although very little wood has come from there for the past 20 years. Aided by publicity and pictures, Circassian walnut became the most highly prized wood yet most of the "Circassian" stock blanks sold for the past 20, or even 30 years, have been selected Spanish and French walnut.

True fancy Circassian is a streaked wood of good color contrast. Rifle blanks almost never have a curly figure, although buttstock blanks for shotguns and single shot rifles are usually cut from crotch or stump and may have any kind of figure. The rifle blank has dark brown lines, sometimes almost black, which assume wavy patterns. Actually, these lines, or streaks, do not stand out, as the stock will be almost half-and-half light and dark. Some blanks you might describe as dark wood with light streaking.

It is because of the slightly wavy figure that Circassian is the choicest stock wood for the light weight rifle. The wood has close texture and great strength yet is lighter in weight than figured American walnut. Weight per cubic foot is between 35 and 40 pounds. A Circassian stock can be beautiful and still be strong and light. Fancy figuring always adds to the weight of any wood, particularly the crotch or burl type of graining. Circassian walnut of the best grades achieves its beauty through contrasting colors in the straight or semi-straight grain wood, rather than from intricate figuring as does American walnut. Occasional fiddleback graining is found in Circassian and stocks made of such wood are perhaps the most beautiful of all as each stock seems to have a life and light of its own.

French Walnut. Most of our imported walnut now comes from France, and blanks now sell from $10.00 up. Nearly all is good wood, and is to be used when available. I prefer French walnut to almost all other woods, as it suits my somewhat conservative tastes. Most of the wood—not all, by any means—is distinguished by fairly narrow black streaks against a relatively light coloring. Hard and strong, with good texture and fine grain, weight per cubic foot is around 40 pounds.

In common with nearly all European walnut, French cuts cleanly, takes checkering very well indeed and also can be carved. The wood takes almost any type of finish quite well, the small pores being easily filled. Stronger than American walnut, French can be used on light-weight rifles to good advantage as slimmer stocks can be fashioned without sacrificing necessary strength. The wood has good resiliency to resist denting, and seems to me to be more inert than even the best American in that once a stock is made it suffers little change in dimensions thereafter from temperature and humidity changes.

A percentage of French walnut—say 20%—does not have the dark streaking we generally consider characteristic, but is a light-brown wood with some slight figure having flesh or even pinkish undertone. I have had several blanks of this type, and one of my own stocks made from one of them shows this trick coloring in the butt. The very fancy figured blanks of this variety of French walnut sell for plenty, the stocks resulting being of course of considerable beauty.

English Walnut. This I know nothing about, having seen only a couple of stocks I was sure were made of it. The British have imported most of their stock wood from Europe for a great many years, and, believe it or not, quite a bit from the U. S. A. The real English walnut is about the color of our lighter-colored American black walnut, but much harder and close grained, in the better grades of course. Good blanks were chosen for figure showing crotch and flame graining, which finished up to give golden highlights, without much contrast.

Spanish Walnut. Another wood with which I am not very familiar, although I have seen some very fancy shotgun stocks on high grade Spanish double barrels which could pass for Circassian. Most Spanish walnut is very similar to French although some very hard, plain wood of light color comes from the arid section of the country. I understand the Germans imported some wood from Spain prior to World War II, probably for military purposes.

Italian Walnut. This I do know about. The wood is good, but mostly plain and straight grained. It is very light in color, with close grain, good strength and light weight. The small quantity of figured wood used for stocks generally has plenty of figure of the burl classification, but little color contrast. The Italians stained the wood to darken it when using it for stocks (not military stocks—these they left light). Texture of the wood is excellent, and will take very fine checkering. I saw an Italian custom shotgun once which must have had 35-line checkering, and the diamonds were all there.

American Black Walnut (*Juglans Nigra*)

American walnut grows across the United States, from the Atlantic to the Pacific, in all but the coldest regions. Altitude limits it to locations below 4,000 feet, which keeps it out of the Western mountain areas. It is found in deep Pennsylvania forests, on the Ozark hills of Missouri, and in the arid southern Arizona country, which means that we can find as much variation in American black walnut as we can in European walnut. The best American—to my mind the fiddleback and mild burl figure of the hardest Ozark wood—compares with French walnut for weight and strength, and very nearly in texture, meaning that it is almost as close grained. Poor American walnut, from the middle western states or from the river bottoms of any state, is quite open grained and light in weight when fully dry. There is great variation in the weight—from 30 to 45 pounds per cubic foot.

The more highly figured, the heavier the weight. The harder the wood, the heavier the stock will be, unless the latter is streamlined. This is no detriment, but rather a good point since a neat, well proportioned stock can be turned out without having to leave considerable bulk at the pistol grip to provide necessary strength.

Wood connoisseurs consider American black walnut more beautiful than European, and spectacular burl figure can be found in stump cuts. Most of this full figured wood does not have sufficient strength for full rifle stocks, and is at its best for shotgun and single shot rifle application. When an occasional rifle blank turns up with full figure yet with grain structure indicating the necessary strength required, that blank sells for as much or more today than fancy imported wood.

Do not sell American walnut short—good wood is good wood, no matter where it grew. Our trouble is, we have very little good to go with a lot of medium and an equal amount of poor. The medium grade of American walnut as furnished by Bishop for his above average blanks may have little figure and color contrast, but does have strength and texture to permit 20-line checkering. These finish up very well and make stocks no man need be ashamed of, providing the stockmaker does not darken and stain the wood to the point of obliterating the natural color and grain marking. Poor American walnut is soft, light and weak, generally dark brown with a reddish cast to it. This should be used for fence posts and firewood, as my old man used to do. We have other woods costing no more which make better stocks.

The better types of our walnut are lighter in color, except for the burl and crotch figurings, which have dark brown and reddish tones predominating. In plain wood, as a rule the lighter the color, the harder the wood. (This does not mean that that white sap-wood showing up on the sides and corners of a semi-inletted blank is good!)

The test of any walnut, however, is its grain texture; if the grain is close, with small pores showing close together on an end grain cut, and a with grain split showing the pores to be both small and individually short—less than ½″—it it okay, brother.

As mentioned earlier, the tougher time a tree has to make a living, the better wood it develops. American walnut grown in rocky, not-too-fertile soil is the best, which is why that from western Missouri, Southeastern Kansas, and parts of Oklahoma, Texas and California is sometimes very good. There are a few walnut trees growing in semi-desert areas in Southern Arizona which might very well prove to have superlative stock wood. They are somewhat gnarled from winds, show evidence of very slow growth and very possibly may have strange color contrasts since the soil abounds in different minerals. So far as I know, no one has ever attempted to cut these trees for stock wood, but I am going to as soon as I can figure out how to slow up air drying of the cut wood. Although of normal trunk diameter, the height of these trees is not over half that of black walnut trees growing in the other localities mentioned.

We have the walnut habit ingrained in us, so that most of us prefer a stock made of the lowest grade walnut to one made of another wood which may really be much better both in strength and appearance. Well, the walnut supply is going down fast, so we had better begin realizing the possibilities of woods to replace and substitute for our cherished favorite. There will always be *some* walnut available, but good grades will get scarcer and scarcer, and prices go higher and higher.

California-English. Could also be called "California-European," as it comes from the planted walnut groves of nut growers, and as previously mentioned, is the European, or *Juglans Regia* type. The supply is limited, as the trees are valuable as crop producers, but the wood is commercially available at not-too-high prices. The wood itself is considerably softer than European walnut, but does have good coloring and figuring. The dark streaking and figuring of imported wood is not found, most of this domestic grown walnut being fairly light in color. It does have a reasonably good color contrast and takes a very good finish. Weight is about the same as European although the grain is not so dense. The wood cuts and checkers satisfactorily. Very handsome stocks can be made of figured wood, in appearance resembling light-colored French walnut. Not all California grown wood of this type is good however, much of it being very light in weight, soft and coarse grained, due no doubt to the tree being grown in good soil and supplied with plenty of water.

Rock Maple. Also known as Hard Maple and Sugar Maple, grows throughout the United States east of the Mississippi in the Northern states. This is the hard wood used quite a bit by colonial riflemakers that has maintained a slight popularity through the years. Custom stock men have always used it occasionally, although none of them ever cared much about working it. The wood is harder than walnut and often as close grained as European walnut. Maple for stocks is always selected for fancy grain, which takes the form of twist, flame or bird's eye, these making a good job of inletting quite an undertaking. I have seen quite a few target .22s stocked with maple selected for straightness of grain in the forend, and some of these had a fiddleback highlight effect. Maple is approximately the same weight as medium grade black walnut, which is to say about 37 pounds per cubic foot. There is less weight variation in maple than in walnut.

"Raw" maple is practically white, seasoned wood takes on a yellowish flesh tinting, and oil-finishing produces a golden, glowing color which is quite pleasing.

I do not believe maple stocks should be stained as the color of the wood is attractive as it is, and delicate color contrast is dulled by careless darkening. Common, cheap burnt umber stains should not be used since they blacken the pores and make the stock look like a fly specked piece of yellow pine.

Maple must be thoroughly seasoned, in the log, in the plank and in the stock blank. It lends itself well to kiln drying, which is a boon. On account of a great deal of maple being used commercially the hardwood lumber outfits know how to handle it.

The wood is hard and tough, with good resiliency. This is amply proven by its use for pins in bowling alleys. It is, however, quite brittle when cut thin, so painstaking care is absolutely necessary in the inletting and final shaping of a stock. Maple takes checkering as well as good walnut. It is difficult to carve well because of the brittle grain characteristic, and I do not consider it well suited to carving because of the slight color contrast in the wood which does not show up carving unless the latter is artificially colored—and I think the latter practice horrible.

Rock maple is definitely a good stock wood. Its light color repels many shooters accustomed to dark walnut, and its cutting characteristics demand a little more care—and more frequent **tool sharpening**—than common walnut. For the good stockmaker, maple usually takes no more time than walnut, as the extra time consumed in inletting is made up in finishing, since maple requires considerably less time in that department.

Pacific Maple. Grows in Oregon, Washington and northern California. This wood is soft, very light, and not to be very highly recommended. Occasional figured blanks have dense enough grain to be worthwhile, but the mine run stuff is little better than white pine, and, to be brutally frank, it even looks like white pine! For featherweight rifles of light recoil, Pacific maple might be okay, but I would hate to use it on any big rifle. The wood is too soft to take checkering, but can be carved and the grain is surprisingly dense, but without the strength we usually attribute to dense wood. Most of it is almost dead white in color, and a stain should be used. This wood will stain evenly, and can take even a walnut color if desired.

Birch. This wood has been avoided, as being too plain in grain to be desirable for gun stocking but some of our factories are now using walnut strained birch on low-priced rifles and shotguns. The public does not seem to kick too much and I gotta hunch there is a little stained beech coming out now, too.

Birch is a dense white wood, seldom having good graining, but of ample strength for any arm. It takes any staining very well indeed—walnut, oak, mahogany or redwood—and birch plaques or furniture so colored and then lacquered or varnished defy identification from the imitated wood from the color standpoint. The tensile strength is good, checkering and carving hold very well, and the wood cuts smoothly and cleanly with sharp tools. Most birch does not present a very good appearance because of the plain graining and even when some figure is present, the lack of color contrast leaves the stock rather flat in appearance. Except for this defect in appearance, birch is an almost perfect stock wood and I would prefer a stained, plain stock of strong birch to a stock made of one of those swamp spruce walnut blanks now so common.

Acacia. I do not believe there has yet been much use of this wood. The trees are planted throughout the country as shade trees for lawns and parks and one of the popular names is "Tree of Heaven." The wood is very similar to American black walnut in weight and color and like walnut, it has a color range, from light to dark. The figure is more of the streaked or wavy grain than burl and I have heard that it is impossible to distinguish from walnut except by taste and smell (walnut has a distinctive taste and odor). Acacia may very well be a popular stock wood of the future as it cuts like very dry, hard walnut and has plenty of strength, although whether it will take fine checkering, I do not know.

Mesquite. This incredibly tough denizen of our western deserts is being used by some California gunmakers, notably Weatherby, for deluxe rifles. I do not know the cubic weight, but would estimate it as close to 50 pounds. The wood is quite heavy, of immense strength, with close grain, and very hard. As for figure, it is all figure. The screw bean mesquite, which we are talking about, does not grow very big, is twisted and gnarled so that any blank with straight grain is a rarity. Because of the small size of the trees, blanks are expensive and to the uninitiate, look very sad—they are full of knots, cracks, checks and small holes. The topnotch stockmaker of course can patch these and make a beautiful stock as the wood will take and hold very fine checkering and finishes up beautifully. It is dark brown, with black streaking and of course variations of burl, crotch and feather figuring, often all in one blank! My only objection to the use of mesquite is its weight. For heavy rifles this is no objection naturally, but for sporter use mesquite adds from six to 16 ounces above the weight of a comparable stock in walnut or maple.

There is a second widespread variety of mesquite, the flat bean tree, which grows to considerable size, particularly in Mexico. This is a brown wood, about the weight and graining of heavy walnut, without very much figure but it is possible that proper cutting might produce excellent blanks. I have seen planks cut of this wood, plain sawed, of fair size, but as they had been chosen for straight grain I could form no opinion as to the possible figure in the rest of the tree. There was no color contrast at all, the wood being an even milk chocolate brown.

Mahogany. This tropical hardwood is imported from Latin America, and possibly from the Philippines. There are several types of mahogany, of varying colors and graining, but all are hard and heavy. African mahogany is figured and fairly close grained, but I do not believe any is imported at this time. I have seen numerous stocks of Philippine mahogany, with several types of finish. This wood is dark red, and does not seem to change color from oil finishing although age darkens it. Grain is straight and plain, weight is considerably heavier than walnut, and the wood will take carving but not checkering, unless the latter is coarse. It is of course extremely strong.

None of the Latin American mahogany has enough figure to recommend it for stock work. The somewhat open grain and lack of color contrast would make for very plain stocks.

Mexican Rosewood. Hard, heavy, tough, and fairly close grained. The color is a yellowish-orange or flesh color, with dark streaking. Streaks are brown turning to black. The wood has good possibilities, but is almost impossible to obtain. Having close texture, the wood is easy to oil finish very well and it takes checkering perfectly. Like mesquite it is too heavy to be desirable on sporting rifles.

Apple. Very close grained and tough, only the heartwood of the tree can be used, this being a dark red-brown, with a wavy figure as a rule. We have a lot of varieties of apples, but I do not know whether the wood varies much. The wood cuts well and is easily finished because the pores of the wood are very small and no filler is required, as a rule. The wood is scarce, but desirable. It will take either fine checkering or intricate carving, and once seasoned, will almost never warp thereafter. Applewood is close fibered enough to resist splitting under almost any circumstances.

Cherry. This was another wood employed by the early American gunsmiths who used the wild cherry tree, which furnished wood superior to that of the cultivated fruit tree. The wood is a reddish-brown, very dense, with almost no color contrast at all and it compares with walnut in weight, although of greater strength. Figured blanks are occasionally seen, and these make very nice conservative stocks— neat but not gaudy is the description. The wood cuts well, but keep the chisels sharp.

Beech. Seldom seen today, beech was earlier used as a substitute for walnut in military arms, particularly in the Civil War era, for contract muskets and rifles. About as heavy as hard walnut, beech is tan colored as a rule, and with a little stain looks like plain walnut. It is strong and tough, though fairly coarse in grain. This grain characteristic is somewhat ambiguous, as the wood is quite satisfactory from the split resistance angle, being very tough. Occasional close grained beech is found, with accompanying increase in weight. It cuts well and takes coarse checkering. There is literally no color contrast, for there is practically no figure to be found. For a plain, tough stock, beech is okay. It does not take stains easily, but requires a penetrating type, however the wood does take a good finish and polish.

Oregon Myrtle. Within the past 15 years this wood has forced its way into the select circle of publicly accepted stock woods. It is difficult to describe as the figure may be wavy or burl and the color may range from a dark yellow to dark walnut, with all variations in between, including a few tinges of green! Myrtle is extremely hard to properly season and few blanks sold are thoroughly seasoned, which leads some stockmakers to believe that myrtle never does stop warping. The wood is very slow to dry out and I do not believe anyone has yet figured out a perfect control for drying. I am told that the best way to handle myrtle is to cut the tree into planks, then sink these planks into mud under water for a couple of years or more, to thoroughly watersoak the wood, after which it can be air dried slowly, cut into stock blanks and these then are kiln dried slowly.

Myrtle is a close grained wood comparable to walnut in weight. It cuts easily, has no tendency to split, and has sufficient strength for heavy caliber rifles. Either checkering or carving is quite easily done, the wood holds even fine checkering and almost any type of finish is acceptable to the wood.

I prefer straight grain myrtle, with a very little figure in the butt. These stocks are light in color and light in weight and resemble plain European walnut in appearance.

THE TREATMENT OF STOCK BLANKS

Stock wood, if received in plank form, should be cut into stock blanks as soon as possible. These blanks must then be stored for future use, and at the same time seasoned further.

The moisture content in the wood varies with seasoning and with environment. Kiln drying is usually regulated to leave a moisture content of from 5% to 7%. This is dryer than normal for the United States excepting the arid parts of Texas, Arizona, New Mexico and California and blanks shipped to these areas will continue to dry out— down to as low as 3% at times while blanks shipped to damp areas will absorb moisture from the air. For most of the country, around 10% moisture content is normal.

It is therefore evident that the stockmaker must use his head when making a stock—the matter of where that stock will go is important, particularly if the wood used is average American walnut. The stock made of wood of average dryness in Pennsylvania will dry out and shrink very noticably if shipped to west Texas. A stock made in southern Arizona and shipped to the coast of Washington is going to pick up moisture and swell up. All the sealing and moisture proofing you can do is not going to completely prevent a stock made of soft wood from changing around due to temperature and humidity. We are all familiar with buttplates hanging out around the edge of a butt, where the wood has shrunk.

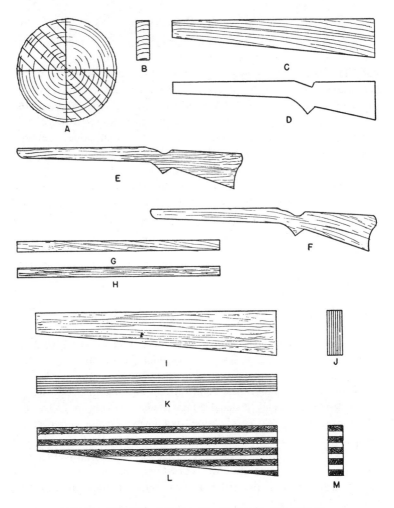

STOCK WOOD - GRAIN & BLANK SHAPING

A. Cross section of a log, lines indicating quarter sawing method productive of the best stock blanks.

B. The choice blank, shown as end grain.

C. Straight grained blank, correctly shaped.

D. Outline blank, cut in this form to save wood.

E. Blank incorrectly cut—grain cuts through the pistol grip, weakening it at this point.

F. Correctly cut blank, grain proper direction through grip.

G. Top view of cross grained blank. No good—will warp.

H. Correct top grain—straight.

I. Side view of laminated blank.

Very hard, thoroughly seasoned European walnut blanks give little trouble, but almost all American walnut is prone to absorb and lose moisture readily. It, therefore, is wise for the stockmaker to make himself some sort of dry room or box in which to thoroughly season blanks. This can be an airtight box with a small light bulb burning constantly. When a stock is in order for a damp climate, take the blank out, rough it into shape, semi-inlet it, *and then allow it to absorb some moisture.* If you do not, and proceed to do a good inletting job on your thoroughly dried, technically perfect blank, your customer is very likely to write you within a few months and ask why the stock is opening up around the metal, with gaps between the wood and the metal, and why he has a strong $\frac{1}{16}''$ of wood overhanging his buttplate, grip cap and forend tip. The opposite condition is even worse, when a stock is sent to a dryer climate and shrinks through moisture loss. Very often the wood cracks as it contracts around the metal parts, buttplates overhang, tips no longer join the forend smoothly and so on.

To check the quality of stock blanks, for grading and pricing, plane one side smooth and wet with water. This will show up the grain. Dry as fast as possible, naturally.

When blanks are cut to one pattern, the stocker or gunsmith can weigh them and so gain some idea of the weight variation of the wood —there is plenty, as much as 25%. This gives an opportunity to classify blanks for lightweight, sporter, and vermin rifle stocks. In the finished stock, there is only about eight ounces maximum variation between the heaviest and lightest of American walnut, but half a pound is plenty when you are trying to build that $7\frac{1}{2}$ pound scope rifle.

If the moisture content is satisfactory, seal the ends of the blanks by dipping in paraffin or pitch. Wood picks up most of its moisture, and loses it, through the butt end, so remember this when you are finishing a stock and really seal the wood under the buttplate.

Blanks should be cut down as close to finished stock proportions as convenient, before storage. This is for insurance against unnecessary warpage after the stock is shaped. If the blank, before being made into a stock, has little greater bulk than the stock it will make, it will

---

J. End view of laminated blank. When laminated vertically, a blank should be made of several thin layers of wood, the thinner the better.

K. Top view of the same blank shown in "I" and "J."

L. Horizontally laminated blank. Thick layers of wood can be used in this construction.

M. End view of "L."

warp the same as it would if made into a stock before seasoning. A blank 4″ thick may have hidden strains which will be released when a stock 2″ thick is made from it.

Blanks must be cut to take best advantage of the grain in order to be sufficiently strong. The grain should run through the pistol grip, not across it and the forend should be free from cross grain figure, in the case of bolt action rifle stocks. As a rule, most stockmakers cut their blanks with the grain angling slightly upward in the forend. This works in with the grain running properly through the pistol grip, and also provides the very doubtful virtue of what possible warping may occur being in the upward direction. It means that the forend is not likely to warp down away from the barrel and leave a gap to insult the stockmaker's reputation. In warping up, pressure against the barrel is increased, but this is easily corrected, if known. The illustration shows the manner of grain selection for strength, and for quarter sawing logs to provide blanks of maximum strength and figuring. By quarter sawing is meant the log is first cut into quarters, each of which is then cut into planks. Lumbermen do not like to do this, because they do not get quite as much footage as they do when straight slab sawing a log right through from the start. There is some wastage by quarter sawing, which runs up the price of blanks a little.

FOREND TIP WOOD

The use of wood for decorative forend tips is becoming widespread. Buffalo horn is very poor, as it checks badly, and plastics do not appear good enough for custom rifles.

Ebony. Long used for forend tips and pistol grip caps, Gaboon ebony (African) is a dead-black wood of extreme hardness with a very dense grain. I prefer ebony tips to all others, but they are hard to handle, for ebony too loves to check. It will crack from temperature change as well as from fast drying—and fast. If ebony is received in small plank form, cut into sizes appropriate for tips and caps immediately and dip each block cut into melted paraffin. Do not allow uncoated blocks to be exposed to dry air, as in a steam heated shop, for longer than 45 minutes, and surface checking can start in one hour.

When shaping tips from ebony, drill for the dowel and pegs without removing the paraffin, face off that side or end of the block and glue to the forend. When starting to shape after the block is attached, try to work fast and steadily and if the tip must be left unfinished for as much as an hour, coat the surface with linseed oil. Whatever moisture is in the block should be retained if possible and regardless of the type

ACKLEY IMPROVED .30-06

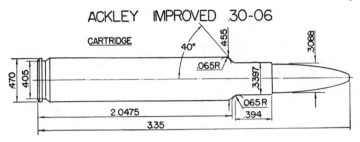

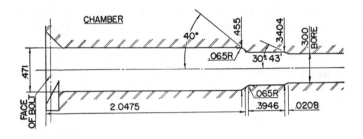

The Improved .30–06 has received quite a bit of attention, as being a cheaply achieved high-velocity .30 caliber wildcat. All sorts of claims have been made for its performance, but P. O. Ackley himself makes no attempt to boost it. It is an improvement on the standard .30–06 in some respects, but by no means rivals the .30 Magnum or the .300 H & H.

A fire-formed cartridge, the cases hold sufficient powder and burn it well enough to increase velocities around 100 FPS over standard .30–06 loadings. Mr. Ackley advises that in rechambering a standard .30–06 rifle to the improved version, the reamer is used only until the bolt can be closed on the minimum (1.940″) gage, for safety in fire-forming. Standard cartridges are fired in the chamber, which allows the case to expand and fit it closely. You will note that in these improved or blown out cases, many case dimensions are the same as corresponding chamber dimensions, since the latter governs the former. In a rifle with close-to-maximum headspace on the standard cartridge, it may be necessary to set the barrel back one thread (turn) in order to rechamber it to the Improved .30–06 and get a clean 40° shoulder. Standard cartridges can be used in the Improved chamber at any time.

of finish the stock is to receive, keep the ebony tip wet with linseed oil for several days. I am not so sure but what raw oil might not be best for this, or, you might heat up a can of boiled oil to the boiling point and hold the tip in it for several minutes. All this trouble is to prevent checking (surface cracking) of the finished tip, of course.

Mesquite. Dark mesquite makes a nice tip on a light colored stock of myrtle, maple or even walnut, as the wood is hard, polishes well and is not subject to checking.

The whole purpose of the tip is to dress up the appearance of the stock, and this is achieved by contrast. Thus, a walnut tip will look well on a maple stock while mesquite is not dark enough to contrast well with dark walnut.

Rosewood. This wood does make a nice contrast with any of cur stock woods and is suitable to nearly everyone as it polishes nicely and will not check.

Lignum Vitae. One of the hardest, toughest and heaviest woods in the world—you will do more filing than chiseling on it. In appearance it is brownish-black with yellowish-green figuring. It will not check as easily as ebony and has great tensile strength.

Desert Ironwood. A variety of the common American ironwood, this grows in the Southwestern desert. For hardness it rivals lignum vitae and ebony, color is solid brown-black and it is extremely heavy and difficult to work, though no harder than the above.

Cocobolo. This South American wood is another of the hard, heavy family, weighing 85 pounds per cubic foot and color is orange to red, with striped effect. There is, I believe, a variety of this wood with a chocolate-brown color that is used quite a bit for knife handles and this type is also excellent for tips.

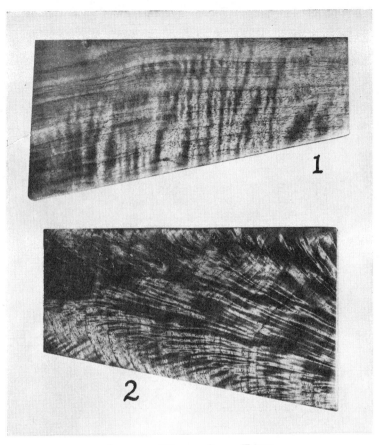

AMERICAN WALNUT GRAIN TYPES

These are examples of fancy graining found in good American walnut, from E. C. Bishop & Son.

1. A rather poor example of fiddleback grain—all that was available at the moment. Fiddleback is characterized by more-or-less parallel wavy color bands running at right angles to the grain.

2. Crotch figure, sometimes called "flame grain," for obvious reasons. This is perhaps the most beautiful grain type in coloring and shading found in American wood.

Not shown is burl figuring, which is basically spirals and curves in reddish-brown shades. A burl is the ancestor of a limb or knot, and while of fine appearance, burl blanks of sufficient length and strength for bolt action rifle stocks are hard to come by. Buttstocks naturally are no great problem, so shotguns and single shot rifles are not hard to accommodate. All of this figured wood is very much harder and heavier than the ordinary stock wood, even when the latter has some attractive figure.

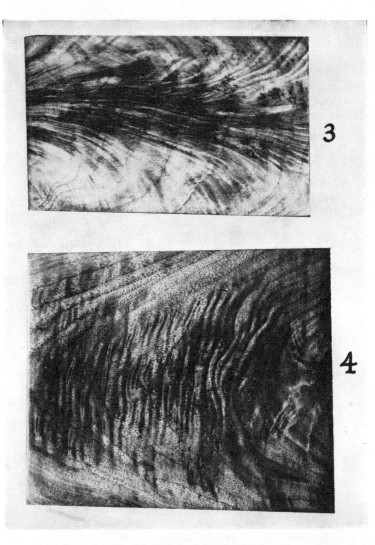

AMERICAN WALNUT GRAIN TYPES
(*Continued*)

3. Also crotch figure, this is the type found at junction of tree trunk and large limbs, or in fork of tree. Such wood is seldom found in sound blanks of sufficient size for rifle stocks, but is almost unbeatable for shotgun stocks.
4. Butt figure. This sample combines some of the features of fiddleback and burl. Stocks can be found in rifle size fairly often. The character is of course found in color contrast.

CHAPTER 23

Design of Gunstocks

IN THIS day and age, the stockmaker, either amateur or professional, should not be overly worried about design, for examples of good stocking are common and pictures of good jobs always being published. There are enough good jobs to be guided by, and so many horrible examples that an intelligent man should seldom go wrong.

Our principal general detriment to good sporting rifle stock design is the influence of the target or vermin rifle type of stocking, featuring heavy, bulky stocks with outlandish pistol grips and cheekpieces. For slow fire or single shot shooting, as done with small bore target rifles and the .22 center-fire vermin rifles having little or no recoil, comfort while aiming is paramount, so bulk and weight is unimportant. The rifles are seldom carried over rough country so weight, balance and ease of handling rarely enter the picture. The majority of vermin hunters shoot deliberately, from rest, or the sitting or prone target positions. The use of target type telescopic sights necessitates ultra high combs, and makes the use of the Monte Carlo type of buttstock advisable.

Unfortunately, most of the features of the target or vermin rifle stock are definitely not suited to the sporting, or hunting rifle. The Monte Carlo buttstock styling is unnecessary for 99% of hunting rifles, it being useful only on the small number of rifles having exceptionally high telescopic sight mounting. It definitely accentuates recoil and muzzle "jump," to make rapid field shooting difficult. The close, deeply curved pistol grips so comfortable for very deliberate slow fire shooting make the sporting arm clumsy to handle—the rifle does not come to the shoulder as smoothly as it should, and the hand is seldom positioned correctly for a quick offhand shot, which is often all a deer hunter gets these days. Weight of course is affected somewhat by the physique of the shooter and by the country in which he will carry the arm.

We are just beginning to get out of the woods on the rifle weight business. A couple of our most highly rated arms writers and editors, now out of the picture or about out of it, practically sold the country on heavy hunting rifles. They advised making them heavy enough to shoot and to hold even when the breath was short, as in mountain hunting. What these boys never bothered to mention was that they were very large, strong men of well above average physique. A 10-pound rifle was no greater burden to them than a 7½ pounder to the average 160 or 170 pound man of normal strength.

Jack O'Connor, our leading sporting magazine arms writer today, has advocated the light hunting rifle for several years. He has written several intelligent articles on it which have been well received. Mr. O'Connor has done more hunting in the Western United States, Mexico, Canada and Alaska than our other gun writers, particularly for big horn sheep, and knows from personal experience about what he talks. And he is by no means undersized—having ample muscles scattered over a six foot frame.

In the matter of stock design for the sporting rifle it is therefore wise to follow the styling of Owen and Linden, whose stocks are graceful and comfortable, with no unnecessary bulk. Of course, the custom stockmakers must very often conform to the customer's desires and specifications, but when stock design is left to men like Shelhamer, Owen, Mews or Hearn, the result leaves little to be desired.

Taking up the individual types and features of different stock jobs:

SHOTGUNS

Few custom shotgun stocks are made, which is a shame. Beautifully figured short buttstock blanks of American walnut are plentiful in comparison with good rifle blanks, and not at all hard to turn into fine stocks. Drop, pitch and pistol grip can be suited to the customer's individual measurements and his most common type of shooting. A small, flat cheekpiece adds to the appearance as well as being a definite aid to positioning the shooter's face when the gun is used. Cast off of ⅜" or even ½" can be made if desired, to make a quick handling arm, but remember that cast off tends to make the muzzle duck to the left when the gun is fired—not much, but enough to delay recovery of aim a little, should a fast second shot be required.

The chapter on shotgun work pretty well covered the matters of pitch and drop and there is not really much to say about the design of shotgun stocks. Make the combs thin, but not too thin. The receiver of the gun involved will to some extent govern the diameter of the pistol grip or small of the stock but, as much as possible, make these small and slightly oval in cross section. Pistol grips themselves should not be close, but gently curved back, with length from 4¾″ to 5″ measuring from the center of the trigger to the front edge of the grip. In the case of double guns, measure grip length from the front trigger, but "pull" or butt overall length from a point between the triggers. Circumference of the grip should be between 4″ and 5″, but as mentioned, the frame or action affects the stockmaker's liberty at this point. Drop at the comb and heel can be 1½″ and 2½″ or more respectively, as these depend more on the shape of the shooter's face than anything else. The wide faced man must have a thin comb or recessed cheekpiece for comfort in shooting. The shooter having a tendency to raise his right elbow will find a very shallow pistol grip curve to his liking, or even a straight, trap style stock with no pistol grip suitable.

In the case of a double or other type of shotgun not having a stock bolt, the blank must be chosen for straight grain through the pistol grip for strength, of course. The guns having stock bolts through the butts can use practically any wood, a cross grain or burl at the grip not eliminating them from use.

Forends. Custom forends for all types of shotguns can be made, although sometimes they require more labor than stocks. Doubles and single shot guns can utilize very fancy wood in either standard or enlarged types of forends, but be cautious about using wood with complicated grain structure in skeet type forends or slide handles on pump guns and for autoloaders, I am inclined to recommend plain grain wood. Of course, French walnut or other wood with color contrast is advisable in order to make an attractive appearance. For doubles, the styling of the forend of the Winchester Model 21 skeet or trap style can hardly be surpassed.

SINGLE SHOT RIFLES

The same types of blanks suited to shotguns are equally well suited to single shot rifles. However it is both possible and desirable to design such stocks to fit a particular purpose and person. Nearly all of these rifles are now rebuilt to modern small calibers, principally for vermin shooting. The action designs more or less call for considerable drop in the buttstock, while the high mounted telescopic sights most often employed call for a high cheekpiece. Action tangs of most receivers can be bent to allow deeply curved close pistol grips, the length of grips to be from 5″ to 6″, measuring from the center of the trigger to the edge of the grip cap. Where the shooter is accustomed to holding the thumb of his shooting hand along the side of the stock instead of crossing it over the small, very thick pistol grips—6″ in circumference —can be shaped. For these rifles, the Monte Carlo buttstock shaping is desirable. In spite of the thick, deep pistol grip, there is no necessity for making the rest of the butt excessively oversize, except for height of the comb or cheekpiece. From 3″ to 4″ of pitch is usually satisfactory, and in consideration of automobile interiors, Pachmayr or Mershon neoprene rifle butt plates should be used.

Because of individual shooting positions and habits of holding, it is not possible to give any set of dimensions to adhere to. About the only generality which can be observed is that buttstocks are customarily more comfortable if from ½″ to 1″ shorter than bolt action rifle buttstocks.

Ballard actions alone defy tang alteration, and though of course permitting any comb variation, require a separate pistol grip. This may be attached to the stock at the bottom of the rear of the action, or may be attached to the lever. Levers can be bent to whatever curve is wished, lengthened by welding on metal, and generally shaped as desired. The pistol grip can be attached to it by screws and serve as a lever handle.

Cast off is almost never needed on a single shot rifle.

Forends. Separate rifle forends are easily made, but attachment without affecting the shooting qualities of the rifle often is a problem. Fourteen inches is as long as any forend needs to be, for a maximum and cross section shape can be whatever the customer prefers, or the rifle usage dictates. For the man who does small vermin shooting from the windows of his car, a perfectly flat bottomed forend is in order. The bench rest shooter will find a very slightly rounded forend bottom easiest to settle on a sandbag or padded rest arm. A reduced size version of the target type beavertail forend will be preferred by the vermin shooters. There is no necessity for a deep forend and 1½″ is sufficient depth to provide a satisfactory cross section dimension and good appearance.

Decorative tips can be used, of course, with attachment by exterior band, encircling both the barrel and the forend. Should it be feared that accuracy will be affected by sling tension in prone and sitting shooting, a metal bar or section of heavy tubing can be brazed to the front of the action, below the barrel, and the forend attached to this only, leaving the barrel floating.

BOLT ACTION RIFLES

At last we are down to the most popular stock job—and in many ways, the hardest.

The sporting rifle, light in weight, designed for hunting either small or large game, is the stockmaker's best means of artistic expression. More than on any other type of arm, the appearance of the bolt action rifle is governed by its stock, so it is fortunate that the demands of the rifle and its sighting equipment does not restrict the stock design to rigid limits. The clean cut stock with graceful lines is very often almost perfect functionally.

We can set up general dimensions for the bolt action sporter stock. Overall length of the blank should be not less than 28½", when a forend tip is to be attached; 30" if no tip is contemplated. Butt length, the center of trigger to the center of the buttplate, varies from 12½" to 14", with 13¼" the general average. Drop, from the line of bore, ⅝" to 1¹⁄₁₆" at comb for low mounting scope use, ¾" to 1" for metallic sights. The ¾" measurement will accommodate either type of sighting so it is suited to rifles to be equipped with both scopes and metallic sights. Drop at heel should be held between 1" and 1⅝" and this dimension is not affected by sighting equipment. Drop at toe is regulated to some extent by size of the buttplate.

A buttplate 5" long, making a butt 5" in height or depth or whatever you want to call it, is sufficiently large to distribute recoil. The Niedner plate is approximately 5¹⁄₁₆" long, and in appearance, shaping and checkering, practically perfect. The plate, and consequently the buttstock, should never be over 1⅝" wide at the thickest point, (not considering cheekpiece of course); except for magnum calibers having considerable recoil, when width can be increased to 1¾" in the interests of comfort. The semi-hard neoprene butt plates made by Pachmayr and Mershon are thoroughly efficient, but do not add anything to the appearance of a good rifle.

Recoil pads should never be used except for rifles of very heavy recoil, or for injured persons or others not able to take normal recoil. The high buttstock—high at heel, I mean—minimizes recoil quite a bit. Recoil pads detract so much from the appearance of a good stock that they should never be used unless absolutely necessary. Their effect on accuracy is totally unimportant on the hunting arm, however, so they do not detract from the performance of the rifle. Shelhamer's comment on recoil pads is very pertinent: "A good rifle with a fine custom stock having a recoil pad looks like a man in evening clothes

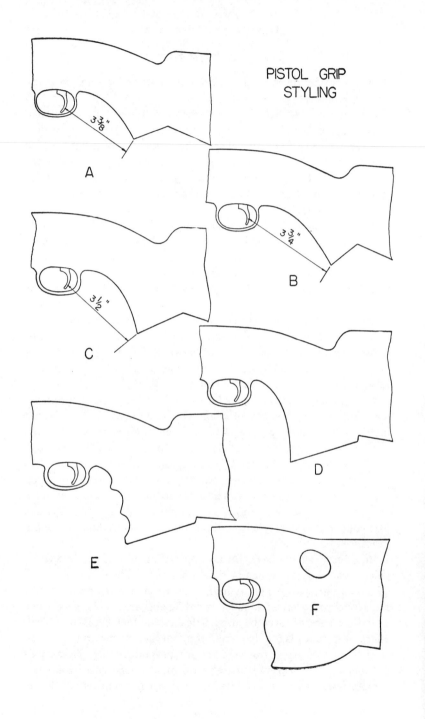

PISTOL GRIP
STYLING

A

B

C

D

E

F

$3\frac{3}{8}"$

$3\frac{3}{4}"$

$3\frac{1}{2}"$

wearing rubber boots."

Bulk of the stock at pistol grip and action is dependent somewhat on the quality of the stock wood. Strong, close-grained wood permits a slimmer stock than softer wood as it has superior strength. Before we get involved, though, we had better take up the specific features of stocks:

Grips. The straight grip is practically extinct, and rightly so. On service Krags and Springfields it was comfortable only in the offhand position and then only when the shooter could elevate his right elbow a little higher than the top of his head! I can think of no reason for making a repeating rifle with a straight grip stock.

The Germans evolved a type of sporting stock of their own, featuring small forends, flat cheekpieces, and skinny little grips usually set too far back. American and British stocks followed the same ideas until Bob Owen, our first great stockmaker, got sick of these uncomfortable gun handles and began designing his own type of stock. The Owen stocks of the 1920s were so obviously superior to earlier efforts that many of his ideas were copied by most stockmakers and factories.

Eventually, the present American sporter stock evolved, with good lines, decently sized forends and comfortable pistol grips. Length of the pistol grip (from the center of the trigger to the front edge of the bottom of the grip, in straight line measurement) can be from $3\frac{1}{4}''$ to $3\frac{3}{4}''$, with $3\frac{1}{2}''$ the average. My own all measure between $3\frac{1}{2}''$ to $3\frac{5}{8}''$, and my hand is quite wide in the palm—$4''$. The width of the hand, not the length of it, regulates the length of pistol grip. The

---

PISTOL GRIP STYLING

A. Short and rather thick grip, suited to stocks made of very soft wood.
B. Long pistol grip, best for general use. Thickness of the small of stock is regulated by the strength and the grain of the wood at that point.
C. Medium, deep pistol grip. Type which is too common today. Makes a stock which handles well for slow fire or deliberate shooting, but clumsy for fast work in the field or forest.
D. Conventional target type profile
E. Special target styling. Grooves are cut for third, fourth and fifth fingers. Such grips usually fit the shooter well in only one position. They must be made to fit the individual hand.
F. Free rifle grip, with thumb hole through the stock. A shelf for the thumb is usually also made on the right hand side of grip, so that shooter has option of two hand positions. The reverse curve for the bottom of the grip is surprisingly comfortable.

COMB PROFILES

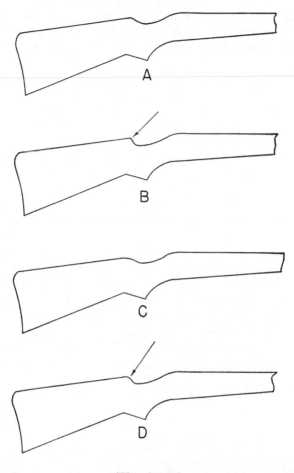

(Thumb cuts)

A poorly shaped comb can spoil the appearance of any stock. The following types, which are exaggerated somewhat, illustrate the common types.

A. Gradual curve—not too bad in appearance, but only suited to those men holding the thumb alongside the pistol grip.

B. Abrupt curve—as above, but suited to the thumb crossing grip.

C. Rounded curve—suited to nothing much, and poor in appearance.

D. Double radius curve—best looking, and can be suited to any hold.

length of the grip is practically constant regardless of the type of rifle or position of the trigger in the guard loop. In the Mauser rifle, the trigger is almost in the center of the guard, while on the Springfield and Winchester it is well to the rear of center. This does not affect the length of grip—if a man needs a 3⅝″ grip on a Mauser, he will also need a 3⅝″ grip on a Springfield.

The curvature of the pistol grip is affected by trigger position, however. The Mauser grip may have a slightly sharper curve than that of the Springfield, although this is not really important. Curvature of the grip depends more than anything else on how the shooter customarily holds the rifle. If he holds his elbow high and crosses his thumb over the small of the stock, the grip should sweep back and be shaped with an ever decreasing curve. If he holds his thumb alongside the receiver tang, the grip should be rather sharply curved, in an even arc, with more of a downward curve.

Circumference of the grip, at the smallest point, is also affected by the two means of holding. For appearance, the slim grip, not over 4¾″ in circumference, is always best and usually the most comfortable for the thumb-across-the-small holder. A 5¼″ circumference is allowable on stocks made of medium grade wood, and is quite comfortable for the thumb-along-side hold. Complicating the picture is the fact that there is a lot of variation in the length of assorted thumbs—as much as an inch, in hands which are otherwise very close in size. There are men with exceptionally short, thick thumbs who cannot find any pistol grip to accommodate them unless the comb of the stock is undercut on the right deeply and the top curve of the grip exaggerated considerably, in order to allow the heel of the thumb to move farther up and over to compensate for the short thumb.

Begins to look as though designing a stock depended a lot on the physical makeup of the customer, doesn't it? It sure as Hell does, bud. We have a few principles to follow, and a set of dimensions with generous tolerances, but styling or designing *A* stock for *A* customer still requires a little specialized thought and individual measurement. Averaging dimensions and shaping a stock to good appearance is not custom stocking.

Combs. We have already mentioned comb heights. Thickness of comb is important. The Winchester 70 stock has a thick comb, of metallic sight height, but, being thick and straight, it allows the use of low mounting telescopic sights very well. I believe the comb should be undercut on the right side, and the pistol grip outlined clearly all the way down, the undercut being carried down and back to accommodate

CHEEK PIECES

the heel of the thumb, if necessary. The profile of the comb is easier shown than described, so look at the drawing. The comb should be carried as far forward as possible when the customer is of the "stock-crawling" type, so that the cheekpiece can be further forward. In stocks with cheekpieces, there is no real "thickness" of the comb to be guided by, the cheekpiece being cut to position the shooter's face properly. On the plain stock, without cheekpiece, the comb of course positions the face and thickness will vary from quite thin for the wide faced shooter, to quite thick for the thin or narrow face. Location of the point of comb is illustrated.

Cheekpieces. Also easier shown than described. The small flat German type, also called the Whelen type, are thoroughly satisfactory if properly located. These must be in the right place. Having the customer hold any comparable rifle in his shooting position will show whether he holds his head forward, back or in between, and a snapshot of him holding a rifle will do as well if he is not on hand. No more horrible example of a misplaced cheekpiece can be found than that shown in Baker's *Modern Gunsmithing*, Fig. 49A, Page 105. This one was fully 3″ further back than it should be for any man having a neck.

Shape of the cheekpiece, from a side view, is of course between you and the customer, any of the varieties shown being okay. Size of the cheekpiece is a pitfall—the majority of them are made too long, being carried back an inch or more too far to the rear. No cheekpiece *needs* to be longer than 5″, but with very long buttstocks, a longer cheekpiece will make a better appearance. However, only with very fat faced shooters will more than 4″ of the cheek be in contact with the

---

CHEEKPIECES

Here is represented the four types of cheekpiece used today. Each of course can be modified greatly, and is. The drawings at right of each represent cross section at the dotted line portion of stock.

A. The standard sporter cheekpiece of most modern stockers, shown in correct position, and flat in cross section. Its face can also be either concave or convex.

B. "Swiss" type cheekpiece, which can be flat or slightly concave across its face. The curved face is shown in cross section. This type is unnecessarily long.

C. Small sporter type with large bevel, shown set too far back from comb.

D. Raised convex type, which is in effect only a high stock comb. These are satisfactory on light recoil rifles, but liable to be uncomfortable on heavy caliber arms.

stock, so the 5″ length is satisfactory on the hunting rifle, accommodating in either offhand or sitting positions.

In the matters of thickness or height of cheekpiece, remember that this must be worked out with the rifle assembled and sighting equipment installed, particularly if a telescopic sight is to be used. When the stock is being shaped, leave the cheekpiece large and high, and finish it last by the old cut-and-try method. After the correct dimension is reached, and feels very comfortable indeed, take off another shave anyway. If the customer has high cheekbones, take off $\frac{1}{16}$″ because in shop trials there is a tendency to "make" the stock fit through slow and careful shouldering and facing the cheekpiece, and it will feel perfect even though a trifle high.

I much prefer the concave face, or hollowed cheekpiece, finding it very comfortable and good in appearance. All cheekpieces must of course slope slightly forward, in toward the center of stock, in order that when the rifle recoils the stock will move back and away from the cheek, not up and into it. The flat cheekpiece is satisfactory in this respect also, when angled correctly. The convex, or rounded-profile cheekpiece is definitely a tricky deal as it raises the face, but does not support it over nearly as much area as does the flat or concave type, and must be very carefully proportioned to fit a particular face. Unless the stock is perfectly straight and the cheekpiece faired forward, recoil will jar your teeth loose on a quick shot. Such cheekpieces merely raise the face in the same manner as a high, thick comb. The cross section views serve to describe the three types of cheekpiece faces. The concave, or hollowed face, has little if any curvature needed in the vertical plane except for rifles with very high sight line.

The edges of the cheekpiece at the bottom and the rear should drop off sharply in a concave cut to the surface of the stock proper. A decorative bevel at the joining point between this cut and the surface of the stock is attractive. Be sure to get down to the proper depth, this being the surface of the stock following the lines from the butt and the bottom of stock. The stock should never go out to meet the cheekpiece. Above all, never forget that the cheekpiece serves a functional purpose—it is not there just for decoration—first you make it fit, then you make it look pretty.

Buttstocks. I figure my base line for determining drops from the line of bore, not the line of sight, since the latter can have a great variation we cannot control. Even when metallic sights only are contemplated, a comparison of Mauser and Springfield will show considerable difference in measurement between heights of lines of sight above lines of bore. When the vast number of telescopic sight and mount combinations is realized, it is evident that to work from the line of sight would give us quite a large set of dimensions to go by on each variety of rifle. With all limiting actual comb height by the position of the cocking piece when the bolt is open, anyway, the idea is somewhat foolish in the first place. However, from the line of bore we can establish a few more-or-less standards to go by.

The dimensions given earlier, of $\frac{5}{8}''$ to $1\frac{1}{16}''$ for drop at comb for scope rifles, and $\frac{3}{4}''$ to $1''$ for metallic sight arms, will stand for almost all large bolt actions. The Remington 721 and 722 actions permit slightly higher combs, but because of low sight line, this is not necessary. The same goes for drop at heel, of $1''$ to $1\frac{5}{8}''$ for all. On the buttplates, Niedner is recommended as these plates are furnished in one size, and are case-hardened. The Niedner people will sell the plates unhardened and it is wise to keep a few of these on hand as you may find a stock blank not quite large enough to take the standard plate and the unhardened plates can be filed down to size and a new border cut as required.

The shape of the butt determines whether the appearance of the finished stock is going to be attractive. Both the top and the bottom lines of the stock should be straight. The bottom line should take off from the highest point of curve of the pistol grip, or from the body of the stock just above and behind the trigger, whichever is higher. From a profile view, the pistol grip is to seem superimposed on a straight grip stock—you do not take the bottom line of the stock back from some point at the rear of the pistol grip, but establish the correct bottom line of the stock, and angle the bottom of the pistol grip up to meet it.

In cross section, the butt at the junction of the grip at the bottom is half round, and tapers back in straight lines to the shape of the buttplate. The top half of the stock goes forward from the shape of the buttplate, straight on top, but tapering in to the comb. It is straight on the top, but curves slightly on the sides.

Pitch should be around $2\frac{1}{2}''$, figuring $30''$ from the buttplate with the pitch line running from the top of the buttplate through the center of the bolt sleeve. This is the only means of standardizing a method of measuring pitch. Taking the pitch from the muzzle is fine, as long as the barrels are all the same length, but locating on the action is something else. If the rear of receiver bridge is used, you can get thrown for a loss in a hurry. The back end of the Mauser bridge is about $\frac{1}{4}''$ lower than that of the Springfield, for one thing. The differences between metallic sights and their settings makes use of the receiver sight a chancy proposition.

Cast off should be from ¼″ to ⅜″, although ½″ is not too much. I prefer a straight cast off of about ⅜″, but the canted version, with ⅛″ more at the toe than at the heel is better for most shooters. I shoot a rifle offhand and sitting with the buttplate on the upper arm, not the shoulder while the majority of modern riflemen keep the butt in the hollow of the shoulder, and the canted buttplate fits a little better.

Laying out cast off is easy except when the stock blank is of minimum thickness. A good many would be stockers do not understand cast off stocks so they angle the stock off and then build on a thick cheekpiece. Cast off does not really affect comb or cheekpiece thickness—it serves to bring the shooter's face a little to the right and closer to the vertical plane of the line of sight—it does not lower his face on the stock. The rifle with a cast off stock simply seems to come to the shoulder easier and the eye to line up the sights quicker. The stock is also more graceful in appearance, which is secondary. With Dunlap the fit is always more important than the looks, but a rifle stock can be made to fit perfectly and also be beautiful. Do not allow yourself to be talked into making a freakish stock with new and doubtful features of comfort and fit, or to sacrifice fit for appearance. Take it from one who has tried, it is not going to work out.

Do not try to be different, just try to be better!

Body of the Stock. This is the portion which encloses the action, from the tangs to the cylinder of the barrel. Here we must consider the caliber of the rifle in some cases as well as the dimensions of the receiver. Most magazine boxes can be cut down ¹⁄₁₆″ without injury to proper functioning, and the 1917 Enfield box can be cut ¼″ and still handle five cartridges of .30–06 diameter. This of course makes possible a well shaped stock. However, if the caliber is such as .30 Newton or the Holland and Holland belted type of cartridge, or any special cartridge based on these large diameter cases, all the magazine depth possible will be needed, to accommodate four cartridges, at most. My .30 Newton on the 1917 action holds only three cartridges in an unaltered magazine.

A thickness of 1¾″ should be minimum on stocks for 1903, 1917, Mauser '98 and the Winchester and Remington rifles, and 2″ the maximum with the minimum allowable only with strong, close grained wood. With the Mauser carbine action and the variants—Vz33 and G33/40, a 1⅝″ minimum is possible with good European walnut on featherweight class rifles. This thickness is measured at both the receiver ring and the receiver bridge location, the stock being straight through the body (viewing from the top or the bottom). When using the 1917 action with full depth magazine box, consider 2" the minimum thickness. This permits the stock to be rounded at sides of the body and give a decent appearance as well as more strength. Less than 2" thickness will mean making the sides of the stock rather flat and give a slab sided appearance.

The sides of the stock should never be paneled. Those flats some of the more backward German stockmakers featured were not supposed to be decorative anyway—they were an excuse to leave enough wood around the action to hold the gun together, while the butt and forend were slimmed down to toothpick proportions to make an exceedingly light rifle.

At the rear of the body, where the pistol grip turns into the body itself, the tang of the receiver decides how the top will be shaped, the Springfield requiring a rather flattened half round section, the Mauser allowing a more curved top and a slimmer body—which is why good stock men often narrow the Springfield rear tang on their own hook. The Winchester has a short wide tang, so it requires the stock to be rather wide at the top while the Remingtons do not have much tang, and what there is can be improved with a little file work, narrowing it for appearance's sake only.

From the tang down and forward to the trigger, a cross section of the stock should be sort of an upside down pear shape: you want to clear a little wood on each side just forward of the pistol grip and reaching forward in a sweeping curve to a point just behind the magazine box location, this on the lower half of stock only—so as to allow the triggerfinger to reach the trigger easily, without having to stretch around a bulge of wood.

There are a number of small details which can dress up a stock through the body portion. On the left side, the wood can be shaped up in a curve to below the distance of projection of the bolt stops, then brought out in a little shelf under the bolt stop. This is almost necessary on Enfield stocks in order to break up the expanse of wood staring you in the face on an unaltered magazine job. It adds to the appearance and shape of a Mauser stock as well, and in the case of plain wood, reveals a bit of grain structure to make it look a little better.

Too, when the body is rounded off to meet the action at the top, a slight flat often looks well, on the left side, where the wood meets the metal. This can be carried on forward through the forend.

On the right side of the stock, the wood can be cut to advantage

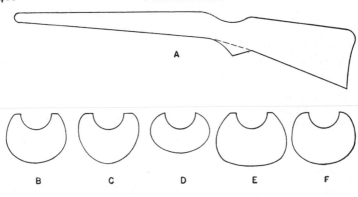

BUTT PROFILE—FOREND SECTIONS

A. The dotted line illustrates how the bottom line of stock should be carried up to meet body of stock at rear of guard.
B. Cross section of usual sporter forend, rounded type.
C. Cross section of deep type sporter forend.
D. Cross section of sporter forend, flattened round. Very good for either lightweight or standard type stocks.
E. Cross section of target rifle forend, rounded type.
F. Cross section of target rifle forend, square type, with sides and bottom flattened.

below the receiver opening—a slight flat at the edge of the metal rounding off into another flat angling slightly downward and faired into the rounded lines of the body.

On the bottom of the stock, most stockers carry a straight line from the rear of the triggerguard forward, but it is sometimes nice to break up this line by following the lines of the guard itself, bringing the stock wood along the curves of the guard loop and perhaps $\frac{1}{16}''$ down with the thicker sections of loop at each end.

Forends. Forends should be full and fairly long. Measuring from the receiver ring to the end of the tip, the length should be from $9\frac{1}{2}''$ to $10''$ for rifles with $24''$ barrels. A $9''$ forend is sufficiently long for a $22''$ barrel, and a $10\frac{1}{2}''$ or even $11''$ forend not too long for a $26''$ barrel. Avoid excessive taper and curving lines in the side and the top views of the forend. Width of the forend at the tip should be $1\frac{3}{4}''$, with $\frac{1}{16}''$ leeway over and under. For the featherweight, make the tip width $1\frac{5}{8}''$—you cannot save more than about an ounce and a half by cutting it down to $1\frac{1}{4}''$, anyway, so leave it big enough for the guy to hold on to. Depth of the stock at the tip, should be from $1\frac{1}{8}''$ to $1\frac{1}{4}''$, and this is plenty. Make the tip itself carry the lines of the forend $\frac{3}{4}''$

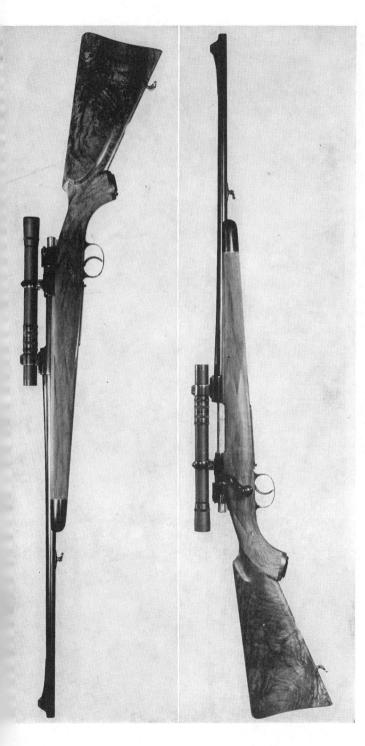

A Lightweight Owen Job

This little rifle is a .257 Roberts on a Mauser action, fitted with a particularly well shaped barrel made by a young comer in the business, Tom Burgess of Spokane, Washington. This outfit, complete with scope and mounts, weighs around 7 pounds 2 ounces, and is now owned by Mr. H. A. Spalding, of Hazard, Kentucky.

The wood in this stock is one of the finest pieces of French walnut that it has ever been my good fortune to get hold of, and was given to me on a visit to Birmingham, England by the late Mr. David Banford who formerly sold gunstocks to the best trade in England. This piece of wood would easily cost a hundred and twenty-five dollars today; it was what was known to the English trade as "Exhibition" quality.

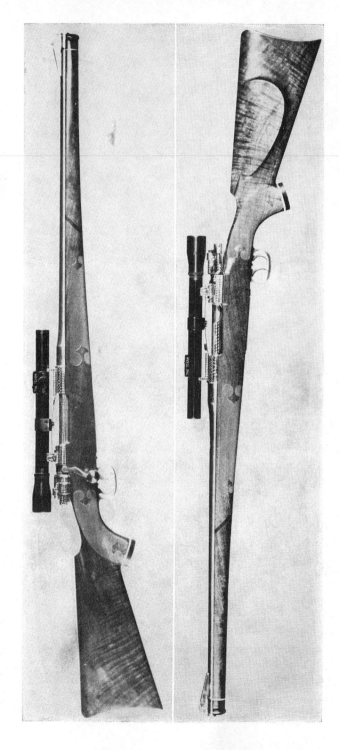

Mauser action stocked in full-length Mannlicher form. Note how the forearm has been cut apart and a thin bit of ornamental material inserted; this to minimize any warping tendencies which so long and thin a forearm is almost certain to have. The checkering patterns were taken from one of Al Linden's pattern sheets.

at least before rounding it off. Do not make the tips, if of contrasting color to the stock, longer than 1¾". The forend feels more comfortable if it is slightly flattened on the bottom rather than rounded. See the cross section outlines. On checking the neatest custom stock I have on hand at the moment, I find the forend to be shaped very much like the wide, target style forend, much reduced of course.

The sling swivel should be from 3" to 3½" back from the end of the forend. In general, take the length of the contrasting tip, if any, and set the swivel back an equal distance from the junction of forend and tip.

Bear in mind you do not absolutely have to have a contrasting tip— or a grip cap. A very handsome stock can be made with no dress up accessories. The forend can be shaped to a decent appearance with either our standard, rounded end, or with the schnabel tip. I do not care for the latter myself, but the customer might like it.

The last word in the stock designing headache is—make the lines of the stock clean. If the curves and shapes of the various portions of the stock will not fair cleanly into each other, make abrupt shape transitions, with definite curves and lines—do not mush the lines into each other. The lines of a stock are straight, definitely angled, and increasing curves. It has been written that a stock is composed of straight lines and circular lines. I checked about a dozen custom stocks, and my own dozen or so rifles, and I could not find an even arc anywhere on any of them.

MANNLICHER TYPE STOCKS

The Mannlicher, or full length sporting stock, is liked by some sportsmen—and no stockmakers. The Mannlicher-Schoenauer carbine is a nice handling little rifle and is responsible for the very limited popularity of the stock type. Most Americans, however, want rifles, not carbines, and their barrels must be at least 22" long. Well, a full length stock, firmly attached to the barrel at the muzzle, has great warping tendencies and usually pulls the barrel around as it does so— which is why good stockmakers almost always refuse to make the Mannlicher type stock. If the guy wants it though, somebody should take care of him.

In the Mannlicher stocked *rifle* the Germans came up with an idea which does away to a considerable extent of the warping bogey. They cut the forend off diagonally at approximately the length of a standard sporter forend, then made a separate continuing forend to reach the muzzle, these two forends joining at the diagonal, with a thin plate, usually of molded horn, in between. The front forend was of course held at the muzzle by the muzzle band, and at rear by either the diagonal alone or by pin or screw from side to side, passing through a small lug sweated to the underside of the barrel.

The Mannlicher stock features slimness and light weight, in spite of the long stock and except for necessary thickness through pistol grip and body, the entire stock is to be made as light as possible. The forend, ahead of the receiver ring, rapidly assumes a cylindrical cross section and carries this to the muzzle, in almost a straight taper on the sides, with a very slight curve on the bottom line. It is smaller in width and depth than the sporter forend at any comparable point. The Mannlicher-Schoenauer action requires a thicker stock than any of the Mauser types and Mannlicher carbines look rather fat. The custom stocked Mauser or Springfield makes a better looking job.

At the muzzle, the Mannlicher stock should not be over 1″ wide and not over 1″ deep, including the barrel of the rifle or carbine.

I do not consider the Mannlicher stock suitable for rifles of heavy recoil, and recommend that no arm for cartridge larger than the .257 or 7mm be accommodated.

CHAPTER 24

Stockmaking: Layout and Inletting*

MAUSER TYPE BOLT ACTIONS

THE first step in making a stock from the rough blank is to make and square a profile stock blank. Make a template, of any suitable material—thin plywood, sheet aluminum, even cardboard will do—of the exact side profile of the projected stock, at least $\frac{1}{32}''$ oversize on all sides (a $\frac{1}{16}''$ tolerance is better). The pistol grip can be sharper and deeper than the final proportions, for protection against dents and edge chipping while inletting. Most custom stockmakers have several plywood templates of minimum and full proportioned stocks for the most popular actions used, and vary the outlines on the blank free-hand to take care of specific dimension requirements.

Make the stock template, check all dimensions carefully, then place it on your plank or rough blank so as to take advantage of the grain structure for strength through the pistol grip, figure in butt, and straight or upward rising grain in the forend. Check both the side and the edge grain of the plank or the blank—a quick planing and wetting with water will show up the grain in a hurry. Draw around your pattern or template with pencil, and then saw the blank out along these lines. A table saw is recommended for the straight cuts and a band saw for the curve of pistol grip or, the band saw can of course be used for the whole job as can a handsaw with plenty of elbow grease.

The blank must be planed smooth on one side, preferably the right, either before or after profiling. It is to be not only smooth, but square, although you do not need the perfect "plane face" demanded by the manual training schoolteacher! With it square, plane the top of the blank square, both on the action barrel section and the comb of the buttstock. This planing removes wood which is an argument for leaving more than $\frac{1}{32}''$ leeway around the actual stock profile, unless you can hold awfully blasted straight with the saw in cutting out the blank!

*See Appendix I, page 713.

The underline of stock should also be quite square, although it need not be trued up by plane. That is why a band saw or table saw is recommended, in order to cut the top and the bottom of the stock in parallel lines.

Next must be considered the thickness of the blank in relation to the design to be executed. A plain straight stock, without raised cheekpiece or offset, can be made from a blank 2" thick, minimum, which will allow a satisfactory outline of cheekpiece, however, and permit a decent overall design. It is best to have a blank not less than $2\frac{1}{4}$" thick, and not over $2\frac{1}{2}$" as thicker blanks mean only more work in shaping the stock later.

Make your center line for the barrel and the action, laid out with pencil on the top and the bottom of the profiled blank, from the pistol grip forward. This line is parallel to the square side of the blank, but not necessarily in the center of the blank. Remember the offset, if you want any, and you do in most cases. A good way to check your leeway on the blank is to cut a rectangular template out of cardboard the length and width of the receiver of the rifle being used, less the length of the tang. By placing this on top of the blank, you can move it toward the left side and check the amount of wood you must leave for the left side wall of the body of stock. Determine your center line for the barrel and receiver through the center line of this small template, carrying the line out to the end of the forend. Run this line down over the end or the tip and back along the bottom of the blank, exactly under the top line.

Now, continue this line, but lightly, back over and around the buttstock, until the line is continuous around the blank. Next, set your offset working center line, by measuring to the right of the line down across the end of butt. An offset of about $\frac{5}{16}$" is almost always possible, and usually more. To get as much as you can, regardless of any specific measurement, measure your intended buttplate, divide this dimension by two, and measure in from the right edge of blank to get your butt center line. Add from $\frac{1}{32}$" to $\frac{1}{16}$" to give yourself working tolerance on the stock.

The offset, or cast off (cast on, in the case of a left handed shooter, and taken in the opposite direction) may be constant or canted. The canted butt is most comfortable to the average shooter. To cant the center line, make your first measurement $\frac{1}{2}$" from the top of the butt, from the right side of course, if the buttplate is governing the amount of the cast off, then $\frac{1}{2}$" above the toe, on the butt, make the same measurement minus $\frac{1}{8}$", and draw your center line through the two points thus located. The top line of the buttstock reaches from the top or the end of the line across the face of the butt to the center line of the stock proper at the tang location of the receiver, and the bottom line of the buttstock goes from the approximate location of the rear guard screw to the line at the toe of the stock. In appearance, on a finished stock of this type, the butt (looking from the rear) appears slightly to the right and slightly twisted, in relation to the body of the stock and the forend.

Now erase the original center line through the butt, to keep from being confused in working as the offset butt line is to be followed from here on out.

We now have a continuous line on which to base our layout for inletting. The first step is to establish the location of the front guard screw hole, which is easy because you can check the action against your stock profile template first and get a measurement from either the front or the back of the blank. Now drill this hole, at right angles to the top of the blank in both directions. With an angle vise and drill-press, the operation is practically foolproof, since you can clamp the blank and check by level against the square top and side to make sure the hole is straight. Drill from the top, with a $\frac{9}{32}''$ bit. If the Mauser action is being used, or any other with parallel guard screws, the rear hole may also be drilled at this time. For the Mauser '98 or Carbine action, the guard screw holes are $7\frac{13}{16}''$ apart, center to center. (Actually, it's a few thousandths over this, but not enough to worry about in woodworking. The hole, or holes, of course locate on the center line of the blank.)

The blank is now turned over for a while, as it is best to inlet the triggerguard first. Another template must be made, of either thin metal or hard sheet fiber, to give an outline of the triggerguard. You can either lay out this template by mechanical drawing, taking all measurements from the triggerguard itself, or by means of carbon paper and plain paper take an impression from the inletting on another stock for the same action. This is transferred to the template material and the template cut out. Check your template by drawing around it on a piece of cardboard, cutting out the scribed portion, and trying the triggerguard in the hole. If okay, lay the template on the bottom of the blank, with the guard screw hole over the hole through the blank, and with a pencil draw the outline of the guard inletting-to-be on the wood.

If the surface of the wood is smooth, a scriber can be used instead of the pencil, or a white grease pencil used, to make a really legible line.

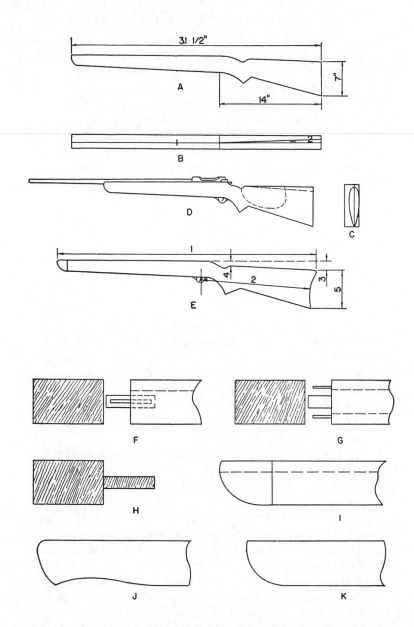

31 1/2"

7"

14"

A

B

D

C

E

1

14

2

3

5

F

G

H

I

J

K

STOCK LAYOUTS & FOREND TIPS

This line will be outside of the inletting, as your template is full size, and the pencil makes an oversize outline. I believe this better than attempting to make an actual size outline, which will be cut away at the first work and so no longer be a guide.

With any of the triggerguards having integral magazine boxes, the first thing to do is to outline the dimensions of the box on the bottom of the stock, inside the guard outline, then remove this wood. You can make templates for this too, if you wish, but simple measurement of the box and comparison with the guard template outline will locate it easily enough. I prefer to use fairly small metal cutting bits in the drill-press to drill out the magazine opening, following the outline of the box closely to leave a minimum of chiseling and filing. The wood should come out in a block, and with chisels and rough files it is easy to clear the opening to admit the magazine box all the way. *It is not necessary and seldom desirable to have the magazine box closely inletted and bearing on the wood at all points.* For rifles of very heavy recoil, the rear of the magazine box can be inletted to bear against the wood, but be sure to

---

STOCK LAYOUT—FOREND TIPS

A. Profile of a stock blank, square on the top and at least one side.
B. Top view of layout, showing the center line of the rifle and offset or cast off in buttstock.
C. View of the butt end, showing the position of the butt plate due to cast off.
D. Represents the rifle inletted into the blank, with dotted lines to indicate finished dimension limits, to which the blank is now cut.
E. Nomenclature of the stock:
   1. Overall length.
   2. Buttstock length, or length of pull.
   3. Drop at heel.
   4. Drop at comb.
   5. Height of stock—determines drop at heel.
F. General method of forend tip attachment, side view. Dowel is cut on or is inserted in end of stock, with small side pins, and the tip drilled to fit on them.
G. Top view of "F." showing position of side pins. These hold the tip from turning.
H. Dowell machined on the tip, the stock end to be drilled to accept it.
I. Profile of sporter tip, showing proper proportions of the tip to the stock. Long tips are poor in appearance.
J. The snobble, schnobble, schnabel tip—(choose your own spelling—everyone else does). Not in favor in America today, but better than a lot of the crummy tip jobs I have seen. Shelhamer is the only top stock man I know of who still occasionally employs this style of forend and tip.

leave at least $\frac{1}{32}''$ clearance at the corners of the box on the sides.

The Mauser guard has a small floorplate, which often exposes the bottom of the magazine box, at the sides, so care must be taken not to enlarge the magazine opening at the bottom. Therefore for the Mauser, keep the magazine box cut at minimum, filing and scraping its sides as the guard enters the stock.

Rasps and files do most of the work in inletting the box. When the guard proper bottoms on the outside of the stock, check its outline against the outline you have drawn by template to see how much inside the drawn outline you must stay, and also check the guard screw hole to be sure it lines up with the hole in the blank, or the stock as we had better call it from now on.

Use straight chisels to cut the outline of the guard in, cutting across the arcs at the ends and at the corners of the magazine, and remove the wood to a depth of about $\frac{3}{16}''$. Then use the curved chisels to cut and finish the full outline and always, if possible, use a chisel or gouge of smaller radius than the cut you wish to make.

Now, there is something of a trick to get the close fit between wood and metal that the master stockmakers achieve. You will find that some guards taper slightly from top to bottom, in cross section being slightly wider at the bottom than at the top, or inner side. If they do not have this taper, or bevel (Tom Shelhamer calls it "draft") put it on with a file yourself, narrowing the tangs of the guards at the top, all the way along on the 1917, fore-and-aft of the box on Mausers and Springfields.

You use a slightly smaller template, the size of the guard (in width and length both) at its top, and are guided principally in inletting by the guard itself. The inletting cut must constantly be scraped or cut wider as the guard goes deeper into the wood, thus a tight fit is practically assured, as long as you do not lose patience.

Bottoming tools are useful in inletting the guard of the 1917 action, but not much help on the other actions. Keep one of your narrow straight chisels with a short bevel on the edge, as, turned over, it is a fast and handy bottomer for the guards.

The guard is inletted until it is approximately $\frac{1}{32}''$ below the surface of the stock at all points on its edges (less floorplate, of course) including the rear tang. During the final half of the inletting it will be necessary to "spot in" the metal to the wood. This consists of coating the underside and edges of the guard with a material which, when in contact with the wood, remains to color the wood at all bearing points and thus indicate where wood must be cut away.

STARTING OFF ON A STOCKING JOB

Leonard Mews shown doing a bit of preliminary measuring and "figgerin out" on a myrtle wood blank intended for a .270 Magnum barrel fitted to a Mauser action.

In starting the work on a plain blank such as this, it does not pay to rush matters in a craze to get working at the actual job. Make haste slowly at this stage and be certain the base lines are correctly placed and that their locations will allow meeting all specifications the customer has stipulated yet at the same time utilize to best advantage all such natural properties and grain figure as may be contained in the wood.

Author checking Bishop's semi-inletting of Mauser stock with separate receiver. Extra stripped receivers such as this are of considerable value in stock work as the action inletting can be checked easily without the weight of a barrel to handicap spotting-in.

Prussian blue, used as layout coloring for metal, is widely used for spotting in. That made by the Permatex Company is the best. Whatever material is used should not dry too quickly, should not build up on the metal from repeated applications and so change dimensions, and should not of course have any ingredients which will damage either wood or metal. Lampblack and oil is an old spotting preparation, as is plain soot from a kerosene or carbide flame, but this is messy and bothersome, as the metal must be smoked thoroughly for each trial.

The best spotting stuff, to my mind, is cream rouge, which a friend brought to my attention a couple of years ago and which I have used since. This is a cosmetic in paste form, and the best ones seem not particularly greasy. A two bit container will last for two or three stock jobs. The stuff comes in varying shades of red, which leave a very legible mark on the wood, to be scraped away on the very lightest cut. It does not soak into the wood. Only one or two applications are necessary, as the spots on the metal left bare by trial contact with the stock are covered by just smearing them over with the finger, carrying more rouge from surrounding areas. You put it on the rifle and guard with the finger in the first place, too. It is less messy than any of the others, and removes instantly from the metal by solvent, alcohol, or even gun oil. I like it most because it leaves a very legible mark on the wood, even in the poorest light.

An essential to good inletting of receivers are headless screws, made to thread into the guard screw tapped holes. Three inches is sufficient length, and you can either make the screws or purchase them from any of numerous advertisers. Cold rolled steel rod, $\frac{1}{4}''$ in diameter, is good enough. The Mauser thread is $\frac{1}{4}$ x 22; the Enfield, $\frac{1}{4}$ x 30; the Springfield, $\frac{1}{4}$ x 25, and the Winchester, $\frac{1}{4}$ x 32. Guard screw thread of Remington 721 and 722 is $\frac{1}{4}$ x 28. Springfield and Mauser are V type metrics, but the above inch pitch measurements serve well enough. The Enfield is a Whitworth type thread, but a V thread usually works out satisfactorily. The Winchester is V type, American thread.

It is not absolutely necessary to inlet the triggerguard first. The only reason for doing this is to use the guard screw holes in the guard as a guide or jig to receive the headless screws placed in the receiver and slid down through the holes in the stock to reach the guard. This process serves to line up the receiver and guard. All the rifles have the front guard screw entering the receiver at right angle, so that it can be used as a guide for all. The Mauser and Winchester also have the rear screw entering the receiver at 90 degrees, so with these actions two guide screws can be used. The Springfield and Enfield have the rear screw entering at an angle, so that only the front guide screw can be used. It is advisable that the guard always be inletted first for these latter two actions.

The Mauser and Winchester actions may be inletted before the triggerguards, as the two guard screws will serve to align the guard after the receiver and the barrel have been fully inletted.

The Winchester Model 70 is difficult to inlet, with the guard being particularly hard to do a good job on unless a special guard unit is made up. The standard 70 guard assembly consists of guard bow, magazine cover hinge plate, and magazine cover, meaning finger loop, floorplate, and front tang. Only the first and last parts are inletted. Trying to inlet and line up the separate parts and do a good job is almost hopeless. So, you buy the three parts listed, assemble them as they would be on the assembled rifle, and solder them together, making a solid, one piece guard unit to work with. Be sure they are in perfect alignment. Trying in a factory Model 70 stock will check it in a hurry. No, you are not through yet. Before using this in actual inletting, file the hinge plate and guard bow on the sides, taking off $\frac{1}{64}''$ all around at the top, and a little less than this on the bottom. Now you can use it as both template and working guard for inletting, setting it to full depth in the stock before attempting to fit the guard assembly belonging to the rifle involved. The latter is easily fitted into the pre-inletting by scraping, and a good tight inletting job is practically assured. And the holes will all line up with the holes in the receiver.

With any type of triggerguard inletting, the only real thing to worry about is canting or tilting the guard, which is not at all hard to do. The possibility of this trouble is the reason why we want the bottom side of the blank square with the top, so that the bottom surface can be used as a check line against the guard during inletting. If both sides of the guard, or rather, top edges, are equidistant from the surface of the wood surrounding, naturally the guard is going straight into the stock.

If the receiver and barrel are to be inletted first, drill the guard screw holes through the stock with a $\frac{17}{64}''$ bit, to give a close fit on the $\frac{1}{4}''$ screws used as guides. Slide the screws (threaded tightly into the receiver, and checked for parallelism between themselves) down through these holes so that the bottom of the recoil shoulder contacts the top of the stock. Mark around the shoulder with a pencil and lift the rifle from the stock blank. With chisels or drill bits remove sufficient wood to leave a hole accommodating the recoil shoulder—just gouge it out in a hurry. There is no need to be neat about this, just do not make the cut any wider than necessary, it will be absorbed in the main receiver cut anyway.

Again try the rifle on the stock. The receiver should bottom at front and at the rear tang, which must be inletted now. The Mauser and Winchester receivers are flat on the bottom, and with the former, only a little circular recess under the rear tang must be cut to make it bottom all the way. Now mark with a sharp pencil or a scriber all around the receiver. This will give you the outline of the bottom of the receiver of course—the part that has to go all the way down. If you care to outline the magazine box opening through the receiver well then drill out this wood, it will save a little time.

Measure from the bottom of the receiver to one half the diameter of the receiver ring. This will be approximately the depth to which the receiver must be inletted. You may with either drill bits or chisels now remove the wood inside your scribed receiver outline on top of the stock to about $\frac{1}{16}''$ above the necessary full depth of inletting. (Or, to be more explicit, $\frac{1}{16}''$ less than the above measurement.) Before doing this, however, you can, with the rifle on the stock, draw the outline of the barrel channel, canting your pencil inward while drawing it along the sides of the barrel to insure a smaller-than-natural dimension.

It will be necessary to cut this channel and keep deepening it as the receiver sinks into the blank, to keep the latter going straight down.

After you clean out your scribed receiver part of the inletting, the receiver will drop into the stock approximately $\frac{5}{16}''$, the downward movement being arrested by the swell of the receiver ring and sidewalls. So far, you have needed only straight chisels for this job. The barrel channel requires gouges, or curved chisels. A very good way to do the preliminary cutting on the barrel channel is to clamp a straight edge along your marked lines on the forend—aside from the curves below the barrel cylinder, you will find most barrels have some straight tapers—and cut straight down about $\frac{1}{8}''$ with a sharp knife point. This is not always possible, but when the wood is reasonably straight in grain it is quite a time saver. With both sides of the channel thus outlined by cuts, a sharp half round outside bevel chisel can quickly shape a deep groove reaching to these cuts. I find it possible to better control the chisel by using a mallet to tap it along on this job, than to use straight hand pressure.

Very fancy wood, with complicated figure and small cross grains or

300 HOLLAND & HOLLAND MAGNUM

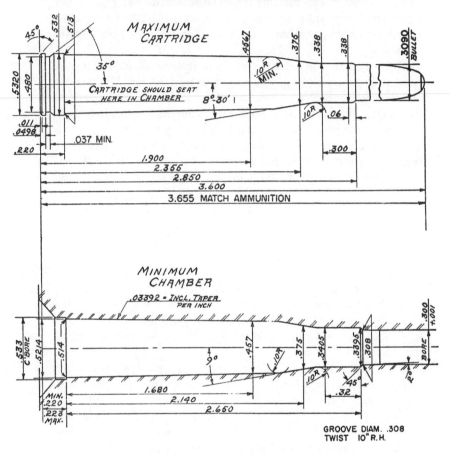

MAXIMUM CARTRIDGE

45° .532 .513

.5320 .480 35° .4567 .375 .338 .338 .3090 BULLET

CARTRIDGE SHOULD SEAT HERE IN CHAMBER 8° 30'

10R MIN.

.011 .0498 .037 MIN. 10R .06

.220

.300

1.900

2.356

2.850

3.600

3.655 MATCH AMMUNITION

MINIMUM CHAMBER

.03392 = INCL. TAPER PER INCH

.533 C'BORE .52/4 .514 9° .457 .375 .3405 .3395 .308 .300 +.001

10R 10R 45° BORE 7°

.32

MIN. .220 1.680

.228 MAX. 2.140

2.650

GROOVE DIAM. .308
TWIST 10" R.H.

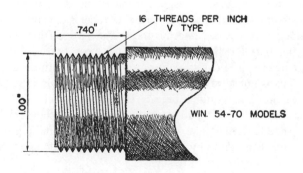

.740" 16 THREADS PER INCH
V TYPE

1.00"

WIN. 54-70 MODELS

little burls, calls for the channel to be cut entirely by chisel—bird's eye maple in particular. To make the outline cut of the channel you use a shallow curved chisel, almost straight across, and about 1″ wide—some call this a "sweep." You cut from each side, making a series of shallow connecting arcs, looking at the stock from the top, then with a very sharp small half round gouge begin in the center and cut a half round channel, gradually making it wider and deeper until the edge cuts are reached.

The preliminary channel cut, the barrel inletting rasp or scraper now enters the picture to smooth out the chisel job and make the channel perfectly half round. Remember always to work with the grain as much as possible, with either knife, chisel or rasp. This may mean changing directions every couple of inches sometimes but go ahead and do it, even if it means variations in depth. A ⅜″ thick piece of board 6″ long, rounded on one edge and used as a backing block for cutting cloth or sandpaper will even out the channel.

The .300 Holland and Holland Magnum

Rimless, Belted

Developed in England for use in sporter rifles built on magnum Mauser actions, this cartridge has become popular in the United States since Winchester put out the Models 54 and 70 rifles for it, and American loading companies began furnishing the ammunition. Abroad, the same cartridge is also made in plain rimmed style for use in double rifles but only the rimless belted case is made in the United States.

Intended as a super .30 caliber hunting cartridge, the .300 Magnum replaced the .30 Newton, which was handicapped by the existence of numerous poor rifles which prevented loading the Newton to its full possible performance.

Previously exciting no great comment, the .300 received its reputation on the rifle range in 1936, when Ben E. Comfort won the 1000 yard Wimbledon match at Camp Perry using a .300 heavy rifle and Western handloaded target ammunition. Proving to outclass the .30–06 at long range, the .300 is now the favorite long range target caliber, as well as an established big game choice.

The long shoulder is not well suited to modern American powders, and velocities can be increased without a corresponding increase in pressure by a sharper shoulder, with consequent greater powder capacity of the case. Weatherby, Ackley and Pfeifer as well as others, have improved .300 chambers.

Winchester loads the 150-grain hunting bullet to 3,090 FPS, the 180-grain to 2,900 FPS and the 220-grain to 2,610 FPS. Western loads the 180-grain boat tailed match bullet to 3,030 FPS for target shooting. (All are muzzle velocities.)

Well, the receiver is into the stock, and the bottom of the barrel part way down in the channel. Scribe around the receiver ring, left side wall—any place you see the surface of the stock holding up the receiver—keeping the scribe handle canted out, to make the new guide lines under the actual dimension of the receiver. Where a straight or slanted section of the receiver is evident, cut straight into the wood to make an accommodating fit. Where the curved sections of the receiver are going, curve your new inletting cuts to match. For the first cuts here, use the short-bent or spoon gouges, straightening out these inner side walls afterward with shallow curved chisels or scrapers.

By now, the assembly is settling deeper into the stock, the rear tang is almost below the surface of the wood, the barrel is touching the edges of the channel so you get out the spotting compound and take a short rest—the easy work is over.

What comes next shows up the difference between a topnotch custom stock and just another gun handle—close inletting. Patience is the most necessary attribute a good stockmaker must have. A man can be either jittery as a healthy three year old boy or stolid and phlegmatic as a stock show bull and become a good stockmaker. But he must be able to force himself to take a scraper and remove a few thousandths of an inch of wood at a bearing point even when he knows that eventually he will have to take off $\frac{1}{32}''$ at the same spot. He must resign himself to trying the rifle in the inletting dozens of times.

There is a considerable difference in the time spent on stocks by good custom stockers. Some men can complete a stocking job in less than four days, others require from 10 days to two weeks. As a rule, Mauser actions require less time than any of the others, possibly excepting the Remington 721–722 models.

I have mentioned scrapers several times, but have not gone into any detail on them. They are sharp edged plates of metal, profiled to desirable shapes at the cutting edges—half round in various sizes, shallow curved, and straight in various widths from $\frac{1}{4}''$ to $1''$. You can make them of any hard, fairly thin bit of steel. Old mill files can be ground on the end to make good scrapers. Hacksaw blades are very good, particularly the wide, hard steel power saw blades. Grind the teeth off, break into short lengths and grind to shape, finishing with a handstoning with oilstone. The edges should be ground at a slight bevel, to give one dependably sharp edge, although if a grinding attachment is available which will permit the end to be ground perfectly straight, two usable edges are provided.

Scrapers are used on the bottoms and the sides of inletting cuts not only to smooth out chisel marks but to remove wood. They are used always with finger pressure only. Make up a batch of them, to help you resist the temptation to use your chisel edges for scraping—there is not a better way to dull a chisel in a hurry.

Getting back to our stock job, check your chisels as some of them will need sharpening—you should have all of them literally razor sharp, so that you can wet your arm and shave hair off with any chisel or gouge on the bench. It will be necessary to take light cuts against the grain sometimes, and across the grain in most cases, therefore only very sharp tools will cut cleanly.

Coat the underside of the receiver and the barrel with spotting stuff, up to half the diameter of the ring and the barrel, and try it in the stock. Inspect the edges of inletting where they contact metal—you may be able to use the scribe again in a few places. Remove the assembly and where the coated steel has marked the wood, use the chisels to clear wood away, in light cuts and shavings. The recoil shoulder has probably already bottomed on the receiver floor in the stock and has had a slight recess cut for it. Now cut the recoil shoulder in the stock, cutting squarely across the stock and straight down, to a depth to accommodate the metal receiver shoulder. If the rifle is of light caliber—no larger than .257 or 7mm—you may spot in the recoil shoulder as you inlet the action, making as perfect and complete bearing of metal against wood as you can. If the rifle is for a cartridge of appreciable recoil, cut the shoulder back to clear the metal recoil shoulder by $\frac{1}{16}''$ right at the start and forget about the bearing for the present.

Repeat the trial spotting and chiseling until the receiver is bottomed on the "floor" in the stock, which you will remember was left about $\frac{1}{16}''$ high. Both barrel and receiver should now fit tightly into the stock, with no gaps between wood and metal. If the guard was inletted first and is in the stock, try the guard screws of the rifle through the guard into the receiver to see if they are in line. If by any mischance the receiver has moved forward or back slightly, now is the time to correct it.

The magazine box should come as close to the receiver as you can get it, without touching—about $\frac{1}{64}''$ is correct, on thoroughly seasoned European or hard American walnut; $\frac{1}{32}''$ on doubtful wood which probably will shrink a little. If your guard and magazine are fully inletted, you are guided more by it than by measurement from now on.

Lower the floor of the stock to the proper relationship with the magazine, or if no magazine is present, to about $\frac{1}{32}''$ beyond the high water mark on the receiver and the barrel, so that both are inletted a little deeper than center. This is where the bottoming tools and straight scrapers come in. If the Mauser action is being inletted, check by short straight edge to see that the tang is not inletted deeper than the floor. Now, with scrapers enlarge the inletting at the sides, and the barrel channel, checking every other minute by spotting the rifle in the stock, until the full depth of inletting is reached. The portion of the right side wall opposite the receiver opening may be cut away with a saw and a chisel to facilitate a close fit of the right side of the action.

The further you go, the more area you will cover with the spotting color each trial, until at the end, the barrel will bear all the way along both sides and bottom of the channel, with full contact the last three inches of tip.

On the matter of decorative tip attachment, we have two schools of thought: One, that the tip block should be set in place on the blank and the channel cut right along with the forend channel; Two, that the tip block should be attached only after the stock has been inletted and shaped on the outside, after which the channel is inletted through the tip. I favor the latter practice, but take your choice.

The bottom of the receiver should bottom solidly from tip of tang to cylinder of barrel, with the recoil shoulder, whether bearing or not, having $\frac{1}{32}''$ clearance at the sides and the bottom.

The guide screws are discarded during the final spotting in, and the receiver and guard assembled in the stock with the regular screws, tightened as much as possible. (To prevent burring new screws, it is smart to keep extra sets of guard screws for the most popular actions on hand just for this purpose.) Check the tension of the forend against the barrel at this time. I prefer a tension of from 6 to 8 pounds (to pull the forend away from the barrel) but customers may order anything from one to 12 pounds. Only, *don't* deepen the channel to give the desired tension now—you have too much bulk in that forend yet. Whatever tension is ordered, double it for your check on the inletted blank and after the stock is shaped you can regulate the tension to order.

With the blank inletted the rifle should be assembled with the bolt in the receiver. Tighten the front guard screw as much as you can, before even starting the rear screw.

Now look at the position of the barrel at the forend tip and the receiver tang, start in and tighten the rear guard screw. The tang should not move down in the stock, nor should the barrel move at all in its channel, either up or down. It cannot go down, but there is a vague

Author in first stages of finishing a semi-inletted Bishop Mauser stock—using a slim round file to clear corners of magazine mortise so that trigger-guard may be inlet.

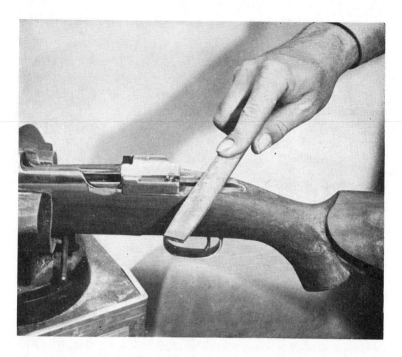

FINAL TOUCH IN FITTING

This shows one of the final efforts in fitting wood and metal, and graphically illustrates why you do not blue the metal until after the stock is completed: the wood is filed right down to metal across the tang as shown, around magazine and guard, and on right side of receiver, at ejection port.

There is no other way to make a perfect fit, either. No scribing, sighting or measuring will make possible cutting wood to correct fit, apart from the metal.

The clip slots on this Mauser carbine bridge have been filed down, in case you are wondering what the action is.

The series of closeup photos and most of the superb rifle pictures were made by Sam Levitz, news photographer and gun nut, who was a little too good here. He did not have to show my dirty fingernails!

possibility the tension might change toward the heavier side.

Should the tang draw deeper into the inletting as the rear screw tightens—which often happens, especially with military Mausers—you are very probably bending the receiver. So, place a shim under the tang, or deepen the floor and barrel channel to compensate, or the rifle will never put two bullets close together.

If close and full contact all along the bottom of the receiver is beyond you, bed on the bottom of the receiver just behind the recoil shoulder and on the tang, giving clearance in the middle—at least the gun will shoot then.

Cut clearance at the tang on the stock to permit passage of the cocking piece, and operate the bolt and while this is not much of a test of a strained receiver, it is better than nothing. You can at this time attach the bolt stop assembly and inlet it, or you can wait until the blank has been rough shaped. Do not cut any notch on the right side for the bolt handle now, just try the bolt back and forth, opened. Inlet for the sear, trigger and floorplate catch at this time, leaving $\frac{1}{32}''$ clearance on the sides of the trigger and the sear cuts.

Except for the floorplate and perhaps the bolt stop, you should be able to assemble the rifle with the guard screws as tight as they will be when the stock is completely finished, and with parts moving freely in their normal functions.

As mentioned earlier, leave a little clearance around the magazine box except at the bottom when any gap will be visible around the floorplate—$\frac{1}{64}''$ is enough.

The 1917 Enfield magazine is difficult to bed tightly and maintain perfect alignment with the guard and the receiver, and as the box is concealed, for ordinary fitting a gap can be left all around the box, from top to bottom of its inletting. However, some very powerful rifles are built on this action, and the customer may specify that the magazine be inletted to assist in absorbing recoil. To inlet the 1917 magazine box closely, first inlet the guard and receiver, making no opening for the box and through the opening in the guard scribe the sides of the future magazine inletting and also the ends, as the box proper fits inside the guard on this rifle. From the bottom, cut straight up along these lines, after removing the bulk of the wood by drill and square out this opening, checking with calipers against the dimensions of the magazine box until it will accept the box. Before the box will enter, you must cut little vertical grooves at the front and rear corners of the box opening, to take the welded or riveted ends. The rivets have little heads on the sides and a vertical groove must be filed to give them passage. The

1917 magazine box goes into the stock at right angles to the receiver and is straight sided; the welded box has no protrusion on the sides, as does the riveted type.

If you have faithfully followed the scribed line made inside the guard, a close fit on the rear of the box is now possible. You do not try to fit the box from the bottom, instead it must be spotted in from the top in order to make the rear wall bear against the wood. The box is a trifle longer above the portion which enters the guard due to light machine cuts made to insure fitting the guard opening, so a little filing both fore-and-aft will be necessary to get the box down into the stock. You put it in through the receiver inletting always, and in assembling the rifle, put in the parts in this order: magazine box, triggerguard, receiver, front guard screw, rear guard screw, floorplate and follower assembly. Because the 1917 magazine box has square corners, it can be inletted to bear against the wood at its rear wall and take some recoil without developing a wedging action to split the stock, as will the other magazines, however, I would always advise that some clearance be left at the sides, to allow for shrinkage of the wood.

In the case of the Remington 721 and 722 rifles, the stamped guard is of no use whatever in inletting, and the receiver should be inletted first, using two headless screws. The squaring of the blank and straightness of the guard screw holes are of vital importance here to keep from canting the receiver in the stock. Strip the receiver of course, before starting inletting and the round receiver means that practically all of your inletting will be done with gouges and curved chisels. In fact, by taking measurements off the rifle's receiver, recoil plate and barrel and transferring them as a penciled outline on the top of the blank, you can do three-quarters of the inletting without further use of the metal parts. Both the receiver and barrel require a half round channel. Leave wood on the tang of the stock to come up flush with the top of the receiver tang, to avoid the drop off so apparent on the factory stock. After the receiver and barrel inletting is completed comes the magazine box and I can think of no way to get this in easier than by inserting it in the receiver opening provided for it and using long guide screws through the guard screw holes in the stock to bring the whole assembly down on the stock wood in proper relationship. Coat the bottom edge of the box with spotting compound and cut and try until the full outline of the box is evident in the receiver channel, then drill and chisel the opening through the stock to dimensions to receive the box. You can leave a wide gap at the rear of the box, or cut a channel back about ⅜″ to provide room for the center guard screw. Of course, if you wish, the box can be inletted fairly closely, and a hole drilled for this small diameter screw whose purpose is to hold the sheet metal guard up to the stock against magazine spring tension.

To inlet the guard, such as it is, hold the stock with the inletted receiver together, and place the guard holes over the headless guide screws, scribe about the outline and complete the shallow inletting necessary for the guard and triggerplate.

For all inletting, it is much easier to use a stripped receiver alone, without barrel, or a polished, slightly undersize triggerguard used as a preliminary working model in inletting. Whenever possible, have the metal parts polished before inletting and for a very good job on a custom rifle, inlet the action before sending it off to the barrelmaker. The barrel channel is not hard to cut later, and the stock can be almost finish shaped before this is done. Be careful about using just any receiver for inletting a rifle with a similar receiver, as there is considerable variation in dimensions. An undersize or minimum receiver and guard, well polished, are of course reliable aids to inletting.

Do not forget to treat the inside of the stock, either. Wet the entire inletting to raise the grain at least twice, using scrapers to smooth the surfaces afterward, then oil the wood with thickened boiled linseed oil. Do not use raw oil or any stains, as they soak into the wood slightly, and in the case of coarse wood, may later go through thin side walls to cause dark spots on the outside.

If guard screw bushings are to be used, they may be installed after the final inletting. A drill with 1″ pilot on the tip should be used, the pilot to be a push fit in the wood hole, and the drill to be of the same size as the bushing. The front screw hole can usually be enlarged with a round file to take the bushing easier than drilling through the short distance involved. Use a hand or breast drill to enlarge the holes, then press in the bushings. I have never considered guard screw bushings worth while on a sporting rifle. The amount of wood they displace makes for weakness in the stock, and with the recoil shoulder of the receiver firmly supported there is no tendency for the screws to split the stock, even if contacting the wood.

In the next chapter we get to the recoil shoulder business, in case you are wondering.

Here is a tip on keeping chisels sharp. Use the polishing equipment and edge the tools as surgeon's knives and scalpels are, by the cloth or soft felt buffing wheels, with a charge of fine abrasive. Polish both sides of the edge. This system makes for extremely sharp cutting edges, superior to the honed edge as a rule. Felt wheels burnish the surface of the steel slightly and make it a trifle harder, though this is a very minor point.

A few files—metal cutting files—are of much use in inletting. A small round file, two or three sizes of flat mill files, and flat and half-round bastard files are enough, but they should be clean and sharp. Do not ever use these files on metal. For cleaning out magazine openings, relieving corners and touching up the edges of barrel channels, files are sometimes handier than chisels. In shaping a stock, files are of course imperative in dressing down and shaping the wood around the action.

Inletting Buttstocks and Two Piece Stocks

The majority of these jobs are easier than bolt action rifle stocks, but a few are much harder. Where a stock bolt is used, drilling the hole for it through the blank is the first step, after profiling the blank to approximate outline of the finished stock and if you want any cast off, center the stock bolt hole at butt end as much left of true center as you want cast off.

The only method of drilling this hole true without special fixtures I know of is to use either a lathe or a drill press and work with centers— meaning you locate both ends of the hole, put a lathe center in one and run the bit in the other end aimed at the center. With the drillpress, the center must of course be clamped directly under the bit, or a hole drilled through the table of the drill to accept the center directly in line with the bit. With the lathe, you reverse the usual drilling system, and chuck the drill in the lathe chuck, not the tailstock chuck. Centering the stock's hole locations between the tailstock center and the bit in the chuck, the stock can be clamped or merely held from turning by the tool holder. The drill is fed by pushing the tailstock center in toward the chuck, moving the stock with it. Only a couple of inches at a time is drilled, the drill bit being fed further out of the chuck as needed and it is best to drill the hole completely from one end if at all possible. Long drill bits can be purchased almost anywhere and they are usually listed as "Electrician's Bits."

The Savage Model 99 is very easy to stock—you can do most of the butt inletting with a saw! The factory stock is the best guide you can have on most of these butt and two piece stock jobs so check the factory stock closely, to see where you can leave extra wood in the inletting, to gain strength.

Probably the hardest shotgun to stock is the side lock, such as the L. C. Smith, having no stock bolt and four tangs of wood at the front end. Always strip the receiver to inlet a double barrel or single shot rifle, (barrels can of course be left on the latter) and remove the lower tang, if you have not done so already and it will come off. Then, square off the butt blank, profiling but leaving the butt end long, and make a template of the upper tang in order to draw the inletting lines on the top. Cut these to the depth indicated by the old stock or the metal parts, plus $\frac{1}{32}''$ anyway. You will start your final inletting on the upper tang by spotting in and moving the stock further forward toward the receiver and eventually you will have to spot the end of stock and cut it to full contact with the rear edge of the receiver on both sides. Now inlet the lower tang, or triggerguard, preferably aligning it with the top by means of headless screws set into the holes in the bottom of the receiver normally taking the lower tang or triggerguard screws. If you cannot find any locating holes, outline the inletting on the bottom by pencil, taking the measurements from the metal parts and making the initial cut undersize and trial and error will set you right before the inletting progresses very far.

After the tangs are inletted, begin the cuts for the action parts, one at a time, checking against their movement in order to not remove too much wood. Give moving parts $\frac{1}{32}''$ clearance on all sides as this minimizes their tendency to get lubricating oil on the wood. Inletting for side plates comes last, these being aligned by their front ends which fit into corresponding cuts in the receiver.

Pump action shotguns are perhaps the easiest of all arms to stock, and examination of the factory stocks illustrates very plainly what needs to be done.

The British Lee-Enfield rifle is one of the more unpleasant jobs—the buttstock is fairly easy, but the forend is terrific. The rear of the receiver is a socket to receive the front end of the butt, and after the perliminary shaping, a little spotting and filing will give a perfect fit. These actions have a very large stock bolt, with the front end cut square for about $\frac{1}{4}''$ back from the tip and when the stock is in place and the screw turned tightly up, this square section should protrude from the front side of the rear receiver wall. You should get it so that it locates with the sides parallel to the vertical line of the action.

The forend comes back around the magazine and action to meet the rear wall of the action, and across its rear end should be a metal plate, pinned or screwed to the wood, with a slot, open on the top, just large enough to engage the square tip of the stock bolt, so that when the forend is moved up on the action and the barrel from the bottom, this plate matches up with the screw and will therefore prevent it from turning. Catch on?—the forend keeps the butt from loosening. Should the butt wood shrink and the stock become loose, the forend must be loosened and lowered enough to permit the stock bolt being turned in ¼, ½, or ¾ of a turn, after which the forend is replaced and will hold the screw in the new setting. Inletting the forend for a Lee-Enfield calls for work. If you have a forend to copy, it is not so hard, otherwise, inlet the barrel and the action first, locating with the front guard screw. The guard is next, the magazine opening last and the magazine must have $\frac{1}{32}''$ clearance on all sides to permit easy removal and insertion.

There is no real recoil shoulder on this action except the rear wall of the receiver, but the British bed the trigger housing (part of receiver which holds the trigger and the magazine catch axis pins) tightly, setting little brass plates into the wood behind it on each side.

On any of the two piece jobs, or buttstocks only, be sure to raise the grain in the inletting, scrape it smooth, then seal against moisture. Linseed oil is not so good here—use spar varnish.

Forends for shotguns are often rather difficult because of intricate design catch housings, but essentially the job is similar on all of them. Inlet the forend iron as best you can in a squared blank, left larger than needed. If you slip somewhere, plane off the top and drop the inletting deeper.

Single shot rifle forends are simple minded affairs—just a barrel channel in a chunk of wood. If the barrel tapers, so much the better. Cut the half round channel to fit the barrel closely a little forward of proper position, then when finally inletted, it can be tapped back with a mallet and really be a tight fit.

Incidentally, when inletting bolt actions, a mallet—rubber or rawhide—is quite a help to getting a clean indication of spotting during the final stages of fitting. You tap the receiver and barrel in by applying the mallet only on the top of the receiver ring. You can beat on triggerguards from end to end if you wish, but do not make too tight a fit earlier as it is possible to split the stock.

CHAPTER 25

Stockmaking: Shaping and Fitting

SHAPING and fitting a stock are allied operations, fitting of course covering the specifications laid down by the customer or gunsmith to make the stock fit an individual shooter, so shaping to some extent must be limited by the fitting dimensions and directions. The design of the stock must be worked out in advance, although some small details can be changed during the course of the shaping.

Pictures and drawings of good stocks are a considerable help in the final stages of shaping, and perhaps the most useful item in this line are the full size stock pattern sheets and drawings of finished stocks drawn by the late Alvin Linden and sold by Samworth in conjunction with the stockmaking booklets authored by Linden. The booklets themselves are highly useful to all but the most expert stockmaker, but if you think you are good enough not to need them, the pattern sheets alone are worth the money asked. Linden was one of the most expert men at shaping a stock we have ever had, and his directions are thoroughly recommended—not only are they useful but they are entertaining as Hell, too.

In using Linden or any other full size stock drawings, do not make the mistake of spreading the drawing or picture out on the bench or table and scrutinizing it closely. That is okay for taking dimensions if you are copying a stock, but to get the effect of the design, tack the drawing on the opposite wall and look at it from at least a distance of 10 feet—you will see the lines then.

I believe in shaping the butt first, keeping the forend square in order to provide a good surface for the vise to clamp against. The first step is to determine the pitch and so be able to set the buttplate. Linden's idea of running a string through the aperture of the peep sight along the pitch line to aid in establishing the angle of the buttplate is fine, when you have a receiver sight on the rifle, otherwise, my straight-edge through the position of the bolt sleeve works best. Consider all buttplates straight, in measuring the angle on the butt for pitch and for the curved ones take a straight line across the high points at the toe and the heel.

Use of another stock with the same type of buttplate being used as a check, held against the blank, helps a good bit and if you have no such stock and are in doubt, grab a piece of soft white pine and mount the buttplate on it, roughly shaping to the dimensions of the projected stock, and use this for a guide.

Recoil pads and the neoprene rifle buttplates are flatbacked and so require the stock to be cut straight, as described for fitting recoil pads on shotguns. However, the first step, after determining the pitch line and cutting the stock accordingly, to the proper length of pull, is to re-establish the center line of the buttplate, line up the screw holes of the buttplate on it, mark them and also draw around the plate with pencil. This leaves a slightly oversize outline to be worked down to in shaping the butt and it is best to go ahead and shape the butt before attaching the plate or pad.

The top center line of the butt gives the line of the comb and should special fitting instructions call for moving the comb line to the right slightly to allow a high cheekpiece, now is the moment to curve the center line to provide room for it.

You may chisel the rear outline of the pistol grip to a depth of $\frac{1}{8}''$ before beginning the shaping of the right side of stock, which comes first.

By using short, slightly tapered pieces of soft pine board it is possible to hold the stock on its side, the pine being used between the vise jaws and the top and the bottom of the forend to protect it, allowing the use of planes and draw knives to remove the wood from the sides of the butt. Very sharp smooth and block planes will cut quite well on all types of wood, even finely figured types, for this preliminary shaping but the draw knives and spoke shaves can be used only on straight grained wood.

Your guides are the penciled comb and bottom center lines, and the outline of the buttplate on the end of the stock blank. Start at one corner of the butt and plane forward to the pistol grip, working this "face" down until within $\frac{1}{16}''$ of the plate outline at the rear. Make it straight, not attempting to taper the cut inward to taper the stock— that comes a good bit later. Do the same on the other corner, which will give you more "corners." Plane these down in turn and eventually, the right side of the butt will be eight or 10 small faces, almost to the outline of the butt.

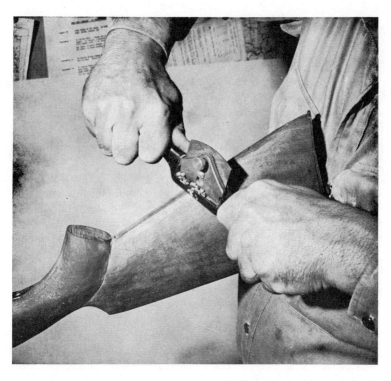

STOCK SHAPING

The tool shown, whether you know it as a cabinet scraper or spokeshave, is about as useful a cutting tool as can be found for shaping a stock. The cut is forward, away from the body, in this illustration. The tool can be used almost anywhere except on curve of the pistol grip. It does faster and cleaner work than a rasp.

Note that buttplate has been roughly fitted, to protect the butt while working. The scraper cuts very well across the grain incidentally, and is of great help in fitting curved buttplates. (You keep it *sharp*, understand?)

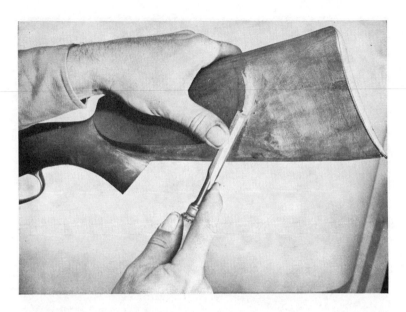

USE OF THE STRAIGHT CHISEL

The straight chisel is used a great deal in stock work, possibly more than any other single style of chisel. Here is a cheekpiece outlining operation, reducing the size of same, or rather, the length, the chisel being used in a paring cut, receiving guidance and some force from the left thumb.

After the reduction to penciled outline, the chisel will be turned over and, cutting straight down against the wood, undercut the edge and shape the bevel.

The penciled line showing final position of the Niedner buttplate is visible on the stock, but most of the fitting of the plate will be done with the cabinet scraper or spokeshave.

Then turn the stock over on the bench or in the vise, to get at the left side—this is the one with the cheekpiece, that takes about five times longer than the other.

First, sketch the full rear line of the pistol grip, then outline the cheekpiece to full, or bottom dimension, at the proper location on the butt. Checking against the center line of the butt, you will see considerably more wood to be removed from the butt in the area behind the cheekpiece than was taken from the right side. Also, there is not room enough to use a plane.

To save time in removing unnecessary wood, use a saw to cut into the left side of the stock behind the cheekpiece, going down as far as you can safely—checking the depth of the cut against the amount of wood to be removed as shown by the buttplate outline. If the grain of the wood permits, most of the area between the saw cut and the end can be split off and if the grain is doubtful, use chisels or saws to remove it. When it is gone, you may outline the cheekpiece with saw cuts or chiseled groove, and proceed to cut out the undesirable wood with gouges but leave the cheekpiece untouched on its face until the outline of the butt is completed. Use a 12″ straightedge from time to time, to keep from cutting hollows too deep to remove when the final shaping takes place.

All this wood eliminating is done in the easiest, quickest and most painless way you can devise. Use saws, chisels, grinders, sanding discs or train a beaver to chew it off. Just be doggoned careful you do not go below closer than $\frac{1}{16}$″ of the finished stock dimension anywhere at any time. This is where you can use outside calipers to good end.

With the butt roughed out, start on the pistol grip and remove its corners. Your blank profile has taken care of the bottom line of the stock, so you can determine the angle of the grip cap. Measurement from the trigger of the rifle set into the stock will give the length but the curvature and depth is something else—something which I have been dodging mentioning on account of it is hard to figure. The best way to lay it out is to use a small try square, one edge in line with the bore, and the other reaching down across the pistol grip. The distance from the bore line to the bottom leading edge of the pistol grip of the grip cap takes care of the depth, and a measurement in the center (from the bore line to the bottom edge of the grip) will determine the curvature. The depth will average $4\frac{1}{4}$″ and the curvature measurement $2\frac{3}{8}$″. Individual requirements for sporting stocks will not as a rule call for more than $\frac{1}{8}$″ variance from these figures in either direction.

.300 H&H – PFEIFER IMPROVED
(.300 PI)

MAXIMUM CARTRIDGE

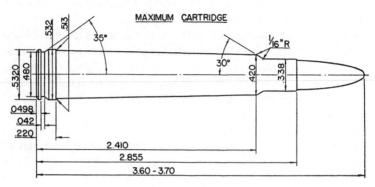

MINIMUM CHAMBER

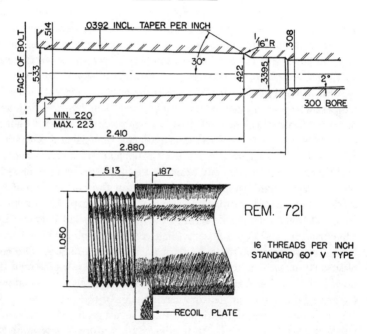

REM. 721

16 THREADS PER INCH
STANDARD 60° V TYPE

One of the best improved versions of the .300 H & H, the only change from the standard case is the sharp shoulder. Body taper of case is not changed, nor is the length of the neck. Case life is long—few cartridge cases ever split at the shoulder. Commercial .300 ammunition may be fired in the

Determining these dimensions, make a final outline of the pistol grip with the proper curvature, and draw it on both sides. Work down either side first, roughing off the corners. Here too, a little saw work speeds things up—use one of the little 6″ hacksaws, cutting shallow corner cuts about ½″ apart from each other along the outline as these cuts prevent splitting off too much wood in the first shaping. As with the butt, remove corner from corner, until the grip is visible as a grip and not as a projection of the blank on one edge.

With planes, draw knife and cabinet scrapers proceed to cut down the sides of the stock as far forward as the cylinder of the barrel, or the swell of the barrel if it has no cylinder. Take the wood off to make a flat sided body first, then with a cabinet scraper round it slightly at the top and the bottom, leaving $\frac{1}{16}$″ above the finished size.

That takes care of the easy work—and it gets harder fast.

Go back to the butt section, and with sharp chisels pare the pistol grip to very slightly above the finished size. You may use a cabinet rasp for this work if you wish although I do not like them myself. Cut the rear line of the pistol grip into the surface of the stock to make a definite outline. The pistol grip cap is now mounted and if a steel cap is to be used, you better make a duplicate in plastic or composition and put it on, for the grip will need a cap from now on during the work, and it is not funny to run a chisel into a steel cap.

Use the cabinet scraper and block plane to clean up the right side of the stock and round it off at the top and the bottom, checking with a straightedge as you shape the wood forward toward the pistol grip. Do not attempt to make the side lines of the stock absolutely straight, though—make them straight for the first 3″ or 4″ ahead of the butt-plate, then curve them inward slightly to the pistol grip. This makes for better appearance in straight grained stocks particularly. A feather-weight stock of hard wood can be cut slim, with straight lines on sides of stock.

On the left side, chisels must be used all around the cheekpiece to outline it right down to the surface of the stock. The stock, behind the cheekpiece and underneath it (below the bottom line of the cheekpiece)

---

chamber perfectly when handloads in fire-formed cases are not available. Velocity is upped about 10% over the standard case, and 14″ twist of rifling is recommended.

The .300 Pfeifer is a very excellent cartridge for long-range target shooting as well as for large game. It is extremely accurate without being difficult to load.

should be the same as on the right side as regards curvature and proportion. Chisels must usually also be used to clear the wood to the proper depth on the left side, although rasps and coarse files help. We still leave the face of the cheekpiece alone.

New mill files will complete the shaping of the body on the sides, but do not cut the stock at the top and the bottom to the correct line of the depth for the rifle and the guard.

The stock is showing its final shape now, and the buttplate should be fitted. Curved plates, such as the Niedner, are naturally considerably more difficult than flat plates. Study the curvature of the plate and draw a line on the butt to correspond and it does not hurt to cut a cardboard profile to fit the plate and so check the line, either. The peak, or pointed bent tip at the top must be inletted very carefully, and about the only way to do this is by trial and error. After the plate is half way fitted, it is coated with spotting compound and the metal is spotted in to a perfect contact with the wood all around its edges.

It is not necessary to have a full contact between the plate and the butt—a contact $\frac{1}{4}''$ wide around the edges is sufficient. After the plate is fitted, with no gaps between the inner edge and the wood, remove it, wet the wood to raise the grain, then again file the butt to perfect contact and seal the end grain, using spar varnish thinned with naphtha. After it has soaked in, put on a coat of thickened linseed oil and screw the plate down firmly.

Wood should project above the edges of the plate all around, about $\frac{1}{32}''$ now—in fact, the whole stock should be from $\frac{1}{64}''$ to $\frac{1}{32}''$ oversize.

This is the moment we get to the recoil shoulder; wood alone is not good enough to support a rifle firing a powerful cartridge. Stock pins and bolts are easiest to install, but really do very little in the way of strengthening the stock against recoil. If pins are to be used, the front one should be $\frac{1}{8}''$ in diameter, and placed through the stock midway between the recoil shoulder cut and the front of the magazine cut and in depth, centered behind the recoil shoulder on the receiver.

Stock bolts are similar, except they have heads and nuts which must be inletted into the sides of the stock. The rear pin or bolt is located behind the magazine opening, below the front of the sear cut in the stock, and centered in line with the front pin if possible, otherwise slightly below it.

The recoil bolt, familiar to us through examples of Mauser military rifles, is a practical and efficient means of controlling recoil, and keeping the zero of the rifle constant. In this, a square, or flat sided bolt is inlet through the stock to directly contact and support the recoil shoulder of the receiver. My only objection to the Mauser bolt is that it looks rather bad and does not take full advantage of the support of the stock.

I prefer a recoil plate, inletted completely through the stock at the recoil shoulder, and, like the Mauser, directly contacting the receiver shoulder—it looks neat, takes in the full width of the stock for support, is comparatively easy to install without special tools, and is easier lined up than the other.

My plates are either aluminum or duralumin, from $\frac{1}{8}''$ to $\frac{3}{16}''$ thick, cut in the form of a rectangle a trifle longer than the stock is wide, and as wide as the recoil shoulder of the receiver involved plus $\frac{1}{32}''$. To install, the recoil shoulder location is first determined (we cut it back to ease the inletting) by placing a small bit of plastic substance on the wood shoulder—putty, plastic wood or wax—and assemble the rifle after oiling the recoil shoulder of the receiver. It will press the soft substance to the correct shoulder location. Removal of the action and barrel leaves this phony shoulder visible so we very carefully mark on the sides of the stock a vertical line to match this shoulder. Measurement with depth gage or plain scale will show on the outside the top and bottom locations of the opening to be made for the plate. The vertical line made is the front side of the plate, and the rear line must be determined by the thickness of the plate being used, being of course that distance to the rear of the first line.

Drill a couple or three small holes through the stock within the small penciled or scribed rectangle you have now outlined and with small chisels and needle files square it out until the recoil plate can be started in from one side with the fingers. After filing and trying until you are sure the opening is large enough for the plate, press the plate into the stock with a vise or an arbor press. Where the plate is visible inside the inletting, now forming a recoil shoulder, take a file and slightly round off or chamfer the edge. The recoil shoulders on the receivers seldom join the latter at a perfect right angle, having a little radius in the corner, which must be accommodated.

You should be able to press the assembly into the stock, the recoil shoulder coming in full and close contact with the recoil plate. If the plate is a little forward, press it out of the stock and file back the front face area to allow the recoil shoulder to move down in front of it. This filing of course is done only on the portion which is presented to the recoil shoulder—you do not file the plate thinner all the way across. Prussian blue can be used to spot the shoulder in. If by mischance or

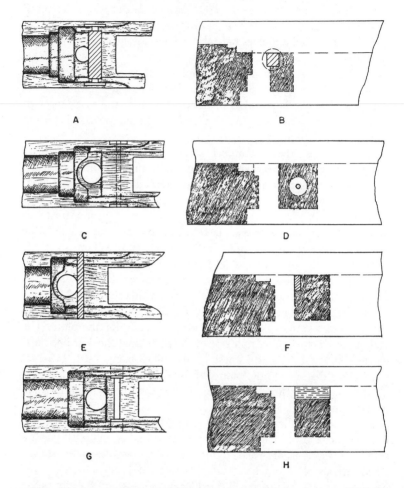

This sketch is an attempt to illustrate three methods of strengthening a bolt action rifle stock at the recoil shoulder—the point where the wood takes the recoil of the receiver and barrel assembly.

The left section of the drawing represents the view of the recoil shoulder area of the stock looking straight down from the top, the right section being a phantom view of the stock from the side. The shaded sections represent solid wood, unshaded sections the areas cut out in the inletting for receiver and trigger guard units.

A. The Mauser-type recoil bolt, square in cross-section, which is to contact the metal shoulder on the receiver. Countersunk screw heads in the sides of stock are not so attractive, and many custom stock men who

misfiguring you got the plate too far back, so that the recoil shoulder does not touch it, put in a metal shim or shims until it does as this affects neither external appearance nor the effect of the recoil plate. The ends of the plate should project a little beyond the sides of the stock, to protect the edges from battering. Filing down to the surface of the wood will leave a small metal rectangle visible.

It has often been said and written that a close inletted stock of good wood requires no recoil bolt or plate—that is not so. Of course, a light-recoil cartridge can be accommodated by a good inletting job in strong, hard wood alone, but for anything stiffer than a .257 you had sure better stick in a plate or a bolt. It insures a uniform, permanent bedding and sight setting. You can assemble the rifle, wind in the screws as tight as you can in the shop, and give the guy his rifle without warning him he will have to fire 20 shots to "settle her down" and tighten the screws every week for the first six years. Also, and more important, the stock will not split unless someone uses an axe on it and you can inlet closely around the rear of the receiver without fear of the tang splitting the stock as the wood behind the recoil shoulder compresses and beats back under recoil.

The Mauser has a shallow recoil shoulder—approximately $\frac{7}{32}$" deep—and a bolt is literally a must for this action. The Springfield and

---

employ such bolts cover screw heads with plastic or contrasting wood inlays.

B. Side view of the Mauser-type bolt, showing its location in the recoil-shoulder section of the stock.

C. The stock pin, as formerly used in 1903 Springfield and other rifles. Serves to hold the stock together in event of splitting, but otherwise is worthless as the wooden recoil shoulder of stock can be beaten back by the metal shoulder of receiver eventually.

D. Side location of the stock pin.

E. My recoil plate, which extends completely through the stock from side to side, thus utilizing the full width of stock to resist recoil. The metal recoil shoulder is bedded solidly against this plate.

F. Side or sectional view of the recoil plate.

G. A modification of the stock pin, used by many stock men. It is located just behind the recoil shoulder, with deeply-countersunk head and nut which are covered with exterior plugs. These are a little better than nothing, but not much. The resisting strength of the stock side-walls is used to only a small extent.

H. No connection to G, but merely a sketch to clearly show the small area in the stock which must support the metal recoil shoulder of the Mauser type bolt action, represented by the dotted-line rectangle. Shallow, isn't it? Shows why a bolt or plate is needed.

Enfield have shoulders about $1\frac{1}{32}''$, and so distribute the jolt of recoil over a wider area. The military minds copying the Mauser '98 in designing the 1903 and 1914 actions thought by deepening the recoil shoulder they could eliminate the recoil bolt used by Mauser. They did, but it did not work out so well. It has become an axiom with American shooters to keep the guard screws tight and watch for the tang to split—Springfield Armory even furnished little metal shims to place between the wood and metal recoil shoulders when the wood beat back!

To get back to our stock again, the next move on the program is to drill the hole for the front swivel. We do this with the forend still in the square, locating on the center line of the bottom and drilling up to the center of the barrel channel, at the proper distance back from the tip, of course. The stock is square on the top yet, so it is simple to drill the hole straight and true into the barrel channel. Make this hole at right angle to the bottom line of the stock.

After this, we proceed to shape the forend. Measure at the tip, on the top, and the sides to get the proper layout, using your own or the customer's specifications as to width and depth. Make these lines straight, and plane down to $\frac{1}{32}''$ all the way around. You can do two-thirds of this job with the smooth plane—my plane is 10" long and does very well. The long jackplane is a little clumsy for stock work, although useful in planing blanks.

The cabinet scraper and block plane just about finish up the forend shaping, cutting the wood to not less than $\frac{1}{64}''$ over finished dimensions. Now you put on the tip block, glueing it with casein glue and of course holding it in line and adding strength to the joint with dowel, tenon or other connection, and pegs or pins as well. After the glue dries, shape the tip with chisels, rasp and files to the approximate shape and size, taking care to oil it well if using ebony or similar very hard close grained wood.

The stock is now completely shaped, but not finish shaped and it is a little oversize all over. Now, Junior, the smart thing to do is to set it on the rack for from two to three weeks, especially if you are using a metal buttplate and grip cap.

Reason? This:

Wood seasons, or dries, from the inside out. Kiln drying is quite a science, and if done right considerably simplifies your stock job before you ever get the wood in the first place. Kilns are huge ovens where wood is baked dry, the natural moisture and water content lowered to a pre-determined percentage, only—heat is not the only factor involved. To get a proper drying, without either surface or inner cracking through too fast or too slow treatment, it is necessary at intervals to humidify the kilns in order to drive moisture back into the surface of the wood to match up with the moisture at the center. Steam is generally used to accomplish this. The moisture thus artificially put into the wood does not reach the center, and a series of treatments gradually reduces the overall water content of the stock. Blanks usually leave the kiln with between 5% and 7% moisture, and pick up 2% or 3% additional from the normal atmosphere in which they are then stored.

What happens is that a stock blank nearly always has more or less— usually more—moisture in the center than on the surface. The moisture content of the surface varies with the humidity of the air in which the wood is stored.

So, you can take a blank which is thoroughly dry on the outside, shape a stock out of it, then watch that stock shrink as it dries out further. Our plan is to let the doggoned thing make up its mind before we finish it to exact dimensions as it is not any fun to try and fix up a custom stock where the engraved steel grip cap and buttplate stick out $\frac{1}{32}''$ above the wood, because the said wood shrunk after shaping. You then must reduce the size of the metal fittings to match.

This shrinkage business depends a great deal on the shop location and environment. A stock is not going to shrink if the shop is damp and humid although it may do the reverse and swell up. If the stock is going to be used in the same type of climate, let it alone, although your nice close inletting may open up a little. But, if you live on the Carolina coast or a similar damp area, and make a stock for some big hat boy who lives in the south end of New Mexico, you had better light up a fire and dry that stock out good because if you do not get the moisture out and shrink the stock down to minimum, it is going to do the job by itself after it hits the desert country in finished form—and all the sealer and filler you shove into the wood is not going to prevent that action.

Very hard, close grained wood such as French walnut thoroughly seasoned, and stored properly in a dry place, will have a minimum of moisture loss and absorption as the texture of the wood makes for very slow action in drying. Wood picks up moisture mainly on the end grain areas, as under the buttplates and the grip caps, and in the inletting for the receiver, therefore you do your best to seal these points. The forend tip takes care of the front end of the stock, which is one practical reason at least for the use of a tip.

Anyway, it is time to get to the final shaping which is done mainly with hand scrapers and files although a small palm plane is sometimes useful, particularly when the wood is fairly straight in grain structure. The cheekpiece can be shaped now, using a plane to remove most of the excess wood from the face. Leaving the face flat and high, but angled correctly, start with chisels to cut the outline of the face, beveling it down to the surface of the stock at the original cheekpiece outline. Make this bevel either straight, or a concave curve (hollowed bevel) but never make a convex curve—as it looks very bad. You may make a little shelf at the lower edges, where the bevel joins the stock lines which sharply outlines the cheekpiece and aids in the appearance somewhat.

Assemble the rifle and check the height of comb and cheekpiece although the comb can hardly be checked until the latter is cut down still further. If the sights have not yet been mounted on the rifle, do this job, making any necessary inletting for the receiver sight bases. The rifle must have the sights in place to correctly shape the cheek-piece, and for a perfect job, you need the rifle owner also, but if he is not available, get one of your local admirers with face shape and physique somewhat similar to those of the customer and get him to act as a trial horse, cutting and shaping the pistol grip and cheekpiece to a comfortable fit as closely as you can in line with the specifications laid down in advance.

With sharp chisels clean up the wood around the bottom and the rear of the pistol grip, then file and scrape to final dimensions. The same is done to the entire stock—and keep the straightedge handy to check the top, the bottom and the side lines of the stock from end to end. Undercut the comb as desired. The wood at the butt now is very slightly over the metal buttplate, and you take your sanding block with o sandpaper and bring it down to meet the metal. Go over the stock from end to end with o, then 2/o sandpaper, backing it with a 6" flat block and sanding with the grain, lengthwise of the stock.

Next, use strips of sandpaper of 4/o grit, or cutting cloth of 180 grit, and work the stock over lightly across the grain, using the shoe shining method which serves to show up inequalities in surfacing and shaping. Then, a light going over with 4/o paper held in the palm, working in all directions to smooth out the wood, will remove most of the tool marks on the wood and the grain will begin to show up well.

After this, set the stock up and very carefully drill the hole for the rear or butt swivel. I locate mine 2⅝" above the toe, but anything between 2¼" and 3" looks okay. It is of course on the bottom line of the stock and at 90° to it. Drill for the body of the swivel screw (inner or core diameter) then run in a ¼″ drill for ⅛″ or ⁵⁄₃₂″ to prevent the threads of the screw pulling up the wood forward of the hole and splitting off little pieces when the screw is turned in. Do not leave the swivel fitted. Finish shaping the forend tip—you already have had to inlet the barrel channel through it in order to assemble the rifle. Put on the permanent pistol grip cap and check the grip to make sure it will not turn. The metal plates are usually hollowed out underneath and they should be spotted in place to make a perfect fit, the wood being left to fill the hollow and so keep the cap from turning.

Most of the pistol grip caps now commercially available are a little large. The Niedner composition caps are about the right size, but steel is better. The pressed steel caps made by Lewis Dodd are okay if dressed up a little—a couple of buck's worth of engraving helps a great deal. I have made a few from Niedner buttplate blanks—the flat, knurled plates. Just cut the cap out, file a border on it, drill the screw hole and cup the cap slightly in a hollowed wooden die by beating the back with a ball peen hammer, which of course, makes a cap to match the Niedner buttplate. Such caps can be either case-hardened or blued. Good caps also can be made of horn.

We are now ready to trim the stock—cut the wood down around the inletting cuts to the proper depth to match the metal parts and it is necessary that the rifle be completely assembled and screws tightened as much as possible. Use the straightedged chisels to cut the bottom of the body even with the lines of the guard, making the cuts straight, or flat, not attempting to angle them upward on the sides. On the tang, chisels also may be used, but mill files will do the work. For the top edges of the body of the stock, around the receiver, use chisels and files both, and for the forend, sharpen the plane bit and plane it down to the half diameter point of the barrel. For Mausers, dress up the slot in the top of the grip at the rear of the tang for passage of the cocking piece with the edge of a mill file.

With files and chisels cut the bolt handle notch in the right side of the body. Spot the handle in all the way, and give it almost ¹⁄₁₆″ clearance fore-and-aft, but do not make the cut any deeper than necessary. Unless you have some very small short-bent or spoon gouges it is difficult to make a neat inletting for some of these deeply curved altered bolt handles. I get around this very easily by using the Handee grinder with a round (ball-shaped) wood carving bit—I should not admit using this gadget on stocks, but this is a very worthwhile means of doing a good job. The bolt cut can be hollowed as indicated by the

STOCK SPECIFICATION SHEET

Name _____

Address _____

Height _____ Weight _____

Arm—Caliber or Gauge, Make & Serial No. _____

_____

Sights _____

Desired approximate weight of completed arm _____

Type of wood _____

Type of finish _____

Length of pull _____ Pitch _____ Type of forend _____

Length of grip _____ Circumference of small _____

Depth of grip _____ Curvature _____

Drop: at comb _____ at heel _____

Cast off: at heel _____ at toe _____

Type of buttplate _____

Type of grip cap _____

Type of forend tip _____

Swivels _____

Bedding of barrel: Contact _____ Floating _____ Other _____

         Tied down (band) _____ Barrel screw _____

Special features _____

_____

_____

_____

(Make up mimeographed sheets on this general order to submit to mail-order customers, and also request photographs of customer, full and quarter-face, preferably holding a gun; sketches of cheekpiece and comb, outline of hand, and letter covering general details of job, with reference and comparison to pictures of similar stocks sent by you, or in books available to customer).

spotting compound until the bolt turns down to full locked position. Do not chamfer the edges of the cut now, but wait until it is finish sanded and then cut a ⅛″ bevel on edges.

Removal of the assembly from the stock allows you to use mill files to round off the stock outside of the inletting cuts around the receiver and the guard openings. Should the guard section now be out of line with the rear section of the forend, a little careful work with the block plane will straighten out the bottom stock line. Use the files to do whatever final shaping is desired at this time, but to smooth off the top of the forend use a flat wood block to back 4/o sandpaper.

The final sanding is now at hand, and the stock is worked over with 6/o paper both by block and by hand, care being taken always not to touch the edges of inletting cuts. If the rifle has not yet been blued, or is to be re-blued, assemble it in the stock and do the sanding with the metal protecting the inletting. Sand the edges of cuts and the matching metal together, to insure a good fit and sand right over the edges of the buttplate and the grip cap.

Remove the rifle from the stock, if you have been sanding with it assembled, and go over the stock alone with 8/o paper, using small pieces—3″ or 4″ square—held in the palm or fingers. This is the final touch.

You are now ready to raise the grain, sometimes called "whiskering." This consists of wetting the surface of the wood to expand the exposed grain structure. The wood will raise only a certain amount and if this is removed, there will be no further raising when the wood is wet later. Whenever you see a stock with little ridges and dots raised on the finish in line with the grain, it is evident that the stockmaker either did not raise the grain or did not do it completely before applying the finish.

Water is generally used, wiped on the wood with a sopping wet cloth and it is necessary to dry the stock rapidly, to keep the water from soaking into the wood below the surface. An open gas flame is not so good—put an old pie tin or piece of thin sheet metal on the grate and hold the stock 5″ or 6″ above it, moving the stock back and forth and turning it to dry all points. After it is dry, you will note the grain has risen and your well sanded stock looks rough all over. Use 8/o sandpaper in the palm or fine steel wool to smooth it down again, then repeat the whole performance two more times.

Grain alcohol can be used instead of water as it dries very rapidly, and no heat is necessary. Remove and refinish the buttplate and the grip cap, then replace them on the stock.

STOCK LAYOUT SHEET

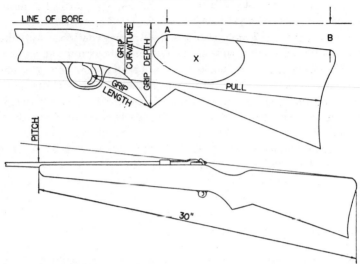

Make up similar drawings to this to submit to stock customers to aid them in giving the correct specifications. Throw in whatever else you can think of to help you figure out *exactly* what he needs.

A. Drop at comb

B. Drop at heel

X. Center of customer's face on stock, to help in figuring size of cheek-piece. You can move this point back to corner of jawbone, if desirable. This is a little easier for most people to determine.

Next comes the finish, and you should start it immediately.

The Wundhammer Bulge

Louis Wundhammer, an old California gunsmith, was among the first to build bolt action sporters in this country, and he liked to put a bulge, or swell, on the right-hand side of the pistol grip, to fill the hollow in the palm of a hand cupped around the grip.

The idea is excellent, especially for a rifle which will be used principally in the offhand position. However, the bulge must very carefully be cut to fit the hand of the individual who will use the rifle. It allows very little leeway between different individuals since it positions the hand rather positively. A small bulge is less limited, but to take full advantage of the feature it is best to make it to fill the palm.

The shooter's hand will return to the same position on the grip each time, as the bulge makes only the proper position comfortable. This is a very excellent idea.

To properly fit the swell it is necessary to have the customer present to try it repeatedly while it is being shaped. Small swells can be put on mail-order jobs, if the customer sketches his method of holding the right hand on the stock. The bulge or swell should always be fully checkered.

I have not gone into the shaping of shotgun stocks, forends, or two piece rifle stocks, as the shaping operations are very similar to those of the bolt action rifle stocks, except much easier as a rule. The same tools are used, and the same spotting in procedure employed to obtain a good fit between the wood and the metal.

The single shot rifle buttstock generally allows more leeway in comb and cheekpiece height, and shaping and fitting can be regulated to conform to unusual customer requirements if necessary.

CHAPTER 26

Stockmaking: Finishing

THERE is more nonsense and misinformation floating around about stock finishes than just about any other item in the gun line, except possibly the "thirty-thirties" the customers used when they werc in the Army.

Especially is this true of the "rubbed oil finish," "dull London oil finish," "French polish" and one or two other glib terms you read and hear about. And half the gun nuts in the country still think that to get a wonderful finish all you need to do is to take raw linseed oil and rub in by hand a dozen coats or so.

Linseed oil has been used for centuries on wood to polish and preserve it but raw linseed oil should never be used in a stock finish as it contains some slow drying vegetable fats which make for a dull, greasy finish that never does really harden. Boiled linseed oil only should be used, when a linseed oil finish is desired. Boiled oil has never been boiled, though—it is raw oil treated with sulphuric acid or caustic soda which reacts upon the impurities in the oil and allow them to be removed from the oil, which is then heated a little and mixed with a bit of drier. Pure bleached linseed oil has this done and also has most of the natural color removed by activated charcoal. We do not need it bleached, though it is okay to use.

Watch out for synthetic linseed oil which is not so good for stocks, although the house painter can use it in his business. The smell of genuine boiled oil is the best guide against imitations.

Tung oil is the only other oil I would recommend for stock finishing, and that to a very limited degree. This oil is hard to get and expensive, but has the advantage of drying about 50% faster than boiled linseed oil. It has two important disadvantages, however. Light applications must be made and rubbed in immediately and thoroughly, as the oil dries fast enough to build up a film on the surface of the wood giving the effect of a plain varnish job, and the oil can flake, check and turn

THE RECOIL PLATE

The recoil plate is a bar of metal passing through the stock full width from side to side, against which the recoil shoulder of the receiver is closely and tightly fitted to prevent shifting or rearward movement of the barrel and receiver. It is installed after the stock is fully inletted and shaped ready for sanding.

FITTING FOREND TIP

This happens to be an ebony tip, but the procedure is the same with ebony, horn or plastic, as well as any contrasting wood, of course. The forend is practically down to finished size, barrel channel fully inletted.

The end of forend and tip block are drilled to size to permit a push fit for the size dowell to be used, then the two side pins accommodated. After this, the final fitting between tip block and end of stock is done with file, until a close joint can be obtained by pushing the tip against the stock by hand.

The end of stock and surface of block are then "nibbled" a little inside the edge surfaces, to allow a little room for both glue and trapped air when the final joint is made.

Not visible are tiny holes drilled from barrel channel and top of tip block into the dowell holes, to permit air and excess glue escape. For this job, casein glue was used to join the tip, and clamps used to hold tip tightly against the forend while drying.

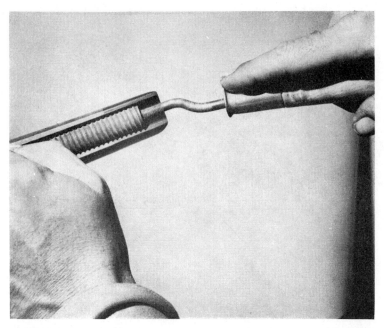

CUTTING THE TIP CHANNEL

This must be done carefully, as usually the pressure of the barrel against the stock is borne mainly by the tip. Ebony cuts well with sharp chisels, but the barrel inletting rasp is best for the final touches. Shown is the Denman two-handed model.

Inletting of the tip channel calls for the spotting-in technique to get a good job.

TIP JOINT

The finished tip shaping, ready for sanding. Note the tiny hole visible in bottom of barrel channel in tip, and also small hole in forend channel, now only a notch in forward edge of swivel countersink recess. These are the air-escape holes previously referred to, and are highly important. The hydraulic action of a close-fitting dowel joint and liquid glue is usually underrated, and many a stocker is unhappily made aware of the fact when something splits!

white, just as a poor varnish job on the office desk will do. Second and more important, about one man in every thousand is violently allergic to tung oil, and will break out in rash, blisters and even running sores wherever he touches it. Japanese rifle stocks were treated with tung oil, and during the war American soldiers of course captured and handled those rifles. Enough men came down with skin trouble to cause a military investigation, which at first declared the wood itself was the cause, the individual soldiers being allergic to it. It was later found that the stock finish was the cause. So, if you are going to use tung oil, try a sample on the customer to make sure he is not one of the allergic boys.

The most common error concerning linseed oil is the belief that it waterproofs wood. Nothing could be farther from the truth. It is true that an oiled stock is *water repellent*, meaning that water will run off it, but any oil will give the same effect, even old crank case drainings. Linseed oil will make a stock shed large drops of water, but by itself will not retard moisture from either entering or leaving the wood.

The next most common error is that you can get a fine finish just by rubbing in linseed oil. Well, you can rub linseed oil on a piece of walnut until your hands are worn off up to the elbows and still not get a finish you would exhibit with pride to your own wife. The wood must be prepared for the finish with sealers and fillers. Oil finishing a properly prepared stock is not a really hard job, nor does it take too long—from four to eight weeks is sufficient to complete a fine oil finish, depending upon the dryness of the climate where the job is done.

I prefer to use a thickened oil, made by adding about 5% Japan drier to boiled oil and letting it set in the sun until it is syrupy. A thick scum forms over the top (you leave the lid off the can or pan while it is thickening), which is removed when the oil has reached the desired consistency. This oil dries a little faster than plain oil and does not soak into the wood to darken it and as I prefer stocks light in color, this works out fine for me at least. Except for cold climates, the same oil also can be used as a filler. Most of the commercial stock finishes are similar mixtures of boiled oil, drier, and a little burnt umber to darken them, except not thickened. The same type of mixture, sometimes with raw instead of boiled oil, was used for the so called dull London finish, which calls for hand rubbing about two weeks between coats for six months or so, the eventual result being a dark finish with a dull sheen in strong light. Except on very fancy wood, it does not look good.

Shellac has been long used for stock finishes, usually in partnership with linseed oil. Shellac itself is a waterproofing agent, but it is also subject to checking, cracking and spotting from temperature changes, since it is not flexible. The French polish employs linseed oil to offset the brittleness of shellac, and allows a high polish, or high gloss stock. It is a fine finish for the gun cabinet, but not so good for the field as water spots it badly and it does not have the quality appearance of a good oil finish. The advantage is that it is very fast—can be completed in 24 hours at most. Most stockmakers wax the stocks after a French polish job.

Varnish finishes are becoming quite popular, and if done properly, compare favorably with the good oil finish. Spar varnishes of the better grades are the only ones to be recommended, for straight finish, but if linseed oil is to be combined with varnish, either spar or good furniture varnish can be used.

Before any type of finish can be considered there is a good bit of work to be done as the stock should be sealed, and in 99% of stock jobs, must be filled.

Sealers are what their name indicates—products to seal the wood—and we use them to moisture proof the stock as best we can. They are liquids carrying water resistant substances which will penetrate below the surface of the wood slightly and fill up the grain somewhat, without being surface fillers. Spar varnish, thinned to water consistency with naphtha (varnishmaker's and painter's type) white gasoline, or some other solvent is good. A fast evaporating solvent is desirable. The sealer is wiped on the wood with a saturated cloth until the wood absorbs all it will take and shows wet. Let it dry before using a filler. You can make a tank and dip the stock in if you care to—the wood will absorb only a certain amount and cannot soak up much if any excess.

Fillers are quite a problem. The silicon filler is the best by far, but it is rough on checkering tools, dulling them very rapidly while the commercial fillers are usually too soft and will not dry thoroughly or stay in the wood. Most of them are composed of solvent, drier, a little fuller's earth, whiting and whatever else was handy to the maker at the time of concoction. The old timers, in turning out a good finish, took their time and used linseed oil as a filler, oiling the stock, letting it gum, polishing down to the bare wood with burlap and pumice or rottenstone, and repeating until the grain was filled. This makes for a good clear finish and one which remains in good shape for years. I prefer this method myself, but would hesitate to recommend it for very cold climates. I have used straight shellac also, mainly in an effort to keep a light colored stock light (fillers slightly darken the wood). This is really the hard way, entailing more work than any other part of stock finishing. The stock is shellacked, allowed to dry, then the shellac is cut off the wood across the grain with 4/0 steel wool. Do this twice and a couple of days are shot and your fingers feel as though they belonged to someone else.

A. Donald Newell's book *Gunstock Finishing and Care* should be kept as a reference, as all types of finishes and preparations for sealers and fillers are described, and countless formulae for mixing your own choice and type. The following filler formulae are Mr. Newell's:

1. High Grade Spar Varnish	10 parts by weight	
Silica, finest grade	40 " " "	
Mineral spirits	to make a thin paste.	

The silica should be ground as fine as flour. Mineral spirits means the solvent or turpentine substitute now generally sold in paint stores as "paint thinner." If you cannot get it, use turpentine.

2. High Grade Spar Varnish	10 parts by weight	
Silica, finest grade	40 " " "	
Boiled Linseed Oil	5 " " "	
Japan Drier	½ " " "	

Japan Drier is a solution of mineral spirits, 1 to 5% lead, and .2 to 1% of either cobalt or cobalt and manganese mixed.

3. High Grade Spar Varnish	10 parts by weight	
Silica or asbestine	40 " " "	
Burnt Umber	3 " " "	
Mineral Spirits	As desired.	

Burnt umber is a dark-brown pigment used to color stains and varnishes. Asbestine, according to the dictionary, seems to be powdered asbestos.

Mix the fillers in a wide mouthed can or jar, using the fingers to thoroughly mix the ingredients and stir thoroughly until a thick paste is formed, which may be transferred to airtight containers. In compounding these fillers, use the spirits for a base, mixing the varnish or oil into it first, then adding slowly the silicon. To use, they are thinned to a thin paste with more mineral spirits or turpentine before application to the stock. Use a clean brush to apply them, brushing across the grain. Only thin out enough for the job at hand, keeping the main supply in the heavy, thick consistency. Stir it at intervals to keep the solids in suspension in the liquid.

Nos. 1 and 3 are very hard fillers which stick to the wood strongly and will not fall out of the grain. No. 3 is stained somewhat by the burnt umber, but the others are to be stained to the color of the stock as used. Only stain to wood color for dark stocks. For light colored wood, the filler can be darkened a little if desired, to somewhat accentuate the grain figure.

No. 2 is a slightly more resilient filler, not quite as hard as the others, but very good at staying put. Many ordinary fillers will dry out and crumble to powder, loosening and falling out of the wood should the finish fail to hold them in and a good finish should not be heavy enough to hold them by itself.

Should the filler turn gray and powdery on the stock after drying, you need more varnish in it.

Fillers should be brushed on the stock, across the grain, using the end of the brush to get it into the pores of the wood. In about half an hour after the application, the filler should be set, or well along in the initial drying. Now take burlap or similar rough cloth and rub the filler off, across the grain. After the whole stock is cleaned, set it away for the filler to dry, which will take from eight to 24 hours. Then you sand it with 8/0 sandpaper or 400 grit wet-or-dry paper, lightly, across the grain. After this is finished, examine the wood closely, preferably under a strong light with a magnifying glass, to see if the pores are not filled cleanly to the surface of the wood. If not, again apply the filler and go through the cleaning and sanding procedure again. If it is now satisfactory, use the fine paper to go over the stock lightly with the grain, and wiping with a clean, dry cloth will show whether any scratches remain. If any, sand them out. It is important that the hands and stock be clean and free of all grease before applying any filler. Even a sweaty hand print on a stock will injure the filler's holding qualities at that point.

Well, the stock is sealed and filled, so let us decide on the finish to be used, and how it is to be applied.

FINISHES AND APPLICATION

Linseed Oil. On a filled stock it is wisest to use—for the first couple of coats anyway—the pure boiled oil with a little drier in, which has been allowed to thicken in the air slightly. This oil has less penetrating action than straight boiled oil and therefore has less tendency to loosen the filler and inasmuch as the stock has been treated with sealer, penetration of the oil is not necessary.

The first coat should be put on a little heavy, and allowed to gum, forming a sticky coat on the stock. While you are still able to push this coat around with thumb pressure, use burlap to cut most of it off, across the grain. Hand rub it with the grain a little, and with rough cotton cloth lengthwise to remove any scratches left by the burlap. Now rub on a coat of the same oil with the palm, using the heel of the hand to work each few drops of oil as far as they will reach. A short cut is to put ample oil all over the stock, wipe it off with paper cleansing tissues, then rub it. The stock should look pretty good after this.

Then you set the stock aside in a cool, dry place for a day at least, after which it is again rubbed, but no more oil applied. If the sun is shining brightly and giving a little dry warmth, you can set the stock in sunshine for a few hours before rubbing.

As a rule, three days between coats is the minimum, and the number of coats is up to you and your time limit. Five coats will give a good finish, and from six to nine the best. Do not ever allow the oil to build up on the surface and should it begin to look rather tacky, take the burlap to it again and cut it down. This treatment does not set you back at the start, however, as another coat will have the stock at its proper appearance for that stage of the finishing. A waxing adds the final touch of protection to the oil finish, but is not always to be desired. The oil finish can be kept in perfect condition by the rifle owner applying a coat of oil every few months to clean it up and disguise any minor scratches and blemishes picked up in the field. If the wax is on, no further oiling can be done unless the wax is wiped off with an alcohol dampened cloth. A straight oil finish can be cleaned at any time by applying a liberal coat of oil and wiping it off with cleansing tissue or a clean cotton cloth.

French Polish. The hardest to apply of all finishes, and in reality, one of the poorest practical gunstock finishes. It is shellac and linseed oil, applied together.

The stock must be well filled and perfectly clean to start with. A pad is necessary for the finish application, and very clean white shellac. Natural, or "orange" shellac is good on reddish American walnut, but for the majority of stocks, the white shellac is much better. Your shellac must be thin—you can thin it a little with grain alcohol before starting the job. Keep the container tightly closed, only pouring out a spoonful at a time into a jar lid or other shallow container you can readily get into with your pad.

Cotton cloth without nap or loose fibers should be used for the pad. It must under no circumstances shed lint on the stock. Years ago,

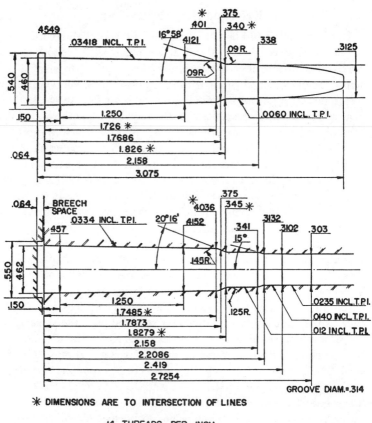

※ DIMENSIONS ARE TO INTERSECTION OF LINES

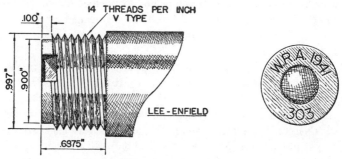

14 THREADS PER INCH
V TYPE

LEE-ENFIELD

GROOVE DIAM.=.314

The .303 British

This is one of the most famous cartridges in existence, and one that is responsible for the coining of two much used words in our ballistic and news reporting language: "cordite" and "dum dum."

The British started evolving this .303 cartridge in 1888, and it originally was intended to be used with black powder, in fact, the case was developed

when I was trying to find out about French polishing, an old timer told me to use a felt pad—that was a near-fatal error.

There are two systems used to combine the oil and shellac, one the reverse of the other. The pad is soaked with oil and then a few drops of shellac put on the pad, or, the pad is soaked with shellac, and a few drops of oil then placed on the pad.

---

to contain a large pellet of compressed black powder. No sooner had experiments on a large scale been commenced than a new and little understood propellant was adopted, a stringlike, smokeless compound known as "cordite."

The British spent the next 20 years trying to develop a satisfactory mixture of this new powder—starting with around 60% of nitroglycerin and finishing up with a 30% mixture. Cordite, in various forms and formulae, is still being manufactured and is today used in a number of British sporting cartridges, and the word is still being used by any number of American writers in describing any smokeless powder—which is wrong as we have never made cordite in the United States.

The .303 bullet has undergone more changes than the powder. In the first 15 years of existence, this bullet was changed six times, officially, and during this same period the famous "dum dum" bullet also was developed, this being only the standard Mark II bullet with its point ground away until the lead core was exposed. The work was done at the arsenal at Dum Dum, India and the bullet was known by that name. The word struck popular fancy and has been used ever since to denote a bullet of the expanding type.

All six of these early .303 bullets were of the same weight, 215-grain, driven at a velocity of around 2,010 FPS. In 1907 the British changed over to the pointed bullet, 174-grain in weight, driven at 2,440 FS, and known as the Mark VII cartridge. The previous 215-grain bullet load was known as the Mark VI.

The British have gone through the motions of dropping the .303 for a more modern cartridge a couple of times, but still have it at present. Quite similar to the Krag in dimensions, British military loadings have boosted ballistic figures considerably higher than those of the .30–40. One high-velocity machine gun loading claimed a speed of 2,800 FS with a 174-grain bullet, which is higher than our .30–06 velocity with the 173-grain military bullet.

I have been told several times that in Australia, South Africa and Canada, back country hunters having old Winchester Model 95 lever action rifles in .30–40 caliber, use .303 ammunition in them, with no trouble whatever, in spite of the .311″–.312″ diameter of the .303 bullet. This M95 rifle was also made in .303 British caliber for export to these countries. It is possible to fire the .303 cartridge in the .30–40 chamber, but not vice-versa.

Here in the United States the .303 is loaded with the 215-grain bullet the same as it was 50 years ago—but the velocity has been stepped up to 2,160 FS. The British and Canadians have a variety of modern loads available, as the cartridge is widely used for hunting.

Newell advises making a small roll of cotton cloth, saturate it with shellac, squeeze out the excess, cover it with another thickness of cotton cloth, then place a drop of linseed oil on the outside and start rubbing. The shellac will be forced through the outer cloth and combine with the oil on the stock.

In French polishing, use boiled oil of thinnest consistency, and a pad about 1½" square or wide. It is moved with the grain on the stock, with gentle pressure. Attempt to make full length strokes, for the pad will leave a mark wherever it is set down on the wood.

Go over the stock once, then allow it to dry, which takes less than an hour as a rule. If possible, examine it in clear sunlight, which will show up areas having too much shellac as shiny spots. Give these a light rubbing with burlap or rough cotton cloth, such as denim, then apply another coat.

Nothing much is gained by putting on more than six coats, as then you are building up shellac on shellac and continued applications will become more difficult, unless the shellac is again thinned out by about 15% alcohol. A very shiny, high polish can be achieved, which looks very fine indeed in a gun cabinet under a soft light. In the field it shows up water spots, scratches and dirt very readily.

To finish the French polish, most stockers go over the stock with an alcohol pad, which cuts the shellac and evens up the appearance and after this, a coat of linseed oil may be rubbed on, or wax can be applied.

The French polish should not be tried on a stock until some time has been spent in practice on odd bits of wood and old stocks. It is difficult to get an even coat of shellac on the wood, and when applying a coat, it is necessary to work rapidly, as the shellac dries fast. The usual cause of failure is not enough oil. When straight shellac gets on a spot, that spot is sealed against the entrance of oil, and when straight oil gets on a spot, that spot darkens, as the oil soaks in a little. This sounds easy to watch out for, but it is not—the catch is, the dark spots do not always show up right away.

Shotgun stocks are much better suited to this finish than bolt action rifle stocks.

Oil and Shellac Finish. This is my own modified version of the French polish. It is very well suited to rifles subject to hard usage and much handling.

The filled stock is first given a complete coat of boiled oil, and while this is still wet, the finish is started immediately. Take two large can lids, pour about ⅛" of linseed oil in one, and about ₁⁄₁₆" of thin, clear shellac in the other. You do not use a pad, you use your hand. Dip the heel in the oil, then dip it lightly in the shellac and rub it on the wet stock, covering as much area as you can, and repeating until the stock is covered. Now wipe the stock with a clean cotton cloth, and let it dry for half an hour. Again oil the stock and repeat the process. Five coats are enough as a rule. Should shellac build up unevenly, it can be cut down with burlap. After the final coat, let the stock set a day or two to dry, after which a coat or two of straight oil can be rubbed in.

This finish is really a speeded up oil job that is durable, fairly weather proof, and can be cleaned and preserved as any oil finish.

Varnish Finish. Good spar varnish or even furniture varnish can be used to put a fair finish on a stock. Varnish can also be used as a filler by itself, being brushed into the grain, then sanded off the surface and while this is considerably more work than a regular filler you do not have to worry about the filler falling out, changing color, or darkening the stock.

The stock should be sealed and filled before the finish coat is applied, which should be put on with a spray gun for best results. Otherwise, a clean brush, applying the varnish rapidly and evenly, must do. Varnish dries very fast, and "laps" show up prominently so after the first coat, use burlap to cut it down and even up the appearance, then again coat. A final burlap rubbing and a coat of linseed oil finishes the job. Varnished stocks take waxing very well, incidentally.

Varnish and Oil Finishing. The procedure is practically the same throughout as the shellac-and-oil finish previously described, except that more time is left between coats, and the stock should be rubbed down with denim after each coating. The varnish—marine spar varnish is best—is mixed with boiled oil half and half for the first three coats, then add more oil. The final coat is with oil alone and when done properly this finish is hard to tell from a straight oil finish. The stock is oiled first, as with the shellac-and-oil method.

POLISHING FINISHES

All the rubbing by hand in the world will not give a stock a high polish, regardless of the type of finish. Cloth buffing wheels on the grinder or polishing head, or, better, dry sheepskin buffs, are now widely used to give a gloss to stocks. Most of the custom stockers polish by hand, using cotton flannel, rubbing by hand for a couple of hours.

Cutting and evening up the polish by rottenstone powder has long been a common practice. A piece of felt about 2″ x 3″, preferably ¼″ thick, should be attached with rubber cement to a ½″ thick piece of sponge rubber, which in turn is cemented to a wooden block. It is best to use the rottenstone dry, sprinkling a little from a salt or pepper shaker on the stock, then rubbing with gentle pressure with the grain. The rubber backing allows the felt to conform to the curves of the stock.

This process removes microscopic irregularities on the finish, and so promotes a good polish. The rottenstone is wiped from the stock after the job is done, and the wood polished by cloth.

Rottenstone can be used wet, the surface of the stock being either watered, or the felt pad being wet and dipped in the rottenstone to transfer it to the stock. This promotes a faster action, but has the disadvantage of wetting the stock, which should be avoided.

A well polished stock should feel dry and slick—it will show fingerprints, of course, as any polished surface will, but you should be able to wipe off prints with a cloth or tissue without pressure or effort.

STAINS

It is sometimes desired to darken a stock completely, or to emphasize the grain for better appearance.

Stains may be added to the finishing material, or applied directly to the wood before finishing in a separate operation and I believe this latter is the best method.

Apply stain with a clean brush, and do not go over the entire stock with one color or one coat. End grain areas—the front of the pistol grip, the bottom line of the stock and the forend, and the receiver inletting around the tang—soak up and show more stain than other areas. They will appear darker than the rest of the stock, unless a lighter color stain is used at these points—darker all over, not just at grain structure variation points. Burls or figured portions also will darken more than surrounding areas, so it is possible and advisable to use more than one shade of stain on one stock, to gain an even color, with the grain showing clearly at all points. For straight-grained plain wood, some improvement in appearance can be achieved by streaking lengthwise with dark and light stains alternately. Spots showing too dark, can be lightened by wiping with a cloth dampened in solvent, but this is liable to pull the filler out of the stock, necessitating re-filling at that point. Alcohol swabs usually help without damaging the filler.

Mix turpentine and thin varnish 50–50 for your stain base, adding color as desired, checking the latter by trying on odd pieces of wood similar to your stock. For hard woods, cut down on the varnish and increase the turpentine.

Hit the paint stores and artist's supply shops for your coloring matter—burnt sienna, raw sienna, burnt umber, and yellow will take care of almost all requirements. Burnt umber can give almost any degree of brown, burnt sienna is red, raw sienna is yellow, but the artist's chrome yellow also should be used, as it mixes well with combinations of other colors.

I will not attempt to give formulae, as it will be necessary in most cases to mix a stain to the desired shade for a particular job. Mix a little at first, and by trial and error, determine what suits your stock best. As a rule, equal parts of solid coloring matter and liquid base must be mixed, to form a thick paste, which is then thinned by turpentine to water consistency, for brushing on the wood. Keep prepared stains tightly closed up, preferably in small jars or cans with minimum air space. Newell gives many staining formulae in his book.

Flame Staining. The Japanese Suigi wood finish treatment received some publicity through the efforts of the late Alvin Linden. It has a limited application on gunstocks and is principally intended to dress up light colored and plain grained woods. Maple takes it very well. An open flame is used to heat-darken portions of the wood.

A blowtorch is probably the best means of doing the job. The flame itself must not be sooty, and the wood must be clean, straight from the sanding, without sealer or filler. Use a broad flame, not much pressure in the tank, and play the flame over the stock at a distance with an inch of flame on the wood. A narrow flame must be handled more carefully, and moved faster over the stock. You make a series of passes, charring the wood brown, not black, in bands or waves or whatever design pleases your fancy. Be very careful at the edges of the inletting and the bottom of the pistol grip, as these char easily—move the flame fast past these points.

After the flame treatment, the stock must be sanded again, using a sandpaper block always. The scorched areas are weaker, and if the hand is used to back the paper, these will cut easier than untouched wood and hollows will be created. After sanding, the grain must be again raised and cut down, after which sealing, filling and finish operations are in order.

This scorching system to darken sections of the stock is an old stunt. American colonial gunsmiths used it to change the plain color of maple stocks. As the old story goes a string or yarn was dipped in oil, tar or pitch, then sometimes rolled in gunpowder (black powder) and wound around the stock in a spiral from end to end and set on fire. As the string burned, the wood immediately underneath was scorched brown. But gun collectors who have tried this trick on old rifles tell me that the stunt can only be used on ramrods, that the impregnated cord will not remain in place on forends or buttstocks, where a particular pattern is required, and that the splendid patterns found on these Colonial rifles were evidently put there by acid stain.

Linden was the only modern top stockmaker to experiment with the flame method of wood staining, adopting the Japanese name "Suigi." There are very definite gunstocking possibilities for it in the use of plain woods which need some adornment such as birch and beech.

CHAPTER 27

Stockmaking: Checkering

CHECKERING the handles of tools and weapons to give a nonslipping handhold is an ancient practice, as even before the invention of firearms sword and dagger handles were checkered or carved. The first hand and shoulder firearms did not have checkering, probably because the heavy recoil of the large caliber guns made a tight hold uncomfortable, and—pistols in particular—most arms were made to slip in the hand under recoil, much in the way the old Colt single action revolver acts. After the percussion cap came into use a wide variety of sporting arms appeared, and checkering began to come into general use and it was then that checkering became decorative as well as useful.

Today, too much checkering is prostituted, put on for a pleasant appearance rather than for functional use. The purpose of checkering is to provide a nonskid grip on the gun, not to make it look pretty. For this reason, checkering finer than 22 lines per inch is not recommended because if it is finer than this, it will feel smooth in the hand after the gun is handled a few times. Decorative patterns need not be intricate to be attractive.

Laying out a pattern on a stock is not difficult, although it is difficult to lay out a pattern on paper and attempt to transfer it exactly to the wood, especially on pistol grip patterns. The curvature of the wood makes exact transference from a flat pattern almost impossible so it is better to use small templates for the front and rear borders of the patterns only, and make the others with a flexible rule and freehand. The thin transparent lucite rules or scales now sold all over the country are very handy for this, as they will bend and twist to follow stock curves and a white grease pencil is best for outlining the pattern as it leaves an easily seen line.

Checkering is very hard on the eyes for most men so always try to do your checkering in the very best possible light.

To lay out the direction and proportions of the individual diamonds is a very simple matter. You make a large diamond of cardboard or thin plastic, exactly the proportions of your desired checkering diamonds. It should never be less than twice as long as it is wide. I prefer one two and one-half times as long as wide, and many stockmakers use a three-to-one or even longer diamond. The pattern can be from 3″ to 7″ long.

It is desirable to have the checkering diamonds point front and rear, in line with the bore, but slight variation from this is often desirable because it is wise to accommodate the borders as much as possible, having the top border of the pistol grip somewhat in line with a row of diamonds.

The pattern diamond is laid on the stock, one point within the outlined borders, and a line drawn along two opposing sides—these lines to converge of course. When a point pattern—the front border of the pistol grip pattern and the ends of the forend pattern—is used, the point of the pattern or template diamond is used to lay out the points. These will then come out even when checkered, containing only full individual diamonds.

After the initial two converging lines are laid out on the stock, the checkering tool, or a single edged grooving tool is used to make them into single grooves, from one edge of the pattern to the opposite. Then the spacer or grooving tool with two edges, spaced properly to give the desired number of lines per inch, is guided by these single grooves to cut a double groove, and the job is on the way. Run the tool over the stock, using one groove to space the next, until the entire pattern is laid out in shallow channels in both directions, with the diamonds outlined. The spacing tool should not cut deeper than $\frac{1}{32}$″.

Now comes the real checkering, using the single edged checkering tool to deepen each individual groove slightly. Go over the pattern in both directions, deepening each line in turn. Do not try to cut full depth at one going over, but just cut a little deeper each time. About three times is necessary before the diamonds should become pointed. Use a magnifying glass if necessary, to check your progress on fine checkering.

The border business is generally overdone or underdone. "Borderless" checkering is excellent on good hard figured wood, and is not really more difficult than the bordered type. Just keep a trifle under the pattern outline, then at the last a little careful work will extend it to an even outline.

The semi-skilled checkerer will find masking tape or even adhesive

CHECKERING CRADLE

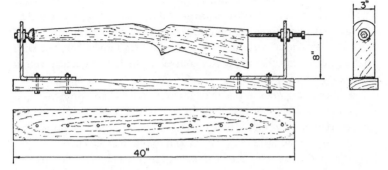

An absolute necessity for checkering, the cradle is also of some value in stock shaping and sanding, and in finishing.

Make it of wood—the base, I mean—and if you can find a piece of gum-wood 2″ x 4″ it is excellent though beech, oak or other hardwood is satisfactory. The end brackets should be made of ⅜″ x 3″ flat steel, bent as shown, and drilled for holding bolts to correspond with a uniformly-spaced set of holes in the base so that either one can be moved toward the other. The left fitting shown is to be arranged for holding the forends, and should be in the shape of a fairly deep cup, lined with sheepskin, wool out. You can turn this out of hardwood on the lathe. The right fitting is a long sharp pointed screw, to dig into the small hole or depression you make for it with a drill bit.

Both fittings, or stock contact points, are to be freely rotating, on good bearings. Get a couple of auto water pump bearings from a junk yard and clean them up, set into the end brackets and hold with set screws or solder on the body, while the shaft is free to rotate and is to be fixed up for the fittings. The stock end fitting (screw) must be tapped through the rotating center of the bearing, so the stock can be turned without the screw either tightening or loosening.

In use, the checkering cradle is clamped by the base in a vise, the stock placed in it, and one hand used to rotate the stock through an arc while the other holds the checkering tool to the wood.

A stop screw, or lock screw can be installed at either end fitting to act as a brake and hold the stock firmly in any desired position, when it is not desired to turn it while working.

tape stuck on the wood to outline his pattern a great aid in preventing overrunning the borders with either spacer or checkering tool. The skilled man will prefer to have the wood bare and work to a penciled outline.

And before I forget to mention it, the word is always "checkering" not "checking" as checking, referring to wood, technically means splitting, or cracking on the surface.

The checkering cradle is a vitally essential piece of equipment, for you must run your lines the full length or width of the pattern while working. The stock is turned to always allow you to bear down on the tool (not hard, of course) so that you do not try to work up and down. Work both spacer and checkering tool with arm movement, not with wrist action as this allows a better control of the tool and keeps you in the groove, literally speaking.

The checkering tool is pushed forward under slight pressure, and moved back in the groove under light pressure. Cutting is done on the forward stroke only, and strokes will run from ½″ to 1½″ in length, the tool being gradually fed forward and extending the cut.

Special bordering tools can be made up, to be used after the checkering is complete in the same way as the checkering tools, or the checkering tool itself can be used to cut a V or double V border. Tom Shelhamer uses a small bent veining tool to cut borders.

As checkering cuts below the cured surface of the stock, it is necessary for a good job to raise the grain in the checkered area by wetting. The checkering tool is then again used to smooth out the diamonds by cutting the raised grain down and give the final sharp outlines. Linseed oil, or linseed oil mixed with varnish, is then brushed into the checkering with a soft toothbrush or similar instrument. Care must be taken not to get too much oil which will gum in the grooves—unless you want to do as John Hearn does, and oil the checkering liberally, letting it gum up, then clean it out with the checkering tool.

Really fine checkering should always be done after the stock is completely finished. It is not possible to checker a plain stock then finish the stock afterward without damaging the checkering to some degree, regardless of how much masking tape or other protection you attempt to give it, during finishing operations.

Only experience can teach checkering, but good tools certainly help in the learning. The illustration and its caption well describe the making of tools. For the file cut checkering tool head, there is a shortcut to spacing the teeth: Get the finest-cut metal checkering file you can locate—probably it will be 50 lines per inch—and use it on the sides of the bevel. The grooves thus cut can be sharpened on their leading edges with a triangular needle file. Leonard Mews, the Wisconsin stockmaker, called this stunt to my attention.

Different textures of woods call for different types of checkering. Hard European walnut, or American rock maple, will take fine checkering—I have seen stocks checkered 28 lines per inch in this country, and some foreign-made stocks with over 30 lines per inch.

PROFESSIONAL CHECKERING

Leonard Mews, in his Wisconsin shop, shown amusing a "museum piece" by scratching its sides and belly with a fine toothed 29-to-the-inch curry comb—and doing it in bodily comfort by sitting on a padded stool, and in visual comfort by wearing an eye saving Magni-Focuser, with a "Flexo" balanced, adjustable fluorescent lamp placed to give a long, glareless area in proper illumination. Knuckle comfort is achieved by the handy little "knuckle duster" finger nail brush, worn as you would wear brass knuckles.

This headband magnifying glass is made by the Edroy Products Company, 480 Lexington Avenue, New York City. It sells for about $8.75, and is called a Magni-Focuser. Carl Zeiss, Inc., New York City, have them in 2¼ power and John Unertl, the scopemaker, made them in 2¼ power some years back and may still do so.

The 2¼ power is too strong and the eye relief is too short for checkering gunstocks, as the tool is rapidly moving about and trying to follow it with the eyes will turn one's stomach, just like trying to read the lettering on the sides of a fast freight train when it rushes past and you are close alongside. A little help is all one needs when checkering; for average eyes the #3 Edroy in 1¾ power, with 12 inch focal length, is just about right—but if the user is over 55 years in age he better try the #5 with a focal length of 8 inches.

The better camera and optical shops handle these magnifiers and if your eyes are not just right you better examine and try out a few different sizes before buying. They run up to the #10, which is about 5X with a focal length under 3 inches—you really have your nose to the grindstone when you get up to these powerful models, which are mostly used by photo engravers and retouchers.

These magnifiers are really worthwhile for checkering if you get fitted out right with one. Al Linden used to use John Unertl's model quite often. They are a great help in filing to scribed lines, when fitting inlays, making and sharpening checkering tools, grinding rifling cutters, sharpening reamers, and similar nose bending operations. Eye glasses can be worn underneath. One source of side light is absolutely necessary but the use of these gadgets make the general lighting much less critical.

Mr. Mews writes:— "Notice the trick gadget fastened to the fingers of my left hand. This is an ordinary five-and-dime store Nylon bristle, oilproof, fingernail brush, having two curled end handles or hooks which enable it to be worn like a pair of brass knuckles.

"This kind of knuckle-duster is just the ticket to dust the little, curly shavings and sawdust out of the checkering. Just a natural, instinctive flick of the knuckles and it's done—quick as a wink and with no risk to the pattern lines. More than once have I snatched up the usual wooden-backed brush and "burnished" the pattern with its back instead of the bristles. Whereas this little fingernail brush is a natural and works perfectly, right off the bat, saves the knuckles, and leaves the left hand free to work with and to help guide the tool, turn the work and the likes. I use my left hand quite a bit helping guide and push the tool, as it saves the muscles of my right hand. I also use my left hand a great deal in turning or rotating the stock while scooting across a pattern which runs "around the bend" when using the right hand and tool to deepen the lines.

"This particular bit of French checkering is 14½ by 29 to the inch; and 29 line checkering requires watchful care with steady and regular breathing all the time the job is being done. The Magni-Focuser relieves eye strain and makes the checkering show up clearly, even if the lighting is not just right or all that it should be—which latter requisites are very necessary when checkering with the naked eye."

A Leonard Mews sporter—.270 Winchester, on their Model 70 action, with Weaver K-6 scope in Buehler mounts. The stock is California black walnut, oil finished, and tipped with African Blackwood. Note that this stock is high at the heel, with the high comb faired down and cheekpiece faired inward at front, to keep the shooter's face from getting beat in from recoil. The recoil pad, a Pachmayr, was heated in hot water and curved slightly to gain more of a rifle shape. Even without any pad, a stock shaped such as this minimizes recoil to a considerable degree. Paul Jaeger's QD swivels and a Mashburn trigger. Now look on other side of this page and find out about the checkering.

In the closeups above, note the "French" or skipcheckering and also the styling of the grip pattern borders, combining curve and diamond effect.

This checkering is $1\frac{3}{2}6$—one line of 13 per-inch spacing, then two lines of 26 to-the-inch spacing. The large diamonds are of course left flat-topped, while the smaller ones are brought to points. This type of checkering is not only decorative, but also a bit more rugged than the standard style, it wears well and in addition slight dents and scratches are less evident.

In discussing this design, Mr. Mews writes:—"This is a forend pattern that I and others have called the 'lightning' pattern, as it looks like a barbed flash of lightning with its many long, slim, jagged points. But it is not one that can be done in a flash. All those points must be formed by the straight and parallel lines of checkering coming out to points and not by short, tapered lines tacked on like thick-butt shingles.

"This pattern is checkered with $3\frac{1}{2}$-to-1 proportion diamonds. It will not have that racy, classy, sharp-as-lightning look with diamonds any shorter or more squareish; they will give it a dead, ungirdled, dumpy appearance—as they do to all patterns. Another reason for long, slim diamonds on this design is that this short pattern is long enough and gives a good enough grip on the entire forearm without smothering all the beautiful polished wood with the checkering of a longer pattern. This is often the case.

"With this pattern it is best to leave the uncheckered strip along the forend bottom; then you will not break up the long flowing lines of a lean, racy rifle or shotgun. This design will not chop the gun into sections as do the run-around patterns, and the uncheckered strip left along the forend bottom will take bumps and dents better than checkering will, also withstands bench-rest use, careless racking and the like much better.

"This is an accomodating pattern that can be modified to fit all sizes and lengths and tapers of forearms. It is a fine pattern for a pumpgun slide handle. If desired, the space between the two side panels can be narrowed up to give checkering almost all-around if one wants it—or the pattern can be run clear around. An inlay or gold or silver monogram, or a multi-pointed diamond shaped patch, can be checkered in center bottom, or in center of a wide strip—all these variations have worked out fine.

"I lay this pattern right out on the stock, or it can first be laid out on paper cut to cover the length and diameter of forend to be checkered. A 6B soft lead pencil is used to draw center line (don't bear down hard) down bottom of forend, then wrap an inch wide or so celluloid or cardboard strip around each side and draw in the ends of the pattern, or the end points, also the points near the center or midway fore-and-aft. Also sketch in at point where front ends of master lines touch border, to keep them even numbers—unless you want the bottom end points shorter than the top ones.

"The grip pattern I sketch right on the stock itself, freehand. Pistol grips vary so much in size and shape that I give each job an individual layout, using curved templates of celluloid or cardboard cut out to fit various curves. A French curve or two is nice to have around the shop to help get nice, full blown, free-flowing lines."

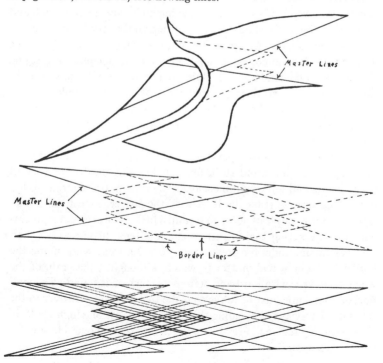

Hard American walnut will take 24 lines per inch, and so will most myrtlewood. Ordinary "good" American black walnut will take and hold 20 lines per inch, providing diamonds are a little shallow. Soft American walnut should have shallow 18 line checkering. I am not familiar with birch as regards checkering, but it should be capable of holding 20 to 22 lines per inch. The closer grained a wood is, the more strength it has to hold small diamonds.

The silicon fillers dull checkering tools quite rapidly, and care must be taken to keep the tool sharp as a dull tool not only will not cut, it will mess up the cut already started. If you can not trust your eye to check the angle of your tool edge, to keep it the same through repeated sharpenings, make a little metal template and use it with a magnifying glass. Just file the proper V in a thin metal plate and hold it over the edge.

There are numerous details regarding checkering which the individual must work out himself, such as the length of the tool, type and size of handle, and curvature of shank. Also, whether he wishes to work with one checkering tool only, or keep several. Many good checkerers prefer to use a single tool, sharpening it as it dulls, while others may keep half a dozen, sharpening all before starting a job and then being able to finish it without working on the tools, using them in turn as they dull. One way you give your eyes a rest, the other you save a little time. No, do not try to do a complete job of checkering at one sitting. Eyes and hands can not stand it. The fingers have quite a bit to do in checkering, and they get tired and shaky after a couple of hours holding and guiding the tool. The best custom stock men spend from one to two days checkering a stock, this meaning from six to twelve hours actual work.

The hardest part of the operation, or rather, parts, come at the start in laying out the lines, and at the finish, in bringing the diamonds up to sharp points and uniform dimensions. The general procedure is to lay out the pattern, cutting the lines with the spacer, then to do something else for a couple of hours to rest up a little. The deepening process with the checkering tool is rather simple after a little practice, and the eyes are not under too great strain. Keeping from overrunning the border is the only real matter to watch, although if the grain of the wood is uneven, with hard and soft spots, such as is found at a small burl or knot, care must be taken that the tool does not ride over to the soft side. Two ways of avoiding this trouble are: use of a high blade on the checkering tool, and use of a tool with teeth cut on one side only for use at such spots.

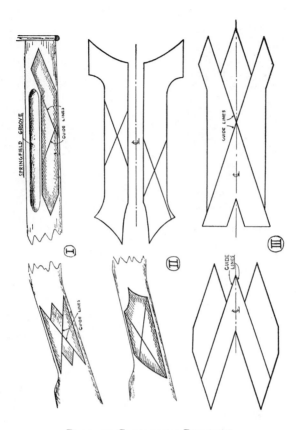

PRACTICE CHECKERING PATTERNS

Here are three simple checkering patterns for the beginner to start off with—and it is very likely that he will have lying around or in the scrap pile material entirely suited for this practice.

These simple patterns are intended for service Springfield, Krag, Mauser and Enfield rifle stocks which have finger grooves in their forearms. With the two latter models these grip patterns will have to be modified somewhat, or other patterns used, as their stocks are not straight gripped.

Such checkering must not be too fine, about 16 or 18 lines to the inch will probably be just right for most of the soft grained wood found in these military rifle stocks.

Pattern No. 3 had better not be attempted until the other two designs have been pretty well mastered—or unless you have a pile of these discarded military stocks lying underneath the workbench.

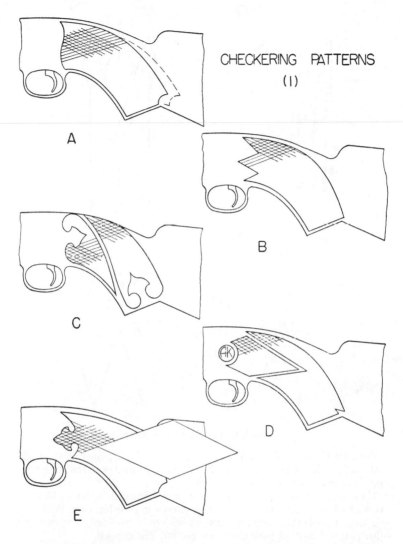

A

B

C

D

E

A. One of my favorite patterns, which looks better on the gun than on paper. It is borderless, and based on curved outlines. The dotted lines show the extent of the checkering on the right hand side of the stock, where the pattern is brought further to the rear to provide support for the heel of the thumb.

B. A conventional pointed pattern. The points on the front outline are almost equal on the gun, but drawing makes them seem out of proportion. Because the stock is curved in two or more directions, it is almost impossible to show a true checkering pattern on a flat plane.

The high-blade tool (at least ¼″ from edge to top) is advisable in any case, since it can be guided or forced slightly to one side or the other by thumb pressure. One hand is used to hold the tool, while the other can hold the stock with its thumb placed so that the side contacts the side of the checkering tool blade.

Use of a large magnifying glass aids considerably in noting the progress of the job, and will of course reveal anything wrong. Get one of the gooseneck glasses, having a long, flexible handle which can be attached to the checkering cradle and moved to any position. An ordinary glass can be attached to a ⅝₆″ rod or bar of lead and give the same result. As good clean wood does not show depth very well, it is wise to use lights to throw shadows across the checkering as a check. A common small flashlight of the fountain pen type is good as anything you can get.

Bright sunlight is ideal for checkering, but we do not have it everywhere all the time, so must work under lights. Use large incandescent bulbs to give a high-intensity light, and if necessary, wear good sunglasses to ease the glare. It does not hurt to wear a hat either. This system is the best I know of to be able to see well without going half-blind in a short time. It works for me and my eyes are terrible.

C. A fancy pattern, of the style used by Tom Shelhamer at times. Checkering runs unbroken over the top of the grip, but it is divided at bottom. Do not try this one until you are able to stop the checkering tool exactly where you want to.

D. A fancy point pattern, with inlaid initial button at front. Considerably easier than it looks, though.

E. Illustration of use of the layout diamond. It should point as parallel to bore of arm as pattern borders permit. Lines in both directions are laid out with the diamond, one each way, with a white grease pencil. Groove each line with the checkering tool against a straightedge for an inch or so, then with the layout or spacing tool, work from these until the whole pattern is grooved, in both directions. The proportions of the large layout diamond determine the proportions of the diamonds in the checkering, exactly. If the layout is 3 to 1 (three times as long as it is wide) each diamond in the pattern will also be 3 to 1.

The white pencil is also used to lay out the borders and details of the pattern. Paper templates are not much use on any but small skimpy patterns, and the flexible lucite rulers not too useful but ⅟₃₂″ thick sheet lead, easily cut with scissors, is about as handy for making border patterns as anything. Make templates, shape them to the general shape of the stock by pressing them over the pistol grip sides of an old stock of similar shape, and trim to the desired outlines.

CHECKERING PATTERNS
(2)

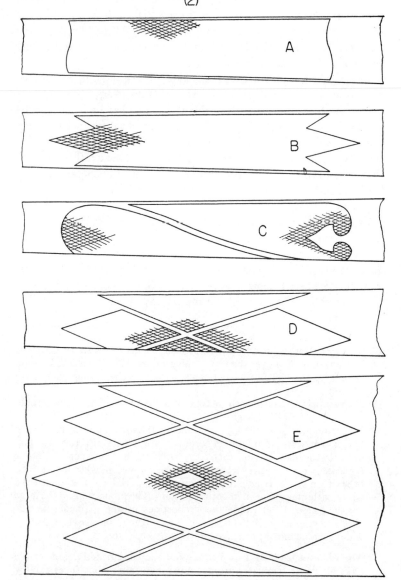

In finishing a checkering job, often the ends of the lines will shallow out a trifle, thus killing the border diamonds. This of course is due to stopping the tool at the edges of the pattern. To touch up these areas, use a straight wood chisel. It should be thin-bladed—the old Swedish "Shark" brand is very good—not over ⅜″ wide (¼″ is better) and ground on a long bevel. Make the bezel ½″ long, to give a thin cutting edge, and sharpen it to a razor sharpness and it will not hurt any to break off the shank and set the handle down to within 3″ of the edge. In use, this chisel of course is used to cut the grooves right out to the border to full depth and sharpness. Naturally it must be used very carefully, under the magnifying glass. Almost no pressure is required for the job, and actually the handle can be dispensed with, for the blade can be handled between thumb and forefinger.

I've been wanting to try some of these 1½ and 2X special spectacles made for tool and die makers on checkering, but have not got around to it yet. These can be worn only for short periods of time, after which a short rest is required, but they should be ideal for finishing up checkering jobs. Since the cost of such glasses is fairly low—from six to twenty dollars—they are worth a trial by anyone contemplating steady stock work.

The bane of checkering, aside from eye-strain, is sweaty hands. Collodion or other coatings on the hands hurt the feel, or sense of touch,

---

CHECKERING PATTERNS

(2)

Forends

A. Curved border type, corresponding with "A" on the No. 1 sheet. Can be continued unbroken around the bottom of the forend if desired.

B. Point panel pattern, to correspond with "B" of the pistol grip patterns.

C. The Shelhamer pattern, as with "C" on No. 1 sheet.

D. A diamond panel pattern, which is not shown too well. Proportion of the panels is correct, however.

E. I attempted to unravel the "D" pattern to show it completely, but could not make an exact drawing. The large center panel is on the bottom of the forend of the rifle, and is an even proportion diamond, though in attempting to transfer the design to a flat piece of paper it came out with a long front point. John Hearn has used this pattern to very good effect.

In laying out the forend checkering, the diamond is also used, but the flexible lucite rule is extremely useful in continuing lines and laying out borders. Templates are valuable in outlining arrowheads or acorns.

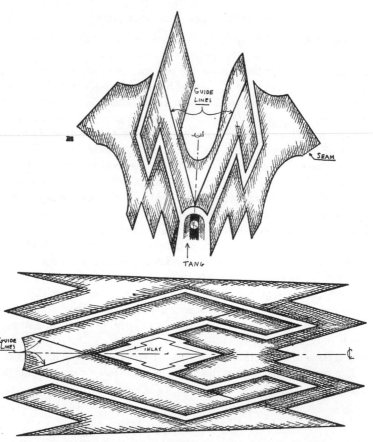

This checkering pattern, shown in better detail on the Plate opposite, was designed by John Hearn to go around the holly inlay in the forearm of the rifle illustrated. It is executed 24 lines to the inch.

The big idea is to make the design on the forearm come out even with the points of the bordering patterns on either side, and use the sides of the diamonds to make the borders of the pattern. This is not a fill-in pattern.

Lay out the guide lines first and then fill in that portion of the pattern. All the diamonds in this section are formed by the guide lines. But it is very important to get the turns true to the desired angle. Then, proceeding very carefully, a guide line can be continued over and across the raised strip and into the upper dovetail patterns along each side of the forearm. This is a complicated pattern, hard to describe and even harder to get on the curved surface of any forearm without squeezing any of the diamonds.

The grip design is a standard over-the-top pattern which is split by the Z-shaped stripe running through the middle. The bottom or forward part of this pattern meets under the grip and is seamed together along an up-and-down line. It is impossible to run the same set of diamonds over the grip and underneath it without a seam.

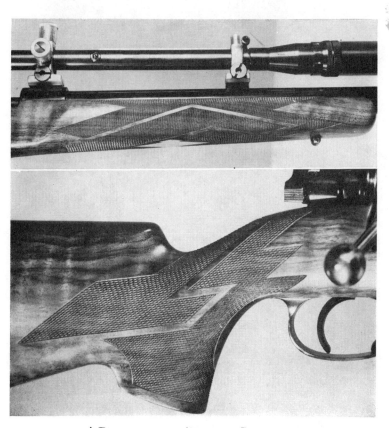

A Design for the Advanced Checkerer

John Hearn sent in the above photographs, with the information that this was the most elaborate and most difficult checkering pattern that he has attempted to date. He calls it his "Mystic Maze" pattern and admits that the checkerer may find himself in a bit of a maze, or possibly a daze, before it is completed.

This design was worked out for a Model 70 rifle, of .220 Swift caliber, made up by O. H. Elliott and having a French walnut stock with holly inlays. It is stocked "target style"—meaning that all dimensions are a bit full and plentiful. Weighs about 10½ pounds without the scope.

The details for laying out and executing this design are shown and explained on the opposite page.

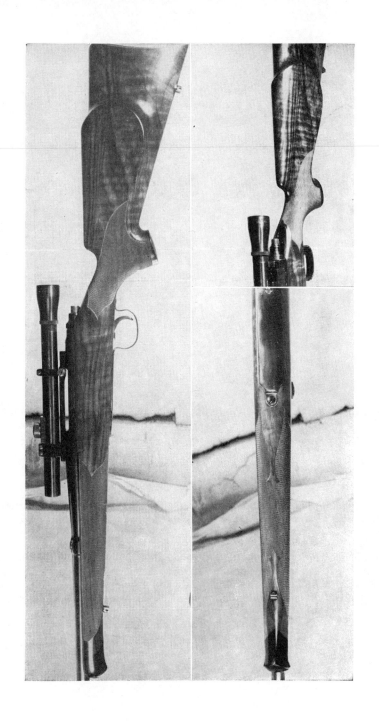

A .300 Magnum, by John Hearn

Above is a Model 721 Remington barrel and action, stocked with the highest quality French walnut. With the scope, it weighs nine pounds even, which is an average weight for a properly built rifle of this caliber. The small views show how the checkering is run over the top of the grip and under the bottom of the forearm in one continuous line in each case. In the grip view, notice that the lines coming up on the left side roll evenly over and go on down on the right side, thus making the diamonds complete.

Mr. Hearn states: "Oddly enough, the forearm checkering pattern started out to follow the curve of the forend tip of this rifle. I decided to complement the sweep back that I used on this schnable tip and started to draw. The pattern is simple in lines, I believe, yet dignified enough for a stock of this quality.

"This grip pattern is a fill-in, except that on this job I ran the checkering down under the grip as well as over the top. At this point, let me say that it is impossible to draw the checkers in one continuous pattern BOTH over and under the grip on the same stock. You can have one or the other, but not both. So it is necessary to use a seam along the bottom of the grip to run the line together.

"Actually, when well done, this has a good looking effect of its own. It shows good workmanship without pretending to fool anyone."

so about the only thing to do is to wash the front feet every fifteen minutes or so in soap and water. If you find a better deal, let me know.

Small brushes, with short, soft bristles, are useful for keeping the checkering cleared while working. Give the local dimestore's cosmetic counter a look and you'll find several useful little brushes.

Repairing a slip of the tool can often mean hours of work. Next to a border it is sometimes possible to dress up the spot with use of the chisel and bent triangular needle file. A crossed line in the middle of the pattern indicates lots of work—it is necessary to cut the entire surface of the pattern down to depth of the crossed grove and so eradicate it. A new 8″ mill file is about the best tool to do this job. The dimensions of the stock are changed slightly, since $\frac{1}{32}$″ or more of wood has to be taken from the surface, but this is to be preferred to a botched-up checkering job. Sand the stock lightly with 6/o and 8/o sandpaper to remove any file marks, and start over. Never, when a tool slips, or a ·line of diamonds breaks off, attempt to get by through merely deepening the grooves at these points. You will not get away with it—the bad spot will show up like a black eye on a blonde.

A good clean cutting spacer goes a long way toward a good job, for the checkering tool does not ride out of a sharp edged groove very easily. Poor cradles can contribute to slips, so make a dependable one and clamp its base tightly.

In soft woods when the lines run parallel with the grain, pressure on the checkering tool must be eased to prevent these grooves from deepening faster than others. The tool must also be very sharp so that it cuts the grooves and does not deepen them by pressure. And for finishing the job—the last going-over, that is—again sharpen the tool, being careful not to change the angle of the edge. This to prevent breaking any diamonds, which a dull tool will do on soft, weak wood.

PATTERN DESIGNS

The average checkering pattern consists of two side panels on both the forend and the pistol grip. These are comparatively easy to lay out and execute, and if not too small, are satisfactory from the practical standpoint. "Point" patterns, having the borders coming to a pointed outline on the front and the rear of the the forend panels and on the front of the grip panels, are easiest to do and the most decorative. S curves as end borders are also rather nice, and permit larger areas of checkering on the forend, which the customer sometimes wants.

There are three refinements possible to dress up a pattern, aside from fancy borders with fleur-de-lis, spearheads, or acorns in the outlines. The first is to use skip checkering, sometimes called French checkering. This is accomplished by using two widths of spacing tools. The main checkering is laid out with the finer tool, say 22 lines per inch, but every fifth or eighth or sixth space is laid out with a coarser tool, perhaps an 18 line. The layout is done this way in both directions, then checkered in the regular way. As the tool points up the fine checkering, the coarse lines of diamonds remain flat on top, and show up very spectacularly, giving a grid effect. This method is best on very good wood, where a 22 or 24 line spacing can be easily contrasted with a coarser one.

The second requires more headwork in laying out and figuring the space to be covered by the checkering. It consists of running the checkering over the top of the pistol grip in an unbroken area, and around the forend in an unbroken pattern. A variation of this is to bring the checkering around on each side of the grip to meet in a straight line on both top and bottom—this is easier.

The third entails very careful work with the spacer and the checkering tool as it involves a pattern within the pattern, with either several borders to watch, or sweeping lines curving through the pattern to leave narrow strips of uncheckered wood. The illustrations show examples of these decorative patterns.

Should you desire to make a fancy pattern, try it out first to see how it looks on an old stock, then be sure you have a good piece of wood in your real stock. A fancy pattern only looks right if the checkering is 22-line or finer.

With the checkering the stock is finished—put in the swivels, give it a final rubdown, and assemble the rifle; it is ready to sight in and go to work.

Machine Checkering. There is now a power driven checkering tool, made by the Dem-Bart Company. This does very excellent work, especially in soft wood, cutting several grooves at each pass although guide grooves must be cut by hand first. Cutters to give the desired spacing are available. The tool is naturally not suited to fancy patterns, but for a quick low cost stock does okay and is much better than trying to do a cheap and fast hand job (there is no such thing).

This tool does its best on plain unfilled, unfinished wood as on finished stocks the cutters dull rapidly and are hard to guide.

Leonard Mews, the Wisconsin gunstocker, does a great deal of this French checkering and he has very kindly sent us illustrations of his work and also pattern layouts, which are shown.

SCORING

Also called "flat-checkering," scoring was used on stocks up until about 1880. Later day European military single shot rifles often had it, the most oft-seen examples in the United States being the Swiss Vetterlin repeater and the Japanese Murata. Some American gun-smiths used it occasionally, but it was never very popular.

Scoring consists of lines scored or shallow grooves cut in forend and on pistol grip, in the areas now sacred to checkering. (Military arms usually had only the forend or forearm scored). Either square or dia-mond outlines could be used, and were. The scoring was done with a large spacer, as used for outlining checkering patterns today. This double edged saw-like tool could be used for just laying out the lines preliminary to cleaning them up with a file or checkering tool, or if shaped well, for the complete job.

Lines, or grooves, were spaced from $\frac{1}{8}''$ to $\frac{1}{4}''$ apart, and seldom over $\frac{1}{32}''$ deep. This made for very large squares or diamonds which of course were merely outlined on the wood of the stock and polished with the stock to show the grain clearly. Diamonds as a rule were much shorter than are used in checkering. Very often the flat-checkered di-amond is only $1\frac{1}{2}$ times as long as it is wide. A refinement used some-times in the early days was to set a little metal inlay, often just a small nail-head, in the center of each diamond.

Scoring preceded checkering as we know it, and some of the early colonial riflemakers used it. The idea applies well to straight-grip arms of all types and to soft woods. There is no possibility of diamonds or squares breaking. One trick can be done, which cannot be done with checkering, and that is to curve lines to follow the contour of the pistol grip. This works out best with squares, rather than diamonds. I have seen a couple of old shotguns with this type of scoring, and once used to the idea, it is not hard to take.

While scoring does not compare to checkering, it is very easy to do, does relieve the monotony of a plain stock, and makes for something different. The latter always appeals to a certain type of individual.

A modified flat-checkering, with deep grooves and fairly well angled sides, can be quite attractive on good wood, as the grain shows up nicely. However, this is a little harder to do, in order to keep the tops of all diamonds uniform in size. Setting in a short piece of silver wire, centered in each diamond, would make a very showy job, and a hard one. Some of the old London guns, with their straight grips, looked exceptionally classy with this type of decoration.

RE-CUTTING OLD CHECKERING

Often a rifle or shotgun will come to the shop for refinishing completely. The checkering as a rule will be worn down, the grooves filled with dirt and oil, maybe a few dents in the pattern and the appearance generally beat down. Remove the old finish and refinish the whole stock, raising dents, sanding out scratches and so on, ignoring the checkering completely. Work right over it.

After the finish is ready for checkering you recut it, using the remnants of the original lines for guides. Make a special tool for deepening these lines, either in the form of a checkering tool with sharp-angled edge (45 degrees) or in the style of a spacer, with single edge. Do not attempt to use a regular spacer even if it spaces correctly with the original spacing, unless the lines evident are reduced to faintly visible marks. Use the single edge grooving tool to lay out the grooves, then make the diamonds come up with the regular checkering tool.

Should the original checkering be in pretty good condition, the tops of diamonds only worn a little, and no scratches or dents messing up the pattern, the checkering tool alone will be sufficient. Clean out the grooves first, using the tool and a bit of solvent or turpentine to soften gummed oil and dirt. One of the little fine-wire brass brushes sold for cleaning suede shoes is highly recommended for assistance in cleaning checkering, too. In extreme cases, a brass bore brush, shotgun size, can be used.

Re-cutting is quite easy as a rule and the best possible training for doing complete checkering. Practice up on all the old stocks you can get hold of which have had checkering, before attempting to do a job on a plain stock. The training in guiding the tools and obtaining the "feel" of the checkering tool as it cuts is invaluable.

CHAPTER 28

Finishing Semi-Inletted Blanks*

SEVERAL years before World War II a few enterprising firms began making semi-finished rifle stocks on production basis, to retail at low prices direct to the shooter for him to finish himself. Stoeger and Bishop were the leaders in this field, and Bishop today is the largest outfit in the business.

Gunsmiths of course can buy semi-inletted stocks and stock blanks wholesale, and most gun shops now carry at least a few on hand, to cover the Springfield, Enfield and Mausers which the amateur gunsmith can finish up.

Bishop—E. C. Bishop & Son—furnish the most complete line of semi-inletted stock blanks, covering Winchester and Remington models as well as practically all the military bolt actions, American and imported, even the two piece Lee-Enfield stock being available. Bishop deals solely in American walnut, having their own logging facilities in southwestern Missouri, and most of their wood is of good quality as regards strength, texture and seasoning. Fancy grades are available at fair prices. I have seen some very beautiful wood from Bishop. Incidentally, they will do the inletting and shaping operations on your own blanks, if you send them to Warsaw, Missouri.

The machine inletting done by Bishop and others is almost as close as can be done and accommodate the variations in rifle actions. As a rule, the inletting for the triggerguard and magazine is almost complete. The barrel channel is not cut to anything like correct size, on account of they do not know what size barrel you may have put on the action. This of course is good, since you can correctly bed the barrel.

If anything, the inletting around the action errs on the oversize side, as the manufacturers attempt to make things as easy as possible for the amateur with little experience and few tools to finish up. Bishop leaves the outside of the stock oversize at all points except at the forend tip, to provide shaping to individual taste. Too many of the pur-

*See Appendix I, page 713.

chasers have no taste, it seems, for mostly they just sand the outside smooth and oil it, leaving a bulky, heavy and lousy looking stock.

Herter's makes quite a line of large rifle stocks, using all available woods, including European walnut. Their plain grade walnut (American) is rather soft and light. The forends are left long as a rule, and can be cut to the desired length. Herter's sells both blanks and inletted stocks, with all variation in between. Buttstocks can be had with or without Monte Carlo. Bishop furnishes only the Monte Carlo, but the heel of the stock is high enough to allow removal of the Monte Carlo comb.

Hutchings supplies semi-inletted blanks, fully-inletted blanks and finished stocks, in American walnut, maple, birch and California walnut, leaving the forend square in the semi-inletted style. He leaves ample wood on the exterior of the butt for correct shaping, and holds inletting dimensions to minimum, so that very close final fitting is possible. Any variation from standard can be made.

Flaig furnishes Pennsylvania walnut rifle semi-inletted stocks, and shotgun blanks of apple and maple. The walnut is rather soft, but the higher grades have good figure. A slight Monte Carlo and long cheekpiece allow considerable leeway in shaping the buttstock.

Any of the semi-inletted stock and blank suppliers will try to accommodate you on special grades at your request, and will make allowances on all stocks for minor alterations such as a narrowed receiver tang on the Springfield, a straightened guard on the Enfield or a commercial Mauser guard tang, which is shorter than the military style.

Inexpensive remodeling jobs on ex-military rifles almost always feature the use of the semi-inletted stock, very often finished by the gunsmith. There is nothing wrong with this practice, as long as he does not call it "custom stocking," which many of them do.

INLETTING

Except for Hutchings' stocks, with their square forends, the first problem with a semi-inletted stock is how to hold it while working. Leather vise jaws are essential, and it is best to clamp at the receiver ring section, centering this in the vise, for the first operations.

Set in the triggerguard first and if the magazine box is separate, leave it out until the last. There is usually very little work—not over 20 minutes worth—in placing the guard. Check with the scale from the top through the magazine opening to get it to the proper depth in the wood, taking measurements from the magazine box if necessary. You want the guard inletted to such depth that the top of the magazine box will be ⅟₃₂″ below the bottom cut for the receiver, showing from the top of the stock.

If there are gaps at the corners of the magazine box or guard ends between wood and metal when you have this done, leave them as you can not repair them at this stage. The guard should fit tightly in the wood, with absolutely no fore-and-aft play. A file and a ⅜″ straight chisel are about all that is needed to inlet the guard on most stocks, with small round files and half-round gouges occasionally needed to clear the corners of magazine openings and the tang ends of guards. It is permissible and possible to bend the guards just forward of the trigger loop up or down ⅟₁₆″, should the bottom line of the stock not conform to the profile of the guard. This particularly applies to the 1917 Enfield and the 1903 Springfield. The angled rear guard screw will still work properly unless the guard is bent ⅛″ or more. Slightly enlarging the guard screw hole in the rear tang of guard by a round file will permit the screw to enter the receiver satisfactorily in this case.

Leave the guard in the stock, tapped in to full depth, and turn the stock right side up in the vise. If the guard is a loose fit, make small wooden wedges to hold it firmly in the wood, glueing these wedges in at either the front or the rear tang, preferably the rear, for appearance sake. Match these wedges to the stock wood the best you can, and make a good joint as they are to stay permanently.

Now install the headless guard screws in the receiver—only the front if Springfield or Enfield, of course—and slide the receiver down on the top of the stock, the screws going down through the holes in the guard, which serve to line them up.

Where the bottom of the receiver rests against wood, mark the outside with either a sharp pointed pencil or a plain scriber, remove the assembly and cut down along these lines with straight chisels, until the bottom of the receiver enters the stock, going at least ⅛″ below the top line. The guide screws or screw remain in the receiver until the stock is completely inletted, of course.

After the receiver will go below the top line of stock, you must use the spotting method from now on, employing cream rouge, Prussian blue, lampblack and oil or whatever you prefer.

When the bottom of the barrel stops further lowering of the receiver, use a pencil alongside the barrel to outline the barrel channel, all the way out to the tip of the forend. By looking straight down on the stock with the barrel in place you can easily tell if your lines are cor-

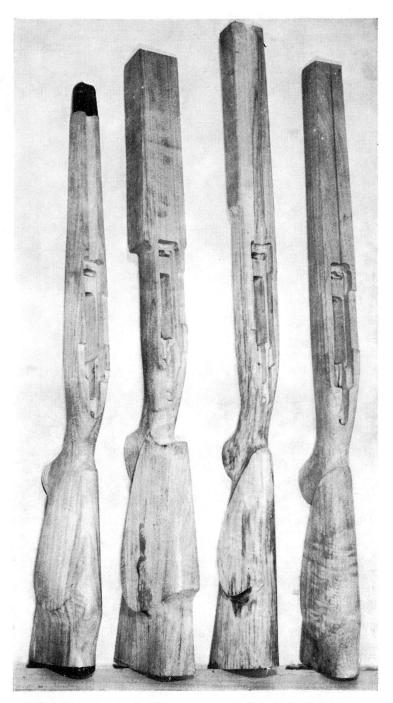

Four makes of semi-inletted stock blanks. Left to right, Bishop, Hutchings, Jaeger (French Walnut) and Win-A-Mer "custom" style. The Hutchings model allows almost any shaping, from large target to slim sporter.

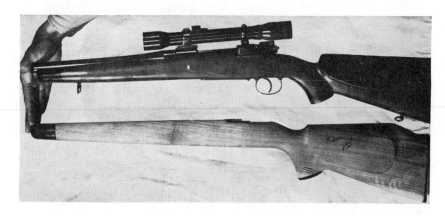

Before and after with Bishop standard sporter semi-inletted blank. The rifle stock was made from blank identical in proportions with that shown.

Two 1903 Springfield target stocks made from Bishop target semi-inletted blanks, to show difference in shaping possible. The lower stock has raised cheekpiece, for telescopic sight use, while that on the rifle is made for competitive shooting in all positions with metallic sights.

Showing what can be done with a standard Bishop blank. A .270 Winchester on FN Mauser action, with 23″ Titus 12″ twist barrel. Unertl 4X Hawk scope in Tilden mounts. Weight, 8 lbs. 6 oz.

Note that butt has been re-shaped and pistol grip pulled back ¼″ from Bishop shaping, also small ledge outlining bolt stop. The slight palm swell, or bulge on the pistol grip is visible in the picture of the right-hand side, though the undercut of comb is not so evident. Niedner buttplate used, and grip cap made to match. The finish is linseed oil. The rifle is not yet completed, although a year old. The Tenite forend tip is to be replaced and grip and forend checkered. The Bishop blanks finish to good stocks. The pistol grip on this illustrated job could be smaller, but in this case the shooter does not cross his thumb over the tang. Made up by the author.

A Lightweight Sporter

Three views of lightweight .257 built by Dunlap for the wife. Action—World War I Mauser '98 carbine, fitted with Springfield trigger-guard. Barrel—21" light Titus, 12" twist. Scope—4X Unertl in Tilden mounts. F.N. safety used. Stock—good American walnut, ebony forend tip, Niedner buttplate and matching grip cap. Weight, 7 pounds 8 ounces. Overall length, 40½", length of stock, 30¾", length of pull, 13".

The stock is of better appearance than indicated in the pictures, as the color contrasts are not sharp enough to register well. I fudged a little in shaping this stock, which accounts for lack of cast off and the rather homely cheekpiece, in order to make the job fit my wide face as well as my wife's narrow one, as I intend to use this rifle myself every now and then. (I have not informed the lady yet, though!)

You will note considerable drop at heel, which is permissible on a .257 or other rifle of light recoil, but not recommended on anything from a .270 up. The right side of pistol grip has a slight swell, to fill the palm, but not an arbitrarily-located bulge. Aside from the narrowed forearm, this stock is full size throughout. It could have been slimmed down more in the butt to eliminate perhaps 4 ounces weight, or, made of good European walnut, cut to weigh from six to eight ounces less, however, the rifle was designed as a lightweight, not a feather-weight. Tightly bedded, with light barrel contact at all points, the accuracy is excellent and the rifle does not change point of impact when fired repeatedly for twenty shots or more. This I consider due more to lucky coincidence than to skill either on my part or Mr. Titus'!

Such rifles as these are very fast-handling and are ideal for deer hunting and for Western varmint shooting.

rect and not oversize. With a straight wide chisel make a cut about
$\frac{3}{32}''$ deep just inside these lines, then with gouges cut a half-round
channel out to these cuts, which should be straight down. An inletting
rasp or scraper will smooth out the channel, and sandpaper on the
edge of a rounded block will finish it up for the present. This preliminary channel must be as true and smooth as you can make it, in
order that the final spotting in will be easier.

Most of the action inletting will be straight chisel work, with a little
scraping and bottoming tools are seldom if ever needed, as the machine inletting pretty well squares the bottom. Bottom the action on
the wood, with as full contact as you can get. Should the rear tang be
inletted too deep before you start, insert fiber plates or shims at this
point or you can use very hard wood. The receiver should go down in
the stock until within $\frac{1}{64}''$ of the top of the magazine box. If you find
that the router boys did not leave quite enough wood from top to bottom to permit this, do not shim under the receiver to raise it, or under
the guard to lower it, but file the top of magazine box off until things
reach the proper distance. Receiver and barrel are inletted to one-half
diameter.

In fitting the magazine box itself, make no effort to gain a close fit
between wood and metal, except at the bottom, which should be close
enough for good appearance. This is not always easy to do, particularly
with Mausers. Allow at least $\frac{1}{32}''$ clearance at the sides and the rear of
the magazine box. *Do not try to take up recoil with the magazine box.* It
sounds good, but does not work out as stocks may crack through the
web.

When the receiver is being inletted, one of the first points encountered is the recoil shoulder in the stock. Cut this back $\frac{1}{16}''$ if
necessary to gain plenty of clearance in your spot-scrape-and-try fitting. The crummiest jobs of inletting are usually done by men trying
religiously to obtain a close and correct bearing on the recoil shoulder.
They usually get a fair fit, after making the receiver ring inletting cut
$\frac{1}{16}''$ further forward than they eventually need, and getting the tang
back and forth an equal distance, and then find out at the last minute
that the triggerguard and magazine box must move forward or back
$\frac{1}{32}''$.

Take care of the recoil shoulder properly, with a recoil plate—no,
not now—later.

With the stock fully-inletted, you hope, you clean up the spotted
wood by light scraping, recoat the metal with your private goo and put
the rifle together with guard screws, winding them in as tightly as you

can and observing whether or not the rear tang moves down any as the screw is tightened, after the front screw is in place. If so, you either relieve the inletting on the bottom at the recoil shoulder, receiver ring, and barrel channel, or shim under the rear tang.

Removal of the assembly from the stock will show what points need further scraping. While still together, try the tension on the forend, pulling the wood away from the barrel. If too much tension, deepen the barrel channel slightly and try again.

With rifles of light recoil—.22/250 and less, or heavy barreled .257s —no recoil plate is needed for good wood, but go ahead and give yourself ample clearance on the recoil shoulder in inletting. Then, square the shoulder in the stock and fit in a plate of aluminum or even lead to make a tight fit between wood and metal. It is considerably easier to make a proper bearing between the metal and wood shoulders by this method than by attempting to fit the recoil shoulder directly against the stock. The latter, while admirable in intent, is very hard to do because usually the metal is bearing against the edges of a couple of chisel cuts, and after a few shots is slapping back and forth.

The inletting completed, set the metal parts in the rack and start cleaning up the outside of the stock, working from the butt forward. The plastic buttplates furnished are not too bad, but to improve the looks of the job, use a steel plate and if you have room, set it as far right on the stock as you can, to give a little offset. Cut the butt to proper length and pitch, inlet or attach the plate, outline the cheekpiece in pencil, both top, or surface, and at the points where it will meet the stock surface and then rough the cheekpiece to the outlines with chisels and gouges. Plane the Monte Carlo off, unless the customer wants it, and slim down the buttstock. *Do not remove any wood from the surface of the cheekpiece.*

Next, the pistol grip. See if you cannot cut the lower line of the butt to line up with the bottom line of the stock at the rear of the guard loop, without leaving the bottom of the pistol grip hanging out in the cold by itself. It is usually possible to cut the bottom of the grip at a sharper angle to allow this shaping.

Now try to cut the pistol grip to the length and curve to suit the customer. On most of the blanks chopping the edge of the grip back from $\frac{3}{16}''$ to $\frac{3}{8}''$ helps a lot—the front edge at bottom that is.

The dimensions of the pistol grip and cheekpiece should be made to suit the shooter or customer, naturally, and his wishes carried out as to shaping and size. As a rule, it is neither possible nor wise to make a grip smaller than $4\frac{7}{8}''$ in circumference at the small, unless a select blank of dense, strong wood has been provided, with the grain running perfectly through the pistol grip. Leave the cheekpiece until the last, so that it can be cut to comfortable height through trial by the shooter.

Shaping of the body and forend are per custom stocking practice, although the use of attached plastic forend tips limits both dimensions and designs here. Bishop's tip is a shell, about $\frac{3}{32}''$ thick at the sides, at most, so you cannot slim down the forend too much.

Rough out the entire stock to about $\frac{1}{32}''$ over the desired final size, then have the customer try it to check the pistol grip and cheekpiece. File or cut these to suit him, then finish the stock down to final size, and do the preliminary sanding with o and oo sandpaper.

One of the small palm planes is useful on these stocks, but a sharp cabinet scraper or spoke shave really gets rid of excess wood and sanding blocks and coarse files take care of the angles, corners and curves.

Now you are ready to install the recoil plate, the same as on the custom stock. Stick a bit of gum or putty on the recoil shoulder in the stock, oil the recoil shoulder of the receiver and set it in the stock. Removal will show where the recoil plate's front edge must be. The recoil plate should be $\frac{1}{8}''$ thick, minimum, so cut the wood back enough to accommodate the recoil plate between the wood and the recoil shoulder of the receiver. Looking down into the inletting, mark the outside of the stock in line with the cut back shoulder of the wood, and run a No. 31 drill through on each side, one hole above the other, in line with the recoil shoulder. Square out this rectangular opening through the stock and press in the recoil plate. It is not at all hard to make a perfect joining of wood and metal, so that only a small upright rectangle of white metal shows on the outside of the stock. Either duralumin or aluminum is satisfactory, both being rustproof and easily worked. Should you find that the plate is a little thick, so that the rifle will not enter the inletting, push the plate out of the stock and file back that part of it which contacts the receiver until the rifle will assemble.

Should by mischance the plate be too far back, and so not support the recoil shoulder, install thin metal shims between the plate and the recoil shoulder until it does support the recoil shoulder. This in no way detracts from the serviceability of the plate.

Try to measure the plate so that it is $\frac{1}{32}''$ longer than the stock is wide. When installed, it projects slightly on each side, and is filed off flush with the wood, then sanded with the wood in the final sanding.

It is sometimes possible to inlet the rifle a little below center in these semi-inletted stocks, so that after the final inletting, the top of the stock can be planed off to the centerline of the barrel and the receiver. This cleans up the top, of course. Never allow the wood to reach above a curve on the receiver or the barrel, as the appearance is injured and nothing at all is helped.

The pistol grip is shaped with the cap in place, if of plastic material, except for the preliminary changing of angle and length.

Install the sling swivels, then remove them again, to keep them out of the way while finishing the stock.

FINISHING

The stock is now inletted, shaped, and sanded. Raise the grain, cut it down, repeat, and dry well.

Most semi-inletted stocks—about 99.8%—require filling. Use whatever filler you choose, the silicon type being best, but rough on checkering tools. The open grained wood takes plenty of sealer and filler.

Assemble the rifle and stock and check the inletting around the receiver and the guard for gaps between the wood and the metal, but if they are not more than .015″ wide, do not attempt to fill them now. The oil finishing or waxing after the stock is completely finished will disguise narrow openings fairly well, and crack fillers do not hold well anyway. For the wider gaps, as at the rear end of the receiver tang (with the recoil plate you do not need to leave clearance behind the tang) and around the magazine box, several fillers are possible. Mittermeier's shellac sticks do well or plastic wood, walnut or mahogany color, will hold if thinned out slightly with alcohol before application and pressed in with the fingers. Shellac and walnut dust, or casein glue and walnut dust make excellent crack fillers. All of them tend to darken somewhat, so it is not a bad idea to slightly darken the stock finish but do not stain it black—the color of dark American walnut is fine. When pressing fillers in between wood and metal, remember always to oil the metal lightly first.

With the stock filled and patched, and stained if desired, put on your finish—shellac and oil, rubbed varnish or whatever is on the ticket.

In checkering, remember that the softer the wood, the coarser and shallower the checkering must be, if it is to stay.

Most American walnut will take 18-line checkering, some of the very softest is better off with 16-line, and good hard wood will stand 20-line. Your pattern can be as elaborate as on the custom stock, but do not forget that your wood will not hold sharp points. It is best to keep the

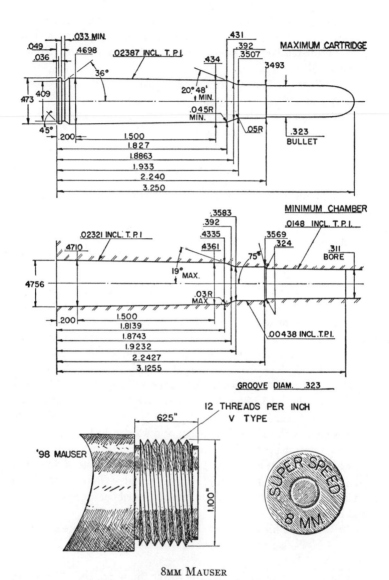

8MM MAUSER

(7.9mm, 7.92, 8 x 57JR)

Known by all of the above names, and generally called the "8mm Mauser," here is the European rival of the .30–06. Used by Germany in the past as a standard military cartridge and by many countries today for small arms, the 8 x 57 is used the world over for sporting purposes. It has never been particularly popular in this country, although both World Wars have repattern conservative as a fancy pattern in coarse checkering does not look so good.

After finishing the stock, install the swivels and assemble the rifle. To further disguise any over cutting on the inletting, wax the inside of the stock, leaving a little line of wax around the top edges of the inletting. After the rifle is assembled, wipe around the gun, at the junction of the wood and the metal to remove any excess. This is not to cover up bum work, either on your part or on that of the stock supplier, really, but is to seal the rifle against moisture. I am taking it for granted that you had enough foresight to raise the grain on the inside of the stock, sand it down, and oil it with linseed oil.

You will be surprised how good a stock can come out of one of these

---

sulted in thousands of military and sporting rifles here in the United States. At the present time, however, a great many rifles are in use, remodeled to some extent or other, and the cartridge sale is about in the same class as the .30–40 Krag, as regards volume.

The 8mm Mauser is one of the very best deer-through-moose hunting cartridges made. It equals or even surpasses the .30–06 for a "meat" gun in some forms of hunting. We are handicapped somewhat by poor factory ammunition, but the handloading men can get some of the superb German hunting bullets and concoct fine cartridges. Bullets weighing from 125 to 250 grains can be used, for every purpose from vermin shooting to big bad bears.

This cartridge does not develop the high pressures of comparable American cartridges, most loadings available being in the 45,000 lb. pressure class. Mauser rifles which therefore are safe and reliable with this cartridge are not necessarily so if rebarreled to hot American calibers.

Most of the ex-soldier owners of Mauser rifles are inclined to consider the cartridge inferior to our top calibers, and usually think they should have them rebarreled for American cartridges. This is definitely a mistake, if the rifle is in good condition internally, but if the guy insists on paying you for a barrel job, do not insult him! It is true that over-the-counter ammunition now available for the 8mm is not all that it could be, but it is certainly equal to the .30–40, which is universally respected.

The barrel shank of the 1898 Mauser (also of the 1924, 1935 and their modifications) is as shown, but considerable care must be exercised in threading. Mausers were made in many different factories, and some slight variations in shank diameters will be found. The Polish arsenal at Radom made some rifles with long receiver rings and consequently long shanks. With any Mauser, the original barrel should be used as a guide in cutting the new barrel shank whenever possible. The thread is approximately 12 per inch, relieved at rear to permit fitting into the receiver diaphragm and at front only for convenience in threading. The thread is not exactly 12 to the inch, but this is thoroughly satisfactory for fitting. It is of course a metric pitch and does not convert perfectly to English measurement.

cheap semi-inletted stocks, when the pocketbook is a little flat. Any-way, do your best—do not hack away at it and excuse yourself with the thought or saying "well, it is not much good anyway, I cannot make a real stock out of one of these abortions," which all too many of us do.

I could never mistake a semi-inletted deal for a custom stock, no matter who finished it, but after all, the customer must be satisfied, and he does not always have from seventy-five to a hundred and fifty bucks for a custom stock. The semi-inletted blanks provide enough wood for almost all custom variation in the buttstock, body and cheek-piece so there is no excuse for making an ill-fitting stock from one of them. It should be possible to fit almost any man not physically handi-capped almost perfectly, if the principles of stock design and custom stock shaping are kept in mind.

The semi-inletted stock makers have really done a great deal to improve the American shooter's taste in stocks, by providing him with cheekpieces, ample pistol grips and forends, and emphasizing the "dress-up" value of forend tips. Everyone can now have a fairly decent looking sporter stock, even with unskilled finishing efforts. The average gunsmith, not skillful enough for custom stock work, can turn out usable and attractive stocks from the semi-inletted stocks, at a rea-sonable price for the average hunter, which are certainly better than standard factory stocks. The amateur at home can shape himself a better proportioned stock from one of these than the best custom stock designers of 40 years ago could turn out.

COMMERCIAL FINISHED STOCKS

Suppliers are going even further today and providing completely inletted and shaped stocks, either with finish and checkering, or sanded smooth for the gunsmith or shooter to finish himself with oil or other means.

Bishop sells stocks both checkered and uncheckered, to order. Frank Lefever sells completely finished rifle stocks, with or without cheek-piece, to retail at less than $30.00. These are well filled, but have only a light coat of oil. For a really fine finish, go over these stocks with oooo steel wool, then apply a half-dozen coats of boiled oil rubbed in—which is very little labor to gain a fine appearance. Lefever will furnish his stocks equipped with either recoil pads or Niedner steel buttplates at the additional cost of the pad or plate ordered. The stocks are full proportioned through the butt, grip and forend. No forend tip is pro-

Remodeled 1903 Springfield, with Lyman Alaskan in Buehler mount, Dahl front ramp. Stock is the ready-made Lefever. Metalwork by the author.

Two Model 70 Winchesters, one with standard stock, the other with standard stock altered by attaching wood and reshaping to cheekpiece high-comb type. Note difference between the two stocks in drop at heel and toe, also heighth above comb of the two cocking pieces in the opened bolts.

This alteration was made to permit use of the standard stock in long-range target shooting, but is also very well-fitting for hunting telescope shooting. Receivers, barrels and bolts of these two rifles were made parallel for the picture.

vided and American walnut is used.

Roy Weatherby should be well established in the stock trade, by the time this book is read. The preliminary samples shown me at his plant were extremely good, the inletting being as close as much of our custom hand work, and the shaping of the stock being very good. Shape of the pistol grip and the forend is designed for completing a good looking streamlined rifle, without excess bulk. All woods available can be furnished. The stocks are sanded smooth, and require only final sanding, grain raising and filling to be ready for the finish.

Where standard military barrels are retained in Mauser, Enfield and Springfield rifles, the makers of these stocks can inlet the barrel channel to reasonably close fit, requiring only scraping for proper bedding. When the original barrels are discarded, it is of course advisable to order the stock with no barrel channel, or with a small channel.

Naturally, all these finished stocks are designed for our "average man,"—that is one 5′ 10″ tall and weighing in the neighborhood of 170 pounds. Without alteration they will fit most men usably well but of course can have the butt shortened for close coupled shooters, or have the butt lengthened by a recoil pad or a thick plate for tall, long-armed men.

CHAPTER 29

Stock Repair and Alteration

T HE general gunsmith does many minor repair jobs on stocks. These range from replacing chipped off butt toes to straightening warped forends. The stock repair job is never to be recommended as other than a temporary measure, for a repaired stock is almost never better than barely passable in appearance and seldom is as strong or efficient as the original or a new replacement.

Taking up the repair end of the chapter first, by types of arms:

SHOTGUN STOCK REPAIRS

Which also includes forends and slide handles. The chipped toe and split tang are the most numerous of jobs. The chipped toe can be replaced by inletting a block of wood per the illustration on the subject, but a much nicer-looking job is to dress the bottom line of the butt up to take out the broken outline and refinish the stock. This can only be done when the chip is shallow. The finished appearance is as good as new, with this method.

Tangs on the Browning-type autoloader chip off at top, when the grain of the wood does not follow the top line of the grip. If saved, the chips can be glued and pinned back on, otherwise pieces of walnut must be cut to fit then attached in the same way, after which they are filed and sanded to conform with the lines of the stock.

A vertical crack in any type of stock at the tang can be nullified by a cross bolt at the most convenient point to strengthen the stock. Head and nut of the bolt should be wide and thin, and should not be countersunk below the surface on either side of the stock, but should be flush with the surface.

Sidelock shotguns, such as the L. C. Smith, throw oil into the small wood tangs of the stock, which weakens the wood and promotes cracking and chipping. Not a great deal can be done, for there is seldom room for bolts or pins. It is necessary to cut and split a chipped tang end back 3″ or 4″ in order to gain holding strength for the replacement patch of wood.

When oil has caused wood to deteriorate and therefore lose its resiliency, which then causes loss of contact with metal parts through lack of resistence to screw tension, cut the spoiled wood away with sharp chisels, glue in blocks of hard walnut or fiber and re-inlet the metal parts to correct contact.

Cracked but still serviceable forends can be helped by inletting a cross bar, or piece of wood, to reach across the crack on the inside, to about ¼″ depth. Just glue the piece in, without pins. If this is considered insufficient, run in two brass or blued screws from the bottom, or outside, of the forend.

Remington M11 forends are prone to split, about which not a great deal can be done, as there is not room for pins or patches. Battering of the wood at either end can affect operation of the gun if not checked in time. Cut useless wood out at the points indicated by wear, to allow insertion of washers or semi-washers made of hard fiber of sufficient thickness to correctly adjust the gun.

The handles on slide action arms split rather readily, and usually there are provisions for holding the split halves in place, by screws on each side, and/or cup-type metal flanges at either end. The only real repair is to replace with a new handle, as these are cheap and not hard to install and replacement should be cheaper than repair. If repair must be done, make two or three spring steel clips, like rings with one-third missing, of the size to fit into the grooves in the handle. Clean the crack out the best you can with a knife and wire scrapers, put in some glue and snap the clips over the handle at front and rear, and perhaps the center, creating eough tension to hold the handle tightly together.

The large skeet and trap forends on slide shotguns are difficult to repair when split without the repairs being obvious. Metal plates can be inletted into the underside of such handles, but must be attached with screws which of course show. Rivets are no less conspicuous. If the forends can be completely removed from the barrels or magazine tube assemblies easily, it is usually possible to glue the split and so restore strength. Before reinstalling it on the gun, check the inletting and make sure it slides freely on its housing. It may have cracked of its own accord through shrinkage.

RIFLE STOCK REPAIRS

Single shot and lever action rifles split stocks at the small, or pistol grip. Very often, when the split is vertical, a cross bolt will restore the arm to years of service. Horizontal cracks the owner usually cures by the time honored method of wrapping friction tape around the grip. The gunsmith can do a neater, if no better job, by inletting and glueing in small blocks of wood inside the inletting and also putting in a couple of small vertical pins. I have found that $\frac{1}{16}''$ brass welding rod is about the best material for such pins. There is not sufficient area for wooden dowels.

Pump action buttstocks are subject to the same trouble and treatment as mentioned above, and the forends also crack. With old guns having small slide handles, it is difficult to do much other than put on spring clips as mentioned for the same type of shotgun. The more modern rifles of this type have sufficiently large forends or·handles to permit pinning and glueing; being larger, they are stronger and less prone to crack, anyway.

Bolt action rifles are more dependent upon the stock than any other type, as regards the effect of the stock upon performance. They are also harder on the wood, and more liable to damage the stock through recoil than other types. The quality of the wood enters the matter also, for softwood requires different treatment in repair than does hardwood.

The warping forend is the most common stock ailment in bolt action sporters. If it warps straight down in a gentle curve, leave it alone if the rifle shoots all right—unless the owner wants it to look like a nice, custom fit at the tip. In which case you file a bit of metal—$\frac{1}{64}''$ or $\frac{1}{32}''$ —an amount equal to that distance which the forend tip has moved away from the barrel, from the top of the magazine box and back, if a Springfield or Mauser, from the bottom of the box if of the separate box type such as the Enfield or Winchester. Then you proceed to inlet the action deeper into the top of the stock, spotting the barrel and the action until a clean fit is reached.

If the customer does not want to pay for this job, give him the old armorer's remedy, charge him a buck, and send him happily on his way. This is to place a washer or shim of hard fiber or soft metal under the rear tang of the receiver, which tilts the rifle in the stock slightly— it works.

Should the forend warp straight up, it is only necessary to deepen the barrel channel to relieve the added pressure on the barrel.

Warping sideways—now we got something! It has been my experience that a stock will warp up or down and usually stay there, but when it moves to right or left it may come back where it was at just the wrong time.

A horizontal warp is of course due to unequal tension in the wood fibers of the forend, one side being of closer grain than the other. Wood can either contract or expand. Naturally, figured wood has all sorts of strains and tensions in it under temperature and moisture changes, and a stock which warps sideways nearly always has some figure on one side or appreciably more figure on one side than on the other.

If the stock blank was well seasoned when the stock was made, which as a rule you must assume to be true, the original position of the forend was correct, and has changed only due to artificial reason such as one side of the stock being exposed to considerable more heat than the other.

Anyway, for the sporting rifle, attempt to bring the forend back to its original position. With the stock off the rifle, clean out the barrel channel if necessary until you can see the run of the grain of the wood at bottom and sides. Now start drilling holes, using $\frac{1}{16}''$ to $\frac{3}{16}''$ bits, making these holes at points where you see a sudden wave or turn of the grain and zig-zagging the pattern of your holes to cut completely through the area of the side of the channel. You do not of course run the drill completely through the stock anywhere! Do the same on the straight grained side of the channel, but do not put as many small holes. The idea is to break up the longitudinal strength of the wood in the forend, so that when it further attempts to expand or contract, the action will be limited by the grain having been cut at intervals. After this, place the stock in a damp place with a weight hung on the forend, or a clamp arrangement to tend to bend it straight. A day is usually all that is necessary, after which the stock is placed in a dry room for a day and observed in its action. Further cutting may be necessary, to obtain the end that the stock will remain straight in either damp or dry environment.

For the target rifle with warped forend, cut the barrel channel out to one side or the other to relieve tension and let it go—probably shoot better full floating anyway.

The bedding of the action causes most other stock troubles with the bolt action. If the recoil shoulder is not solidly supported, it will slam back when the rifle is fired, with the result of causing the stock to split at the tang, back of the receiver, unless considerable clearance has been provided for it at that point. Should the wood be soft, it may be compressed and batter back under repeated firing, to cause the same damage. This setting back of the wood at the recoil shoulder is a cause of much inaccuracy in rifles which lack a recoil bolt fitted at this point.

If the stock is of decent wood, and the shoulder (wood) only reduced in contact through long pressure and shrinkage, a hard fiber or copper

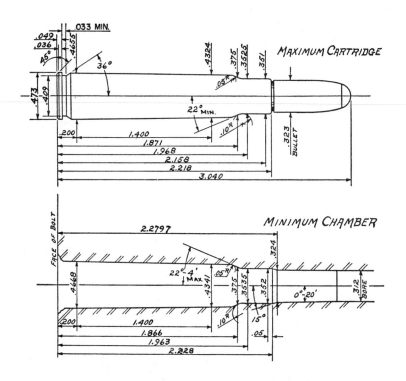

MAXIMUM CARTRIDGE

MINIMUM CHAMBER

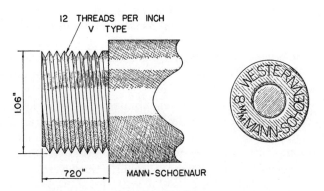

12 THREADS PER INCH
V TYPE

1.06"

.720"   MANN-SCHOENAUR

WESTERN 30-08
8 M.M. MANN-SCH.

THE 8MM MANNLICHER-SCHOENAUER (8 X 56)

This drawing is intended principally to show the difference between the 8mm Mannlicher-Schoenauer cartridge and the 8mm Mauser cartridge. Mauser rifles outnumber the Mannlichers probably more than 100 to 1 in this country. Kindly note that headspace is considerably different between

shim may be placed before it, to carry the action forward slightly—there is no other necessary treatment. The crack in the tang usually is only the depth of the metal receiver tang. Fill it up with plastic wood, or inlet a decorative plate to disguise the split. Should the split be serious—through the small of the stock vertically, a through bolt is necessary, and two small bolts are better than a single large one.

Should the recoil shoulder in the stock be split or broken, a recoil plate should be installed. The recoil bolt is not too good for repairing damage to the recoil shoulder itself and the plate, with its holding or recoil resisting area spread across the full width of the stock, is much better.

There should be some slight clearance at the sides of the magazine box between wood and metal, to offset the tendency of the stock to split itself vertically in the inletting through shrinkage. The Model 70 Winchester rifle is a bad offender here, as in a hot or dry climate the wood contracts enough to split behind the front guard screw and forward of the trigger. Target models suffer worse than sporters from this, in the factory arms.

Occasionally a stock will shrink enough in all dimensions to cause the guard screws to lose their power of holding the rifle rigid in the receiver inletting. The cure is introduction of shims under either guard or receiver, or cutting enough metal from the magazine box to permit the correct tight fit of the wood to the metal.

Going back a little, the splitting of the small bit of wood connecting the walls of the stock ahead of the trigger and behind the magazine box is apparently not very serious. Here in the dry Southwest, 90% of large bolt actions split their stocks at this point through wood shrinkage. Accuracy and bedding does not seem to be affected so I consider no repair necessary. The only repair would be installation of a stock bolt at this point, to hold the sides of the stock tight against the metal.

---

the two and that the Mannlicher cartridge in the Mauser rifle has considerable excess headspace.

The Mannlicher barrel shank dimensions are similar to the Mauser, except for length, but in the fitting of a barrel, take measurements from the old barrel if at all possible. A Mannlicher barrel will screw freely by hand into a Mauser receiver, which of course is not right.

The Mannlicher case is called the 8 x 56mm, while the Mauser is the 8 x 57mm, meaning the neck is approximately 1mm longer. Do not confuse the 8 x 56 Mannlicher with the 8 x 60 Mannlicher Magnum, which is a longer case with ballistics similar to the .30–06.

As they are too tight anyway, this means clearing out the sides of the magazine cut in the stock and as the bolt is always unsightly it should not be used unless requested by the rifle owner.

REPAIR OF STOCK FINISHES

Factory varnish-type finishes chip and spot rather badly, and the only real cure is to remove the objectionable or scarred finish all over the stock and refinish the wood to the customer's desires. Use varnish remover first of all.

Oil finished wood is of course easy to clean up. Wiping with raw linseed oil usually removes most of the dirt and to some slight extent equalizes color differences. Varnish remover can also be used on oiled stocks, incidentally.

With the stock cleaned, sand it lightly with the grain, using 4/o sandpaper, to show up the dents and scratches. Dents can be raised through steaming, which is done by laying a wet cloth or bit of blotting paper on the dent, then putting a hot iron on top, to create steam and drive it into the wood fibers of the dented area and expanding them. For small dents, an old screwdriver blade makes an excellent iron for the job. A furniture workman told me that he used wet gauze pads and an electric soldering iron for dent removal, which sounds like a good idea if you have plenty of dents.

Scratches and cuts cannot be raised, but must be filled. The old "stock putty" made of shellac and wood dust, can hardly be beaten. No, Junior, you do not make up a potful and apply with a putty knife. You clean out the scratch or cut with a knife point or a wire brush, put a bit of shellac in it, then sand the stock over the whole area with sandpaper from 4/o to 8/o. Very soon the gouge is filled up and close to the color of the stock. Use only white shellac, thinned out, for the job. For deep abrasions, several applications of shellac may be necessary, and about two hours' time allowed between each separate application and sanding.

To clean an oil finished stock, wipe with a cloth wet with ethyl alcohol, then coat with boiled linseed oil. Wipe the oil off immediately with clean cloth or cleaning tissues. Varnish, shellac or lacquer finishes may be damaged by alcohol, so experiment at some not too prominent part of the stock before giving it the works. In many cases the alcohol will cut the finish very slightly, which is usually good, since it will smooth out the surface and remove minute scratches in the finish itself. If the stock has deep scratches or gouges, do not use the alcohol for it will work under the finish and injure it at the edges of the abrasions. For such stocks, your best bet is plain warm water with a little Oakite in it. Wash it with a rag and dry it with cloths and cleaning tissues immediately. The finish can be touched up with a small brush and spar varnish, or coated with linseed oil mixed with drier. If in really bad shape, you will not help the appearance a great deal, but you will weatherproof the stock somewhat.

Do not use any of the "scratch removing" furniture polishes. These contain powerful solvents which partially dissolve almost any type of finish.

Changing Drop of Buttstocks. The factories will not like me for mentioning this, but it is possible to either raise or lower the height of butt at heel as much as $\frac{1}{8}$", with some models of modern repeating arms. With shotguns like the Remington 31 or Winchester 12, you disassemble the receiver parts until you have the receiver stripped, then alter the angle of the receiver shank, bending up or down as desired. If it is not integral with the receiver, remove and bend in the vise, without the necessity of completely dismantling the gun. This tang bending deal can be worked on a number of lever and slide action rifles as well as shotguns and it is possible on autoloading shotguns of the Browning type, although care must be taken to bend the receiver tang right at the receiver. The tang on the triggerplate must be bent to compensate, and usually must be heated although it is possible to bend upper tangs cold.

When the drop is changed by altering the angle at which the butt joins the receiver or frame, the stock inletting must of course be made to conform, usually ending up about $\frac{1}{8}$" shorter than it was before—the buttstock length, I mean.

It is possible to bend full length or one piece stocks at the pistol grip, but not wise to guarantee that they will stay bent. Several days or even weeks are required. The finish is removed from the stock at the small of the grip, where the bend is to occur. Either oil, water or steam can be employed, and I do not know which to recommend. The oil is used hot, and boiled linseed oil generally used. Raw oil is as good, however. Water takes the longest time, steam the shortest. Both have the serious defect of waterlogging the wood. Oil soaks in deeply and darkens the wood; also will keep coming out for the next 30 years on hot days.

Bending clamps have been made for altering buttstocks, usually in the form of a frame which clamps solidly on the small of the stock and providing a turn screw to exert tension on the toe or the heel of the butt,

For bolt action rifle or shotgun stocks a wooden frame can be made to hold the forend and receiver sections solidly and extending to the rear enough to provide a screw fitting or just a support for wedges between it and the butt. If you have a corner vacant, with a table or bench you will not be using for some time, just place the stock on it with the butt hanging over the side. Clamp the stock to the table with ordinary C clamps and wooden protecting blocks, then hang a heavy weight on the butt. For hot oil you might make rubber flanges to place over the stock at either side of the bend area, as it will be necessary to pour the oil over it many times. A gauze pad wrapped around the stock at the bend point retains oil. The pad is also used when steam is involved, the easiest method being to place water in a can with a small spout on a gas plate under the stock, so that steam constantly permeates the gauze and eventually, the wood.

With water, soak a strip of bath towel and wrap one end around the small of the stock, letting the other end rest in a pan of water. Capillary action will keep the water moving up the towel and onto the wood. Weeks are required for much of a bend to develop.

After a bend has been achieved, the stock should be cleaned and dried, then replaced in the clamp or weight set up for several days in a dry room. It is then removed and refinished, with special attention being paid to a good job of sealing the surface. A varnish or rubbed shellac finish is best, and the stock should be thoroughly waxed for a final touch.

STOCK ALTERATIONS

Shotguns. The matter of increasing or decreasing butt length and the installation of recoil pads has already been covered, as has the angle-of-buttplate or pitch business.

Over shooting can sometimes be corrected by placing a small lead weight—two to six ounces—in the butt, right ahead of the plate or pad. It has the effect of changing the balance of course, and in practice, the shooter positions the gun a little higher on his shoulder. In a very long stock, however, the weight may have the opposite effect, and make the man shoot higher.

The high, thick combs on present day shotguns do not fit all faces and many a shooter finds his cheek bruised after shooting. Also, on fast shots, he may undershoot. A file or small cabinet scraper or spokeshave will quickly remove the offending wood. Get the shooter to grease his cheek with cold cream or similar substance and throw the gun to his shoulder, using his regular shooting stance. The stock will be plainly marked for the cutting down where his puss deposits grease. Go easy, not removing over ⅛″ for the first go, then sending him out to shoot a number of shots. If he still complains, take off more, a little at a time, and having him shoot at each stage. Remember, shooting a shotgun and handling a shotgun without shooting are distinctly not the same acts, and the feel of a shotgun "dry" does not mean it will feel the same way when fired at game. On a .22 target rifle, a stock can be made to fit practically perfect without any shooting, but on any other type of firearm—pistol, revolver, rifle or shotgun—the proof of the fit is determined only by shooting, not by measuring in the shop.

In cutting the stock, hollow out a "cheekpiece"; do not cut down the top of the stock.

For the reverse condition—when comb is too low—either the entire comb can be raised by glueing on a piece of wood, or a cheekpiece can be inletted into the side of the stock. The illustration shows both principles. I think all shotguns should have cheekpieces, for the position of the cheek is more important on the shotgun butt than on any other type of arm. The cheekpiece of course tends to bring the gun to the same sighting point every shot, regardless of whether shooting is fast or slow.

Pistol grips can be lengthened by spacers between the end of the grip and cap, or by making a new and thick cap.

Stocks for handicapped shooters are naturally special items, to be individual designs for the men involved. The commonest job is altering a stock for a righthanded shooter who must sight with his left eye. I do not believe the offset stock is a very good solution as recoil throws the muzzle of the gun violently to the left. (The offset stock is one which is given a sharp S-curve at the pistol grip to place the comb around 4″ to the right of its normal position. The buttplate or pad is therefore approximately 4″ to the right of the line of recoil, or the line of bore.)

The cutaway comb is a more practical solution. In this alteration, the stock is cut deeply at the comb to allow the shooter to lay his head across the stock in order to align his left eye with the front sight. Such cutting of course weakens a stock greatly, and it is always best to make an entire new stock, selecting a blank which has the grain deeply curved down and back from the grip. More bulk can be left at the bottom, also. However, since the amount of wood in the buttstock is decreased by the cutting, it is possible and practical to make the stock of harder, stronger and heavier wood than walnut and still not have it weigh any more than a normal walnut buttstock.

The one armed shotgunner poses several problems. If he has an arti-

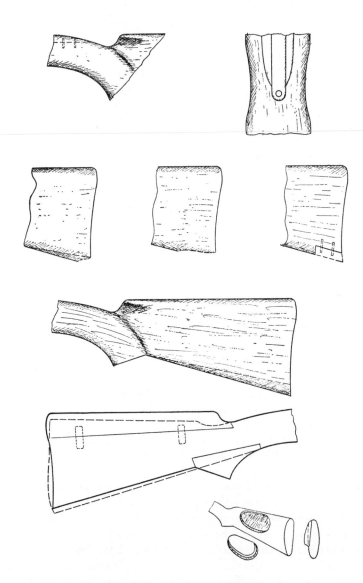

Stock Repair and Alterations

At upper left we have the split off tangs repaired by attachment of replacing wood by glueing and pins. This job will be common on automatic shotguns, Browning patent.

Upper right, the old rifle ailment, stock split or chipped by recoil. If split badly, make a new stock, on account of the bedding is probably so bad nothing will help the original very much. If chipped, cut wood away to clean

ficial hand, provision to use it can usually be worked out. When I was a small boy my father had a large slough which provided fine duck hunting for he and his cronies, one of whom had only the old fashioned hook for an artificial left hand. This man used a pump shotgun exclusively, having had a metal fixture attached to the slide through which he could engage his hook. As I remember it, he could operate the gun as fast as any two handed hunter.

The shooter who has lost either arm above the elbow has a much harder row to hoe. The remaining arm always becomes much stronger than normal, since it must do double duty, which makes it possible for a shooter with his right arm only to both hold and shoot with that arm. In other words, the man gets along without a left hand to support and point the gun. Shifting the balance back helps. Barrels not longer than 26", and lead weights in the buttstock to make the gun butt heavy aid such handicapped shooters in pointing the gun. Many of these men need no pity, either—they get along pretty well. Jack O'Connor told me several anecdotes about a southern Arizona shooter of years back who was so handicapped, but could shoot flying quail, with a rifle! He did not get 'em every shot, but he used a .22 Winchester autoloader and shot fast, to run up a respectable average.

The righthanded shooter minus his right arm taxes the gunsmith's ingenuity. He must hold and point the gun with his left arm, the left hand not only supporting the forend or slide handle but also firing the

---

surface and inlay wood or plastic wood to replace it, leaving clearance on the end of the tang, and shimming the recoil shoulder of the receiver to prevent the action moving back again.

Next we have buttstocks, with the toe chipped off. Occasionally, correction may be made as at the left—cut the whole bottom of the stock to new line. This shortens the distance between the toe and the heel, so it is possible only for slightly chipped stocks. Center, line at which figured buttstocks usually chip, and right, method of repair, by cutting in a definite shoulder at the front of the repairing piece, which is held by glue and wooden pins. The shoulder is necessary to holding strength of the patch.

Below these three sketches, we have a side view of a buttstock, with the dotted line showing area at the bottom which can be either removed or added to increase or decrease the drop. The top line of course can be altered in the same manner.

Next, drawing of military rifle buttstock, the dotted lines here represent the original outlines; the light solid lines the outlines of pieces added to the stock by glueing, pinning or both; and the heavy lines the final possible outline, for sporter use.

Bottom is a small sketch of the buttstock cut for inlaying a cheekpiece.

gun in some manner. Sliding rod extensions for the trigger have been devised, to present a front trigger to the extended left hand, but these are not very practical on pump or double guns. It seems the one-winged hunters all love repeaters, too.

One shooter of my acquaintance, having only his left arm, worked out a system which seems to work very well indeed for him. He says he has used it on automatics as well as single shot and pump guns. A spring supported butt section, from 1" to 2" long, is attached to a rod along the right side of the buttstock. This rod is hinged to a short lever attached to the right side of pistol grip at one end, the other end of the lever being hinged to a shorter rod which is attached by pin to the trigger. When the butt is pressed back against the shoulder, the lever mechanism pulls the trigger back and fires the gun. The shooter aligns the gun with his left hand, and when ready to shoot, pulls the entire gun back against his shoulder. The idea is illustrated, to better convey it.

Rifle Stock Alterations. Military rifle stocks can have blocks inletted and attached with pins, screws, and glue, to provide higher combs and usable pistol grips. These are more amateur jobs than professional, for a working gunsmith would today have to charge as much for altering the shape of a stock in this manner as to discourage the average flat pocketbook shooter, when the latter realizes he can purchase a semi-inletted stock blank from Hutchings or Herter and worry it into a better stock than he can obtain by patching up the issue club, at little or no greater cost.

The Krag and service Springfield stocks can be made to fit very well by attaching comb and pistol grip, per the illustration, but the appearance will not be very pleasing. Finger grooves in the forends can be deepened slightly and given sharp edges by means of a router bit in the drill press or by plain careful chisel work, so that bits of wood can be inlaid to round out the stock and improve its appearance.

When a full length Krag is altered to a sporter, the stock being cut off ahead of the swivel band, a gap below the barrel is left since one of the lightening recesses below the barrel channel is exposed. Take the cut off section of the forend and saw off the portion at the tip, formerly concealed by the upper band, and shape a plug from it to fit into the gaping hole in the end of the forend. Before fitting, use sharp straight chisels to square this opening, cutting away any oil soaked wood. Fit and glue the plug in and after the glue has set, correctly, inlet the barrel allowing it to rest against the bottom of the channel now formed by the plug, then shape the forend tip.

Enfield and some Springfield stocks show a large gap between the barrel and the channel when stocks are cut to sporter length. In most cases the rifles shoot very well with the barrel left floating, but occasionally a block must be inlet into the channel to support the barrel at the forend tip.

The matter of cutting off a stock back of the pistol grip and shaping it into a large tenon to fit into a buttstock blank is not so practical. The idea of glueing a piece of wood large enough to make into a well shaped buttstock onto the stub of the military stock is okay, but the amount of time and labor involved make the job uneconomical, especially so when you consider poor inletting, plain wood, exposed stock bolts and sorry proportions of the military stock. You do not have anything worth keeping when you are finished. To make a stock from one of the semi-finished blanks commercially available costs little more in either money or labor, to my mind.

Shooters occasionally want to lighten their guns a little by removing stock wood, and a little is about all they can lighten them, too. Slimming down the exterior removes at most about four ounces, unless of course the stock is much more bulky than normal. Only about three ounces can be deducted from the stock weight by hollowing out the butt, if lightening is done by drilling large holes in the butt. Two 1″ diameter holes, the top one 6″ deep and the lower 5″, take out from two to three and one-half ounces, depending of course on the density and weight of the wood. The strength of the stock is not affected by this means of lightening.

On rifles having full floating barrels, another two or three ounces can be removed by cutting deep recesses in the bottom of the barrel channel in the forend. Under no circumstance, however, do you cut these channels on a rifle having forearm contact with the barrel as they weaken the forend enough to allow sling tension to bend it while shooting, and therefore affect accuracy and the point of impact.

To add weight, holes can be drilled in the butt and lead weights inserted under the buttplate. Full floating barrels can have channels cut under them and weights installed in these channels. Heavy cast brass or bronze buttplates or grip caps also can add a good many ounces to a rifle's total weight. The contact barrel stock must have forearm weights carefully installed, preferably on the exterior of the stock at the tip. If of the target type with adjustable front swivel base, a lead or brass weight can often be attached to the front holding screw of the base, or a heavy hand stop cast of brass or bronze to replace the usual plastic or aluminum one.

Most of our present model target rifles come with very bulky stocks which are not very comfortable to full faced shooters because of high, thick combs and thick pistol grips. The factories provide plenty of wood so that the thin faced shooter will be comfortable and the fat guy can always whittle off enough to accommodate himself. The job is the same as for reducing the shotgun high comb—file or cut the wood away to reduce the thickness of the comb. The pistol grips on most stocks are too thick at the right rear point, and the recesses may be hollowed out to allow the heel of the right thumb and palm to reach a comfortable holding position. Wide forends can of course be narrowed with a plane if desirable.

The shape of the bottom of the target rifle forend can stand a little change for some shooters. In the prone position many shooters, including myself, suffer considerable pain from firing more than a few shots, through the stock pressing against the heel of the left thumb. Heavily padded gloves do not seem to help much, but a small recess cut in the bottom of the forend to receive this portion of the hand does help a good bit.

Rifle stocks can be lengthened at the butt the same as shotgun stocks. Narrow forends can be widened fairly easily, by planing the sides smooth and glueing on pieces of wood. Cheekpieces can be attached to buttstocks to raise the head when telescopic sights are to be used with a low comb stock. Plane a flat surface on the side of the stock, angling it up to the center of the comb, then glue on a flat piece of walnut from ½″ to ¾″ thick. Shape the cheekpiece out of this attached patch. Do not attempt to make a complete separate cheekpiece and then attach it to the stock as it will not work so good, for in most cases the comb does not need to be thickened, but only raised a bit.

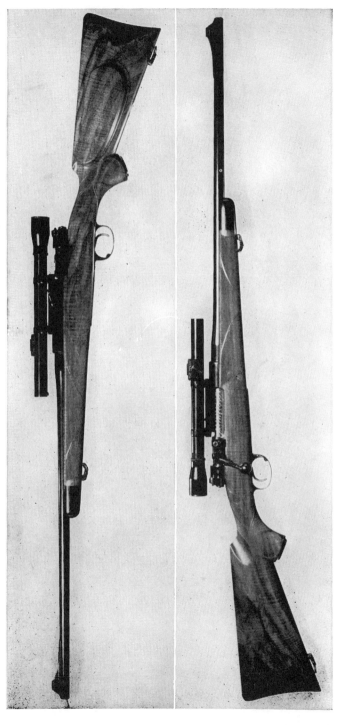

AN OWEN-STOCKED .270 MAUSER

This .270 Mauser was made on a prewar action with hinged floorplate, barreled with an Elliot 8-groove barrel which shoots beautifully. Sighting equipment is a Williams "fool proof" receiver sight, with a gold bead on Molnar front ramp; the rifle is also fitted with Texan scope and Jaeger detachable mount.

This stock was made of a fine piece of French walnut, having some fiddleback intermingled with the dark "veins." Note particularly the way the grain runs with the grip.

Gun now owned by Mr. Moore, of Midland, Texas.

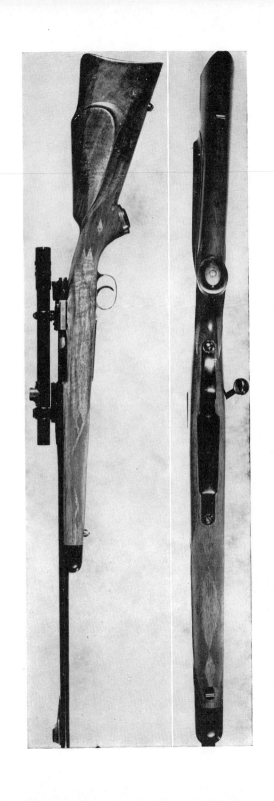

Custom lightweight .257 on G33/40 Mauser carbine action. Barrel and metalwork by Sukalle, stocked in European walnut by Leonard Mews. Stith scope in Tilden mounts. Weight of rifle is 7 lbs. 7 oz. Barrel length, 21".

Mr. Mews writes—"This cheekpiece stock was made from a French walnut blank only 1 13/16" thick, which was furnished by the customer who thought that a cheekpiece could be had by giving the butt a lot of cast off. So it got 3/8" cast off and a cheekpiece. The rear part of this cheekpiece *is* quite thin and flat but it gave full support to the face of this shooter as he is quite a tall fellow and uses only the forward part —the rest being only for appearance.

"Grip cap and forearm tip are of ebony; stock has a 13 1/2" pull; a 3 1/6" reach from grip cap to trigger; level comb with a 1/2 inch drop to the heel from rear of the Monte Carlo; Niedner steel checkered buttplate slightly flattened. This forearm is slightly swelled in order to take away that 'stiff look' and to give a more natural fitting handful.

"The checkering patterns are matched with a bit of open work in each. The open diamond of polished wood showing out from the grip checkering breaks the plainness of this simple pattern and also appears to reduce the depth of the grip, a trick especially useful to know when checkering deep-hanging or close-up target pistol grips. This disillusionment of cutting down appearance of depth or length by the checkering pattern is similar to the trick practiced by our women for years past in the clothing they wear—the tall, skinny ones wear belts and ruffles and horizontal stripes while the fat ones wear the up-and-down embellishments. Ever notice that?

"All this sort of open work makes the checkering job look like the most painstaking work—which it is. It gives one a real headache as all lines *must be kept in line*."

CHAPTER 30

Styling the Custom Rifle

THIS is a what-to-do rather than a how-to-do-it chapter. The custom rifle is one which is made up on a prescribed action to the specifications of an individual. If the individual knows rifles and has had them made up before, he probably can lay down definite dimensions for the stock and for the barrel and set a weight limit of sorts. If the man does not know exactly what he wants, you must help him determine the stock dimensions at least. The hardest guy of all to handle is the one who says "You know more about it than I do—you figure everything out and it will be all right." Very seldom can you turn out a perfectly satisfactory job, because the man invariably has in mind some particular stock shaping, sights, or checkering pattern he does not bother to mention until the rifle is finished.

Pin the customer down on the main points, making him give his consent to general stock shaping, checkering pattern, sights and total weight of the rifle. On the latter point, first check over your stock blanks and estimate the weights of the finished stocks they will provide. Do not promise a 7½ pound rifle unless you can make a light and strong stock for it. It is not hard to estimate stock weights once you have made a stock from a particular batch of walnut. Make a practice of weighing profiled blanks and the stocks made from them, with notes on type, density and origin of the wood and the list thus made will be quite a valuable guide in the future.

The best way of finding out the customer's preferences and dimensions is by means of examples. Show him pictures of stocks to illustrate different checkering patterns, cheekpiece shapes and stock outlines. Samworth's pattern sheets are very useful for such comparisons. Show the different sights, telescopic sight mounts, buttplates and such accessories. Have him handle and try for fit similar rifles already made up. You can tell a lot from the manner in which he holds the rifles and positions his head and hands.

If it is a mail order deal, make up and send him form sheets similar to the sample illustrated, for him to fill out. Direct him to check as closely as possible on other guns which he can handle for trial. Ask him to be particularly careful as to determining his butt length, or pull. If he says he wants a 14″ stock and gives his height as 5′ 8″, something is wrong—tell him to either find a rifle with a 14″ stock and handle it, or take a more standard stock and tape a block to the butt to increase the length to 14″ and try that—and to not forget to tell him to make his trials with his hunting clothing on, not in the living room in his shirt-sleeves. Sketches should be made and submitted of special patterns and stock features, as well as of metal alterations.

List what action and guard alterations you recommend, explaining each. Should engraving be ordered, get the engraver to describe his proposed designs, and the areas to be engraved. Make your recommendations on metallic sights, telescopic sights and mounts, giving the customer a choice of at least two. On the barrels, you and the barrel-maker should decide on the proportions for the caliber involved, considering also the proposed total rifle weight—and try to give yourself three ounces leeway on the latter point. As with stocks, weigh actions before and after barreling, to gain an idea of the weights of various barrels. The Springfield 1903 action weighs approximately 2 pounds 12 ounces; the 1917 Enfield, unaltered, 3 pounds 5½ ounces; with receiver remodeled, around 3 pounds 2 ounces; the Mauser '98 around 2 pounds 10 ounces; and the Winchester 70 about 3 pounds.

Use whatever custom metal alterations are appropriate and desirable, drill and tap for sights if advisable, have the action barreled, polish it, inlet the stock, then send to the engraver if to be engraved. After its return, finish the stock, mount the sights and test fire. Make whatever alterations are necessary, if any, to make the sight or sights line up correctly, then blue the metal parts and give the stock the final touches.

When a trap buttplate is to be fitted, first fit it to the butt with full underside contact, then outline the recess to be cut. A Forstner bit (wood bit without lead screw) or endmills are best for cutting the cavity, although metal cutting bits in the drillpress will do the job. The size of the cavity is regulated by the size of the trap door in the plate, and the purpose for which the cavity will be used. A ⅝″ drill is about the largest useful for a trap cavity, and three complete holes give about enough vertical length to the recess. Linden's "half-hole" method is easiest, drilling first one end hole, driving in a dowell to fit, then drilling another hole at the edge of the first, removing half the diameter of the dowell, then driving in another dowell and repeating until the desired butt recess is outlined, after which the dowell pieces are pulled out and only small projections mar the long, round ended recess. Bastard files, rifflers and bottoming tools will make the hole smooth sided.

I do not believe these recesses should just be cut to as full size as possible, but rather that they should be cut to fit some particular item and serve as a receptacle for that item. In the case of a full sighted rifle, a recess can be cut to take an emergency rear sight or a Lyman 48 sight arm, to be carried when the scope is mounted, or a hood for a ramp front sight to keep from losing it, or to hold two or three emergency cartridges.

For either hood or cartridges, the job is simple—you need only drill round holes approximately $\frac{1}{16}''$ larger in diameter than the item to be held, making separate holes for the cartridges. I do not think much of the cartridge deal, as they are too easy to get at and the shooter usually shoots them and forgets to refill the butt. The old habit of cutting butt recesses to carry cleaning equipment is disappearing due to our present non corrosive ammunition which does not require constant bore cleaning. However, it is not a bad idea to put in a hole for one of those little round metal oil containers as furnished for the United States Carbine M1, which are often available from war surplus parts dealers. As a rule these do not leak.

I advocate cutting recesses to just accept the article to be carried, plus enough tolerance to allow a felt or baize lining to be glued to the inside and to both prevent oil from metal objects getting into the stock wood and keeping down rattles. It is a simple matter to cut wooden forms or plugs to hold the material against the walls of the recess while glue is drying. Dowels can be used as forms to line round holes. Cement cloth or neoprene pads to the underside of the trapdoor, to eliminate rattles.

It is not a bad idea to drill recesses for a couple of cartridges under a plain buttplate, for an emergency measure, and slot the buttplate screws wider so that a dime can be used to unscrew them, or if the guy does not have a dime, the rim of an empty cartridge case.

The matter of screw slots deserves attention on a fine rifle—keep them pointing the same way, preferably in line with the bore. Buttplate screws should have parallel slots, either vertical or horizontal because they do not always line up correctly when pulled down tight, it may be necessary to cut the countersink in the plate a little deeper, or cut down the head of the screw underneath, to allow it to turn to the desired position. The plate countersink can be deepened by means of a metal cutting drill bit if not case-hardened, or lapped deeper if hardened. Naturally only a little metal is removed. A number of screws usually allow a selection and by trial-and-error correct lining up can be accomplished with little effort. For Niedner plates, I usually use Phillips screws and checker the heads. However, the special screwdriver needed for the screws makes this practice not too practical should it be desired for any reason to remove the plate in the field.

Straightening out the screw slots on the guard screws and the sight-mounting screws calls for cutting the underside of the head down a little, and should the screws be hardened, this is intriguing at times. If not hardened, just chuck the screws by the shanks in the vise and hold a pillar file against the flange formed by the head; if hardened, use one of the thin rough Arkansas "file" stones, or the pillar file backing a strip of cutting cloth.

On rifle guard screws, unless you are absolutely sure that there will be no shrinkage of the stock wood, fix them to come within about one-eighth of a turn from lining up. Then, as the stock shrinks, the screws can be tightened and will be approximately in line and parallel with the bore when in final position.

Lightening a stock is rather difficult. The largest holes you can bore in the butt and still retain the necessary wall-strength will hardly ever remove more than three ounces of weight. Cutting grooves in the bottom of the barrel channel only takes out an ounce and a half or so more, and should never be done unless the barrel is attached to the forend by a band.

It is not considered poor practice to tie the forend and barrel together on a sporting rifle. The Winchester 54 and 70 have this system, and while it does not make for 10 shot group accuracy or a lifetime uniform point-of-impact, a stronger overall assembly of rifle and stock is gained. Some custom stockers claim that continued carrying of a rifle by the sling will pull the forend away from the barrel, lessening the forearm tension and thus affecting accuracy. The simplest method of holding the forend to the barrel, or vice-versa, is to insert an 8–40 screw through the forend, inletting an escutcheon for the head, and threading into the barrel approximately $\frac{1}{8}$". Shelhamer advocates this system, and there are few men who know as much about bedding a sporter for accuracy as he does. I have tried rifles with barrels so tied down, and with the screws removed, without finding apparent difference in accuracy or grouping. In hunting rifles, there is a distinction. They should be judged on the first three shots, firing from a cold barrel rapidly, with little regard for size of 10 or even five shot groups fired from a warm, fouled barrel.

The Winchester rifles will vary the height of the point of impact very considerably with screw tension on the barrel, but custom rifles with closely inletted barrel channels and the screw cut to exact length, bottoming its head in the escutcheon countersink, are not affected, since the screw cannot tend to bend the barrel by pulling it down at the point of contact. The bottom of the barrel is supported solidly by the contacting channel in the forend. The barrel and the forend are unified, the forend tending to smother barrel vibration to some extent. In light barreled arms, the system sometimes makes for better grouping ability than either floating or light contact bedding. When the hold down screw is used, the barrel channel should be full contact, and the screw located approximately 4″ ahead of the receiver ring.

Forend swivels should have machine thread shanks and screw into ferrules, escutcheons or plain nuts inletted into the barrel channel— never attach a front swivel with an ordinary wood screw shank. The detachable swivel seems to be losing popularity, although Jaeger's present type is attractive. The older ones were heavy and rattled— one big game guide I know is violently opposed to such swivels, claiming they make enough noise to scare game before it is seen. The standard Winchester swivels are quite good and easily obtained. I prefer the foreign type with flattened bands, to take a ⅞″ or 1″ sling, but they are hard to get. These are light and very good in appearance.

Slings themselves can be made to order, of tooled leather, to dress up a fine rifle, and either leather or sheepskin lined cases furnished with the rifle or recommended strongly to the customer. Canvas cases tend to wear both the blueing and the stock finish. We now have treated sheepskin which is sometimes impregnated with oil or grease to protect the metal parts of the rifle. No case should ever be air tight, however, or sudden temperature changes may cause condensation on the steel inside the case and so rust will be formed unless the arm is immediately removed from the case, dried off and oiled, and the case allowed to dry out.

It is a very good idea to provide the customer with two or three good screwdrivers, shaped to fit the guard screws and sight or scope mounting screws. Otherwise he will be trying to tighten them—whether they need it or not—with incorrect drivers and mar up the slots. Then you get the rifle back to fix up the screws or make new ones.

Almost every variation from standard practice in the shaping of rifles, particularly stocks, has been tried. The present styling, the principles shown by the illustrated Owen, Shelhamer, Hearn and Mews stocks, has evolved as modern sights and shooting habits have guided it. Every man has his individual ideas in shaping, and even if you attempt to copy exactly a stock made by another man, your stock will be in some way different. Be guided by the ideas of Owen and Linden, but do not feel you must copy their stocks as closely as possible. On the matter of overall shaping, do not attempt to be radical and different—it has been tried before, often, and the names of those trying are long forgotten—only minor changes in dimensions are worthwhile considering. If the customer insists he has to have a weird job, try to talk him into line, and if he will not hold still then, make up a sample stock of soft wood along his ideas and let him see how his brainchild really looks and find out how it fits. Ten to one he will change his mind then.

Photographs are the best possible aid to both gunsmith and customer. Get pictures of fine stocks, and take pictures of your own jobs, to use in conferring with customers either in person or by mail. Dimensions of each stock—that is, circumference of the pistol grip, the drop at comb and heel, and the depth and the width of forend—should be noted on the back of each photo. This helps the customer visualize his own stock. The pictures should be of assembled rifles, not of stocks alone. Ideas can be taken from different rifles—comb shaping and curvature from one, checkering pattern from another, pistol grip detail from another, and so on, and these individual features can be combined to form an entirely different, yet conforming stock. Individualized checkering patterns of course serve to make similar stocks different.

I do not care at all for inlays and do not believe they have any place in a good custom job, where the stock is made of good wood—however, that is just my opinion. If the customer wants something flashy, go ahead and inlay contrasting wood diamonds or other designs on the right side of the butt or on the sides of the body or even the forend. Bright colored plastic inlays and white inlays are even used, though it seems they would be more popular in the Congo than in the United States. If the man with the money wants such decoration and you can bring yourself to do the job, that is it. Remember, the custom rifle is to be built as much to the customer's individual wishes as sound and safe functional limitations permit—you can recommend, but he gives the orders.

CHAPTER 31

Custom Metal Work

THERE are quite a number of alterations possible on most rifles and a few handguns and while most of them improve the appearance of the arm, there is usually a practical reason for the change.

PISTOLS AND REVOLVERS

Nearly all handgun alteration jobs concern hammers and grips, aside from ramp sight and rib sight attachments. The stunt of cutting the front half of revolver triggerguard loops is falling into the discard somewhat, as the exposed trigger creates quite a hazard. More than one character has shot a groove across his fanny or belly when shoving such an altered gun into a pocket or a holster in a hurry and catching the trigger against the pocket or the holster edge. Now the FBI method of narrowing the right edge of the guard forward of the trigger is more popular.

Wide hammer spurs on target revolvers and .45 auto pistols are easily made, by packing the bottom half of the hammer in wet asbestos and welding metal on the tangs, in quantity to permit shaping as required. The tang of the grip safety on the .45 is, on older models, too short to protect a meaty hand from the slap of the hammer as the gun cocks. This also can be lengthened and reshaped by welding on steel.

Revolver grips, particularly on S & W revolvers, are short and small for large hands. When length only is desired, a small rectangle of metal can be sweated or screwed to the bottom of the grip, and the stocks lengthened to match. If the hump at the top is objectionable, do not try to file or grind it away completely—weld steel on the backstrap below the hump and reshape it to a comfortable curve, making stocks to match. Almost any desired shaping of a revolver handle can be acquired by making a special set of stocks alone, except when the customer wants a grip made smaller for a pocket arm. Then it is necessary to cut and reweld the bottom to shorten the grip and to grind and file down the front and back straps.

RIFLES

Single shots. Not a great deal can be done on the single shot rifles. Some slight degree of speedlocking can be accomplished by skeletonizing hammers, cutting the notch forward, and employing stronger mainsprings. Levers can of course be altered to almost any desired shape, and lower tangs bent to conform to the desired pistol grip curve. Most of these jobs can also be done on Winchester lever action repeaters.

I can not think of much to do to the Savage 99 except to put on one of Anderson's tang shotgun type safeties, or anything to slide and auto rifles, which leaves us bolt actions, on which we can do plenty.

Bolt Actions. The easiest and simplest job is to narrow the trigger-loop of the guard to about $\frac{5}{16}''$ which not only improves the appearance considerably, but also permits the finger to reach the trigger easier in arms where the trigger positions close to the rear of the loop. The loop can be narrowed all along the bottom, although it looks better if tapered, wide at front, narrow at rear. Commercial Mauser sporters almost always have these tapered loops, the width of the guard at the front, and narrowed to about $\frac{3}{8}''$ at the back.

Files and the bench grinder do the work very well, although of course if a number of guards are to be worked over, the milling machine saves wear and tear on the fingers. If you have a good eye, the narrowing can be done without guide lines, otherwise, scribe a centerline and use it as a guide, grinding each side of the loop to an even distance from it. Exact side lines outlining the proposed shape of the guard are not much use as the metal will burr over during grinding and obscure them anyway.

After narrowing the loop to exact dimensions, use narrow pillar files and round files to round off the corners and shape it up at the rear end of the loop where it joins the guard. Cut a sharp curve to reduce the width just below the guard, to that of the narrowest dimension—it is surprising how much this dresses up a sporter.

The bolt handle and knob alterations are rather completely explained by the drawing, so we need not go into it much, except that a cross matting all over the knob, if round, makes for a good appearance, disguises any dents and pits in an ex-army rifle, and gives you a good no slip surface. Use a fine checkering file and make passes in opposing directions until the knob has somewhat of a basket weave appearance and when blued, this looks very nice. Checkering a bolt knob is a real job, and approaches engraving in the work involved. Panels of checker-

BOLT WELDING – CUSTOM HANDLES

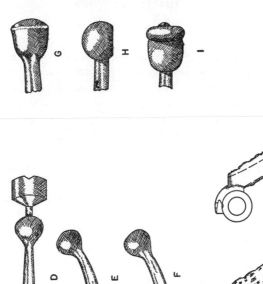

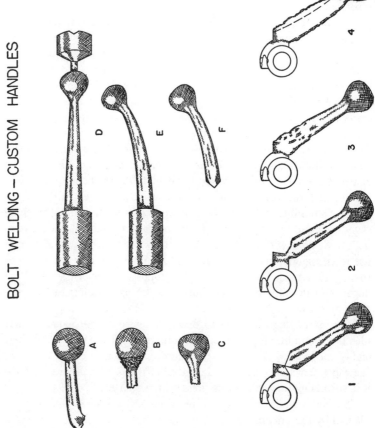

ing should be laid out on the top and the bottom of the knob, round, diamond, or shield shape. Cut the borders first, using a sharp triangular file for square lines, and chisels to bring them to corners. For the round, make a tool to cut a circle in the steel. A tubular or circular hollow bit, with saw teeth on the edge, can be made up, or the bolt handle chucked in a four jaw lathe chuck and the circle cut on the lathe by mounting the knob off center. Metal checkering files will cut the central portion

---

CUSTOM BOLT HANDLES

Often a gunsmith will find that the original bolt shank and knob are not desirable and will want to make up a new one. Also, it is sometimes wise to make a longer bolt handle than standard, for increased leverage in the operation of heavy caliber rifles, for the same reason on target arms, or for convenience in manipulation when a very large telescope ocular cell takes up extra room and limits the holding area on the bolt knob.

A. Mauser bolt handle, with round knob. Shank is a little thinner than it should be, for reality. Issue shanks are pretty thick at the knob.

B. Mauser or Springfield knob, joint at knob and shank thickened by welded on steel, so that the pear shaped knob shown as

C. is a considerable improvement in appearance. Note that the end is flattened slightly.

D. Illustration of complete new bolt handle turned out of round stock on the lathe. The knob end is cut clear and polished smooth before proceeding to

E. The handle is bent to the desired shape before cutting free from the metal stock.

F. The finished handle, cut from the stock, and the end chamfered for welding to the bolt.

G. Decorative bolt knob—this is my favorite, and I call it a modified acorn type.

H. Round knob, flattened on the bottom, per the Mauser '98 carbine style, or the FN modern version—not particularly good, but allows the bolt handle to be turned down to a considerable degree and still provide clearance for getting hold of the knob when the bolt is closed, even when the stock is left fairly thick.

I. The old German acorn knob.

Steps in welding handles:

1. A Springfield bolt shown. Positioning of the handle and the bolt before starting determines the lowness of the alteration and the position of the knob against the stock when the bolt is closed.

2. First weld, the bolt and the handle fused, with very little metal added to the top and the bottom until the sides are also welded.

3. Finished weld, showing the amount of metal necessary.

4. Finished weld, with dotted lines showing the finished outline of the bolt handle after filing and grinding away the unnecessary metal.

FLOORPLATE HINGING

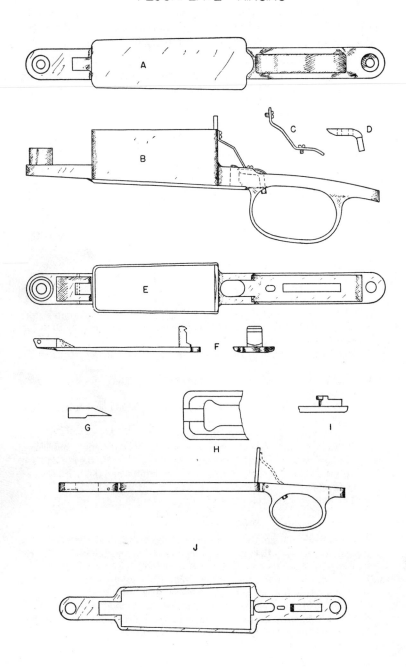

of the pattern, but chisels and graving tools must be used to cut the grooves to the borders without overrunning them. An easier way all around is to have the bolt knob engraved in a deep cut floral design!

The hinged floorplate is a definite improvement to my mind. I like to get the loaded cartridges out of the magazine without working them through the action. It looks good too, and makes the magazine instantly available for cleaning. All kinds of stuff gets into magazine boxes, and I dislike the idea of allowing cartridges to carry it into the chamber.

The principles of the hinging systems are illustrated and obvious. My own system is very neat, I believe, but the Mauser system has many adherents. The Newton catch system, now used by the Winchester 70, requires a fairly stiff spring. The jolt of recoil tends to move these catches and disengage them if a weak spring is used.

Hardest part of a hinge job as a rule is welding the hinge part to the front of the floorplate so the joint does not show. In cutting the notch

---

FLOORPLATE HINGING

A touch of "deluxing" which has considerable merit, in that it permits quick unloading of a rifle without the necessity of working the cartridges individually through the action, with the possibility of accidental discharge. It can also permit changing cartridges in magazine without scaring away the game.

A. Bottom view of the hinged plate in the triggerguard.

B. Side view of the Springfield guard with hinged plate showing the method of the spring attachment and position of the release button. Drawing is incorrect in that it shows the spring attached too high up on the rear wall of the magazine box. The spring must be attached low enough not to interfere with the sear movement.

C. The catch spring, with screws to attach to the guard and the catch.

D. The floorplate catch, side view, showing approximate shape.

E. Top view of the guard showing the slots for the floorplate hinge and the catch button.

F. The floorplate, with hinge piece welded to the front and the catch seat built up and shaped for the new catch.

G. Profile of hinge piece before welding to plate.

H. Top of the Springfield plate, showing seat for hinge piece filed through the raised front portion of the plate. The engaging lip is filed away completely at the front.

I. Standard catch seat: Must be built up by welding on the steel at the top, to a height of approximately $\frac{3}{8}''$, and shaped as shown in F.

J. Side and top views of the 1917 Enfield guard altered for a hinged floorplate. A vertical plate is welded or brazed to the guard as shown, for attachment of the catch and its spring.

in the guard tang for the hinge, angle the front of the cut back on the top to give clearance to the end of the hinge as it pivots upward when the floorplate is opened, otherwise, a gap between the end of the hinge and the end of its recess is necessary. Because the hinge will contact the end of this opening when the plate is fully opened, and so wear the blueing off in a line across the hinge, put a pin or plate in the guard or on top of the underside to arrest the movement of the plate before the hinge can hit the guard.

The Japanese M38 rifles have the same type of floorplate release, in appearance, as the large and magnum Mauser commercial actions do for the hinged plates. The Jap plate is not hinged, however, but it is a comparatively simple job to hinge the plate, narrow the guardloop, reduce the size of the release button inside the loop and fit the guard to the Remington 722 action, which certainly needs a decent guard. The front guard screw hole is drilled in the tang, and the end of the tang cut off behind the original hole. In custom stocking a 722, this idea should be seriously considered.

Bullet guides should be installed in magazines, even in the .22 center-fires or Wasp size or larger, to protect the pointed soft point bullets now in wide use—or any factory load except the Remington bronze point! Use cartridges in the magazine box to locate the guides, which are strips of steel or brass, soldered to the walls of the box to prevent the cartridges moving forward under recoil to batter their points against the front end of the box. They should allow at least $\frac{1}{32}''$ movement of the cartridge back and forth to permit easy loading. The guides contact the shoulder of the cartridge case, and should be rounded off at the point of contact, and of course are rounded off on the inner edge at the top so as not to obstruct loading the magazine or the passage of the cartridge from the magazine into the chamber.

When the take up or first pull of a military trigger is unnecessarily long, a pin can be set through the guard from side to side to limit the forward movement of the trigger. Most triggers can be improved in shape of the curved finger section by a little filing, and all of them are helped by checkering. If you can not get a narrow checkering file, anneal a wide one, saw out a strip with two or three rows of teeth, re-harden this strip and use it. Another method is to grind two hacksaw blades to give the edges a pointed profile in cross section, clamp these blades together and use them as a spacer in laying out the checkering lines. A triangular needle file then deepens the grooves. Or, a very passable job can be done with the needle file alone, using your eye and fingers to space the individual grooves. When blued, the appearance

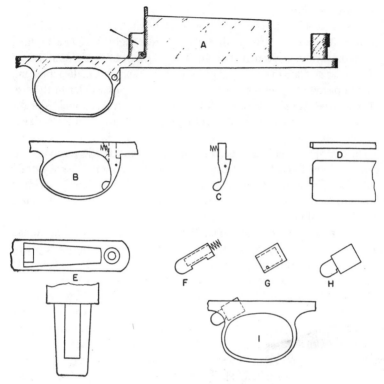

FLOORPLATE HINGING

(Continued)

A. Profile of Mauser military guard, with an arrow pointing to the catch housing which must be cut away for installation of the catch as illustrated for the Springfield, though other details of hinging are on the same principle.

B. Mauser floorplate catch, as formerly used in commercial sporters.

C. Mauser type catch, with a spring to show the direction of tension.

D. Rear end of the floorplate for use with the Mauser style catch, the small lip being engaged by the catch.

E. Sketches to show the appearance of the guard from the bottom and the front when equipped with this style catch.

F. Variation of the Newton style catch for a hinged floorplate, composed of parts "F," "G" and "H." "F" shows the plunger and spring,

G. The plunger housing, with the hole for a pin to hold and limit the plunger movement.

H. The assembled catch, which can be held with screws or pins or any other method in the guard.

I. Sketch of the guard, with this type catch installed. The Winchester M70 utilizes this style catch for its hinged floorplate.

is improved 100%.

The barrels leave little alteration work possible. On the Winchester 70 and Remington 721–722 barrels, the rear sight base can be filed down on the sides when custom stocking. This swell, very reminiscent of a snake swallowing an egg, not only looks lousy but makes inletting a good barrel channel much harder so file it off *on the sides* to the size of the barrel, thus permitting a straight edged barrel channel. The appearance is aided considerably, as the rear sight base then looks like a special job.

On the Springfield 1903 barrels, the spline cut at the receiver ring can be either filled by electro welding, or an inch long sleeve turned out of an old military sight base to cover it. I do not like the welding business here, not so much because of the heat angle but because usually it will not blue to match the rest of the rifle.

Receiver and Action Alteration. Very little needs to be done to the Mauser '98 receiver, except to file or grind down the raised clip slot portion of the bridge down to the level of the rest of the bridge. This also can be done to the '98 carbine and to the Vz–33 receiver.

The 1903 Springfield receiver should have the rear tang narrowed when custom stocked, and have the cut off housing streamlined by shaping it like a torpedo or coffin. The rear edge of the left receiver wall can be modified into a neat S curve to help the appearance.

The 1917 action allows considerable receiver remodeling, aside from just cutting the "ears" off. The bridge can be shaped to almost any desired dimensions, per Mauser, Remington 30–S, or M70, in cross section. The front profile of the bridge can be cut down to reach the sidewall in a concave curve, cutting back to remove the clip slots, and bringing the right sidewall down in a straight line or a gentle curve. Do not cut back this sidewall at the bottom, for the extractor just reaches it when the bolt is closed, and if it is cut back, the rear end of the extractor is not supported in the receiver and this can mean interference when the bolt is opened, and when it is moved to the rear. The left rear wall of the receiver can be cut down to remove the bolt stop spring rest (the button), to end the sidewall just behind the bolt stop hinge on the receiver and the spring is then cut and bent around the hinge to conceal the slot visible from the rear. The hole in the top of the bridge of Winchester and early Eddystone 1917s can be welded up or plugged and welded at the edges of the plug and hole. Cut the left sidewall down and back in whatever degree of curve or straight line you wish if the wall is not to be shortened to the rear of the bolt stop. The bolt stop itself can be improved somewhat by cutting off the lip at the

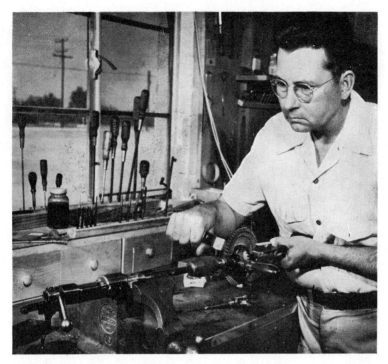

The author lapping the face of a bolt to get it at right angles to bore, as well as to eliminate tool marks in the original machining.

A barrel butt is threaded tightly into the receiver as a guide for the cast-iron rod lap. It is of course bored out concentrically to insure accuracy in the lapping.

The row of small drawers along rear of bench is invaluable in storage of small parts, tools, screws, springs and so forth. The action is another shortened FN Mauser, though why the bolt handle looks straight, I don't know. It ain't.

ALTERED BOLT FACES

Here are several bolts, showing alteration for various purposes. From left to right—U. S. Krag bolt, extractor lip lengthened and face bushed for .218 Bee cartridge; next, a standard Krag bolt, to show the difference. Center is an Enfield bolt, as used for large rimmed cases, and next to it, one altered for .300 Magnum cartridge. On right end is standard 1917 bolt, for contrast.

top and then checkering the front end, to give a holding surface for its operation. The Mannlicher type bolt stop used on the Remington 720 can be adapted to the 1917, if you can get them loose from Remington.

The Enfield bolt alteration, to cock on the opening movement of the bolt, is illustrated. On the other rifles—Mauser and Springfield, that is—only speedlocking is ever desirable, and I personally do not desire it. However, should the customer be an admirer or the Model 70 and still want a Mauser or Springfield fixed up, shorten the length of the cocking notch which will increase the angle as the width of the notch at the base of the bolt must be retained. This makes for easy cocking, until you get in a super mainspring to insure good ignition. Keep the firing pin fall $5/16''$ long anyway, and be sure the safety works. Either the cocking piece nose can be lengthened, and firing pin the same distance, to maintain the original relationship between safety and cocking piece grooves or position, or the top of the cocking piece altered to correctly cooperate with the safety.

On the Winchester Model 70, you do not do anything except maybe smooth out prominent tool marks before refinishing and on the Remington 721, throw away the original triggerguard and fit Winchester 70 guard parts.

Magazines and receivers often need alteration when large or long cartridges are to be used. One of the common jobs is altering the Winchester 70 in .257 caliber to take handloaded ammunition of $3''$ overall length. The long magazine box is blocked by a false rear wall forward of the real wall and held by studs engaging in slots in the sidewalls of the box. These slots are crimped on the wall, and can be uncrimped by putting them in the vise and using pressure to straighten them out. Then push the false wall or blocking plate up and out of the box. With hacksaw and files cut new slots further back, to position this wall a little over $3''$ from the front of the box, and replace the wall, crimping in the corners of the slot. It will be necessary to slightly file down the top portion of this plate to avoid interference with the bolt, then remove the extractor from the bolt and take the extractor collar and attached bolt stop extension from the bolt. Note that the extension is cut away on the bottom rear corner up past the front edge of the collar. The full width section of this extension is approximately $17/32''$ long so with files and saw shorten it from the rear to $5/16''$, pulling the cut on the bottom forward. This permits the bolt to travel further to the rear to pick up cartridges from the lengthened magazine box. Now the ejector also must be moved further back and in removing it from the receiver, you will note the pin hole and section at the rear relieved

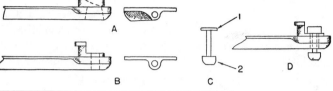

FLOORPLATE BUTTON RELEASES

A minor improvement on the military floorplate release system, the button allows easier removal of the plate, for cleaning or for unloading the magazine without the necessity of working loaded cartridges through the action. Sketches are applicable to Springfield or Enfield. For the Mauser '98, only the button needs to be made and clearance for it in the plate.

A. The standard military plate and catch.

B. Same, altered for button release system.

C. The button: can be made with solid top or bottom one must be removable so that it can be placed through the hole in the floorplate. The top part is to be thick enough to support the catch in the same position as before alteration. 1. Top, can be a nut threaded on the shank of the button. 2. Button, can be threaded or soldered to the shank, but should be integral and should be checkered lightly.

D. Sketch of rear portion of floorplate with button assembly installed. The button must have clearance to move upward far enough to disengage the catch.

to allow room for the spring. The unaltered ejector is $2\frac{3}{16}''$ long overall, and the distance from the front tip to the pin hole is $1\frac{7}{8}''$. Measure $\frac{1}{4}''$ ahead of the hole, locate a center, and drill with #38 drill for the new pivoting point. Shorten the ejector on the rear to an overall length of approximately $2''$, and cut the rear profile to correspond with the original, in order to allow room for the ejector spring. On the one side of the ejector will be seen a shallow, rounded cut with sharp shoulder on the front end. This shoulder is $3\frac{1}{32}''$ from tip of ejector so pull it forward with pillar file until it is about $2\frac{3}{32}''$. That finishes the job, and the ejector will operate properly. The throat of the barrel must be reamed to allow shallow seated bullets.

Next most familiar job is opening up '98 Mauser receivers and magazine boxes to take .30-06 or .270 cartridges. Clamp the magazine upright in the vise and file the inner rear wall of the box back until you cut into the floorplate catch recess at bottom. Then file the front end of box forward until a .30-06 military cartridge can be passed through freely, even when canted at rather sharp angles. Be careful not to file all the way through the box, when making this front cut and you must not cut back the lip at the bottom of the guard which retains the floor-plate. Short strokes with a sharp file, and careful work with the hand grinder allow metal to be removed above this area. Fit the guard to the receiver, and use the hand grinder to cut away the feed lip machined into the bottom of the receiver until its rear wall is even with the magazine inner front wall, then smooth it up until cartridges will feed freely.

It has become common practice to build magnum rifles on Springfield, Mauser and Enfield actions, cutting the receivers as described above to permit long cartridges. The length of the .300 and .375 H & H cartridges is 3.60"—add for clearance and a magazine box $3^{11}\!/_{16}$" long, inside measurement is needed. As they come, the Mauser box is $3^{5}\!/_{16}$", and the Springfield and Enfield approximately $3^{13}\!/_{32}$". The boxes themselves are minor, as they can be cut and welded to any desired length, to extend the front of the box portion and cutting back the rear of the box and cutting on the bolt stop will not give over $\frac{1}{16}$", so we must cut the remaining clearance from the front. If the Enfield action is being used, do not attempt to extend the magazine box feed lip forward but cut the lip from the box, and you will not have to cut a great deal of metal from the receiver. You do not want to because the right locking lug of the bolt seats right ahead of here, and you want *plenty* of metal behind the lug seat.

A steep slope is necessary for the new feed lip in the receiver, to preserve strength, although as a rule the rifles feed quite well in spite of this. Winchester 70 magnum magazine boxes can be fitted to take the place of 1917 boxes. For the Mauser and Springfield, cut back along the top line of the tang into the box, sawing at least $\frac{1}{4}$" back, then saw down to remove this upper front corner of the box. Weld in pieces, or rather strips, of thin flat stock of sufficient width to give the length box desired, then weld on the front section of the box, thus giving a long magazine. Brazing instead of welding can be employed, since no part of the work is exposed but if brazing is preferred, first build out the bottom corners of the box at the guard juncture to the length of the long one by welding on steel, to permit a good inletting job, then lengthen the box. The box is only longer above the depth of the guard tang, which is sufficient, since the magazine follower and spring take up this space and no cartridge room is lost.

Bolt Face Alterations. When the standard actions are altered for use with belted magnum or for rimmed cases, it is necessary to enlarge the counterbore or recess on the bolt face to allow it to accept the larger cartridge base. As a rule this cutting can be done on the lathe, using a

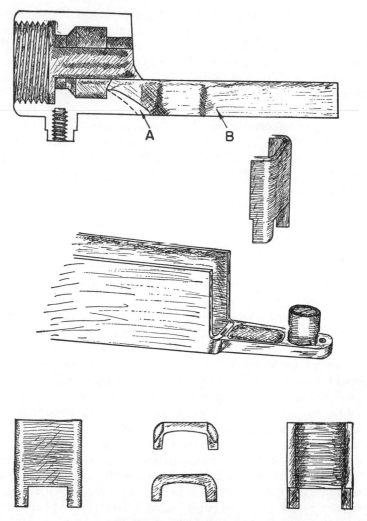

MAUSER ACTION ALTERATIONS

These are standard alterations for equipping the '98 action to handle longer and larger cartridges. They can of course be applied to other receivers and guards.

To enable the standard 8mm '98 action to handle the .270 and .30–06 cartridges, it is only necessary to file or mill the inside ends of the magazine box to accept .30–06 military ammunition freely, at a test, but to make the '98, 1917 or 1903 handle magnum cartridges, the box must be extended forward, and the feed lip on receiver cut forward as indicated by the dotted line on the drawing. The extension piece for the front of magazine can be

Carballoy cutter, but if too hard for this, use the hand grinder with a small cylindrical stone to do the job, spinning the bolt in the lathe and holding the grinder in the milling attachment. Make the cut .010″ greater in diameter than the specified shell base, to allow a .005″ clearance at all points and so provide for occasional oversize bases.

Square all bolt faces and make the counterbore or section which supports the cartridge base at 90° to the line of bore. You will need a couple of gadgets, made of old barrels, to handle this job. Cut both of these old barrels off 2″ or 3″ ahead of the thread area, and bore one of them out to ½″ diameter, and cut the front end square on the lathe. Clamp the lathe chuck on the threads to do this as it will act as a gage to check the bolt face and the end of the receiver is not to be depended upon as a base for checking. So, wind in this barrel section and use a dial indicator against the bolt face, basing the indicator on the squared end of the barrel shank. If you do not have an indicator, it is possible to check the bolt face by covering the said face with Prussian blue and using a depth gage to scrape across the face of the bolt from side to side and so indicate the high and the low side but this takes time. The bolt during checking is always to be in the locked position.

The other barrel stub is to be cut and squared, but bored out and polished to the diameter of the counterbore of the bolt face involved and it will probably be necessary to make two or three of these eventually. Now make cast iron cylinders to fit the bored hole or holes. These are laps, and are used through the barrel stub fitted to the receiver with oil and lapping compound to cut the face of the bolt square so make them as long as possible. It is necessary to square the working end in the lathe every so often, twice during each job anyway, so the longer they are the longer they will last. Use the breast drill to turn them, threading the back end or turning it down so as to allow the drill to accept it and only a *very* small amount of metal is ever removed

---

made of ⅟₁₆″ cold rolled steel. If a long floorplate is made to extend forward and cover the lengthened box, the piece can be soldered or brazed on, but if the regular floorplate is to be used, weld the box together and fill in the front corners so they may be smoothed off, polished and blued.

The side-rail alteration is advisable when fat, sharp-shouldered cases are to be accommodated. The insides of the rails must be relieved to allow the right and left top cartridges to move up in the magazine without being canted inward before the feeding movement of the bolt. Occasionally it is necessary to slightly widen the space between the two top edges of the rails, but this should never be done until careful examination proves it necessary. A hand grinder will take care of these jobs.

from a bolt face.

For large base rimmed cartridges, the bolt head is often cut off square, removing the rim of the original counterbore. It is best to leave a little metal, if only a ¼″ wide section, on the left side, to support the cartridge against the extractor and so insure good extraction and ejection.

Bolt Lug Fit. On all actions to be rebarreled, polish the rear faces of the locking lugs with crocus cloth, then spot them in, coating them with spotting compound and closing the bolt in the receiver while holding the bolt handle to the rear to set the lugs against the supporting wall in the recesses. Removal of the bolt will reveal the contact of the lugs in recesses and you now polish the recesses with crocus cloth held on the end of a bent rod and again spot. Do not worry much about the cam surfaces or leading surfaces in the recess as all you want is full lug contact when the lugs are in fully locked position—and *do not polish out a lot of metal to fit a balky bolt*—get another bolt and try it. On some actions, particularly Mausers, the heat treatment is a type of case-hardening not very thick and if cut through the receiver strength is lost, as in firing the metal will set back and increase headspace progressively.

Action Shortening. This calls for highly skillful welding. The receiver should be stripped of course, the barrel removed and case-hardened actions must be treated carefully, it being necessary to anneal before cutting. I will not shorten any action I can not saw through without preliminary annealing, myself, preferring nickel-steel 1903 actions.

During welding or annealing it is necessary to protect the receiver ring against heating, which might change the strength of the locking lug recesses. Stuff wet cloths or asbestos inside the ring and keep the stuff soaked while welding or annealing.

First make a mandrel, bolt diameter, which will be around .700″, to be a slide fit through the receiver all the way, then in the center of this mandrel turn it down to about ⅜″ diameter for about 1½″. The purpose of the mandrel is to act as a jig and line up the two sections of the receiver for welding after cutting and shortening and aside from one milling cutter, this is the only special gadget needed.

Then saw the receiver in two, preferably with a power hacksaw, in order to cut squarely across it, but if a hand hacksaw is used, afterward check and file square. For the 1903 action, make the rear cut 3½″ from the front edge of the receiver ring and the front cut as much in front of this cut as you desire to shorten the action, less ⅟₁₆″. Saw cuts and filing the contacting edges will use up this $\frac{1}{16}$". For Mausers, make the first cut just in front of the receiver bridge, in the thumb cut for clip loading.

The two sections of receiver can now be placed on the mandrel and pushed together and if cut square, the edges will meet all around—if not, you file them until they do. Then with a file or a grinder chamfer the outer edges, to form a V-bevel where the weld will be made.

Place the receiver on the mandrel, edges touching, then set the receiver on a brick or other flat surface to line up the bottom receiver surfaces and tack, or weld at intervals around the receiver. Then change the setup, clamping the tang end of the mandrel in the vise, leaving the action hanging out the side in the air and now you will probably need to spoon a little more water into the asbestos packing in the receiver ring around the mandrel.

The vise will draw off much of the heat through the mandrel in the succeeding welding, in which the receiver is fused together again, and steel added to fill the bevel and make the full joint. If you are in doubt as to whether your rod is suitable, take the pieces of receiver you cut out in shortening, saw these into strips, weld them together by fusing, and use this for your rod.

Fuse the receiver well together before adding metal, then add on the inside surfaces first, building them out a little and cooking the steel in good. Corners are hard to fill and sometimes steel must be flowed into them, then go over the outside exposed areas and weld them. Renew the dampness of the receiver ring packing whenever it begins to steam profusely.

Let the receiver cool naturally in the air, then remove the mandrel —it should push out fairly easily. Now you clamp the front end of the receiver, again pack it with wet material, and weld the two points formerly protected by the mandrel—the inner walls. Weld the left side first, as it has more bulk, then weld the right, holding at red heat until the left side cools down below red, to prevent warping and that is all the welding for now.

If possible, shape a milling cutter to clean out the inside of the left receiver wall, otherwise do the job with files and rifflers. Clean the inside surfaces until you can slide the unaltered bolt all the way in freely.

Now cut the bolt. If a Springfield, cut the desired amount, less $\frac{1}{8}$", centered between the front of the safety lug and the extractor collar cut. On the Mauser, shorten the rib area and fit the two pieces of bolt in the receiver, holding the front half in locked position tight back against the lug recesses, and the front half in proper position to give clearance to safety lugs. Shorten the bolt by turning in the lathe until the correct length is established, and bevel the cut all the way out from inside edges to leave the wide V necessary to a good weld.

V-blocks are sufficient to hold the bolt in line for the welding. On the Mauser, the rib serves as a guide, but on the Springfield it is wise before cutting to make a longitudinal scratch on the bolt to serve as an index mark for lining up the two pieces for welding in correct relation to each other. This line is to be made before cutting. Fuse the two sections of bolt together, then add steel to build up the weld, above the surface of the bolt taking care to melt in the edges and blend the outlines. Protect the locking lugs with a wad of wet asbestos.

Turn the bolt in the lathe to remove the excess, then check for straightness. It should be reasonably straight, but if it is curved, heat to a dull red at the weld location then cool the outside of the bend faster than the opposite side. This is done by placing a piece of copper against the bolt first, then as it cools a little, holding a wet cloth to that point.

Try it in the receiver and if it requires a little effort to get it all the way forward, do not try to straighten either receiver or bolt. The considerable amount of polishing and filing necessary to clear out marks of welding and toolmarks of the original machining will go a long way toward making the bolt fit the receiver smoothly but should the bolt be tight after polishing, straighten it as necessary.

Tip: on the '03 action, receiver modifications such as narrowing the tang and streamlining the cut off housing can be done very conveniently while the receiver is cut in two pieces, as the separate rear section is easily handled.

To clear the receiver runways, the milling machine is best, but in a pinch you can do it with files. The bottom of the receiver is your best check for straightness of the shortened receiver. It is usually necessary to use grinders to pull the cartridge shoulder recess in the walls of the magazine opening further forward, but this can be done later, after the action is completed and the feeding tested.

Lap the face of bolt to a right angle with line of bore, as previously described, screw in an old barrel and test fire. For the Springfields, use an old '03 .30–06 barrel; for the Mausers it is preferable to use an '06 barrel also, as the 8mm cartridges are hard to load to high pressures and test cartridges should build up around 65,000 pounds pressure. There should be no appreciable increase in headspace beyond the initial set back when a new receiver has been shortened, and none at

Set-up of shortened FN Mauser action for welding. The receiver has been cut, section removed, and placed on the mandrel for correct alignment in the tacking, or first welding operation. Both ends will be protected by wet cloth packing for the actual welding, in all stages.

After the two sections have been joined by fusing at two or three points, the mandrel is removed, and the receiver unit checked for straightness. If all right, the receiver is screwed onto an old barrel lightly, repacked with wet cloths, and the complete welding job done.

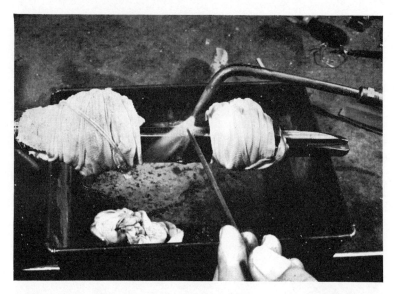

The actual finish-welding of the short action alteration. The pan of water is kept handy so that the protecting cloths can be moistened anew should they dry out.

The receiver bridge is protected only against heat discoloration, while the front receiver ring must be protected against any possible change in temper of the metal.

The milling machine is a great time-saver in clearing off excess metal after the welding is completed. Note that the marks of heat discoloration extend only about one-half inch to either side of the weld.

There is absolutely no change in strength of the receiver through the alteration.

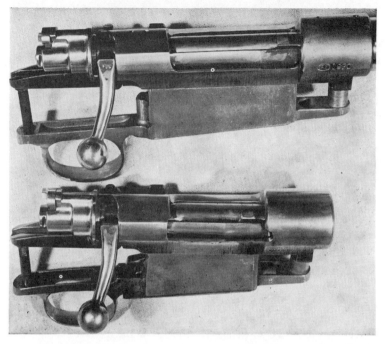

Standard and shortened FN Mauser actions, to illustrate difference in dimensions. Both actions have yet to be polished up for finishing.

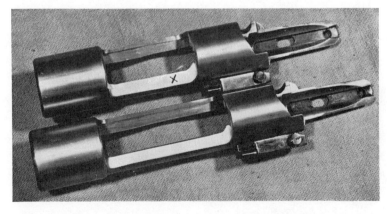

The finished and polished shortened FN Mauser receiver, shown alongside an unaltered one. The X indicates point of weld.

all on a used action.

After giving the action the works with proof cartridges, take off the barrel and fit the triggerguard. This is easy—cut with saw down the sides just ahead of the rear box wall, file the sides of this wall down the distance of the approximate thickness of the sidewalls, then spring the sidewalls out over this vertical rear wall and assemble the two pieces of guard to the receiver with the guard screws and the two sections will assume their correct relationship. With a scribe mark along the rear edge of the rear wall on the inner sides of the sidewalls, and saw these off, with the front section removed from the receiver. Again assemble and tack weld the guard together while it is on the receiver, remove and finish weld, making the seam on the back edge, not the corner.

The floorplate should be shortened in the middle if the military-style catch is to be used, cutting each end back from the center until it assembles on the guard to the proper length and it is best to hinge the floorplates. If the original magazine follower is to be used, cut it from the rear end and solder a little flat shoulder on the underside of the rear, to keep the magazine spring in proper position. Use Win. 70 .250/3000 magazine springs.

Springfield firing pins are shortened from the front. Shorten to the proper distance to accommodate the regular striker, cutting the new striker assembly button on the front to a tight fit in the striker. Shorten Mauser firing pins in the middle, cutting and welding. The insides of bolts are easily cleared out with large drills fitting the inner bore diameter, and polished with cutting cloth on mandrels.

Shorten the magazine box from the top $\frac{1}{8}''$ or so, to narrow the vertical height of the action. All refinements as to trigger and bolt are made as desired—low bolt for scope, and such—as on a deluxe regular action. Two-piece scope mounts such as the Tilden are easiest used. A single base mount, such as Redfield Jr. or Buehler, must of course be shortened, by cutting in the middle and rewelding to the correct length.

This about cleans up the short action job. You also could make long actions, if desired, by cutting in two, setting in pieces of steel, and rewelding to add $\frac{3}{8}''$ or $\frac{7}{16}''$ to the overall length of the action. I have not done this myself yet, but there is absolutely no objection that I can think of to the idea. So long as the receiver ring and bolt head are protected against heat during welding, there can be no loss of strength no matter what is done to the receiver and the bolt behind these parts.

Wait a minute, we forgot the extractor on the short action. The

Springfield extractor in particular must be shortened to a length to clear the safety lug so first cut to length to contact the front of the lug on the bolt. Now take the little piece you cut from the back end and file away the top portion, leaving a little curved section to fit the bolt curve, perhaps ¼″ long, and of course, full extractor width. Clean off the bottom of the cut extractor at rear, then with silver solder sweat the little piece to the underside of the receiver. File from the rear to give a little less than ⅟₃₂″ clearance of the safety lug, and polish. Extractors altered in this manner look very good as from the side no alteration is visible, and from the rear, only a thin line of silver at the joint; when the extractor is left in the white it is difficult to see the alteration at all.

These "custom" alterations on metal parts are operations which are sometimes necessary and usually decorative. They serve to make a rifle somewhat distinctive and give the owner something in which to take pride. The short action is worthwhile only on a featherweight .22/250 or .250/3,000 rifle for sporting use. Less than four ounces of weight is eliminated, but the short bolt throw makes the job practical. Cutting the clip slots from Mauser receivers, and streamlining the Springfield cutoff are about the only alterations made solely for appearance's sake, and good stockmakers consider the latter practical as it eases a good inletting job. You can find a reason, rather than an excuse, for most custom metal work.

CHAPTER 32

Ornamentation of Wood and Metal

CARVING and coloring are about the only things I can think of to do in connection with ornamenting a gun stock—aside, of course, from checkering and inlaying.

Wood Carving. Concerning carving, the most important point is not to get too much of it on a stock. A leaf pattern at the ends of the checkering patterns and under and in back of the cheekpiece is enough for most tastes. Floral designs on the forends and both sides of the buttstocks are sometimes done, as well as animals and hunting landscapes, but these always seem overdone. All stock carving must be low relief work, therefore, it is not particularly difficult.

The stock should be sanded and filled but not finished before carving. The design must be carefully outlined in lead pencil or white grease pencil, and tools prepared. Small veining tools and short bent, or spoon, gouges are used. Very probably a couple of very small gouges will have to be made up, although possibly some model and hobby shops may be able to supply them. For chip carving, straight shank chisels and gouges are used. Chip carving is a type of work sometimes done in place of checkering, and consists of cutting small depressions, rounded or V-type, of similar size in geometric patterns.

For soft but close grained woods such as soft maple, carving is better than checkering, and oak leaf patterns on the pistol grip and the forend of a stock are considerably better than fragile checkering.

Backgrounds may be chip cut or scraped clean. The carving is "dressed up" by either pressure or staining, or both. A design cannot be sanded so small irregularities and tool marks must be scraped out. Burnishing the wood by pressing with small, rounded end tools helps a lot, both on the design and background. The designs can be shaded and accentuated by using light and dark stains, applied with small camels hair brushes. The background should be finished the same as the rest of the stock, to the same color and care must be taken to keep this area from becoming darker as the dark background is satisfactory only when very small, in which case it makes the carving stand out.

Inlays. To inlay wood, or other material in a stock, first determine the design on the inlay and cut it to perhaps $\frac{1}{64}''$ oversize in all dimensions. Then lay it against the stock and scribe around it with a sharp lead pencil. Cut the outline, staying well inside the outlined border and remove the wood to the desired depth. You always leave the inlaid design a little high, compared to the surrounding surface, so that it may be sanded down to meet it perfectly. Make the inlay cut in the stock straight down, and file the inlay until it will push in. Then slightly undercut the recess. Good wood glue, or casein glue, is best for most organic materials, but for some plastics special cements may be necessary, which no doubt will be recommended by the maker. Set the inlay in with glue or cement, clamping with a C-clamp and leather protectors and allow to dry thoroughly. The inlay is then sanded and finished. Be sure to raise the grain over the full area and cut it down.

Metal designs can be inlaid also, with a fairly wide range of coverage, from initials, initial or monogram shields, to complete game scenes. Almost any metal which is easily worked and polished will do—aluminum and brass, as well as precious metals. Gold is best of all because of its resistance to corrosion, but silver is cheaper, more available, and shows up even better.

This type of ornamentation has been popular since rifles were invented. Colonial shooters were not happy unless their stocks had brass tacks, silver stars and similar gimmicks in the wood. I have seen modern rifles in the border country with Mexican and United States silver coins inlet into the stocks. In this connection, if you do not know it already, please be advised that it is illegal to mutilate or alter any United States silver coin.

Initials or monograms can be filed out of sheet silver or other metal, the stock inlet to accept them, then two small and short pointed pins soldered to the underside of the metal to drive into the wood and hold in the inlay. Cigar box nails make excellent pins for this purpose as only about a $\frac{5}{16}''$ length is needed. The inlay is sanded just like the wood or plastic job, though crocus cloth can be used for a final polish. A little lacquer over the metal will protect against corrosion and weathering—get the type used for musical instruments, which comes in clear, gold and silver.

Shields are inlet as above, polished, then engraved on the stock. For a good job you do not have the shield engraved and then try to put it in the stock.

A crude form of old fashioned stock decorating was the inlaying of brass or silver wire, to form simple designs and pictures. This is not so good on account of it being hard to keep the wire in the stock. Square wire silver solder stock might be used to better advantage, although I have never tried it, or small pins could be soldered to the underside to keep it in the wood.

The easiest method is to use the quick setting amalgams used by dentists for gold and silver fillings. This is kept in the form of powder, to be mixed with mercury into a thick paste as needed. It sets up quite fast, so do not mix more than you need. Your dentist can perhaps supply you, or will order amalgam, mercury and the little mixing bowl and pestle for you from the S. S. White Company or other dental supply wholesale houses. One part mercury to six or seven of silver powder is about right—you will get directions with the stuff—but get the dentist to show you how to mix it, test for enough mercury, how to get rid of too much mercury and so on. At the proper consistency, the amalgam is sort of like fresh putty. Do not mix the silver until the design is completed and the stock ready for the inlaying, for the amalgam will set up in 10 minutes, thereafter becoming too hard for shaping and forcing into the inlay cuts. (I have mentioned silver only, because it is much better suited to wood than gold, which does not show up well.)

The design is cut into the wood in the form of lines and solid openings, by chisels, hand or flexible shaft grinder or Vibra-Tool. When a solid space is cut, provide an anchor for the silver, by driving in cigar box nails until the head is below the top surface of the stock. The silver will be forced over and under and around the head and therefore will be held very well. Lines must be slightly undercut at sides, for the silver will not adhere to the wood and must be held by a dovetail system. Make the lines and other cuts at least $\frac{1}{16}''$ deep, to provide room for undercutting, although the design can be greatly aided by spiking. This consists of forcing a large needle or sharp scribe point down at an angle in the lines and spaces of the design, so that silver can flow into the holes thus made and create its own holding "nails." Spiking can be used instead of undercutting for short lines.

The stock must be completely finished before this type of inlaying can be done. The grain should be completely filled, with a very strong holding filler, and the closer the grain, the better the job will be.

Designs can be laid out freehand, transferred with tracing paper, or cut directly from book or magazine illustrations. In the case of the latter, tape or paste the picture to the stock and cut the desired lines through the paper into the wood. Rubber cement is recommended for

Examples of engraving layout, by Paul Showalter, of Patagonia, Arizona. The block or panel is simply an illustration of a type of design figure, with parts of the figure illustrated separately above and below the block con-

holding the paper to the wood. Remove the pattern, clean up the lines, add shading lines where desirable, spike the design and put in the amalgam, working along each line and using a smooth metal surface to force the silver down into the pattern. Use heavy pressure to insure the metal entering the spike holes and undercut areas, and apply enough silver to completely fill the design cuts and build up a little over the surface. Allow the silver to harden for an hour, then use a sanding block to cut it down to the surface of the wood, then with 8/o paper sand silver and wood together. If a small line pulls out or if some spot is not properly filled, mix up a little more amalgam and patch it up.

About the only warning on this method—do not make too heavy a pattern, with too many lines too close to each other. Outline drawings, with light shading, look best. Edward Damon's article on silver inlaying in the August 1949 issue of *The American Rifleman* covers this method very well, and the illustrated patterns are in excellent taste.

Filigree inlaying is all right for pistol and revolver stocks, but of not much suitability for rifle and shotgun decoration. In this system, which really requires engraving to be attractive, the design is cut out of thin silver stock—around .030″ thickness—in the form of an interconnecting leaf, floral, or figure design, and this plate then peened around the curve of the stock or grip. It is attached with small pins or screws, and looks very good against ebony or other dark wood. As a rule, there is no necessity for inlaying the silver in the wood, for the design itself provides a rough surface (comparatively speaking) for the hand to hold. If the silver is inlet into the wood, simple designs are necessary and considerable practice required for a good job since the filigree plate must be shaped to the stock and then inlet to fit. Smaller designs are required, to match the smaller area of the stock, than if the plate is to go *over* the stock.

METAL DECORATION

Etching. This is done by using acid to eat away the surface metal of specified areas. The procedure is simple and anyone can do it, but some artistic talent is required in laying out the design. The steel is pro-

---

siderably enlarged. The floorplate is a simple scroll layout, with center left blank, the space to be used for game figure or monogram, as desired. The two narrow lines of graving are two types of border, and the last drawing showing the bottom of a triggerguard, narrowed somewhat at rear. It shows still another type scrollwork.

tected by an acid proof coating which is cut and scraped away in the shape of the desired pattern. Wherever the coating is removed, the acid will attack the metal. This produces intaglio etching which is well suited to firearms work. Relief etching is the opposite procedure—the design is placed on the metal with acid proof varnish and the surrounding metal eaten away, leaving the design raised.

The protecting varnish is also called "ground," "stopping varnish" and "stopping out varnish." Several formulae are available, the best of which are given. These protective coatings must be definitely acid proof, be easy to cut through, and yet not be brittle enough to chip when cutting—and must stick to the steel very closely. Plain shellac, thinned a little with alcohol and colored with methyl violet dye to give a Prussian blue effect, can be used, though not too good. (It is best to color the ground in order that the design will be easier cut out with the tools—a colorless varnish on polished steel is almost impossible to use.)

Asphalt or asphaltum, thinned with benzol, makes a better varnish for etching. A one-to-five mixture is about right.

A more complicated mixture can be made with mastic for a base. Formula:

Mastic	4 parts
Burgundy pitch	12 parts
Beeswax (melted)	30 parts
Asphalt (melted)	50 parts

After mixing, add an equal amount of turpentine.

This is a somewhat soft coating well suited to pistols and revolvers.

Another formula, which I believe was used by Kornbrath, uses beeswax:

Mastic	1 part
Beeswax	1 part
Pulverized Syrian Asphalt	2 parts

Melt the beeswax and mix in the mastic, then add the pulverized asphalt and stir until the mixture is dissolved. Pour into water (at room temperature) and mould into bars or cakes by hand as it cools. Small pieces are cut off and dissolved in turpentine to make the varnish as needed.

Lampblack or other coloring matter may be added to any ground to aid in definition of the etching. Use small brushes to apply to the metal, and let it dry before trying to cut through with the etching tools.

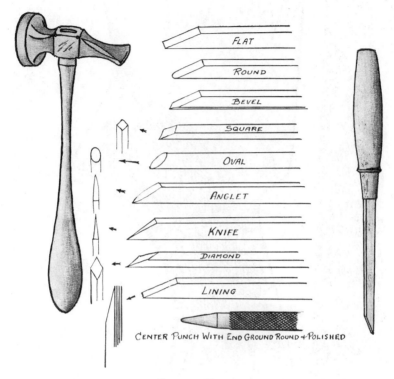

FLAT

ROUND

BEVEL

SQUARE

OVAL

ANGLET

KNIFE

DIAMOND

LINING

CENTER PUNCH WITH END GROUND ROUND + POLISHED

GRAVING TOOLS

The remodeled center punch is used for making dots, usually in border designs. Point must be rounded a very little and polished very smooth, preferably on lathe. The chasing hammer is held back at the large end of the handle, so that the spring action of the slender section can be employed. Points of the graving tools are illustrated as shaped for working in steel, by Paul Showalter. Some engravers use greater or smaller angles, of course—techniques vary considerably. Many men use the gravers without handles for chasing, in direct chisel style, while others use the full-handled tool, as illustrated, for both chasing and hand engraving. Handle shapes also are a matter of individual choice, whether the rounded palm type, or elongated knife-style such as shown.

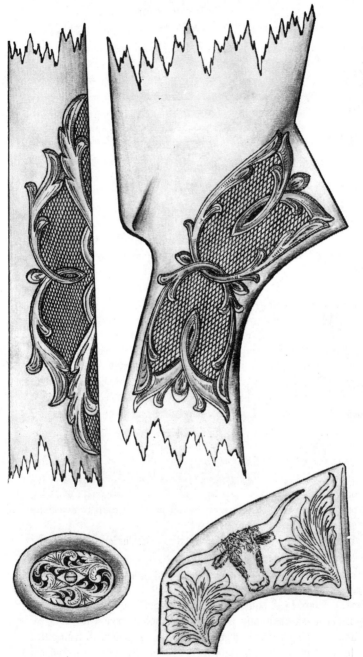

These drawings, by Paul Showalter, show carving as applied to rifle and pistol stocks. Used as an ornate border for a checkering design the carving is quite attractive. The pistol stock, meant to be of very hard wood or of ivory, employs an elaborated leaf and steer head. Note that the stock is not crowded, while the design arrangement provides for a non-slipping gripping area at proper points.

Nitric acid is the principal steel etchant, in solutions varying from one part acid to four parts distilled water, to half-and-half solutions. As the acid absorbs steel when in action, solutions used for tank etching (when the whole gun or part is submerged in acid) become progressively weaker and it is best to mix a new batch when needed, rather than attempt to bring the old one up to strength by adding acid. Remember always to use the water for a base, putting it in the bottle first, then adding the acid. Very hard steel may react better to hydrochloric acid, mixed two parts to one with commercial acetic acid. Pure nitric can be used for touching up a design, but is not satisfactory for straight etching undiluted, as it works furiously, absorbs steel fast and so quickly "kills" itself.

After the design is cut through the ground, the acid can be applied in drops with glass rods or eyedroppers with neoprene bulbs. Wear a neoprene or rubber apron when working with acid, and keep a pitcher of water handy to pour on a shoe or pants leg should acid be dropped or spilled there. This protects you, but not the shoes or clothing as ammonia is necessary to really counteract nitric acid, and a bottle should be kept handy at all times. The fumes are none too pleasant to inhale, but about the best you can do is provide cross ventilation and keep the jar or dish of acid downwind, so to speak. To remove the acid from the gun after it has acted the desired length of time, wash it off in warm water having a little ammonia in it. If the design is finished, also scrub it with a nylon toothbrush while washing.

Etching to be good at all is never a one operation job—it is necessary to allow the acid to eat deeper into the metal at some points, which calls for repeated applications and considerable time. It is best to cut the design through the ground only at these points first, and etch this area before completing the design and etching the whole area outlined, rather than doing the whole outline then blanking off parts of it for further action. However, the latter method must be used to some extent, to properly finish a fancy design.

The skill and the work come in cutting the design through the varnish or ground. Numerous small tools must be made up, in the form of little scrapers; needles set into handles are used for making fine lines, and little pointed chisels with different bevels and shapes of points made from $\frac{1}{16}''$ square rod. A triangular pointed scraper is perhaps more used than any other single tool—curve the faces in, rather than bringing them in straight to a sharp point. A triangular needle file with $1''$ of the point broken off and the teeth ground off can be shaped into this scraper. Polish all the scraper tips and harden them if convenient. They will from time to time contact acid, for you will occasionally find it necessary to touch up a design while the etching acid is working, so it is necessary to keep polishing them.

After the ground is dry, sketch the design on the metal, using a crow quill pen and whatever colored ink that shows up well. (A crow quill pen is not made from a crow feather—it is a type of fine point pen used by artists for shading drawings, and makes a very narrow line.) You will not be able to really make a detailed drawing, so a considerable part of the design will be freehand with the etching tools, in scraping and cutting the ground from the steel in the desired design. After the decided design is ready for etching, stop and study it carefully through a magnifying glass. Any slips of the tools can be found and repaired by putting on more varnish at such points and recutting the design properly. The tools should cut the varnish cleanly, but do not use enough pressure to scratch the steel. If this is done the acid may work under the ground where it is scratched and so spread and spoil the design at that point.

With the design completed, apply the acid, preferably using glass rods. Should it be feasible to apply quite a large amount of acid at a time—meaning about three drops—a small glass tube can be used, with about $\frac{1}{16}''$ inside diameter. This is set in the acid to the depth necessary to pick up the desired amount, and a finger placed over the top end. While the finger is held to the opposite end of tube, acid will remain in the other end. By trial and error you can determine how much to pick up at a time, but make your trials and errors on old practice guns and stray pieces of steel. Practice etching on such test items before attempting even the simplest job on a good gun.

Should a design "run," or be spoiled by acid getting where it should not, only changing the design at that point, or the outline, to take in the furthest point of the run, is possible for correction. Keep a bit of ammonia instantly available for mishaps such as getting acid on unprotected parts of the gun accidentally. If acid does get on the wrong place, a quick wetting with ammonia will neutralize it enough to prevent damage.

Etching for decoration is really not too good by itself. An etched design cleaned up and emphasized by a good engraver is very good. Etching can really be of service in dulling shiny surfaces on guns and for touching up backgrounds in engraved designs, though the latter calls for steady hands and great care. Etching acid will blur engraving itself and spoil its appearance.

Matting and Stippling. These are similar hammer-and-punch opera-

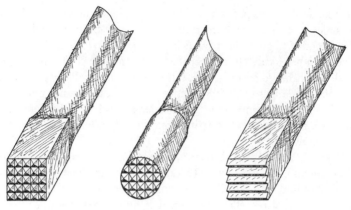

MATTING TOOLS

These punches are used to break up a flat surface, as on a sight ramp, or the top of a receiver, to provide a nonreflective surface. They cannot be used for much of an ornamentation job, to decorate a gun, however.

tions, stippling being a specific type of matting job in the general definition. In the machine tool business, the decorative burnished zig zag marks on tool guides and runways are sometimes called stippling. I have done a bit of this on radial drill and special press dovetails and such, but never have figured any application for firearms. The gunsmith's stippling is a prick punch roughing of a metal surface to afford a nonslip hold, to reduce or eliminate light glare from smooth surfaces, or to accentuate the shading in background areas of decorative designs.

Matting can take the form of embossing in checkered, dot, or line form, depending upon the business end of the matting punch of course. Punches are usually small—seldom over ¼″ square—and about 5″ long. The working end is shaped by needle file (triangular) across its face in diamonds, or squares, this being just plain checkering. Checkering files of 50 or 60 lines per inch are excellent for laying out the lines, but a sharp needle triangular file is needed to sharpen the small diamonds. It is often necessary to grind or stone one face of the file smooth, to sharpen the two edges and so permit a finer cut for finishing. The checkering files also serve to lay out the lining punch, making the face a series of parallel lines. Such punches are good for matting front sight ramps and the tops of barrels and barrel ribs.

Do not make deep cuts on the face of the punch; make these cuts sharp pointed or sharp edged, but keep the grooves shallow, to make the tool as strong as possible. Make the punches of chisel steel if at all possible, or of tool steel of the type made for power punching die tools. You can always get a cheap cold chisel, anneal it, shape and reharden, if you can not locate chisel steel stock. Matting punches must be very hard, to be able to impress steel, but must not be at all brittle as there must be no danger of the tool shattering under a hammer blow. The punches naturally work only on unhardened steel. Case-hardened surfaces can be worked with matting punches only after the hard surface is ground away.

Engine Turning and Damaskeening. The two terms are almost synonymous, but not quite. Engine turning can be referred to as Damaskeening, but all Damaskeening is not engine turning. Damaskeening is also spelled Damascening, and comes from the appearance of ancient Damascus made swords.

Engine turning involves the use of abrasives applied to a revolving tool which, when pressed against a smooth surface, cuts a bright circular spot. A series of overlapping spots makes a showy appearance on polished steel. On rifles, the most common use is for decorating bolts and magazine followers, and this is strictly decoration. However, on flat parts, such as shotgun hammers and other working parts, and revolver innards, engine turning is definitely practical. The polished rings left by the operation really are slight depressions in the steel and they tend to retain oil and cut down friction through reduction of contacting surfaces. Engine turned flat parts are much less likely to rust than plain parts—that is why the insides of good watches show engine turning.

The tools, called laps, are rods of hard rubber, or hard fiber, and are chucked in the drill press, which is to be run at medium speed although a lathe with a milling attachment is as good or better, holding the lap in the lathe chuck and the work in the milling attachment vise, which can be moved precisely in uniform steps to allow a regular pattern. When working on bolts under the drill press, V-blocks are desirable, although drilling vises can be used quite well.

The abrasive is emery flour, oilstone powder, or any very fine lapping powder, which is mixed with oil—olive, cutting, or a highly refined thin mineral oil—into a fairly stiff paste which is spread on the metal to be turned. The lap is brought down on the metal—a test will show how much pressure is required for that particular job—and the first metal spot turned. The following spots are governed by the first, as for spacing and usually they are slightly overlapped. I do not believe the diameter of the lap should ever be over $\frac{1}{4}''$, or less than $\frac{1}{16}''$, for gun work. After doing perhaps a half dozen spots, hold a patch dampened with solvent to the bottom of the lap to clean it.

Bolts are the most difficult parts to handle, because to get a perfect circle it is necessary to rotate it slightly under the lap in order for the flat lap face to contact the rounded bolt.

Damaskeening by burnishing a series of wavy, zig zag or even parallel lines is possible as an alternative. To do this you use a small tool with a large handle. The blade is chisel-shaped, or better, square in cross section at the tip, and flat across the face. This gives you four working edges, which should be between $\frac{1}{16}''$ and $\frac{1}{8}''$ across. The tool must be strong—$\frac{3}{8}''$ square or round stock is about right, with a fast taper to the tip to conserve strength—and should project from the handle about 3″. The handle should be about $1\frac{1}{2}''$ in diameter and at least 18″ long.

You clamp the work solidly, supporting it from underneath, place the tip of the tool on it, grip the handle with both hands close together at the bottom, rest the top of the handle over a shoulder, pull the handle downward to create pressure on the tip and then begin a full body waggle to the rear, pulling the tool toward you. The more wave you want in the pattern, the wider your waggle! Zig zag patterns are easy, and with little practice very uniform patterns may be achieved. The surface to be burnished should be polished, oiled with light machine oil, and this oil wiped off with a lint free cloth. The tool tip should be very hard, and be polished and the corners of the square tip should be sharp, and the tool moved across the steel while held at about a 45° angle. It cannot cut the steel, since it is drawn back, rather than pushed forward and the design is burnished, not cut.

This system will not work on hardened steel, but will on ordinary rifle bolts.

Neither method described will stand blueing—that is, if done properly, blueing will practically eradicate them. It is of course possible to engine turn a design rather deeply into steel, which can show up under any refinishing, but you should not go that deep on any gun part.

Engine turned bolts are quite spectacular in appearance, but rather sad in use. The bright surfaces reflect sunlight and in the case of bolts, just a little bolt operation puts longitudinal scratches right through the design and makes it look rather sick. I prefer blued bolts, but then my rifles get year around use while for the man who can only use his rifle perhaps a week out of the year and who gets much of his gun pleasure through just looking at his arms, appearance can mean a great deal. These are the boys who appreciate Damascene jobs and good engraving.

Metal and Metal. Contrasting metals can form attractive decoration —brass, gold, silver and platinum all are excellent against blued steel. Inlay was the original method of attachment, and is still used today to some extent. In inlay work, channels are cut in the base metal, the edges undercut by chisels, and the softer decorative metal peened into the channels, which are cut in the desired design. This system is well adapted to initials and geometric designs, but the toughness of gun steel limits its application considerably. Its greatest advantage is that no heat is necessary, so that heat treated parts can be handled safely.

The attachment of metal to metal through soldering is easier and permits all sorts of latitude in designs. One very simple system which the beginner can practice with is a sort of combination of inlay and solder. The design, letters, or numbers are stamped, engraved, or chiseled into the steel surface, then flux the surface and apply brass, gold or silver. On parts where brazing heat cannot injure the arm, such as triggerguards, bolt handle knobs, grip caps and buttplates, ordinary brazing technique is used, flowing the brass or other metal onto the steel and into the design cut. Metal is deposited over the surface, then filed and polished down to bare steel, revealing the design alone against the steel, which is then blued. Ordinary alphabetical stamps can be used to put initials or names on triggerguards or floorplates, and brass flowed on for a simple, low cost decoration and identification. Serial numbers and receiver ring stamping can be inlaid with ordinary soft solder at low heat, if desired, but a blueing system which does not attack lead must be used afterward. Ordinary silver solder does for silver inlays of this type, but do not use it on receiver rings.

The overlay method of attachment is that used by engravers in producing raised game figures or other relief items in fancy pictorial designs. The projected figure is cut to a rough outline, then soldered to the firearm with soft or silver solder. (There are also brass alloys for soldering gold.) The engraver then cuts this soldered-on plate to the finished figure. Initials can also be attached, to leave raised letters, and by having an engraver make up a good monogram in silver or gold, a little careful soldering can produce an attractive result. Formerly, overlay figures were attached by semi-inlaying them into the steel, with the undercut system of holding the edges into place.

Naturally, the system of turning out pictorial designs employing gold or silver overlay calls for artistic talent, because the figures must literally be sculped from the metal. There are very few men who can do a decent job. Griebel, of Chicago, is a worthy successor to the great Kornbrath, and there are a couple of others who do creditable work.

There are many expert engravers who cannot do good pictorial overlay.

Decorative overlay does not have to be combined with engraving, though it generally is. I have seen quite passable Mexican work of this sort on firearms with little or no engraved background. Usually taking the form of eagles, cougars, horses or sombreros; good looking figures sometimes combine gold, silver and copper to give color to the work.

Engraving. The real backbone of gun decoration is engraving. Deep relief forms the best looking type, except when fine scroll designs are used although good engraving combines both deep and shallow cuts to shade and emphasize parts of the design.

There is not much good engraving on foreign guns. In Europe, particularly Germany, gunsmiths under the apprentice system learned engraving so that they might be able to engrave their own products. The gunsmith practiced engraving as he practiced stockmaking or sightmaking, just as part of the job—much of the time the gunsmith had no interest in guns, but was merely a tradesman working at a bench and this was the reason for so much crummy German engraving. The law of averages did of course produce some expert German engravers, who usually gave up gunsmithing and concentrated on engraving only, often working for one of the larger manufacturers.

In the United States engraving has been a separate art, few gunsmiths being able to engrave at all unless they came from abroad, and our engravers are usually ignorant of gunsmithing. One thing in our favor, though, is the engraver's temperament—once he tries to engrave a gun, he never gives up. A man skilled in working in silver and gold finds steel a challenge to his ability, so he works at it. He finds he must change the shapes of his graver tips and learn the techniques of chasing, rather than graving. Specifically, "graving" means using hand pressure on the tools, while "chasing" means using the tools with hammer pressure to cut the steel. Both are employed on gun work, border and scroll designs being possible to engrave while using the engraver's block, or hand moved vise.

The engraver must be something of an artist before he ever starts work, for he must be able to sketch his designs on the metal, freehand as templates cannot be used.

To lay out engraving, the metal is coated lightly with Chinese white, a substance available from jeweler's supply houses, usually in the form of a stick, and applied to metal with a small brush or finger, wetted, first applied to the stick, then to the metal. A thin white coating is left, on which the design can be drawn with a sharp lead pencil and the graving tools are guided by these lines.

Generally, the gun is polished and buffed bright before the engraving, then blued afterward, however, a modern departure, of doubtful virtue, is to blue the gun and then engrave it, which leaves the engraving bright. Rust attacks such jobs unless constant care is taken or a wax coating kept on the metal.

When a firearm is polished bright and engraved, it may be cleaned for blueing by a degreasing solution, such as Oakite, and may have a very quick acid solution cleaning, to help the blueing take evenly. No mechanical polishing is possible, excepting light touchup work at points outside the engraved areas. The engraving must not be blurred by polishing or by the etching action of acids, or the final appearance will suffer.

The Burgess Vibra-Tool can be used to matt or rough up backgrounds in engraving designs quite well, and a skilled man can even shade areas with it. Engravers usually use both graving tools and matting punches to work on backgrounds, sometimes even using acid etches.

There are jeweler's touchup plating solutions, available in different shades of gold and silver, and also platinum, which I believe could be used to plate engraving backgrounds. On a raised surface these would rapidly wear away, but on a protected sunken area they should be quite durable.

Swartchild & Company, of Chicago, about the largest of jeweler's supply houses, could furnish these materials. They carry literally everything in the line of jeweler's, watchmaker's and engraver's tools and supplies—get your jeweler to show you their catalog. A bench is a necessity for engraving, and the watchmaker's (or engraving) bench is handy for revolver work also—general gunsmithing, I mean. From 38" to 44" high, the tops are about 20" by 40", and the benches have a multitude of small drawers.

Engraving blocks are really small universal vises, with round bottoms which usually seat in a round ring pad. The work (if small enough) is clamped on top of the block and the engraver holds the block with one hand and the graver against the work with the other. Both hands work together, the block being turned against the graver while the latter is forced into the metal and also moved. Special jigs or holding clamps are easily made for holding floorplates and magazines, these being the principal rifle parts which can be engraved by use of the block. A good block, with attachments, will cost about 50 bucks as it is

An example of Arnold Griebel's engraving on a Ballard action rifle made up by the Niedner Rifle Corporation some years ago. Mr. Griebel is our finest engraver. Note that pattern consists of panel and decorative border, but that no attempt was made to cover the entire action with engraving. This job is in perfect taste. Loop lever is nicely case-hardened.

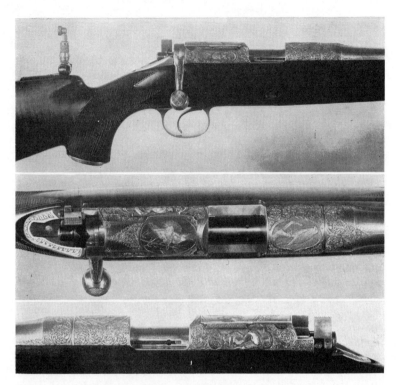

KORNBRATH ENGRAVING

Three views of a magnificent Winchester 52 sporter made by Thomas Shelhamer and engraved by the immortal Kornbrath quite a few years ago. This was Mr. Shelhamer's personal squirrel and small game rifle, until talked into selling it one sad day. Note how the engraver emphasized the small-game motif, and that while the work is ample, it is neither florid nor overdone.

quite a mechanism in itself.

Gravers are almost entirely made abroad, France, Switzerland, and England producing most of them. E. F. B. (Ezra F. Bowman, Lancaster, Pennsylvania) gravers are made in America. If you want to experiment, try making up a few gravers yourself. They must be file hard, but not brittle, which means the finest tool steel hardened as much as possible, then drawn very slightly and for working in steel, graver points must be cut to a wider angle (side profile) than for soft metal work—this to make them stronger. For the same reason, some of the standard jeweler's gravers are not suited to gun work. Knife gravers are of little use in gun work, as they constantly tend to dig in deeper. Round gravers have limited application, and really work only on soft steel while bent gravers of any shape are not too practical.

The gun engraver does 90% of his work with three shapes, in two or more sizes each; flat, square, and oval. The flat graver is generally used for deep cuts and the bolder parts of the design since the engraver can, by changing the angle of the tool while working, shade lines and give depth to emphasize detail. Gravers come in different sizes in the same shapes, and for steel the larger sizes are used, although regardless of size, in a given type all cut the same shape of furrow, so a large one can be used to give the same depth of cut as a small one, by not digging it in so deep at the start. Line gravers, which are practically the same as flat gravers, except available in different widths and with grooves cut in the edges to give a line effect, are used to shade designs sometimes and a very fine checkered effect can be made with them. Most engravers use handles on the gravers, even when using the chasing hammer to drive the tool along in the metal. Chasing hammers have small heads, shaped somewhat like a shoemaker's hammer, and flexible hickory handles. To sharpen gravers, a little sharpener attachment is sold, this being a small frame which clamps on the graver at the top and has rollers at the bottom; the graver is clamped and set on an oil stone, then moved to sharpen, the roller moving on the stone, and the clamp, which is adjusted to the desired angle, holding the point at the same angle during the operation.

If you want to take up gun engraving, go ahead. You need from 40 to 90 buck's worth of equipment to start—block, gravers, Chinese white, stones, sharpener, several old guns, a course in freehand drawing, good eyes, firm hands and practice. About five year's practice, eight hours a day would be right, but eyes and hands cannot stand it, so work about three hours a day, half an hour on, half an hour rest.

No one, least of all me, can tell anyone how to engrave, and nobody can teach you very much, except mechanical operations and movements. The only way is to watch an expert engraver, note his movements and techniques, and then practice, attempting to follow his actions. You will develop your own style.

Wavy border lines are not hard to master, with the straight square graver, and simple scroll designs should be practiced first. Simple does not mean just a few lines, but fairly shallow lines so that shading can be learned. Engraving must hold to a middle course to be attractive— a design with just a few lines looks amateurish and half done, and a design with crowded lines all over the place looks over elaborate and rather flat, since no particular theme can be emphasized. Shading means an angled cut, of varying depth and therefore width, defining the major lines of the design.

If you run across a fine example of engraving and overlay work which you wish to copy, there is a method of transferring the design to another arm. This is by using transfer wax, which comes in different colors—red, yellow, white and black—for contrast against the metal or other substance to be engraved, I presume. Pressed over a design, the wax can be stripped off in strips or small sheets, placed over the new job and used as a guide, the impression being visible enough to follow.

The jeweler's supply houses can offer quite a few useful items to the gunsmith, as a considerable number of special tools and supplies are made specifically for that trade and are not advertised outside to the general public. Dunmore makes a geared utility tool which certainly will handle any dental engine job, being a flexible shaft electric tool, with speeds from 500 to 2000 RPM, variable with a foot operated rheostat and with a small chuck to take tool shafts from ⅛" down to a No. 80 drill. Every type of file ever designed is, I think, available in miniature form. Eye loupes, or magnifying glasses to attach to the head or regular glasses frame can be highly useful in all phases of gunsmithing. Special soldering alloys, blocks, coppers, solutions for fluxing and other metal items are of considerable value at times. Polishing items such as white, black and green rouges are useful on hard metals, and of course tripoli is an old standby for soft metals. They have all kinds of stuff we gunsmiths can use, even diamond dust, if you really want to cut something down in a hurry!

CHAPTER 33

Target Rifles

A NUMBER of factors have combined during the past few years to lead me to believe that a particular phase of gunsmithing deserves detailed mention. This is the construction of center-fire rifles for target use, and the alteration of existing rifles for the same purpose. In this country, practically all big bore competitive shooting involves the .30 caliber, the .30–06 being almost the "standard," supplemented by various larger .30 caliber cartridges for long range shooting. When the government declared the 1903 Springfield obsolete, the shooters were left to their own devices regarding rifles for general competition. The M1 (Garand) autoloader is the service rifle at present and so will be used in all matches requiring the service rifle, but since private citizens may not purchase these rifles, civilian shooting remains dependent upon the bolt action rifles.

With the Springfield no longer in the "required" class, an issue National Match 1903 rifle is no longer the limit of the .30 caliber rifleman's desires. The field is open, with few holds barred, excepting of course for weight and trigger limits. As the M1 rifle weighs from 10 pounds 4 ounces up and is the official service rifle, it sets the weight limit for rifles to be used in military target courses. Most states (state rifle associations) have realized this and now set the maximum weight for rifles in regular competition at 10½ pounds. We can therefore build precision arms for our .30 caliber matches.

The resuming of international competition has aroused some interest in free rifle competition and in the special rifles used. Whether the United States will become a serious participant in future matches depends to some extent upon whether American gunsmiths can furnish capable rifles to the shooters. At one time U. S. riflemen commanded high respect in the international shooting game, and the same standing can be reached again if shooters and gunmakers can get together. It will take a bit of time but can be done.

TYPES OF TARGET RIFLES

There are two types of target rifles, the first being the plain target arm, the second being the free rifle.

The target rifle is that which meets competitive rules with regard to weight, sights and trigger, and can be any arm from the issue Springfield or Enfield with target sights to the custom built job, or the Winchester Model 70 National Match, which is the standard M70 in a target stock with target sights. The weight limit may be 9½, 10 or 10½ pounds (minus sling) depending upon local ruling. Sights are metallic, but they are not limited to any particular type, and the bases for target type telescopic sights may be installed, so that the rifle can be used with the telescope in specific matches allowing it. Palm rests are not allowed in American competition, nor is the Swiss or Schuetzen buttplate. Trigger pulls must not be less than three pounds weight.

The free rifle was originally that made possible under the rules for international competition, but American shooters and gunmakers have produced a different type. The international match rifle has a weight limit of 19 pounds 13 ounces (9 kilograms, to be exact) metallic sights only, and is constructed for use in all positions, the required ones being offhand, kneeling, and prone. Set triggers, palm rests and special buttplates are allowed, and buttstocks are sometimes hinged so as to be adjustable for all positions. The longest range at which these rifles are fired is 300 meters, or 328 yards, and they must be capable of grouping all their shots within four inches. Any caliber goes.

The American version of the free rifle is radically different. There is no weight limit I have ever heard of, and many custom rifles weigh well over 20 pounds. The matches open to these rifles in this country are generally at 600 and 1000 yards, with telescopic sights permitted. I would say that the majority of "bullguns," as we call them, have no metallic sights on them at all. Set triggers are permitted, as are any special features or accessories. Since the shooting is all in the prone position, the rifles are stocked accordingly so they are generally uncomfortable in other positions. As with the international rifle, there is no caliber limitation and the accuracy minimum should be nine inches at 600 yards or around seventeen at 1000 yards.

Each of the three types described must follow some particular rules although of course the rifles somewhat overlap their classes—the target rifle could be used in either free or international competition, although at a disadvantage; the international rifle could be used in American free rifle matches, but would be outclassed by the bullgun;

and many bullguns could be used in international shooting, but the addition of palm rests will not make them well suited to position shooting.

Taking up each in turn:

Competitive Target Rifles. Maximum weight limit, 10½ pounds. Metallic sights, 3 pound trigger pull.

Actions: Because the rifle will be used in all positions and in rapid as well as slow fire, the five round magazine must be used, the receiver must have clip slots in the receiver for clip loading, and of course be very smooth and easy in bolt operation. All standard actions mentioned must be polished at the points of friction in the receiver runways and on the bolt, and all the cams involved in cocking made to work smoothly. Magazines must feed cartridges reliably and without effort. Triggers of course should be as crisp in letoff as they can be made, the initial takeup of the military double pulls shortened slightly, and trigger stops installed to eliminate movement of the trigger after disengaging the sear when pulled. It is highly commendable to sandblast the tops of the receivers, to cut down light reflections. For the same reason all bolts should be blued after polishing.

Polish all points in the trigger-sear-cocking piece assembly, and limit the trigger in movement so as to cut down the trigger travel in the first pull, but do not stop the trigger back enough to remove the first pull, or cut down the sear to make a single stage pull. Doing so naturally cuts the sear and the cocking piece engagement to the minimum, and to the danger point in actions where any play is present in the fit of the cocking piece, or firing pin, bolt sleeve, bolt, and receiver. In rapid bolt manipulation all tolerance in movement of the bolt in the receiver is used up and it may be possible to lift the cocking piece over the sear when closing the bolt. If the double stage military trigger, even refined in action, is definitely objectionable to the customer, use one of the sear release trigger mechanisms made by Mashburn, Timney, Dayton-Traister or others. If the standard trigger is used, either fine checker it sharply or cover it with one of the trigger shoes such as made by Henshaw and others. These broad plates serve to distribute finger pressure and so seem to make the pull feel lighter and smoother.

A very helpful idea is to put a nonskid surface on the bolt knobs, and even on the shank of the bolt handle above the knob. *Do not* do a nice job of sharp checkering—it is too hard on the fingers during rapid fire shooting. Use a fine checkering file (50 lines per inch) and cover the entire knob with it, to your own desires as regards design. I have used both a sort of spiral lining and a sort of basket weave effect, making a pass with the file in one direction, then in another, without crossing the lines. This surface is wire brushed before blueing, to remove any sharp edges or burrs.

Do not attempt to make short action speedlock ignition systems. These are not uniform in ignition unless extremely strong mainsprings are used, which make for harder cocking. Because of the rapid fire courses, the action must cock very smoothly.

1903 Actions. Springfield actions with serial numbers of 800,000 or higher are suitable. The double heat treated ones between 800,000 and 1,275,767 make the best target arms, as the hard surfaced bolts and the receiver runways cooperate with little friction. The nickel-steel actions above 1,275,767 can be polished to work very smoothly, although the softer metal has some binding action. Rock Island actions are also satisfactory, those mostly being of the double heat treated type. Some, not all, of the actions numbered above 319,921 were of nickel-steel, according to General Hatcher. World War II 1903 models made by Remington can be used, especially when good Springfield or Rock Island bolts can be installed. The Remington 1903 A3 and A4 models and the L. C. Smith rifles have actions too poorly machined to make decent target arms.

Use of the headless firing pin and the reverse safety is often advisable. This assembly adds very little to achievement of faster ignition, but it provides considerable comfort and moral support to stock crawling shooters. They can park their snoots an inch further forward than with the standard pin and safety. Disadvantages of the headless pin are failure to deflect gas coming back through the bolt—of little importance today, as we have good primers and use shooting glasses almost universally—and inability to cock the firing assembly manually without opening the bolt. Hangfires or misfires are not common, but sometimes in rapid fire a man will brush the bolt sleeve lock against his clothing and so allow the firing pin to slide down into the cocking notch while the bolt is open. With the headed pin, it is possible to seize it and cock the assembly instantly and continue firing.

The separate striker and the firing pin of the 1903 action should be made into a rigid assembly by installing little discs of steel shim stock between the ends of the two parts where they butt together. The tip of the striker should be polished with crocus cloth to glass smoothness.

Machined triggerguards only should be used, however, the war production stamped magazine followers are satisfactory. During the war I discovered that we had fewer magazine jams with it than with the machined type. No alteration beyond polishing the tops should be done to the followers. Magazine springs are unnecessarily strong, and may be weakened by compression to set at approximately 3″ in height, or the Winchester M70 .30–06 magazine spring substituted. Use only the service or National Match mainsprings, in good condition. Specifications of the service spring are as follows:

Length	5.58″
Diameter	.40″
Diameter of Wire	.049″
Cocked Length	1.8285″
Coils	33½–6 per inch
Strength	To sustain load of 16 to 19 pounds at cocked height.

Extractors should be polished and filed until they move freely on the bolt, do not drag against the receiver wall when the bolt is operated, and will engage the cartridge head without forcing or cutting brass whether the cartridge is fed from the magazine or placed in the chamber and the extractor sprung out over the rim when the bolt is closed. Most American shooters have the deplorable habit of placing the cartridge in the chamber instead of in the magazine when single loading for slow fire. The 1903, 1917 and Winchester actions permit this. Many Mausers do not, as no clearance is provided for the extractor to spring outward when the bolt is forward.

1917 Actions. Enfield actions make excellent target jobs, when the bolt is altered to cock on the opening movement. The same polishing procedure as for the 1903 is desirable, as is the use of a weaker-than-issue magazine spring. The magazine box may be narrowed vertically ³⁄₁₆″ and retain a five round cartridge capacity, while permitting the use of the better shaped 1903 trigger. The forward tang of the triggerguard should be straightened in order to provide greater strength of the stock at that point. Alteration of the cocking system gives excellent fast ignition when the stronger Remington 720 or 30S mainspring is used.

There is no magazine cutoff on this action, so that the bolt will be held open in the rear position by the follower when the magazine is empty. Do not alter the follower so that the bolt will close over it. Provide an extra follower so altered, for the man to practice bolt manipulation.

Bolt handles should be bent slightly forward and up, which makes them easier to handle in rapid fire. Knobs should be lined, checkered lightly, or otherwise roughened to give a better hold.

Remington actions are most desirable, Winchester next, and Eddystones last. Do not use Eddystones so hard as to be possibly brittle. One of my friends had one of these crack at the receiver ring through firing, with the original military barrel in use.

Winchester Actions. The Winchester 54 action has a very poor trigger system which makes good pulls extremely difficult to maintain. Substitution of a patent trigger makes these as desirable as any and better than most, for the ignition system is a reliable speedlock one. The pressed steel triggerguard is no objection, as the magazine is very reliable in feeding and a removable floorplate not absolutely necessary. Bolts should be polished and cams cleaned up, as for the military actions, to reach the smoothest operation.

Winchester Model 70 actions are excellent, requiring only a polishing to be ready for rapid fire. Trigger pulls are easy to adjust by file and stone, and a stop is builtin. Postwar triggers are not hard and can be filed, if necessary and both sear and triggers can be hardened at points of contact, if desired, although they will maintain a uniform pull for a considerable length of time in standard form.

The followers used allow the bolt to close when the magazine is empty, but the rear left corner of the follower can be cut down a little on the left edge to allow the follower to rise and block the bolt, should the customer be afraid of closing the bolt on an empty chamber during rapid fire.

TARGET BARRELS

The center-fire target rifle will be for the .30–06 cartridge in all probability, so that existing military barrels can be used, if of sufficient accuracy. These are made with rifling twist of one turn in ten inches, which is suited for accuracy at velocities of 2700 fps and less with 150-, 173- and 180-grain bullets. The minimum standard of accuracy for .30 caliber target work should be a 6″ group—20 shots—at 300 yards, fired from bench rest or prone with sandbag rest under the left forearm—and fired in twenty minutes. Due to the fact that many full power handloads make the long boattail bullets corkscrew to some extent through overstabilization because of the 10″ twist of rifling at short range, .30 caliber testing at 200 yards may be misleading. One such case I remember covered a load which gave 6″ groups at 200 yards and 5″ groups at 300! I was the guy, and it was my rifle and my load, too.

Should the rifle fail to hold its point of impact for the 20-shot string, check the stock bedding first, experimenting with the forearm tension,

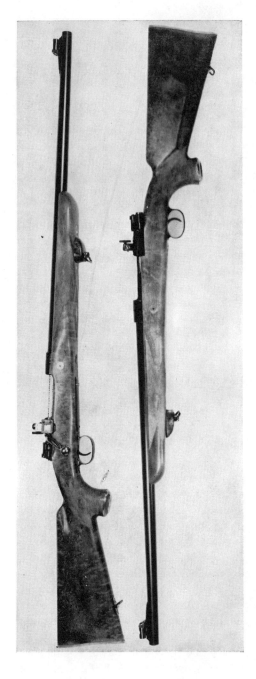

A Leonard Mews target job. This .30–06 rifle weighs 12 pounds and is built on an 1898 Mauser action. It has a birdseye maple stock with beavertail forend and a "close and deep" pistol grip with a thumbrest.

The checkering is hard to see in this illustration but it is ample and runs 26 lines-per-inch.

Note that the cheekpiece is long and comparatively flat, while the comb is high, yet there is no Monte Carlo effect. This stock is well designed for its job.

The recoil bolt is covered on each side with decorative plugs in the form of miniature targets, made by Mews of bronze with an ebony "bullseye" in the center. Mews also did the metal work on this rifle, which included a trap grip-cap. The rifle has a special barrel made by Wm. Staege, Omro, Wisconsin and the job was built for Mr. L. F. Masche, of Loveland, Colorado.

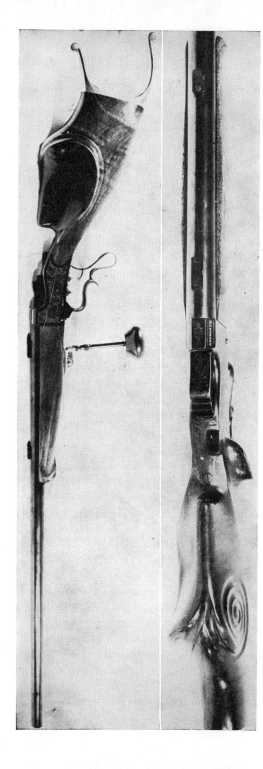

A Recently Naturalized American

Clifford Christopherson, of Appleton, Wisconsin, wanted his liberated Schuetzen action restocked so it would be real "foxy" looking, as he put it, mit scrolls und schnabels und all those other hallowed whorls and lines as befitting these old German and Swiss rifles.

So Leonard Mews schnitzelled and schnabbled away until he gained the above (and desired) effect.

He writes:— "It is actually fun to let oneself go and really work on these beautifully done actions that naturally suggest scrolls and curved lines. Now some of these curved lines are for a reason. Bullseyes! That pot bellied sag on the buttstock, considered so improper on modern gunstocks, really belongs on these old-timers. It rests on the chest muscles and steadies the holding greatly. Which was a well-liked feature of the old Schoyen Schuetzen rifles. This is really a 'fittin' stock and it wraps itself around you like a beagle pup's tongue."

P. O. Ackley rebarreled this action with a .32/40 barrel. This Pope type palm rest is handled by Chester Nickodym Industries and the Schuetzen buttplate by P. J. O'Hare. There is the word "Concurrenx" and the letters "D.R.G.M." stamped on the receiver ring. The stock and forearm are American black walnut, obtained from Howard Clark, Stevens Point, Wisconsin.

sling tension and floating the barrel. If the stock is not at fault, the barrel is definitely disqualified for target use, even though it may keep the first three or four shots well grouped. A barrel straightened during manufacture usually warps from heat in firing and changes the point of impact.

Winchester target barrels are excellent, although handicapped by being rifled with the 10″ twist. A 12″ twist of rifling stabilizes bullets sufficiently since our .30–06 velocities have gone up 10% since 1906, and also permits better velocities with slightly lower pressure. My personal theory is also that the 12″ twist barrel will last a little longer than the 10″ through less torque pressure of the bullet against the lands, although this is a minor point I cannot prove.

Custom match barrels are to be preferred, made by a reputable maker—Ackley, Pfeifer, Sukalle or Titus, listing alphabetically the best men I know. Length should be 28″, for maximum ballistic performance with minimum target weight contour and rifling twist, one turn in twelve inches—fourteen can be used for maximum accuracy of the 152- and 164-grain present government bullets. The chamber should be rather tight, though not of minimum headspace. Diameter should be close to the minimum in order to minimize cartridge expansion at the base which to a large degree governs the condition of the fired cases for repeated reloading. Headspace should be between 1.944″ and 1.946″. Closer headspace may make for difficulty in closing the bolt upon oversize factory or issue ammunition, as well as to increase breech pressure without increasing velocity.

As a practical measure, the entire top of the barrel should be matted, or the barrel sandblasted before blueing, in order to make it less reflective. Telescopic sight bases may be mounted so that target telescopes can be used in testing ammunition or in "any sight" rifle matches. No dovetail slots should ever be cut in a target barrel, of course.

The barrelmakers regard the six groove barrel as slightly more accurate than the four groove, however many very accurate rifles have had the four groove barrel. It is known that the four groove has slightly longer life than the six groove barrel—the difference, from what few records I have seen, is around 10%. Barrel life is not a major problem to the target man, since he can get several seasons of shooting with any of them, as the barrelmakers use the very best steels for target barrels.

Very often when accuracy begins to fall off, a barrel can be restored for another 1000 rounds by cutting off an inch at the breech, refitting and rechambering. This is especially true of barrels through which boattail bullets are used, as the bullet bases cause erosion, or gas cutting, principally at the throat, right ahead of the chamber. Flat based bullets are easier on the barrels at this point, and so give slightly longer barrel life. Barrels used to be quite spotty in this respect—of two National Match Springfield barrels I have had, one went out in less than 1400 rounds, and one went 5000, using boattail bullets exclusively in both rifles. The present-day target barrel can be expected to give from 3000 to 4000 rounds before accuracy begins to leave. No set figure can ever be given, as some powders are more erosive than others and some bullets give more bore wear than others.

The barrelmaker should of course lap match barrels so that there will be no "breakingin" firing necessary. A barrel with prominent tool-marks may not give full accuracy until three or four hundred bullets have passed through it. Naturally, this is highly undesirable to the target man.

The two barrel contours listed are the most practical; the lighter will permit rifles of total weight under 9½ pounds if necessary, with the 1903 action, and the heavier, rifles under 10½ pounds with any of the actions mentioned. Weight of the rifle is regulated by the stock.

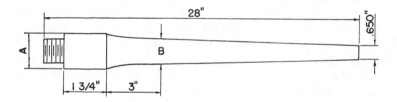

```
LIGHT  TARGET  BARREL     A = 1.125"   B = 1"
HEAVY  TARGET  BARREL     A = 1.2"     B = 1.0625"
       STRAIGHT  TAPER  FROM  POINT  "B"
                   TO  MUZZLE
```

It will be noted that the muzzle diameters of both barrels is .625″ or ⅝″, which is the same as the 1903 military barrel, allowing for tolerances in arsenal manufacture. This permits use of the Springfield 1903 front sight base, for which commercial target sights are made.

The 12″ rifling twist is the main thing, for it permits loading 180-grain match bullets to better than 2800 fps with maximum accuracy in the .30–06 cartridge, as well as handling the 150-grain bullets better than the 10″ twist. For higher velocity .30 calibers, such as the .300 H & H and assorted wildcat .300s, the 14″ twist should be used. A good compromise might be the 13″ twist, but the rifling machines in general use require special guides to cut other than even number inch twists.

TARGET SIGHTS

The target rifle should have target sights of course, and the commercial selection is somewhat limited, as compared with the many types and combinations possible on the .22 target rifles. The die hard Springfield man with good eyes may be satisfied with a plain blade which can be set in the '03 movable stud per the service sight. The blade should be between $\frac{1}{16}$″ and $\frac{3}{32}$″ in width, for best definition at all ranges. A wider blade is okay at 200 and 600 yards, but leads to large groups at 300 and 1000 yards, and a narrower one leads to elevation trouble through poor definition of its top at long range.

Redfield, Lyman and Griffin & Howe offer target type front sights with interchangeable reticules which will fit the Springfield front sight band special dovetail The front sight must be attached by a band or by screws to the barrel. The detachable model front sights are rather heavy, and the Redfields and Lymans of this type offer no advantage over the fixed type. The standard Vaver large globe detachable front is not heavy, but not suited to .30 caliber work as it permits use only of apertures, and both apertures and posts are necessary for military target shooting; unless the shooter is good enough to use the aperture offhand, which few are. Modification of the Vaver to use large reticules of the Lyman or Redfield style makes it a very fine front sight. The large diameter of the globe, or hood, is of great benefit in allowing the shooter to check his target number through the sight without having to move the rifle from firing position. The removable Vaver attaches to a small dovetail base which fixes to the barrel with two small screws, and makes for a low mounting. The size of the sight and the possibility of its being damaged while the rifle is in transit make the detachable feature worthwhile in this case.

The post reticule, like the plain blade, should be between $\frac{1}{16}$″ and $\frac{3}{32}$″ in width. The apertures, used for long range shooting principally, come in assorted sizes to suit individual preferences. They are rather thick walled for good definition on small distant bullseyes, an unnecessarily large one being required for practical use. A thin walled aperture, presenting a narrow ring around the bull, taking in most of the four ring on the target, gives better results. The reticule arms supporting the aperture should be horizontal so as not to obstruct the vision of the target number board.

Rear sights must be of the receiver type, with micrometer adjustments. The Vaver, with one quarter minute clicks, is to be recommended for the Winchester rifles. For Springfield and Enfield actions, the Redfield 70 or Lyman 48 are best. On these receivers the sights mount on the righthand side, just forward of the bolt handle when the bolt is closed, and if the Vaver is used, its large protruding knob does an efficient job of tearing knuckles during rapid fire. The Redfield comes with quarter minute adjustment, and the sight arm is not readily detachable. The Lyman comes with either quarter or half minute click adjustments, and has the sight arm readily removable. The Lyman "takedown" screw must be loosened for each adjustment in elevation, and must be constantly checked during shooting to be sure it remains tight. I have used both the quarter minute and the half minute type and prefer the latter.

Marble-Goss is producing a bolt sleeve sight for the Springfield with builtin spring plungers to return the sight to uniform location each time the bolt is operated. This looks like a good idea, and on a well fitted bolt should be quite reliable. It brings the peep aperture a little over an inch closer to the eye, which aids definition somewhat. Extension rear sights, popular on small bore target rifles, are dangerous on big bores, because of the possibility of recoil driving it into the eye or glasses.

Excepting a proper mounting job, no special work needs to be done on the receiver sight beyond a little file work on the windage scale plate. These plates are usually graduated with rather coarse lines, making it difficult to read the exact setting at a glance. Stoning down the top of the plate to reduce the thickness of the metal and consequently narrow the indexing marks is quite a pious thought, particularly with Redfield sights.

The peep disc itself is quite important since if it is of improper size it can nullify the effect of a good front sight. The adjustable Merit disc is to be highly recommended. Of the standard type discs, the Vaver is perhaps the best in definition with its thin diaphragm centers, having different aperture sizes available for different light conditions. However, it is no match for the Merit as a practical sight for competition, as the latter can be adjusted instantly while on the firing line, without effort or change of position of the shooter.

STOCKS

Good target stocks are easier to make than good sporter stocks. A few rules must be followed in construction, but there is little need for the very careful inletting and the artistic shaping desirable on the fine hunting rifle. A well fitting target stock is not particularly beautiful to anyone but the owner as a rule.

The stock blank should be absolutely straight grained forward of the pistol grip and of course be as well seasoned as it is possible to get and no forend tip of plastic, horn or wood should be attached. Hard, plain American walnut is as good wood as can be desired.

Inletting. Inletting of the stock for either target rifle, free rifle or bullgun requires first that the receiver be carefully bottomed in the stock so that all points on the bottom of the receiver will be supported. To achieve this, a slight clearance at the sides of the receiver is necessary in order to check the bedding. In other words, do not attempt to make the tight fit between wood and metal which is proper on the custom sporter. This is not to mean that wide gaps are to be left, but only enough tolerance to permit the receiver to fit into the stock without force. The sides of the stock must not exert tension against the sides of the receiver. Whenever possible it is best to inlet the receiver and triggerguard before the barrel is installed, the receiver first.

The recoil shoulder on the receiver should have ample clearance during inletting, after which the metal recoil plate is inserted through the stock and filed to full contact with the shoulder on the receiver, as for the sporter rifle.

The magazine and the triggerguard may be as carefully inletted as is possible, for good appearance and care must be taken that the underside of the guard tangs bottoms on the stock inletting so the screws will exert no bending action when tightened. Should ferrules be used in the guard screw holes through the stock—they do not need to be— shorten them enough so that they will not contact either the receiver or the guard when the rifle is assembled. Correct inletting of the guard is difficult only in its depth in the stock, for the magazine box should not exert any pressure against the bottom of the receiver when assembled. The top of the magazine box should be as close to the receiver as it can be without touching as no gap wider than $\frac{1}{64}''$ is possible without the possibility of the bottom edge of the magazine follower catching on the edge of the box and hanging up, particularly on the 1903 action.

Using the metal recoil plate in the stock practically eliminates danger of the stock cracking under recoil, so only slight clearance at the rear tang of the receiver is required.

Inletting the barrel is quite easy with any of the available barrel channel rasps. The cylinder of the barrel should be in full contact with the wood for all types of target arms. For the standard military barrels

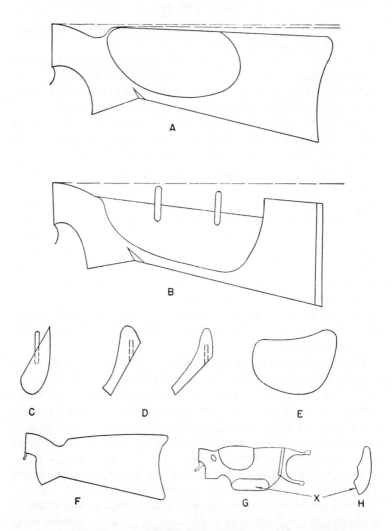

Target Buttstocks

On the target buttstock, the stockmaker and shooter must work out the best possible fit for the position the rifle is to be used in, or the best compromise for a rifle to be used in all positions.

A. The conventional target butt, with high comb and large cheekpiece. The top dotted line is parellel with the bore, and the lower line indicates the highest line at the heel.

B. Buttstock cut back from grip and pins or dowels installed for use with interchangeable cheekpieces to position the face as desired for different shooting positions.

it may be best to float the barrel from here on out to within two inches of the end of the forearm, clearing the wood to leave a gap of $\frac{1}{32}''$ between forearm and barrel at all points. The two inch section at the tip of the forend should be inletted to the bottom of the barrel closely, supporting the barrel for perhaps one quarter of its circumference and going away from the barrel on the sides. Put the front swivel in place and with one of the old spring type hand scales check the tension of the barrel against the forend when the rifle is assembled. Keep scraping the bottom of the channel at the tip until from eight to ten pounds will pull the forend away from the barrel.

More or less tension may be necessary for best performance of the individual barrel. Quite often Springfield barrels shoot very well when full floated, not contacting the forearm at any point forward of the cylinder at the breech. The wide $\frac{1}{32}''$ gap between barrel and wood facilitates barrel cooling.

The heavier target barrels, such as the two dimensions given, require less forend tension, or none. Most of them shoot best full floating, but it is wise to try the rifle out with some forend tension before going ahead and clearing the barrel all the way. If the rifle shoots very well and holds its point of impact with a little tension on the barrel, leave it alone.

International or bullgun barrels, which are still heavier, as a rule are full floated, although the inletting may be close on the barrel channel, since these rifles are used in slow fire only and cooling is not a problem. Also, these rifles may be made single shot only, with the magazines eliminated completely and no cuts made for them in the stocks. Straight strap triggerguards should be used, however, rather than individual receiver holding screws.

C. Cross section of buttstock at center, showing the maximum amount of wood which can be removed without too great a weakening effect.

D. Profiles of possible cheekpieces. These are of course to be cut to the individual's comfort.

E. Side view of cheekpiece.

F. Target stock with a deep cut top of grip, and reverse curve on the bottom of the grip.

G. A free rifle butt with all the trimmings: thumbhole, high cheekpiece, adjustable offhand buttplate, and—"X"—another rest, not for the cheek, but for the breast. Shooters with thick chests can park the butt across the body and gain additional support. Do not laugh—I saw a stock once which had this feature, and it was built around 1885.

H. Cross section of "G," showing approximate shape of such a stock.

Shaping of the Target Stock. Here again a few principles must be followed, but the shooter's individual requirements and preferences cover most points.

First, no Monte Carlo buttstock is ever to be used—keep the heel of the stock as high as possible and as straight in line with the comb as possible. The Monte-Carlo type is abominable in prone shooting and accentuates recoil. The straight stock is the most comfortable all around design. Pitch of the buttplate is to be figured slightly differently than as for the shotgun. Place the assembled rifle, with rear sight at approximately the 200 yard setting (peep disc removed) against a wall or your pitch cradle, and measure 36″ forward of the butt, marking the barrel with pencil at that point. Now, the correct pitch will be found to be 2″ from the top of the barrel to the straight edge of the wall or cradle, the buttplate contacting the floor or the end of the cradle at both the top and the bottom.

Second, do not use any form of recoil pad, unless of course the shooter is physically unable to withstand recoil of the .30–06 cartridge. The recoil of a 10-pound rifle with the 180-grain bullet loaded to maximum velocity is approximately 15 pounds and the rifle recoils approximately ⅛″ before the bullet leaves the barrel. A recoil pad will double this movement, with the effect of giving high and low shots, depending on varying sling tension during shooting. The Pachmayr and Fray-Mershon nonslip neoprene rifle plates are excellent, and the Niedner steel sporter plate is very good. I prefer it to other steel plates because it is curved in both directions and is sharply checkered. The factory target buttplates are not too good, for they are flat across and the edges seem to dig in under recoil.

Third, put around ⁵⁄₁₆″ or ⅜″ castoff into the buttstock. This makes the straight buttstock very adaptable to offhand shooting, without affecting comfort in the other positions.

Fourth, shape the cheekpiece to the customer's face, noting his position when holding the rifle in the offhand position, and cutting the cheekpad from there forward, making it slightly hollowed out but sloping forward a little. When the rifle is fired the stock should recoil away from the face, not into it. The head is held farthest forward in the prone and kneeling positions, back a little in sitting, and farthest back in the standing or offhand position. The cheekpiece should be comfortable in all.

Except for these "rules" there remains nothing but your and the shooter's ideas as regards the bulk of the stock, the size and the shape of the pistol grip, and the forearm detail. Generally, the stock should

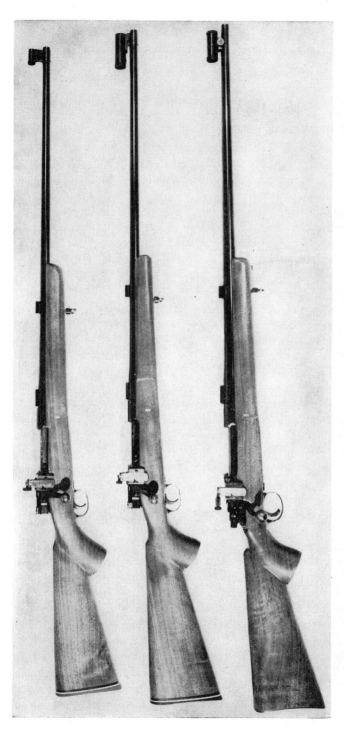

Three target .30–06s, upper two on 1903 actions, lower on 1917. All have 28″ Titus 12″ twist barrels, straight stocks, target sights. Receiver sights are Lyman 48s with Merit discs. Front sights, top, Lyman 17A, center, Goss, lower, Vaver W-11-B, modified for post or aperture reticules. All three rifles make the 10 lb. weight class. Note straightness of buttstocks. Stocks are of American walnut, the center one being stained, other two natural. All three rifles have trigger shoes.

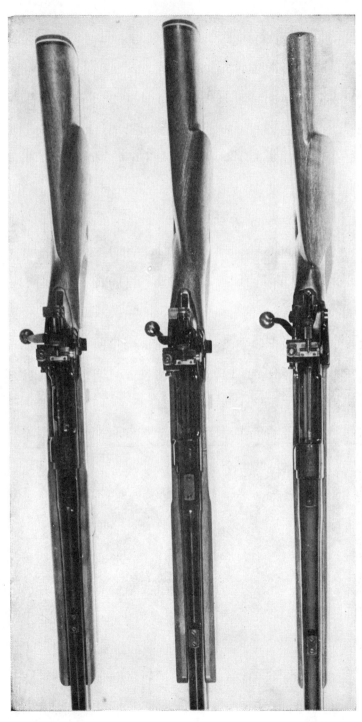

Top view, illustrating relative widths of forends and showing the concave cheekpieces faired forward. The rifles are comfortable to shoot in all positions. The two 1903s have headless cocking pieces and reverse safeties, and their bolt handles are shaped to allow the use of target telescopic sights. All three barrels are bedded to light contact at tip of forend, and are almost floating. Top of 1917 barrel is matted. Bolt knobs are matted. Top of 1917 barrel is matted.

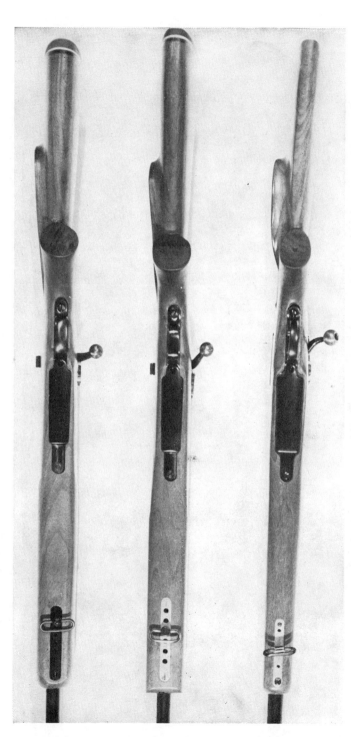

Bottom view of the rifles, showing clearly the differences in pistol grips, forends and lengths of stocks. The 1917, at bottom, has pronounced cast-off. The forend is quite slim, while on the other two definite target-type forends are evident. Note that bolt knobs are out from the stock, positioned for good handling in rapid fire.

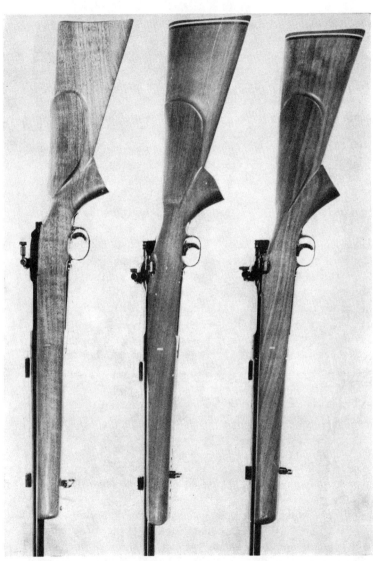

Left side view of same three rifles, showing individual cheekpiece and pistol-grip detail. These rifles were made to exact specifications to fit the individual owners, and while similar in design are definitely not alike. The recoil plates are clearly visible.

be about ⅜″ shorter in the butt than the shooter thinks he wants it, and the forearm and pistol grip a little smaller. Only shooting can tell, so have him try out the rifle with stock shaped as requested but only rough sanded. A large pistol grip which seems comfortable in slow fire will be a trifle clumsy in rapid fire. Coarse checkering is beneficial to the pistol grip and to the sides of the forend. The adjustable front swivel base is needed, for three positions of swivel will be used—forward for slow fire prone, central for rapid fire prone, and back for rapid fire sitting. The weight limit of the rifle may require the stock being slimmed down at all points possible, which to my mind improves the appearance considerably.

The very wide beavertail forend often is not too good for rapid fire shooting when the shooter has short fingers. However, some depth must be left in the forend, to keep the shooter's fingertips from contacting the hot barrel.

Handguards to prevent this can be made, being hollow shells of wood attached to the barrel cylinder by an inside narrow band—wire is satisfactory—and by an outside band or a clip at the forend. It must not be attached to the barrel or contact it ahead of the cylinder. Contact with the barrel may affect adversely the accuracy through interference with the whip or vibration during firing.

Finish of the target stock must be practical rather than decorative. A stock with a finish so smooth as to be slippery when the shooter starts to sweat is no help. I am not even sure it is wise to fill the grain on target stocks for this reason, although I have always done it in the past. Use linseed oil and shellac on the inside of the stock, and anything else you may have to seal the wood against moisture, except oil or grease. The outside finish can be plain oil, used conservatively (if repeated coats of linseed oil are applied, oil will cook out of the wood on hot days during rapid fire), oil and shellac, spar varnish, or one of the new plastic varnishes. If in a damp climate, wax it for a final touch. The whole idea is to maintain the status quo of the wood—keep its normal moisture content from drying out or more moisture from getting into it.

With the full floating barrels this is not too important, but should the forend warp slightly on a tip contact bedding job, accuracy suffers. Should the forend warp to one side, use the system of drilling small holes into the wood in the barrel channel as explained for sporter stocks, and scrape the channel at the tip to proper bedding. Should it warp up, cut the channel down. And if it warps down, away from the barrel, you may have to put in an inlay of wood at the tip, to restore proper tension on the barrel. In the great majority of cases, when a stock warps, it will remain warped to a large degree, even should atmospheric changes tend to sometimes bring it back where it was originally.

BULLGUNS

The bullseye rifle for long range prone shooting is considerably easier to construct than the all around target rifle. The barrel can be as heavy and as long as desired, with caliber anything the shooter fancies, from wildcat super 7mms up. The .300 H & H is popular, although the cartridge is poorly designed for modern powders. Various sharp shouldered cases—Ackley's super .30, long type; Weatherby's .300 case; the .30 Newton; and others offer higher velocities. High velocity is essential to the super accurate long range work these rifles are used for and the 14″ twist of rifling is to be recommended, with barrel lengths up to 32″.

Stocks need to be perfect fitting in the prone position only, with only one front swivel location needed—it is wise to install an adjustable base, however, because you will not know that one correct location without considerable trial.

A single stage trigger mechanism should be used, adjusted to about 2 pounds pull. Set triggers can naturally be used if the customer can use them. The rifles can be made without magazines, as they are used for single shot shooting only. Stocks should be bedded as for the target rifle.

INTERNATIONAL FREE RIFLES

Design of the true free rifle is rather difficult, in spite of the only ruling being that the rifle weigh less than 19 pounds 13 ounces. The rifle must be completely comfortable in offhand, kneeling and prone positions, for competition calls for 40 shot strings in each—it is a real grind, and for keeps.

The barrels should of course be as accurate as barrelmaking skill can make them, for the ten-ring of the target used is only 10 centimeters (3.937″) in diameter. This means close to one minute of angle accuracy at the standard 300 meter (328 yard) range. Because of the short range, in .30–06 caliber, the 10″ twist of rifling is appropriate, since ammunition need not be loaded to maximum velocity, as for 600 and 1000 yard shooting. Any caliber can be used although in this country we are handicapped by not having good target bullets available except in .30 caliber. Swedishmade 6.5mm match bullets are now being imported, so that rifles can be made up for this caliber. The 7mm and the .270 are also good calibers for such rifles, if suitable bullets could be found. High intensity magnum cartridges are not suitable, as recoil of the rifle must be held to a minimum, in consideration of the number of shots fired in each position.

The holding ability of the shooter governs to some extent the bulk of the barrel. The rifles should be muzzle heavy, but not so much so as to cause early fatigue. Lengths of from 26″ to 28″, with muzzle diameters from ¾″ to 1″, straight taper to the receiver diameter at the breech, or up to ⅛″ less, will cover nearly all individual preferences.

Front sights can be any of our standard target types suitable to the shooter. The Redfield Olympic mounts rather high, but it is otherwise satisfactory. Large hood front types are to be preferred. Apertures must of course be suited to the large—19″ plus—bull of the international target. Posts of ⅛″ width can be used, if the shooter does not wish to use the apertures at all times.

Rear sights can be the same as on the target rifles, except that possibly the ⅛ minute click adjustment Vaver might be found most desirable. It can be used on all actions, regardless of mounting position, since all shooting is slow fire. Vaver and Merit discs should be used. Extension rear sights can be used—both the Vaver extension type and the Redfield Olympic rear can be fitted to the Winchester 54 and 70 actions.

I would advise installation of target scope blocks, so that telescopic sights could be used in checking ammunition. These can of course be removed at any time. Cartridges for these rifles must naturally be not only very carefully loaded, but suited to the individual rifle and considerable experimentation is often necessary.

Triggers—set or not set—that is the question. I believe positively that set triggers are an asset, particularly in the offhand position. I also believe positively that a man to be skilled with the set trigger should not shoot rifles without set triggers. A shooter cannot expect to use a three pound trigger one day and a three ounce one the next and do so well. The trend today is away from the set type and toward the light single stage trigger with pull between one and two pounds. Whatever type of trigger is chosen, the shooter should practice with it only. I know of no first rate set trigger mechanisms available at this time. The Mauser and FN double set jobs are usable in a pinch, but that is about all. Occasionally a good trigger will turn up on a war souvenir rifle—I took an excellent three-lever trigger from a German 9 x 62mm sporter once. Only the rear-trigger-setting double set type is

OFFHAND BUTTPLATES

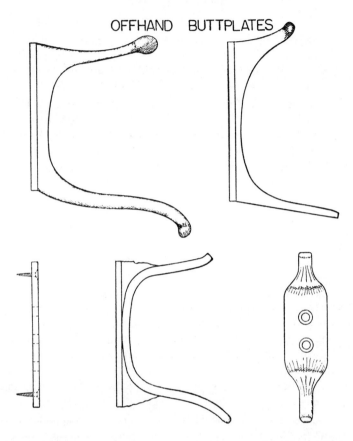

This style of plate is of practical use, in that it permits the use of heavy rifles in offhand shooting without producing rapid fatigue.

Upper left is the conventional Swiss, schuetzen, or free rifle plate.

Upper right, a modification of the same type which can be held at the shoulder joint as well as on the upper arm.

Bottom left, side view of the stock plate for attachment of various types of buttplates. It is fastened permanently to the stock with wood screws, and has a series of holes drilled and tapped in its rear face for the attachment of the buttplate proper.

Bottom center, sketch of fabricated offhand plate—a straight plate for a base is joined by welding to the curved arm piece. This plate can be made of brass rather than steel, if desired.

Bottom right, sketch of the rear face of the plate, showing the holes for the attaching screws. Perhaps the easiest method of making a special plate is to carve a model out of wood for use as a pattern, give it to a foundry and have them cast it in brass or bronze. It is desirable that these plates be rather heavy.

worth having for range use. With the single set or forward setting double type, the shooter must move his hand from the firing position on the stock to set it, which is highly undesirable.

Speedlock firing mechanisms with short striker fall and strong mainsprings are desirable on the free rifle. Any refinement of this type which is well engineered is beneficial. It must be remembered that any target arm, the free rifle in particular, will fire from ten to fifty times as many shots as will the sporting rifle and will be dry fired, or snapped empty, far more than it will be shot, by the serious rifleman. So trigger and firing mechanisms must be of the finest steels, to withstand much wear.

The stock of the international rifle is quite a special type. Not only must it be comfortable in three positions, but it needs to be equipped with adjustable Swiss buttplate, which can be moved up and down for offhand and kneeling and replaced by a conventional type for prone shooting. Also, provision must be made for the palm rest. The prone plate can be used for all positions, but the hook Swiss job greatly lessens fatigue in offhand shooting.

About 1930 the Europeans began to go in for the special pistol grip, featuring the hole through the stock for the thumb. This makes a very comfortable position for the righthand, but the real advantage is that such construction permits the cheekpiece to be carried farther forward. As with the target stock, some offset is desirable in the buttstock. Cheekpiece details are to be made as for the target stock, to provide comfort in all positions. Since the free rifle is to be used at one range only, 300 meters, the sights can be set and the cheekpiece accommodated to the shooter almost perfectly. With the target rifle, to be used at from 200 to 1000 yards, with a consequent rear sight raise of around $\frac{5}{16}''$, this is not possible.

A possible method of providing stock comfort and fit in the three positions is to use separate interchangeable comb pieces, including cheekpieces. These may be attached on slide pins, as shown in the drawing, and combined with an adjustable buttplate can be made to suit practically any shooter. I do not consider the German system of adjustable comb height suitable for the free rifle, as more than height is involved. Making by cut-and-try it will probably be found that three separate combs quite different from each other will be produced, each suited to but one shooting position.

The free rifle should be checkered wherever the hands will hold it. In the thumb hollowed pistol grip type, it is not possible to checker without great difficulty and in this area it is permissible to use a checkering punch or woodcarver's background tool to roughen the

PALM RESTS

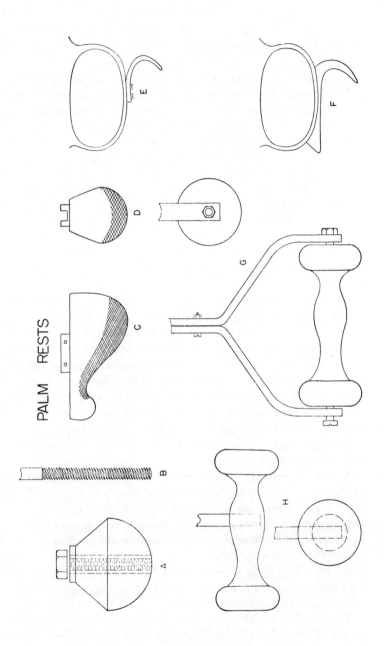

surface. The adjustable front swivel base is advisable for the prone shooting, and the type made by Remington for their Model 37 .22 match rifle is very appropriate.

Palm rests are a necessity, and range from a descending portion of the stock, ahead of the trigger, to detachable types of all descriptions. I am considering only free rifles built on bolt actions, incidentally. The single shot Haemmerli-Martinis formerly popular seem to be out of favor.

For the bolt actions it is wise to eliminate the magazine cuts and use a solid steel guard. Utilization of the standard guards, with removable floorplates, and using a separate floorplate as a base for the palm rest is not too good—the floorplate catches are not any too strong. The most common complaint about palm rests is lack of rigidity. With a straight one piece guard, made of $\frac{1}{4}''$ x $\frac{3}{4}''$ steel, palm rests can be attached by strong screws. Three of the most popular types of palm rest are illustrated. The ball type is made of wood or cork and turned to a

---

PALM RESTS

The palm rest is an old accessory to offhand and free rifle shooting. It was at one time used in the kneeling position as well as offhand. The idea is to put something on the rifle so that it is comfortable to hold, with the sights leveled at bullseye height, while the elbow of the holding hand is rested on the hip. Depending upon the individual shooter's physical makeup, the rest may be located from 2″ to 7″ below the bottom of the rifle, and from the triggerguard to a point several inches forward.

A. The round type rest, made of a wooden sphere 3″ in diameter, tapered from its diameter up to the top fitting, and with threaded sleeve and lock nut to allow up and down adjustment.

B. The threaded rod used with "A."

C. Close rest, or forend extension type, which is attached to the bottom of the triggerguard ahead of the trigger loop.

D. End view of "C," showing proportions. American shooters would be wise to try this type when first taking up free rifle shooting, as it is the next logical step from our standard hip rest offhand stance with standard target rifles.

E. Middle finger rest, which is sometimes beneficial to offhand shooting, particularly with set triggers.

F. Same thing, with rest run forward and the bottom checkered for the thumb. I saw a guard like this on a German .22 free rifle and thought it a good idea.

G. Dumbbell type palm rest. Made of wood, with steel strap frame and through bolts for locking in any desired position.

H. Dumbbell rest, with straight rod, which must be between the third and fourth fingers. These dumbbell rests are very comfortable.

3″ sphere, or the bottom half to a 3″ hemisphere, the top tapered off as in the drawing. Wood is better to use, as it is strong enough to hold the threaded fitting for the support rod. This type has an inch or more up-and-down adjustment. The butterfly nut serves to hold the rest tight on the rod and prevent it turning. Prevention of movement in the base fitting is by set screw in the fitting engaging in detents in the flattened portion of the support rod. The bottom of the ball should be checkered or carved to roughen it up.

The supplemental forend type of rest allows the greatest leeway for individual design. Depth is not adjustable, but can be made to suit the individual shooter. These should be checkered well where they contact the palm of the hand. This type is best suited to the extra floorplate type of attachment.

Last and perhaps newest version of the palm rest is the dumbell type, two of which are shown. Fitting the No. 1 to the stock can be done by installing a pin through the stock, or even several pins—these to be threaded sufficiently to take lockwashers and to hold butterfly nuts; or a vertical rib can be made integral with bottom strap of the guard and a base housing used. Adjustment can be had by swinging the rest forward and back, or a single rod used as with the ball with corresponding housing. Vertical adjustment can be had easiest by moving the upper section of the support in its housing. The No. 2 type is handled in this way. The vertical rib protruding from the bottom of the guard is of course highly useful on any type of palm rest for attachment reasons. Someone will no doubt go me one better and dovetail it, like an inverted scope rib, and so make things even easier.

I would like to make a few of these rifles, to experiment with different sights and ideas, but probably will never have time.

GENERAL NOTES

A few points to be mentioned—Mauser actions can be used for bullguns and free rifles, although only the newer types without the thumbcut in the left receiver wall are to be recommended. Mausers are too sloppy in bolt travel to be well suited to the all around target rifles.

When actions are to be rebarreled, use crocus cloth on the backs of the locking lugs to polish them, backing the cloth with a small mill file.

It is not usually necessary to use lapping compound on the bolt and work it in the receiver to smooth it up, if flat polishing is done at all the required points. There is no objection to its use, and it is practical to lap the extractor collar on the bolt that way. Valve grinding compound should never be used, as it is too coarse, and do not try to lap 1903 nickel-steel bolts with anything. The soft surface just will not cooperate with lapping procedures well enough to bother with. Polish dry, with #320 cloth strips, followed by crocus cloth and buffing wheel.

A Swiss gadget, now not used much but which free rifle experimenters may desire to play with is the barrel cooler. These are made of copper rod as close to bore diameter of the rifle barrel as they can be and still slide in, entering the barrel from the muzzle and reaching to the throat of the barrel, with from two to four round thin sheet copper discs attached to the upper end. These may be soldered very lightly to the rod. The idea is, the rod is slid into the barrel after a shot and the rifle stood in an upright position so the heat of the barrel runs up the rod and is dissipated rapidly from the copper flanges, or discs. Formerly these were used quite a bit in foreign matches, as the shooting was very slow and the shooters desired to maintain a more-or-less uniform temperature of the barrel, in order to prevent change of impact.

Use of the electric bedding device is quite practical on large bore rifles, and if all conventional bedding methods fail, or should it be desired to bypass the labor involved in trying them, the electric device is to be recommended. The two point support furnished will correct bedding troubles with heavy barrels in particular.

BENCH REST RIFLES

Since the end of World War II a highly specialized form of recreational marksmanship has developed, in the form of shooting from bench rests to achieve the highest accuracy possible. This has naturally resulted in the development of rifles designed expressly for the purpose. These rifles are either single shot falling block types, or bolt actions, the latter being by far the most numerous. Since most of the shooting is done at 100 yards, (rather an insult to a center-fire rifle!) high velocity .22 wildcat cartridges are used almost universally. The .22/250, .219 Wasp, .219 Improved Zipper and the Pfeifer .224 are popular.

Most of the information given in regard to construction of bullguns and free rifles is directly applicable to the bench rest rifle. Stocks are of course quite different as a rule, since they are to be used from a rest. Bulk is of no importance in the buttstock or pistol grip—cut them to fit the customer's comfort. Cheekpieces should be carefully shaped to sup-

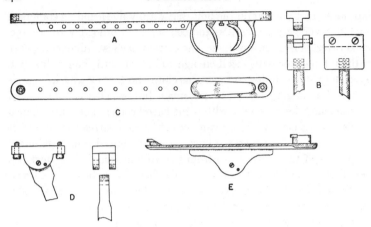

PALM REST ATTACHMENT

A few ideas on attachment of free rifle palm rests. The one piece straight triggerguard base is to be preferred, and the method of adjustment and locking may be worked out to the best advantage of the individual gun and shooter.

A. The double set guard, for a single shot rifle of bolt action type, with vertical rib on the bottom drilled for locating and locking holes.

B. Style of clamp for use on the above, showing locking screws.

C. A straight strap guard, with holes drilled and tapped at regular intervals to provide attachment and adjustment of the palm rest clamp.

D. The style of clamp and hinge fitting used on the above guard. Small screw is to lock rod in position.

E. Hinge fitting or rod housing sweated to the bottom of the floorplate for use on a rifle with regular magazine and triggerguard. The small screw is to lock the rest rod in position.

port the shooter's face in the high position necessary with the target-type telescopic sights used. Forends can be longer than for normal use by as much as 4″—and size is immaterial. Naturally, they must be large enough in width and depth to resist any outside force, and I believe a square type with rounded corners is perhaps the most practical. Bottoms can be either flat or slightly rounded and no sling swivel should be attached. Bedding should be the same as for the bullgun, since the barrels will as a rule be of equal weight.

The gunsmith should install all the mechanical improvements he can on these guns, such as single-stage triggers; tighten bolts, sleeves and cocking pieces in the receiver; make speedlock ignition systems, and so on.

While I do not consider a single shot bolt action any more accurate than one that repeats, assuming bedding to be perfect on both, there is no real reason for having a magazine in them. All shooting is single loading, therefore, the magazine well may be omitted in the stock, and straight strap style triggerguards made up. Do not cut off most of the box from Mauser and Springfield guards and inlet the rest—this gives a poor appearance and is a lot of extra work in addition.

Care must be taken with Mauser actions to bed them very evenly on the bottom so that there will be no tendency to bend the receivers by tightening the guard screws. A third guard screw is sometimes used, threading into the bottom of the receiver in front of the sear, but this is unnecessary if the bedding is right.

Should a magazine be desired, it can be made to operate reliably with the short cartridges in long, unaltered, bolt actions. The .22/250 and other rimless cartridges offer no problem, as blocking the box from the rear and using a short follower often is all that is required. Sometimes metal must be ground from the siderails of the receiver to permit proper placement of the cartridge shoulder in feeding from the magazine, but not always. (Same as altering the Mauser or other actions for cartridges larger than the military sizes, as in this case you are moving the cartridge further forward in the receiver well and so contact the heavy portions of rails designed to guide the original cases.)

The Wasp and other rimmed cases will not feed reliably from the Mauser-type magazines furnished for rimless cases. It is possible to make a double row magazine to feed rimmed cases fairly well—the British and Russians have done it for a long time—but to be sure, use the single row feed system, as the Mannlichers do. A single column magazine can be either curved or slanted to allow room for the rimmed cases to stack up. To build such a magazine, use the original box for a housing, then install a single width box fabricated of sheet steel and with lips shaped and bent like those of a .22 rifle box magazine, or a Winchester M43 clip. Your follower and spring design are obvious. Such magazines are easiest loaded if placed to the rear of the original box, which surrounds and supports the working magazine. Four cartridges are about all there is room for.

Bolt faces should be squared and polished, and in the matter of chambering, stick close to the minimum on the rimmed cases. Get the guy to make up his mind what brand of cases he wants to use and work accordingly; and tell him not to mess around with odd cases which vary in rim thickness—not if he wants to put all the bullets in one hole. Chamber necks should be minimum and case necks reamed if necessary to gain a close fit between the loaded cartridge and the chamber at this point. The usual fitting and polishing of firing pin tips is okay.

Because most of the shooters are very careful of their fired cases, strong and positive ejectors and extractors are not desirable. Stone the sharp inner edges of the extractor lips smooth, and remove entirely or block the ejectors so that the fired case may be easily removed from the receiver when the bolt is opened by hand, and not get slung out in the sand 10 feet away!

CHAPTER 34

The Garand Rifle

THE United States service rifle will of course be used by civilian marksmen in military rifle training programs and in government sponsored matches. Through the Director of Civilian Marksmanship, rifle clubs affiliated with the National Rifle Association can now obtain M1 rifles on loan for the use and training of civilian members. Naturally, the individual club men will want these rifles to be as reliable in functioning and as accurate as it is possible to make them, and this chapter is intended to be of assistance to these men. It is by no means authoritative, for we have just begun to seriously use the M1 rifle in match shooting and I expect the next few years to teach us much about the little details which mean accuracy. However, the tips on tuning up the M1 will be of definite value to the civilian just being introduced to this rifle. The information is taken from instructions by Mr. Garand, the inventor, and from Marine Corps data on adjusting the rifle for most accurate shooting, as well as from my own experience.

I will cover the M1 only from the rifle range point of view, for the rifle is not now open to individual ownership. The rifles legally in civilian hands are for instruction and competition on the target range only and do not belong in the hands of the hunter. If the 11 pounds plus of a loaded Garand with sling does not discourage hunting with the rifle, most state laws will.

The M1 is known to most civilians as the Garand, so we too will call it that. Unloaded, without sling, weight of individual rifles varies between 9 pounds 12 ounces and 10 pounds 3 ounces. Rifles as light as 9 pounds 8 ounces—the listed weight—are scarce.

Gas operated, this semiautomatic, or autoloading rifle balances quite well for offhand shooting and the stock shaping is excellent. The rifle "fits" nearly all shooters satisfactorily. Only long necked and long armed men will have much real discomfort in shooting, and they can lick this by lengthening the butt by a slip on or laced type recoil pad.

In the early days of its public life the Garand rifle received considerable adverse comment by the NRA and shooters in general, regarding its accuracy in particular. The military handling of the situation was characterized by the sterling stupidity so familiar in prewar brass, which did not help things. They claimed finished performance for the rifle before it was perfected or even thoroughly tested, and it was of course quite simple for experts to use the arm and disprove their claims. Most of the experts of course were sentimentally attached to the 1903 Springfield with its famed but untrue reputation of being the world's most accurate military rifle. The Springfield's reputation was made at Camp Perry's National Matches, with the National Match Springfield, which was definitely superior in every way to the Springfield *Service Rifle*. As an army range sergeant, I saw too many service 1903s which had difficulty staying in a 10" group at 200 yards, fired from a sandbag rest.

True, a good percentage of service Springfields could be rebedded and tuned up to match standards, but, as was, issued to line soldiers, they were distinctly not the rifle the civilian thought they were.

The issue M1 rifle is certainly no less accurate than the issue 1903 was, and civilians were able to make the Springfields perform to their satisfaction, so why not the Garand?

The sights of the M1 are far better than those of the 1903. The front sight is protected by wings or ears against being burred or bent by accidental dropping, the rear aperture being close enough to the eye to be practical and of decent size for all around shooting. No, it is not too big. In 1939 or 1940—I cannot remember which—the Ordnance Department provided a number of rifles for civilian marksmen at Camp Perry, equipped with different widths of front sights and different sizes of rear aperture. Together with military tests, that shooting determined the present size of the sights, which, I believe, is practically the same as specified by Mr. Garand in the original model.

With decent ammunition, the M1 rifle can be capable of shooting in three minutes of angle, which means perfect scores on any of the military targets. The M2 ball ammunition used today is third rate, and not productive of match accuracy in any type of rifle. A very few lots of wartime manufacture were reasonably accurate, but that is about as much as can be said for it. With good cartridges, the rifle will deliver. I know of several excellent long range scores credited to the M1, including a possible at 1000 yards, fired with match ammunition.

Early M1 rifles would not take too many high pressure cartridges, the action parts taking a beating from the recoil and fast functioning, but the rifles have been improved so that they will now handle heavy match bullets loaded to maximum velocity. The M2 Armor Piercing military cartridge is as rough as any handloaded target loading on the rifle, and apparently does not harm it.

Getting on to the rifle, and its maintenance:

FUNCTIONAL DIFFICULTIES

As with most repeating rifles, there can be two or more reasons for every type of failure it seems. While in the war I did considerable repair work on Garand rifles and found that there was a definite pattern to the maintenance problem. First, lack of cleaning of the gas cylinder sent most rifles to the armorer. In the damp climate of the Pacific islands, the chlorate priming compound of the cartridge promoted rust at a fast rate, and soldiers often were unable to clean the piston (the front end of the operating rod) so that it rusted and corroded undersize, this meaning that gas would leak past the piston. The result was that the operating rod did not receive sufficient impetus to the rear and would not recoil the bolt far enough back to pick up another cartridge. Substitution of a new operating rod usually corrected this failure-to-load malfunction. If new rods were not on hand, we would either repair the old one or, for a rush job, weaken the operating rod spring by shortening it slightly from the front end, so that the amount of gas being delivered was enough to function the mechanism; this by cutting the spring off about ⅜″ at a time and trying the rifle out. To repair the worn piston, the edges are ground on a bevel at front, then steel is welded on to build up the end, to sufficient amount necessary to permit cutting the end of piston square and smooth, to a diameter of about .527″.

Oversized gas cylinders occasionally turned up, which give the same malfunction even with perfect pistons at times. The remedy is substitution of another cylinder of correct boring, or building up the piston to fit it. Ordnance specifications call for an inside diameter of not over .5320″. There should be not over .005″ difference between diameter of the piston and the inside diameter of the gas cylinder. Do not attempt to make a close fit as a certain amount of gas leakage is necessary to prevent too abrupt action of the operating rod.

Second, in my observations in importance in causing trouble, was the bent follower rod, which caused the clip to be ejected on the seventh round. Some of these particular jobs were also affected by sticking follower slides.

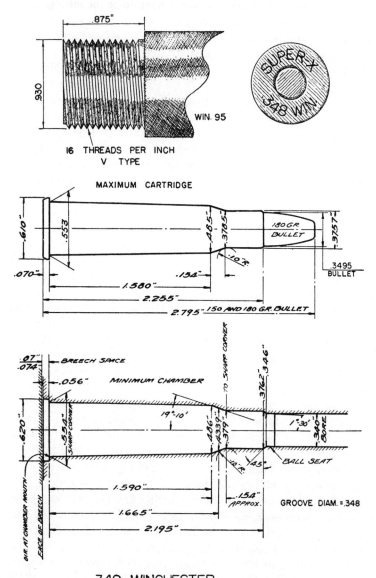

.348 WINCHESTER

The most powerful lever action rifle cartridge now made with a rifle to match it, the .348 is capable of stopping almost any soft skinned game animal on earth. Winchester's Model 71 rifle in this caliber is a modernization of the old 1886 action and is fast, reliable and strong.

The two above mentioned troubles I found to be the most common functional complaints from front line service rifles. Neither should be encountered in the civilian maintained M1, which should be kept clean and reasonably lubricated at all times.

Mechanical Troubles. The most annoying mechanical trouble with the Garand I found on rifle ranges in this country, and it has not anything to do with the rifle's performance. It was the excessive and energetic cleaning from the muzzle by range personnel, causing the wearing away of the rifling and consequently greatly impairing the accuracy. The rifle *must* be cleaned from the muzzle, which is not good, but is not very bad either. Use a smooth, clean steel rod, making only one or two passes with the wire bore brush and two or three passes with patches. There is no necessity for pumping a rod back and forth through the barrel a dozen times. With military ammunition, the G.I. bore cleaner is about as good a cleaner and light preservative as you can get. With handloaded or commercial ammunition no cleaning is needed for the noncorrosive primed cartridges unless the rifle is to be laid away for some time. Of course, the bore should be inspected for metal fouling and this removed by brush if found. The rifle should be taken down (the stock removed) and the operating rod and the gas cylinder assembly removed before cleaning. The end of the rod, (piston) should be wiped with bore cleaner or washed in water and dried, and the cylinder wiped out. The cylinders will not rust or corrode themselves but if not cleaned will affect the piston. The piston should be smooth, with sharp edges.

Mechanical failures due to the human element are reasonably common in military service, but should be few and far between with civilian M1 shooters—the latter will be better able and more inclined to keep his ammunition clean. He can disassemble the entire rifle for cleaning, keep the critical points sufficiently lubricated and if necessary, smooth up rough parts to insure reliable functioning.

The M1 rifle requires a certain amount of lubrication to operate

---

If the action were strong enough, the .348 could be necked down to .30 caliber or 8mm and surpass the .30–06 in velocity and energy. Pfeifer is making .270s and 7mm rifles on this case, using the best single shot actions.

The .348 is a knock down big game rifle for use up to 250 yards with the 150-grain bullet, at 2,880 FPS. The 200-grain bullet is perhaps the best heavy game bullet, with velocity at the muzzle of 2,520 FPS. The 250-grain loading, with only 2,320 FPS, has too much trajectory for ranges over 175 yards, unless the hunter is an accurate judge of distance and knows where to hold.

reliably for any length of time. If bone dry, the arm will function for a short time (24 to 48 rounds as a rule) but camming surfaces receive undue wear under this condition. The most critical points from the lubrication angle are the locking lugs on the bolt, the rear end of the bolt, and the cocking lug recess in the operating rod handle. These should have a light oil film whenever practicable although under very dusty or sandy conditions, leave them dry as much as possible, for the oil will pick up foreign matter and be worse than no oil at all.

Taking up the possible malfunctions in outline form:

Rifle Fails to Fire. Check to see if the bolt is fully closed as very often a very tight clip or dirty cartridge will slow up the feeding operation so that the bolt is not brought completely forward. Either hit the operating rod handle a glancing forward blow with the heel of the hand, or draw the rod back approximately two-thirds of the bolt travel and let it slam forward. Hold the hand palm up and use the little finger to move the handle. As with the Browning machine gun, on the M1 it is necessary to be on watch against the handle striking the hand by an unexpected firing. Whenever contacting the handle, do so in such a manner that no part of the hand or wrist is behind the handle in a position to obstruct the rearward movement of the protruding part of the handle.

If the bolt seats forward correctly and the rifle fails to fire, the hammer being heard to fall, examine the cartridge to see if the primer is indented in the normal manner—you may have a defective cartridge. If the primer is not indented or shows a shallow indentation, check the firing pin and the trigger housing parts for possible blockage or breakage of the pin or the hammer. If the trigger releases easily, and the hammer is not heard to fall, glance through the opening in the right side of the receiver to see if the hammer has not followed the bolt forward. If it has, check first for breakage or damage to the hooks on the hammer and for a broken sear. Damaged parts may possibly be filed and ground to operating shape, but they should be replaced by new ones if at all possible. Very occasionally, the safety may be loose enough to move of its own accord to lock the hammer. I met this condition once. Such a safety is defective and should be replaced by a new one.

Dirt or other foreign matter in the locking recesses of the receiver can prevent the bolt from closing sufficiently to permit firing, but this is usually obvious at a glance. A misshapen or battered cartridge also can cause the same trouble and is also obvious to the shooter, and, if the rifle has a worn piston and is not recoiling enough to pick up a cartridge from the clip, your chamber may be empty! Correct as mentioned for the first functional failure.

Failure to Feed Properly. Seventy-five percent of the time due to short recoil, as mentioned earlier. However, not only insufficient gas can cause the trouble, but also dirty or rusted moving parts without lubrication can cause sluggish functioning. Too, the gas cylinder may have been forced out of alignment so that it bears against one side or the other of the operating rod and interferes with its free movement to the rear and return.

In the matter of insufficient gas, the usual cause is as previously mentioned—a worn piston or an oversize cylinder. However, any blockage of the gas port in the barrel also can create the same condition—most often this is carbon building in the walls of the port and decreasing the diameter. The army method of cleaning the port in a hurry without taking the gas cylinder from the rifle is to run a few drops of oil down the muzzle so that it contacts the gas port, then fire a couple of shots, and repeat. This usually clears the port. When there is no objection to removing the cylinder group, the port can be reamed clean very easily. This gas port is .0805″ in diameter, and must not be enlarged because if the port is enlarged the movement of the operating rod will be speeded up on the rearward move and punish the action parts through too abrupt action. This may or may not affect the feeding, as the operating rod spring regulates the return movement. In some cases the spring seems to gain strength through the extra rapid compression and so causes the bolt to pick up the next loaded cartridge in a hurry and jam the bullet point against the edge of the chamber. To ream the gas port, take your micrometer and start measuring No. 46 drill bits. These are .0810″ in diameter if perfect, but more often than not will be undersize and you want one not over .0805″ in diameter. Touch the point to a grinder, or make a little collar to fit on the drill ¼″ back from the point to prevent the drill from marring the rifling of the barrel opposite the port.

A long ejector or one whose movement is blocked by foreign matter can prevent a cartridge from feeding properly. Unless the ejector can be forced flush with the face of the bolt, it will cant a loaded cartridge up, possibly jamming the bullet point against the rear of the barrel above the chamber. If protruding beyond the front of the bolt (rim or ring on the front) it will prevent a cartridge from rising to be engaged in the bolt.

If the eighth cartridge fails to feed properly, while the preceding seven have been handled properly, check the follower slide. If too loose, too tight, or blocked by foreign matter, the last round may not feed correctly. Very occasionally the follower itself may be worn to the point of binding or cocking in the guide ways in which it slides in the receiver, but as a rule, the follower slide is at fault.

In rifles having the valve type gas cylinder lock screw, any defugalty with the valve can affect operation by diverting gas from the piston. Check the valve spring to be sure that it closes the valve tightly in its seat, keep it clean and free of burrs. This type screw was made so that rifles could be used with grenade throwing attachment.

Loading Difficulties. If a clip of cartridges refuses to enter the receiver with normal pressure, first try another clip; the first may be bent or misshapen in some way. If the clips are okay, check the clip ejector as occasionally the point of the clip ejector is too long and will not depress sufficiently to permit ready insertion of the clip. More often, foreign matter will be found blocking movement, or the ejector will be found broken. A long point on the ejector can be ground down.

In a damp climate, the stock may swell and bind on the clip ejector. Bullet guides can be bent enough to interfere with the movement of the follower arm, but this is highly unlikely outside of military service. Prying or poking around in the action with any sharp instrument can raise burrs on the follower and sides of the receiver, to possibly cause parts not to work properly.

To load the M1 (right handed shooter) the right hand is held straight, fingers together, and the clip forced into the action with the thumb while the fingers are pointed downward, the heel of the hand being presented to the operating rod handle, so that if the operating rod should fly forward, it will be stopped painlessly before moving far and fast enough to injure the fingers. As the clip is seated, the heel of the hand presses against the handle, and prevents movement. After the clip is loaded, the hand is brought to the rear of the handle to allow the palm or the heel to be pushed forward and up on the handle and therefore allow it to fly forward, loading the rifle. This is not always necessary, as the handle may move forward as soon as the movement of loading the clip is completed and the hand removed. As the clip is engaged by the latch and held in the action, the bolt and operating rod should be free to move forward, but often the clip may be tight enough on the cartridges to cause the two to hang back. The slight tap or pressure upon the rear of the handle allows the bolt to move forward okay.

Failure or defect of the clip latch or its spring may cause the loaded clip to pop up out of the receiver, or may cause the operating rod to hang in the rear position. The clip latch cams the operating rod catch out of the engagement when the loaded clip is forced to the bottom of the magazine section of the receiver, to permit the operating rod to travel forward, closing the bolt and loading the first round into the barrel. Sometimes. Should a rifle give repeated trouble in failing to load the first round properly, check the accelerator and the operating rod catch and spring. It is very seldom that the hooks on the catch or rod are worn or damaged to the point of improper engagement or disengagement.

Ejection Trouble. A very rough chamber can bind on a fired case and cause difficult extraction and ejection. Keep the M1 chamber clean, using the special tool provided, or make a swab holder out of copper wire to allow thorough cleaning as the chambers are prone to rust much more than those of bolt action rifles.

If the bolt is not recoiled sufficiently to the rear, the fired case may be replaced in the chamber. A broken or jammed ejector can cause the rifle to jam, as the empty case is not thrown clear of the action. A broken, chipped, or jammed extractor will cause the same trouble.

Bolt Troubles. A rough bolt may have a binding action in movement and be sluggish in functioning, to cause failure to load properly. The rear section can be polished smooth with crocus cloth, and the front lugs stoned smooth with a slip-stone—(hard Arkansas white).

Should the bolt fail to remain in the open position after the last shot, several things may be wrong. The gas assembly may be carboning up so that an insufficient amount of gas is acting upon the piston; the operating rod catch may be bent, broken or blocked in its movement; or the clip latch may be out of shape. Rough, unlubricated camming surface on the hammer delays bolt functioning also.

If the empty clip remains in the gun, while the bolt is free in travel forward and back, the clip ejector is broken or jammed. If the empty clip is partially out of the receiver and jammed by the bolt, either the operating rod catch is at fault; the movement of the rod to the rear is being limited by insufficient gas, binding action upon the rod at some point; or the last cartridge was of insufficient power.

Sight Troubles. The front sight on the M1 can hardly go wrong, except that the gas cylinder, on which it is mounted, may not be a close enough fit on the barrel to keep the sight in one place. A light peening of the spline cuts in the barrel usually serves to tighten the cylinder and so prevent movement of the sight. The gas cylinder must not be fitted rigidly to the barrel, for best performance. Under rapid firing the barrel heats and expands much more rapidly than does the gas cylinder, and must have a slight clearance to permit this expansion.

There have been numerous modifications of the rear sight knobs, screws and pinions. The first model was held in adjustment by spring tension only, and it was found that under recoil the sight would "jump" and get out of setting. A nut was then installed over the windage knob, in the form of a cross bar to lock movement. This was okay, but required that the nut be loosened for each adjustment of the sight. In 1947 a new click system was worked out, and the cross bar dispensed with. The modern sights can be readily adjusted to any setting and will remain at that setting until manually changed.

Both windage and elevation adjustments click in one-minute-of-angle changes, meaning approximately 1″ per hundred yards—one click changing the point of impact 2″ at 200 yards, 4″ at 400 yards, and so on. Actually, because of the curved base of the aperture, the clicks have slightly less than one minute value at less than 300 yards, and slightly more at ranges of 900 yards or more.

The elevation knob may be zeroed at any desired short range—the rifle may be sighted in and, without moving the aperture, the knob may be loosened and moved to read 0 or 100 or 200 yards, whatever is wanted, then tightened so that the sight can be moved and returned to that setting at any future time.

A windage scale is stamped into the receiver below the rear sight, graduated into "points" which represent four minutes, or four clicks each on the windage knob.

TUNING UP THE GARAND FOR MATCH SHOOTING

No production rifle is satisfactory for match target shooting as it comes, save in very rare instances. We have to smooth up the trigger, check the sights and do what we can to improve accuracy through bedding and choice of ammunition. The fundamentals of making the Garand shoot to range standards have been worked out, but I am sure we will find out more of the fine points during the next few years.

First, we must have reliable sights, the front returning to the same position for each shot, its blade profile sharp and square, and the rear with round aperture, having no slack or play in movement.

Very little stock alteration is possible or permissible, excepting a slip on type of recoil pad for comfort in informal shooting and perhaps fitting the stock ferrule to better engagement in the lower band.

Triggerpull should not be cut to less than 4 pounds by the individual shooter, and he should carry a trigger weight around to check any loss

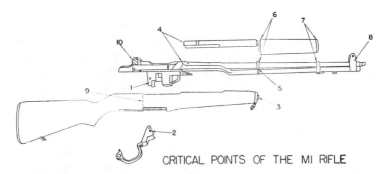

CRITICAL POINTS OF THE MI RIFLE

For maximum accuracy with the Garand, the rifle must be tightened at some points, and freed at others.

1. The little lug recesses in the receiver at point indicated must be in good shape, not battered or burred. It is seldom that these are damaged.

2. The small round lugs on the triggerguard, which engage in the recesses mentioned above. These must also be in good shape, for they engage in the receiver to hold the rifle tight in the stock, which is necessary to accuracy. As they are not of hardened steel, they do wear to the point of allowing the action to become loose in the stock.

3. The stock ferrule, the tip of which engages in the lower band. The tip should be a fairly close fit laterally, but should not contact on the end or shoulder. In other words, there should be a slight clearance—.020″ is sufficient—for movement back and forth of the tip in the band.

4. Junction of rear handguard and receiver should not be tight. Allow a slight clearance for fitting, and spread the clip so that it does not bind the guard too tightly to the barrel.

5. The lower band seems to be an important factor in the accuracy of these rifles: It should not fit too tightly on the barrel, but the holding pin should be tight enough to provide firm holding strength, to maintain its position.

6. The fitting of handguard to band is quite important. Enough clearance to offset expansion of the barrel must be provided.

7. As for 6, the ends of handguard must be relieved sufficiently to allow the barrel to expand without restriction from the heat generated in firing. The front handguard should be free enough to be moved back and forth perceptibly by hand.

8. The gas cylinder, holding the front sight, should be a tight fit at front, where the splines fit in the cuts in barrel, but should not be tight at rear band-barrel junction. The rear band of the cylinder is not to be a tight fit on the barrel, but the cylinder should be tight at front to prevent the sight from assuming more than one position.

9. The shoulders in the stock which support the rear side walls of the magazine portion of the receiver. These are as close to a conventional recoil shoulder as can be found in the MI, and should be in full contact with the metal when rifle is assembled.

10. The rear sight must be without side or knob play. It should be as tight and difficult to change as is possible without definite effort.

of pull weight. At less than 4 pounds weight, the hammer may jar out of contact when the bolt closes. Military specifications call for a minimum of 4½ pounds. Work with needle files and slip stones on the front hooks of the hammer to either alter the weight of the pull, or to reduce creep—(by "front hooks" is meant those in the front position when the hammer is cocked). The triggerpull of the M1 does not last forever, and should be checked fairly often.

Mr. Garand advises that a stronger mainspring improves accuracy, through cutting down lock time (increasing speed of hammer fall).

Should the shooter receive a new M1, I believe it wise to clean the metal parts in gasoline or solvent, and with the action parts completely dry and free of lubricant, fire two or three clips of ammunition. Disassembly of the rifle will reveal the points of friction on the moving parts, which can then be polished by stone and crocus cloth, after which the rifle is to be again cleaned in gasoline or solvent, dried and lubricated with light oil. It should then function smoothly and reliably.

Check the sights, and smooth up the triggerpull. In adjusting the pull on the M1, strive to achieve a crisp, clean letoff rather than a light pull.

The most noticeable improvement in accuracy is usually due to the attention given the handguards and the lower band in relation to the barrel. Neither of the handguards should ever touch the barrel, in fact, a clearance between the barrel and the guards of not less than ⅟₃₂″ at all points should be considered minimum.

The lower band should be fairly tight on the barrel, with the holding pin a very close fit in its hole and groove.

Neither of the handguards should be tight on the rifle—it should be possible to slide either of them back and forth slightly, and the ends which engage in the band should not be at all a tight fit.

The stock ferrule should not engage tightly in the lower band, and in particular should not be so long as to contact the sides of the band. There must be fore-and-aft clearance, to make sure that any barrel expansion in firing simply moves the band further forward on the ferrule without any tension of the stock being affected ot transmitted to the barrel.

The heat generated by rapid firing of the M1 rifle is enough to expand the barrel and lengthen it almost ⅛″. This means that if the thin barrel is under any tension from the handguards or band before firing, the tension will very probably be relieved as the barrel heats and stretches out—the result is change of impact during firing.

The gas cylinder may fit closely over the spline portion of the barrel, and should fit well enough to prevent any loss of gas between the barrel and the cylinder at the gas port area, but should be a loose fit at the rear ring, close to the front handguard.

Peening the spline cuts in the barrel is the old armorer's method of tightening the gas cylinder, but it is somewhat temporary—removal and replacement of the part for cleaning eventually loosens the joint again. Mr. Garand has advised plating the barrel with hard bronze or nickel to obtain a close fit between the barrel and the cylinder and with any electro plating setup the job would be simple. Neoprene plugs for the muzzle and gas port would be necessary, after which the muzzle end of the barrel could be lowered into the bath for 3″ for the plating to take.

Bedding the receiver in the stock may require the use of shims. No lateral movement of the rifle in the stock should be perceptible, and if at all possible, the rear walls of the lower portion of the receiver— sometimes referred to as the "magazine"—should bear solidly and equally against the wood. This is where the shims come in. The rifle should require some little strength to engage it in the stock, without involving the stock ferrule and the lower band tolerance. In other words, the rifle does not just fall into the stock, but should require a little pushing!

The trigger housing group holds the rifle together, the little lugs on the triggerguard locking in recesses in the receiver at the bottom rear, on each side. These lugs are soft steel and wear out of shape fairly rapidly, so that they exert less holding tension. They may be peened back into shape a couple of times, but eventually the guard must be replaced with a more serviceable one. In an emergency, small pieces of thin hard fiber could be used to make shims for installation between the guard and the stock, to keep the rifle tight in the stock.

The Garand rifle can be made accurate enough for satisfactory target work—at least enough so that the shooter or the ammunition can be blamed for poor scores, rather than the rifle.

Handloading M1 shooters can work up satisfactory short-range loads with 150-grain hunting type bullets, such as the A.B.C. which is capable of much better accuracy than the military M2 bullet. The M1 clip holds the cartridges more firmly than does the bolt action magazine, so that the points of soft nose bullets do not batter excessively. Also, short cartridges can be loaded and used as well as standard lengths. In experiments, 110-grain bullets have been loaded in .30–06 cases, seated to a very short overall length, and fired satisfactorily in

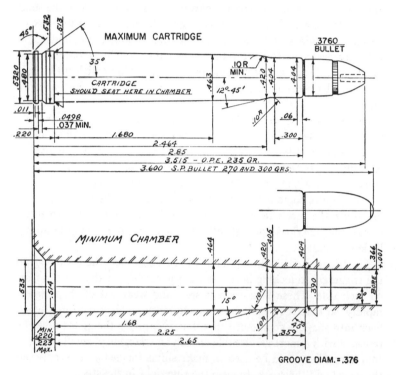

MAXIMUM CARTRIDGE

.3760 / BULLET

45° .632 .513

35°

CARTRIDGE
SHOULD SEAT HERE IN CHAMBER

.530 .480

.530

.011

.0498
.037 MIN.

.220

1.680

.463

12° 45'

.10 R
MIN.

.420 .404 .404

.10 R

.06

.300

2.464

2.85

3.515 − O.P.E. 235 GR.

3.600 S.P. BULLET 270 AND 300 GRS.

MINIMUM CHAMBER

.464

.420 .405

.404

.366
+.001

.533 .514

15°

.10 R

.390

2°

BORE

.10 R

45°

1.68

2.25

.359

2.65

MIN.
.220
.223
MAX.

GROOVE DIAM. = .376

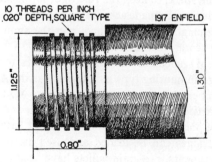

10 THREADS PER INCH
.020" DEPTH, SQUARE TYPE

1917 ENFIELD

1.125"

1.30"

0.80"

the M1 rifle. Long loaded 180-grain match ammunition can be fired satisfactorily by single loading.

In single loading the M1, the cartridge is inserted full depth in the chamber by the fingers, with the bolt held open and then the hand positioned as for clip loading, so that the thumb will be able to depress the follower and release the operating rod catch. The bolt will usually hang on the follower after the hand is removed, but will close readily when the operating rod handle is touched.

MATCH SHOOTING WITH THE M1

The civilian rifleman must do the best he can with the four or five rifles assigned to his club. He does not have a large number of rifles to disassemble and match individual parts for the best fit desirable for match accuracy, nor an assortment of new parts for replacement of

---

THE .375 H & H MAGNUM

This British-developed belted cartridge is the most powerful commercial cartridge loaded in the United States. It is popular all over the world in big-game areas, having quite a successful record on all heavy game, including elephants. Very fine game bullets have been made for it in Europe and England, while American bullets, designed for soft-skinned animals, are unsuitable for most African and Asiatic heavy game. The cartridge is low-pressured, by American standards, and requires a reasonably fast-burning powder.

Developing quite respectable velocity, the .375 has a practical hunting range of 250 yards. Recoil is not objectionable to most men, in spite of the heavy bullets used. Not generally known is the fact that the .375 is extremely accurate. It is rated with the .22 Hornet and the .250/3000 Savage as the most accurate factory-loaded hunting cartridges made today. As a rule a commercial .375 rifle will outshoot a commercial .30–06 rifle, both using over-the-counter hunting ammunition.

The length of the cartridge makes it require either a Magnum Mauser or Winchester 70 Magnum action, or a lengthened-out ex-military action. Neither the 1903 Springfield or 1898 Mauser are very suitable, though they can be used. The 1917 or 1914 Enfield is very suitable and requires a minimum of receiver alteration to accept either .300 or .375 cartridges. Headspace is governed on the belt of the cartridge head, of course, and there is very little trouble in headspace with the .375.

The only commercial arm made in this country for the .375 today is the Winchester Model 70. British bolt action rifles for the cartridge were formerly made on special Mauser actions, but at present the British makers are using 1917 or 1914 military actions. (These are the same, basically, the 1917 being originally .30–06, the 1914 either .276 or .303, although only a thousand or so rifles were ever made in the .276 caliber.)

worn or unsatisfactory ones. The rifle is to be tuned up as previously mentioned:

1. Front sight reasonably tight and maintaining the same position for each shot.
2. Rear sight without slack or free movement. (Spring steel shims can be used under the base sometimes, if the cover does not keep it fairly tight.)
3. Handguards and stock ferrule sufficiently free to not affect barrel vibration and expansion.
4. Action lubricated and clean.
5. Triggerpull smoothed and adjusted to not less than 4-pound let off. (The sear provides the stop, or final pull tension of the two stage pull, and it is possible to lessen the final pull by working on the sear as well as by cutting down the engagement area of the hammer hooks.)

In shooting the M1, the offhand or standing position is the same as with the bolt action rifle, except that the right elbow cannot be elevated as high as with the Springfield with comfort, due to the shape of the M1 pistol grip. In all positions with the Garand, the position of the left hand must be governed by the operating rod—the hand must either be forward against the sling swivel, or the fingers must be closed somewhat, so that the tips position below the operating rod.

For shooting in the kneeling position, a more forward position than that used with the bolt action rifle is recommended. The weight is shifted or leaned forward.

The same is true for the sitting position—lean forward as much as possible. A slightly longer sling loop is possible, as compared with the Springfield in this type of shooting.

In the prone position, better results with the M1 are obtained by a straighter position—having the body at less of an angle to the line of fire to the target. A slightly higher position than that used for the bolt action rifle usually is more comfortable and adds a point or two to the score.

The .30 caliber rifleman is more dependent upon a good firing position with the Garand than the bolt bolt action rifles. He seldom realizes it, but he is accustomed to regaining his position after each shot in rapid fire to some degree by the act of operating the bolt. With the M1 semi-automatic functioning, any incorrection in the position—wrong angle to target, left elbow not under the rifle, or right elbow too far out—must be corrected consciously during firing, for the recoil will push the shooter off the target in just a couple of shots. During rapid fire with a correct position, the front sight should at each shot rise the width of the bullseye above the bull, then drop to approximately half the width of the bull below it. The motion should be vertical—if the sight moves to either side, by the end of the clip the position will have been changed so that conscious effort and side tension on the forearm will be necessary to align the last shot or two.

A good rapid fire shot is a good rapid fire shot, but the best bolt action man will need some practice with the Garand before he begins to shoot possibles.

We are going to have to learn perfect positions first of all—16 rounds a minute instead of 10 does not sound bad when you remember there is not any bolt manipulation involved, but it is too blasted fast if you are off balance in any way at all!

CHAPTER 35

Testing Facilities and Apparatus

E VERY gunsmith should have some way of test and proof firing
repaired arms and remodeled or custom jobs. Some sort of range
or butt should be right in or alongside the shop, for many repeating
arms, particularly .22 rifles and pistols, cannot be well tested for functioning with dummy cartridges, and in the case of an autoloader which
occasionally malfunctions, it is sometimes necessary to fire 60 or 80
rounds during a job.

A simple indoor butt or backstop can be made of empty wooden shell
boxes filled with sand. First throw an old sack or piece of cloth in the
box, then put on a two-inch layer of sand, another cloth or rag, then
more sand, and repeat until filled. Nail the lid back on, and tack a
cardboard cover on the bottom as well. You shoot into the bottom, and
keep replacing the cardboard as it gets shot up enough to allow sand to
leak out. The cloths are to help keep sand in the box. A 10″ backstop of
this type is sufficient for .22 rifle and all pistol testing. If you must
proof fire large rifles in the shop, tear a hole in the floor over in the
corner of the room and run a 4″ metal pipe from the floor into the
ground underneath. If there is a basement, put a barrel of moist earth
or sand underneath the pipe to catch the bullets and tack cloth of some
sort over the top of the barrel to keep the contents from splashing out
when the bullets hit it.

Indoor and short range bore sighting was covered pretty thoroughly
earlier so now let us talk about outdoor sighting. The gunsmith should
belong to rifle clubs which have all caliber ranges; make arrangements
with some farmer for a shooting area; or rent, lease or buy sufficient
land for a private range. A bench rest should be set up to allow sighting and testing up to 200 yards at least. Very often a customer who
has new metallic sights or a telescopic sight mounted wants the gunsmith to adjust them or it for a specific range with a specific cartridge
and sometimes wants to go along himself for instruction in adjust-

668

ment; so as long as he is willing to pay for the ammunition and your time, that is okay.

On the bench rest, use one large sandbag and keep three or four small ones handy. These will allow comfort in position for almost all rifles and customers who are not used to the low position of proper bench rest procedure. Keep a couple of pieces of cotton blanket to throw over the bags and the top of the rest to protect the finish of new rifles, and remember that the small bags can be arranged to support either one or both hands in testing handguns.

If any doubt exists that the rifle will be on the 200 yard target at the first shot, set up a target at 25 or 30 yards first, and shoot at it because when a rifle hits close to center at this short range it is practically always on the 200 yard target unless muzzle velocity is very low.

The custom gunsmith, or any gunsmith who fits barrel blanks, should use the bench rest to test rifles for accuracy, particularly when wildcat calibers are involved and should the bench rest be considered not accurate enough, the shooting rests illustrated can be made up, at low cost. These are made to give the most perfect performance possible for a complete arm, the only human error which might occur being in the sighting. However, differences in holding are eliminated, and the natural tensions on the arms are simulated exactly each time. On the rifle rest, sling tension is exactly the same for each shot, and with the pistol, the gun is free to recoil exactly the same for each shot. For ammunition testing, these rests are highly recommended and shots can be fired quite rapidly, with little fatigue to the shooter. I made up and used one of the rifle rests about 15 years ago for testing match rifles and ammunition and found it very worthwhile. When a target telescopic sight of considerable power is used, the error of aim is almost eliminated and true accuracy tests can be made. The genuine machine rest allows only comparable accuracy tests between different varieties of ammunition within a caliber, and high accuracy tests are made with the Mann type rest which calls for a very heavy cylindrical round barrel. Completely assembled rifles cannot be tested very well. The shooting rest illustrated can be made by any gunsmith or rifleman without straining the bank account, it can be portable, and it delivers the goods.

The rifle rest must be instantly adjustable, so the rifle can be mechanically aimed for each shot, in accordance with the shooter using the sights on the rifle at an established aiming point. The pistol rest needs less refined adjustments as shooting will generally be at short ranges and you will find that it will be necessary to sight the pistol

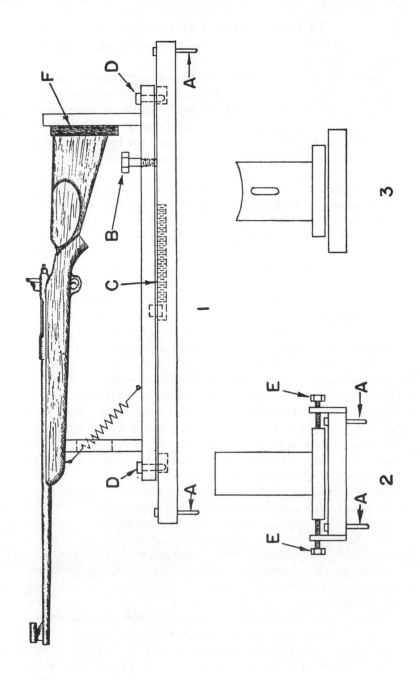

1

2

3

from 6" to 18" below the grouping point in most cases, since handguns "jump" when fired, and the barrel moves upward before the bullet leaves. The rest arm can be weighted to correspond to normal arm "hold down" tension if desired.

Both of the rests must hold the arms under simulated human tensions to some extent. The rifle must have its recoil arrested both by the spring tension on the sling swivel and the spring and rubber butt support and the whole carriage or supporting arrangement should be able to recoil with the rifle as one unit at the same time. This movement should not be over 2", as a man shooting in the prone position, to which the shooting rest corresponds, does not move further than this when a shot is fired, even with a heavy rifle—anyway, the bullet is out of the barrel after the rifle moves a very small fraction of an inch, so this is really a minor point. The carriage really does not have to slide, this is only to prevent possible straining of the rifle stock through repeated recoil absorption. Accuracy will not be improved through the sliding carriage, so for rifles of light recoil, a fixed carriage is satisfactory, using only the sling tension and tension supported buttplate to take up recoil.

Pistol recoil is absorbed mainly by the inertia of the arm itself and

---

RIFLE SHOOTING REST

As described in the text, this is a sort of jig for holding a rifle for accuracy tests. The rest is adjusted to sight the rifle correctly for each shot, should recoil throw it slightly out of alignment. Which it will. The rest simulates the position of the rifle when held in a normal prone position. This type of rest will give a true check of either rifle or ammunition accuracy.

A. These are large bolts or pins in the fixed base of the rest, to engage in holes in the bench rest or shooting table.

B. This is a large screw or bolt threading through the movable base and bearing against the fixed base, to give elevation adjustment. Two should be used, one on each side.

C. A heavy recoil spring in recess in fixed base, to resist movement of the entire movable assembly through stud or projection in the latter.

D. These are bolts or studs moving in slots in the fixed base, to keep the movable assembly in line when moved to rear under recoil.

E. On Figure 2, these are bolts threading through fixed brackets on base to bear against the movable base and give lateral adjustment. This is a rear view of course.

F. Socket for butt. Should be made of heavy leather lined on sides and rear with sponge rubber.

G. Figure 3 shows only the front outline, illustrating the top of forend support, and slot for spring which gives sling tension.

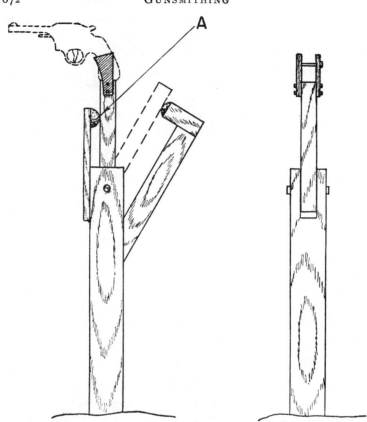

A

PISTOL SHOOTING REST

the swinging support arm moving back. The only pitfall with this rest is failure to secure the frame of the gun to the arm tightly. It is absolutely necessary to inlet separate clamp jaws for each different revolver or pistol butt and the stocks must always be removed.

Should it be necessary or desirable to get rid of possible human error in pressing the triggers, a rubber tube with bulbs on each end, one to fit into the triggerguards in a partially collapsed condition, can be used. You put one bulb in the guard and squeeze the other and this moves the trigger without quivers, shakes or jerks.

The general gunsmith will have little use for a chronograph, but the man working on cartridge development in either the interests of customers or himself should definitely have one. The Owen chronograph, sold by Hollywood Gun Shop, is priced low enough to be within the reach of any interested party. We would not have half the wildcat cartridges now kicking around if the originators had had chronographs available to find out just what they had without optimistically estimating the velocities they thought were present by shooting across the canyon, lake, or other typical "practical" test.

There are many factors affecting velocity of a bullet. The shape is not of much importance in muzzle velocity tests, but the temperature of the air, of the cartridges and of the gun does affect velocities. The bore and groove diameters are also important, and to some extent, the tolerance of the chamber as a tight bore and tight chamber will give a higher velocity reading with the same cartridges than a worn barrel and loose chamber. The length of the barrel is important, even $\frac{1}{2}''$ being enough to increase or decrease velocities. Different lots of the same powders react differently, and even different primers can show a change of velocities. Bullet jacket hardness, and bullet compressibility (overall hardness of the bullet) as well as diameter differences affect velocity readings—and the chronograph must be kept regulated.

The portable Owen chronograph opens up an opportunity for the gunsmith and the private firearms investigator. Not only can muzzle velocities be determined, but large screens can be set up for various ranges and velocities at 200 or 600 yards can be found, so that different bullet shapes can be tested to see how each maintains velocity. The word "screen" is perhaps wrong, as the Owen set up calls for breaking two current carrying tapes with the bullet. However, any arrangement which allows a bullet to break two light electrical contacts cleanly can be used. Most testing will be done with the tapes 20 feet apart—and be sure they are just exactly 20 feet, too, not an inch over or under.

RELOADING ITEMS

The practice of reloading ammunition is now so widespread that all gunsmiths should be familiar with it to some extent. Tools, accessories and components—bullets, powders and primers—will be fairly profitable items to carry in stock, but the gunsmith must be able to advise customers starting out in the game. The handbooks published by Lyman and Belding & Mull are valuable, but there is no real textbook on reloading worth having at the moment. All now on the market are rather obsolete, being principally devoted to components no longer available.

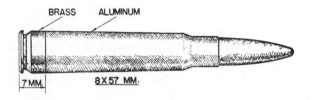

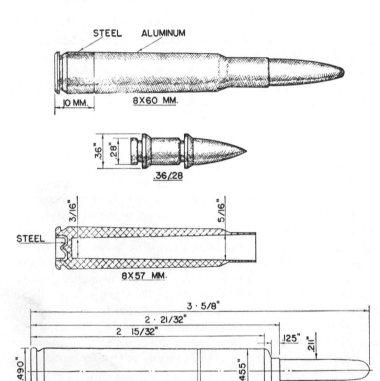

NEW AND OLD IDEAS

Just a few advanced cartridge case experiments.

Top, a German military experimental with aluminum case and brass head. The overall dimensions are the same as for their standard 7.9mm, however, the case has a central flashhole, as for American primers.

Next, another German aluminum body case, with steel head. This had their regular Berdan primer pocket. Case body dimensions are the same as the standard 7.9mm, but the neck is made 3mm longer.

A two diameter projectile, or bullet, made for a taper bore high velocity

There are a number of small gages and tools which the gunsmith can make up quite easily for individual handloaders, such as overall snap gages for cartridge lengths, the same for bullets, diameter gages for bullet selection, punch sets for reshaping government .30–06 primer pockets so they can be reloaded, and such. The illustration shows these simple gadgets.

The snap gages are sawed out of flat stock and filed to the correct inner dimension and they can be either blued or plated to resist the rust caused by handling. The bullet gages are harder to make, as each hole must be lapped to the correct diameter desired. Letter drills work out for a few calibers, and fractionals can be sharpened with the point off center to cut close to other desired calibers. Always cut the hole a little undersize, bevel both edges then lap the hole to the correct size. Bullets can often be chucked in the drillpress, coated with oil, and lapping powder, and used to lap out the holes. To check diameters, pound lead slugs into the holes, push them out and mike them. I have made several calibers on one piece of metal, but believe it best to make one gage for each caliber, say for .257 loading, one hole with diameter of .2570", the other two, say, .2568" and .2572", to check for bullets over and under the desired size.

The punch sets are very useful to those who use G.I. ammunition and wish to reuse the empty cases, which are very strong and durable.

---

rifle. This was made before World War II in an American factory, incidentally, and it is solid bronze.

The sectioned case is another German idea, this being all aluminum, with a steel cup pressed into the head for a primer pocket. Note the shape of the combustion chamber. You could use a fast burning powder in it, if you did not mind losing rifling rapidly.

At the bottom is a drawing of the 5.5mm Mondragon cartridge, thrown in to confound Californians and other sharp shoulder addicts who think they are ahead of the times. Note the dimensions of this case, think of the powder capacity, then look at that shoulder—and the date on the head of the case is 1894!

This cartridge is little known, even among collectors, and several stories about it are told, one being that it was designed for a machine gun or machine rifle, with the bullet seated deep in the case—a cardboard or other wad being held below the cannelure on the case, after which the case was necked down and the bullet seated, forced all the way back to this cardboard, so that only the nose protruded from the case. Another is that it was loaded as shown, for rifle use, but that at that time they had no powders which would make the cartridge perform without devouring the rifling rapidly. I do not know whether the Mexicans or the Swiss worked out the cartridge, or why.

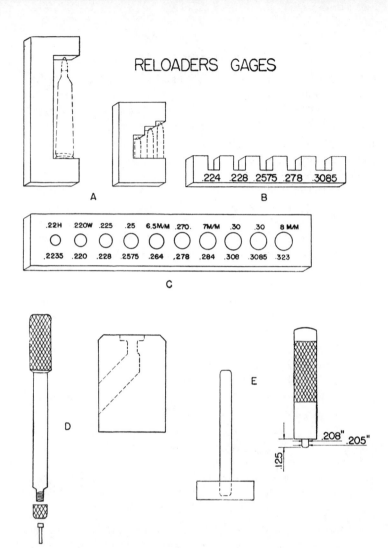

RELOADERS GAGES

.224 .228 .2575 .278 .3085

A   B

.22H	220W	.225	.25	6.5M/M	.270	7M/M	.30	.30	8 M/M
.2235	.220	.228	.2575	.264	.278	.284	.308	.3085	.323

C

D   E

.208" .205" .125

Reloader's Gages

These are a few items which can be made up for handloaders. All can be varied to individual prescription of course.

 A. Length gages for cartridges and bullets, made of ¼″ flat stock. Can also be made for cases only.

 B. Diameter gage for bullets.

 C. Diameter gage for bullets, with holes lapped to desired diameters. Harder to make than "B," but easier to use.

 D. Punch and base set for removing crimped-in primers from fired government cases.

 E. Punch and base set for reshaping primer pockets of decapped government cases.

Con Schmidt used to furnish these, but I have been led to understand he will not make any more, so the general gunsmith can perhaps supply the demand. The bases and anvil are simple turning jobs, the primer pocket punch not so simple. When turning the tip of this punch, try to get the little taper on the lathe, using a pillar file for the final shaping. Make the radius at the top, between the tip and the body of the punch, very small because if much of a radius is left, the punch will tend to force the case metal down around the edges and tighten it on the tip of the punch. File until within .0002″ of size, then use fine cutting cloth and crocus to polish the tip and cut it to size. Try it in a few cases, hammering it in and wriggling out, and then prime those cases to make sure that the primers go in without undue pressure. Then harden and repolish. An unhardened punch made of plain drill rod will last for a couple of thousand cases.

Bullet seating punches can also be made without great effort, to suit a particular bullet nose and it is not necessary to harden these. Straight line bullet seaters can be made from old barrels, if the correct chambering reamer for the caliber is available. About a 7″ length is right, this barrel section of the same caliber as the one the seater is for. Ream out the rifling until the bullets are a slide fit through it, then run in the chambering reamer to accommodate the cartridge. The chamber may be cut to completely accept the cartridge, or about ¼″ short, in which case a separate metal base is turned and counterbored to take the protruding base of the cartridge and support it. The bullet seating rod is turned from drill rod or other steel rod, counterbored to accept the desired bullet point on one end and slip into the bored out barrel section. The other end is threaded and a thick washer threaded on it first, then a short cylindrical handle or knob threaded to also screw down. The rod can be adjusted up and down to allow for different bullet seating depths, or overall cartridge length, whichever you want to call it. These seaters are theoretically the most accurate and so are fairly popular with handloaders.

There are many small items the gunsmith can make for testing various points on arms—bore gages for checking barrel diameters or degrees of breech wear in a hurry, button gages for checking headspace in rimmed or belted cartridge rifles, sets of pins for checking firing pin hole diameters, and so on. Bore gages are short cylinders of polished steel of the desired diameters. It is a good idea to thread a smaller rod into one end, so that they can be pushed slowly through a barrel, and successively smaller ones into the breech end to check bore wear.

Make any tool you are sure you can use, but do not become a gadget happy gunsmith, whose greatest delight is finding an excuse to make a new jig, tool or gage. There are too many boys who are always willing to spend a day or two making some such doohickey to take care of a five dollar job, when another such job will not turn up for 10 years. There are usually more gadgets in gunshop drawers now which the maker has forgotten the use of than there are worthwhile tools.

METAL TESTING EQUIPMENT

With today's high pressure cartridge developments, the gunsmith is wise to check the hardness and strength of the steels used in the assorted actions and parts he must use. The Rockwell Hardness Tester is perhaps the most common bit of equipment used in this connection but as the instrument is expensive, only large shops will have enough call for its services to warrant purchase. The small gunsmith can usually make arrangements with some local machine or tool shop which has the equipment to take care of his occasional job.

All of the hardness testing machines tell only the surface hardness of the metal tested, which is often misleading. Mauser receivers are particularly troublesome to check, because of the great variation in the steel and the heat treatment. Some are exceedingly hard on the surface yet quite soft under the case-hardening or carburized skin, others are soft, but tough, and still others are just plain soft. When a Mauser receiver checks out on the soft side, do not throw it away before putting in a barrel and running a batch of proof loads through it to see if it sets back. If it would seem to be too hard and therefore possibly brittle, stick on a barrel and try to blow it up. If it takes 10 proof loads, it will undoubtedly be safe for any standard cartridge. If at all possible, use the .30–06 cartridge for proofing actions. I consider 58 grains of 4320 behind a 180-grain bullet a decent proof load. Test the receivers for hardness on the receiver ring, and the bolts on the locking lugs and the body of the bolt between the two front lugs.

The Rockwell machine C scale is used for hard metals, with a conical diamond point backed by a load of 150 kilograms. A weight at the rear of the machine on a compound lever applies the pressure at first, then it is removed and the small initial load left on the penetrating point. The depth of the impression is read on a built in dial gage as a scale of hardness.

For soft metals, a $\frac{1}{16}''$ ball point is used with an initial load of 100 kilograms, and the hardness read on the "B" scale.

ROCKWELL HARDNESS TESTER

This instrument as set up at the Pfeifer plant to determine hardness and co-related strength of rifle actions. Illustration shows an FN mauser action being checked for hardness of receiver ring and lug wells.

THE BENCHREST

Indispensable to the experimental shooter and hand-loader, a benchrest is very worthwhile for the gunsmith as a means of final sight checking and setting, particularly when telescopic sights are involved. I designed this one and consider it the best type. The separate seat eliminates much of the human element—weight shifting, involuntary muscular movements of the legs, and similar tremors. Bench legs are set a foot or more into cement-hard Arizona caliche earth. The rest is of course quite rigid.

A conversion table is given for the four hardness machines. The Brinell and Vickers systems have been widely used in Europe, while the Rockwell seems to be gaining popularity in this country. The Rockwell is fastest and easiest to use, and by far the most practical for gun work.

HARDNESS CONVERSION TABLE

Rockwell C 150 kg.	Brinell 3,000 kg. 10 mm	Vickers	Shore Schleroscope
70	780	1150	106
68	745	1050	100
66	712	960	95
64	682	885	91
62	653	820	87
60	627	765	84
58	601	717	81
57	578	675	78
56	563	654	76
54	530	615	73
52	514	567	70
50	495	540	67
49	477	515	65
48	462	501	64
46	444	472	61
44	415	437	57
42	401	420	55
40	375	389	52
38	363	375	51
36	341	350	48
34	321	327	45
32	302	305	43
30	285	287	40
25	255	256	37
20	223	223	32

To give a few hardness readings—(Rockwell C):

Nickel-Steel Receivers	40 to 44
Nickel-Steel Bolts	43 to 47
Carbon Steel Receivers	34 to 39
Carbon Steel Bolts	36 to 40

This is a safe range for high pressure cartridges.

MUZZLE BRAKES & COMPENSATORS

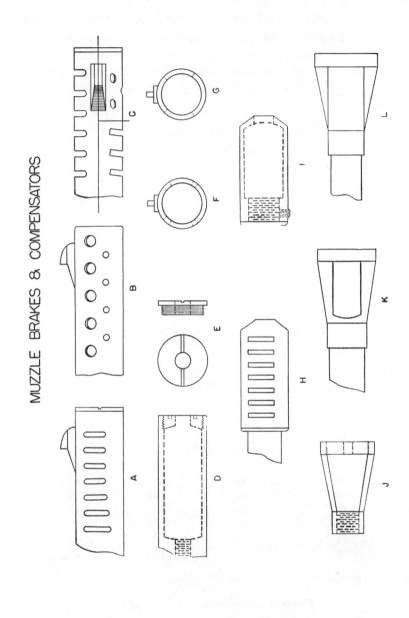

The Brinell apparatus uses a hardened steel ball, 10mm in diameter, which is forced with a pressure of 3,000 kilograms into the metal to be tested, on a flat surface. The pressure is held for 10 seconds. The impression made is measured by a microscope, the hardness reading being determined by dividing the pressure (3,000 kg.) by the area of the impression. For soft metals, a 500 kilogram pressure is maintained for 30 seconds. The Brinell system is not suited to testing irregularly shaped objects such as gun parts. I have had no actual experience with it at all.

The British Vickers Pyramid Hardness Testing machine uses the same idea as the Rockwell, but using a pyramid shaped diamond point only, and the depth of the impression is taken with a calibrated microscope built into the machine.

The Shore Scleroscope is somewhat different, and while used as a hardness tester, is really for measuring tensile strength of the metal

---

MUZZLE BRAKES AND COMPENSATORS

Mean the same thing. Shown at the top rows of this drawing is my idea of a built in compensator, machined into the end of the rifle or the pistol barrel (pistol barrel shown). I believe there is a limited application for this principle in .22 autoloading pistols for use in rapid fire matches of the Olympic type.

A. Side view, showing slotted sides, the slots being above center so that escaping gas has a tendency to hold the muzzle down.

B. Side view, showing gas escape ports round, made with drills. Holes arranged to hold the muzzle down in firing.

C. Composite top view, showing styles of gas ports—round holes, square slots, and raked slots.

D. Sectional view, showing how the barrel is bored out. Walls should be left approximately 1/16" thick. The muzzle plug is threaded in—with a spanner wrench in this case.

E. Easier made muzzle plug, with slot across the face for installation and removal. Bullet escape port should be approximately .003" larger than diameter of the bullet.

F. End view of "B," showing approximate hole positions.

G. End view of "A," showing approximate slot positions.

H. Conventional muzzle brake attachment, side view.

I. Sectional of same, showing the threaded section at the rear for attaching to the muzzle of the rifle barrel, and set screw for holding it.

J. Sectional of modified artillery type muzzle brake, applicable to rifles.

K. Side view of same.

L. Top view. This type brake has been used abroad on special types of small arms, such as antitank rifles. It has the advantage of being very light in weight.

STRAIGHT LINE BULLET SEATER

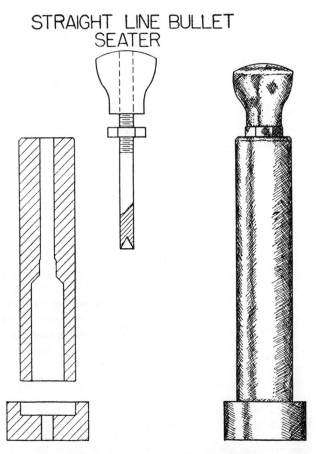

The straightline bullet seater is beloved of painstaking reloaders, and you can pick up odd dollars now and then making them. Make one every time you have to check a chambering reamer after sharpening. Regular chambering reamers are used, but in some cases it is necessary to lap the seater out to take unsized cases freely. The seating rod is to be cut to fit the bullet nose involved, though as a rule only the cavity for the spitzer bullet is necessary for any type. The bore of the seater should be reamed and polished until the proper bullets are a slip fit in it. Bases may be turned to form a socket seat for the base of the seater, or just be a flat plate to support the cartridge base in the chamber. A small cut may be milled at one point of base of seater to allow use of a screwdriver to pry out an occasional stuck cartridge.

tested. A glass tube is held vertical on the work, with a steel cylinder having a hardened steel point inside. This is called the hammer, and it is dropped down the tube against the work. It rebounds, and the distance of this rebound, gaged against a scale on the tube, gives the reading. The scale is divided into 140 equal parts, and the hardest steel will not read over 115. Mild steel will read from 25 to 32. To find the tensile strength, multiply the Scleroscope reading by four, then subtract 15, which gives the strength in thousands of pounds per square inch.

The gunsmith must often do the best he can with a poor gun, and often he cannot make a job look pretty, but he can always test a gun for safety. On the matter of a firearm of doubtful safety, tell the owner so and advise a thorough prooftest to be made at the risk of destroying the gun. On the matter of safety, be honest to the point of brutality— if you hurt his feelings, too bad, but do not be kindhearted enough to send him out with a gun which may take off a couple of fingers or ruin an eye.

Every firearms accident which occurs anywhere hurts *your* business, through increasing insurance rates, over emphasized and usually incorrect newspaper stories and the resulting unfavorable opinion of the nonshooting public, with its consequent perennial and invariably stupid attempted restrictive firearms legislation. Do your part to keep your slice of the public safety conscious.

There are easier and more remunerative ways of making a living than gunsmithing I am sure, though I doubt if I ever get very far away from it. While few gunsmiths get in the upper brackets of the income tax forms, fewer still ever quit gunsmithing for a different profession. So, brother, if you are in it now, you are in for good and you had better make the best of it, literally!

I hope this volume is of genuine value to all men interested in gunsmithing, professional and amateur, and that American gunsmiths will continue to work on improving arms, ammunition and accessories as they are doing at this time.

CHAPTER 36

Tables of Mechanical Reference

DECIMAL EQUIVALENTS

Fraction	Decimal Equivalent	Fraction	Decimal Equivalent	Fraction	Decimal Equivalent	Fraction	Decimal Equivalent
1/64	0.015625	17/64	0.265625	33/64	0.515625	49/64	0.765625
1/32	.03125	9/32	.28125	17/32	.53125	25/32	.78125
3/64	.046875	19/64	.296875	35/64	.546875	51/64	.796875
1/16	.0625	5/16	.3125	9/16	.5625	13/16	.8125
5/64	.078125	21/64	.328125	37/64	.578125	53/64	.828125
3/32	.09375	11/32	.34375	19/32	.59375	27/32	.84375
7/64	.109375	23/64	.359375	39/64	.609375	55/64	.859375
1/8	.125	3/8	.375	5/8	.625	7/8	.875
9/64	.140625	25/64	.390625	41/64	.640625	57/64	.890625
5/32	.15625	13/32	.40625	21/32	.65625	29/32	.90625
11/64	.171875	27/64	.421875	43/64	.671875	59/64	.921875
3/16	.1875	7/16	.4375	11/16	.6875	15/16	.9375
13/64	.203125	29/64	.453125	45/64	.703125	61/64	.953125
7/32	.21875	15/32	.46875	23/32	.71875	31/32	.96875
15/64	.234375	31/64	.484375	47/64	.734375	63/64	.984375
1/4	.25	1/2	.5	3/4	.75	1	1.

TABLES OF DECIMAL EQUIVALENTS

7ths, 14ths, and 28ths of an Inch

7th	14th	28th	Decimal	7th	14th	28th	Decimal
		1	.035714			15	.535714
	1		.071429	4			.571429
		3	.107143			17	.607143
1			.142857		9		.642867
		5	.178571			19	.678571
	3		.214286	5			.714286
		7	.25			21	.75
2			.285714		11		.785714
		9	.321429			23	.821429
	5		.357143	6			.857143
		11	.392857			25	.892857
3			.428571		13		.928571
		13	.464286			27	.964286
	7		.5				

6ths, 12ths, and 24ths of an Inch

6th	12th	24th	Decimal	6th	12th	24th	Decimal
		1	.041667			13	.541666
	1		.083333		7		.583333
		3	.125			15	.625
1			.166666	4			.666666
		5	.208333			17	.708333
	3		.25		9		.75
		7	.291666			19	.791666
2			.333333	5			.833333
		9	.375			21	.875
	5		.416666		11		.916666
		11	.458333			23	.958333
3			.5				

INCHES INTO MILLIMETERS

In.	0	1/16	1/8	3/16	1/4	5/16	3/8	7/16	1/2	9/16	5/8	11/16	3/4	13/16	7/8	15/16
0	0.0	1.6	3.2	4.8	6.4	7.9	9.5	11.1	12.7	14.3	15.9	17.5	19.1	20.6	22.2	23.8
1	25.4	27.0	28.6	30.2	31.7	33.3	34.9	36.5	38.1	39.7	41.3	42.9	44.4	46.0	47.6	49.2
2	50.8	52.4	54.0	55.6	57.1	58.7	60.3	61.9	63.5	65.1	66.7	68.3	69.8	71.4	73.0	74.6
3	76.2	77.8	79.4	81.0	82.5	84.1	85.7	87.3	88.9	90.5	92.1	93.7	95.2	96.8	98.4	100.0
4	101.6	103.2	104.8	106.4	108.0	109.5	111.1	112.7	114.3	115.9	117.5	119.1	120.7	122.2	123.8	125.4
5	127.0	128.6	130.2	131.8	133.4	134.9	136.5	138.1	139.7	141.3	142.9	144.5	146.1	147.6	149.2	150.8
6	152.4	154.0	155.6	157.2	158.8	160.3	161.9	163.5	165.1	166.7	168.3	169.9	171.5	173.0	174.6	176.2
7	177.8	179.4	181.0	182.6	184.2	185.7	187.3	188.9	190.5	192.1	193.7	195.3	196.9	198.4	200.0	201.6
8	203.2	204.8	206.4	208.0	209.6	211.1	212.7	214.3	215.9	217.5	219.1	220.7	222.3	223.8	225.4	227.0
9	228.6	230.2	231.8	233.4	235.0	236.5	238.1	239.7	241.3	242.9	244.5	246.1	247.7	249.2	250.8	252.4
10	254.0	255.6	257.2	258.8	260.4	261.9	263.5	265.1	266.7	268.3	269.9	271.5	273.1	274.6	276.2	277.8
11	279.4	281.0	282.6	284.2	285.7	287.3	288.9	290.5	292.1	293.7	295.3	296.9	298.4	300.0	301.6	303.2
12	304.8	306.4	308.0	309.6	311.1	312.7	314.3	315.9	317.5	319.1	320.7	322.3	323.8	325.4	327.0	328.6
13	330.2	331.8	333.4	335.0	336.5	338.1	339.7	341.3	342.9	344.5	346.1	347.7	349.2	350.8	352.4	354.0
14	355.6	357.2	358.8	360.4	361.9	363.5	365.1	366.7	368.3	369.9	371.5	373.1	374.6	376.2	377.8	379.4
15	381.0	382.6	384.2	385.8	387.3	388.9	390.5	392.1	393.7	395.3	396.9	398.5	400.0	401.6	403.2	404.8
16	406.4	408.0	409.6	411.2	412.7	414.3	415.9	417.5	419.1	420.7	422.3	423.9	425.4	427.0	428.6	430.2
17	431.8	433.4	435.0	436.6	438.1	439.7	441.3	442.9	444.5	446.1	447.7	449.3	450.8	452.4	454.0	455.6
18	457.2	458.8	460.4	462.0	463.5	465.1	466.7	468.3	469.9	471.5	473.1	474.7	476.2	477.8	479.4	481.0
19	482.6	484.2	485.8	487.4	488.9	490.5	492.1	493.7	495.3	496.9	498.5	500.1	501.6	503.2	504.8	506.4
20	508.0	509.6	511.2	512.8	514.3	515.9	517.5	519.1	520.7	522.3	523.9	525.5	527.0	528.6	530.2	531.8
21	533.4	535.0	536.6	538.2	539.7	541.3	542.9	544.5	546.1	547.7	549.3	550.9	552.4	554.0	555.6	557.2
22	558.8	560.4	562.0	563.6	565.1	566.7	568.3	569.9	571.5	573.1	574.7	576.3	577.8	579.4	581.0	582.6
23	584.2	585.8	587.4	589.0	590.5	592.1	593.7	595.3	596.9	598.5	600.1	601.7	603.2	604.8	606.4	608.0

MILLIMETERS TO DECIMALS OF AN INCH
From 1 to 99 Units

Millimeters	0	1	2	3	4	5	6	7	8	9
	0	0.03937	0.07874	0.11811	0.15748	0.19685	0.23622	0.27559	0.31496	0.35433
10	0.39370	.43307	.47244	.51181	.55118	.59055	.62992	.66929	.70866	.74803
20	.78740	.86614	.90551	.90551	.94488	.98425	1.02362	1.06299	1.10236	1.14173
30	1.18110	1.22047	1.25984	1.29921	1.33858	1.37795	1.41732	1.45669	1.49606	1.53543
40	1.57480	1.61417	1.65354	1.69291	1.73228	1.77165	1.81102	1.85039	1.88976	1.92913
50	1.96850	2.00787	2.04724	2.08661	2.12598	2.16535	2.20472	2.24409	2.28346	2.32283
60	2.36220	2.40157	2.44094	2.48031	2.51968	2.55905	2.59842	2.63779	2.67716	2.71653
70	2.75590	2.79527	2.83464	2.87401	2.91338	2.95275	2.99212	3.03149	3.07086	3.11023
80	3.14960	3.18897	3.22834	3.26771	3.30708	3.34645	3.38582	3.42519	3.46456	3.50393
90	3.54330	3.58267	3.62204	3.66141	3.70078	3.74015	3.77952	3.81889	3.85826	3.89763

HUNDREDTHS OF AN INCH TO MILLIMETERS
From 1 to 99 Hundredths

Hundredths of an Inch	0	1	2	3	4	5	6	7	8	9
	0	0.254	0.508	0.762	1.016	1.270	1.524	1.778	2.032	2.286
10	2.540	2.794	3.048	3.302	3.556	3.810	4.064	4.318	4.572	4.826
20	5.080	5.334	5.588	5.842	6.096	6.350	6.604	6.858	7.112	7.366
30	7.620	7.874	8.128	8.382	8.636	8.890	9.144	9.398	9.652	9.906
40	10.160	10.414	10.668	10.922	11.176	11.430	11.684	11.938	12.192	12.446
50	12.700	12.954	13.208	13.462	13.716	13.970	14.224	14.478	14.732	14.986
60	15.240	15.494	15.748	16.002	16.256	16.510	16.764	17.018	17.272	17.526
70	17.780	18.034	18.288	18.542	18.796	19.050	19.304	19.558	19.812	20.066
80	20.320	20.574	20.828	21.082	21.336	21.590	21.844	22.098	22.352	22.606
90	22.860	23.114	23.368	23.622	23.876	24.130	24.384	24.638	24.892	25.146

METRIC CARTRIDGE CONVERSION DATA

Metric	Inches	Metric	Inches
4mm	.157480	7.7mm	.303149
4.3mm	.169291	7.8mm	.307086
4.5mm	.177165	7.9mm	.311023
5mm	.196850	7.91mm	.311416
5.5mm	.216535	7.92mm	.311809
5.6mm	.220470	8mm	.314960
6mm	.236220	8.15mm	.320855
6.35mm	.249999	9mm	.354330
6.5mm	.255905	9.1mm	.358267
7mm	.275590	9.3mm	.366141
7.5mm	.295275	9.5mm	.374015
7.56mm	.297637	10.35mm	.407479
7.6mm	.299212	10.75mm	.423227
7.62mm	.299998	11.15mm	.438965
7.63mm	.300093	11.2mm	.440940
7.65mm	.301180	11.25mm	.462201

TABLE OF TAPERS
Diametrical Variation for a Given Length

Length of Tapered Portion Inches	Taper per Foot-Inches					
	1/16	3/32	1/8	1/4	3/8	1/2
1/32	.0002	.0002	.0003	.0007	.0010	.0013
1/16	.0003	.0005	.0007	.0013	.0020	.0026
1/8	.0007	.0010	.0013	.0026	.0039	.0052
3/16	.0010	.0015	.0020	.0039	.0059	.0078
1/4	.0013	.0020	.0026	.0052	.0078	.0104
5/16	.0016	.0024	.0033	.0065	.0098	.0130
3/8	.0020	.0029	.0039	.0078	.0117	.0156
7/16	.0023	.0034	.0046	.0091	.0137	.0182
1/2	.0026	.0039	.0052	.0104	.0156	.0208
9/16	.0029	.0044	.0059	.0117	.0176	.0234
5/8	.0033	.0049	.0065	.0130	.0195	.0260
11/16	.0036	.0054	.0072	.0143	.0215	.0286
3/4	.0039	.0059	.0078	.0156	.0234	.0312
13/16	.0042	.0063	.0085	.0169	.0254	.0339
7/8	.0046	.0068	.0091	.0182	.0273	.0365
15/16	.0049	.0073	.0098	.0195	.0293	.0391
1	.0052	.0078	.0104	.0208	.0312	.0417
2	.0104	.0156	.0208	.0417	.0625	.0833
3	.0156	.0234	.0312	.0625	.0937	.1250
4	.0208	.0312	.0417	.0833	.1250	.1667
5	.0260	.0391	.0521	.1042	.1562	.2083
6	.0312	.0469	.0625	.1250	.1875	.2500
7	.0365	.0547	.0729	.1458	.2187	.2917
8	.0417	.0625	.0833	.1667	.2500	.3333
9	.0469	.0703	.0937	.1875	.2812	.3750
10	.0521	.0781	.1042	.2083	.3125	.4167
11	.0573	.0859	.1146	.2292	.3437	.4583
12	.0625	.0937	.1250	.2500	.3750	.5000
13	.0677	.1016	.1354	.2708	.4062	.5417
14	.0729	.1094	.1458	.2917	.4375	.5833
15	.0781	.1172	.1562	.3125	.4687	.6250
16	.0833	.1250	.1667	.3333	.5000	.6667
17	.0885	.1328	.1771	.3542	.5312	.7083
18	.0937	.1406	.1875	.3750	.5625	.7500
19	.0990	.1484	.1979	.3958	.5937	.7917
20	.1042	.1562	.2083	.4167	.6250	.8333
21	.1094	.1641	.2187	.4375	.6562	.8750
22	.1146	.1719	.2292	.4583	.6875	.9167
23	.1198	.1797	.2396	.4792	.7187	.9583
24	.1250	.1875	.2500	.5000	.7500	1.0000

NUMBER SIZES OF DRILLS

Drill No.	Deci.	Drill No.	Deci.	Drill No.	Deci.	Drill No.	Deci.
80	.0135	60	.0400	40	.098	20	.161
79	.0145	59	.0410	39	.0995	19	.166
78	.0160	58	.0420	38	.1015	18	.170
77	.0180	57	.0430	37	.1040	17	.173
76	.0200	56	.0465	36	.1065	16	.177
75	.0210	55	.0520	35	.1100	15	.180
74	.0225	54	.0550	34	.1110	14	.182
73	.0240	53	.0595	33	.1130	13	.185
72	.0250	52	.0635	32	.116	12	.189
71	.0260	51	.0670	31	.120	11	.191
70	.0280	50	.0700	30	.129	10	.194
69	.0292	49	.0730	29	.136	9	.196
68	.0310	48	.0760	28	.141	8	.199
67	.0320	47	.0785	27	.144	7	.201
66	.0330	46	.0810	26	.147	6	.204
65	.0350	45	.0820	25	.150	5	.206
64	.0360	44	.0860	24	.152	4	.209
63	.0370	43	.0890	23	.154	3	.213
62	.0380	42	.0935	22	.157	2	.221
61	.0390	41	.0960	21	.159	1	.228

LETTER SIZES OF DRILLS

Drill No.	Deci.	Drill No.	Deci.	Drill No.	Deci.	Drill No.	Deci.
A	.234	H	.266	O	.316	V	.377
B	.238	I	.272	P	.323	W	.386
C	.242	J	.277	Q	.332	X	.397
D	.246	K	.281	R	.339	Y	.404
E	.250	L	.290	S	.348	Z	.413
F	.257	M	.295	T	.358		
G	.261	N	.302	U	.368		

METRIC DRILLS AND DECIMAL EQUIVALENTS

Diameter mm.	Diameter Inches	Diameter mm.	Diameter Inches	Diameter mm.	Diameter Inches
0.30	0.0118	2.75	0.1082	6.70	0.2637
0.35	0.0137	2.80	0.1102	6.75	0.2657
0.40	0.0157	2.90	0.1141	6.80	0.2677
0.45	0.0177	3.00	0.1181	6.90	0.2716
0.50	0.0196	3.10	0.1220	7.00	0.2755
0.55	0.0216	3.20	0.1259	7.10	0.2795
0.60	0.0236	3.25	0.1279	7.20	0.2834
0.65	0.0255	3.30	0.1299	7.25	0.2854
0.70	0.0275	3.40	0.1338	7.30	0.2874
0.75	0.0295	3.50	0.1378	7.40	0.2913
0.80	0.0314	3.60	0.1417	7.50	0.2952
0.85	0.0334	3.70	0.1456	7.60	0.2992
0.90	0.0354	3.75	0.1476	7.70	0.3031
0.95	0.0374	3.80	0.1496	7.75	0.3051
1.00	0.0393	3.90	0.1535	7.80	0.3070
1.05	0.0413	4.00	0.1574	7.90	0.3110
1.10	0.0433	4.10	0.1614	8.00	0.3149
1.15	0.0452	4.20	0.1653	8.10	0.3228
1.20	0.0472	4.25	0.1673	8.20	0.3230
1.25	0.0492	4.30	0.1692	8.25	0.3248
1.30	0.0511	4.40	0.1732	8.30	0.3268
1.35	0.0531	4.50	0.1771	8.40	0.3307
1.40	0.0551	4.60	0.1811	8.50	0.3346
1.45	0.0570	4.70	0.1850	8.60	0.3385
1.50	0.0590	4.75	0.1870	8.70	0.3425
1.55	0.0610	4.80	0.1889	8.75	0.3444
1.60	0.0629	4.90	0.1929	8.80	0.3464
1.65	0.0649	5.00	0.1968	8.90	0.3504
1.70	0.0669	5.10	0.2007	9.00	0.3453
1.75	0.0688	5.20	0.2047	9.10	0.3583
1.80	0.0708	5.25	0.2066	9.20	0.3622
1.85	0.0728	5.30	0.2086	9.25	0.3641
1.90	0.0748	5.40	0.2126	9.30	0.3661
1.95	0.0767	5.50	0.2165	9.40	0.3701
2.00	0.0787	5.60	0.2204	9.50	0.3740
2.05	0.0807	5.70	0.2244	9.60	0.3779
2.10	0.0826	5.75	0.2263	9.70	0.3818
2.15	0.0846	5.80	0.2283	9.75	0.3838
2.20	0.0866	5.90	0.2322	9.80	0.3858
2.25	0.0885	6.00	0.2362	10.00	0.3937
2.30	0.0905	6.10	0.2401	10.50	0.4133
2.35	0.0925	6.20	0.2441	11.00	0.4330
2.40	0.0944	6.25	0.2460	11.50	0.4527
2.45	0.0964	6.30	0.2480	12.00	0.4724
2.50	0.0984	6.40	0.2519	12.50	0.4921
2.60	0.1023	6.50	0.2559		
2.70	0.1063	6.60	0.2598		

TAPER PIPE TAP SIZES

Tap Size Inches	Threads per Inch NPT	Drill Size Inches
$\frac{1}{8}$	27	$1\frac{1}{32}$
$\frac{1}{4}$	18	$\frac{7}{16}$
$\frac{3}{8}$	18	$\frac{37}{64}$
$\frac{1}{2}$	14	$\frac{23}{32}$
$\frac{3}{4}$	14	$\frac{59}{64}$
1	$11\frac{1}{2}$	$1\frac{5}{32}$
$1\frac{1}{4}$	$11\frac{1}{2}$	$1\frac{1}{2}$
$1\frac{1}{2}$	$11\frac{1}{2}$	$1\frac{47}{64}$
2	$11\frac{1}{2}$	$2\frac{7}{32}$
$2\frac{1}{2}$	8	$2\frac{5}{8}$
3	8	$3\frac{1}{4}$
$3\frac{1}{2}$	8	$3\frac{3}{4}$
4	8	$4\frac{1}{4}$

COMMON METRIC THREADS

Diameter of Screw mm.	Pitch mm.
3	0.5
4	0.75
5	0.75
6	1.0
7	1.0
8	1.0
8	1.25
9	1.0
9	1.25
10	1.5
11	1.5
12	1.5
12	1.75
14	2.0
16	2.0
18	2.5
20	2.5
22	2.5
22	3.0
24	3.0

COMPARISON OF ENGLISH AND METRIC PITCHES

Common English Pitches			Common Metric Pitches		
Threads per Inch	Pitch		Pitch		Threads per Inch
	Inches	mm.	mm.	Inches	
4	0.2500	6.350	8.0	0.3150	3.2
4½	.2222	5.644	7.5	.2953	3.4
5	.2000	5.080	7.0	.2756	3.6
6	.1667	4.233	6.5	.2559	3.9
7	.1429	3.629	6.0	.2362	4.2
7½	.1333	3.387	5.5	.2165	4.6
8	.1250	3.175	5.0	.1968	5.1
9	.1111	2.822	4.5	.1772	5.6
10	.1000	2.540	4.0	.1575	6.4
11	.0909	2.309	3.5	.1378	7.3
11½	.0870	2.209	3.0	.1181	8.5
12	.0833	2.117	2.5	.0984	10.2
13	.0769	1.954	2.0	.0787	12.7
14	.0714	1.814	1.75	.0689	14.5
16	.0625	1.588	1.50	.0591	16.9
18	.0556	1.411	1.25	.0492	20.3
20	.0500	1.270	1.00	.0394	25.4
24	.0417	1.058	.90	.0354	28.2
27	.0370	.941	.75	.0295	33.9
28	.0357	.907	.60	.0236	42.3
32	.0312	.794	.45	.0177	56.4
36	.0278	.706	.42	.0165	60.5
40	.0250	.635	.39	.0154	65.1
44	.0227	.577	.36	.0142	70.6
48	.0208	.529	.33	.0130	77
56	.0179	.454	.30	.0118	85
64	.0156	.397	.27	.0106	94
72	.0139	.353	.24	.0094	106
80	.0125	.318	.21	.0083	121
			.19	.0075	134
			.17	.0067	149
			.15	.0059	169
			.13	.0051	195
			.11	.0043	231

TAP DRILL SIZES
(FRACTIONAL SIZES)

Nominal Size of Tap in Inches	Threads Per Inch NC	Threads Per Inch NF	Tap-Drill Nominal Size	Tap-Drill Decimal Equiv.	Actual % Full Thread Tap-Drill Will Give
¼	20		#8	.1990	79
			#7	.2010	75
			13/64″	.2031	72
¼		28	#3	.2130	80
			7/32″	.2187	67
5/16	18		F	.2570	77
			G	.2610	71
5/16		24	I	.2720	75
			J	.2770	66
3/8	16		5/16″	.3125	77
			O	.3160	73
3/8		24	Q	.3320	79
			R	.3390	67
7/16	14		U	.3680	75
			3/8″	.3750	67
7/16		20	W	.3860	79
			25/64″	.3906	72
			X	.3970	62
½	13		27/64″	.4219	78
			7/16″	.4375	62
½		20	29/64″	.4531	72
9/16	12		31/64″	.4844	72
9/16		18	½″	.5000	87
			33/64″	.5156	65
5/8	11		17/32″	.5312	79
			35/64″	.5469	66

A Chronograph for Gunsmith Use

This is Hollywood Gun Shop's Owen Chronograph, which takes the guesswork out of experimental cartridge testing. The outfit shown is complete—
the instrument, tape-holders, batteries and wire. Portable and economical,
equipment such as this is of great value to gunsmiths specializing in "wildcat" rifles.

Showing a set of chambering reamers and headspace gages, together with one of the drawers from the reamer cabinet at Pfeifer's plant. Chambering reamers are put away carefully, in this fashion, after being properly cleaned and greased.

TAP DRILL SIZES
(FRACTIONAL SIZES)
(Continued)

Nominal Size of Tap in Inches	Threads Per Inch		Tap-Drill		Actual % Full Thread Tap-Drill Will Give
	NC	NF	Nominal Size	Decimal Equiv.	
$\frac{5}{8}$		18	$\frac{9}{16}''$	.5625	87
			$\frac{37}{64}''$	.5781	65
$\frac{3}{4}$	10		$\frac{41}{64}''$	.6406	84
			$\frac{21}{32}''$	.6562	72
$\frac{3}{4}$		16	$\frac{11}{16}''$	.6875	77
			$\frac{45}{64}''$	.7031	58
$\frac{7}{8}$	9		$\frac{49}{64}''$	.7656	76
			$\frac{25}{32}''$	.7812	65
$\frac{7}{8}$		14	$\frac{51}{64}''$	.7969	84
			$\frac{13}{16}''$	.8125	67
1	8		$\frac{7}{8}''$	.8750	77
			$\frac{57}{64}''$	.8906	67
1		14	$\frac{59}{64}''$	.9218	84
			$\frac{15}{16}''$	.9375	67

TAP DRILL SIZES
(MACHINE SCREW SIZES)

Nominal Size of Tap Mach. Screw Nos.	Threads Per Inch		Tap-Drill		Actual % Full Thread Tap-Drill Will Give
	NC	NF	Nominal Size	Decimal Equiv.	
0		80	3/64″	.0469	81
1	64		#53	.0595	66
1		72	#53	.0595	75
2	56		#51	.0670	82
			#50	.0700	69
2		64	#50	.0700	79
			#49	.0730	64
3	48		5/64″	.0781	77
			#47	.0785	75
			#46	.0810	66
3		56	#46	.0810	78
4	40		#44	.0860	80
			#43	.0890	71
4		48	3/32″	.0937	68
5	40		#39	.0995	79
			#38	.1015	72
			#37	.1040	65
5		44	#37	.1040	71
			#36	.1065	63
6	32		#36	.1065	78
			7/64″	.1094	70
			#33	.1130	62
6		40	#33	.1130	77
			#32	.1160	68
8	32		#29	.1360	69

TAP DRILL SIZES
(MACHINE SCREW SIZES)
(Continued)

Nominal Size of Tap Mach. Screw Nos.	Threads Per Inch		Tap-Drill		Actual % Full Thread Tap-Drill Will Give
	NC	NF	Nominal Size	Decimal Equiv.	
8		36	#29	.1360	78
			9/64″	.1406	65
10	24		#26	.1470	79
			#24	.1520	70
10		32	5/32″	.1562	83
			#21	.1590	76
			#20	.1610	71
12	24		11/64″	.1719	82
			#17	.1730	79
			#16	.1770	72
			#15	.1800	67
12		28	#15	.1800	78
			3/16″	.1875	61

AMERICAN NATIONAL SPECIAL (N.S.) SCREW THREAD PITCHES AND RECOMMENDED TAP DRILL SIZES

Sizes	Threads per Inch	Outside Diameter of Screw	Tap Drill Sizes	Decimal Equivalent of Drill
¼	24 27 32	0.250	4 3 $\frac{7}{32}$	0.2090 .2130 .2187
$\frac{5}{16}$	20 27 32	.3125	$\frac{17}{64}$ J $\frac{9}{32}$	.2656 .2770 .2812
$\frac{3}{8}$	20 27	.375	$\frac{21}{64}$ R	.3281 .3390
$\frac{7}{16}$	24 27	.4375	X Y	.3970 .4040
½	12 24 27	0.500	$\frac{27}{64}$ $\frac{29}{64}$ $\frac{15}{32}$	0.4219 .4531 .4687
$\frac{9}{16}$	27	.5625	$\frac{17}{32}$	.5312
$\frac{5}{8}$	12 27	.625	$\frac{35}{64}$ $\frac{19}{32}$	.5469 .5937
$\frac{3}{4}$	12 27	.750	$\frac{43}{64}$ $\frac{23}{32}$	.6719 .7187
$\frac{7}{8}$	12 18 27	.875	$\frac{51}{64}$ $\frac{53}{64}$ $\frac{27}{32}$	.7969 .8281 .8437
I	12 27	1.000	$\frac{59}{64}$ $\frac{31}{32}$	.9219 .9687

SIZES OF WIRE NAILS

Size (d = penny)	Length (Inches)	Number per Pound
2-d	1	900
3-d	1¼	615
4-d	1½	322
5-d	1¾	250
6-d	2	200
7-d	2¼	154
8-d	2½	106
9-d	2¾	85
10-d	3	74
12-d	3¼	57
16-d	3½	46
20-d	4	29
30-d	4½	23
40-d	5	17
50-d	5½	13+
60-d	6	10+

TABLES FOR COMPUTING WEIGHT OF STEEL
Weight in Pounds of a Lineal Foot of Round, Square and Octagon Stock

Size in Inches	Round	Octagon	Square
1⁄16	.010	.011	.013
⅛	.042	.044	.053
3⁄16	.094	.099	.120
¼	.168	.177	.214
5⁄16	.262	.277	.334
⅜	.378	.398	.481
7⁄16	.514	.542	.655
½	.671	.708	.855
9⁄16	.850	.896	1.082
⅝	1.049	1.107	1.336
11⁄16	1.270	1.339	1.616
¾	1.511	1.594	1.924
13⁄16	1.773	1.870	2.258
⅞	2.056	2.169	2.618
15⁄16	2.361	2.490	3.006
1	2.686	2.833	3.420
1⅛	3.399	3.585	4.328
1¼	4.197	4.427	5.344

WEIGHTS OF SHEET STEEL AND IRON
U. S. Standard Gage

Gage Number	Approx. Thickness (Inches)	Pounds per Sq. Ft.		Gage Number	Approx. Thickness (Inches)	Pounds per Sq. Ft.	
		Steel	Iron			Steel	Iron
0000000	.5	20.4	20.	17	.05625	2.295	2.25
000000	.46875	19.125	18.75	18	.05	2.04	2.
00000	.4375	17.85	17.5	19	.04375	1.785	1.75
0000	.40625	16.575	16.25	20	.0375	1.53	1.5
000	.375	15.3	15.	21	.03438	1.403	1.375
00	.34375	14.025	13.75	22	.03125	1.275	1.25
0	.3125	12.75	12.5	23	.02813	1.148	1.125
1	.28125	11.475	11.25	24	.025	1.02	1.
2	.26563	10.838	10.625	25	.02188	.8925	.875
3	.25	10.2	10.	26	.01875	.765	.75
4	.23438	9.563	9.375	27	.01719	.7013	.6875
5	.21875	8.925	8.75	28	.01563	.6375	.625
6	.20313	8.288	8.125	29	.01406	.5738	.5625
7	.1875	7.65	7.5	30	.0125	.51	.5
8	.17188	7.013	6.875	31	.01094	.4463	.4375
9	.15625	6.375	6.25	32	.01016	.4144	.4063
10	.14063	5.738	5.625	33	.00938	.3825	.375
11	.125	5.1	5.	34	.00859	.3506	.3438
12	.10938	4.463	4.375	35	.00781	.3188	.3125
13	.09375	3.825	3.75	36	.00703	.2869	.2813
14	.07813	3.188	3.125	37	.00664	.2709	.2656
15	.07031	2.869	2.813	38	.00625	.255	.25
16	.0625	2.55	2.5				

SURFACE SPEED OF WHEEL IN FEET PER MINUTE

Speed of Arbor	DIAMETER OF WHEEL								
	2″	4″	6″	8″	10″	12″	14″	16″	18″
800	420	850	1250	1680	2150	2500	2900	3250	3700
900	470	950	1400	1900	2400	2800	3250	3700	4100
1000	525	1050	1575	2100	2600	3100	3600	4100	4550
1200	630	1260	1950	2550	3200	3750	4400	5000	5550
1400	730	1470	2250	2950	3650	4400	5100	5800	6500
1600	840	1680	2550	3400	4200	5000	5900	6600	7500
1800	940	1890	2900	3800	4750	5650	6600	7500	8500
2000	1050	2100	3200	4200	5250	6250	7300	8400	9300
2200	1150	2300	3450	4550	5750	6900	8000	9100	10300
2400	1260	2500	3750	5000	6300	7500	8800	10000	11200
2600	1360	2700	4100	5450	6800	8200	9600	10900	12200
2800	1470	2950	4400	5900	7400	8900	11000	12500	13200
3000	1570	3140	4700	6250	7900	9400	11000	12500	14100
3200	1680	3350	5000	6650	8400	10000	11800	13400	15100
3400	1780	3560	5250	7000	8900	10600	12500	14300	16000
3600	1880	3780	5600	7500	9500	11300	13200	15100	17000

FUNCTIONS OF NUMBERS

Number	Square	Cube	Square root	Logarithm	Number	Square	Cube	Square root	Logarithm
1	1	1	1.0000	0.00000	51	2601	132651	7.1414	1.70757
2	4	8	1.4142	.30103	52	2704	140608	7.2111	1.71600
3	9	27	1.7321	.47712	53	2809	148877	7.2801	1.72428
4	16	64	2.0000	.60206	54	2916	157464	7.3485	1.73239
5	25	125	2.2361	.69897	55	3025	166375	7.4162	1.74036
6	36	216	2.4495	.77815	56	3136	175616	7.4833	1.74819
7	49	343	2.6458	.84510	57	3249	185193	7.5498	1.75587
8	64	512	2.8284	.90309	58	3364	195112	7.6158	1.76343
9	81	729	3.0000	.95424	59	3481	205379	7.6811	1.77085
10	100	1000	3.1623	1.00000	60	3600	216000	7.7460	1.77815
11	121	1331	3.3166	1.04139	61	3721	226981	7.8102	1.78533
12	144	1728	3.4641	1.07918	62	3844	238328	7.8740	1.79239
13	169	2197	3.6056	1.11394	63	3969	250047	7.9373	1.79934
14	196	2744	3.7417	1.14613	64	4096	262144	8.0000	1.80618
15	225	3375	3.8730	1.17609	65	4225	274625	8.0623	1.81291
16	256	4096	4.0000	1.20412	66	4356	287496	8.1240	1.81954
17	289	4913	4.1231	1.23045	67	4489	300763	8.1854	1.82607
18	324	5832	4.2426	1.25527	68	4624	314432	8.2462	1.83251
19	361	6859	4.3589	1.27875	69	4761	328509	8.3066	1.83885
20	400	8000	4.4721	1.30103	70	4900	343000	8.3666	1.84510
21	441	9261	4.5826	1.32222	71	5041	357911	8.4261	1.85126
22	484	10648	4.6904	1.34242	72	5184	373248	8.4853	1.85733
23	529	12167	4.7958	1.36173	73	5329	389017	8.5440	1.86332
24	576	13824	4.8990	1.38021	74	5476	405224	8.6023	1.86923
25	625	15625	5.0000	1.39794	75	5625	421875	8.6603	1.87506
26	676	17576	5.0990	1.41497	76	5776	438976	8.7178	1.88081
27	729	19683	5.1962	1.43136	77	5929	456533	8.7750	1.88649
28	784	21952	5.2915	1.44716	78	6084	474552	8.8318	1.89209
29	841	24389	5.3852	1.46240	79	6241	493039	8.8882	1.89763
30	900	27000	5.4772	1.47712	80	6400	512000	8.9443	1.90309
31	961	29791	5.5678	1.49136	81	6561	531441	9.0000	1.90849
32	1024	32768	5.6569	1.50515	82	6724	551368	9.0554	1.91381
33	1089	35937	5.7446	1.51851	83	6889	571787	9.1104	1.91908
34	1156	39304	5.8310	1.53148	84	7056	592704	9.1652	1.92428
35	1225	42875	5.9161	1.54407	85	7225	614125	9.2195	1.92942
36	1296	46656	6.0000	1.55630	86	7396	636056	9.2736	1.93450
37	1369	50653	6.0828	1.56820	87	7569	658503	9.3274	1.93952
38	1444	54872	6.1644	1.57978	88	7744	681472	9.3808	1.94448
39	1521	59319	6.2450	1.59106	89	7921	704969	9.4340	1.94939
40	1600	64000	6.3246	1.60206	90	8100	729000	9.4868	1.95424
41	1681	68921	6.4031	1.61278	91	8281	753571	9.5394	1.95904
42	1764	74088	6.4807	1.62325	92	8464	778688	9.5917	1.96379
43	1849	79507	6.5574	1.63347	93	8649	804357	9.6437	1.96848
44	1936	85184	6.6332	1.64345	94	8836	830584	9.6954	1.97313
45	2025	91125	6.7082	1.65321	95	9025	857375	9.7468	1.97772
46	2116	97336	6.7823	1.66276	96	9216	884736	9.7980	1.98227
47	2209	103823	6.8557	1.67210	97	9409	912673	9.8489	1.98677
48	2304	110592	6.9282	1.68124	98	9604	941192	9.8995	1.99123
49	2401	117649	7.0000	1.69020	99	9801	970299	9.9499	1.99564
50	2500	125000	7.0711	1.69897	100	10000	1000000	10.0000	2.00000

TABLE OF THE CHEMICAL ELEMENTS WITH THEIR SYMBOLS, ATOMIC NUMBERS AND ATOMIC WEIGHTS

Name	Symbol	Atomic Number	Atomic Weight	Name	Symbol	Atomic Number	Atomic Weight
Aluminum	Al	13	26.97	Molybdenum	Mo	42	95.95
Antimony	Sb	51	121.76	Neodymium	Nd	60	144.27
Argon	A	18	39.944	Neon	Ne	10	20.183
Arsenic	As	33	74.91	Nickel	Ni	28	58.69
Barium	Ba	56	137.36	Nitrogen	N	7	14.008
Beryllium	Be	4	9.02	Osmium	Os	76	190.2
Bismuth	Bi	83	209.00	Oxygen	O	8	16.000
Boron	B	5	10.82	Palladium	Pd	46	106.7
Bromine	Br	35	79.916	Phosphorus	P	15	30.98
Cadmium	Cd	48	112.41	Platinum	Pt	78	195.23
Calcium	Ca	20	40.08	Potassium	K	19	39.096
Carbon	C	6	12.010	Praseodymium	Pr	59	140.92
Cerium	Ce	58	140.13	Protoactinium	Pa	91	231.
Cesium	Cs	55	132.91	Radium	Ra	88	226.05
Chlorine	Cl	17	35.457	Radon	Rn	86	222.
Chromium	Cr	24	52.01	Rhenium	Re	75	186.31
Cobalt	Co	27	58.94	Rhodium	Rh	45	102.91
Columbium	Cb	41	92.91	Rubidium	Rb	37	85.48
Copper	Cu	29	63.57	Ruthenium	Ru	44	101.7
Dysprosium	Dy	66	162.46	Samarium	Sm	62	150.43
Erbium	Er	68	167.2	Scandium	Sc	21	45.10
Europium	Eu	63	152.0	Selenium	Se	34	78.96
Fluorine	F	9	19.00	Silicon	Si	14	28.06
Gadolinium	Gd	64	156.9	Silver	Ag	47	107.880
Gallium	Ga	31	69.72	Sodium	Na	11	22.997
Germanium	Ge	32	72.60	Strontium	Sr	38	87.63
Gold	Au	79	197.2	Sulfur	S	16	32.06
Hafnium	Hf	72	178.6	Tantalum	Ta	73	180.88
Helium	He	2	4.003	Tellurium	Te	52	127.61
Holmium	Ho	67	163.5	Terbium	Tb	65	159.2
Hydrogen	H	1	1.0080	Thallium	Tl	81	204.39
Illinium	Il	61	?	Thorium	Th	90	232.12
Indium	In	49	114.76	Thulium	Tm	69	169.4
Iodine	I	53	126.92	Tin	Sn	50	118.70
Iridium	Ir	77	193.1	Titanium	Ti	22	47.90
Iron	Fe	26	55.85	Tungsten	W	74	183.92
Krypton	Kr	36	83.7	Uranium	U	92	238.07
Lanthanum	La	57	138.92	Vanadium	V	23	50.95
Lead	Pb	82	207.21	Xenon	Xe	54	131.3
Lithium	Li	3	6.940	Ytterbium	Yb	70	173.04
Lutecium	Lu	71	174.99	Yttrium	Y	39	88.92
Magnesium	Mg	12	24.32	Zinc	Zn	30	65.38
Manganese	Mn	25	54.93	Zirconium	Zr	40	91.22
Mercury	Hg	80	200.61				

704 GUNSMITHING

MELTING POINTS OF COMMON METALS

Metal	° Fahr.
Mercury	−38
Sulphur	236
Tin	450
Bismuth	520
Cadmium	610
Lead	621
Zinc	787
Antimony	1166
Magnesium	1204
Aluminum	1218
Silver	1761
Gold	1945
Copper	1981
Manganese	2300
Silicon	2588
Nickel	2646
Cobalt	2696
Chromium	2768
Pure Iron	2800
Wrought Iron	2700–2750
Stainless Steel	2400–2700
Carbon Steel	2400–2750
Cast Iron	2100–2350
Cast Steel	2600–2750
Palladium	2820
Zirconium	3090
Vanadium	3128
Platinum	3191
Molybdenum	4595
Tantalum	5252
Tungsten	6152
Carbon	6332
Brass	1700–1850
Bronze	1675
Solder (50–50)	450
Babbitt Metals	350–450
Zinc Die Casting Alloy	715–720

APPROXIMATE MELTING POINT OF COMMON SALTS
(Used for Tempering Baths)

Sodium Chloride (Table Salt)	1480° F.
Sodium Nitrate	590° F.
Sodium Sulphate	1620° F.
Potassium Nitrate	640° F.

CONVERSION OF FAHRENHEIT AND CENTIGRADE SCALES

Cen.	Fah.	Cen.	Fah.	Cen.	Fah.	Cen.	Fah.	Cen.	Fah.	Cen.	Fah.	Cen.	Fah.
0	32	230	446	460	860	690	1274	920	1688	1150	2102	1380	2516
5	41	235	455	465	869	695	1283	925	1697	1155	2111	1385	2525
10	50	240	464	470	878	700	1292	930	1706	1160	2120	1390	2534
15	59	245	473	475	887	705	1301	935	1715	1165	2129	1395	2543
20	68	250	482	480	896	710	1310	940	1724	1170	2138	1400	2552
25	77	255	491	485	905	715	1319	945	1733	1175	2147	1405	2561
30	86	260	500	490	914	720	1328	950	1742	1180	2156	1410	2570
35	95	265	509	495	923	725	1337	955	1751	1185	2165	1415	2579
40	104	270	518	500	932	730	1346	960	1760	1190	2174	1420	2588
45	113	275	527	505	941	735	1355	965	1769	1195	2183	1425	2597
50	122	280	536	510	950	740	1364	970	1778	1200	2192	1430	2606
55	131	285	545	515	959	745	1373	975	1787	1205	2201	1435	2615
60	140	290	554	520	968	750	1382	980	1796	1210	2210	1440	2624
65	149	295	563	525	977	755	1391	985	1805	1215	2219	1445	2633
70	158	300	572	530	986	760	1400	990	1814	1220	2228	1450	2642
75	167	305	581	535	995	765	1409	995	1823	1225	2237	1455	2651
80	176	310	590	540	1004	770	1418	1000	1832	1230	2246	1460	2660
85	185	315	599	545	1013	775	1427	1005	1841	1235	2255	1465	2669
90	194	320	608	550	1022	780	1436	1010	1850	1240	2264	1470	2678
95	203	325	617	555	1031	785	1445	1015	1859	1245	2273	1475	2687
100	212	330	626	560	1040	790	1454	1020	1868	1250	2282	1480	2696
105	221	335	635	565	1049	795	1463	1025	1877	1255	2291	1485	2705
110	230	340	644	570	1058	800	1472	1030	1886	1260	2300	1490	2714
115	239	345	653	575	1067	805	1481	1035	1895	1265	2309	1495	2723
120	248	350	662	580	1076	810	1490	1040	1904	1270	2318	1500	2732
125	257	355	671	585	1085	815	1499	1045	1913	1275	2327	1505	2741
130	266	360	680	590	1094	820	1508	1050	1922	1280	2336	1510	2750
135	275	365	689	595	1103	825	1517	1055	1931	1285	2345	1515	2759
140	284	370	698	600	1112	830	1526	1060	1940	1290	2354	1520	2768
145	293	375	707	605	1121	835	1535	1065	1949	1295	2363	1525	2777
150	302	380	716	610	1130	840	1544	1070	1958	1300	2372	1530	2786
155	311	385	725	615	1139	845	1553	1075	1967	1305	2381	1535	2795
160	320	390	734	620	1148	850	1562	1080	1976	1310	2390	1540	2804
165	329	395	743	625	1157	855	1571	1085	1985	1315	2399	1545	2813
170	338	400	752	630	1166	860	1580	1090	1994	1320	2408	1550	2822
175	347	405	761	635	1175	865	1589	1095	2003	1325	2417	1555	2831
180	356	410	770	640	1184	870	1598	1100	2012	1330	2426	1560	2840
185	365	415	779	645	1193	875	1607	1105	2021	1335	2435	1565	2849
190	374	420	788	650	1202	880	1616	1110	2030	1340	2444	1570	2858
195	383	425	797	655	1211	885	1625	1115	2039	1345	2453	1575	2867
200	392	430	806	660	1220	890	1634	1120	2048	1350	2462	1580	2876
205	401	435	815	665	1229	895	1643	1125	2057	1355	2471	1585	2885
210	410	440	824	670	1238	900	1652	1130	2066	1360	2480	1590	2894
215	419	445	833	675	1247	905	1661	1135	2075	1365	2489	1595	2903
220	428	450	842	680	1256	910	1670	1140	2084	1370	2498	1600	2912
225	437	455	851	685	1265	915	1679	1145	2093	1375	2507	1605	2921

CONVERSION FORMULAE

From—° Cen. to ° Fah. → Degrees Centigrade $\times$ 1.8 + 32 = degrees Fahrenheit

From —° Fah. to ° Cen. → $\dfrac{\text{Degrees Fahrenheit} - 32}{1.8}$ = degrees Centigrade

S.A.E. STEEL SPECIFICATIONS

CARBON STEELS

SAE Number	Nominal Chemical Ranges			
	Carbon Range	Manganese Range	Phosphorus Max.	Sulfur Max.
1008	0.10 max.	0.30–0.50	0.040	0.050
1010	0.08–0.13	0.30–0.50	0.040	0.050
1015	0.13–0.18	0.30–0.50	0.040	0.050
1016	0.13–0.18	0.60–0.90	0.040	0.050
1020	0.18–0.23	0.30–0.50	0.040	0.050
1022	0.18–0.23	0.70–1.00	0.040	0.050
1024	0.20–0.26	1.35–1.65	0.040	0.050
1025	0.22–0.28	0.30–0.50	0.040	0.050
1030	0.28–0.34	0.60–0.90	0.040	0.050
1035	0.32–0.38	0.60–0.90	0.040	0.050
1036	0.32–0.39	1.20–1.50	0.040	0.050
1040	0.37–0.44	0.60–0.90	0.040	0.050
1045	0.43–0.50	0.60–0.90	0.040	0.050
1050	0.48–0.55	0.60–0.90	0.040	0.050
1052	0.47–0.55	1.20–1.50	0.040	0.050
1055	0.50–0.60	0.60–0.90	0.040	0.050
1060	0.55–0.65	0.60–0.90	0.040	0.050
1066	0.60–0.71	0.80–1.10	0.040	0.050
1070	0.65–0.75	0.70–1.00	0.040	0.050
1080	0.75–0.88	0.60–0.90	0.040	0.050
1085	0.80–0.93	0.70–1.00	0.040	0.050
1095	0.90–1.05	0.30–0.50	0.040	0.050

MANGANESE STEELS

SAE Number	Nominal Chemical Ranges				
	Carbon Range	Manganese Range	Phosphorus Max.	Sulfur Max.	Silicon Range
1320	0.18–0.23	1.60–1.90	0.040	0.040	0.20–0.35
1330	0.28–0.33	1.60–1.90	0.040	0.040	0.20–0.35
1335	0.33–0.38	1.60–1.90	0.040	0.040	0.20–0.35
1340	0.38–0.43	1.60–1.90	0.040	0.040	0.20–0.35

FREE CUTTING STEELS

SAE Number	Nominal Chemical Ranges			
	Carbon Range	Manganese Range	Phosphorus Range	Sulfur Range
Bessemer				
1111	0.08–0.13	0.60–0.90	0.09–0.13	0.10–0.15
1112	0.08–0.13	0.60–0.90	0.09–0.13	0.16–0.23
1113	0.08–0.13	0.60–0.90	0.09–0.13	0.24–0.33
Open Hearth				
1115	0.13–0.18	0.70–1.00	0.045 max.	0.10–0.15
1117	0.14–0.20	1.00–1.30	0.045 max.	0.08–0.13
1118	0.14–0.20	1.30–1.60	0.045 max.	0.08–0.13
1132	0.28–0.34	1.35–1.65	0.045 max.	0.08–0.13
1137	0.32–0.39	1.35–1.65	0.045 max.	0.08–0.13
1141	0.37–0.45	1.35–1.65	0.045 max.	0.08–0.13
1145	0.42–0.49	0.70–1.00	0.045 max.	0.04–0.07

NICKEL STEELS

SAE Number	Nominal Chemical Ranges					
	Carbon Range	Manganese Range	Phosphorus Max.	Sulfur Max.	Silicon Range	Nickel Range
2315 2317	0.15–0.20	0.40–0.60	0.040	0.040	0.20–0.35	3.25–3.75
2330	0.28–0.33	0.60–0.80	0.040	0.040	0.20–0.35	3.25–3.75
2340	0.38–0.43	0.70–0.90	0.040	0.040	0.20–0.35	3.25–3.75
2345	0.43–0.48	0.70–0.90	0.040	0.040	0.20–0.35	3.25–3.75
2515	0.12–0.17	0.40–0.60	0.040	0.040	0.20–0.35	4.75–5.25

NICKEL CHROMIUM STEELS

SAE Number	Nominal Chemical Ranges						
	Carbon Range	Manganese Range	Phosphorus Max.	Sulfur Max.	Silicon Range	Nickel Range	Chromium Range
3115	0.13–0.18	0.40–0.69	0.040	0.040	0.20–0.35	1.10–1.40	0.55–0.75
3120	0.17–0.22	0.60–0.80	0.040	0.040	0.20–0.35	1.10–1.40	0.55–0.75
3130	0.28–0.33	0.60–0.80	0.040	0.040	0.20–0.35	1.10–1.40	0.55–0.75
3135	0.33–0.38	0.60–0.80	0.040	0.040	0.20–0.35	1.10–1.40	0.55–0.75
3140	0.38–0.43	0.70–0.90	0.040	0.040	0.20–0.35	1.10–1.40	0.55–0.75
3141	0.38–0.43	0.70–0.90	0.040	0.040	0.20–0.35	1.10–1.40	0.70–0.90
3145	0.43–0.48	0.70–0.90	0.040	0.040	0.20–0.35	1.10–1.40	0.70–0.90
3150	0.48–0.53	0.70–0.90	0.040	0.040	0.20–0.35	1.10–1.40	0.70–0.90
3240	0.38–0.45	0.40–0.60	0.040	0.040	0.20–0.35	1.65–2.00	0.90–1.20
3312⎱ 3310⎰	0.08–0.13	0.45–0.60	0.025	0.025	0.20–0.35	3.25–3.75	1.40–1.75

MOLYBDENUM STEELS

SAE Number	Nominal Chemical Ranges							
	Carbon Range	Manganese Range	Phosphorus Max.	Sulfur Max.	Silicon Range	Nickel Range	Chromium Range	Molyb. Range
4023	0.20–0.25	0.70–0.90	0.040	0.040	0.20–0.35	....	....	0.20–0.30
4027	0.25–0.30	0.70–0.90	0.040	0.040	0.20–0.35	....	....	0.20–0.30
4032	0.30–0.35	0.70–0.90	0.040	0.040	0.20–0.35	....	....	0.20–0.30
4037	0.35–0.40	0.75–1.00	0.040	0.040	0.20–0.35	....	....	0.20–0.30
4042	0.40–0.45	0.75–1.00	0.040	0.040	0.20–0.35	....	....	0.20–0.30
4047	0.45–0.50	0.85–1.00	0.040	0.040	0.20–0.35	....	....	0.20–0.30
4063	0.60–0.67	0.75–1.00	0.040	0.040	0.20–0.35	....	....	0.20–0.30
4068	0.64–0.72	0.75–1.00	0.040	0.040	0.20–0.35	....	....	0.20–0.30
4119	0.71–0.22	0.70–0.90	0.040	0.040	0.20–0.35	....	0.40–0.60	0.20–0.30
4125	0.23–0.28	0.70–0.90	0.040	0.040	0.20–0.35	....	0.40–0.60	0.20–0.30
4130	0.28–0.33	0.40–0.60	0.040	0.040	0.20–0.35	....	0.80–1.10	0.15–0.25
4137	0.35–0.40	0.70–0.90	0.040	0.040	0.20–0.35	....	0.80–1.10	0.15–0.25
4140	0.38–0.43	0.75–1.00	0.040	0.040	0.20–0.35	....	0.80–1.10	0.15–0.25
4145	0.43–0.48	0.75–1.00	0.040	0.040	0.20–0.35	....	0.80–1.10	0.15–0.25
4150	0.46–0.53	0.75–1.00	0.040	0.040	0.20–0.35	....	0.80–1.10	0.15–0.25
4320	0.17–0.22	0.45–0.65	0.040	0.040	0.20–0.35	1.65–2.00	0.40–0.60	0.20–0.30
4340	0.38–0.43	0.60–0.80	0.040	0.040	0.20–0.35	1.65–2.00	0.70–0.90	0.20–0.30
4615	0.13–0.18	0.45–0.65	0.040	0.040	0.20–0.35	1.65–2.00	....	0.20–0.30
4620	0.17–0.22	0.45–0.65	0.040	0.040	0.20–0.35	1.65–2.00	....	0.20–0.30
4640	0.38–0.43	0.60–0.80	0.040	0.040	0.20–0.35	1.65–2.00	....	0.20–0.30
4815	0.13–0.18	0.40–0.60	0.040	0.040	0.20–0.35	3.25–3.75	....	0.20–0.30
4820	0.18–0.23	0.50–0.70	0.040	0.040	0.20–0.35	3.25–3.75	....	0.20–0.30

CLASSIFICATION OF TOOL STEELS

This information is taken from the book on "Tool Steels" by James P. Gill, published by The American Society for Metals.

	C	Si	Mn	Opt.	W	Co	V	Cr	Ni	Mo
10. Carbon Tool Steels *(With or without Vanadium or Chromium up to .50%)*										
11. Carbon Tool Steel	.60–1.40	.25	.25							
12. Carbon-Vanadium Tool Steel	.60–1.40	.25	.25				.15–.50			
13. Carbon Tool Steel with Chromium up to .50%	.60–1.40	.25	.25					.10–.50		
20. Chromium & Chromium-Vanadium Tool Steels *(Carbon from .50 to 2.50% with or without Vanadium)*										
21. Chromium Tool Steels (A)	.40–.60	.25	.60					2.00–2.50		
(B)	.90–1.10	.25	.25					1.00–2.00		
22. Chromium-Vanadium Tool Steels (A)	.50–1.10	.25	.25				.20	.75–1.50		
(B)	.50–1.10	.25	.65				.20	.75–1.50		
30. Low Chromium Steels with Nickel, Molybdenum or Manganese *(Chromium .40–.75% Chromium less than 2.50%)*										
31. Chromium-Nickel Steels	.40–.75	.25	.40					.75–2.25	1.00–2.00	
32. Chromium-Molybdenum Steels	.40–.65	.25	.40					.75–1.50		.20–.50
33. Chromium-Nickel-Molybdenum Steels	.40–.70	.25	.40					.75–1.50	1.00–2.00	.20–.50
34. Chromium-Molybdenum-Manganese Steels	.50–.70	.25	.70–1.00					.75–2.00		.20–.50
40. Oil Hardening Non-Deforming Steels *(Low alloy types)*										
41. Manganese type	.95	.25	1.60	.25 Mo & .25 V						
42. Low Manganese type	.95	.25	1.20	.25V	.50			.50		
43. Tungsten type	1.20	.25	.25		1.75			.75		
44. Chromium type	.90	.25	.25		.45		.20	1.60		.25
50. Silicon Tool Steels *(Predominating alloy in Silicon)*										
51. Silico-Manganese with or without Chromium and Vanadium	.55	2.00	.80	.30 Cr & .25 V						
52. Silico-Manganese with Molybdenum	.55	2.00	.80	.40V						.40
53. 1.00% Silicon Type	.50	1.00	.40	.25V						.50
60. Tungsten Finishing Steels										
61. Tungsten type	1.30	.25–.50	.25	.35 Mo	3.25–4.00					
62. Tungsten-Chromium type	1.30	.25	.25		3.50–4.25			.50–1.00		

CLASSIFICATION OF TOOL STEELS

(Continued)

	C	Si	Mn	Al	W	Co	V	Cr	Ni	Mo
70. Graphite Steels (*Containing free Carbon*)										
71. Carbon-Silicon Steels	1.50	.80	.30							
72. Carbon-Silicon-Molybdenum Steels	1.50	.80	.30							.25
73. Carbon-Silicon-Tungsten Steels	1.50	.65	.30		2.80					.50
74. Carbon-Aluminum Steels	1.50	.20	.25	.18						
75. Carbon - Silicon - Manganese - Nickel Molybdenum Steels	1.50	1.25	1.25					.35	1.75	.50
80. Air Hardening Die Steels (*Intermediate Alloy content*)				Opt.						
81. Chromium-Molybdenum Type	1.00	.30	.40-.70	.30-.60 V				5.00		1.00
82. Chromium - Manganese - Molybdenum type (A)	1.00	.30	2.00					2.00		1.00
(B)	1.00	.30	3.00					1.00		1.00
90 to 130. Die Steels for Hot Work (*Not including Die Steels used for Drop Forging which are under Class 30*)										
90. 1.00% Carbon-4.00% Chromium Types				Opt.						
91. 4.00% Chromium type	.95	.25	.25					3.25-4.25		
92. 4.00% Chromium type with Molybdenum	.95	.25	.25	.50V				3.25-4.25		.50
100. .35% Carbon-5.00% Chromium Type with Silicon, Molybdenum or Tungsten				Opt.						
101. Chromium-Molybdenum Type	.35	.90	.25					5.00		.50-1.50
102. Chromium-Tungsten type	.40	.90	.25		4.50-5.50			5.00		
103. Chromium-Tungsten-Molybdenum type	.35	.90	.25	.25 V	1.25			5.00		1.25-1.75
110. Chromium-Tungsten Types				Opt.						
111. 7.00% Chromium-7.00% Tungsten type (A)	.35	1.50	.60		7.50			7.50		
(B)	.45	1.50	.60		7.50			7.50		
(C)	.60	.90	.60		7.50			7.50		

A DELUXE CHECKERING CRADLE

Monty Kennedy, of Pfeifer Rifle Company, checkering a gunstock in the special type of cradle used there.

This is a most flexible design of cradle, easily and quickly adjustable for any angle or position. The rig can be moved about to meet varying lighting conditions or to obtain elbow room and freedom of operation. Operator can sit or stand. The seat can comfortably be straddled, also used as a shelf for tools not in immediate use. All in all, quite the best arrangement so far seen for gunstock checkering or finishing.

GUN BARREL REAMING MACHINE

Purpose of this tool to properly ream bored hole to desired size and finish. Photograph of one of Pfeifer's machines.

CLASSIFICATION OF TOOL STEELS

(Continued)

	C	Si	Mn	Opt.	W	Co	V	Cr	Ni	Mo
120. Tungsten Types										
121. 10.00% Tungsten Type with 3.00% Chromium	.30	.25	.25		9.00-11.00		.40	3.25		.40
122. 10.00% Tungsten Type with 2.00% Chromium	.45	.25	.25		11.00		.40	2.00		
123. 15.00% Tungsten Type (A)	.30	.25	.25		15.00		.40	2.75		
(B)	.45	.25	.25		15.00		.40	2.75		
124. Nickel-Tungsten type (A)	.33	.25	.25		14.00			4.00	2.50	
(B)	.33	.25	.25		11.00			3.00	1.50	2.10
130. Molybdenum Types										
131. 6.00% Molybdenum type	.35	.25	.25		1.00		.75	3.50		6.25
140. High Carbon High Chromium Die Steels										
141. 2.25% Carbon Oil Hardening type	2.25	.25	.30	.30-.80 V				11.50		
142. 2.25% Carbon Oil Hardening type with Silicon and Tungsten	2.25	1.00	.30		1.00					
143. 1.25% Carbon Air Hardening type	2.25	.25	.30	.30-.80 V				11.00		.80
144. 1.50% Carbon Air Hardening type	1.50	.25	.30	.30-.80 V				12.00		.80
145. 1.00% Carbon Air Hardening type	1.00	.25	.30	.30-.80 V				12.00		.80
146. 1.40% Carbon Air Hardening type with Cobalt	1.40	.25	.30			3.50	.30-.80	12.00		.80
150-200. High Speed Steels										
150. Tungsten Types										
151. 18-4-1 Type	.50-.80	.25	.25		18.00		1.00	4.00		
152. 18-4-2 Type	.80	.25	.25		18.00		2.00	4.00		.80
153. 14-4-2 type	.75	.25	.25		14.00		2.00	4.00		
154. 18-4-3 type	.95	.25	.25		18.00		3.00	4.00		
160. Tungsten-Cobalt Types										
161. 18-4-1 type plus 5.00% Cobalt	.75	.25	.25	.75 Mo	18.00	5.00	1.00	4.00		
162. 18-4-2 type plus 8.00% Cobalt	.75	.25	.25		18.00	8.00	2.00	4.00		
163. 14-4-2 type plus 5.00% Cobalt	.75	.25	.25		14.00	5.00	2.00	4.00		
164. 20-4-2 type plus 12.00% Cobalt	.75	.25	.25		20.00	12.00	1.75	4.25		
170. Molybdenum Types										
171. Molybdenum-Tungsten Type	.75	.25	.25		1.50		1.00	4.00		8.50
172. Molybdenum-Vanadium Type	.80	.25	.25				2.00	4.25		8.25

CLASSIFICATION OF TOOL STEELS

(Continued)

	C	Si	Mn	Opt.	W	Co	V	Cr	Ni	Mo	Cu
180. Molybdenum-Cobalt Types											
181. Molybdenum-Tungsten type with 5.00% Cobalt.	.80	.25	.25		1.50	5.00	1.25			8.50	
182. Molybdenum-Tungsten type with 8.00% Cobalt.	.80	.25	.25		1.50	8.00	2.00			8.50	
190. Tungsten-Molybdenum Types											
191. Tungsten-Molybdenum Type	.80	.25	.25		5.75		1.50	4.00		4.50	
192. Tungsten-Molybdenum-Vanadium Type	1.25	.25	.25		5.75		4.00	4.25		4.75	
200. Tungsten-Molybdenum-Cobalt Types											
201. Tungsten-Molybdenum with 5.00% Cobalt	.80	.25	.25		5.75	5.00	1.50	4.00		4.75	
202. Tungsten-Molybdenum with 8.00% Cobalt	.80	.25	.25		5.75	8.00	1.50	4.00		4.75	
500-600. Miscellaneous Types											
510. Die Irons for Hobbing and Carburizing											
511.	.05	.05	.15								
512.	.05	.05	.15					0.50	1.20		
520. Low Alloy Tap Steels											
521.	1.25	.25	.60					.50			
522.	1.25	.25	.85					.50			
523.	1.25	.25	.25		1.50					.50	
530. Non-Tempering Chisel Steels											
531.	.33	.65	.40					.75		.75	.75
532.	.35	.25	.70					.75	1.00	.45	
533.	.40	.25	.70								
540. Tungsten Chisel Steels (also used for hot work)											
541.	.50	.25	.25		2.10			1.50			
542.	.40	.90	.25		2.00		.25	1.00			
543.	.50	.25	.25		1.00			1.00			
544.	.50	1.00	.25		1.00						
550. Wortle Die, Wire Drawing Die Steels and Self-Hardening Steels											
551.	2.25	.25	.25		.50			.50			
552.	2.00	.25	.75		4.50		*or*	2.00			
553.	2.00	.25	.75		3.50						
554.	2.25	.25	1.50		11.00			2.00			
555.	2.00	.25	1.50		3.75			3.75			

APPENDIX I (1963)

Synthetic Bedding

Since 1950, considerable experimentation—with success—has been conducted involving the use of various materials to aid bedding of rifles, primarily to improve accuracy.

Various synthetics are now available, nearly all of the self-hardening resin types—either the common fiber glass or epoxy—and used with various fillers. This is over-simplification, but the alternative would be almost a catalog listing of probably over a hundred variations of the two! There are types which set up fast, slow, hard, medium, flexible, electrically conductive, nonconductive, etc., etc. For firearms use in bedding we are concerned only with a material which will not require special equipment to use, which will not harm either metal or wood, and is strong enough to hold the rifle against recoil, without shrinking so much as to defeat its purpose.

Plastic or "moldable" bedding is not a new idea, of course. Probably gunsmiths have always tried to do something of the sort—I've seen old muzzle loaders with nooks and crannies in the inletting filled with hardened mixtures of sawdust and glue. In the 1930's we tried to use plastic wood to bed bolt action rifles with fair success, although it didn't get hard enough to do a really good job and of course had considerable shrinkage. Every man who has ever cut and scraped for hours on an inletting job has dreamed of just cutting out enough wood to allow the action to drop in, then putting in something that will mold closely to the metal and give a perfect inletting job.

As mentioned earlier, for bedding purposes we need material which can be used without special equipment, in small quantities at a time without undue waste and expense, and without danger. The ordinary fiber glass and simpler epoxies are therefore most practical for us.

For any synthetic bedding substance, the following rules *must* be followed for successful applications:

713

1. The wood must be free of oil of any type, for material to adhere.

2. The clearance between wood and metal must be uniform, so that the bedding material forms a layer of uniform thickness between wood and metal on the bottom of receivers, etc. Sides are not so important except where receivers are round, of course.

3. The release material (used to keep metal from sticking) must not contaminate the bedding substance.

4. All "locks" must be avoided—any pin-holes, slots, etc., into which the bedding material could flow, then harden to prevent removal of rifle from stock without damage should be filled with modeling clay.

5. The resins must be properly and thoroughly mixed, and fillers be well mixed in, if used.

FIBER GLASS

The fiber glass mixture is most popular and if properly done, should give as perfect a job as can be had. Most of the resins now come from the manufacturers with a cobalt "accelerator" already mixed in—this is to speed up hardening. Such resins have a purple tint from the cobalt. The catalysts used are practically all some form of high-powered industrial peroxides, or ketones. These have to be handled carefully—the flashpoint on the one I use is 100 degrees F. Neither resins nor catalysts are poisonous to handle, though not pleasant for the fumes aren't too nice to breathe. Always have some ventilation going when bedding.

I prefer to use a colored glass, and buy ordinary artists' dry pigment, brown, of which a very little goes a long way. It is mixed in with the straight resin, before mixing with catalyst of course, and with a little practice you can get almost any shade of walnut color you wish. The best filler is a 1/32″ length glass fiber, commonly called flock (with or without the "K") and appearing as little white fuzzy balls. This seems literally to dissolve in the resin and make a very smooth paste for application. Glass wool, cloth, etc., comes in all forms down to the 1/64″ fiber, which is in effect a gritty powder. If any of these fillers are used, you have a fiber glass, and a "glass" bedding. However, many other fillers are used in various applications— powdered chalk, asbestos, and wood dust, to name a few. I do not think these have any use in stock bedding, though I have used wood dust to make patching material for repairing outside stock defects.

Modern resins are much improved over those of just a few years ago when they came into general use in rifle bedding. One I have used is a Reichold resin which is wax-free and also has a "run inhibitor" in it—meaning the resin won't run and drip off a vertical surface quite so readily. Wax-free means that the glass will stick to itself, should you have to build up two layers to get uniform bedding depth, or re-doing a defective job, etc. The release agents are also easier to handle now—the silicone greases originally used are hard to apply uniformly over irregular surfaces, and contaminate the surface of the glass. Oils should not be used on any direct bearing surface, though it is well to have a very light film of oil inside the receivers, slots, magazine boxes, etc., to prevent any stray bits of glass from sticking too hard. The release agent I consider best is Johnson's "Stride" floor wax. It is thin as water; you wipe it on with a little wad of cloth or tissue, and put it in the screw-holes and on screws, of course. And watch what you're doing—it dries in a couple of minutes to an invisible film and you can't see where you haven't been! The coating is so thin you get a perfect bedding and the glass is not contaminated. It does not come off easily—even a hot caustic blueing solution doesn't take it. You have to rub it off with patches, tissue, or a fine wire brush, all kept wet with lacquer thinner or acetone, which will cut it. It can be left on, of course, and probably would make a fine rust preventive.

All of the *unhardened* resins can be dissolved by either lacquer thinner or acetone. Keep a small can handy when bedding in which to wash brushes and paddles, and to wet tissue to wipe glass off your hands. The lacquer thinner is cheaper, does not evaporate as rapidly and is therefore better for general clean-up duties, but acetone is easier on the hands, not drying out the skin as badly. Either will attack hardened resins, but very, very slowly, not enough to worry about. You can wipe finished in-letted jobs with pads wet with acetone to clean them up, if you wish. Also you can clean and dry out the inletting prior to using glass resins, to make sure of adhesion. Even wood with a fair amount of oil in it can be glassed, if the surface is roughed up well and washed and dried several times with acetone or lacquer thinner.

The procedure is to have the stock and metal all prepared, held in a vise with all the components ready for instant use— and with the release agent on all screws and metal parts that will contact glass. You don't gain a thing by going very slowly and you've got to be right the first time. It is best by far to have special guard screws with long T-handles—I have drilled out many screws for shooters who tried to glass-bed their own rifles and used regular guard screws, but didn't get release agents in screw threads or screws, and ended up with the rifle firmly glassed together, which they were unable to disassemble. Standard screws can be used of course, but you must check them during time of set-up (hardening of the glass) loosening a bit every now and then and re-tightening, to keep them from locking in place.

I prefer to work very fast, mixing my glass to set up in four or five minutes. The resin is colored to suit—or taken from a container of resin already colored—catalyst added and stirred rapidly but thoroughly, then the inletting is painted with this mixture, using a small brush—a very little of the glass flock can be mixed in if desired—then sufficient glass flock is added and mixed, adding more as needed, to get the desired consistency. For the M1 rifle and others with deep vertical surfaces to be glassed, a fairly thick liquid paste is used, just thick enough not to run out of the vertical areas before the rifle can be placed in its stock. For bolt action rifles, particularly those with round receivers, a thinner mixture is used, and a considerable amount placed in the bottom of the receiver and barrel-breech area, so that it will flow up around the metal when the rifle is bedded and screws are tightened. You do not use excessive pressure on the screws, just snug them up uniformly. In mixing the fiber glass mixture, you stir it well, but don't "beat" it, slapping the mixing paddle in and out rapidly. This will put air bubbles in it, which turn into holes in the finished bedding. I usually get the rifle together only a minute or so before set-up begins. In a few minutes the glass which has extruded around the action is rubbery and no longer very sticky to the fingers. It is now possible to trim it away from the metal with very light cutting with a sharp wood chisel, pick out lumps from the action, and otherwise make finishing up easier. Theoretically, it is not wise to use a fast-hardening glass, as the more catalyst used, the greater the shrinkage. However, the marine fiber glass resin I use, together with the thin cross-section of glass actually involved, seem to offset this technicality. It's quite a job to get the rifle either in or out of the stock!

With normal resins, set-up time is controlled by two factors— temperature of the resin at time of mixing and amount of catalyst. If the resin is warmer, it will work faster—I'd say set-up time about a third less with resin at 90 degrees than at 65. Five drops of catalyst to an ounce of resin (liquid measure) will mean perhaps a twenty-minute time to set-up, while say, eight drops means five minutes. A little experimentation will teach you a lot with your own particular components. Incidentally, the resins and catalysts do not need refrigeration, though they should not be exposed to unnecessary heat. My shop is probably around 90 degrees for six months of the year, and I keep the glass in a gallon jug under the bench, the catalyst in glass bottles on top of it. The prepared resins—those with accelerators, etc., mixed in—should be shaken up a little before pouring out for use. Most of the poly-resins will deteriorate somewhat from age, however. This can be seen as sort of a straw color showing up. They can be used in this condition for most purposes, though I understand some tensile strength is lost.

Gunsmiths and armorers who expect to do much glass-bedding should try to locate industrial firms in their areas using fiber glass—plastic forms, boat builders, and repair yards are the best sources. Most of them will sell resin by the quart or gallon, with catalyst thrown in at fair price, and either have or can get you whatever flock is wanted, and most important, can tell you how to handle the specific resin you get and what its characteristics are: The prepared fiber-glass "kits" and such sold by hardware stores and auto supply houses are not much good. First, they are usually paste or of putty consistency and won't adhere to wood well enough; second, they are usually an ugly gray color; and third, they are usually an expensive one-shot deal—you have to use the whole works at once. Commercial stock-bedding kits are fine for the individual, of course.

Preparation of stock and rifle are most important to a really good job. The uniformity of inletting cannot be over-emphasized —you must watch this. The resins shrink—all of them, no matter what the sellers claim. So, if you have a clearance of say about 1/16″ under the receiver, and ⅛″ under the barrel cylinder, you've got trouble. After bedding, the ⅛″ thick area of glass will shrink twice as much as the 1/16″ area, and the barrel will not be supported at all, or not until the rifle is fired about ten shots fast and the barrel expands enough to touch the glass. Then it doesn't shoot in quite the same place! It is a simple matter to mix a little glass ahead of time and build up any really deep cuts in the wood so you will have a uniform depth for finish bedding. This shrinkage I am concerned about is very little, probably much less than a thousandth of an inch, but it can be sufficient to affect rifle performance.

EPOXIES

The epoxy resins are similar in treatment to the fiber glasses, though the molecular actions are different, and too hard for me to explain, even if I knew anything about them. Even explaining the difference is a little hard to do, but as I see it, the fiber glass is a single resin which will create its own heat and harden when a very small amount of catalyst is added, while the epoxies are also synthetic resins but harden in a different manner, actually merging molecules with a "partner" or "hardening" agent, which is practically another epoxy itself. The finished result has really a different composition than either of its components. The epoxies are almost unbelievable in some respects—there are epoxy cements which will stick metals together with great strength—greater than if they were soldered or brazed together. Tensile strength of joints runs above 4,000 pounds per square inch in some cases, greater than that of the metals themselves. Different metals can be joined, also. And if you want to go to the trouble to get the right kinds you can make figures lie and win bets—such as two and two don't necessarily make four. Thus with some epoxies you can take a gallon, say, and add a gallon of its component. And then you don't have two gallons of mixed epoxy; you still have just one gallon. Don't write me letters about it—a letter costs me almost a dollar to answer. I'm not interested in the least in the matter or whether you believe it or understand it, and I am not about to start studying up on things like this!

There has been considerable experimentation with epoxies in bedding, but the advantages are doubtful. There is very little shrinkage, which is good, but there are so many different epoxies used in industry, all with quite special characteristics, and so few available for general experimentation that little is really known. They are both harder and easier to use than glass, harder in that even more care must be used in preventing "locks"; easier in that set-up time is usually very long and material is both easier to apply to inletting and to pull up slowly and extrude into all points of stock and metal for complete fitting.

The only epoxy bedding material I have used, and I believe it is the only one of any wide use at all in bedding by others, is the Devcon "Plastic Steel," made for industrial use by the Devcon Corporation, Danvers, Mass. Several types are handled by most mill supply houses, large hardware firms, tool firms, etc., but the only one I consider usable for bedding is the Type B, Liquid Type. The putty types are too thick for gun use. When mixed, the Type B forms a thin paste which is just right for bedding. It is mixed according to directions, which are quite specific and simple; has a "pot life" of 45 minutes at 70 degrees, less at higher temperatures, more at lower; is listed as containing 80% powdered steel; and can be used as a bonding agent for practically anything, from wood to concrete, inclusive. The small package costs three or four dollars, will do as many rifles. For bedding purposes, it can be considered as having no shrinkage, which is desirable, but it also means you must take great care in use of the release agent, which is apparently a silicon grease. Before applying the release agent, use a fine, sharp file to clean up the sides of the receiver walls, all sides of the recoil lug, etc. I do this on all actions before glass bedding also, as a little burr or deep tool marks, especially on the M70 Winchester receiver with its deep straight walls and deep lug, can form a lock and make disassembly rough. You can chip and scrape glass or Devcon, if it lets the receiver out of the stock at all. With the Devcon, it's a good idea to put a coat of the release grease all over, allow it to dry, then put another coat on the *front* of the recoil lug, to give it a little clearance. In disassembly, you have to try to get the action straight up out of the stock, rocking it as little as possible, whether glass or epoxy is used, to avoid disturbing the fit. The Devcon B should be allowed about eight hours to set-up hard, before attempting to disassemble the rifle; and you should positively have T-handle bedding screws. It has a beautiful clean surface when hard, and will show every tool mark on the receiver. The fitting will be so close you can have only the lightest film of oil on the metal before final rifle assembly—there isn't clearance for any heavy oil or grease.

I consider the best thickness of bedding material to be around .050″—call it between 1/32 and 1/16″ and you'll be OK. With a thinner bedding coat, you won't support the rifle, as the wood can compress too easily under the glass or steel; with a thicker one, you can run into shrinkage troubles with glass. I have found best results, with all types of rifles from .22 rimfire target models to the heaviest long-range magnums, and including sporters, to be to bed the receiver and the breech of the barrel approximately 2″ ahead of the receiver. The bedding, or final glass or steel bedding, must be complete—both receiver and barrel area at the same time. The bottom area is the important one—the sides don't matter too much on the Mauser type actions, including the Winchester, Springfield, etc. With actions having more than two guard screws, you use only the front and rear to pull down during set-up, running in the others just enough to keep bedding material out of holes.

A constant problem is keeping the unhardened resins from flowing into magazine cuts and trigger slots in the stocks and other places where it is very definitely not wanted. Magazine boxes can of course be thoroughly coated with the release agents—any magazine rifle should be glassed with the magazine in place, of course. I am doubtful whether it is beneficial that the box be glassed tightly, however. The simplest way to handle the trigger slots and such in the stock is to pack them full of modeling clay. With .22 target rifles I find the most practical method is to use strips of Scotch tape—cut to just cover the magazine and trigger slots in both the receivers and stocks. Release agent is applied to the outer tape surfaces. The tape is pulled or cut out after disassembly of the bedded rifle. (With 52 Winchesters, you better pack the receiver safety cut full of modeling clay, too.) Linseed oil, painted on the wood carefully with a small brush, will keep material from sticking to the wood in undesired spots. It will stick, but come off at a touch of the chisel or fingernail. This is also to be done when glass-bedding a finished rifle, as the resins will attack and remove any but oil finishes. Linseed oil can be wiped all over the receiver area (outside) of a finished stock, to prevent the bedding material from damaging the finish when it runs down, etc. Trigger guards can be bedded separately, if wanted, and in many cases without even putting the rifle in the stock—just pressed in to correct depth by hand. I do M1 stocks in two operations—the bottom rail areas, etc., first, with the floorplate assembly clamped to the stock.

Quite often either guards or receivers will go below the desired depths in the oversized inletting needed for synthetic bedding—in most cases the resins will have sufficient body to oppose the metal parts and permit any degree of compression allowed by the screw pressure in the bedding assembly. If not, small bits of wood of the correct thickness can be placed in the inletting to support the metal parts. These will be imbedded in the resin and should be allowed to remain.

Sporter barrels can be bedded the full length of the fore-end if wanted, though they seldom shoot so well. Many men prefer the more accurate floating barrel, but don't like big gaps around them—so barrels can be wrapped or stripped with masking tape, the tape given a good coat of release compound, and the barrel bedded—when the tape is removed, there is of course barrel clearance.

Glass or steel bedding won't keep a stock from warping—I've even had one multiple-lamination glass-bedded target stock warp through the action area! It was the only one I've had or even heard of. However, the synthetic beddings do give a far more uniform bedding than is possible except by the very highest skilled custom stockmakers using very hard and well-seasoned wood. With the ordinary stock woods we have today, some form of help is needed to hold any centerfire rifle in the stock, and bedding with glass or steel should be considered essential to even reasonable performance. The average sporter needs it more than it does a butt plate and sling swivels. Bedding won't make a rifle more accurate than its barrel and sights will allow, but it will keep a poor stock from detracting from that accuracy.

APPENDIX II (1963)

Cartridge and Chamber Drawings and Data Sheets

For the convenience of the interested gunsmith, on the following pages (and interspersed within the book on pages 4, 14, 44, 52, 58, 62, 72, 82, 96, 112, 124, 127, 164, 274, 282, 307, 308, 356, 372, 382, 400, 410, 430, 436, 446, 469, 498, 512, 532, 564, 572, 654, and 664) are shown maximum cartridge and minimum chamber drawings and specifications for many popular cartridges.

These drawings and data are *not* manufacturing specifications; they are furnished only to show the fit of the cartridge in the gun. Therefore they indicate only recommended limiting values with respect to the maximum cartridge and minimum chamber dimensions and are *NOT* to be construed as *product drawings*. For this reason no tolerances are shown.

Numerous other factors, not shown on these drawings and data sheets, must also be considered, such as outside dimensions of barrels, material, ammunition pressures, etc., each of which is of extreme importance from the standpoint of both safety and performance.

The following are shown earlier in the book:
.22 Long Rifle, page 4
.22 Hornet, page 14
.218 Winchester Bee, page 34
.219 Winchester Zipper, page 44
.219 Gipson Wasp, page 52
.219 Ackley Improved, page 58
22/250 page 62
.220 Swift, page 72
.25/35 Winchester, page 82
.250/3000 Savage, page 96
.257 Remington Roberts, page 112
.256 Newton, page 124
.257 Ackley Improved, page 127

6.5mm Mannlicher-Schoenauer, 6.5x54, page 164
.357 Magnum, page 274
.38 S & W Special, page 274
9mm Luger, page 274
.38 Super Auto, page 282
.45 Auto Colt Pistol (ACP), page 282
12 gauge Shotgun (2¾″) shotshell, page 307
16 gauge Shotgun (3″) shotshell, page 307
20 gauge Shotgun (2¾″) shotshell, page 308
410 gauge Shotgun (3″) shotshell, page 308
.270 Titus Savage, page 356
.270 Winchester, page 372
.270 Ackley Magnum, page 382
7mm Mauser 7x57, page 400
.30/30 Winchester, page 410
.300 Savage, page 430
.30/40 Krag, page 436
.30/06 Springfield, page 446
.30/06 Ackley Improved, page 469
.300 H & H Magnum, page 498
.300 H & H, Pfeifer Improved, page 512
.303 British, page 532
8mm Mauser, 8x57, page 564
8mm Mannlicher-Schoenauer, 8x56, page 572
.348 Winchester, page 654
.375 H & H Magnum, page 664

The cartridge and chamber drawings and data sheets listed below follow on the pages indicated.

RIM FIRE:
.22 Winchester Magnum Rim Fire, page 725

CENTER FIRE, PISTOL AND REVOLVER:
.22 Remington Jet C.F. Magnum, page 725
.256 Winchester Magnum, page 726
.44 S & W Special, page 726
.44 Remington Magnum, page 727

CENTER FIRE, RIFLE:
6mm Remington, page 727
7mm Remington Magnum, page 728
.222 Remington, page 728
.222 Remington Magnum, page 729

.243 Winchester, page 729
.244 Remington, page 730
.256 Winchester Magnum, page 730
.264 Winchester Magnum, page 731
.280 Remington, page 731
.284 Winchester, page 732
.300 Winchester Magnum, page 732
.308 Winchester, page 733
.338 Winchester Magnum, page 733
.458 Winchester Magnum, page 734

SHOTSHELL:
20 gauge, Shotgun (3″) shotshell, page 734

22 WINCHESTER MAGNUM RIM FIRE

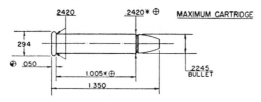

MAXIMUM CARTRIDGE

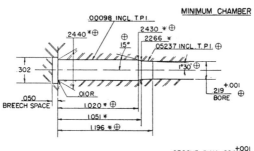

MINIMUM CHAMBER

GROOVE DIAM. .224 +.001

* TO SHARP CORNERS
⊕ BASIC

22 REMINGTON JET CENTER FIRE MAGNUM

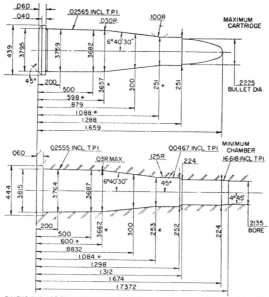

* DIMENSIONS ARE TO INTERSECTION OF LINES

GROOVE DIAM.=.2225

256 WINCHESTER MAGNUM

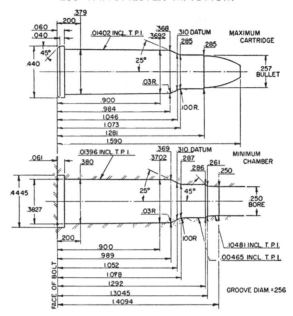

44 SMITH AND WESSON SPECIAL

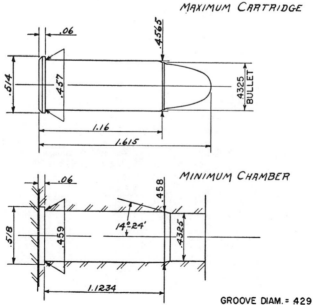

44 REMINGTON MAGNUM

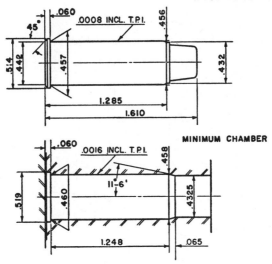

MAXIMUM CARTRIDGE

MINIMUM CHAMBER

GROOVE DIAM. = .429

6MM REMINGTON

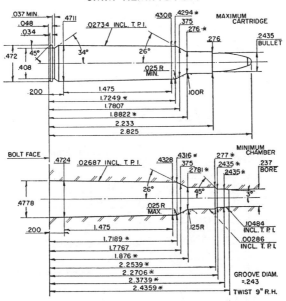

MAXIMUM CARTRIDGE

MINIMUM CHAMBER

GROOVE DIAM. = .243

TWIST 9" R.H.

* DIMENSIONS ARE TO INTERSECTION OF LINES.

7MM REMINGTON MAGNUM

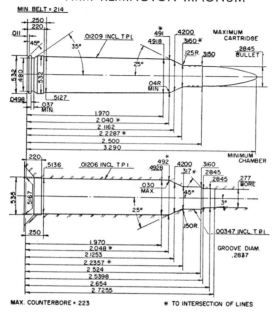

MAX. COUNTERBORE = .223   * TO INTERSECTION OF LINES

222 REMINGTON

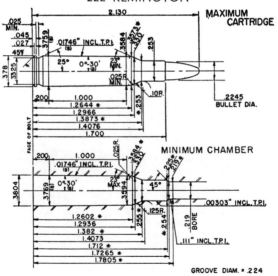

(a) INDICATES BASIC DIMENSION
* DIMENSIONS ARE TO INTERSECTION OF LINES.

222 REMINGTON MAGNUM

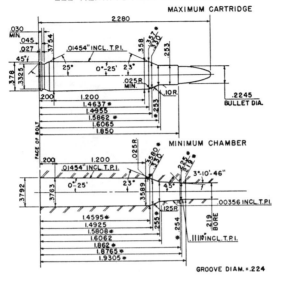

MAXIMUM CARTRIDGE

MINIMUM CHAMBER

GROOVE DIAM.=.224

* DIMENSIONS ARE TO INTERSECTION OF LINES.

243 WINCHESTER

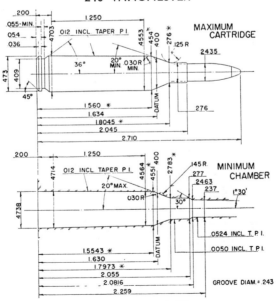

MAXIMUM CARTRIDGE

MINIMUM CHAMBER

GROOVE DIAM.=.243

* DIMENSIONS ARE TO INTERSECTION OF LINES

244 REMINGTON

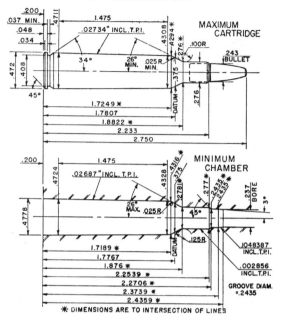

✳ DIMENSIONS ARE TO INTERSECTION OF LINES

256 WINCHESTER MAGNUM

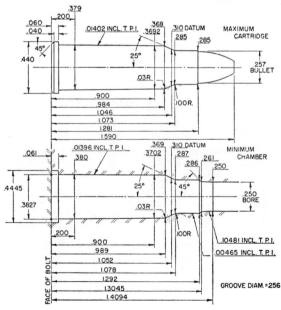

264 WINCHESTER MAGNUM

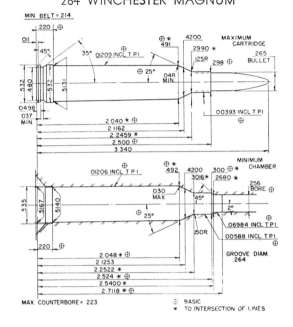

280 REMINGTON

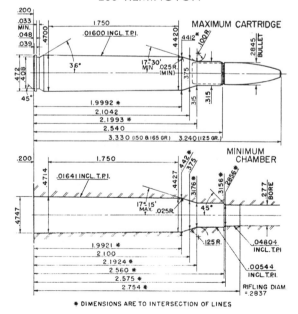

* DIMENSIONS ARE TO INTERSECTION OF LINES

284 WINCHESTER

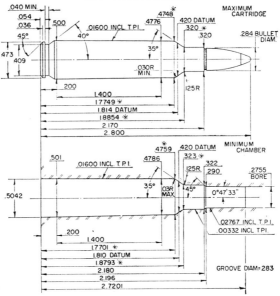

✳ DIMENSIONS ARE TO INTERSECTION OF LINES

300 WINCHESTER MAGNUM

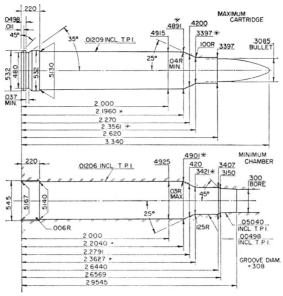

✳ DIMENSIONS ARE TO INTERSECTION OF LINES

308 WINCHESTER

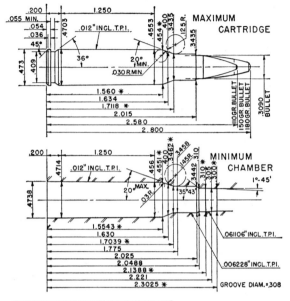

* DIMENSIONS ARE TO INTERSECTION OF LINES.

338 WINCHESTER MAGNUM

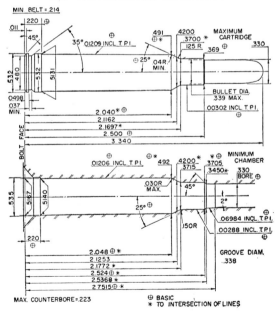

458 WINCHESTER MAGNUM

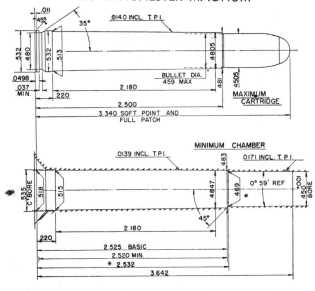

* TO SHARP CORNER

GROOVE DIAM.=458

20 GAUGE 3"

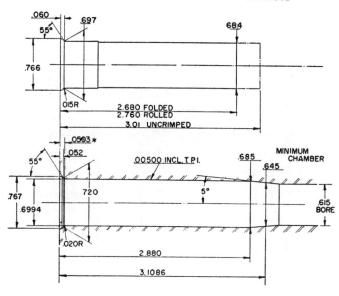

INDEX

A

Acacia, 462
Accuracy, altering pistols to obtain, 275-281
Ackley, Improved cartridge
.219, 58
.257, 127
.270 Ackley Magnum, 382
.30/06 Ackley Improved, 469
Ackley, P.O., 54-55
Action shortening, 604-608
Actions
M1917 Enfield, 629
Winchester M54, 630
Winchester M70, 630
Alignment, screw slots, proper, 586, 587
Alloys of copper and zinc, Table, 100
Altering
Pistols to increase accuracy, 275-281
Police arms for speed, 284
Springfield bolt, 250-254
American black walnut, 452, 459, 460
Annealing, controlling, 119
Aperture rear sights, rifle, 413-418
Apple, 464
Arc welding, 102, 103
Assembly, disassembling
Handguns, 78
Rifles, bolt-action, 77, 78
Rifles, pump or slide-action, 78
Rifles, single shot, 78
Shotguns, 75
Shotguns, autoloading, 77
Shotguns, double-barreled, 75
Auto Colt Pistol cartridge (ACP) .45, 282
Autoloading pistols .22, 363
Auxiliary aperture rear sights, 418

B

Ballard breechblock, 231
Barnes, Fred, 263
Barrel
Bands, 140-142
Breech diameters, high pressure cartridges, 183
Bedding controls, 361
Blank specifications, Table, 193
Characteristics, 186
Cleaning, 80, 81, 83
Contour, 183, 632
Cutting and crowning, 222, 223
Dimensions, 182
Drill and reamers, 189
Fitting, 214
Information, 180
Lapping, 217
Leading, shotguns, 332, 333
Making, 180
Measurement, 206, 207
Obstructions, removing, 228-230
Problems, springing or bending, 187
Shank and receiver diameters, Table, 265
Steels, 180, 181
Straightening, 188
Target rifles, 630

Treatment, when accuracy begins to fall, 631
Vibration, 183
Vises, 216
"Whip," 183
Basic tools, 9
Bedding
Moldable, 713
Plastic, 713
Steel, 721
Synthetic, 713
Beech, 464
Belgian pistols, 278
Bench rest
Rifles, 647-650
Shooting, 669
Beretta pistols, 280, 281
Birch, 462
Blacking metal, 366, 395, 399, 401, 402
Blowtorch, 19
Blueing metal, 366, 385, 386, 387
Boat-tail bullets, 170
Bolt handles
Altering, 106
Custom, 592, 593
Bolt lug fit, custom work, 604
Bolts, engine-turned, 618, 619
Books, reference, 37
Bore sighting, 404-406
Bottoming tools, 28
Brazing, 97-99
Breech protector, 138
Brinell metal testing system, 679, 681
British Cartridge, 303, 532
British shotgun specifications, Table, 343
Broken springs, 147
Browning metal, 366, 379
Buckshot sizes, 341
Bullet seater, straightline, 682
Bullguns, 640
Burnishing, 166, 618, 619
Butt pads, shotgun, 320
Butt plates and pistols grip caps, 142
Butt plates for trap guns, 143
Buttstocks, changing drop of, 575, 576

C

California-English walnut, 460
Caliper
Micrometer, 9
Vernier, 9
Carbon steels, handling, 116, 117
Cartridge
Cases, 168
Information, 167
Shoulder slopes and body tapers, 175-177
Wildcat, .22/250 cartridge, 62, 63
Case-hardening, 123
Catalogs and handbooks, 38-56
Catalyst, bedding, 717
Chamber and barrel work, 206
Chambering, 210, 211, 224-227
Chambers
Lapping, 227
Polishing, 226
Charcoal, in case-hardening, 123

Chasing, 621
Checkered triggers, making, 241, 242
Checkering, 539-555
  Cradle, 29, 541, 542
  Laying out, 540
  Machine checkering, 553
  Machine inletting, 556
  Pattern designs, 552
  Purpose of, 539
  Re-cutting old, 555
  Scoring (in checkering), 554
  Semi-inletted blanks, 556-567
  Tools, 29, 31, 32, 542-552
Checking barrel straightness, shadow-line method, 188
Cherry, 464
Chinese white, 621
Chisels, 16, 505
Chronograph, Owen, 653
Circassian walnut, 453, 457
Clamps, parallel, 36
Clausing lathes, 6
Coil springs, 151-153
Color case-hardening, 125
Colt revolvers, 268
.38 Colt Super auto cartridge, 282
Commercial finish stocks, 566, 567
Comparison
  Of American and foreign shot sizes, Table, 346, 347
  Of metric and British units, Table, 342
Contact barrel bedding, 360
Crane joints, loose, 271
Cross-firing, shotgun problems, 337-339
Custom metal work, 590
Custom rifles, styling, 584-589
Customs rates and regulations, 61-64
Cutting dovetail slots, 408
Cyanide hardening, 126

D

Decorating with contrasting metals, 620
Decorations with metal overlays, 620
Dent removal, shotgun barrels, 335, 336
Design of gun stocks, 471
Desirable rifling twist, 213
Devcon "Plastic Steel" bedding, 719
Dies, 18
Disassembling
  Bolt, 77
  Guns, 75
Dovetail
  Sights, fitting to ramp, 409
  Slots, cutting, 408
  Slot sights, 406
Dowels, wood, 22
Drill, breast, 13
Drill-grinding attachments, 27
Drill
  Presses, 3
  Rod, 22, 24
Drilling, 86
Drilling jigs, 88
Drills, 18, 19
  Care of, 69
Dutch Mannlicher, 6.5mm, rimmed cartridge, 164-165

E

Electric welding, 103
Enfield
  Actions, alterations, 242-250
  Cartridge, 665
  Floorplates, how to hinge, 249
  Guard, straightening, 247
  Improvements, 248, 249
Engine turning, Damaskeening, 618
English walnut, 458
Engraving, 621-624
  Laying out, 621
  Layout, example, 612
Epoxies for synthetic bedding, 718
  Devcon "Plastic Steel," 719
Etching, 613-616
Etching varnish, 614
European walnut, 453, 456

F

Farquharson, Gibbs, 52-53
Farquharson, Jeffery, Westley Richards, Bland and Belgian, 53
Federal Firearms Act, 56-61
Fiber glass bedding, 714
  Kits, 717
File
  Card, 12
  Shapes, 11
Files, 9, 10
  Care of, 67, 68
  Use in inletting, 506
Filigree inlaying, 613
Fire forming cases, 173, 174
Firearms Act, Federal, 56-61
Firing
  Pins, 153-155
  Pin gages, 160
  Tips, 155-158, 161
  Tip shapes, 158
Fitting sights, 404
Fixed barrel bedding, 360
Flame staining, 537
Flexible shaft tools and accessories, 25
Floating barrel, 360
"Flock" filler, 714
Floorplate
  Hinged, 593, 594
  Hinging, 597
  Loose, 247
  Release, Japanese M38, 596
Flour of emery, 221
Foreign handguns, appraisal of, 266
Forend tip wood, 468
  Cocobolo, 470
  Desert Ironwood, 470
  Ebony, 468
  Lignum Vitae, 470
  Mesquite, 469, 470
  Rosewood, 470
Form sheet, custom orders, 585
Free Rifle competition, 625
French
  Polish, 531-536
  Walnut, 457, 458
Functional difficulties, Garand rifle, 653
Furnaces, heat treating, 119, 121
Furnace temperatures, 119

G

Gages
"Go," "no-go," 212
Headspace, 33
Miscellaneous, 675-677
Starrett, 9
Gas cylinder problems, Garand rifle, 653
German shotgun chamber dimensions, Table, 344
German shotgun shells, dimensions, Table, 345
General shotgun repair and alteration work, 318
Gibson Wasp, .219, 52
Glass bedding, 717
Gouges, 16
Gravers, 623
Graving tools, 615
Grinder accessories, 26
Grinders
Hand, 26
Power, 3
Grinder stones desirable, 3
Guns, cleaning, 79
Gunsmithing costs, small work, 129
Gunsmithing specialists, 129
Gunstock
Design, 471
Wood for, 452

H

.300 H & H Magnum cartridge, 498
.300 H & H Pfeifer improved cartridge, 512
.375 H & H Magnum cartridge, 664
Hacksaws, 13
Haemmerli-Martinis, rifles, 645
Hammers, 17
Handgun improvements
Colt .45 semi-automatic M1911, 275
Colt Super, .38, 277
Handgun springs, 267
Handguns, reassembly of, 267
Handling broken taps, 71
Hardening carbon steels, 121
Hardening "kinks," 128
Hardening steels, 120
Hardness conversion Table, 679
Hatcher, Maj. Gen., 628
Headspace, 171, 208-213
Headspace gages, shotgun, 339
Heat treating baths, barium chlorid, 122
Heat treatment of metals, 116
Helical springs, 153
Hidden screws, 75
Holes, depth control, 72, 73
.22 Hornet cartridge, 14
Hunting scopes
Defective scopes, 428, 429
Hensoldt, 426, 427
Lyman Alaskan, 427
Maxwell Smiths, 427
Texas, 427
Unertl 4X Hawk, 6X Condor, 425, 426
Weaver K-4, K-6, 425
Zeiss, 427
Hunting scope mounts, 429-450

Hunting scope mounts, top
Ackley-Turner—King-Pike, 445
Buehler, 444, 445
Hill-Lehman, 445
Kesselring, 447, 448
Mashburn-Williams, 445
Redfield, 443
Stith, 449, 450
Tilden, 441-443
Weaver, 448, 449

I

Improving handgun sights, 284-286
Inlays, custom rifles, 589
Inlays, wood, 610-613
Inletting target rifle stocks, 635
Installation
Cutts compensator, 325-328
Metallic sights, 404
PowerPac, 328
Weaver or PolyChoke, 323, 325
International Free rifles, 640
Accessories for, 641
Firing mechanism, speedlock, 643
Offhand shooting, buttplates, 642
Italian walnut, 458

J

Jacket composition, metal-jacketed bullets, 169
Japanese rifles, alteration, 263
Japanese 6.5mm cartridge, Model M38, 82-83
Japanese 7.7mm cartridge, Model M99, 430-431

K

Kiln drying, 465
Krag Jorgensen .30/40 Krag cartridge, .30 USA, 436-437
Knowledge, helpful gunsmithing, 75

L

Lathe, 5
Lathe chucks, 6
Lathe dimensions, desirable, 6
Layout and inletting rifle stocks, 489
Lee Enfield, British cartridge, .303, 532-533
Level, 10
Linden, Alvin, 537
Linseed oil finishes, 526, 530, 531
.22 Long Rifle cartridge, 4
Loose crane joints, 271
Loose sights, correcting for, 89, 90
9mm Luger cartridge, 274
Luger pistol, 270

M

Magnum cartridge, .357, 274
Mahogany, 463
Mainspring comparisons, Colt vs S&W, 269
Making Mauser sporters, 257-262
Malleable iron, case-hardening, 125
Mannlicher-Schoenauer cartridge
6.5mm, 6.5 x 54, 164
8mm, 8 x 56, 572, 573
Matting and stippling, 616-618

Matting tools, 617
Mauser
    Alterations, 257
    Cartridge
        7mm (7 x 57), 112, 400, 401
        Small Mauser (1908, Mexican and
            commercial), 400, 401
        8mm (7.9mm, 7.92mm, 8 x 57 JR),
            564, 565
    Guard change, 246
    Mexican cartridge, 1908 Mauser, 400-
        401
    Rifle actions, 646, 647
    Small, 112-113
    Triggers, 247
Measuring chambers, 207, 208
Measuring tools, 9
Mechanical reference, Table, decimal
    equivalents, 685, 686
Mercury hardening, 127
Mesquite, 463
Metal browning, blueing, and blacking
    Barrel sanding, 374
    Basic principles, 366
    Blacking, 395-402
    Blueing, cold solutions, 385, 386
    Blueing, Old American acid blue, 387
    Brass, blacking, 402, 403
    Browning, 379
    Browning formulae, 381-385
    Copper, blacking, 402
    Degreasing, 376
    Deplating, 368-370
    Distilled water, in browning, 381
    Du-Lite, 396
    Finishing non-ferrous metals, 402
    Hand polishing, 374-376
    Hazards of over-polishing, 371
    Heat blueing, 392, 393
    Hot blueing, 391, 392
    Houghton, 397
    Lathe, in cleaning barrels for blueing,
        371, 372
    Mixing acid solutions, 381
    Mixed blacking formulae, 398, 399
    Nickel, blacking, 403
    Niedner cold blue, 388-390
    Ordinary polishing, 370-374
    Phosphatizing, 393-395
    Preparation of steel for finishing, 367
    Quick Acid Blue, 388
    Silver, blacking, 402
    Stripping old finish, 367
    Tanks and heating, 376-379
    Use of flexible-shaft tools, polishing,
        370, 371
    Heat treatment, Chart, 120
Metal decoration, 613
Metal hardness testing system, Brinell,
    Vickers, 679
Metal inlays, 620, 621
Metal-jacketed bullets, 169
Metals, melting points of, Table, 114, 115
Metal
    Overlays, 620
    Testing equipment, 678
    Work, custom, 590-608
Metals, physical properties of, Table, 111

Metallic sights, fitting, 404
7mm Mexican Mauser, 7 x 57 cartridge,
    400
Mexican Rosewood, 464
Micrometer calipers, 9
Micrometer receiver sights, 413-418
Miscellaneous supplies, 22
Monte Carlo buttstock, 471
Mounting
    Scope blocks, 420-424
    Side scope mounts, 434-441
Muzzle protectors, 137

N
.256 Newton cartridges, 124
Newton catch system, 595
Niedner rifle actions, 234
"Normalizing" steels, 118

O
Oakite, 622
Odd gun parts, 162-165
Off-shooting, 328-331
Oils, in heat treatment of metal, 122
Open rear sights, 412, 413
Oregon Myrtle, 464, 465
Ornamentation of wood and metal, 609
Oxyacetylene welding, 103-114
Owens Sporters, 7

P
Pacific maple, 462
Parts
    Fitting, 146
    Heat treatment, 146
    Making, 146
    Storage, 3
Pennsylvania walnut, 453
Photographs, in custom rifle work, 589
Pistols and revolvers
    Custom metal work, 590
    Sights, 134
    Work, 590, 266
Pistol
    Cartridges, 177
    Grip caps, 144
    Recoil absorption, 671, 672
    Stocks, 281
Planes, 12
Pliers, 36
Plungers, 139
Power grinders, 3
Proof-firing, 178, 179
Punch, automatic center, 35
Punches, 18
    Bullet seating, 677
Purchasing accessories and small parts, 129
Pyrometer, 119

R
Ramp sights
    Attaching, 131
    Front sights, 130, 409-412
    Hoods, 132, 133
    Making, 131
    Sweating on, 132
Rasps, 28, 29
Ratios, bore to barrel diameter, 184
Rear sights, micrometer receiver, 413-418

Receiver and action alteration, custom work, 598-604
Receiver wrenches, 218, 219
Reconditioning rifle actions, 235
Reference and technical books, 37, 38
Release agent, bedding, 715, 720
 Johnson's "Stride" floor wax, 715
Reloading items, 673
Remington cartridge 721, 512
Remington cartridge 722, 62-63
Remington 37 chamber, 4, 5
.22 Remington Jet C.F. Magnum cartridge, 725
.222 Remington C.F. cartridge, 728
.222 Remington Magnum cartridge, 729
6mm Remington C.F. cartridge, 727
.244 Remington C.F. cartridge, 730
.257 Remington Roberts cartridge, 112
7mm Remington Magnum cartridge, 728
.280 Remington C.F. cartridge, 731
.44 Remington Magnum cartridge, 727
Removing barrel from action, how to, 214-217
Removing obstructions, 228-230
Repair and adjustment, .22 rifles, 348-365
Repair and alteration work, shotguns, 318
Repair of stock finishes, 574
Repairing handguns, 266
Replacement parts, making, 146-166
Resin, synthetic bedding
 Epoxies, 718
 Hardened, 714
 Reichold, 714
 Temperature, 717
 Unhardened, 714
Re-soldering ribs, 336, 337
Rest, for pistol shooting, 672
Reticule, post, 633
Reticules, front interchangeable, 633
Revolver
 Alterations illustrated, 270
 Sights, converting, 136
 .22 Revolvers, 362
Rifflers, 10, 11
Rifle action alterations, 231
Rifle barrels, comments by specialists
 Ackley, P. O., 195-197
 Buhmiller, J. R., 195
 Pfeifer, Joseph, 200-201
 Sukalle, W. A., 202-205
 Titus, Bliss, 198-200
Rifle, Garand M1, 651-667
 Bolt troubles, 659
 Ejection troubles, 659
 Failure to feed properly, 657
 Failure to fire, 656
 Functional difficulties, 653
 Gas cylinder problems, 653
 Loading difficulties, 658
 Mechanical troubles, 655
 Sight troubles, 659
 Tuning up for match shooting, 660-665
 Using in match shooting, 665
Rifle ranges for test or proof firing, 668
Rifle range, indoor butt (or backstop), how to make, 668
Rifle repair problems, .22
 Cartridge feeding malfunctions, 355
 Correcting burred chambers, 348, 349

Ejection troubles, 350
Extraction troubles, 350
Firing pins, 351
 Miscellaneous problems, 352, 353
 Springs, 351
Stuck or ruptured cartridge case, 349
Takedown joints, 354
Rifle rests, 669
Rifle stock blanks, desirable dimensions, 452
Rifle stocks
 Buttstocks, 482-484
 Cheekpieces, 480-482
 Combs, 478, 479
 Desirable dimensions, 484-488
 Forends, 486, 487
 Layout and inletting, 489
 Mauser-type actions, 489-505
 Mannlicher-type, 487, 488
 Stock bodies, 484-488
Rifles, custom metal work, 591
Rifles, target, 625
Rifling
 British system, 192
 Cutters, 190, 191
 Six-groove vs four-groove, 631
 Twist, 213
Rim fire arms, .22, 348
Rock maple, 461, 462
Rockwell machine, metal testing, 678
Round ball sizes, shotguns, 341
Rule, steel, 9
Rules for synthetic bedding, 713
Ruptured cases, removing, 228, 229

S

Sanders, 3
Savage, Model 1899
 Solid frame rifle, 97
 Take-down, 97
.250/3000 Savage cartridge, 96
.300 Savage cartridge, 430
Saws, sharpening, 67
Saw, wood, 15
Scope blocks, mounting, 420-424
Scope mounts
 Echo, 434
 Griffin and Howe, 434
 Jaeger, 434
Scope sights, cleaning, 450, 451
Scopes, rings or mount-clamping bands, 432, 433
Screw-threading gear for lathes, 6
Scribers, 35
Semi-floating barrel, 360
Semi-inletted blanks
 Finishing, 563-566
 Inletting, 557-563
"Set back" of new actions, 179
Set-triggers, 263, 640
 Adjustment of, 264
Shaper, 36
Shapening chisels, 505
Sharps-Borchardt
 Actions, 232
 Model 1878 Sharps, 58
Sharpening stones, using, 65, 66
Shellac finishes, 527
Shells, 178, 307, 308

Shims, 90
Shop practice, 65
Shore Scleroscope, metal testing, 681
Shortening or lengthening shotgun stocks, 321, 322
Shot sizes, 340, 341
Shotgun barrel
    Dent removal, 335, 336
    Work, 323
Shotgun
    bore diameters, Table, 340
    Cartridges, 177
    Choke alterations, 331
    Corrections, off-shooting, 328-331
    Firing pins, 159
    Forends, 473
    Shotgun, 12 gauge (2¾") shotshell, 307
    Shotgun, 16 gauge (2¾") shotshell, 307
    Shotgun, 20 gauge (2¾") shotshell, 308
    Shotgun, 20 gauge (3") shotshell, 734
    Shotgun, 410 gauge (3") shotshell, 308
    Repair, 287, 336
    Repairing
        Browning shotguns, 313
        Fox shotguns, 314
        Ithaca shotguns, 314-316
        Marlin shotguns, 316
        Miscellaneous shotguns, 317
        Parker shotguns, 314
        Remington Model 10, 299
        Remington Model 11, 289-295
        Remington Model 11-48, 288
        Remington Model 12, 302, 303
        Remington Model 17, 299
        Remington Model 29, 299
        Remington Model 31, 295-298
        Remington Model 32, 298-299
        Remington Model 97, 300-302
        Savage shotguns, 312
        Smith, L. C., shotguns, 316
        Stevens bolt-action shotguns, 311
        Stevens double barrel shotguns, 311
        Stevens, Models 520, 521, 620, 620A and 621; 309-311
        Stevens single barrel shotguns, 311
        Winchester Model 01, 306
        Winchester Model 11, self-loading, 306
        Winchester Model 20, 309
        Winchester Model 24, 304
        Winchester Model 24, 305
        Winchester Model 37, 305
        Winchester Model 40, 309
        Winchester Model 42, 303
        Winchester Model 1893, 306
    Stock measurements, Table of Proportions, 320
Stocking, cast-off, cast-on, 472, 473
Stocks, 472
    Work, 287
Sights, 144, 145, 333, 334
    Accessories, 129
    Adjustment
        Fixed sight revolvers, 271
        S&W revolvers, 273
    Base bands, 142
    Drilling and tapping for, 86
    Fitting metallic, 404

Mounting telescopic, 419
Peep disc, 634
Rear, micrometer adjustable, 633, 634
    Target, 633
Side mounts, telescopic, 433
Silver soldering, 99, 100
Single shot action alterations, 231
Smith and Wesson revolvers, adjustments, 273
.357 S&W Magnum cartridge, 274
.38 S&W Special cartridge, 274
.44 S&W Special cartridge, 726
Smith, L. C., re-assembling, 76
Soldering, 92-97
Solders
    Table of, 93, 94
    White, hard, 101
Spanish
    Handguns, 266
    Walnut, 458
Speedlocks, 264
Sporting rifles
    Pistol grip styling, 476, 477
    Recommended barrel dimensions, Table, 185
Springfield
    Action, 1903, 628
    Alterations, 250-257
    "Star Gage," 206
Springfield, .30-06, 1906 Springfield cartridges, 446
Spring, Service specification, 629
Springs, 76
    Tempering, 148-150
Steel jacketed bullets, 170
Stevens 44½ rifle action, 14, 15, 232
Stock
    Alteration shotguns, 576-580
    Alterations, rifle, 580-583
    Blanks, E. C. Bishop & Son, 556
Stock and metal ornamentation, 609-624
    Fillers, 528
    Finishes, 530, 574
    Repairs, rifle, 569-574
    Repairs, shotguns, 568, 569
    Sealers, 528
    Staining, 536-538
    Warpage, 570, 571
    Weaknesses, 568-574
    Wood, 452
Stockmaking
    British Lee-Enfield, rifle, 507
    Checkering, 539
    Final shaping, 520-525
    Finishing, 526-538
    Fitting, 509
    For Savage M99, 506
    Inletting Enfield magazine, 503
    Inletting stock bolt hole, 506
    Inletting trigger guard, 491
    Layout, 489
    Mauser and Winchester actions, 496
    Recoil shoulder, 514-518
    Sample specification sheet, 522
    Seasoning before finish shaping, 518, 519
    Shaping and fitting, 509
    Shaping for cheekpiece, 511

Stocks
Blanks, checking quality of, 467
Blanks, treatment of, 465
Bolt-action rifles, 475-488
Commercial finish, 566, 567
For single shot rifles, 473, 474
Target rifles, 634
Stones, sharpening, 16, 17
Storage, tools and parts, 3
Styling custom rifle, 584
Sukalle, W. A., 38
Sulphur cast method, chamber measure-
ment, 207, 208
Suppliers, semi-inletted stock blanks, 556,
557
Sweating, 94-95
.220 Swift cartridge, 72
Swivels, 140
Synthetic bedding, 713
Epoxies, 718
Fiber glass, 713
Plastic, 713
Resin, 713
Rules for, 713

T

Table
Common metric threads, 692
Comparison English and metric pitches,
693
Inches to millimeters, 687, 688
Metric cartridge conversion data, 688
Metric drills and decimal equivalents,
691
Number and letter sizes of drills, 690
Tapers, 689
Tables
American national special screw thread
pitches and recommended tap drill
sizes, 698
Chemical elements, 703
Classification of tool steels, 709-712
Computing weight of steel, 699
Fahrenheit and centrigrade conversion
scales, 705
Functions of numbers, 702
Mechanical reference, 685
Melting points of common metals and
salts, 704
S.A.E. steel specifications, 706-708
Surface speed of wheel in ft. per min-
ute, 701
Tap drill sizes, 694-697
Taper pipe tap sizes, common metric
threads, 692
Weights of sheet steel and iron, 700
Wire nail sizes, 699
Tape steel, 9
Taps, 18
Renewing edges, 70
Using, 70, 71, 73
Target
Sights, 633
Telescopic sights, 419
Target rifle
Actions, competitive, 627
Barrels, bullgun, 637

Bullguns, 640
Buttstocks, 362, 636
Martini repair problems, 359
Palm rests for, 645
Receiver wall cracks, 358
Securing proper headspace, 357
Stevens, M417 Walnut Hill, 359
Stock bedding, .22 bolt-action rifles,
359-362
Stocks, 634
Trigger adjustment, M52, 358
Types, 626
Target rifle stocks
Finishing, 639
Handguards, 639
Inletting, 635
Shaping, 638
Types, 626
Telescopic sights
Hunting, 424-429
Target, 419
Testing
Hardness, Mauser receivers, 678
Rifles, 668-673
Tightening a loose
Sight, 407
Barrel, 90
Titus, Bliss, 39
.270 Titus Savage cartridge, 356
Tool
Basic, 9
Cabinet, 3
Carbon steels used in Table, 117, 118
Extra, 25
Sharpening, 65-68
Storage, 3
Table, carbon percentage, 91
Woodcarving, 609
Transfer wax, 624
Trap guns, grip caps, 144
Trigger adjustment, military double-pull,
trigger, 238
Trigger changes, two stage to single stage,
conversion, 365
Trigger
Pull adjustment, 236, 272
Pulls, 235
Weight, 235
Triggers and sears, typical, 240, 241
Tung oil, 526
Turning down barrels, 184

V

V springs, 153
Varnish finishes, 528
Vaver target sights, 633
Vickers metal testing system, 679, 680
Vise jaws, lining, 27
Vises, 2
Barrel, 215
Drilling, 3
Machinist's, 2
Pin, 36
Smaller, 3
Swivel-base, 2
Swivel-base vs rigid base, 2
Weights, 3

W

Walther pistol, 279
Water, in heat treatment of metal, 122
Weaver side mounts, 438
    Detachable, 441
    U & Q, 440
Welded work, expansion and contraction of, 113
Welding, 102
    Bolts, 114
    Electric arc welding, 102
    Equipment and accessories, 19, 105
    Flame, regulation, 105
    Forge, 102
    Gas, 102
    Gas tanks, bottles, 104
    Hose, 104
    Protection of gun parts in, 108
    Regulators, 104
    Rod, 21
    Scale control, 108, 109
    Torches, 104, 105
Wildcat .22/250 cartridge, 62
Winchester 52 chamber, 4-5
    Model 54 rifle, 72-73, 262
    Model 64 Rifle, 45
    Model 65 rifle, 34, 35
    Model 70 rifle, 72, 498-499
    Model 71 rifle, 654
    Model 1892 rifle, 34-35
Winchester single shot actions, 232
Winchester single shot
    No. 1 & No. 2 Models, 44-45
    No. 3 Model, 45
Winchester target rifle barrels, 631
.218 Winchester Bee cartridge, 82
.219 Winchester Zipper cartridge, 44
.22 Winchester Magnum Rim Fire cartridge, 725
.22 Winchester Magnum C.F. cartridge, 732
.243 Winchester C.F. cartridge, 729
.25/35 Winchester cartridge, 82
.256 Winchester Magnum C.F. cartridge, 733

.256 Winchester Magnum C.F.
    Pistol and revolver cartridge, 726
    Rifle cartridge, 730
.264 Winchester Magnum C.F. cartridge, 731
.270 Winchester cartridge, 372
.284 Winchester C.F. cartridge, 732
.30/30 Winchester cartridge, 410
.300 Winchester Magnum C.F. cartridge, 732
.308 Winchester C.F. cartridge, 733
.338 Winchester Magnum C.F. cartridge, 733
.348 Winchester cartridge, 654
.458 Winchester Magnum C.F. cartridge, 734
Widening hammerspurs, 283, 284
Wildcat cartridges, 171-175
Wire springs, 151-153
Wood
    Carving, 609
    For gunstocks, 452
    Ornamentation, 609
Woodworking tools
    Illustrated, 22
    Sharpening, 65
Workbench
    Bracing, 1
    Dimensions, 1
    Low bench, disadvantages, 2
    Material used for, 2
    Stockmaking, 6
    Weight, 1
Workshop
    Blueing equipment, 7
    Cabinets, 7
    Considerations, 1
    Library, 37
    Lighting, 7
    Location, 1
    Polishing equipment for blueing, 7
    Racks, 7
    Shelves, 7
Wrenches, receiver, 218, 219
Wundhammer Bulge, 524